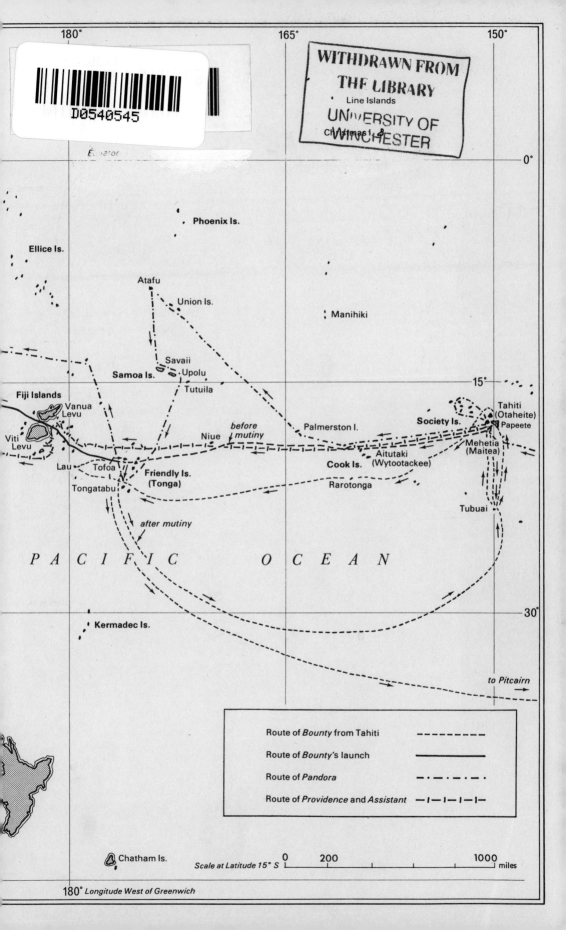

180°　165°　150°

0°

Line Islands
Christmas I.

Equator

Phoenix Is.

Ellice Is.

Atafu

Union Is.

Manihiki

Savaii
Upolu
Samoa Is.
Tutuila

15°

Fiji Islands
Vanua
Levu

Niue
before mutiny

Palmerston I.

Society Is.

Tahiti
(Otaheite)
Papeete

Viti
Levu

Mehetia
(Maitea)

Lau　Tofoa
Tongatabu

**Friendly Is.
(Tonga)**

Aitutaki
(Wytootackee)
Cook Is.

Rarotonga

Tubuai

after mutiny

P A C I F I C　　O C E A N

30°

Kermadec Is.

to Pitcairn

Route of *Bounty* from Tahiti	– – – – –
Route of *Bounty*'s launch	——————
Route of *Pandora*	–·–·–·–·
Route of *Providence* and *Assistant*	—ı—ı—ı—ı—

Chatham Is.

Scale at Latitude 15° S　0　200　1000 miles

180° *Longitude West of Greenwich*

BLIGH

BLIGH

Gavin Kennedy

Duckworth

First published in 1978 by
Gerald Duckworth & Co. Ltd.
The Old Piano Factory
43 Gloucester Crescent, London NW1

© 1978 by Gavin Kennedy

ISBN 0 7156 0957 2

Photoset by
Specialised Offset Services Ltd., Liverpool
and printed in Great Britain by
Redwood Burn Limited, Trowbridge & Esher

Contents

Illustrations

For Patricia

Preface

William Bligh's name was assured of immortality by the mutiny that took place on His Majesty's armed vessel *Bounty* just after 4.30 a.m. on 28 April 1789. The ship was about thirty miles from the Pacific island of Tofoa. This was one of the least sensational of mutinies, though it is probably now the most famous mutiny in history. There were other, more bloody, more dramatic mutinies in the Royal Navy. Not eight years later in 1797, for example, the entire British fleet in home waters was paralysed by mass mutinies at Spithead and the Nore in the middle of a war. For brutality we need only look to the mutiny on H.M.S. *Hermione*; Captain Hugh Pigot drove his men so hard with senseless floggings that they rose and murdered him and nine other officers, including a thirteen-year-old midshipman. By contrast, the *Bounty* mutiny was a placid and minor affair, remarkable only for having no obvious cause. Posterity has credited it with far more importance than it deserves.

Bligh had to pay a heavy price for this fame. He carried the mutiny on his back for twenty-eight years, and never managed to live it down. At the Nore, during the great mutiny of 1797, his own ship, H.M.S. *Director*, was strike-bound. The loyalists on the *Director* tried unsuccessfully to seize control of the ship from the mutineers on two occasions and the official reports described the mutineers as holding the ship by 'terror'. One author has used these reports as if they referred to the 'terror' of Captain Bligh (Ellis, 1955, pp. 256-7). In fact, when the mutiny was over and the entire fleet was preparing to return to the war with the Dutch, Bligh's behaviour was magnanimous in the extreme; he spoke up for nineteen of his crew accused of mutiny by his First Officer, and secured their release.

In 1805 he was court-martialled by one of his junior Lieutenants for 'oppression'. Bligh had charged Lieutenant Frazier with malingering and Frazier counter-charged that Bligh used abusive language and was tyrannical. Bligh was reprimanded and advised to use less emotional language. His critics have used the *Warrior* court martial to prove that he was a 'tyrant', though a close reading of the case suggests less dramatically that he had a hot temper and high standards, and was harsh on those he thought were not pulling their weight.

Bligh's toughest job was as Governor of New South Wales from 1806 to 1810. This was an unruly and troublesome penal colony; the officers of the British regiment there had enriched themselves by irregular trafficking in rum and the acquisition of land. Bligh's task was to break up the commercial activities of the army officers and stop the rum trade. In setting about it with his normal enthusiasm he clashed repeatedly with John Macarthur, former Captain in the New South Wales Corps and the colony's most notorious troublemaker, especially when it came to protecting his own interests. The result of their altercations was a conspiracy between Macarthur and his friends in the army to depose Bligh, which they succeeded in achieving in January 1808. In the build-up to this military mutiny reference was made to the _Bounty_ mutiny and the _Warrior_ court martial in order to personalise the quarrel with Bligh and blame him for what happened. The _Bounty_ was a stick with which to beat him. The way the military officers and other merchant friends of Macarthur enriched themselves in the period of their rule between Bligh's deposition and the arrival of the new Governor, Lachlan Maquarie, is proof enough of the real motivations of the 'Rum Rebellion'.

The unwelcome notoriety the mutiny brought to Bligh in his lifetime came about because of the public campaigns against him by the relatives of Fletcher Christian. It was not possible to exculpate Christian from mutiny except by attempting to prove that Bligh had driven him to it. This is what Edward Christian, Fletcher's brother and Professor of Law at Cambridge, set out to do in 1792 after the trial of some of the mutineers. He collected together several influential friends, assisted by Fletcher's friend William Wordsworth, and conducted an 'enquiry' into the mutiny, the results of which were published in 1794. His 'Appendix' made numerous charges and allegations against Bligh. After an exchange of pamphlets between Bligh and Edward Christian the controversy died down; but, on the dubious assumption that a charge is proven once made, the allegations began to appear in books on the _Bounty_ without regard to their veracity.

Peter Heywood, midshipman on the _Bounty_, was one of the mutineers captured by the Navy and brought home for trial in 1792; he was found guilty and sentenced to death but was pardoned by the King on the Court's recommendation. He was responsible for the second public assault on Bligh's reputation. He had formerly been a friend of the Bligh family but never forgave Bligh for not clearing his name and thereby jeopardising his life. Heywood had acquired a manuscript by James Morrison, Boatswain's Mate of the _Bounty_, written in 1792-3. He too had been convicted but reprieved. This manuscript (now in the Mitchell Library, Sydney) was quoted by Heywood in a biography of himself published in 1825. It was violently anti-Bligh and was intended to show how unsuitable a commander he was, accusing him of theft, stinginess, fraud and bad management (we might note, in passing, that Bligh was never accused by anybody who served under him of brutality by violence of any kind – he was a 'soft' commander in this respect). Morrison's charges were repeated in books on the _Bounty_ throughout the nineteenth century. Almost all books on the subject accept them uncritically.

Lady Belcher (Heywood's step-daughter) used Morrison's manuscript to attack Bligh in her book published in 1870. She also made many mutilations in the original text. The Morrison charges were repeated in Sir William Clowes' history of the Royal Navy (1877) and set the standard for the presentation of

the *Bounty* controversy in later years. Sir Basil Thomson in his introduction to
the 1915 edition of the *Voyage of H.M.S. Pandora* gave credence to Morrison's
charges against Bligh. Attacks on this anti-Bligh bias were lone voices amidst
the crowd. Bladen in 1908, Mackaness in 1931, Montgomerie in 1937 and
Evatt in 1938 were among the few authors who challenged the credibility of
Morrison's charges and the way that popular authors (and later film
scriptwriters) used them. Although much of the documentary evidence was
made available by Owen Rutter (1931, 1934, 1936, 1937), unsatisfactory
accounts of the *Bounty* mutiny still proliferated. Among the more recent
distortions of the historical evidence, Richard Hough's *Captain Bligh and Mr
Christian* (1972) must be remarkable for its acceptance of the absolute truth of
everything that Morrison wrote. Even as distinguished an historian as Peter
Mathias asserts that Bligh was guilty of 'monstrous cruelty' (1974), which is
about as major a travesty of the facts as the assertions made by Lady Belcher a
century before.

I did not begin the research for this book with any particular view of Bligh
or Christian in mind. I took up the subject because it interested me and I did
not plan to be partisan. What I found altered many ideas I had, in common
with most people, about the legends of the *Bounty* and the character of Bligh.
Books and documents on Bligh are crowded with misrepresentation and
outright falsehood, and to get through to the essential person it is necessary
to comment on the literature that purports to represent his life. The motives
of the writers must be looked at and nothing accepted uncritically. The
controversy over Bligh has produced some fierce polemic, and to understand
its causes we must go back to the authors who had a personal interest in
condemning him – Edward Christian, James Morrison and Peter Heywood.
In some ways this book is about the growth of the *Bounty* legend, and what
Bligh was not, as much as about what he was.

Bligh cannot be judged alone. It is necessary also to judge the men who
opposed him. If we are asked whether Bligh was a tyrant we must also look at
the actions of the mutineers when they were free of him. I think the bloody
sequel and murderous actions of the mutineers, Christian included, must
weigh heavy in the balance of right and wrong in this controversy. We must
also put Bligh into perspective as a man of immense personal courage and
determination. The epic open boat voyage of 3,900 sea miles across the
Pacific with seventeen men, little food and inadequate navigational aids
cannot be dismissed as irrelevant. He also fought as a commander at
Camperdown and at the bloody battle of Copenhagen. Nelson thanked him
on his quarter-deck for remaining in action when he decided to ignore,
through his blind eye, Admiral Parker's signal to cease the action.

George Mackaness, in his 1931 biography of Bligh, said: 'As a biographer
worthy of the name is bound neither to extenuate nor to set down anything in
malice, so we cannot blink certain less pleasing features of Bligh's character.'
I have tried to bear this in mind. My accounts of his conduct are not attempts
to 'extenuate'; they are attempts to set the record straight. Certainly nothing
has been written in malice. But some readers are bound to feel that I have
offended on both counts.

The most important single source for archival material relating to the life of William Bligh is undoubtedly the Mitchell Library in Sydney, Australia. I am extremely grateful to Miss Suzanne Mourot of the Mitchell Library for her considerable assistance while I was researching this book, and to her staff for their personal assistance and many kindnesses on my visits to the Library and in correspondence since. I would also like to thank the Librarians and staffs of the Public Record Office, London; the National Maritime Museum, Greenwich; the Admiralty Library, Fulham; the British Library, London; the National Library of Scotland, Edinburgh; the Alexander Turnbull Library, Wellington; the Bernice P. Bishop Museum, Honolulu; and the Folger Museum, Nantucket. Acknowledgments for permission to reproduce material for illustrations are gratefully offered to the following: the Dixson Galleries, Sydney for 3, 20, 21 and 23; the Hydrographic Office of the Ministry of Defence, Taunton, for 2 and 11; the Mitchell Library, Sydney, for 4, 5, 6, 7, 10, 12, 14, 15, 22 and 24; the National Library, Canberra, for 8; the National Maritime Museum, Greenwich, for 13; and the National Portrait Gallery, London, for 1. Photographs 25 and 26 are by Ray Davies.

In the four years that this book took to write, many individuals have helped me in my researches. Among these I may mention, without discredit to those who remain anonymous, the following: Terry Martin, Edinburgh; Alexander Smith, Dumfries; Edouard Stackpole, Nantucket; Cynthia Timberlake, Honolulu; Betty Goodger, Yvonne Brown and Jenny Broomhead, Sydney; Herbert Rees, Bradford-on-Avon; Stephen Walters, Oakley; and Joy Hughes, Sydney. Lieutenant-Commander Andrew David, of the Hydrographic Department, Taunton, has been extremely helpful both from a technical and historical point of view and I have benefited enormously from many comments he made regarding several aspects of the book. Emma Fisher, of Duckworth, undertook the labour of editing the manuscript and such merit as the book has in its finished form owes much to her. She also contributed to some of the research work.

It is appropriate here to acknowledge the scholarship of Professor George Mackaness of Sydney. I have been consciously influenced by the work of Mackaness (1931), and I hope that in the places where I disagree with his assessments, this will be put down to the benefits of an additional forty years of archival accumulation and not to any fault in Mackaness's scholarship.

Lastly, the contribution of my family must be clarified. Authorship is a great consumer of time and patience. I can best describe my debts to Patricia and Florence by asserting that I gave them more cause to mutiny than William Bligh ever gave to Fletcher Christian.

Edinburgh   G.K.
February 1977

1

Young Bligh

William Bligh was born in Plymouth on 9 September 1754 to Francis and Jane Bligh. His father, the fifth son of John Bligh who held the Manor of Tinten in St. Tudy, came of a distinguished Cornish line which in the years 1505-88 provided Bodmin with five mayors.[1] More recently it had produced General Edward Bligh (1635-1775), who distinguished himself in Britain's foreign wars, though he retired amidst controversy; and Admiral Sir Richard Rodney Bligh (1737-1821). Of the same line came the Earls of Darnley, who won favour through an Irish peerage, 'promoted' not long after to an English peerage.[2] The Darnleys were active in the Customs and Excise service in Plymouth from 1648 to 1663; Bligh's father was a Customs Officer in Plymouth all his life, and named his son after the William Bligh who had held the same post and fathered the Darnley line.

William Bligh's mother, Jane, was a widow before she married Francis Bligh. Her nephew, John Bond, was a surgeon in the navy, and Bligh was close to his Bond cousins and exchanged family 'news' throughout his life. On his second 'breadfruit' voyage in H.M.S. *Providence*, he made a point of taking a relative, Francis Godolphin Bond, as his First Lieutenant.[3] Bligh's mother died before he was 16; his father made two later marriages and died on 27 December 1780.

Bligh's formative years were spent in the naval centre of Plymouth, where his father's post as Customs Officer assured the family a modest standard of living and family connections were available to open doors in the navy. It is not known where William Bligh learned his basic mathematics, but that he was gifted in this subject we know by his rapid progress when he came to apply himself to the problems of navigation. Traces of his early career in the

---

[1] See Mackaness, 1951, pp. 2-3; *Notes and Queries*, 8th series, Vol. II, pp. 30, 94, and 9th series, Vol. IV, p. 217; Polwhele, 1831, Vol. 2, p. 19; *Dictionary of National Biography*, entries under Bligh; *Western Antiquary*, Vol. IV, March 1885, p. 214; Gilbert, 1838.

[2] See Darnley (Peter Stuart Bligh) in *Debrett: Burke's Peerage 1970*, pp. 729-30; there is a portrait of General Edward Bligh by Gainsborough (*c.* 1770) in the Metropolitan Museum of Art, New York. William Bligh used the coat of arms of the Earl of Darnley as a personal seal for his correspondence (an example is in the Mitchell Library, Sydney); he was on social terms with the Darnleys, as can be seen from his correspondence with them in the Mitchell Library.

[3] Bligh and Bond quarrelled on this voyage. The quarrel did not prevent Bligh from using his influence to get Bond promoted some years later; see Bligh's letter to Sir Joseph Banks, 6 December 1798, Mitchell Library (ML) MS, Bligh Correspondence, C218.

navy include the appearance of his name as 'Captain's Servant' on the muster roll of H.M.S. *Monmouth* in 1762. Bligh was only seven years and eight months old at the time. This kind of arrangement was not unusual for the sons of well-connected parents. The practice of having very young 'Captain's Servants' did not mean that the navy countenanced child labour on its ships. The parents would persuade captains to place their sons' names on the books; the captain could draw extra rations for them if they did not actually go to sea, or, if they did, they would be taught by a schoolmaster and could familiarise themselves with life on board. Captain James Cook on his voyages to the Pacific placed his sons' names on the roll once the ship had left port and removed them abruptly when he was near home on his return; he was thus able to claim rations for them. It was a harmless fiddle and fairly common. Naturally, this arrangement was only open to boys from families of higher social class than those of seamen, and it tells us something about the social standing of Bligh's father that he was able to arrange this for his son. It is not known for certain whether Bligh actually went to sea at this early age. That his name went on the roll he owed to a friend of the family, Captain Keith Stewart;[4] it remained there for six months.

On 27 July 1770, at the age of 15, after his mother died, Bligh was entered on the roll of H.M.S. *Hunter*, a small ten-gun sloop. His rating was Able Bodied, or A.B. After Bligh's death it was sometimes argued that this rating 'explained' his later proneness to mutiny, since promoted seamen make the worst masters. The argument was first advanced in 1831 by Sir John Barrow, Secretary to the Admiralty, in his book on the mutiny on the Bounty. Barrow wrote: 'It is indeed a common observation in the services, that officers who have risen from *before the mast* are generally the greatest tyrants. It was Bligh's misfortune not to have been educated in the cockpit of a man-of-war, which is to the navy what a public school is to those who are to move in civil society'.[5]

A quick look at the regulations and practice of the time will put Bligh's rise from 'before the mast' into perspective. The first rung on the ladder to the Quarter Deck was the office of midshipman, or 'Young Gentleman'. The regulation which was in force, but more or less avoided, was that the Young Gentlemen should have at least two years' experience at sea and be at least 13 years old, or 11 in the case of sons of naval officers.[6] The Admiralty did

---

[4] Mackaness, 1951, pp. 5-6. Keith Stewart helped Bligh in later years, particularly in the all-important promotion to Lieutenant; see Banks Papers, Brabourne Collection, ML, A78-4, p. 29, Lord Selkirk to Sir Joseph Banks, 14 September 1787; also Bligh to Admiral Campbell, 1782; 'From Mr Kieth Stewart's partiality to me from my services I have since gained promotion as a Lieutenant' (quoted in Mackaness, 1951, p. 29). The *Monmouth* was stationed at Plymouth and made an occasional Channel cruise. Bligh may not have actually sailed in her. See Rutter, 1936, p. 14 and PRO Adm. 51/3916. This letter is quoted in full by Bligh in his letter to Duncan Campbell 28/4/1782 – ML MS, Bligh Correspondence, Safe 1/40.

[5] Barrow, 1854, p. 292. The 1831 edition of his book was anonymous; various editions have appeared over the years (*see* Bibliography). For an account of the life of Barrow see Lloyd, 1970.

[6] The most common form of entry to midshipman's rank was by personal invitation of a captain in command of a ship. About 90 per cent of entrants followed this route. The other method was by attendance at the Naval Academy in Portsmouth from the ages of thirteen to sixteen. This system was introduced in 1733 but provided only forty recruits a year. *See* Lewis, 1939, pp. 84-6; 1960, pp. 159-60.

not control the recruitment˙of Young Gentlemen, but it did lay down the establishment of the ships. The number of midshipmen was rigidly fixed per ship, and if a captain wanted to take more than his quota of Young Gentlemen he could only do so by temporarily rating them as A.B.s. When a vacancy occurred among the midshipmen, through death, desertion, dis-rating, transfer or promotion, the captain was then able to re-rate one of the Young Gentlemen A.B.s as a midshipman. This is what happened in Bligh's case, and in those of Cook, Nelson and thousands of others, including, we might note, that of Fletcher Christian (see p.14).[7] In practice these men were treated like established midshipmen. They messed with the officers and took on supervisory duties almost immediately. Bligh was never 'before the mast' in the literal sense implied by Barrow. Confirmation of his real status is seen in the *Hunter*'s muster roll only six months after he joined her: on 4 February 1771 he was discharged from the ship by order of Admiral Sir Richard Spry and re-entered the next day as midshipman. A vacancy had appeared, and the Captain had promoted him. There is no question of Bligh having managed this transformation on his own. His family background and sponsorship through interest[8] had carried him over the first hurdle; the rest was now up to him. Bligh joined 'the cockpit of a man-of-war' from the start of his career; what Barrow claimed that he missed, Bligh in fact had the good fortune to enjoy.

On 22 September 1771 Bligh was transferred to the larger H.M.S. *Crescent*, a 36-gun, on which for the next three years he learned his navigation and seamanship. In 1774 he was paid off the *Crescent* and entered H.M.S. *Ranger*, first as an A.B. volunteer, a nominal and temporary rating, and then, in September 1775, once again as a midshipman. H.M.S. *Ranger* was employed in searching for contraband among the ships in the Irish Sea, based at Douglas in the Isle of Man. The time Bligh spent on this duty completed his six years as a midshipman. He must have shown outstanding promise, for Captain James Cook, then fitting out his Third Voyage, passed over more senior and experienced men and chose Bligh to be his Master on the *Resolution*.

The appointment was a remarkable one. Bligh was unknown, yet he was offered the senior post of Master, with responsibility for seamanship and navigation. Cook, who never suffered fools gladly, must have formed a high opinion of the young man's capabilities.[9] The post was the highest, short of full commission as Lieutenant; Bligh would be extremely close to Cook on

---

[7] Nelson was rated A.B. with Troubridge (both became admirals) in H.M.S. *Seashore*, 5 April 1774; Cook volunteered as an A.B. on 17 June 1755 and was posted to H.M.S. *Eagle*.

[8] Interest was an important eighteenth-century mechanism for distributing the fruits of patronage. Careers in public service required sponsorship ashore, and the wider and more influential the interest a person could set to work on his behalf, the more assured he was of advancement. Family ties could be crucial; if these were lacking, patrons were sought among the high-ranking families. Bligh's family got him started and he found a firm friend in Sir Joseph Banks, who kept his career afloat at difficult moments in his life.

[9] Bligh's chart of Lucea, illustrated (plate 2), is undated; up to now it has been assumed that Bligh prepared it while working for Duncan Campbell in 1783-7. But it or similar ones could well have been done by Bligh for his midshipman's journals while in the *Crescent*, 1771-4, sent to the Admiralty, and there seen by Captain Cook as he fitted out his third voyage.

the voyage, too close for the liking of some. The opportunity to acquire experience would have been sufficient incentive to join the *Resolution* without promotion; to go as Master was a very creditable beginning to his senior training, and a pointer to future success. With Cook's voyage behind him he could look forward to the next posting as Lieutenant, and was assured eventual promotion to Post Captain if he proved himself capable.[10] Once a Post Captain, a man was on the ladder to seniority; even if he did nothing of note and had no help from then on, he would gradually rise through the lists to Flag Officer's rank. The King himself could not move a man up the Post Captains' lists above men senior to him, or hold him back. As men on the list died or were promoted, everyone below moved up. It was a ghastly progression; news of tragedies at sea and loss of Captains signified a general move towards Flag Rank for others on the list.

At 22 Bligh was a long way from Post Captain, but he was much nearer a Lieutenant's commission than he could have hoped when he was posted to the *Ranger*. To complete the formalities of the termination of his midshipman's time he sat his Lieutenant's examination some time before joining Cook on the *Resolution*. He had to demonstrate his competence in the basic skills of navigation and seamanship; the neatness and detail of his Midshipman's Journals (kept by each midshipman on the ship he served for eventual presentation to the examiners after being signed by his Captain) were probably above average, if his later Journals and Logs are anything to go by. His certificate of passing is dated 1 May 1776.[11] William Bligh was ready for the first major test in his turbulent career.

[10] The use of 'Captain' can be confusing. If an officer was in command of any vessel he was its captain and would be addressed as such by the crew. He might not, however, hold the rank of Captain – he might not be Post Captain, as it was known. Bligh commanded the *Bounty* and was addressed as Captain Bligh though he was in fact ranked as Lieutenant Bligh at the time. Whether the person commanding a vessel held the rank of Captain was related to the size of the ship. The main stepping stones to the rank of Captain were being rated midshipman; after six years, passing the lieutenant's examination; and finally a posting as a Lieutenant (which did not automatically follow the passing of the examination; some midshipmen were in their late thirties and a few were over forty).

[11] Bligh's certificate states: 'He produceth Journals kept by himself in the Crescent and Ranger, and Certificates from Captains Henshaw, Morgan, Thompson and Lieutn Samber of his Diligence Sobriety & obedience to command. He can splice, Knott, Reef a Sail, work a Ship in Sailing, Shift his Tides, keep a Reckoning of a Ships way by plain Sailing and Mercator, observe by Sun or Star, find the variation of the Compass, and is qualified to do the duty of an Able Seaman and midshipman.' Quoted in Rutter, 1936a, p.31; PRO Adm. 6/50 (Appointment Book).

2

The Voyage with Cook

James Cook had entered the Royal Navy as a temporary A.B. after a career in the merchant service. Once in the Royal Navy, he at first made rapid progress, moving from A.B. to Master in a month (July 1755), but he then stood still for twelve years and was not commissioned as a Lieutenant until 1768 when he was forty years old. In that rank he made his first two voyages to the Pacific. On his first voyage he took with him a young botanist, Joseph Banks, who was to play a crucial role in William Bligh's life.

It was for his third and final voyage that Cook chose Bligh. On this expedition were several other men whose names later became linked with Bligh's. Among these was Lieutenant James Burney (later Admiral Burney) who became a close friend of Bligh's and edited his narrative of the mutiny on the *Bounty* in 1792.[1] But for the moment we are concerned with two main aspects of this voyage: Cook's conduct of the expedition, and his death. The former throws light on Bligh's actions on the *Bounty*; the latter is relevant because of recent attempts to hold Bligh responsible for what happened to Cook, and because it affected his chances of promotion.

The facts of the first are straightforward. Cook had a remarkable record in preserving the life of his crews on long voyages. It was not uncommon to lose a dozen or more men on an Atlantic crossing, yet Cook managed to sail for years with very few deaths. The basis of his management was regular and reasonable food combined with personal cleanliness. He overcame resistance by example and discipline, and on one occasion had two seamen flogged for refusing to eat meat. Cook also introduced a three-watch system on his ships, giving the seamen eight hours' rest between duties instead of the traditional four. He was elected to the Royal Society in 1776 for his improvements to health at sea, and was awarded the Copley Gold Medal for a paper on the subject. Yet his recommendations were not widely adopted. Bligh was one of the first to institute Cook's methods on all his ships, meeting with similar resistance to new diets and habits. He learnt much from Cook about naval management; he may also have been influenced by his personal mannerisms, for Cook's violent fits of rage on this voyage were notorious, and Bligh later exhibited similar behaviour.

The major discovery of Cook's third voyage was the Hawaiian island group in the north Pacific. Cook named them after the Earl of Sandwich and they were known as the Sandwich Islands into the nineteenth century. It was

[1] *See* du Rietz, 1962.

here that Cook was killed by Hawaiians on the morning of Sunday, 14 February 1779. The story of the death of Cook is one of misunderstandings between sailors and Hawaiians, hasty decisions, and violent disagreements afterwards about who was to blame; but Bligh comes out of it well. I will give only the bare bones of the episode here, highlighting Bligh's part and the effect on his subsequent career.[2]

Cook's ships, the *Resolution* and the *Discovery*, had come upon the Sandwich Islands on the way north to the Bering Strait in 1778, and after a fruitless search for the fabled North-West Passage to Europe he brought his ships back to the islands for a rest, and to survey his new discovery. On this visit the ships stayed at the eastern end of the island group, on the large island known as Hawaii, at a place called (today) Kealakekua Bay. After a stay of some weeks they left the bay and went exploring, but heavy storms forced them to return to Kealakekua for repairs to the *Resolution*'s foremast.

Initially Cook had been welcomed by the Hawaiians. He was identified by them with the legendary god Lono, who had disappeared to sea in ancient times and who, they believed, would return to them bearing gifts in canoes decorated with white streamers.[3] But relations between Polynesians and Europeans deteriorated. The sailors ate large quantities of the local produce, and were pleased to discover that the local women would have sex for an iron nail. Iron and other objects that could not be bargained for were often stolen by the Hawaiians. On 13 February some Hawaiians began to roll large lava stones down the hillside to the well where some sailors were drawing water for the ships. A little later a Hawaiian stole some tongs from the *Discovery*; he was caught and flogged. Then another stole them again, and this time got away. He was chased ashore, and the result was a mêlée on the beach between a few unarmed Europeans and several hundred Hawaiians with clubs and stones. By the time things were sorted out, a ship's boat had been ransacked and its oars broken.

During the next night, some Hawaiians removed one of the *Discovery*'s boats from its anchorage in the bay. This was a very serious loss for an expedition that used the ships' boats for work near uncharted shores. Lieutenant Clerke, captain of the *Discovery*, informed Cook of the theft at approximately 6.30 a.m. Cook had been extremely vexed by the previous incidents and this was the last straw; he decided to show the Hawaiians how dangerous it was to trifle with him. He issued orders to blockade the bay and seize the Hawaiians canoes. On previous occasions he had taken both islanders and property hostage to recover stolen items, usually with success. Accordingly he ordered Captain Clerke to send two boats 'well manned and armed' to the southern point to stop any canoes escaping,[4] and sent two of

[2] The full story, with a close discussion of the various accounts, is told in my book *The Death of Captain Cook*, where I conclude that Captain Cook's failure to think ahead, his irritable temper, and his belief that one shot would clear the beach of Hawaiians, are largely to blame – in contrast to the official version by Lieutenant King which tried to exonerate Cook and was followed by many subsequent authors. *See* Beaglehole, 1794; Gould, 1935.

[3] Daws, 1968.

[4] Captain Clerke, *Log and Observations*, 14 February-26 July 1779; PRO Adm. 55/22-3 and 51/4561/217.

his own boats from the *Resolution* to the northern point with the same orders. While the orders were being passed on, a large ocean canoe was sighted making its way out of the bay. The only boat ready manned and armed was the *Resolution*'s cutter, commanded by William Bligh. Cook ordered Bligh after the canoe, and he set off immediately. He soon caught up with it and tried to persuade it to go ashore, but no notice was taken, so Bligh ordered his men to fire their muskets at it. No-one was hit, but the noise of the muskets caused the canoe to veer towards the southern shore. There the Hawaiians beached their canoe on some rocks and ran off inland.

Soon after this, Cook decided to go ashore to visit the Hawaiian King, Terreeoboo, with the intention of getting him on board and using him as a further hostage for the return of the boat. This did not fit well with his first plan, as the gunfire in the bay would have alarmed the Hawaiians, and the men needed to take Terreeoboo by force were scattered about the bay keeping in the canoes. But at about 7 a.m. he left for the shore with a Marine Lieutenant, two NCOs and seven armed marines. Just before he left his attention was drawn to Bligh's boat, which had chased the canoe to the rocks. It was suggested by an unnamed officer that if Bligh had the same trouble as the boat party the day before he would be in difficulties. Cook dismissed the idea, saying that Bligh was armed and one shot would clear the beach.[5] Once on shore, Cook found Terreeoboo just getting up, and invited him to accompany them to the boats with a view to going on board. At first Terreeoboo agreed willingly, but on his way to the shore he was persuaded not to go by his wife and some of the crowd which was rapidly gathering.

Cook insisted and the crowd resisted. The situation worsened; news came to the Hawaiians that one of their chiefs had been killed in the bay while trying to penetrate the blockade. Cook refused to abandon his plan. The Hawaiians became more and more insolent and threatening, and Phillips, the Lieutenant of Marines, asked permission to line up his marines along the shore in case fire was needed. Cook agreed and this was done. The sequence of events at this point is not clear, but it is fairly certain that a Hawaiian threw something at Cook – a stone or breadfruit – which struck him on the face;[6] either then or shortly after, he fired, first small shot and then ball shot, and killed at least one Hawaiian, either in rage at this insult and with the intention of making an example of one of the islanders, or – as some suggest – in self-defence. A general assault now began; the marines fired once, then turned and fled into the water, abandoning their muskets. Phillips and the Sergeant soon followed.[7] The pinnace that had brought the shore party was waiting near the shore, but could not give a good supporting fire. Cook and some of the party were left on the rocks, and quickly overrun by Hawaiians. Captain Cook was struck down by a Hawaiian club and stabbed repeatedly with knives. Four marines who could not swim were dragged out of the water,

[5] James Burney, *Journal of Lt Burney with Captain Cook 1776-1780*, BM Add. MS 8955; also ML MS, 2 vols, safe 1/64.

[6] Lieutenant James King, *Log and Proceedings*, 4 February 1778-25 August 1779, PRO Adm. 55/122.

[7] Phillips to Clerke, quoted in Clerke's Log.

stabbed and beaten to death with clubs. The Hawaiians were dispersed for a short time by fire from the ships' guns of the *Resolution*, but some quickly crept back and dragged off the corpses, which were dismembered and stripped of flesh.

One person who could have helped and did not was Lieutenant Williamson of the *Resolution*, who had gone to the north point with an armed party of seamen in the launch, as part of the blockade, and then been ordered by Cook to back up the shore expedition. Instead of coming in closer and giving supporting fire at the crucial moment, he moved his boat further out, and would not allow his men to fire, even though they wanted to. He also made no attempt to recover the bodies, although at one point the shore round them was empty.[8]

With Captain Cook dead, Captain Clerke of the *Discovery* immediately took command. His immediate problem was to safeguard the shore camp in the southern part of the bay, where Lieutenant King was guarding the *Resolution*'s foremast; he sent Bligh in the *Discovery*'s cutter to inform Lieutenant King of what had happened, with orders to break up the camp and bring on board the ship's timekeeper, essential for navigation. King departed for the *Discovery* in the cutter, leaving Bligh in charge of the camp, and while he was away Bligh's party was attacked by stone-throwing Hawaiians.[9] He ordered his men to fire and repelled them successfully. Reinforcements soon arrived, with all the available armed men from both ships, and orders from Clerke to bring everything on board as quickly as possible.[10] This was managed; once Bligh had demonstrated that they were prepared to stand and fight, the Hawaiians left them alone. By 11.30 everything was safely on board. It took several days to recover parts of Captain Cook's body, and these were committed to the deep before the ships left Hawaii.

Surprisingly, Williamson was promoted on the voyage and eventually became a Post Captain. His behaviour was covered up by his fellow Lieutenants, and the Admiralty was given a distorted account of what happened. Lieutenant King was awarded the prestigious task of completing Cook's account of the voyage, which was published in 1784. His influential account admitted Captain Cook's over-confidence in dealing with the Hawaiians as a contributory cause of his death, but suggested that the 'fatal turn in the affair' was provided by the news of the death of the chief, killed by Lieutenant Rickman's boats at the southern point. Samwell, perhaps more convincingly, called Williamson's conduct 'the fatal turn in the affair'. Rickman was made a scapegoat for Cook's death and never progressed beyond Lieutenant in the Navy. King did not mention Williamson's part; he ignored the criticisms made at the time and recorded in the Logs and Journals of the crews. Recently, it has been suggested[11] that Bligh's action

[8] Samwell, 1786, and his Journal, 10 February 1776-29 November 1779, BM Egerton MS 2591.
[9] Cook and King, 1784, Vol. III, p. 58.
[10] *ibid.*
[11] Hough, 1972, p. 49.

led to the killing of a chief and that this made the crowd turn murderous, so that Bligh was really responsible for Cook's death – an idea based on a distortion of the evidence.

William Bligh marked in the margins of a copy of King's account many bitter comments on the accuracy of what King had written, not just about the death of Cook but about the whole voyage.[12] King had edited Bligh's contribution to the voyage out of the book. As Master of the *Resolution*, Bligh had done much of the navigation, and also drawn a large number of charts under Cook's supervision. Some of these were excellent examples of Bligh's skills as a cartographer. King infuriated Bligh by using some of the charts in the book and ascribing them to Henry Roberts.[13] But Bligh's most caustic comments were reserved for the account of Cook's death. He wrote: 'The Marines fire[d] & ran which occasioned al[l] that followed for had the[y] fixed their bayonets & not have run, so frighte[ned] as they were, they migh[t] have done all before t[hem].' Bligh described the conduct of Lieutenant Phillips, presented by King as a hero, as a 'most ludicrous performance', and called King's version of what Phillips did in the attack 'a most infamous lie'. His criticism of King is no less harsh. King writes of Cook: '... my feelings, on the death of a beloved and honoured friend, may be suspected to have had some share in this opinion' (namely, to use firm measures against the Hawaiians to secure the return of Captain Cook's body), at which Bligh boils over with the remark: 'A most Hypo[cr]itical expression, [for his] death was no more atten[ded] to in the course of [a few] days than if he n[ever] existed.'

If, as seems likely, Bligh had expressed these views to King and Phillips during the remainder of the voyage, it explains why he was excluded from the general promotion on the ships' return to Britain in 1780. If King could cover up for Williamson (whom even Phillips could not excuse; the recriminations flared up into a duel between them later in the voyage, at the Cape of Good Hope), could shift the blame implicitly onto Rickman and could mis-credit charts and drawings of Bligh's to Roberts, he was capable of blocking Bligh's promotion. King's version became the official and authoritative version of the voyage, and Bligh could only fume in private. He was apparently intending to draw up a detailed reply to King's version after the *Bounty* voyage, but all his charts and other evidence were taken by the mutineers, and his claims were never made public.

[12] This copy of King's *Voyage*, with Bligh's comments, was rediscovered in the Admiralty in the 1920s by the biographer, Rupert T. Gould (*see* Gould, 1928). It is not certain when he wrote these comments; he could have written them on his own copy, which might have been among the books and papers handed back to the Admiralty when royal naval ships visited Pitcairn in 1814. Among Bligh's books taken by the mutineers was a copy of King's *Voyage*, see Rutter, 1936a, p. 118. Another possibility (suggested to me by Andrew David) is that Bligh wrote on an Admiralty copy while working in the hydrographic office at various times between 1800 and 1805. A careless binder cropped parts of Bligh's comments and the reconstructions are those of Gould (1928). See Staines and Pipon, n.d.

[13] Bligh wrote on the title page: 'None of the Maps and Charts in this publication are from the original drawings of Lieut. Henry Roberts; he did no more than copy the original ones from Captain Cook, who besides myself was the only person that surveyed and laid the coast down, in the *Resolution*. Every plan & Chart from C. Cook's death are exact Copies of my Works' (Gould, 1928).

If Bligh was disappointed at his failure to be promoted on his return, he found one consolation when he revisited the Isle of Man. He had probably met the Betham family when he was stationed at Douglas before the voyage. The Bethams had an unmarried daughter, Elizabeth, aged 27, and William and Elizabeth became engaged. The Bethams were rich and influential: Elizabeth's father, Richard, was an intimate friend of the Scottish philosopher, David Hume, and the Scottish economist, Adam Smith. Her grandfather, Dr Neil Campbell, had been a Principal of Glasgow University and Chaplain to the King. Her uncle, Duncan Campbell, was a wealthy and successful merchant, who owned several merchant ships plying between the West Indies and Britain, and also acted as a contractor to the Royal Navy. Bligh married Elizabeth at Douglas on 4 February 1781. He gained the loyal and lasting support of a strong-willed, educated woman, and was also brought into touch with important interests in and around the Royal Navy.

3

A Plum Job

When the *Resolution* and the *Discovery* returned in 1780, Britain was fighting another decisive war with her continental rivals. There was the added complication of the revolt of the American colonies. In a sense it was a world war, which was being fought in Europe, in America and in the Atlantic. Though Britain was forced out of America she remained premier power in Europe. Her attention was on Europe, its competitive neighbours and their designs, rather than the colonies. Rodney's great victory in the Caribbean against the French, in 1782, following the British surrender of Yorktown, was regarded as more significant than the loss of a continent, because it gave command of the Atlantic to the British navy once again. But in a day when serious debate took place over whether to settle for Guadeloupe Island in exchange for Canada, it is perhaps less surprising that an empty ocean was preferred to an empty continent.

Bligh participated in two of the naval events that took place at the tail end of the war; he missed a third by being delayed in port. The first was with Admiral Parker in the North Sea at Dogger Bank. On 14 February 1781 Bligh was appointed Master of the *Belle Poule*, a captured French frigate put into the King's service. The main duty of the North Sea fleet was to keep an eye on the Dutch and also to escort British merchant ships from the Baltic to the home ports. As Master of the *Belle Poule*, whose Captain was Philip Patton, Bligh spent some time crossing and recrossing the North Sea. In April, the *Belle Poule* captured a small French prize, *La Cologne*, which was taken to Leith in Scotland.

Admiral Parker had served in the West Indies and had been publicly criticised for his conduct during one of Rodney's engagements. The dispute was over a new tactic that Rodney had devised for a battle with a large Dutch fleet in the West Indies. Standard naval practice at the time was to engage the enemy line all the way along its length, each British ship closing with one enemy ship. Rodney's idea was to concentrate the attack on nine of the enemy's ships instead of the whole line of twenty-three, so that there would be two or three British ships for each enemy ship attacked, and superior fire-power would ensure success. Rodney might have won a victory on Nelsonian lines. But because of insufficient planning, little practice, and a general lack of initiative (Rodney implied that it was lack of courage), there was confusion and misunderstanding and the plan failed. Parker was rebuked, but was widely known to be more than usually angry (his nickname, Old Vinegar, suggests something of his personality); he was in a mood to prove his worth at the next opportunity, where he could show the advantage of the old tactics over the new-fangled ones that 'nobody understood'.[1]

His opportunity came on 5 August 1781. A British convoy, escorted by seven line-of-battle ships and five frigates, including the *Belle Poule*, met a Dutch convoy, escorted by eight Dutch warships, near the Dogger Bank. The Admiral directed the merchant ships to cut and run for home. The wind, a north-easterly, favoured the British squadron, with the Dutch lying to the south-west. In the rush to catch the Dutch the Admiral misjudged the pace of the ships, and they approached the enemy in some disorder. Frigates by convention did not engage line-of-battle ships, so the *Belle Poule* did not take part in the main assault, but would have been nearby, ready to give assistance, pass on signals, and act as a support if needed.[2] As Master, it was Bligh's job to control the sailing of the ship, and the fact that he was promoted after the battle to a larger ship suggests that he distinguished himself in command of the crew when other ships were sailing around in confusion.

Admiral Parker described the battle as follows: 'I bore away with a general signal to chase ... the enemy formed their line consisting of eight two-deck ships on the starboard tack ... Not a gun was fired on either side until within the distance of half musket shot. The *Fortitude*, being then abreast of the Dutch Admiral, the action began, and continued with unceasing fire for 3 hours and 40 minutes. By this time our ships were unmanageable ... the enemy appeared to be in as bad a condition.'[3] Behind the simple phraseology of the report there was a lot left unsaid. The British ships were old – Parker had denounced them as 'rotten' – and extremely difficult to handle. The British crews were relatively untrained in battle manoeuvres and their disorderly approach could have been fatal. For some reason, as the British ships went past them, the Dutch held their fire. The French would never have missed the chance that Parker presented to the enemy with the opening pass, but the Dutch preferred close in-fighting. If they had been able to close at this point they could have raked the British decks with murderous broadsides. As it was, they let the British come round again unmolested, and the old tactics of line against line, with Admiral engaging Admiral, were carried out, showing that what Parker lacked was not courage but imagination. The ships stood off a short distance and fired at each other for over $3\frac{1}{2}$ hours causing about equal damage and casualties. The British lost 104 killed and 339 wounded and the Dutch 142 killed and 403 wounded. A Dutch ship later sank in shallow water; but apart from this the damage was minor.

His first battle was useful experience for Bligh; wartime was normally a period of promotions, to staff the extra ships needed and to replace casualties. The careers of men on a voyage of discovery stood still for the three or four years they were away; if they were not promoted immediately

[1] For an account of the controversy *see* Laughton, 1907, pp. xliv-li.
[2] *See* Kemp (ed.), 1969, p. 120; Mackaness, 1951, pp. 27-8. Bligh's log as Master is in PRO Adm. 52/2171; extracts in Rutter, 1936a, pp. 62-7.
[3] Quoted in Padfield, 1973, p. 109.

on their return, then they had to wait for the next war before they were likely to be promoted. Bligh had returned home just in time to get a chance at some action. On 5 September 1781 Bligh was transferred from the *Belle Poule* to the *Berwick*, and also promoted Lieutenant, owing to the influence of Captain Keith Stewart (see p.2, n.4). This was an important step for him, as by gaining his commission at last he was qualified to proceed to Post Captain.

The *Berwick*, under Captain John Fergusson, had been one of the line ships in the battle of the Dogger Bank, and Bligh served on her for only a few months before being transferred again, as Fifth Lieutenant, to the *Princess Amelia*, another ship of the line at the Dogger Bank battle. He served on her from 1 January 1782 to 19 March 1782, and was then transferred to the *Cambridge*. In the *Cambridge* Bligh was Sixth Lieutenant, and he served in her until 13 January 1783.

The *Cambridge* was assigned to Vice-Admiral Barrington's fleet, but during April 1782 she was undergoing repairs. Owing to what Bligh considered to be a 'want of effort' on the part of the shipwrights and other artificers, the *Cambridge* was held in port while the fleet under Barrington captured a convoy of supply ships.[4] Such an action had financial consequences for those who took part; officers and men received prize-money in proportion to their rank. Prize-money was always a controversial issue in the navy. It was a supplement to the income of officers in an age when wages were not generous. It sometimes took years to settle the sums, and litigation between commanders over their shares was not uncommon. Nelson fell out with his commanders over his share and bitterly contested the issue, eventually winning a settlement over Lord St Vincent.[5] Bligh thought his missed prize-money would have been about £200.

The *Cambridge* did, however, take part in the relief of Gibraltar, which was under siege from a combined force of French and Spanish ships and troops. The Governor, General Elliot, had successfully held them off but was in desperate straits from want of supplies and provisions. Lord Howe's fleet left Spithead on 11 September 1782 and reached Gibraltar on 13 October. The French and Spanish fleets came out to meet him but, being careless in stationing themselves and possibly daunted by the size of Howe's fleet (149 ships and thirty-four ships of the line), they remained too far off to present any obstacle to Howe's entrance into Gibraltar. He brought enough provisions to last a year; Gibraltar was secured for another two centuries. When Howe left, the French and Spanish fleets came within sight and battle was prepared for, but the only result was a long-distance cannonade before the enemy made off again.[6]

The fleet returned to Spithead on 14 November, and on 13 January 1783

[4] Mackaness, 1951, p. 29.
[5] *See* Oman, 1947, p. 415. On prize-money in general *see* Lloyd, 1968, pp. 252-3; the Admiral on a station got a sixth of everything taken in prize, irrespective of his own absence from the action (or even from the station), and this could mean fabulous sums. Parker, the Admiral in the West Indies, took £122,697 in 1762 while the seamen got £3 each; he returned to Britain from the West Indies a very rich man indeed, *see* Pope, 1970, Chapter 1.
[6] Mackaness, 1951, p. 30; Kemp (ed.), 1969, p. 99.

Lieutenant Bligh was paid off and placed on half-pay, along with thousands of other officers, as the great war fleets were stood down for the peace. In the months after his return Bligh was with his wife and his new baby daughter, Harriet Maria, at Douglas, Isle of Man. His half pay was 2s. a day, hardly enough to feed and clothe his family. Elizabeth's uncle, Duncan Campbell, had a number of merchant ships for which he needed experienced and reliable officers, and he advised Bligh to get a written clearance from the Admiralty to go into merchant service and leave the country.[7] Bligh completed the formalities by July 1783, and shortly afterwards embarked on a mercantile career which was to last four years, commanding various vessels, acting as Campbell's agent in Jamaica and learning about mercantile practice. This last was to be of use to Bligh as his career progressed. When his time in merchant service ended Bligh knew how to manipulate bills of exchange, make claims on the British Government in foreign stations, and handle finances.

With his new income (about £500 a year) Bligh was able to move his family to London. He was close enough to the Admiralty to walk there when he was at home – a frequent chore for an ambitious officer. Here Elizabeth had two more daughters, Mary and Elizabeth, during these four years.

Bligh commanded the *Lynx*, then the *Cambrian* and then, in 1787, the *Britannia*. It was in the *Britannia* that he took on as a volunteer the young midshipman Fletcher Christian, following recommendations from Captain Traubman and persuasion from Christian himself. Although Bligh had his establishment completed and had declined to take Christian as a Master's Mate, according to his brother, Edward, Fletcher wrote to Bligh with the following offer: 'Wages were no object, he only wished to learn his profession, and if Captain Bligh would permit him to mess with the gentlemen, he would readily enter his ship as a foremast man, until there was a vacancy among the officers. "We midshipmen are gentlemen, we never pull on a rope; I should be glad to go one voyage in that situation, for there may be occasions when officers may be called upon to do the duties of a common man".'[8] Christian made at least two voyages with Bligh to the West Indies and they became close friends.

On the last voyage of the *Britannia*, Bligh was unhappy about the value of the cargo he had brought across for Campbell and wrote apologising for it: 'It is the best that could be done and I have been as attentive as possible in all respects.'[9] A few days later he arrived home to find some good news awaiting him: under the patronage of Sir Joseph Banks, he had been appointed to command an expedition to the South Seas.

The Government had decided upon an expedition to Tahiti to procure

---

[7] Bligh carried on a life-long correspondence with Duncan Campbell. Many of the letters are extant in the Mitchell Library, Sydney. See Letters, Bligh to Campbell, 2/4/1782-10/11/1805, Bligh Correspondence, Safe 1/40; Letters, Campbell to Bligh, ML MS A3228-9, Duncan Campbell Letter Books. Bligh had been stationed for three years in the West Indies, 1771-1774, which probably influenced Campbell to employ him; PRO Adm. 51/204.

[8] *See* Edward Christian, 'Appendix', 1794, p. 77.

[9] Quoted in Mackaness, 1951, p. 32.

breadfruit plants for transport to the West Indies. The breadfruit was a Pacific island plant that explorers had reported on over the years. The islanders ate it regularly and it was the closest thing to bread that Europeans had discovered in the Pacific communities. The seamen became accustomed to it when they made landfall there and, as it grew in abundance without cultivation and was easy to cook, it attracted the attention of plantation owners in the West Indies as a possible food for slaves. In 1786 Hinton East, a West Indian planter, was in Britain lobbying Sir Joseph Banks, who soon became convinced of the case. He had been under pressure from planters in the West Indies for some years to persuade the Government to undertake the scheme. The idea had the backing of the scientific community and of commerce, a powerful combination; it was also the right time for it politically, as British attention shifted from the losses in America to the possibilities of the Pacific. Sir Joseph put it to King George III at one of their meetings, and the King made the necessary orders for a ship to be assigned to the task. Sir Joseph, having been a prominent member of Cook's expedition to Tahiti, and being an eminent botanist and President of the Royal Society, was placed in charge of the arrangements for the expedition, which included the appointment of the commander. It would be a plum job for a young officer. The small size of the proposed ship precluded sending an established Post Captain, but the nature of the expedition would make it attractive to an unemployed Lieutenant. A voyage lasting two years or more, with the opportunity of discoveries, would mean almost certain promotion.

Why was Bligh selected? Since the demands for the expedition were coming from the West Indies, and since Bligh had been sailing to and from the West Indies for the previous four years, meeting planters, Government officials and Admiralty personnel, his name was no doubt mentioned in discussions. He also knew Tahiti, having been there with Captain Cook, and he had sailed the greater part of the route the ship would take. The other officers on Cook's voyages were either dead, or too senior, or they were engaged in other work. Bligh's navigational skills were fairly well known among his contemporaries, and he was junior enough to regard the voyage as a prize. Perhaps for these reasons, the Admiralty agreed to Sir Joseph's recommendation. It had been a possibility since May,[10] but Bligh only received the news in August, a few days before the official confirmation of his appointment. He wrote immediately to Sir Joseph Banks to thank him:[11]

August 6, 1787

Sir,

I arrived yesterday from Jamaica and should have instantly paid my respects to you had not Mr Campbell told me you were not to return from the country until Thursday. I have heard the flattering news of your great

[10] We can deduce this from a letter written by Duncan Campbell to his cousin in Jamaica, dated 2 May 1787, in which he refers to Bligh: 'I wish him home soon, as thereby he may stand a chance of employment in his own line, but of this more by and by', quoted in Mackaness, 1951, p. 37.

[11] Quoted in Mackaness, 1951, p. 37.

goodness to me, intending to honour me with the command of the vessel which you propose to go to the South Seas, for which, after offering you my most grateful thanks, I can only assure you I shall endeavour, and I hope succeed, in deserving such a trust. I await your commands, and am, with the sincerest respect, Sir, your much obliged and very Hmble Servant,

Wm Bligh

4

His Majesty's Armed Vessel Bounty

On 5 May 1787 Lord Sydney, a Principal Secretary of State, wrote on behalf of King George III to the Lords Commissioners of the Admiralty and officially informed them of the King's intentions about a South Sea voyage for breadfruit. I shall quote this letter at length because it is important to see what the Admiralty's orders were and what the Government had in mind for the expedition.

The Merchants and Planters interested in His Majesty's West India Possessions have represented that the Introduction of the Bread Fruit Tree into the Islands in those Seas to constitute an Article of Food would be very essential Benefit to the Inhabitants, and have humbly solicited that Measures may be taken for procuring some Trees of that Description from the place of their present Growth, to be transplanted in the said Islands.

His Majesty desirous at all Times to promote the Interests of so respectable a Body of his Subjects, especially in an Instance which promises general Advantage, has thought fit that Measures should immediately be taken for the procuring some Bread Fruit Trees and for conveying them to the said West India Islands, and I am in Consequence to signify to your Lordships His Majesty's Command that you do cause a Vessel of proper Class to be stored and victualled for this Service, and to be fitted with proper Conveniences for the Preservation of as many of the said Trees as from her Size can be taken on Board, giving the command of her to some able and discreet Officer, and when she shall be ready for sea, your Lordships are to direct the said Officer to proceed in her to the Society Islands, situated in the Southern Ocean in the Latitude about 18 Degrees South and Longitude about 210 Degrees East from Greenwich, where according to the accounts which are given by the late Captain Cook, and Persons who accompanied him during his Voyages, the Bread Fruit Tree is to be found in the most luxuriant state.

It is proposed that the Vessel which your Lordships are to dispatch upon this Service should proceed round Cape Horn and after she shall have arrived at the Society Islands and as many Trees and plants have been taken on Board as may be thought necessary, to proceed from thence through Endeavour Streights (which separate New Holland from New Guinea) to Princes Island in the Streight of Sunda, or if it should happen to be more convenient, to pass on the East Side of Java, to some port on the North side of that Island, where any Bread Fruit Trees which may have been injured or have died may be replaced by Mangosteens, Duriens, Jacks, Nancas, Lansas, and in short all the fine fruits of that

Quarter, as well as the Rice Plant which grows upon dry Land. From
Princes Island she should proceed round the Cape of Good Hope to the
West Indies, calling on her way thither at any Places which may be
thought necessary, and deposit one half of her Cargo at His Majesty's
Botanical Garden at St Vincent for the Benefit of the Windward Islands,
and from thence to carry the other half down to Jamaica.

As from Analogy it appears that the Monsoons prevail in the Seas
between New Holland and New Guinea, the easterly Winds will commence
in March or April. It is therefore judged proper that the Vessel should sail
from hence in the month of September next.

Mr David Nelson and Mr William Brown, Gardeners by Profession,
have from their Knowledge of Trees and Plants been hired for the Purpose
of selecting such as appear to be of a proper Species and Size and it is His
Majesty's Pleasure that your Lordships do order those Persons to be
received on board the said Vessel and to be borne for Wages and Victuals
during the Voyage.

I shall shortly transmit to your Lordships a List of such Articles of
Merchandize and Trinkets as it is supposed will be wanted to satisfy the
Natives of the South Sea Islands for such Trees and Plants as may be
obtained from them with an Account of the number of Ducats which will
be necessary to pay for such Trees and Plants as may be purchased from
the Inhabitants of Java, in order that the same may be procured and put
on Board the Vessel for the purpose above mentioned. I shall also forward
to your Lordships for your Information a copy of the Instructions which
will be prepared for guidance of the Gardeners, as well in procuring the
said Trees and Plants, as in the Management of them after they are put on
Board, and your Lordships will give Directions that the Officers and Crew
do afford the said Gardeners every possible aid and Assistance not only in
Collecting of the said Trees and Plants, at the Places before mentioned,
but for their Preservation during their Conveyance to the West Indies.[1]

The *Bounty* voyage was unambiguously a botanical 'collect and carry'
mission. The Admiralty had some experience of combined expeditions of this
kind, such as the voyage of H.M.S. *Paramour*, commanded by a civilian,
Halley (the Astronomer Royal), where discipline had become a serious
problem.[2] After this the Admiralty had insisted that one of their own
commanders should be in complete charge of such expeditions, as with, for
example, the voyages of Captain Cook. For this exercise, to collect plants,
there was no question of anyone but their own commander having complete
control, and the somewhat careless direction that the navy should give 'aid
and assistance' to the gardeners was not likely to win the wholehearted
enthusiasm of the Lords Commissioners. This may explain why the
preparation and planning of the expedition, though punctual in response to
the King's orders, also showed a lack of consideration of its requirements.

Within a week of receiving Lord Sydney's letter the Lords Commissioners,

---

Quoted in Knight, 1936, pp. 183ff. Much of the information in this chapter comes from
Knight's article which uses original sources and is one of the foundations of much of the *Bounty*
story, though not always acknowledged by those who have used it.

[2] *See* Campbell, 1936, p. 46.

having no suitable vessel available, had issued instructions to purchase a vessel of not more than 250 ·tons. The Navy Board opened tenders for purchase of a ship, and requested that the various offerings should be inspected by a person who was to sail on the ship, as well as by their own officials. This was a sensible suggestion. In the event, however, it was Sir Joseph Banks and David Nelson, the gardener assigned to sail on the voyage, who inspected the short list of two vessels, the *Bethia* and the *Harriet*, the other vessels having been rejected by the inspectors. This incident underlines the predominantly botanical aspect of the voyage; the naval inspectors would certify the ship's seaworthiness and value, and the botanical interest could remark on its capacity for carrying plants, but the commander was the only person competent to judge its suitability for a voyage of the length proposed. Bligh's appointment was not yet confirmed, however, and his views were not available until a great deal of expense had been undertaken and the purchase decision was irrevocable.

On 23 May 1787, the Deptford Yard officers reported on the value of the *Bethia* and estimated it at £1820 12s. 8d. against the price of £2600 that the owners[3] were asking. A negotiated price of £1950 with the approval of Sir Joseph Banks was agreed, and the *Bethia* passed into the Navy's hands and was moved into Deptford Dock for extensive alterations and fitting out. The Admiralty ordered that the wooden sheathing be replaced with copper (to combat the notorious pest *Terado navalis*) and also gave directions as to the masts and rigging, it being necessary to shorten the sail area for a voyage in the South Seas. They also asked for the opinion of the Deptford officers on the number of men that the ship could accommodate. On 6 June, the reply was sent that the ship would accommodate 20 men in addition to the officers. On 8 June, the Admiralty informed the Navy Board that the *Bethia* was to be listed 'as an Armed Vessel by the name of the *Bounty*' and was to have an establishment of 45 men – 25 A.B.s in addition to the officers.

On 25 June, Deptford reported to the Navy Board on the work in progress and the proposals of Sir Joseph Banks to arrange accommodation for the plants. The *Bounty* was ready for service on 14 August. Bligh's appointment as commander was confirmed on 16 August 1787. When Sir Joseph Banks visited the ship at Deptford and met Bligh, he thought him a 'very deserving man'; but he was somewhat put out to find that 'he knew he was to go to the S. Seas & some other places but he knew little or nothing of the object of his voyage had no Idea of going to the East Indies or to the West Indies in short he was about to sail the latter end of this month with little or no information or knowledge of the Object of his Voyage'. In the same letter to Sir George Yonge he offered the advice: 'I will not suppose but that Mr Nelson the Gardiner may have had Full instructions but you will excuse me for saying that unless you do

---

[3] Welbank, Shairp and Company, the owners, were long established traders in hemp; *see* Pool, 1966, p. 99. Some authors (e.g. Mackaness, 1951, p. 37) have suggested that the *Bethia* originally · belonged to Duncan Campbell, but the documentation to support this is not given. The suggestion may be due to a confusion, in that Duncan Campbell did tender one of his ships, the *Lynx* (the first ship Bligh commanded for Campbell in 1783), but it was rejected by the inspectors. It was much bigger than the *Bounty*, weighing 300 tons; *see* Knight, 1936, p. 185.

interest the Captain himself or instruct him & inspire him with the spirit of the undertaking it is to very little purpose the vessel would sail.'[4]

Bligh must have known something about the voyage, if only from Duncan Campbell, from conversation with David Nelson, and from observing the alterations of the main cabin to take the plants. But he seems to have chosen to appear ignorant until he was informed officially by his superiors. He would naturally have been polite to his new patron the first time they met, waiting for Banks to give information rather than volunteering the port gossip himself; but reading between the lines of Banks' letter, there is a hint that Bligh's ignorance about the voyage was connected with the Admiralty's lack of interest in the voyage. They were carrying out the King's instructions to the letter but not the spirit. The navy had been ordered to provide a ship and a commander and they did just that, without officially informing the Captain of the purpose of the voyage. Banks discovered this state of affairs by accident. He was annoyed, but pleased with the willingness of Lieutenant Bligh to become enthusiastic about the enterprise. Banks' letter continues:

> I had above an hours discourse with him, he enterd into the plan with Spirit was delighted with the Idea of rendering such service to his Country & mankind but declared if it had not been for my visit he never should have known any thing of it … I have promised him extracts from all my official papers on the subject he enters into it with pleasure has even begd to be assisted in studying the subject.

The relationship that Bligh built with Banks lasted his entire life, and Banks never failed as a friend and sponsor. That bond was established from this first meeting.

Due to the parsimony of the Navy Board and the ignorance of the botanists, an extremely small ship had been foisted on Bligh. The *Bounty* weighed only about 215 tons; in comparison, among Cook's ships the *Endeavour* weighed 368 tons, the *Adventure* 336 tons, and the *Resolution* 462 tons. In fact the *Bethia* had been the lightest of the ships offered to the navy. It was about 91 feet long, 11 feet 4 inches deep in the hold, and 24 feet 4 inches wide. On the bowsprit was the inevitable figure, in this case a woman in riding habit. But the major feature was its smallness, whose consequences were twofold. It meant, first, that the ship's company lived on top of one another even more than usual, and secondly that the ship's complement was reduced below the minimum needed for such a voyage; in particular the officer structure was diluted and no marines could be carried. The ship was in effect to be overcrowded and at the same time undermanned.

Although the Admiralty had chosen a small ship and obviously did not think the voyage very important, it spent a great deal of money converting the ship. The total cost of the alterations was £4456, more than twice the cost

---

[4] Sir Joseph Banks to Sir George Yonge, 7 September 1787, in Banks Papers, Brabourne Collection, Vol. 5, ML A78-4. Unless otherwise noted, letters to and from Banks quoted here are from this collection. Partially quoted in Mackaness, 1951, p. 39.

1. Portrait of William Bligh by J. Smart.

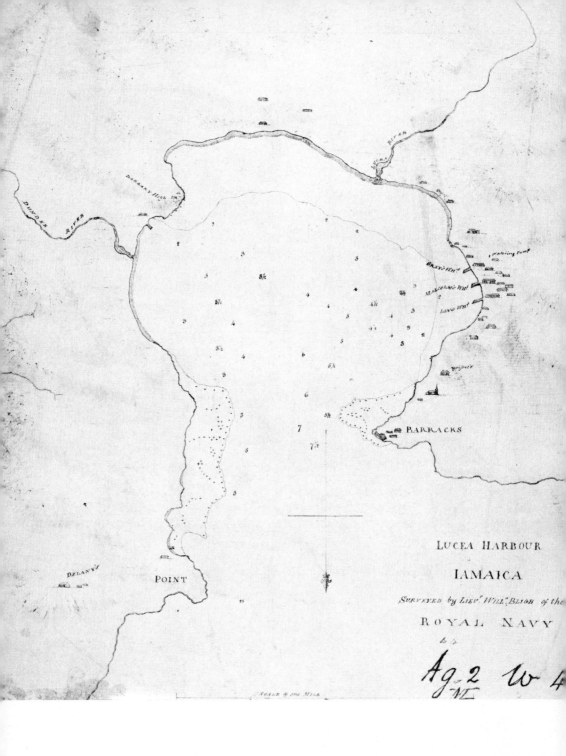

2. Bligh's chart of Lucea harbour. See p. 4, n. 9 for the possible date of this chart.

of purchase.[5] The unreasonableness of all this did not escape attention. It appears to have been hotly debated between the principals involved in the preparation, but in spite of representations to the Admiralty little or nothing could be done.

In September Bligh wrote to Lord Selkirk on the subject of manning, and Lord Selkirk took up his points with Sir Joseph Banks. He wrote to Banks:

> ... an officer of the navy ... happens to be here just now on a visit; who tells me that this Establishment of Blighs vessel is that of a Cutter & says it is highly improper for so long a voyage; only 24 Able Seamen & 21 of all others, without a Lieutenant, or any Marines, with only a Surgeon without a surgeons Mate, which arises from it being considered as a Cutter, whereas in a Sloop of War they have besides Lieut a Surgeon & his Mate, tho they be but on the Channel Service, where if a Surgeon dies, they can have help at every Port but if Blighs Surgeon meets with any accident they must wait all Medical assistance God knows how long ... And for this Establishment of a Cutter poor Bligh must be deprived of his preferment, for it seems a Lieut. cannot command a Sloop, & a Master & Commander is above taking command of a Cutter.[6]

Bligh was anxious to be promoted before sailing. He was being sent away on a long voyage on the promise of Lord Howe that he would be promoted on his return, but Lord Howe might not be in a position two years later to fulfil that promise. And his anxiety was not entirely from selfish motives; he could see, from the size of the *Bounty* and its establishment, the problems that might arise on a two-year voyage. He was the only commissioned officer on board, the rest being warrant officers and midshipmen. He had no marines to maintain discipline. He felt in these circumstances that he should be made Post Captain and (as would be automatic if this happened) that a Lieutenant should be appointed below him. This would extend the officer structure and partly make up for the deficiencies in the ship and its establishment. Earlier in the same letter to Banks, Lord Selkirk had written:

> But I was sorry to find by it, that Mr Bligh himself is but very indifferently used, or rather realy ill used: for he seems to have lost hopes of getting any preferment at going out, & God knows who may be at the head of the Admiralty at his return. It would have been scrimply Justice to him, to have made him Master & Commander before sailing; nay considering that he was, I believe, the only person that was not in some way or other preferd at their return, of all who went out with Capt. Cook, it would be no unreasonable thing to make him Post Captain now: more especially as Ld How made Captain Hunter Post when he went out lately to Botany Bay with Commodore Phillips. Hunter & Bligh were in very similar situations, they had both been Masters & both were refused by Sandwich to be made Lieutenants and it happend that both of them were made Acting

---

[5] Knight, 1936, p. 193.
[6] Lord Selkirk to Sir Joseph Banks, 14 September 1787.

Lieutenants by Keith Stewart & afterwards confirmed not with
Sandwiches goodwill.

Bligh persisted in his quest to be made Post Captain, or failing that Master
and Commander. A month after Lord Selkirk's letter to Banks, Bligh wrote
to Banks on the same subject:

> Pray Sir, could I not hope that my Lord Howe as promotion would take
> place, might be prevailed on to give me rank as Master & Commander,
> considering that I was going out of the immediate chance of promotion,
> and the great advantage of being in the beginning of a War. I have taken
> the liberty to suggest this matter to you as you are not immediately on the
> spot, and to ask your opinion if you thought any thing might be done. I have
> been constantly in service for 18 years and I hope that may have some
> weight with his Lordship ... As you have already been so great a Friend to
> me I thought I might just mention this circumstance.[7]

Throughout November and December 1787, Bligh's letters to his patron
invariably return to this question; but the eighteenth-century system of
interest failed him on this point. Banks could not get him what he wanted
and he had to reconcile himself to the situation, which he did with a good
grace.[8]

Although small, the *Bounty* was an armed vessel and therefore carried some
small armament. Four four-pounders and ten swivel guns were placed on her
with ordnance sufficient for 'Foreign Service' under the charge of a Master
Gunner. To assist in maintaining these weapons the establishment had been
altered to put an armourer on board, making one seaman the less. The rest of
the ship's equipment included three boats, which the Navy Board had
ordered to be built at Deptford, namely a launch of 20 feet, a cutter of 18 feet
and a jolly-boat of 16 feet. This was standard equipment for a vessel on this
kind of mission. However, Deptford was too busy at the time to make the
boats, so the order was placed with John Burr, a boat contractor, to build the
launch, and the other two boats were ordered from the Navy office at Deal.
These were presumably delivered before Bligh was appointed, as the order
was placed in June with a delivery time of two weeks. Bligh, for an unknown
reason, asked the Navy Board to exchange the 20-foot launch for a larger one
23 feet long, which would hold four more men. After the mutiny Bligh was to
travel with 17 companions for 3,900 miles in this launch.[9]

On 20 August the first appointments of warrant officers were made; first
the Master, John Fryer, who was the same age as Bligh. He had been a
Master in the navy since 1781 (in H.M.S. *Camel*) and had worked his way to
the grade of 3rd Rate.[10] He never rose above Master, though this did not

[7] Bligh to Sir Joseph Banks, 3 October 1787.

[8] Bligh to Sir Joseph Banks, 5 November 1787; 6 December 1787; 10 December 1787; 12
December 1787.

[9] *See* Knight, 1936, pp. 190-1, 192.

[10] A summary of John Fryer's career is given in Rutter (ed.), 1934, Introduction. For the
duties of a Master *see* Lewis, 1939, pp. 226-30; also Masefield, 1971, Chapter III. Details of the

prevent him aspiring to a Lieutenant's commission. To him, this voyage was a great (and perhaps last) opportunity of promotion. The other warrant officer appointed on this day was Thomas Huggan, the Surgeon, who turned out to be a drunkard. Probably somebody in the Admiralty wanted to get rid of Huggan and regarded the *Bounty* as the best place for him, which would explain his early appointment. Bligh tried to get him removed, but failed; instead he asked for an Assistant Surgeon, which he eventually got just before the ship sailed, though he had to be entered on the books as an A.B., again making one seaman the less.

With the two warrant officers appointed on 20 August there were two A.B.s. The first was William Brown, who came recommended by Sir Joseph Banks. Bligh complained later when he was taken out of the Bounty on Lord Howe's order, because he was 'the best uncommission'd officer I had'.[11] Brown was sent to the *Ariel*. The other appointee was Thomas Hayward, aged 20, from Hackney. He came in as A.B., but he must have had some interest because he moved up to midshipman on 1 December 1787. He turned out later to be lazy and untrustworthy. So far Bligh was not getting the best and brightest of the navy for his mission.

A week later, 27 August, the next batch of appointments was made. William Cole, Boatswain, came from the *Alecto* fireship, and William Peckover, Gunner, came from the *Warspite* receiving ship. He had sailed on all three of Captain Cook's voyages and knew Bligh. He knew Tahiti from Cook's visits, and is reported to have been fairly fluent in the language. His usefulness apart from his naval capacities as a gunner made him an excellent choice. William Purcell, Carpenter, on the other hand, was a disastrous acquisition. He was to become the bane of Bligh's life on the *Bounty*, as he married insubordination with sheer bloody-mindedness, and in his position as warrant officer was protected from being disciplined by the Captain. Lawrence Lebogue, Sailmaker, came with Bligh from the *Britannia*; he was 40 years old and very loyal to Bligh.

Two A.B.s were appointed, Henry Hillbrant from Hanover and Michael Portman from Birmingham. Hillbrant was 24. Portman was on the *Bounty* for two months and was discharged on 18 November at Deptford. John Samuel, from Edinburgh, aged 26, was appointed Clerk; Bligh had a high regard for him and later publicly acknowledged his debt to him. The last person appointed in this group was George Stewart from the Orkneys, aged 21. Bligh had met his family when the *Resolution* stopped there on the way back from Cook's third voyage. Bligh was later to write that because of the reception he had received from Stewart's family in 1780 he would 'gladly have taken him with me; but, independent of his recommendation, he was a seaman, and had always borne a good character'.[12] He came onto the books as a midshipman but on 30 November was re-rated A.B. This did not mean

---

dates of appointments, ages and places of origin of the crew come from the *Bounty*'s muster and pay books, quoted in Smith, 1936, p. 212a.
  [11] Bligh to Sir Joseph Banks, 5 November 1787.
  [12] Bligh, 1792 (1965), p. 121.

he was dis-rated, for he kept his position as a Young Gentleman, as was the custom of the day. It was simply an adjustment to the ship's books; the extra midshipmen above the allowance of the establishment were rated A.B. This reduced the number of effective A.B.s yet again, because Young Gentlemen did not 'pull on a rope', as Christian put it, so there were fewer seamen to carry out the ship's duties.

The last of the enlistments which were made on 27 August was that of Peter Heywood, aged 15, from Douglas in the Isle of Man. The Heywood family were close friends of the Bethams, and it was through this connection that Bligh was persuaded by his father-in-law to take Heywood with him. Richard Betham, Elizabeth's father, wrote to Bligh in the following terms:

> I'm much obliged to you for your attention to young Heywood, and getting him a berth on board the vessel. He is an ingenious young Lad and has always been a favourite of mine and indeed everybody here. And indeed the reason of my insisting so strenuously upon his going the voyage with you is that after I had mentioned the matter to Mrs Bligh, his family have fallen into a great deal of distress on account of their father's losing the Duke of Atholl's business. And I thought it would not appear well in me to drop this matter, if it could possibly be done without any prejudice to you; as this would seem deserting them in their adversity; and I found they would regard it as a great disappointment. I hope he will be of some service to you, as far as he is able, in writing or looking after any necessary matters under your charge.[13]

By these earnest entreaties, Bligh was persuaded to take on board a young boy with no experience of the sea or ships, too young to be much use as a seaman, too inexperienced for responsibility. It was magnanimous to do so with the ship already undermanned with experienced and useful seamen. Heywood stayed with Bligh's family while the *Bounty* was fitting out; Bligh took charge of him and let him accompany him to the ship and about the ship's business. Heywood came on the *Bounty* as an A.B. and moved up to midshipman on October 23.

Two important posts were filled on 29 August. William Elphinston from Edinburgh became Master's Mate. He was 36 years old. Peter Linkletter, from Shetland, became Quartermaster. He was 30. Elphinston was old for the post he held; he was older than both Bligh and Fryer. The Mate's job was to assist the Master in the more routine tasks such as heaving the log, watching the rate of the chronometer, attending the galley to stop 'wrangling', checking on the crew's work to maintain cleanliness. Elphinston settled into his post as Master's Mate and probably would have remained one for the rest of his sea time. Linkletter, the Quartermaster, was young for the job. This was normally given to an older man because the duties, while responsible, did not require a lot of exertion. His role was to oversee the specialised work of others such as the helmsman, the work of stowage, the ringing of the ship's bell, and the weighing out of provisions by the purser.[14]

---

[13] Quoted in Mackaness, 1951, p. 42.
[14] Descriptions of tasks taken from Masefield, 1971, Chapter IV.

Here then were two other 'misfits', reflecting the shortage of proven men available to Bligh.

In the batch signed on 29 August came several A.B.s. The first ones were Thomas Hall, aged 38, from Durham, John Charlton, aged 23, from Sunderland, and John Cooper, aged 28, from Suffolk. Hall became the *Bounty*'s cook and the other two men went absent, Cooper within a week at Deptford and Charlton in November at Portsmouth. This was to happen several times before the *Bounty* finally got away and we can assume that as the nature of the voyage became obvious – though the men were not officially told where they were going until the *Bounty* was well into the voyage – some men changed their minds about the prospect of a long absence from home, especially as the general mobilisation of the fleet commenced in September in anticipation of war, creating many other opportunities for service nearer home.

Four more A.B.s signed on a couple of days later. Among these was Isaac Martin, from Philadelphia in America and aged 30. The three others changed their minds and left the ship, two a month later when she was still at Deptford, and one two months later at Portsmouth. Joseph Coleman joined the ship as Armourer; as we saw the Admiralty had decided not to carry one, but changed its plan. He was from Guildford and aged 36.

The recruitment of the A.B.s continued into September, by now competing with a general mobilisation. On 7 September Charles Churchill, 28, from Manchester joined the ship, and was made Ship's Corporal, which task included assisting in the maintenance of order among the crew – a singularly inappropriate choice in this case, as Churchill was one of the worst troublemakers on the voyage. With him Richard Skinner, 22, from Tunbridge Wells and Alexander Smith from London were recruited. Smith, or Adams as he came to be known, was 20. Samuel Sutton, 28, from Hull came on board with these men as an A.B. but he deserted four weeks later at Deptford.

Lord Selkirk's son, the Hon. Dunbar Douglas, was also signed on as an A.B. and efforts were made by Lord Selkirk to get his son's tutor, Mr Lockhead, taken on board as well! Bligh, while solicitous of the favours that Selkirk could do for him, was in no mood to dilute his crew even more with inexperienced men, and he politely but firmly refused to consider him, using Lord Howe's establishment for the ship as the excuse.[15] Whether this played any part in changing the mind of the Hon. Dunbar Douglas we do not know, but within a month he had been discharged into H.M.S. *Royal Sovereign*. Naturally there would have been no question of Douglas working as an A.B. if he had sailed with the *Bounty*: he would have been a Young Gentleman.

Along with Douglas came Fletcher Christian, 22, from Cockermouth in Cumberland. He was rated Master's Mate and in view of his youth it was clear that he was regarded as someone with a future in the navy. He had, of course, sailed as a midshipman before he joined Bligh in the *Britannia*. This

---

[15] *See* Lord Howe to Sir Joseph Banks, 22 September 1787: 'Application had been made to obtain admission for the Client of Lord Selkirk. But Lieut Bligh had expressed his inability to make room for him, in terms of very laudible civility; and his exceptions were entirely approved.'

voyage would assure him of a Lieutenant's commission. He had left the *Britannia* on its last voyage with Bligh in August. His friendship with Bligh from the two voyages they had completed to the West Indies assured him of consideration for the *Bounty*, and his naval service made this a simple matter of the commander's preference as far as the Admiralty was concerned. Thus from a career point of view he was indebted to Bligh; this is an example of the kind of help that Captains could give to their friends.

The batch of recruits appointed on 7 September was the largest to join the *Bounty* in one day. Probably the most important of the men who came on board was James Morrison, 27, from London, rated Boatswain's Mate. His job was to work for William Cole, the Boatswain. It was an exacting job in many ways. His charge was directed towards the ship's rigging. It had a supervisory element in it, checking on the sailmaker and on the condition of the sails in the ship's locker. Another of the duties of the Boatswain's Mate was conducting punishments of the crew. Morrison must have been an above average seaman to get appointed to this post; his Journals show that he had a considerable talent for description and exposition, though often wasted in invective and general moaning. With Morrison came Thomas McIntosh, Carpenter's Mate, from North Shields, and John Mills, Gunner's Mate, from Aberdeen.

Robert Tinkler, 17, rated A.B., came on the recommendation of the Master, Mr. Fryer; he was his brother-in-law. Bligh would hardly refuse the Master's request in this respect. Though he was an A.B. he was considered a Young Gentleman in the making and messed with the midshipmen; indeed, after the mutiny, Tinkler went on to become a Commander in the navy. Other A.B.s were Thomas Burkitt, 25, from Bath; John Millward, 21, from Plymouth; John Sumner, 22, from Liverpool; and John Williams, 26, from Stepney. Five others joined as A.B.s in this batch but jumped ship before she sailed.

John Hallet came aboard as the second midshipman, recommended by Bligh's wife as the brother of a friend. He was 15, from London, and combined loyalty to Bligh with a capacity for sleeping on the watch. Bligh asked John Norton to join as a Quartermaster, having known him in the merchant service, possibly in the *Britannia*. He was appointed on 13 September and joined the ship a month later on 13 October. He was 34 and came from Liverpool.

Four more men arrived on 23 October: William Musprat, 27, from Maidenhead, Matthew Thompson, 37, from the Isle, of Wight, Luke Dods, 20, from London (another man who left the *Bounty* at Deptford) and Edward Young. Edward Young was 21 and came from St. Kitts in the West Indies. He was the nephew of Sir George Young. He was rated A.B. but was another of the Young Gentlemen. The fact that very little is known about him, and that his activities on the *Bounty* did not warrant a mention in the Log, has inspired some people to attribute to him a special, and sinister, role in the mutiny.[16]

[16] *See* Darby, 1965, 1966; Du Rietz, 1966.

During October other men joined the ship, some to replace those who had left, and others to complete the complement. James Valentine, 28, from Montrose, was among these. Another Scotsman came on board, Alexander Tyre, 23, from Arbroath, but he jumped ship at Deal within four weeks. George Simpson, 27, from Kendal, Westmorland, came as an A.B. but was promoted to Quartermaster's Mate a few days later.

Robert Lamb, 21, from London, joined as an A.B. on 8 October and young Thomas Ellison, aged 19, from Deptford, a former crew member of the *Britannia*, joined with him. The last few men came aboard during October: John Smith, A.B., 36, from Stirling, and Charles Norman of Portsmouth, were among the late entrants; so was Michael Byrne of Kilkenny, rated as A.B. but in fact so nearly blind as to be of little use. He was a fiddle player and Bligh recruited him to keep the men exercised by regular dancing sessions. The *Bounty* was still short of A.B.s, so four men were sent from the *Triumph*, two as volunteers and two as pressed men. The two pressed men, John McTargett and Alexander Johnston (presumably Scotsmen), both made off on 5 December in Portsmouth. The last man to join the ship was Thomas Daniel Ledward, rated A.B. but taken on as Assistant Surgeon in view of the nature of the voyage and the incapacity of Huggan. This completed the ship's company. The final list was as follows:[17]

		Age
Lieutenant	William Bligh	33
Master	John Fryer	33
Boatswain	William Cole	
Gunner	William Peckover	
Carpenter	William Purcell	
Surgeon	Thomas Huggan	
Surgeon's Mate	*Thomas Ledward	
Master's Mate	William Elphinston	36
Master's Mate	Fletcher Christian	22
Midshipman	John Hallet	15
Midshipman	Peter Heywood	15
Midshipman	Thomas Hayward	20
Midshipman	*Edward Young	21
Midshipman	*George Stewart	21
Midshipman	*Robert Tinkler	17
Quartermaster	John Norton	34
Quartermaster	Peter Linkletter	30
Quartermaster's Mate	George Simpson	27
Boatswain's Mate	James Morrison	27
Gunner's Mate	John Mills	39
Carpenter's Mate	Charles Norman	24
	Thomas McIntosh	25
Sailmaker	Lawrence Lebogue	40

[17] Positions and personnel are taken from composite sources; *see* Mackaness, 1951, pp. 39-40; Bligh, 1792 (1965), pp. 120-1.

Armourer	Joseph Coleman	36
Corporal	Charles Churchill	28
Cooper	*Henry Hillbrant	24
Steward	*William Musprat	27
Clerk	John Samuel	26
Cook	*Thomas Hall	38
Commander's Cook	*John Smith	36
Butcher	*Robert Lamb	21
A.B.s	Richard Skinner	22
	Alexander Smith	20
	Thomas Burkitt	25
	John Millward	21
	John Williams	26
	John Sumner	22
	Matthew Thompson	37
	James Valentine	28
	Michael Byrne	26
	William McCoy	23
	Matthew Quintal	21
	Isaac Martin	30
	Thomas Ellison	19
Gardener	David Nelson	
Assistant	William Brown	25

The names with an asterisk are those men who were rated as A.B. although they were either Young Gentlemen, or were assigned tasks by Bligh which meant they did not actually work as A.B.s. In the end, instead of the 25 A.B.s the Admiralty had allowed for in its Establishment, there were only 13 to see to the actual working of the *Bounty*, and one of these was a nearly-blind Irish fiddler.

Nineteen men assigned to the *Bounty* did not sail with her; three were transferred to other ships, and the other sixteen 'ran'. Their replacements included six of the eventual mutineers, three of whom – Young, Quintal and McCoy – were to become hardliners who went on to Pitcairn. The whole *Bounty* episode might very well have different if the preparatory stages at Deptford and Portsmouth had not been so long and less men had deserted. Desertion before a long voyage was quite common; for instance, during the preparations for Cook's third voyage sixty men deserted![18]

This then was His Majesty's Ship *Bounty*, small, overcrowded and undermanned, with a crew that in many ways was a second or third choice enlistment. Where it did not recruit incompetence it recruited potential dissent. Bligh's command structure was fragile, his support almost non-existent. He made many attempts to alter the conditions laid down by the Admiralty for the prosecution of the voyage, but with one or two exceptions his recommendations failed. He was left to get on with it.

[18] Beaglehole, 1974, p. 503.

5

Deptford to Cape Horn

The *Bounty* left Deptford on 9 October and after a stop at Long Reach made
for Spithead, which it reached on 4 November 1787. Bligh had had the
opportunity to observe his men under the difficult conditions of the passage
down the channel – the weather almost drove him onto the French coast –
and he set down his views in letters to Sir Joseph Banks and Duncan
Campbell. Of the Master, John Fryer, he wrote that he was 'a very good man
and gives me every satisfaction'. He was less complimentary about Huggan,
the Surgeon, who while 'a very capable man' was 'unfit for the Voyage' owing
to his 'indolence and corpulency'. On the whole, however, he thought it
would not be long before he got the crew in 'very good order'.[1]

If Bligh had been expecting a speedy departure from Spithead he was to be
disappointed. The Admiralty had not yet sent Bligh's final orders to Lord
Hood at Spithead, and without them he could not sail, although the weather
for the next three weeks was near perfect for getting down the Channel and
into the Atlantic. Good weather was followed by bad, and every day lost was
adding unnecessary difficulties to the voyage. The final sailing orders arrived
on 24 November and after paying the men two months' wages in advance
Bligh attempted a quick dash down the Channel; but he was driven back to
Spithead on 3 December. He tried again on 6 December but was again
beaten back by the weather. By this time he was fuming at the bureaucrats
who had kept him idle while the ideal weather prevailed. On December 10,
after his two attempts to get away, he wrote to Duncan Campbell:

> If there is any punishment that ought to be inflicted on a set of Men for
> neglect, I am sure it ought on the Admiralty for my three weeks detention
> at this place during a fine fair wind which carried all outward bound ships
> clear of the Channel but me, who wanted it most. This has made my task
> a very arduous one indeed for to get round Cape Horn at the time I shall
> be there I know not how to promise myself any success & yet I must do
> it if the ship will stand it at all or I suppose my character will be at stake.
> Had Lord Howe sweetned this difficult task by giving me promotion I
> should have been satisfied ... The hardship I make known I lay under is,

---

[1] Bligh to Sir Joseph Banks, 5 November 1787. Banks made a note on Bligh's letter stating
that he offered his interest (which would guarantee the appointment) to any Surgeon's Mate
who would go as Able Seaman with Bligh. But in another letter to Banks (November 1787)
Bligh noted: 'I had got a Person to go out Surgeons Mate & to be rated Ab but Adl Drake would
not discharge him into my Ship and I am going without one.' He eventually got Ledward out of
the *Triumph* from Captain Bertie; *see* Bligh to Banks, 5 December 1787.

that they took me from a state of affluence from your employ with an
income five hundred a year to that of Lieuts pay 4/- Pr Day to perform a
Voyage which few were acquainted with sufficiently to insure it any degree
of success.[2]

On 17 December he wrote to Sir Joseph Banks for advice on whether to apply
for discretionary orders in case it proved impossible to get round Cape Horn.
His original orders made it mandatory to approach Tahiti from the Horn
and return via the Cape of Good Hope. This was the quickest way there but,
with the season so far advanced, Bligh was concerned that the voyage should
not end prematurely in impossible waters at the Horn. He needed advice on
this point before he made an approach in case it caused trouble for him.[3]

Banks contacted Lord Howe on Bligh's behalf and it was agreed that Bligh
should be allowed discretion between the Horn and the Cape. Banks advised
Bligh, however, that he was not to give up the attempt to get round the Horn
without a trial. Bligh replied by return 'I assure you Sir I will do all that it is
possible for a Man to do to get round Cape Horn'.[4] The discretionary orders
were only partly helpful. Bligh calculated that the uninterrupted voyage to
Tahiti would take seven months via the Horn and nine or ten via the Cape.
The difference was between arriving in Tahiti in July or in October. By
insisting that Bligh try the Horn route in winter, the orders implied the
possibility that he would fail and therefore have to double back across the
South Atlantic, with an even greater delay, which indeed was what
eventually happened.

In one of his last letters before he left, Bligh told Duncan Campbell how he
had managed a last visit to his wife and family (one of the children had had
smallpox) and how Lord Hood had 'winked at my absence'. Of the Horn he
wrote: 'I shall endeavor to get round, but with heavy Gales, should it be
accompanied with sleet & Snow my people will not be able to stand it, and I
shall not then hesitate to go to the Cape Good Hope. Indeed I feel my Voyage a
very arduous one, and have only to hope in return that whatever the event may
be my poor little Family may be provided for.' He added, after this melancholy
plea, that the ship was 'in the best of order and my Men & Officers all good &
feel happy under my directions'.[5]

A word should be said here about the evidence I shall use for what
happened on the voyage before the mutiny. I shall rely on the Log of the
Bounty, written daily by Bligh. The ship's Log was a legal document, and the
legal presumption was that it was an accurate reflection of what went on
during a voyage. Captains were obliged to keep a Log and record all events;
punishments, the weather, any sailing orders such as changes in the sails,
and any work the crew was ordered to carry out. It was a faithful record of
everything, momentous and trivial, and with the Captain's remarks written

[2] Bligh to Duncan Campbell, 10 December 1787, quoted in Mackaness, 1951, p. 48.

[3] Bligh to Banks, 17 December 1787.

[4] Banks wrote a note of his advice on the back of Bligh's letter; Bligh's reply is dated 19
December 1787.

[5] *See* Betham to Bligh, 21 September 1787; Bligh to Duncan Campbell, 22 December 1787.
Quoted in Mackaness, 1951, pp. 45, 49.

alongside provided the Admiralty with a legal picture of what had happened.

There are two major sources for the Log of the *Bounty*. The original Log and Journal, Bligh's private copy, in his own handwriting, is in the Mitchell Library and consists of two volumes, one from December 1787 to October 1788 (Safe 1/46) and the other from 4 April 1789 to the arrival of Bligh's party in England in 1790 (Safe 1/47). This is the most detailed version, containing some additional comments excluded from the official copy deposited with the Admiralty. The latter corresponds closely with the Mitchell Library original, and appears to have been a copy made for Bligh by his Clerk, John Samuel. It was not unusual for the Captain to have a copy of his Log made for official purposes, rather than handing in his own hand-written copy. As the two copies are almost identical, and the sections Samuel was instructed to leave out did more discredit to Bligh's officers than to Bligh himself, it is clear that Bligh did not doctor the official copy of the Log after the mutiny to justify his actions. Until the mutiny, Bligh had no knowledge that his remarks would later become important evidence for or against him; there can be no question about the authenticity of the Log's contents. I therefore allow Bligh, in the neutrality of his undoctored Log, to present his version of the proceedings before the mutiny. The journals and pamphlets written after the voyage, which most authors on the subject have used in describing this part of the voyage, will be discussed fully in their proper context: the factional retributions of the Christian and Heywood families directed at Bligh after the news of the mutiny was made public. I shall leave till then detailed discussion of the so-called Journals of James Morrison, which I contend were written in 1792-3 after the trial of the mutineers, not on board the *Bounty*.[6]

On 23 December 1787 Bligh finally got the *Bounty* away and into the Channel. The ship was lashed by gales and heavy seas; this was the second test of the ship and its crew, and Bligh was pleased by the performance of both. Two days later it was Christmas day, and rum was issued with beef and plum pudding. The storms began to build up and soon everything and everybody was wet. Bligh tried to minimise the discomforts of the weather, but the best that could be done for the crew at the moment was the issue of more grog 'to make up for their Wet uncomfortable Situation'.[7] Uppermost in Bligh's mind would have been the desire for the voyage to be a success, and he believed that a healthy crew was essential for that success – a connection many of his contemporaries seemed unable to make. The *Bounty* had too few seamen for ill-health to be an acceptable risk. Bligh had learnt about the benefits of crew welfare from Captain Cook, and he implemented Cook's policies consistently on this voyage.

In the storms the *Bounty* suffered a good deal of damage. The ship's boats

[6] Most of my quotations from the Log are from the private Log in the Mitchell Library. The PRO Log (PRO Adm. 55/151) is available in an edition by Rutter (1937) which contains selected quotations from the private Log; it has also been published in facsimile (Bligh 1975). For quotations from the period between the end of October 1788 and 4 April 1789, and for some others, I have used Rutter (1937). Where differences between the ML Log and the PRO Log are important I have made it clear which I am quoting from.

[7] Bligh's private Log, 27 December 1787.

were stove in and almost lost overboard; only the determined action of the crew saved them. Seven barrels of beer were washed away and a large part of the 'bread' (biscuit) store was destroyed by seawater. The hands were set to work to salvage what remained of the biscuit by picking out the uncontaminated pieces. This task was so important that everybody was kept at work on it for several days. Bligh decided to ration the remainder of the biscuit store by cutting the daily allowance by a third. Given the uncertainty over the time needed to get to Tahiti, even by the Horn, and the possibility of further losses in storms or from vermin, this was a sensible decision, and it was accepted by the men. It proved a prudent move, because not only did the *Bounty* eventually have to take the longer route, but hundreds more pounds of biscuit were damaged by seawater in the South Atlantic. Some critics have made an issue of this decision, implying that Bligh had some ulterior motive; but when he logged the decision the Admiralty became liable for short allowance money to the men, and Bligh had nothing to gain one way or the other.[8]

When the storm abated, as soon as he could get the ship's stove alight, Bligh organised the drying of clothes. Two men were assigned from each watch to do nothing else. The fires provided hot water for washing clothes, and when the weather permitted the hatches were opened to let air into the ship. Until Tenerife was reached on 5 January, the daily routine consisted of washing between decks and cleaning clothes. Vinegar was used to wash the beams; the bedding was aired on deck, and everybody was inspected by Bligh on Sunday musters for personal cleanliness. These methods combatted the combined effects of dirt, foul air and cramped living conditions, which proved fatal on so many eighteenth-century ships.[9]

At Tenerife, the *Bounty* interrupted its journey to take on fresh supplies, but it was a bad time of year for what was most wanted, such as fresh fruit and wine. Bligh noted the various prices for what little that there was on offer:

As there was a great surf on shore, I bargained for everything I wanted, to be brought off by the shore boats, and agreed to give 5s per ton for water. Very good wine was bought at £10 per pipe, the contract price; but the superior quality was £15; and some of this was not much inferior to the best London Madeira. I found this was an unfavourable season for other refreshments: Indian corn, potatoes, pumpkins, and onions, were all very scarce, and double the price of what they were in the summer. Beef also was difficult to be procured, and exceedingly poor; the price nearly six pence farthing per pound. The corn was three current dollars per fanega, which is full 5s per bushel; and biscuit at 25s for 100 pounds. Poultry was so scarce that a good fowl cost 3s. This is therefore not a place for ships to expect refreshments at a reasonable price at this time of year, wine excepted; but from March to November supplies are plentiful particularly

[8] See Lady [Diana] Belcher, 1870; Morrison, 1935.
[9] *Log of the Bounty*, 28, 29, 30, 31 December; 1, 13, 15, 19, 20, 23, 24, 25, 27, 30, 31 January; 2, 4, 5, 7, 9, 11, 13, 14, 15, 16, 18, 19, 20, 21, 24, 25 February and so on.

fruit, of which at this time we could procure none; except for a few dried figs and some bad oranges.[10]

Without substantial fresh supplies at Tenerife, the *Bounty* had to fall back on its own resources, which were meagre.

One important innovation by Cook, which Bligh copied, was the three-watch system (or four hours in twelve). On most ships at that time the rule was two watches, which meant that seamen were on duty four hours in eight. The effects of their general alacrity can be imagined; moreover, since the entire crew would be needed in an emergency, such as a storm, efficiency could rapidly deteriorate. Interrupted sleep, constant effort, exhausting work aloft, and the normal effects of rain and wind, all led to a weary crew, and a weary crew led to accidents and perhaps disasters. Three watches did not remove all the defects of the two-watch system, nor did it turn a dangerous and difficult job into a safe and easy one. But it helped the men to cope with their work and minimised additional dangers. Bligh's defence of his decision in his Log is worth quoting:

> I have ever considered this [three watches] among Seamen as Conducive to health, and not being Jaded by keeping on Deck every other four hours, it adds much to their Content and Chearfulness.[11]

For most of his crew this was an innovation, and no doubt several of them considered it an imposition or a new-fangled idea. Others who had sailed with Bligh before would have accepted it as a normal practice in his ships.

The creation of three watches instead of two automatically called for three watch officers. Bligh decided that the watch officers would be Fryer, the Master, Christian, the Master's Mate, and Peckover, the Gunner. For Christian this was an important step towards promotion. If a midshipman had had charge of a watch it was a powerful argument in his favour at the examination for Lieutenant. On a long voyage such as the breadfruit expedition the practical experience to be gained was invaluable. This is another instance of the assistance that Bligh was giving to Christian in his career. More was to follow. Christian took over the watch on 11 January 1788, and seven weeks later Bligh issued a written order, which was read out to all hands, making Christian an Acting Lieutenant.[12] This virtually assured Christian of promotion on the return of the *Bounty*.

Two problems emerged from the decision. First, Bligh would expect Christian to justify this public expression of faith in him, because a failure would reflect not merely on Christian but on Bligh's judgment. Christian's subsequent failure to meet Bligh's standards goes some way to explain the

[10] Bligh, 1792 (1965), pp. 25-6; *see* also *Log of the Bounty*, remarks at Tenerife, 6 January 1788. This was Bligh's third visit to Tenerife; he had been once with Cook and once in the *Crescent*.

[11] *Log of the Bounty*, 11 January 1788.

[12] The dates are of significance here only because Morrison, in his supposed Journals, got them wrong. He placed the announcement of Christian's appointment and the establishment of a three-watch system on the same day, when in Bligh's Log they were separated by seven weeks.

gradual decline in their relationship. Secondly, and of greater immediate significance, Bligh's choice of the Master's Mate for the position of Acting Lieutenant was bound to injure the passed-over Master, John Fryer. Fryer was of a different background from Christian. His hope of a commission depended on the patronage of someone in a position to help him. We do not know what ambitions he had for himself after the *Bounty*, but as second-in-command he would have entertained some hopes. Even when hope is futile, it still persists; Christian's appointment ended Fryer's hopes within the first ten weeks of the voyage. He had had every reason to believe he was performing well; Bligh had written in praise of him before the *Bounty* left Spithead. We know from what happened later that this promotion marked the turning-point in Fryer's commitment to the voyage and to Bligh. We have no reason to believe that he thought Christian undeserving, but he brooded about his position and lost interest in the whole enterprise.

Bligh needed support, but it might have been better for him if he had not arranged it in the way he did. He could have made Fryer Acting Lieutenant and given him a chance to show what he could do; or, if he felt it was so important to give Christian his chance, he could have made both Fryer and Christian Acting Lieutenants. Or he could have gone on as he was, without an Acting Lieutenant. He cannot be accused of excusing incompetence on the grounds of friendship; Christian himself was to crumble under Bligh's criticism after leaving Tahiti. If Bligh was at fault it was in being blind to the consequences of his choice of a man junior to the ship's Master.

Fryer was connected with much of the subsequent trouble on the *Bounty*. He was apparently involved in the first incident in some way, though details are not available. Eight days after Christian's promotion, on 10 March 1788, Fryer had a quarrel with one of the seamen, Matthew Quintal. According to the ship's Log Fryer reported Quintal to Bligh for 'insolence and contempt' (in Bligh's personal Log this is recorded as 'insolence and mutinous behaviour'). Whether the altercation was trivial or serious, in the eighteenth-century navy punishment was inevitable once a man had been reported to the Captain. Bligh had to back Fryer, if only because the action of which Quintal was accused contravened the Articles of War. Quintal was alleged to be in breach of Articles 22 and 23, relating to quarrelling with a superior officer.[13] Bligh ordered punishment, but from his Log we can see that he was not very happy about it: 'Untill this Afternoon I had hopes I could have performed the Voyage without punishment to any One, but I found it necessary to punish Matthew Quintal with 2 dozen lashes for Insolence and Contempt.'[14]

Whereas Fryer's loss of interest was occasioned by his grievance about his treatment on the voyage, the Surgeon's carelessness was brought with him.

---

[13] The Articles of War governed all the King's ships and set down severe penalties if they were broken, in some cases a mandatory death sentence. It was obligatory for the Captain to read through the Articles at musters, and Bligh followed this practice at Sunday musters, recording each reading in his Log. For a full list of the Articles *see* MacArthur, 1813, Vol. I, Appendix 1, pp. 325-36.

[14] *Log of the Bounty*, 10 March 1788.

Bligh wrote in his personal Log of Thomas Huggan: 'I now find my Doctor to be a Drunken Sot he is constantly in liquor, having a private Stock by him which I assured him shall be taken away if he does not desist from Making himself such a Beast.' Huggan's behaviour did not improve. To have a senior officer so conspicuously incapable right from the start was hardly conducive to a respect for discipline.[15]

From Tenerife, the *Bounty* set out for the Horn. Bligh informed the crew of the purpose of the voyage, its destinations and its probable duration. He also committed himself to a public assurance 'of the certainty of promotion to everyone whose endeavours should merit it'.[16] The *Bounty* headed south for the hot weather and the equator. Since many of the crew had not crossed the line before, the traditional ceremony was held, but without the practice of ducking, for Bligh thought that 'of all Customs it is the most brutal'.[17] To make life more comfortable during the hot weather, Bligh ordered that whenever possible the men were to work under awnings. A daily programme of cleaning, drying and airing of clothes was organised, and the hatches were opened to get air into the ship. Bligh ordered the pumps to be used until the water coming out was as clean as the water going in; this not only cleared the air of putrid smells, but also exercised the men.[18]

Once past the tropics, the *Bounty* approached the colder southern regions, and Bligh prepared the crew and the ship for the rigours they were likely to face in the next weeks. He was determined to try to double the Horn. On 22 March, the day before landfall, Bligh reported that the air was 'very sharp' and that some of the men were complaining of rheumatism. The next day they sighted Staten Island, of which he wrote: 'I am fortunate perhaps in seeing the Coast of Terra del Fuego at a time when it is freest of snow, however I cannot help remarking that at this time it has not shewn itself with all the horrors mentioned by former Navigators.'[19] Bligh had not been to the Horn before, and his knowledge of it came from the navigational journals which he had brought with him, including an account of the ill-fated Anson expedition of 1740-4.[20] Nevertheless he regarded the passage round the Horn as the 'most difficult and grand part of our passage'.[21] He ordered hot breakfasts for the men, consisting of wheat with sugar and butter, and a few days later he ordered portable soup boiled in pease to be served with their

---

[15] *ibid.*, 23 January 1788.

[16] *ibid.*, 11 February 1788; Bligh, 1792 (1965), p. 29.

[17] *ibid.*, 9 February 1788.

[18] *ibid.*, 22 February to 20 March, 1788.

[19] *ibid.*, 23 March 1788. This date is one of the few that Morrison got right in his Journals, and some authors (e.g. Mackaness, 1961, p. 55n) have argued that this proves that Morrison kept a diary while on the *Bounty*. But the landfall happened to coincide with a specific allegation by Morrison about the killing of a sheep (*see* p. 196,n.) and this could have been enough to fix it in his mind. He got other landfalls wrong by weeks.

[20] George Anson, later Lord Anson, circumnavigated the world in 1740-4 in the *Centurion*, with five warships and two supply ships. He intended to defeat the Spaniards and open up the Pacific for Britain. Anson lost 1,300 men and seven ships on the voyage, but captured bullion worth over a million pounds. In his book (Anson, 1748) he described the passage of his squadron round the Horn.

[21] *Log of the Bounty*, 25 March 1788.

hot dinners. By 29 March they had to batten down fore and aft as the seas began to break over the ship. Bligh recorded that the seas at the Horn exceeded anything he had seen before, and his earlier scepticism about Anson's accounts was abated by his own experience.

From 2 April the gales continued to batter the small ship. In his Log Bligh leaves us a testimony to his sheer determination to perform his duty as he saw it. A lesser man would have succumbed at the first change in the wind and used his discretionary orders to turn away from the Cape of Good Hope route to Tahiti, having made a token gesture. But it was not in Bligh's character to give up. He kept the *Bounty* hard at it, even though the gales blew him back to where he started.

Bligh was worried about the privations that his course was creating for the men, but still confident that his methods could counteract them. He wrote in his Log:

> The Sails & Ropes were worked with much difficulty, and the few Men who were obliged to be aloft felt the Snow Squalls so severe as to render them almost incapable of getting below, and some of them sometimes for a While lost their Speech; but I took care to Nurse them when off duty with every comfort in my power. The Invalids I made attend and dry their Cloaths and Keep a good fire in every Night, so that no Man when he took his Watch had a Wet Rag about him. They were at three Watches, and When lying too, I would only suffer two Men on Deck at a time. I gave them all additional Slop Cloaths, and I made their Meal pleasant and wholesome as may be Observed in the different days Occurrences.[22]

It was unfortunately necessary for men to be aloft in these conditions. A sudden change of wind could have rent the sails or placed too great a strain on the masts, and men were needed to take in or let out the sails. It was an appalling task, but none the less a necessary one if the *Bounty* and its crew were to survive.

The ship leaked quite badly, and men had to work on the pumps every hour for most of the time. The damage was severe, but the toll on the men was as severe as on the ship. Day and night the gales blew, and what progress the *Bounty* made it soon lost again by being blown back. Even with fires and dry clothes, the damp got in everywhere. Bligh tried to help by moving some of the men to the great cabin to give them somewhere drier to sleep and to leave more room for their companions in the fo'c'sle. The hot breakfasts were supplemented with a concoction of diluted malt to strengthen resistance to colds.

On 13 April Bligh wrote: 'I cannot expect my Men and Officers to bear it much longer, [n]or will the object of my Voyage allow me to persist in it.'[23] William Peckover, the officer of the watch, went down with rheumatism, along with Charles Norman, Carpenter's Mate. Thomas Hall, the crew's cook, fell and broke a rib, and the Surgeon fell and dislocated a shoulder

[22] *ibid.*, 22 April 1788.
[23] *ibid.*, 13 April 1788.

(whether by the motions of the ship or from drunkenness is not recorded). To keep himself steady on deck, Bligh lashed himself with a rope to the ship.

The casualties rose steadily. On 18 April two more men went down with colds, making five in all. Four days later this had risen to eight, which was 'much felt in the watches, the ropes being worked with much difficulty from the wet and the snow'. It was here that the shortage of working A.B.s was felt the most. The watches were turned out with men short, and while there is no record of this, with up to eight seamen off duty out of thirteen there must have been a crisis in manning, and some of the spare, but nominal, A.B.s were probably drafted in.[24]

On 17 April Bligh gave up the hopeless task and turned the *Bounty* for the Cape of Good Hope. But a turn in the wind changed his mind and encouraged him, incredibly, to try again. He battled on for a few more days until, on 22 April, he made the final decision to give up: 'I ordered the helm to be put round to the universal joy of all hands.' It must have been a popular decision. For the record he felt obliged to write his reasons in detail in his Log, in case he was questioned about the decision by the Admiralty. We might speculate what he would have done if discretionary orders had been refused: from his conduct, his numerous attempts, and his character, it is likely that he would have kept trying until the *Bounty* made it or sank.

---

[24] The anonymous writer of Peter Heywood's obituary claimed that Bligh had kept the 15-year-old Heywood aloft for eight hours in a snowstorm at the Horn. Heywood himself, as far as we know, never made a public statement of this during his lifetime, neither did Morrison or Fryer; if it had happened they would certainly have mentioned it to blacken Bligh. It is unlikely that Heywood could have survived such an ordeal. If Heywood and other 'A.B.s' were sent on deck to assist the few men available, during snowstorms when 'the ropes were worked with difficulty', this could have evolved into a mastheading story. 'Mastheading' was a traditional punishment for errant midshipmen, but no Captain would have permitted a mastheading in a blizzard at the Horn. For the original mastheading claim *see* anon., 1831; for an authoritative rebuttal *see* Smith, 1936, pp. 207ff. This myth persisted through repetition by authors such as Sir John Barrow, and was included in the highly fictional MGM film in 1960.

6

Cape Horn to Tasmania

The *Bounty* anchored in False Bay at the Cape of Good Hope on 22 May and stayed there for 38 days. The beating the ship had taken at the Horn necessitated considerable repairs, including the re-caulking of the entire hull. The carpenter and his men were kept busy and needed help from local tradesmen. Bligh made courtesy calls on the Dutch officials in the local settlement and, as always, spent time on navigational observations. Everybody took the opportunity to rest and eat fresh food.

Bligh made an extensive entry in the Log on what he termed his 'Mode of Management'. He was clearly pleased with the *Bounty*'s performance and proud of the fact that he had brought the ship through the attempt on the Horn without loss of life:

Perhaps a Voyage of five Months which I have now performed without touching at any one place but at Tenarif, has never been accomplished with so few accidents, and such health among Seamen in a like continuance of bad W[eather] ... Having never had a symptom of either Scurvy, Flux or Fever, and as such a fortunate event may be supposed to have been derived from some peculiar Mode of Management it is proper I should point out what I think has been the cause of it ... We have it much in our power to act against the latter by taking care of the Men in their cloathing, and the rest will generally be prevented, by the timely distribution of the necessaries that Ships may be supplied with, and a strict regard to cleanliness. Seamen will seldom attend to themselves in any particular and simply to give directions that they are to keep themselves clean and dry as circumstances will allow, is of little avail, they must be watched like Children, as the most recent danger has little effect to prevent them from the same fate. The Mode I have adopted has been a Strict adherence to the first grand point, cleanliness in their persons and bedding, Keeping them in dry Cloaths & by constant cleaning and drying the Ship with Fires, to this I attribute their having kept free of Colds so wonderfully as they have done. A Great nuisance which is in general an attendant in ships in a long continuance of bad weather is dirty Hammocks and Bags, this I think I perfectly got the better of, by having two sets, one of which ... is in charge to be got cleaned and dryed as a general Stock or property whenever they were done with, and by this Means I had it in my power to deliver Clean Hammocks and Bags as often as I saw it necessary. One Person of a Watch was appointed to dry Cloaths by the Fire and a Man never came on Deck or went to sleep in wet apparel. No foul Cloaths were ever suffered to be kept without airing, and

in cleaning Ship all dark holes and Corners the common receptacles of all
filth were the first places attended to.

After all that can be done perhaps Ships may be subject to Fevers and
Fluxes; but the Scurvy is realy a disgrace to a ship where it is at all
common, provided they have it in their power to be supplied with Dryed
Malt, Sour Krout, and Portable Soup. With these articles properly issued,
I am firmly convinced no Scurvy will appear. Chearfullness with exercise,
and a sufficiency of rest are powerfull preventitives to this dreadfull
disease, a calamity which even at this present period destroys more men
than is generally known. To assist in the first two particulars every
opportunity I directed that the Evenings should be spent in dancing, and
that I might be secure in my last I kept my few Men constantly at three
Watches, even in the Worst of Weather, and I found them additionally
alert on a call when their immediate Service was required ...

... Hot breakfasts are particularly to be prefered in Stormy and Wet
weather to eating a Scrap of Salt Meat or a peice of biscuit, but very
common[ly] Seamen do their duty without any breakfast at all, and this
has a pernicious tendency.

... I am thoroughly convinced that had I been a fortnight sooner there I
could have made my passage round the Cape into the South Sea with the
greatest ease.[1]

Bligh wrote to his patrons, Banks and Campbell, in the same vein; in a letter to
Campbell he pointed out that, in contrast with the *Bounty*, 'a Dutch Ship came
in to day having buried 30 Men & many are sent to the Hospital, altho they
have only been out since the last of January'.[2]

Bligh's own picture of his almost parental care for his men, the good
results of which he was anxious to have credited to him, is backed up by a
letter written by Ledward, the Assistant Surgeon. He reports on the violent
seas at the Horn and adds: 'The Ship laboured so much that there was
danger of rendering her unfit for the further prosecution of the Voyage. The
Captain was therefore obliged to bear away, & I have no doubt will gain
much credit by his resolution & perseverance & by the extreme care he took
of the Ship's company.'[3] Being a young medic, Ledward was more likely
than the others to understand the reasons behind Bligh's mode of
management and see that it was directed at the health and welfare of the
crew.

While at False Bay Bligh also had the time to make notes on the slave
trade:[4]

Slaves are a property here as well as in the West Indies, and the number
imported by the French (to whom that Trade has been confined) from
Madagascar,   Musambique,   Sumatra   and   Mallaca   have   been

---

[1] *Log of the Bounty*, 24 May 1788.
[2] *See* Bligh to Sir Joseph Banks, 24 May 1788, and Bligh to Duncan Campbell, Letters from
False Bay, May 1788, Mitchell Library.
[3] *See Notes and Queries*, 1903, 9th Series, Vol. XII, p. 501.
[4] *Log of the Bounty*, Remarks at False Bay, 1788.

considerable, but it appears there is in some degree a Stop put to this Trade, for the seller has now only permission to part with as many as can pay for the supplies he absolutely is in need of. To this if the Police could oblige the owners of these Poor Wretches consigned to constant drudgery, to cloath and feed them properly it would be much to their honour and humanity, for it is distressing to see some of them carrying Weighty burdens naked, or what is worse in such rags that one would imagine could not fail to reproach the owners of a want of decency and compassion in not relieving such a degree of wretchedness of which they were the cause, and had every call on their humanity to remove. Several of these poor wretches I have seen pick up the most offensive offals and claim them for food.

The repairs to the ship and the victualling were nearing completion, and Bligh now made arrangements for the next leg of the voyage. The next landfall was expected to be Adventure Bay, so named since H.M.S. *Adventure* had called there on Cook's second voyage, in Tasmania, known then as Van Diemen's Land and thought to be part of the Australian mainland. This was a journey of about 6,000 miles across an empty sea to an empty continent. Turning the corner, so to speak, at the Cape meant entering a barely known world. While they were at the Cape Bligh recorded in his Log the report of the destruction of a European ship on the coast of South Africa, not far from the Dutch settlement but too far to allow any attempt to rescue the European survivors, who were taken by local tribes. The *Bounty* was going not just up the coast of Africa, but out across an enormous ocean and past a whole continent up into the Pacific to a tiny island not visited for a decade. Disaster on any scale here was final. The rest of the voyage would be a test of the ship, the crew, and above all the social structure that bound the small band of Europeans together. If authority crumbled, support was distant and retribution uncertain. From this time on the *Bounty* would be entirely dependant on its own resources.

This aspect of the *Bounty* voyage has been neglected by many authors. Yet it is a most important aspect of the dilemma that Bligh eventually faced in command of the little bit of Britain that was the *Bounty*. At home, among familiar surroundings, the naval hierarchy was reinforced by the presence of large numbers of people among whom the habit of deference was firmly established. Seamen who were punished at home or near home were isolated and impotent; the power of those over them was near-absolute. But at sea, on a long voyage across the world, the bonds were loosened. The officers were themselves isolated, and brought down to the same level as the men; the social distance between the commander and the men was abbreviated, and the hazy indefinable line between fear and contempt, which is the threshold of mutiny, was easily broken. The *Bounty*, a small overcrowded ship captained by an unsupported Lieutenant, alone and out of sight of the known world, was particularly vulnerable. True, other single ships had sailed the same waters, but not all of them were heard of again; some may have been casualties of poor navigation or seamanship, but we will never know how many of the others succumbed to a failure of discipline and the breaking up of the accepted social structure on board ship.

Two days before he left False Bay Bligh wrote his final report to Sir Joseph Banks:

> I am now ready for sea with my little ship once more in most excellent order and every man on board in very good health. I flatter myself with a speedy passage to Otaheite as I apprehend there will be no want of wind.
>
> I might wood & water at Botany Bay with little loss of time and it may be imagined I will do so, but I cannot think of putting it in the power of chance to prevent my accomplishing the object of the Voyage. I shall therefore pass our Friends there but could I have taken in any considerable supply it would have been for the good of the service for me to have done it and I should – In the present case I can render them no service, and Government will hear of them before any accounts could be brought home by me. Should any unforseen accident drive me there I have a great many seeds and some fruit plants which I shall leave with them ... I wish you to enjoy the most perfect health & happiness and to see you satisfyed with my conduct on my return will give.[5]

The 'friends' at Botany Bay were the first British settlers sent there in 1787 under the command of Captain Phillip. Bligh, and the rest of his countrymen, had no knowledge as to what had happened to them, as news had not yet returned from the new colony. He did not even know whether they were still there. From this letter to Banks, he clearly thought that a visit to Botany Bay would add risks to the voyage and serve only to satisfy curiosity; and in fact he did not call in there. The colony at Botany Bay had opened up that part of the world to Britain, and its existence was some comfort to the increasing number of British ships that entered the Pacific; a visit might have had a useful psychological effect on the crew, particularly on the 'troublemakers' – a reminder that while Britain was far away its reach stretched across the world. It might also have been helpful to Bligh if he had gone there and met Captain Phillip, as his life was to be bound up with the colony at a particularly turbulent period.

For the 'good of the service' Bligh set out on 1 July for the most southern tip of New Holland (Australia), with the intention of sailing even further south round New Zealand. The passage from the Cape to Adventure Bay was uneventful. The routine of cleaning below, drying clothes by the fires, inspecting the hands and serving 'hot breakfasts', malt extract, flour and raisins, was strictly adhered to. The Log monotonously records this routine. The weather did not change much for the better; squalls and rain were interspersed with gales as the *Bounty* ploughed on towards Adventure Bay. The strong winds pushed the ship along at a fair rate and the seas broke over the ship, causing more discomfort than injury, though the man at the wheel on one occasion was knocked off his feet and 'much bruized'.[6] This was an isolated incident.

Bligh was a fastidious navigator. The small ship, with what would be

[5] Bligh to Sir Joseph Banks, 28 June 1788.
[6] *Log of the Bounty*, 22 July 1788.

regarded today as primitive navigational aids, aimed for a small rocky island, St Paul, a month out from the Cape. Bligh wanted to fix the position of the island accurately, and he stated his reasons for this quest in his Log:[7]

> It is strange that the Publishers of these Works should not have made themselves acquainted better with the latitude of these Islands particularly as real information might surely have been got from our Indiamens Journals in their route to China, some ship or other seeing them every Year. But a Rage seems to have got among these publishers of errors about fixing places in their true longitude, (which if they can do to one degree is sufficient for all ships), and in the mean time they have neglected the grand point, the latitude, which they err as much in, when it might be known to five Miles.

After St Paul, the next point aimed for was another three weeks' sailing away, the Mewstone Rock off the coast of Tasmania. Bligh brought the *Bounty* to the exact spot and got his measurements, but not before he had 'carried much Sail by which means every one got thoroughly Wet with the Sea making a fair breach over us'. This discomfort was justified by Bligh on the grounds that 'I got a good Noon Observation and likewise very good ones for the Long[itude] by the Time Keeper'.[8] Positioning tiny rocks in vast oceans and getting 'thoroughly wet' in the process may not have seemed to the men the welcome challenge it was to their Captain. For the midshipmen it was a difficult exercise in navigation under the stern eye of Bligh, a better navigator than any of them. After the cold weeks at sea, with these uncomfortable manoeuvres, the monotony of the diet, and the compulsory dancing in the evening, everyone probably yearned for a landfall.

On 20 August 1788 the *Bounty* neared Adventure Bay and the next day anchored there. Having secured the ship, Bligh went ashore to look around. It was eleven years since he had been there with Captain Cook. Nelson and Peckover were no strangers to the bay either, and for the three of them it must have been an exciting day – the more so, because the bay was practically as they had left it. The next day work parties were organised to get wood, collect water, make some alterations in the cabin, and hunt and fish for food. Nelson and Brown set to work to collect botanical specimens. The shore party was placed under the command of Fletcher Christian, assisted by Peckover. Fryer was left in command of the ship to supervise the work of loading supplies. One man was directed to wash clothes. Everybody had a job to do of some kind. All co-operated in the work programme, except for Purcell, the Carpenter.

Purcell was the centre of two serious incidents at Adventure Bay, and his conduct was obstructive. What caused the first incident is not known. Bligh hints at what happened in his Log but does not give further details, and in his

[7] *ibid.*, 28 July 1788. Bligh refers to the books which he had with him on the voyage, which were taken away by the mutineers. Some of them were recovered by Bligh at Tahiti on the second breadfruit voyage, and others by the Admiralty from Pitcairn in 1814.
[8] *Log of the Bounty*, 19 August 1788.

published *Narrative* there is no mention of the incident. From the Log it appears that Bligh criticised the way Purcell was carrying out his work and that Purcell was imprudent enough to reply. Naval captains did not expect anybody on their ship to answer back, and, indeed, even midshipmen reported men for punishment for less. Normally, a warrant officer who did not carry out the orders of a superior officer, or was disrespectful or disobedient, would be arrested and confined until he could be brought before a court martial. But the *Bounty* was not due home for fifteen months, and to confine an officer for that length of time was out of the question. Bligh wrote in his Log:[9]

> My Carpenter on my expressing my disapprobation of his Conduct with respect to orders he had received from me concerning the Mode of working with the Wooding Party behaved in a most 'insolent and reprehensible Manner, I therefore ordered him on board, there to assist in the general duty of the Ship, as I could not bear the loss of an able Working and healthy Man; otherwise I should have committed him to close confinement untill I could have tryed him, the prospect of which appears to be of so long a date made me determine to keep him at his duty, giving him a Chance by his future Conduct to make up in some degree for his behaviour at this place.

If a seaman was in the same situation, the Captain could order a punishment of a dozen or more lashes and that would be the end of the incident, but Purcell could not be punished by flogging without the authority of a court martial. If Purcell could not be punished and could not be confined he could not be intimidated by the Captain's authority. If he chose not to recognise that authority, and specifically chose to argue with the Captain, what could the Captain do about it? Purcell had accidentally discovered something about Bligh's position which might not yet have been obvious; while Bligh had the authority of the King's commission he had no means of enforcing it. This discovery was the first step on the road to mutiny.

In sending Purcell back on the *Bounty* Bligh had placed him under Fryer's command. On board with Fryer were William Elphinston, Master's Mate, and one of the Quartermasters.[10] The incident happened on Saturday 23 August and as there was no work on the next day, Sunday, it was not until the Monday that Fryer was able to direct Purcell to assist in loading the ship. The entry for Tuesday in the Log makes the following point: 'As My Ships Company when divided into three Boats and others cutting Wood, made the Working Party on board very small, I repeated my injunctions to the Comm[andin]g Officer Mr Fryer that he would take care to keep all Officers employed as well as Men ...'[11] Reading between the lines, it seems likely that when Bligh returned from his shore duty on Monday he enquired about the work that Fryer was supervising and discovered that Fryer had not allocated

---

[9] *ibid.*, 23 August 1788.
[10] *ibid.*, 26 August 1788; the Quartermaster is not named.
[11] *ibid.*

general work to Purcell, on the grounds that he was an officer, or that he had simply directed him to some carpenter's work on the ship. Bligh was undoubtedly annoyed at this breach in his intentions, and accordingly he wrote out his instructions, specifically naming the officer to whom they were given. Purcell was to assist in general, i.e. labouring, duties as a punishment, and Fryer was enjoined to see to it.

Bligh recorded what happened when Fryer tried to carry out the Captain's instructions: '... he was opposed by the Carpenter who refused to assist in hoisting Water into the Hold ... On my coming on board Mr Fryer acquainted me of this circumstance, but my directions and presence had as little effect.'[12] This was a direct refusal of duty, the most serious offence, short of mutiny, on a naval vessel. In home waters Purcell would have been at risk of his life. This fact has been neglected by some of Bligh's critics, who have mainly concentrated on his reaction to this offence, not the offence itself.[13] There was no question of such an incident passing unnoticed, and no doubt it was the main topic of conversation that evening among the men when they returned from their work. They would have been watching Bligh to see what he did. Bligh's response was a stratagem which weakened his position irretrievably. He wrote his decision into the Log:

> I therefore Ordered the different Persons evidence to be drawn out and attested, and then gave Orders that untill he Worked he should have no provisions, and promised faithfully a severe Punishment to any Man that dared to Assist him, which immediatly brought him to his senses.[14]

Bligh presumably took the evidence with a view to Purcell's eventual court martial. It was a formal legal step and a perfectly proper one, forcing Purcell at least to consider his probable fate. Instead of confining Purcell for the duration of the voyage to await a court martial, Bligh used the stopping of provisions as a means of persuasion; Purcell could not hope to last out that kind of sanction. He did not appear willing to rely on help from any friends he might have, and from what we know of him, he does not seem to have had many friends on board anyway. Thus he was forced to capitulate on the issue of work. But he had managed to strike a blow against Bligh's position.

The Log continues:

> It was for the good of the Voyage that I should not make him or any Man a prisoner. The few I have even in the good State of health I keep them, are but barely sufficient to carry on the duty of the Ship, it could then answer no good purpose to lose the use of a healthy Strong Young Man in

---

[12] *ibid.*

[13] For instance, Lady Belcher, Peter Heywood's stepdaughter, who simply says Bligh 'also put the carpenter in confinement' as if this was yet another example of arbitrary tyranny. If Purcell was 'confined' at all, he would merely have been sent to his cabin until he capitulated a few hours later. Lady Belcher wrote her version of the mutiny from the family copy of Morrison's journal – she did not have Bligh's Log – and Morrison is not specific about what was at stake. See Lady [Diana] Belcher, 1870, p. 24.

[14] *Log of the Bounty*, 26 August 1788.

my situation. I therefore laid aside my power in the particular for the good of the Service I am on, altho it continued in force with equal effect.[15]

It is a sign of realism to consider the wider issues in any situation, and Bligh sets them out convincingly. But he was wrong in his conclusion. By not imprisoning Purcell for the rest of the voyage, Bligh surrendered the power to punish anybody else who might chose to disobey his commands. Apart from two dozen lashes on the A.B.s, Bligh now had no punishment to offer, and without a power of punishment, immediate and certain, or the consent of the men concerned, the Captain's authority could not 'continue in force with equal effect'. Management by consent was hardly a typical management style of the eighteenth-century navy. Nelson's leadership has often been romanticised, but even Nelson, who at periods in his career had men scrambling to fight alongside him, was a severe disciplinarian. We know that Cook was never loath to order a flogging and other great seamen were the same or worse. There were the floggers, the men who ruled by sheer terror, and if ever tyranny meant anything their ships were floating exhibitions of it at its worst. But William Bligh was never a flogger in anything remotely like that sense. He expected discipline as manifestation of duty. Perhaps another captain would have had Purcell flogged in spite of his status and would have risked a court martial on return if the man brought one against him. It may be that in the circumstances the court would have admonished him and left it at that. But this was not Bligh's way. The rule forbade flogging, and that was that. Bligh tried his superior intelligence against the man, but in winning the issue he lost something he could never recover. Immunity for Purcell was immunity for everybody else.

[15] *ibid.*

7

Refusal of Duty

The *Bounty*, wooded and watered, sailed from Adventure Bay on 4 September 1788, intending to go southward past New Zealand, out into the east Pacific, and then northward to Tahiti, approaching it from the east. This roundabout route was necessary to catch the prevailing winds. After two weeks at sea, Bligh discovered a group of rocky islands south of New Zealand which he named after the ship, Bounty Isles, a name they have to this day. The weather was again wet and uncomfortable and the Bligh routine of fires, cleaning and health foods was resumed. But with every day's sail warmer weather was approaching. The men were put through regular exercises with the small arms. Bligh was taking no chances. He had no reason to think that the Tahitians would not welcome him as they had when he was last there, but he had been scarred by the events at Hawaii and had no intentions of being caught off-guard or ill-prepared.

The situation on the *Bounty* was by no means happy. Bligh was still smarting over the Purcell incident. It is worth quoting Morrison's version of the situation, although one has to remember that for his own purposes (see pp.195-208) he slants everything to emphasise Bligh's inadequacy as a commander: 'Here also were sown seeds of eternal discord between Lieut. Bligh and some of his Officers. He confined the Carpenter and found fault with the inattention of the rest, to their duty, which produced continual disputes every one endeavouring to thwart the others in their duty, this made the men exert themselves to divert the storm from falling on them by a strict attention to their duty and in this way they found their account and rejoyced in private at their good success.'[1]

We can accept it as likely that, after Purcell's challenge to his right to criticise the work of a warrant officer, Bligh found opportunities to exercise his right with others, and possibly also that Bligh was doing this sufficiently to cause tension among the officers and attention to duty among the ship's company. But Morrison ignores the fact that Purcell's action had provoked the whole situation and made Bligh's position as a commander nearly impossible.

Fryer's reactions to tauter supervision of the ship's officers created the

---

[1] James Morrison, Journal, Mitchell Library MS, Safe 1/42, p. 16 (in quotations from this Journal I have used the MS page numbers throughout). From the context, Morrison places the confinement of Purcell after the *Bounty* left Adventure Bay. Again, if Morrison was writing some years later this vagueness about dates is not surprising.

second challenge to Bligh's authority. The Fryer episode has been given more attention than the incident with Purcell; yet it arises from a similar refusal to obey and, insofar as it was provoked by Bligh's behaviour, it arose indirectly out of the altercation between Bligh and his Carpenter. It is remarkable that previous accounts of the incident have missed the real causes of the dispute, even though these are present in the Log when it is read carefully.

On 9 October 1788, Bligh was presented with the Boatswain's and Carpenter's expense books. By signing them he approved their contents, and when they had been signed by the Master, John Fryer, it was formally established that the books were correct. Upon this authority, and only upon this authority, at the end of the voyage the Admiralty was to pay the Warrant Officers concerned their wages and make allowance for the expenses claimed. This was the routine on naval vessels every month or so, and by involving several officers, except in the unlikely event that every one of the officers was corrupt, the admiralty ensured that moneys claimed were not falsified. Bligh records in his Log what happened on this occasion:

> The Clerk was then returned with a Certificate for me to Sign, before the Books could, the Purport of which was that he [Fryer] had done nothing amiss during his time on board. As I did not approve of his doing his duty conditionally I sent for him and told him the Consequence when he left me abrup[t]ly saying he would not sign the Books upon such conditions. I now ordered the Hands to be turned up. Read the Articles of War, with particular parts of the Instructions relative to the Matter, when this troublesome Man saw his error & before the whole Ships Company signed the Books.[2]

Why should Fryer have wanted a certificate of his good behaviour on the *Bounty*? Most authors have ignored this question and asked only why it was that he would not sign the books. But the two are connected, and it is worth going back and trying to understand what Fryer's motives could have been. Three days before this incident, on 6 October, something had happened which might have had a bearing on Fryer's conduct. Bligh had had a furious row with Huggan, the Surgeon. In Bligh's private Log (but not in his official Log; he instructed his Clerk, John Samuel, to leave it out when writing the official Log, by putting a pencil line through the entry) we find the following:

> Mr Elphinston, one of the Mates of the Ship came and told me this morning that Jas. Valentine (who had had an inflamed arm after some blood being taken from him some time since) was delirious and had every appearance of being in a dying state. This shock was scarce equal to my astonishment, as the Surgeon told me he was getting better, and had never expressed the least uneasyness about him. I therefore sent for the Surgeon and was perhaps severe for his remissness – However, all I could get out of him was that he intended to have told me of it last night ... that he must now inform

---

[2] *Log of the Bounty*, 9 October 1788; Bligh added in his personal Log 'Here again I forgave him'.

me that he had not many hours to live. – The strangeness of this declaration, as the Man had been daily fed from our Table and he not knowing the tendency of his symptoms gave me very unfavourable ideas.[3]

Bligh was shocked that he had not been informed that a seaman was dying, although he was under the care of Huggan and Huggan dined with Bligh in his mess. When he said he was 'perhaps severe' Bligh probably understated his reaction. For this meant that his much vaunted 'mode of management', which went to great lengths to keep the crew healthy in contrast to most other naval vessels of the time, was undermined by the incompetence of one of the instruments of health on board, the ship's Surgeon. To lose a man through scurvy was unthinkable – Bligh called it 'a disgrace' – but to lose a man through blood poisoning brought on by the Surgeon himself was even worse. It would certainly reflect on Bligh's record and probably speak against his management. The fact that it was one of the Mates, Elphinston, who brought him the news of Valentine's condition, not the Surgeon, nor the Assistant Surgeon, nor the Acting Lieutenant, Christian, nor the Master, John Fryer, implicated them all in the neglect. Bligh was probably extremely 'severe'; he would not be slow to tell the officers what he thought of them.

As Fryer was the other member, with Huggan, of the Captain's mess, he would be a particular butt of Bligh's temper. Fryer was already in trouble over the Purcell affair. On that occasion Bligh had thought it necessary to repeat his instructions to Fryer about what Purcell was to do while on board, and also to log this second issue of orders. The fact that Fryer had not complied with these orders the first time was probably taken by Bligh as an affront. As a Warrant Officer himself, Fryer probably sympathised with Purcell's refusal to do a seaman's duty, and possibly felt that it was Bligh's fault that Purcell had got into a mood of non-cooperation. Whether because of this earlier occasion, or because of Bligh's outbursts about Huggan's incompetence and his need to rely on one of the junior Mates for information, or a combination of the two, Fryer began to feel threatened by Bligh's opinion of him. Not only had he been passed over when Christian was made Acting Lieutenant, but he might now end up with a bad character from his Captain.

The Log records the death of Valentine on 9 October, the same day as Fryer's refusal to sign the books. This suggests that Fryer knew Valentine's death was imminent, and anticipating Bligh's outrage was driven into a panic, perhaps reacting to threats made by Bligh about what he would do if Valentine died. By the morning of 9 October Fryer had devised a scheme, though a hopeless and desperate one, for getting Bligh to sign a certificate of good conduct for him as an insurance for the future. The only lever he had on Bligh was a refusal of duty, and for this he chose the sensitive area of finance, where even a whisper would spread gossip.

The gambit could only have succeeded if there had been some irregularities on the books which Bligh would fear being brought out into the

---

[3] Private Log, 6 October 1788.

open. A charge of falsifying the books would, if established, finish Bligh's career.[4] One could argue from this that there must have been irregularities, on the grounds that if there were none, Fryer's action can only be seen as an ill-judged emotional outburst, the behaviour of an unstable and petty-minded man. But Fryer could be said to be both these and more without stretching the facts. The intensity of feelings on a small ship, with irritable men in close contact, and the pettiness to which they sometimes devote an alarming proportion of their time, are not unknown phenomena.

Morrison's version of what happened contained a strong hint that Bligh had falsified the books, and this construction of the incident has been followed by many of Bligh's critics. Morrison wrote:[5]

> ... Previous to making Taheiti, a dispute happened between Mr. Bligh and the Master Mr. Fryer relative to signing some books, which the Master had refused to sign, for reasons best known to himself, Upon which all Hands were Calld aft, and the Articles of War read, and some part of the Printed Instructions, after Which the Books and papers were produced with a Pen and ink and Mr. Bligh said Now Sir Sign them Books. The Master took the Pen and said 'I sign in obedience to your Orders, but this may be Cancelled hereafter.' The books being signed the People were dismiss'd to return to their duty.

Morrison makes no mention of the certificate of good behaviour, and it is unlikely that he would have known about it, as Bligh did not make this the issue when he assembled the crew. Bligh simply read out the legalities of his order and left Fryer to consider his position. Morrison also claims that Fryer signed the books conditionally, with a threat to withdraw his assent later, presumable in Britain. Rather than making his accusation outright, Morrison implies it in this bit of dramatic dialogue.

Outside the Logs, we have one surviving reference by Bligh to this incident, a manuscript he wrote in 1793 on his return from the second breadfruit expedition, when called upon to comment on the charges made by Morrison in his Memorandum. Sir Joseph Banks had sent him a copy of it and the 1793 manuscript notes are evidently the basis of his reply to Banks (the original reply has not been found among the Banks papers). Bligh claims that he gave Fryer the opportunity to write down his reasons for a refusal: 'Captain Bligh ordered the Master to sign the Books, or to express his reasons (for not complying) at full length at the bottom of the Page where his signature was to have been made – The Master thought proper to sign the Books.'[6]

---

[4] *See* MacArthur, 1813, Vol. 1, Appendix I, p. 335, Article **XXXI**: the penalty for signing a false muster book was to 'be cashiered, and rendered incapable of further employment in His Majesty's naval service'.

[5] Morrison, Journal, p. 17a; note again the vagueness in the phrase 'previous to making Taheiti'.

[6] William Bligh, 'Captain Bligh's Remarks on Morrison's Journal', unpublished MS in Mitchell Library, Bligh, Bounty Mutineers, Safe 1/43, p. 48; note that though this refers to a Journal, it was the Memorandum Bligh was replying to and not the Journal (*see* also pp. 209-21). The charge was the same.

Who was telling the truth? Fryer's action appears to have been a bluff, for Bligh's response was to call Fryer out in front of the entire ship's company and give him the opportunity to make his charges known, or declare the conditions he insisted upon before doing his duty. If Fryer had something on Bligh, why did he not say so to the crew? It would have been the end of Bligh if he had done so publicly; Christian would have had to take command and take the *Bounty* to Botany Bay, which was the nearest British authority. Was Fryer persuaded to give in by Bligh's possession of his proposed certificate of good conduct? We cannot be sure, but on balance it does not seem likely that Fryer had evidence against Bligh. He never mentioned the incident in his own Journal, written in 1790 with the express intention of blackening Bligh, when he was under threat of court martial from his Captain for his conduct during the boat voyage. Even if this was because he had no evidence at the time – the account books may have been lost in the mutiny – he might have had a witness in Purcell, who kept one of the books. But there is silence from him. It seems more likely that his gambit to get his certificate of good conduct signed failed because he had no reason to refuse duty. Bligh entered the incident in the official Log, and it was therefore official in the eyes of the Admiralty; they could question him if they wanted to and if there was a smell of corruption he would suffer accordingly.

Other factors in Bligh's favour are the riskiness of the behaviour he is charged with, and the silence of his possible accomplices. One of the books was kept by William Cole, the Boatswain, and the other by Purcell, the Carpenter. If Bligh had adjusted Purcell's books he would have had a most unreliable accomplice in the event of an Admiralty enquiry; Purcell would have been the first to expose Bligh and Bligh would not have been foolish enough to trust him in this matter. In fact, Purcell was eventually court-martialled in England for offences on the *Bounty* and in the open boat voyage; one word from him at the court martial about the books would have placed Bligh in a difficult position, but he never mentioned them. Cole's Mate was James Morrison, whose passionate dislike of Bligh was to keep him busy in the condemned cell and for several months afterwards collecting together all the charges he could think of against Bligh. Yet Morrison does not mention anything about Cole's book being improperly presented. His only remark on the subject was the innuendo, quoted earlier, that Fryer refused to sign the books 'for reasons best known to himself'.

In one of his Journals Morrison did, however, make a charge against Bligh about irregularity in the accounts at False Bay when the *Bounty* was there in May and June.[7] The books Fryer refused to sign were for the months of August and September.[8] The system operated something like this: Bligh's accounts would show all provisions and their values, and as the provisions were used, or lost, whether they were food or ship's materials, he would

---

[7] *See* James Morrison, 'Memorandum and Particulars respecting the *Bounty* and her crew', October 1792, ML, Safe 1/33, p. 39; these charges were not repeated in the more detailed Journal.

[8] *Log of the Bounty*, 9 October 1788.

deduct the value concerned from the total taken on the ship at the beginning of the voyage. Purchases made while *en route* would be added to the total. Thus every item would be accounted for, and at the end of the voyage the stock remaining would, in theory, be equal to the original amount less those items used up in one way or another. (This is one reason why Captains were concerned about losses due to thefts; the Admiralty took a poor view if these losses were large, considering it to be a result of slackness on the part of the commander.) Thus in the carpenter's case, stocks of wood, iron, tools, etc. used would be listed and, with Bligh's and Fryer's signatures supporting the claim, the total remaining would be altered by that amount. Similarly the Boatswain's stores would have to be accounted for and the books balanced accordingly. If any fiddling was going on in either case, the amounts involved could not be considerable, and could not be 'adjusted' without the knowledge of the two Warrant Officers concerned. To complete the deception it would be necessary to carry over the false entry throughout the voyage. It would have been an extremely risky business for very little reward.

In sum, it is likely that the whole incident was caused by recent events in the ship: the 'seeds of eternal discord' sown by the behaviour of Purcell, Huggan and Fryer, and Bligh's justifiable anger over the approaching death of Valentine and the way it had been hidden from him.[9] The situation on the *Bounty* was worsening all the time, and there was very little Bligh could do about it. Two officers, Purcell and Fryer, had now refused duty against direct commands from their Captain. Both incidents were public knowledge and neither man was punished in the usual way. A third officer, Huggan, was manifestly incompetent and had contributed to the death of a seaman. Nothing was done about him, and his public inebriation, apparently unrestrained by the Captain's disapproval, was a daily exhibition of insubordination. Bligh may not have realised the extent to which his position was being undermined, but his impotence was exposed to all. Within a few weeks the entire crew had seen two men challenge the Captain and live, an extraordinary state of affairs on a British naval vessel.

[9] Among authors who have missed the significance of Valentine's death are Mackaness, 1951, Chapter 7; Danielsson, 1962, pp. 53-4; Hough, 1972, pp. 101-2.

8

The Alcoholic Surgeon

As the ship left the southern route for the warmer climates of the approach to Tahiti, Huggan became increasingly incapable through drunkenness. After nine months at sea it was to be expected that some men would report sick. The prolonged period of managed diets and sea duty had an effect on the crew's health. Cook's reforms in health and hygiene were primitive by modern standards, though they were revolutionary in the eighteenth century. Bligh was completely committed to Cook's reforms, and the appearance of any illness in his men was enough to alert him and invite his personal intervention in their treatment. It was at this time that Huggan, in his medical report to Bligh, listed three men as suffering from scurvy.

They may really have had scurvy; but the report can be read more convincingly as another blow in Huggan's battle with Bligh. There was nothing more calculated to enrage Bligh than the charge of scurvy on his ship. He had declared unequivocally at the Cape that the appearance of scurvy was a 'disgrace', and he had advertised the measures that he was taking to prevent it. Huggan, who had been messing with both Bligh and Fryer for most of the journey out, knew Bligh's views on scurvy. He was already smarting under the lash of Bligh's tongue and temper for his neglect of Valentine. His professional competence had been castigated, and he struck back at his commander's professional reputation by claiming that his reforms had failed. Taking one look at three seamen complaining of 'the Rheumatism' on 14 October 1788, he saw his chance to put one over on Bligh, diagnosed them as suffering from scurvy and then promptly joined them on the sick list himself.

Bligh was furious at this new turn in his row with Huggan, but he did not make the elementary mistake of rejecting an officer's assessment merely through lack of faith in his competence. He promptly put the three men on a concentrated diet 'of the decoction of Essence of Malt'.[1] He did not believe they had scurvy, and directed his next efforts to establishing this; but in case Huggan was right he took the necessary steps.

Over the next few days the battle of wills between Bligh and Huggan continued, though it was in many respects an unequal contest. Huggan, unlike Purcell or Fryer, did not have his wits about him. His personal disintegration through drink left the way open for Bligh to take over the medical treatment of the men who were claiming to be ill from rheumatism,

---

[1] *Log of the Bounty*, 14 October 1788.

3. Portrait of Sir Joseph Banks by Thomas Phillips.

4. Sketch by George Tobin of the wooding place at Adventure Bay, Tasmania, used by the *Bounty* and later by the *Providence* and *Assistant*. Here Purcell and Bligh had their first row on the *Bounty*. This and other sketches by Tobin were made on the voyage of the *Providence*

and he directed the *Bounty*'s resources towards them. As the ship was running out of malt, he stopped the issue of malt and Sweet Wort to all hands and confined it to the sick men. On 18 October he wrote in his Log: 'Served decoction of Malt as Yesterday and on examining the Men who the Doctor supposed had a taint of the Scurvy it appeared to be nothing more than the prickly heat. However their decoction I desired to be continued.'[2] He went at his general health programme with a renewed vigour. Diet, cleanliness and exercise, the three main ingredients of his campaign, were enforced rigorously over the following days. Any man complaining of rheumatism was to be given decoction of essence of malt, 'the doctor to issue it himself if able'.[3] At the Sunday muster of all hands on 19 October, Bligh made the perhaps exaggerated claim that 'I think I never saw a more healthy set of Men and so decent looking in my life.'

On the same Sunday, Bligh supervised the dancing session in the evening. As he was worried about the crew's health, not only would they have to dance as usual but they would have to do so with an extra relish; he attended the session to make sure this order was carried out. But two men, John Mills and William Brown, took the extraordinary step of refusing to dance. Bligh immediately ordered their grog to be stopped, 'with a promise of further punishment on a Second Refusal'.[4] William Brown was the assistant to the Kew Gardener, David Nelson, and was a supernumerary on the ship's books. He was technically a civilian, though he had been a midshipman previously in his career.[5] Mills was an ordinary seaman and more deferential towards an officer. Brown spoke up and complained that the reason why he was not dancing was because he had 'rheumatic pains in his legs'. Huggan immediately backed him up and declared, moreover, that Brown had scurvy. Bligh examined Brown himself and wrote in his Log: 'I can discover no Symptoms to lead me to be apprehensive.'[6] In his private Log, Bligh noted his doubts about the professional competence of Huggan, especially over Brown's claim to be ill. He wrote: 'The doctor's opinion likewise to me, is of little value as has been constantly drunk these last four days and is ever so when he can get liquor. I do my endeavour to prevent it, but all has no effect.'[7] On the 20th Bligh confided in his Log: 'The Doctors Intoxication has given me much trouble these last five days having been obliged to be attentive with much anxiety to complaints of four men who complain of the Rheumatism, with some difficulty I got a Sick list from him to day with only Jno. McIntosh in it under a Rheumatic complaint, the others he now seems to think nothing

[2] *ibid.*, 18 October 1788.

[3] *ibid.*, 19 October 1788. The words 'if able' appear only in the private Log and were omitted in the official Log.

[4] *Log of the Bounty*, 19 October 1788.

[5] Brown had served his time at sea and had been an acting Lieutenant in H.M.S. *Resolution* (Captain Lord Robert Manners) at Rodney's action of 12 April 1782; D. Bonner Smith, 1936, p. 211. The little that we know about Brown's early career suggest that he was of above average ability, but why he graduated from a naval career to that of botanist is not at present known.

[6] *Log of the Bounty*, 19 October 1788.

[7] Private Log, 19 October 1788.

about.'[8] It is significant that Brown's name does not appear on this list. Perhaps he had been trying it on, taking advantage of the obvious discord between Surgeon and Captain. Overnight he may have listened to advice from his shipmates (who no doubt had a good laugh over the whole business), and desisted from continuing with his 'illness'.

Huggan's drunkenness was reaching embarrassing proportions. His position as an officer was being undermined by his condition. He was clearly in breach of the Articles by his behaviour.[9] Bligh sent for him on 21 October 'and in a most friendly manner requested him to leave off drinking, but he seemed not sensible of any thing I said to him and it had little effect'.[10] Bligh now arranged for the Assistant Surgeon, Thomas Ledward, who had been signed on for this job (though rated as A.B.), to take on several of the official duties of Huggan. On the same day Huggan went back on the Sick List, which was signed by Ledward.

Why did Bligh not confiscate Huggan's liquor store? We have a statement of his reasons set out in the private Log on 21 October:

> The Surgeon kept his Bed all this day and always drunk, without eating an ounce of food. If it is ever necessary this should be publickly known, I may be blamed for not searching his Cabbin and taking all liquor from him; but my motive is that, altho Every person on board is acquainted with his ebriety, yet hoping every day will produce a change in him, I forebear making a publick matter of My disapprobation of his conduct, in expectation as he has done many times this Voyage, he may turn sober again.[11]

Was Bligh being candid about his reasons for not exercising his authority to confiscate the liquor store? It may be that he was using Huggan's drunkenness to make it easier to assert his own control over the medication of the men on the sick list. The more drunk Huggan was, the more his diagnosis of scurvy would be discredited. While he was incapable under alcohol he could not judge the condition of anybody else and if, as Bligh probably suspected, he was maliciously diagnosing scurvy to embarrass the record of the voyage, it made sense for Bligh to let him wallow in a state of incapacity, whatever other problems this might cause for discipline.

The sick list for 22 October had McIntosh, Milward and Huggan on it under rheumatism, and some other men complained of rheumatic pains. On this day Bligh ordered the issue of portable soup, barley and malt to the complainants and for the entire crew he ordered a 'medicine' of elixir of vitrol in water to be taken half an hour before breakfast. Some of the crew objected,

---

[8] *Log of the Bounty*, 20 October 1788.

[9] 'All flag officers, and all persons in or belonging to his Majesty's ships or vessels of war, being guilty of profane oaths, cursings, execrations, drunkenness, uncleanness, or other scandalous actions, in derogation of God's honour, and corruption of good manners, shall incur such punishment as a court martial shall think fit to impose, and as the nature and degree of their offence shall deserve', MacArthur, 1813, Vol. 1, pp. 325-6.

[10] Private Log, 21 October 1788.

[11] *ibid.*

including Purcell, but they were threatened with loss of grog, and this forced compliance.[12]

In Bligh's opinion it was the warmer weather that was causing illness in the crew. For most of the voyage they had been in cold climates. Some men claimed that they felt faint around noon, and Bligh naturally took this to confirm his views about the heat. He ordered the salt provisions to be stopped and introduced portable soup, barley, flour and raisins into the diet of the whole crew. On 24 October he wrote optimistically about the medical condition of the men:

> It is with much pleasure I find the few Invalids recovering very fast. The faintness which they complained of is totally gone away and their Spirits and looks are good, but most of them still complain of the Rheumatism and they all say it is particularly troublesome when they go to bed. This with their having no eruptions or swellings, convinces me that their complaint is not scorbutic. Their Gums also are as sound as any can be expected after such a length of Salt Diet and their breath is not offensive neither is their teeth the least loose.[13]

The sick men were on the mend, at least in Bligh's opinion, and he now turned to deal more effectively with Huggan. On the same day, Bligh ordered Huggan's cabin to be cleaned out and his liquor store removed. The cabin was so filthy that Bligh was prompted to record that the 'operation was not only troublesome but offensive in the highest degree'. The drunken surgeon was naturally disturbed by the commotion in his cabin, and when he was sober enough to understand what had happened he tried to get his own back. He put himself down as suffering from 'Paralytic Affection' – a diagnosis occasioned by having 'lost the use of one side' of his body, as Bligh described it. He also re-diagnosed McIntosh and Milward as having the scurvy, and Matthew Thompson as having 'lumbago'. Bligh was naturally once again furious. He demanded to know why the diagnosis had been altered when 'every Man was recovering and almost well'.

But to this question he received no satisfactory answer from Huggan. All he could do was shout at his surgeon, who sent him into further paroxysms of rage by acting stupid. The childish tussle may have been amusing to onlookers – it was certainly undignified for two officers to behave in this manner – and in such a small ship as the *Bounty* everybody could watch Huggan baiting the Lieutenant. Amusing or not, the fact remains that the verbal altercations between the offended Lieutenant and the drunken surgeon were serving to undermine still further the credibility of the Commander.

The *Bounty* passed Maitea, the first of the Tahitian group of islands, on 25

---

[12] *ibid.*, 22 October 1788; later the medicine time was changed from before breakfast to 11 a.m. at the crew's request.

[13] *Log of the Bounty*, 24 October 1788; soft gums, loose teeth and bad breath were well-known symptoms of scurvy.

October 1788. The sick men were even fitter, according to Bligh, and even the Surgeon had lost his paralytic disorder, which, Bligh wrote, 'has been perfectly cured in 48 hours by giving him no Spirits to make use of, and only a little Wine and water'.[14] After 27,000 miles, the approach of landfall was of major interest for everybody. It was an opportunity to get out of the cramped ship and away from the incessant rows of the past weeks. The *Bounty* arrived at Matavai Bay on 26 October.

Surprisingly, in view of what had been going on between them, Bligh ordered Huggan to make a medical inspection of the entire crew to check for venereal disease before landing. Ledward could have been directed to the task, but Bligh, as a person imbued in the ways of the service, considered it only proper that Huggan, if he was sober, should carry out the duty. And Huggan had sobered up just in time to obey the order.

The reason for the inspection was largely diplomatic. The mission required peaceful relationships between the islanders and the Europeans, to ensure a smooth transfer of the breadfruit. The relationship between the *Bounty*'s crew and the island women was hardly likely, in Bligh's tactful phrase, 'to be of a very reserved nature'. Quite the opposite, indeed, if previous experience was a precedent. If they could be accused of infecting the islanders, this might prejudice the success of the expedition, although it is certain that venereal disease already existed on the island by this time.

Huggan's verdict was that they were all clean of venereal disease. Bligh accepted the verdict and recorded it in the Log; and it also appeared in the published *Narrative*. But from other evidence, this verdict is suspect. The medical records of the *Bounty* up to the time of the mutiny have survived and we may note some interesting points.[15]

When a man caught VD he reported to the doctor who gave him a 'cure', which was recorded and charged against his wages. A cure cost £1.10s. a time. The date of the cure was not recorded. Both Ledward and Huggan dispensed cures, and their names are also recorded against each man they treated. In Huggan's case, eight men are listed as having purchased cures from him. These are William Cole, Boatswain; John Swan, A.B.; Alexander Smith, A.B.; Fletcher Christian, Master's Mate; James Valentine, A.B.; Robert Lamb, A.B.; Matthew Quintal, A.B.; and William Brown, Assistant Gardener. Another twelve names are listed by Ledward, and he also treated Quintal and Brown; in other words, nearly half the ship's company had had venereal disease by the time the *Bounty* left Tahiti.

From Huggan's list we can establish that he prescribed at least two cures before the *Bounty* arrived at Tahiti. We know this from the presence on his list of the names of John Swan and James Valentine. Swan did not sail from Britain but deserted at Portsmouth on 27 November 1787; Valentine died after leaving Tasmania. The other six on Huggan's list must have had the disease at some time between the signing on of Huggan as Surgeon and his death on 9 December 1788 at Tahiti. Bligh's Log, which recorded the

[14] *ibid.*, 25 October 1788.
[15] Smith, 1936, pp. 216-17.

medical reports and sick list on a daily basis, tells us that between 26 October and 9 December five people (unnamed) were treated for VD. He recorded this in detail because he was concerned to rebut any suggestion that his ship brought the disease to the island; he hoped to show that they caught it while they were there and were promptly treated. If only five men were treated at Tahiti before Huggan's death, and all were Huggan's patients, this leaves one of the six unaccounted for, who must have been treated by Huggan on the voyage out. If, as seems possible, some of these five were Ledward's patients, then more than one of them was treated by Huggan before the arrival at Tahiti.

Fletcher Christian's bout of venereal disease has been a matter of minor controversy since its discovery in the ships documents. If he was treated before the *Bounty* got to Tahiti he must have caught it somewhere else, perhaps on his West Indian voyages in the *Britannia*. If he caught it at Tahiti, his family's denials that he had sexual relations at Tahiti are undermined (see p.234).

It seems that Huggan's inspection was perfunctory and that at least one, if not more, of the crew had the disease before they got to Tahiti. Why would Huggan want to give a false impression of the state of the men's health the day before the *Bounty* anchored? Partly because it would not suit the men if he pronounced any of them to have VD. The men would have been confined to the ship while they were being 'cured'. It can also be seen as an extension of his quarrel with Bligh. If he kept the diseased men on board, Bligh might achieve a clean record in respect of this disease on the island. If any of them had it, Huggan could pronounce them clean and hope that their relationships on the island would spread it, thus embarrassing Bligh. This view is supported by subsequent events on the island; on the few occasions on which Huggan was fit enough to go ashore, he diagnosed venereal disease as being responsible for the bodily sores of several of the women, though Bligh expressed his own doubts about this and noted that by treating these sores with clean bandages they were cleaned up. Bligh went to considerable lengths to enquire about venereal disease among the women, and he notes on numerous occasions the answers to his questions from the islanders. The fact that Huggan diagnosed VD whenever he was called upon to give an opinion regarding a limb with sores on it suggests that he diagnosed it as often as possible to blacken the *Bounty*'s and Bligh's reputation with the islanders, as a last pathetic gesture of sabotage.

9

Matavai Bay

On his previous visit to the South Seas with Captain Cook, Bligh had seen at close hand the fragility of relationships between islanders and Europeans. On this visit he hoped to prevent incidents that might disturb the collection of the bread fruit, and before the *Bounty* reached Tahiti he had made arrangements to ensure the security of the mission.

One of the main sources of conflict between the islanders and the Europeans was, as we have seen, the islanders' proclivity to steal anything they could lay their hands on from the ship and from the seamen. It was theft that had led to Cook's death, and the practice was apparently universal throughout the Pacific. Attempts by the seamen to recover their property, or to purloin in return the property of the islanders, always led to trouble. Relations between seamen and island women, however, were not a source of conflict, as they might have been at other ports of call. The women were always willing to engage in sexual relations with the Europeans, and their menfolk did not seem to mind. Trade was the other area of potential trouble. The *Bounty*'s need for fresh provisions could only be met by trade. Food could be exchanged for the petty items of European manufacture that were popular with the islanders – iron objects, adzes, axes, nails, mirrors, beads and cloth. The *Bounty* had taken on a large stock of these items. The main problem that could arise was a depreciation of the 'currency' through illegal entrepreneurial activity by the seamen. The seamen knew that local curios would fetch a good price back in Britain, and might be tempted to indulge in the rash purchase of items offered by the islanders, particularly if they could purloin the ship's stores to use as currency.

These problems were not unique to the *Bounty*. Cook on his three voyages had also encountered them, and he had developed a sensible policy to deal with them. He enforced some rules of conduct to govern the relationships between the seamen and the islanders, and Bligh had learned the efficacy of these rules from experience. Bligh was not, therefore, being unusually tyrannical when he copied Cook's policy. The day before landfall Bligh posted his Rules of Conduct for the Officers and Men of the *Bounty*. They were similar to the rules set out by Cook, though more lenient in some details. They were aimed at 'the better establishing a trade for supplies of provisions, and good intercourse with the natives of the South Seas, wherever the ship may be at'.[1]

---

[1] Bligh, 1794, p. 4.

The first rule was: 'At the Society, or Friendly, Islands, no person whatever is to intimate that Captain Cook was killed by Indians; or that he is dead.' Bligh did not know that a ship had called at Tahiti just before the *Bounty* and that the visitors had already told the islanders that Cook was dead, although apparently they had not been indiscreet enough to say how he died.[2]

The next rule was that 'no person is ever to speak, or give the least hint, that we have come on purpose to get the bread-fruit plant, until I have made my plan known to the chiefs'. Careless talk might disclose that the plants were valuable to the visitors, and this could encourage the islanders to demand payment for the plants from the ship's stores. Bligh's plan was to get the plants as a gift to the King of Britain and concentrate the barter trade on provisions.

The third rule specified the nature of the conduct of the seamen towards the islanders. It stated: 'Every person is to study to gain the good will and esteem of the natives; to treat them with all kindness; and not to take from them, by violent means, any thing that they may have stolen; and no one is ever to fire, but in defence of his life.' This instruction sums up the conclusions Bligh had drawn from his experience with Cook in the *Resolution*. Captain Cook had written on the habit of theft by the islanders: 'I must bear my testimony that the people of this country, of all ranks, men and women, are the arrantest thieves upon the face of the earth.'[3] Given this kind of behaviour, Bligh was concerned to prevent incidents arising from the seamen's reaction to it. The stricture against violence and opening fire with their weapons, except in defence of life, was meant to be a general rule to govern their conduct both when they were supervised by an officer and when they were on their own.

Cook also made the following point about thefts by the Tahitians: '... we must not hastily conclude that theft is a testimony of the same depravity in them that it is in us, in the instances in which our people were sufferers by their dishonesty; for their temptation was such, as to surmount what would be considered as a proof of uncommon integrity among those who have more knowledge, better principles, and stronger motives to resist the temptations of illicit advantage: an Indian among penny knives and beads, and even nails and broken glass, is in the same state of mind with the meanest servant in Europe among unlocked coffers of jewels and gold.'[4] The best policy to deal with theft was to try to prevent it by 'locking the "coffers"'. If the ship's fittings and fixtures were left carelessly about, or the tools and implements of the shore party were not looked after, the islanders would be less able to resist temptation. The men must be made to look after the equipment that

[2] Bligh in his published *Voyage* (1792) mentions that the islanders told him that Lieutenant Watt was an officer on the ship that had called before the *Bounty* with the news of Cook's death; Watt had been on the *Resolution* with Bligh, as a midshipman. From subsequent events it seems that the *Bounty* men convinced the islanders that this was a misunderstanding and Cook was still alive.

[3] Quoted in Barrow, 1961, p. 28.
[4] *ibid*.

was in their charge and therefore 'every person employed on service, is to take care that no arms, or implements of any kind under their charge, are stolen; the value of such things being lost shall be charged against their wages'.

The parallel problem to theft by the islanders was, of course, the possibility of theft by the *Bounty*'s crew. The islanders wanted European goods and, deprived of access to them, they could induce the seamen to steal for them by offering them things that they might want. To counter this, Bligh ordered that 'no man is to embezzel, or offer for sale, directly, or indirectly any part of the King's stores, of what nature soever'. In contrast to Cook, he did not threaten a court martial for offenders.

If theft could be stamped out, and Bligh believed that it could, then all trading would be channelled into official hands. Bligh, like Cook, appointed an official trader: 'A proper person or persons will be appointed to regulate trade, and barter with the natives; and no officer or seaman, or other person belonging to the ship, is to trade for any kind of provisions or curiosities; but if such officer or seaman wishes to purchase any particular thing he is to apply to the provider to do it for him. By this means a regular market will be carried on, and all disputes which otherwise may happen with the natives will be avoided.' The man appointed as 'provider' was William Peckover, the Gunner, and he was an obvious choice: he knew the islands and the language, and his three voyages with Cook had given him a lot of experience of what was required.

With these preparations completed, the *Bounty* entered Matavai Bay, Tahiti, on 26 October 1788. Their welcome was tumultuous even by Tahitian standards. As the ship swung inside the reef and into the calmer water off Point Venus,[5] hundreds of canoes put off from the shore towards her, and within minutes the deck of the *Bounty* was covered with smiling and laughing near-naked islanders. It must have been a bewildering experience for the seamen who were visiting the island for the first time. Unfortunately the ship was endangered by this exuberant welcome, as the anchor was not clear and the sails were not reefed. Bligh noted that 'in less than ten minutes the deck was so full that I could scarce find my own people'. He shouted out orders to stop the ship drifting aimlessly towards the shore, and the *Bounty* dropped anchor safely at the end of its 27,000-mile journey. The first stage of the expedition was completed.

The Tahitians quickly established that the ship was from Britain – 'Pretanee', as they called it – and many of them recognised Peckover, Nelson and Bligh. They asked eagerly after the others whom they knew and remembered. Bligh wrote: 'Captn. Cook was the first person asked after, and they said a Ship had been here who had told them he was dead ...'. The situation was saved by David Nelson, who in a fit of over-enthusiasm declared loudly, pointing at Bligh, 'This is the Son of Captain Cook'; as Bligh noted, 'It seemed to please them very much'.[6] The islanders also asked after Joseph Banks who had been very popular with several of the women

---

[5] Named Point Venus because of the Observatory that had been set up there on Cook's first voyage to observe the transit of Venus.

[6] *Log of the Bounty*, 26 October 1788.

and was known widely among the islanders from his role as Cook's trader, and also after Dr Solander and others from the *Endeavour*.[7]

Bligh also had questions for the Tahitians. He asked for Omai, the Tahitian taken to Britain by Cook on his second voyage and returned to Tahiti with Cook on the third voyage, a very friendly person and a great favourite at the British court, and for the two young Maori boys whom Cook had taken to Tahiti and left there. The news about the three friends was unhappy: all three were dead. Bligh was told that they had died from natural causes.

Bligh asked for the Chief, Otoo, because it was only through the Chief that he could arrange his real business. Otoo was away, but when he heard that Bligh had returned he sent presents with a message that he would arrive at the Bay the next day. When Otoo arrived, with his family and the retinue of servants that accompanied him everywhere, he told Bligh that he had a new name, Tinah. The Chiefs often changed their names, which could be confusing. He sent on ahead of him the framed portrait of Captain Cook, which had been painted for him by Webber, the official artist of the third voyage, as a symbol of friendship to show to other European ships that might visit Tahiti. Bligh, who had gone ashore with another local Chief, Poeeno, inspected the site of Cook's 1777 shore camp with a view to using it for the *Bounty*'s shore party, but he reserved his best attentions for the arrival of Tinah.[8] The celebrations following the Chief's arrival and the exchange of presents went on for two days. Tinah was apparently not quite the powerful personage that Bligh had been led to believe from his previous visit. Much had happened in the Tahitian power-game in the intervening years.[9] But Tinah was nevertheless capable of an imposing style of life. Whereas other Chiefs, like Poeeno, took their own canoes out to meet the *Bounty*, Tinah, when he arrived at the shore, demanded and received one of the *Bounty*'s boats to pick him up and carry him across to the ship. Bligh became very attached to Tinah during his stay and clearly enjoyed his company.

Naturally, nothing had been said so far about the purpose of the visit, and to the Tahitian mind nothing was needed to justify a visit of this kind. They themselves went on regular tours round the islands merely to see friends. Bligh, nevertheless, was looking for a chance to raise the issue of the breadfruit plant, and an opportunity came quite early on in a conversation with Tinah. From Bligh's Log and his 1790 and 1792 accounts we can

---

[7] James Morrison, in his Journal, p. 101b, claimed that Matte – the Chief when the mutineers returned to Tahiti – was angry with Bligh for keeping the news of Cook's death from them and for claiming to be Cook's son. This conflicts with Bligh's Logs and his published *Narrative*, but has influenced some critics; Hough, 1972, pp. 106-7, does not mention that the islanders knew of Cook's death. Bligh records in his Log that the Tahitians asked after Williamson of the *Resolution*, although Williamson was his bitter enemy – a small point, but it supports the veracity of the Log. Criticism of Bligh by Hough and others over this trivial incident originating in the chance remarks of David Nelson seems unnecessary. When Bligh returned to Tahiti in H.M.S. *Providence* Matte was friendly to him.

[8] During the first visit ashore an islander was caught trying to steal a pot. The thefts had begun.

[9] *See* Danielsson, 1962, p. 62 for an analysis of the power structure at the time.

Bligh

reconstruct the interview. Tinah asked how long Bligh intended to stay at Matavai and he was told that the *Bounty* would stay a while and then visit other islands. Tinah's own 'kingdom' had been plundered recently by rivals from across the island, but the arrival of the Europeans gave him a great opportunity to re-assert himself. He expressed horror at the thought of his European friends leaving Matavai, as he hoped that their presence would deter any further trouble from his enemies. 'Here,' said Tinah, 'you shall be supplied plentifully with everything you want. All here are your friends, and friends of King George: if you go to the other islands you will have everything stolen from you.' Bligh realised that this was the opening for his request, and he pointed out that King George knew of Tinah's friendship and had sent out valuable presents for him. The next step in the argument was the important one, for having got Tinah to state what he wanted – the presence of the *Bounty* – and having introduced the subject of presents from King George to Tinah, there was a chance that Tinah might then offer some present to King George in return. The question was what would he offer? Bligh asked Tinah: 'Will not you, Tinah, send something to King George in return?' Tinah immediately said yes and then listing everything he could think of, began to enumerate the different articles that he might send to King George. Among these he mentioned breadfruit.

Bligh had finessed the offer he wanted. He described in his book, with obvious pleasure, how he closed the deal between them on the spot: 'This was the exact point to which I wished to bring the conversation; and seizing an opportunity, which had every appearance of being undesigned and accidental, I told him the Bread Fruit trees were what King George would like; upon which he promised me a great many should be put on board, and seemed much delighted to find it so easily in his power to send anything that could be received by King George.'[10] No doubt Tinah considered that he had cause to be 'much delighted' with his negotiations. He had ensured the presence of the *Bounty* for some time ahead, from which alone he would extract enormous prestige, and he had done this at the 'cost' of a plant that grew in abundance everywhere in the island. His enemies could have made the same deal. Bligh, though he had no intention of getting embroiled in any of Tinah's plans of conquest, not only because it would interfere in his mission but also because involvement in local wars could prejudice future visits by the King's ships, was also 'much delighted'. And so were the crew, for the ship's rules allowed Tahitian women to stay on the ship for the night; only men were required to go ashore.

Some authors, such as Hough and Danielsson, have raised the question of why Bligh kept the *Bounty* at Tahiti for a full five months, thus allowing the men to grow slack and their indiscipline to increase. It is argued that he should have left a small shore party to collect and tender the plants and have taken the *Bounty* on a cruise of the islands, charting and discovering, until the plants were ready to be loaded. We do not know the answer to this question, nor even whether Bligh had considered other possibilities. I can only suggest

[10] Bligh, 1792 (1965), p. 63.

some possible reasons why Bligh lingered at Matavai. First, the transplanting of the breadfruit involved some serious technical problems. The plants had to be carried over 12,000 miles and delivered fit for re-planting. Dr Solander, the man who had noted the nourishing properties of the plant, had suggested in 1776 that everybody should be encouraged to 'bring it over, either by young plants properly rooted, or by seeds collected in the proper season, and sown during the passage'.[11] But by 1787 nobody had made a proper study of the breadfruit plant and its characteristics, and nobody knew for certain that it could be 'brought over' without considerable loss. Bligh therefore had to rely entirely on the professional judgment of David Nelson, the Kew botanist. Nelson's recommendation was that the plants should be transplanted into pots, and that when they were observed to be firmly rooted, and only then, they should be placed in the *Bounty*. This meant the *Bounty* would need to be in the Pacific for several months at least. If Bligh risked a hasty transplant operation and an early departure from Tahiti, and it was discovered when well on the way home that the plants were not thriving, it would be necessary to return to Tahiti, with strain on the ship's provisions and a possible long journey to catch the prevailing winds. Secondly, the shore party had to be secure. Before the *Bounty*'s arrival the Matavai kingdom had been attacked and laid waste by a rival chief. Even if the local Chiefs were friendly to the Europeans, there was no guarantee that islanders from elsewhere would not take advantage of the absence of the ship to harass and attack the shore party and its encampment. Anything like a mêlée among the potted plants would have been a serious set-back. Bligh was, as we know, never loth to go out of his way in pursuit of geographical knowledge or accurate charting. The idea of sailing round the islands for several months would have been attractive to a man of his temperament and devotion to navigation. He had made meticulous measurements and descriptions while en route for Tahiti, at Tenerife, False Bay, Tristan da Cunha, St Paul's Island, Mewstone Rock, Penguin Island, the Bounty Isles and Maitea. It seems likely that it was not the want of a spirit of exploration and adventure that kept him at Tahiti while the plants matured, but devotion to the task in hand.

Danielsson has suggested a further possible reason for the delay.[12] The Admiralty's original sailing orders directed Bligh to return through the Torres Straits (known to Britain at the time as Endeavour Straits, after Cook's first voyage through them in H.M.S. *Endeavour*). Because the *Bounty* had been delayed in departing from Britain and had lost the chance of getting round the Horn, it had arrived at Tahiti more than six months later than anticipated, dropping anchor in October instead of March. Danielsson suggests that a quick departure from Tahiti for a passage through the Endeavour Straits was not feasible because the prevailing winds at that time of year are westerly, making the straits even more dangerous than with the wind assisting. This may have been a factor in Bligh's decision to wait for the

[11] Edwards, 1818-19, Vol. 1, p. 293.
[12] Danielsson, 1962, pp. 68-9.

plants to be ready, though it does not explain why he did not make a tour round the islands in the meantime; he could have gone in an easterly direction.

Bligh made administrative arrangements for the stay at Tahiti. He put Fletcher Christian in charge of a shore party consisting of William Peckover, the Gunner and Official Trader, the Botanists David Nelson and William Brown, midshipman Peter Heywood and four seamen. We can speculate on the reasons for this decision and its consequences. Fryer had been left continuously in command of the *Bounty* at Matavai while Bligh was ashore engaging in his numerous meetings with the chiefs and general diplomatic work, and had exhibited an alarming degree of incompetence. Bligh needed a reliable man in charge of the collection of the breadfruit plants. He apparently did not trust Fryer to do this job properly, and he probably thought that if he himself was on the *Bounty* most of the time he could keep an eye on Fryer more effectively than if he allowed him to exercise his incompetence on shore. During the following months Fryer's failures on the ship were to drive Bligh into rages, which spilled over onto the heads of others; but Christian on the shore was out of the way of this growing bitterness. When he returned to ship duty the following April, he was taken from a relaxed and pleasant life where he was his own boss, respected by the islanders and diverted by the attractions of Tahiti, and replaced in a command structure that was collapsing under personal conflicts. His commander had been transformed from the friend of the *Britannia* into a bad-tempered man with no confidence in those around him, who was indulging in verbal thuggery at the slightest provocation. This probably helped to push him over the brink into mutiny.

In the months that the *Bounty* spent at Tahiti, Bligh made copious notes in his Log on what he observed of the customs of the islanders. His accounts are in many ways a brilliant and moving testimony to his scientific objectivity, but unfortunately they cannot detain us here.[13] We must press on to the events that led up to the mutiny.

[13] Readers interested in anthropological details should consult Bligh's *Narrative* (1790 and 1792, 1965) and *Log of the Bounty* (ed. Rutter, 1937) and Morrison's Journal (Morrison, 1935).

10

The Move to Oparre

Inevitably the first troubles on the *Bounty* were associated with a spate of thefts. The first row was on 30 October 1788, within four days of the *Bounty*'s arrival. Bligh made it an issue with the Chiefs following the theft of hooks and thimbles which had been cut out from their places on gun carriages. 'These were the first thefts I thought it necessary to take notice of,' wrote Bligh, 'and therefore ordered every Man except the Cheifs Attendants out of the ship.' Following this order to clear the ship, there were many rows and recriminations, probably due to the roughness with which the seamen carried out the order and their scanty knowledge of the Tahitian language. In one of these rows an islander attacked an armed sentry who, according to the Rules of Conduct, was not permitted to open fire. But the incident created such a commotion that Bligh was brought to the scene. By the time he got there the islander had fled into the escaping crowd. Bligh was satisfied with his policy, however, because 'Every one was excessively alarmed at my determination, and I hope it will be the last provocation'.[1] But the next day the buoy of the bow anchor was stolen.

If chastisement of the islanders for their thefts was an insufficient deterrent, the alternative policy of chastisement of the seamen responsible for the property was the only other remedy. When the thefts continued, Bligh decided to punish the next seaman he considered to be guilty. On 4 November, a seaman, Alexander Smith, was brought before him charged with negligence for letting an islander steal the gudgeon of the large cutter. The Log explains Bligh's reasoning: 'Several petty Thefts having been committed by the Natives owing to the negligence and inattention of the Petty Officers and Men, which has always more or less a tendancy to alarm the Chiefs, I was under the necessity this afternoon to punish Alexn. Smith with 12 lashes for suffering the Gudgeon of the large Cutter to be drawn out without knowing it.'[2] The alarm felt by the Chiefs at these incidents was based on the fear that following a theft the British would exact some retribution upon them or their people, but they also expressed real grief at the punishment of Smith. When the Chiefs and their wives saw the preparations for his punishment – in the Navy of the time punishment followed a specific drill – they attempted to intercede on Smith's behalf and pleaded with Bligh to cancel the punishment. He could not do this; naval

[1] *Log of the Bounty*, 30 October 1788.
[2] *ibid.*, 4 November 1788.

protocol would not allow it. But he was deeply moved by the reaction of the islanders. His Log records the incident and concludes with the remark that 'seeing it had no effect they retired, and the Women in general showed every degree of Sympathy which marked them to be the most humane and affectionate creatures in the World'.[3]

The punishment of Smith did not stop the thefts. With the work continuing both on board and ashore and the constant stream of visitors plying between the ship and the shore, it was a difficult task to police all the ship's property. What to do about the thefts presented a dilemma: 'Frequent disputes with Indians have a dangerous tendency, as all altercations produce threats on our side without being able, or perhaps not convenient, to put them in execution, it is therefore better to put up with trifling losses unless the Offender can be detected.'[4] The incident that prompted this entry was the 'remissness of my Officers & People at the Tent' leading to the theft of the boat's rudder. Punishment was not ordered, because Bligh was not sure exactly who was responsible. He mentions the officers without naming them, but we can take it that the man concerned – Christian, Peckover or Heywood – was at least verbally reprimanded by Bligh. Again the discriminatory treatment, though inevitable in the eighteenth-century Navy, must have rankled; while Smith had received twelve lashes after the theft of the boat's gudgeon, the officers with the 'soft' jobs at the tents went scot free after losing the boat's rudder. A couple of days later one of the (unnamed) officers had a pair of sheets stolen from his hammock. Again no punishment followed.

The day after the theft of the 'gentleman's sheets', Purcell again proved difficult and disobeyed Bligh. Bligh was asked by one of his visitors if he could give them a stone to sharpen the hatchets that they had received as presents. He agreed immediately, and ordered Purcell to prepare a stone for that purpose. To his astonishment, Purcell refused, saying: 'I will not cut the stone for it will spoil my Chissel, and tho there is law to take away my cloaths there is none to take away my Tools.' Purcell evidently knew there was little that Bligh could do about his insolence. The carpenter was in great demand at this part of the voyage, getting the cabin ready for the plants and doing the kind of work that accumulates on a ship after any long voyage: Bligh simply could not do without him. He was only able to confine Purcell to his cabin for the day and to apologise to the islander, who was no doubt confused by what had happened.[5] On the same day, a gale suddenly blew up and hit the bay with alarming fury. It lasted a couple of anxious days. The shore camp was almost flooded, and the plants there were secured from being washed away only with great difficulty. During the gale Matthew Thompson fell foul of Bligh or one of the officers and was ordered to punishment for 'insolence and disobedience of Orders'.[6] We do not know whom Thompson offended or

---

[3] *ibid.*

[4] *ibid.*, 1 December 1788.

[5] *ibid.*, 5 December 1788. Bligh added: 'Altho I can but ill spare the loss of a Single Man, but I do not intend to lose the use of him but to remitt him to his duty to Morrow.' Danielsson, 1962, p. 66, states that Purcell was in 'guard room arrest for a few days'.

[6] Danielsson, 1962, p. 68.

exactly what he did, but the contrast was again noticeable between the punishments. It was probably a talking-point below decks that evening. Purcell, a Petty Officer, had been 'insolent' and had disobeyed orders, and had been sent to his cabin; Thompson, a seaman, was charged with the same offence and got twelve lashes.

The next day the carpenter was returned to his duty. The islanders told Bligh that at that time of year storms were fairly frequent, and he decided to move the ship and the camp to somewhere safer. Chief Poeeno's wife displayed such an 'excess of Greif for the danger the Ship had been in, that would have affected the most dispassionate creature existing', wrote Bligh.[7] But it was not possible to move the *Bounty* immediately. Nelson advised that the plants be kept ashore for a few days to see if they had been damaged in the storm. Meanwhile, the men were put to work to prepare the ship for sea, and it became a hive of activity as the shore camp was dismantled and the ship's stores were stowed.

During this work, a young boy playing near the ship's boat, which was being run up onto the shore, fell under one of the wooden rollers and was injured. Some islanders present immediately set off in their canoe to the *Bounty* to tell Bligh what had happened. Bligh hurriedly summoned all medical assistance only to find that Huggan was once again drunk in his cabin and incapable of moving. He then called for Ledward to take over and to get ashore quickly but Ledward was apparently unable to find instruments 'or any thing necessary for some time'. Fortunately the boy had no broken limbs, but Bligh admits that when he got ashore himself he was very angry with the man hauling the boat for letting the accident happen. He was concerned in case the boy had internal injuries, and he had him taken on board to receive medical attention.[8]

Later that day Ledward reported to Bligh that Huggan was in a deep alcoholic coma, and he recommended that they move him to the main cabin to get fresh air. Bligh ordered Fryer with some men to attend to the removal and reported Fryer's astonishment at finding Huggan already unconscious on the deck.[9] Huggan was eventually moved to the main cabin and offered some coconut milk, but at 9 p.m. he died. This was the second death on the *Bounty*, and Bligh wrote in his Log:

This unfortunate Man died owing to drunkeness and indolence. Exercise was a thing he could not bear an Idea of, or could I ever bring him to take half a dozen of turns on deck at a time in the course of the whole Voyage. Sleeping was the way he spent his time, and he accustomed himself to breath so little fresh Air and was so filthy in his person that he became latterly a nuisance ... In the Morning the News of the Surgeons death became known to all the Natives. Most of them particularly the Cheifs knew him very well and without hesitating a moment pronounced his

---

[7] *Log of the Bounty*, 8 December 1788.
[8] *ibid.*, 10 December 1788.
[9] *ibid.*; this is a mystery. No one can explain how Huggan got up on deck or who moved him there.

death owing to his 'not working and drinking to much Ava no Pretanee', for this was the literal meaning and they had Often remarked before that every person was employed but himself.[10]

The Surgeon was buried at Point Venus, and Ledward was promoted from A.B. to Acting Surgeon. Huggan's effects were 'disposed of'[11] by auction among the crew. On Huggan's death his cabin was locked, and two days later, on 12 December, Bligh spent the best part of a day making an inventory of his effects for the auction. This was normal on the death of an officer away from home waters, and sometimes for a seaman, though with a seaman the effects would not usually amount to much and would simply be divided out among his friends. Valentine's effects, for instance, were given to the men who tended him while he was sick. Because of the lack of personal hygiene of the Surgeon, his effects were not sought after and Bligh held back 33 shirts because 'not one half of the Value was Offered for them'.[12] There must have been a lot of property on offer if it took Bligh nearly a day to list it. Ledward was naturally interested in acquiring the medicines and instruments, and he bought the lot at Bligh's valuation less £5. He may not have been too pleased with his 'bargain', because Bligh decided that the instruments could not be valued properly except at their purchase price. On the other hand, he did well out of Huggan's death, as there was a good chance of his promotion being confirmed on the return of the ship to Britain.

During the following week the men were busy bringing out sails, stowing stores and picking the bread (this involved cutting the rotten pieces out and throwing them into the bay). Tinah, having noticed this activity, tried to persuade Bligh not to depart from his kingdom, and he suggested an alternative anchorage just along the coast at Oparre. To the delight of Tinah and the other chiefs, Bligh decided to move to Oparre rather than further away. This was bound to be popular with the men who had made good friends among the Tahitians. The decision has been criticised because it bound the *Bounty* and its crew deeper to the people of Matavai. So it did, and this was probably what it was meant to do. Tinah's people were not interfering with the collection of the breadfruit plants, and in fact were proving helpful in this and other respects. There were powerful arguments, therefore, against going elsewhere and risking poor relations with the inhabitants.

Joseph Coleman, the Armourer, set up his forge to make some iron parts for the ship, and by accident Bligh discovered a popular way to please the islanders. They brought large numbers of pieces of iron for Coleman to fashion into something useful for them, which he gladly did (in contrast to Purcell's attitude). Some of the iron pieces dated from Cook's visits to the island. Bligh told Coleman to continue this public relations work along with his ship's work.

---

[10] *ibid.*; 'Ava no Pretanee' was Tahitian for British liquor; ava was a local brew drunk by the Chiefs.

[11] Bligh, 1792 (1965), p. 83.

[12] *Log of the Bounty*, 13 December 1788.

On Christmas Eve, Fryer was sent to sound the channel from Matavai and the anchorage at Oparre. He reported a depth of 16 to 17 fathoms all the way. The plant pots were then brought on board. Because somebody (unnamed) had told Bligh that it would take two days he supervised the operation himself and it was completed in one day.[13] With the pots on board, the *Bounty* was ready to sail, and Bligh made arrangements to conduct the ship safely between the two bays.

In spite of these precautions the *Bounty* ran aground on the journey. Bligh's 1792 *Narrative* suffers here from Burney's editing. The public was not made aware of the ineffective role of Fryer, and the incompetence of Fletcher Christian, in this accident. The *Narrative* states: 'At half past ten, we got the ship under sail, and ran down under top-sails; when we were near the launch, it fell calm, and the ship shot past her. We immediately let the anchor go, but, to our great surprise, we found the ship was aground forwards. She had run on so easy, that we had not perceived it at the time. This accident occasioned us much trouble ...'[14] The ship's Log tells a different story and locates the blame for the accident.

The ship's launch had been sent to Oparre with the tents and the property from the shore camp at Point Venus. Bligh gave instructions to the launch party to return to the opening in the reef and await the arrival of the *Bounty*.[15] Christian, as commander of the shore party, was almost certainly the man in command of the launch. The *Bounty* weighed anchor at 10.30 a.m. and moved slowly towards the new harbour, arriving near the opening in the reef at 11.15, where the launch was waiting to guide it through the channel. John Fryer was sent aloft by Bligh to the foreyard to get a good view of any obstructions and to shout a warning if he saw any. He had already sounded the channel and given it a clearance for safety, but Bligh had decided not to rely on an ordinary seaman for this job, and as he sent the Master aloft it was obvious that he considered it an important task.

As the *Bounty* approached the entrance to Oparre, the launch, which was waiting there, let the *Bounty* get between it and the wind. This becalmed the launch and allowed the *Bounty* to slide past unattended. If, as seems likely, Christian was in charge of the launch, this was a fault in his seamanship. Bligh immediately ordered the anchor to be dropped and also called to the men waiting aloft to shorten the sails. He was not going to try to enter the harbour without the launch showing the way. The *Bounty* slowed to a halt, which Bligh naturally attributed to the action he had taken, but Fryer came

[13] *ibid.*, 25 December 1788. The unnamed officer could have been Christian, Fryer, Peckover or Nelson.

[14] Bligh, 1792 (1965), p. 87.

[15] *Log of the Bounty*, 25 December 1788. See also Edward Christian, *Appendix*, in which there is reference (p. 71) to a claim by Bligh that Fletcher had allowed the *Bounty* to go aground after they left Tahiti. Edward Christian may have misunderstood Bligh's criticism of his brother; Bligh may be referring to the grounding after leaving Matavai, not Tahiti. According to Andrew David (private communication to the author, December 1976) the conditions on the day were extremely difficult for good observation from the foremast – overcast sky, muddy bottom because of heavy rain – though this does not excuse the coxwain in the launch. Bligh named Fryer but not the coxwain, which indicates either that he believed Fryer to be negligent or he was protecting the coxwain.

down from the foremast and told him that the ship had grounded. Bligh was astonished at this report: 'I have been in many situations,' he wrote, 'of this Nature much more hazardous and I thought my precautions were abundant to carry me safe. A Lead in the Chains, a Boat sent to be ahead, and the Master on the Fore Yard to look out. Yet with all the Ship went on shore.' Bligh was probably severe in his criticism of the two officers who had let him down. He must have wondered what he needed to have in addition to his officers in order to move the ship in coastal waters on a calm day a distance of three miles. It certainly did not augur well for the treacherous Endeavour Straits.

The *Bounty* was grounded mid-ships on a small rock. Bligh acted quickly to get the ship off by ordering Fryer to send a kedge anchor out astern into deep water. He decided to do the next bit himself. He took over the launch, got the bower anchor out, took it astern in the launch and dropped it in thirteen fathoms of water. The ship was now anchored by the bower and the kedge astern; by hauling on the kedge anchor line the ship could be moved to deep water. Experienced officers and seamen ought to have been able to manage this manoeuvre, but once again there was an 'accident'. Bligh was in the launch supervising the dropping of the bower anchor and at a distance from the *Bounty*. Fryer and Christian were on the *Bounty* supervising the men heaving on the kedge anchor line; but nobody on the ship was directed to haul in the other line, which was slackening as the ship moved off the rock. The inevitable happened: the lines got entangled, and one of them fouled some rocks on the sea-bed. The operation of heaving the ship off the rock took thirty minutes, but the entangled lines took hours longer to get clear. Fryer, as sailing master, should have been more attentive, and if he was too busy he should have asked Christian to organise the hauling in of the slack line.

When the *Bounty* was cleared and the anchor lines retrieved, the ship anchored for the night in deep water. Mercifully for Christian, he and his shore party were sent ashore to prepare for the reception of the breadfruit plants the next day. He thus escaped the atmosphere created by Bligh's anger at Fryer and himself for their repeated failures. For Fryer, on the other hand, there was no respite from Bligh's anger. But these verbal onslaughts on Fryer had little positive effect on his performance, and they simply made the relationship between the men apparent to everybody on board.

When the *Bounty* was secured in Oparre the next day the plants were taken ashore to Christian's shore party and Peckover set up his trading post. Christmas day was celebrated on 28 December, a Sunday, instead of the working day, 25 December. The new anchorage was, according to Bligh, 'a delightful situation', and safe from sudden storms. He ordered that everything not needed should be stowed below, including the rigging and the booms. The *Bounty* was to remain at Oparre for another three months.

Two days after Fryer and Christian had displayed their own remarkable neglect of duty and received no punishment other than a verbal one, William Musprat received a dozen lashes on 27 December for 'neglect of duty'.[16] It is

---

[16] *ibid.*, 27 December 1788.

not stated on what day the offence was committed; it could have been during the anchor incident – perhaps he was on the anchor line. There was another punishment on 29 December; Robert Lamb, the ship's Butcher, was thought to have been negligent in respect of the theft of his cleaver, and received twelve lashes in front of the assembled crew and the local chiefs. Bligh announced that if any islander was caught stealing in future he would receive the same punishment as the seamen; Tinah promised to get the cleaver back and, much to Bligh's surprise, he did return it a few days later.

The contrast apparent between the failures of the petty officers and punishments among the seamen is quite marked; as we have noted, John Mills and William Brown had their grog stopped over the dancing incident during the time when Huggan's drunkenness was notorious; Alexander Smith received twelve lashes for failing to prevent a theft just before officers at the shore camp lost items in their care and another officer lost his sheets. Earlier, Huggan's negligence over Valentine and Purcell's insolence had gone unpunished, while Quintal had been punished for 'insolence' and John Williams had been punished at False Bay for not heaving the lead with alacrity. The number of punishments on the *Bounty* was comparatively small, but there must have been many seamen who now felt it was unfair that they should suffer when much greater negligence was obvious among the petty officers. I am not suggesting that this was sufficient grounds for mutiny, but it may have been a contributing factor when Christian gave them the opportunity.

11

Desertion

The first week of the *Bounty*'s stay at Oparre passed uneventfully. The work parties on shore included Coleman, the Armourer, who had set up his forge again and was inundated with work both for the ship and for the islanders. The carpenters were busy repairing the small cutter, and Peckover was engaged with his trading activities, though he also reported increasing difficulty in getting supplies. On New Year's day double grog was issued to all hands and, as on all working days, two seamen were permitted ashore free of all duties for 'their own amusement', while the rest were employed, at least nominally.

Some authors – Danielsson and Mackaness for instance – have given the impression that the time spent at Tahiti was one long holiday for everybody, with no work done, and nobody stirring themselves except to eat fruit or fresh pork, to converse with their friends or make love to the women. This lotus eaters' picture is incorrect, though it is true that Tahiti must have seemed a paradise after life at sea. Work assignments were given out every day by the officers – though much of it was not as strenuous as work at sea – and they had to be completed each day. As with much 'military' activity, we can assume that some of the work was not really necessary, but the men still had to look busy when an officer, especially the Lieutenant, was in sight. Nominal work can be even more irksome than hard labour, especially when there are other diversions to hand.

Sunday, 4 January 1789, was a day of rest for everybody. In the early hours of Monday morning three men deserted the *Bounty*: Charles Churchill, the Corporal; William Musprat, who had been flogged for 'neglect' on 27 December; and John Millward.

Desertion from European ships in the South Seas was a fairly common occurrence in the eighteenth and nineteenth centuries, and was not always motivated by negative pressures such as bad treatment. It could also be positively motivated by the sharp contrast between the uncomfortable lives that seamen led in European ships and the life that they thought they could lead in the idyllic splendours of the islands of the Pacific. With a pleasant climate, little need for exertion, an abundance of food and the availability of obliging women, Tahiti and other islands had a powerful attraction for seamen from the cold and crowded ports of Europe. Desertions were attempted on Cook's ships, and in one case 'the only successful argument against it was getting a certain disease and dying rotten'.[1] In the records of the

---

[1] James Mario Matra, quoted in Mackaness, 1951, p. 126.

London Missionary Society there is a fair number of reports of seamen deserting their ships or being shipwrecked and refusing rescue.[2] The presence of European seamen among the missionaries' flocks created confusion in the minds of those converted from 'licentiousness', when they observed 'Christian' seamen behaving without the restraints advocated by the missionaries. On at least one occasion a missionary deserted his mission and joined the ex-seamen and their way of life.

The fact that desertion was common and easy presented the Navy with a problem. Ships were often manned by prisoners, criminal or political malcontents, misfits – anyone who had fallen foul of the law or was a victim of injustice: all these had every incentive to desert. To deter all but the most persistent, punishment for desertion was extreme: 'Death, or such other punishment as the circumstances of the offence shall deserve'.[3] From the records of the decisions of courts martial for the period 1750-1783 we can see the sentences on the deserters who were captured – 170 in all: 'found guilty, death' or less often 'found guilty, 500 lashes'.[4] All His Majesty's ships were bound by the Articles wherever they sailed, and as the Captain had to read the Articles at least once a week to the crew, nobody could plead ignorance.

It is worth quoting Bligh's account of the desertions and his reactions.

a.m. at 4 on the relief of the Watch found the small cutter missing. Mustered the Ships Company, when Charles Churchill, the Ships Corporal, Willm Muspratt and Jno. Milward, Ab. were found absent, the latter being the Centinel from 12 to 2 O'Clock in the Morning – Also eight Stand of Arms and Ammunition were taken away by them all owing to the Mate of the Watch being asleep on Deck.

It was not untill a half past four that the above circumstance was found out and I acquainted of it. Not the least knowledge had we of which way the Boat was gone, I therefore went on shore to the Cheifs who soon got me information that they had proceeded to Matavai and were sailed for Tetturoah in a Sailing Cannoe. – As the Boat was the most of my concern, I returned to the Ship with Tynah, Oreepyah & Moannah and sent them away with the Master to search for her. – They had but just got to One Tree Hill[5] when the Boat was rowing towards them with five Natives who were bringing her to the Ship, and as a thorough knowledge of the Deserters plan

[2] For example the shipwrecked Englishmen found living on Tahiti by missionaries in 1791 (Haweis papers, ML MS 21a, Seymour; *Daedalus* voyage, 1791, A1963). Another report in the same MS tells how a missionary went to the Sandwich islands (Hawaii) and found two Englishmen there; two of the crew of the ship he was in deserted to join them, and only one was recaptured. There are many other examples.

[3] MacArthur, 1813, Vol. I, p. 330, Article XVI.

[4] *ibid.*, the sentences ranged from 50 lashes upwards and were imposed on hundreds of men. In some cases the men would simply be listed as, for instance, '28 seamen, different ships' and the verdict covered them all. In other cases the prisoner was named: 'W. Mickleburgh, Seaman, *Flying Fish*, found guilty, death'. Mickleburgh was sentenced on December 20, 1781.

[5] One Tree Hill had been so named by Captain Wallace of H.M.S. *Dolphin* on his visit to Tahiti in 1768. This was the first British ship to call there and it was attacked in Matavai Bay by the islanders. Order was restored and peace began only after the ship's guns were fired. At the southern end of Matavai Bay there is a small promontory and on this at the time there was a single tree. Paintings of Wallace's visit, and others, clearly show the tree.

was with certainty known, they returned to the Ship and I rewarded the Men for their fidelity.

As the object now was to adopt means to get the people I told Tynah and the other Cheifs I looked to them for that Service, and that therefore without delay they must proceed to Tetturoah and get them taken and brought back to me – that I would not quit the Country without 'them, and that as they had always been my Friends, I expected they would show it in this instance, and that unless they did I should proceed with such violence as would make them repent it.

It was therefore agreed that in the morning Oreepyah and Moannah should set off in two Canoes and take the Deserters, but they appeared afraid on account of the Arms. – This, however, I was obliged to get the better of by describing to them for the Natives to collect round them as friends, and then to seize on them and their Arms, and bind them with Cords, and to show no mercy to them if they made resistance. Oreepyah was very desirous to know if they had Pocket Pistols like mine, for with such he said they might kill him while they were held, but as I assured him they had only musquets, all fears and doubts were laid asside but one, which was whether I would not serve them as Capt Cook had done at Tootahah; confine them on board, however they laughed when they asked this question, and I showed them they had no reason to fear, the Boat being manned to carry them on shore when they liked. –

As I have never shown any violence or Anger at the trifling Thefts that have been committed, because it was our own faults, and having lived among them with so much harmony and good will, they place every confidence in my word and are faithfull in return to me – I have therefore no doubt but they will bring the Deserters back, but in case of failure I shall proceed to no extremities until I have the Plants on board. –

Had the Mate of the Watch been awake no trouble of this kind would have happened I have therefore disrated and turned him before the Mast.[6] Such neglectful and worthless petty officers I believe never was in a Ship as are in this – No Orders for a few hours together are Obeyed by them, and their conduct in general is so bad, that no confidence or trust can be reposed in them – in short they have drove me to everything but Corporal punishment and that must follow if they do not improve.[7]

Morrison gives an account that squares with Bligh's in all important respects but includes extra details not mentioned by Bligh. He says that a search was made of the possessions of the deserters, and a paper was found in Churchill's chest 'Containing his own Name & that of three of the Party on shore, which Churchill had written, on which Lieut. Bligh went on Shore to the House & informd Mr. Christian of the Business calling the men and challenging them with being concerned with Churchill and intending to disert. They persisted in

[6] The Mate of the Watch was Thomas Hayward, one of the midshipmen. By disrating him, Bligh made him an A.B. and reinforced this by 'turning him before the mast', i.e. placing him with the seamen whose quarters were at the front of the ship. Hayward appears to have been re-rated midshipman some time after his confinement for he was assuming the duties of a watch officer on the night of the mutiny, when he fell asleep again.

[7] *Log of the Bounty*, 5 January 1789.

their Innocence, and denyd it so firmly, that He was inclined from Circumstances to believe them and said no more to them about it.'[8]

The deserters went untraced for some weeks, and in the meantime the rest of the crew continued with their work schedules. The vulnerability of the plants prevented Bligh from making strenuous efforts to recapture the deserters. He could not use the hostage gambit straightaway, though he was prepared to consider it once the plants were safely aboard. The longer the men were free the more it might tempt some of the others to follow suit; he set down his clear determination to get them back whatever happened: 'When I have got the Plants on board I shall take an Opportunity of confining them [the Chiefs] to the Ship – untill then I think the Plants are of more Value than the Men, and is the most material Circumstance I have to Attend to, however I may put my Plans in execution earlier if I find they [the Chiefs] do not exert themselves when the fair W[eathe]r comes.'[9] While waiting for an opportunity to get the deserters back, Bligh set the crew to work on picking the store of bread 'to free it from vermin', and two days later John Fryer reported that another 1,754 pounds of bread were unfit for consumption. Hundreds of pounds had been damaged by seawater at Tenerife, the Horn, on the passage to False Bay and at Matavai Bay, and vermin had ruined the rest. Hops and tobacco were issued to all hands and were welcome all round.

The next problem arose with the shore party under Christian. Apparently one of the officers – once again not named by Bligh in his Log – had plucked a branch of a tree (the Tutuee tree) and had taken it into the tent where the shore party was camping. At the sight of the branch all the islanders got up and left the area, as this particular tree was taboo to the islanders and was associated with one of their religious festivals. Notwithstanding this reaction, someone, presumably the unnamed officer, then bound the branch to one of the posts in the camp, thus keeping the islanders away from the area altogether. This was a severe affront to the Tahitians, and Peckover's trading activities ceased as a result. Bligh was called to the beach, probably by Peckover, who would have had more sense, from his long experience of Tahiti, than to indulge in such a silly prank. After discovering what had happened Bligh got Tinah to remove the taboo; the islanders then returned to the camp and trading recommenced. The actions of the officer concerned was irresponsible in the extreme, and Bligh was angry with him, but he did not mention his name, at least in the PRO Log. This is most strange, and interesting; for Bligh had suppressed an officer's name before, when we have had reason to believe that the officer concerned was Christian. He did not identify the officer in the launch when the *Bounty* grounded, nor did he identify the officer responsible for the loss of the boat rudder at the shore camp. The only other officers on the shore camp were Peckover and

[8] James Morrison, Journal, pp. 26-7. He again gets the dates hopelessly wrong; according to the Log, the desertions were on 5 January and the deserters were recaptured on 22 January; Morrison gives 24 January and 15 February for these two events. His memory had slipped over the years. He had Bligh's account of the mutiny, published in 1790, but this did not give details of the desertions; if he had had the 1792 *Narrative* he would have got the dates right.

[9] *Log of the Bounty*, 6 January 1789.

Heywood; Peckover is unlikely to have behaved so stupidly, while Heywood was a young man of about sixteen at the time and could have been dealt with by Christian as commanding officer if he had done it. It is possible that Bligh was protecting his friend. Christian was letting Bligh down, though he was the only man Bligh still had any faith in. The other officers on the ship were useless to the point of exasperation, and Bligh may have been trying not to face the fact that his entire command was either incompetent or obstructive, or both.

Two weeks later Fryer made another mistake. Bligh was on shore making observations to check the rate of his time-keeper. He was doing this in preparation for new discoveries and corrections to contemporary charts on the homeward voyage. Fryer was on the *Bounty*; he sent a message to Bligh that the islander who had canoed the deserters from Matavai to the island of Tetturoah was on board the ship, and asked for Bligh's instructions on what to do about this. Bligh was furious that Fryer should waste time finding out what he already knew his instructions to be: to arrest the man and keep him for questioning. 'As he knew perfectly my determination in punishing this Man,' wrote Bligh, 'if ever he could be caught, it was an unnecessary delay in confining him, but what was still worse, while the Messenger was absent, which was about 10 Minutes, he [Fryer] suffered this Offender to jump overboard and escape without hoisting the Cutter out which was on deck, so that I now lost an Opportunity of securing the return of the Deserters without disturbing my friendly intercourse with the Chiefs.'[10]

What made the islander jump overboard? One of the crew may have warned him that the boat had gone ashore to arrange his capture. Or Fryer may have made it so obvious what he was doing that the man was alarmed. Why did Fryer not simply arrest him? We do not know the answers; but if one is looking for signs of a conspiracy, which in the light of later events is a possibility, they could be found here. One or more of the three men on Churchill's 'list' could have been sent for by Churchill who wanted to make contact with them, because he wanted something from them or wanted them to join in some other plan he might have had. In the course of trying to find the men, the islander might have alerted Fryer accidentally, and as soon as Fryer's attention was occupied in getting a message to Bligh the conspirators might have warned the messenger and then obstructed the cutter.

The incident passed without further comment from Bligh. But the next day he exploded into another rage with Fryer, this time over a more serious example of his incompetence. The sailroom was ordered to be cleared so that all sails could be taken ashore and given an airing. While this was being done it emerged that the new and spare sails for the fore topsail, the foresail, the main topmast sail, the staff sail and the main staysail were mildewed and rotten. Without spare sails the ship was at the mercy of the weather. The direct responsibility for this neglect belonged to the Sailing Master, John Fryer, and to some extent to the Boatswain, William Cole. According to Bligh both had reported to him on previous occasions that all the sails had

---

[10] *ibid*., 16 January 1789.

been taken out and aired and that they were all in good order. 'Scarce any neglect of duty,' writes Bligh, 'can equal the criminality of this, for it appears that altho the Sails have been taken out twice since I have been in the Island, which I thought fully sufficient and I had trusted to their reports, Yet these New Sails never were brought out, [n] or is it certain whether they have been out since we left England, yet notwithstanding as often as the Sails were taken to air by my Orders they were reported to me to be in good Order.'[11]

It has been suggested[12] that the responsibility for the state of the sails was Bligh's alone, and in a formal sense this is true. The Log entry recorded the matter for the Admiralty, and therefore Bligh was not covering anything up even though the responsibility would ultimately be his. But in all fairness it is hard to see how Bligh can be blamed for the incompetence of the officers. Short of acting as sentry, being personally in charge of every item of the ship's equipment, opening the sailroom himself, climbing the foremast to act as lookout, sailing the launch, and preventing incidents with the islanders and their customs at all times of the day and night and also doing the jobs of all his officers combined, it is difficult to see how Bligh could have acted more 'responsibly'. He had a right to expect that his officers would be competent and that their reports would be truthful and candid.

Bligh would have liked to sack both Fryer and Cole for the neglect of the sails – he wrote in his Log on 17 January 1789: 'If I had any Officers to supercede the Master and Boatswain, or was capable of doing without them, considering them as common Seamen, they should no longer occupy their respective Stations' – but he knew he could not. This was the central dilemma of the *Bounty*, as we have seen. It was understaffed and no man could be replaced or done without. The petty officers were too young and inexperienced, or in disgrace. Hayward had been disrated for sleeping on the watch; Heywood and Hallet were only boys on their first voyage; and Elphinston, still a Master's Mate at the age of thirty-six, was clearly incapable of replacing the Master. All Bligh could do was admonish the officers and supervise the work himself. This he did, and Lawrence Lebogue, his sailmaker friend, tried to salvage what was left of the sails.

For the next week life returned to normal. Then the news arrived by Tahitian messengers that the deserters had left their island refuge and were within five miles of the *Bounty*. Bligh decided to arrest the deserters himself and accordingly left the ship near dusk on Friday 23 January with an armed party.

> I had Odiddee with me and by his Advice I had landed at a convenient place for the Boat but at some distance from where the Deserters were. That being the residence of my Friend Teppahoo from whom the information came. I therefore represented to Odiddee that my Boat must be within my call, and that unless there was a good landing and Safety for her at Teppahoo's House she should remain where she was. As he assured me of

---

[11] *ibid.*, 17 January 1789.
[12] Hough, 1972, p. 126.

it, I desired the People to pull along shore with a Native for their guide and that I would proceed along the beach ... but my walk to them was very near being interrupted by some fellows who wanted to get what I had, and were closing upon me for that purpose, until I dispersed them by threatening to destroy them, and clearing the Beach with my Pistol.

... The first thing I did was to enquire about the deserters and I was told that they were in a House just by. I therefore determined to get hold of them if possible and in proceeding towards the House, they heard of my Approach and came out without Arms and gave themselves up. By this time the native from the Boat swam on Shore and I sent a Message back by him for one of my People to come to me and the Boat to proceed to where I first landed and wait for my return.[13]

This quote is from his Log; in his 1792 *Narrative* the incident is played down – his courage in approaching the deserters alone, when for all he knew they were armed and desperate, is made less obvious: 'At the time they delivered themselves up to me, it was not in their power to have made resistance, their ammunition having been spoiled by the wet.'[14] He did not know this at the time, and it was lucky for him that it was so. He and his party spent the night on the beach, the deserters and two guards in a hut and the rest out in the boat.

On his return with the prisoners to the *Bounty*, Bligh discovered that the useless Fryer had let the time-keeper go down; he had not wound it during the night when he had the command.[15] By now, it appears, Fryer was totally indifferent to anything Bligh wanted on the voyage, and where he was not negligent through indifference he was negligent through incompetence. The timepiece was crucial for Bligh's charting work, as Fryer well knew.

The punishments ordered were lenient by the Navy's standards. The men were guilty of desertion and also of theft of ship's property, and they could have sabotaged the mission by forcing Bligh to use violence against the Chiefs. The men were ordered into irons: Millward and Musprat received two dozen lashes and Churchill a dozen. The punishment was repeated on 4 February. Millward, who had been sentinel on the night of the desertions, was considered to be more blameworthy than the others; Musprat had already been punished for 'neglect of duty', and this second breach would ensure he was punished heavily. But why did Churchill receive only half the punishment of the other two? After all, he was the ship's Corporal and therefore responsible to Bligh for the discipline of the ship. We do not know why this difference was made. Neither Bligh, nor Morrison, nor anybody else explains it.

The deserters themselves were conscious of their precarious position. They wrote the following letter to Bligh between their punishments:[16]

---

[13] *Log of the Bounty*, 23 January 1789.

[14] Bligh, 1792 (1965), p. 94.

[15] Again, in Bligh's published *Narrative* (1792), the incident of the timepiece is glossed over as if it was nobody's fault in particular.

[16] Quoted in Bligh, 1794 (his reply to Edward Christian's defence of his brother).

On Board the *Bounty*, at Otahéite, January 26, 1788

Sir,

We should think ourselves wholly inexcuseable if we omitted taking this earliest opportunity of returning our thanks for your goodness in delivering us from a trial by Court Martial, the fatal consequences of which are obvious, and although we cannot possibly lay any claim to so great a favour, yet we humbly beg you will be pleased to remit any further punishment and we trust our future conduct will fully demonstrate our deep sense of your clemency, and our steadfast resolution to behave better hereafter.

C. Churchill
Wm. Muspratt
John Milward

To Captain Bligh

The 'fatal consequences' they mentioned were the death penalty, or a punishment by a gross or more lashes if they were tried in Britain. Bligh, however, was not moved by this appeal, and after the Fryer incident this is not surprising. He had failed to get Fryer to behave better by clemency, so he had no reason to believe it would work in this case.

There was another matter arising from the desertions waiting for settlement: the question of Hayward, the officer of the watch, who was asleep on duty. Bligh blamed Hayward for the whole incident, and Hayward was also in breach of the Articles. He was publicly rebuked by Bligh for his neglect on the two punishment musters, and in between times was held below in irons. This was as far as Bligh could go without inflicting a flogging. It was also of little deterrent value: in the crucial hours of the mutiny Hayward again fell asleep on his watch.

At the first punishment muster Bligh addressed the officers on their conduct. He believed the desertions were 'solely caused by the neglect of the Officers who had the Watch', and he told them plainly that 'however exempt they were at present from a like punishment, yet they were equally subject by the Articles of War to a condign one'. He went on to speak about the officers' responsibilities: 'An Officer with Men under his care is at all times in some degree responsible for their conduct; but when from his neglect Men are brought to punishment while he only meets with a reprimand, because a publick conviction by Tryal will bring both into a more severe and dangerous situation, an alternative often laid aside through lenity, and sometimes necessity, as it now is in both cases; it is an unpleasant thing to remark that no feelings of honor, or sense of shame is to be Observed in such an Offender.'[17] We should note this strong affirmation of both his humanity and his sense of command.

Evidently Hayward was displaying no remorse, and this helps to explain why Bligh punished him as he did. Hayward was apparently indifferent to

[17] *Log of the Bounty*, 24 January 1789.

the fate of the men for whom he was responsible, and Bligh decided to curb his arrogance by confining him below decks. One author describes Hayward's punishment as 'a savage sentence on a boy still in his 'teens'.[18] But Hayward was in fact twenty-two, and the punishment was far less savage than he would have been liable to receive from a court martial.

After the confinement of Hayward, during the night of 6 February, the *Bounty*'s anchor cable was cut through. To make sure that it did not happen again, a stage-walk was erected for the sentries to walk along so that they could inspect the cables from the deck. At the time nobody could say who had cut the cable. Every seaman and officer had a native *tyo*, a special friend, and was adopted by him into his family, sharing his hospitality and his wife; Morrison claimed in his Journal that Hayward's tyo had the cable cut, because he was so incensed at Hayward's confinement, and that the tyo had decided that if Hayward was flogged he would kill Bligh.[19] Bligh believed that the cable had been cut by one of the islanders, and his belief was strengthened when he went ashore to question the Chief and Tinah's parents ran off into the mountains, although it was pouring with rain. According to Morrison's account, Hayward's tyo was a young brother of Tinah. Morrison also states that the crew did not believe at the time that the cable was cut by an islander. Later, Bligh came to the opinion that it was cut by one of the subsequent mutineers, who wanted to remain at Tahiti, and hoped that by cutting the cable he would cause the *Bounty* to founder on the shore.[20]

In the last weeks before departure, thefts and trouble continued. At the end of January, a few days before the second punishment of the deserters, Isaac Martin had a fight with an islander whom he suspected of stealing an iron loop. Martin was in breach of Bligh's Rule that nobody was to use violence on the islanders, even when a theft of property was involved; this was a difficult rule to keep, as the seamen were flogged if they allowed anything to be stolen, but were at the same time prohibited from retrieving stolen property by force. Martin's physical altercation appears to have been the only one that occurred between the seamen and the islanders during the stay of the *Bounty* at Tahiti when it was under Bligh's command. Martin was sentenced to twenty-four lashes, but the Chiefs intervened strenuously with Bligh, and in a gesture of conciliation he reduced the punishment by five lashes.[21]

After the deserters were returned to duty, the *Bounty* began to bustle with

---

[18] Rawson, 1932, p. 50. Rawson's work is very unreliable on dates and chronology, as well as other facts; for instance, he dates the desertions before Huggan's death on 9 December 1788, when according to the Log they occurred on 5 January 1789.

[19] Morrison, Journal, p. 101a; Hough, 1972, pp. 125-6, claims that Hayward's tyo swam out himself to the *Bounty* and cut the cable, but Morrison's version is that he had this done for him.

[20] *Log of the Bounty*, 6 February 1789; Bligh 1792 (1965), p. 98. The idea that the damage was accidental was discussed by Barrow, 1961, p. 61. Though he is alleged to have had access to Morrison's version from the Heywood family, he concluded that 'the damage done to the cable was, in all probability, owing to its chafing over the rocky bottom'.

[21] Bligh, 1792 (1965), p. 94.

activity as the ship was fitted out for the voyage home. The Armourer, Carpenter and Boatswain were all extremely busy. The ship was caulked, planks were sawn and the rigging got up from below. Cats were taken on board to chase out rats and cockroaches. Storms hit the island and lasted for days on end, slowing down the work and, as always, threatening the breadfruit plants, which had been collected together in 774 pots (over a thousand plants in all were being tended at the shore-camp).

On 2 March 1789, a thief stole an empty water-cask, 'part of an Azimuth Compass' and 'the Bedding out of Mr. Peckovers Hammock while he had the look out'.[22] The heavy rain gave the thief enough cover to sneak past Peckover and into his tent. Bligh was informed in the morning and he went ashore to berate the Chiefs, who, sensing his mood, had left Oparre to avoid him. They reappeared later, with the thief and the stolen items, and demanded that Bligh kill the guilty islander. Bligh had no wish to impose capital punishment, or even the barbaric ear-cutting ordered by Captain Cook; but he did impose the severest punishment that he is known to have ordered, namely one hundred lashes. With this punishment Bligh had now tried everything against theft but the seizing of hostages. He was surprised, he records in his Log, by the islander's capacity to take the punishment; his back did not cut until the last few lashes were delivered. As was customary, James Morrison, the Boatswain's Mate, swung the cat.

Bligh tried to fit in as many navigational observations as he could before leaving, and he spent much time measuring and charting Matavai and Oparre, even sending Fryer to carry out surveys that he had not the time to do himself; for he still had diplomatic duties with the local Chiefs that involved much activity in dining and gossiping. His geographical work was hampered by the weather, as the rain continued to fall day after day, hiding the sun and stars which were used in measurements.[23]

During one of the rainy nights, George Stewart, while he had the watch, allowed the islander who had been flogged for the thefts, who was still confined on the ship, to break his irons and flee over the side. Bligh was both angry and saddened by this latest example of indifference to his orders. 'I had given in Written orders', he wrote, 'that the Mate of the Watch was to be answerable for the Prisoners and to visit and see that they were safe in his Watch, but I have such a neglectfull set about me that I believe nothing but condign punishment can alter their conduct. – Verbal orders in the course of a Month were so forgot that they would impudently assert no such thing or directions were given, and I have been at last under the necessity to trouble myself with writing what by decent Young Officers would be complied with as the Common Rules of the Service.'[24] The necessity for written orders to the midshipmen is the surest sign there could be of Bligh's collapsed authority and of the dangerous slackness and indifference that were everywhere on the ship. It also suggests that Bligh may have been collecting

[22] *Log of the Bounty*, 2 March 1789.
[23] *ibid.*, 4 March 1789.
[24] *ibid.*, 7 March 1789.

written evidence for a report on the conduct of the midshipmen for use back in Britain.

The rain eventually cleared, and the preparations for departure got under way again. The caulking was resumed and the masts and rigging were checked over. Bligh noted that hogs were getting scarcer; Peckover was trying to buy them for curing and storing, as well as for daily use. Thus his demands increased at the time when the supply was falling, owing in some measure to the prolonged stay of the *Bounty* in the area. Peckover was forced to go further into the country to get supplies. The ship needed these stocks to provide meat for the diet on the return voyage, and the men themselves added to the complications by trying to buy meat independently to form their own personal sea-stores. Bligh instructed that all pigs brought on board should be registered by the watch on a list, so that there would not be arguments later about whose pig was which. Morrison later used this as an example of Bligh's harshness; he described in his Journal how the men and their tyos went to considerable lengths to avoid detection by Bligh when they brought personal food supplies on board. Bligh's actions may have seemed at the time to be directed against the liberty of the individual seaman, and critics galore have seized on Morrison's charges in order to dramatise Bligh's apparent tyranny. Yet it is obvious that Bligh's concern for the ship's stores – which were for all hands – was an example of good management and providence rather than personal tyranny.

It was in connection with the pig shortage that Fryer once again crossed swords with his commander. Peckover came to Bligh to say that he had been warned by his islander friends not to go out on one of his purchasing tours, for fear that he would be beaten and stripped. Bligh, through his relationships with the Chiefs, was able to get to the bottom of the problem. The source of the trouble was Fryer. He had taken a mat and a piece of cloth from a Tahitian woman who had been staying with him on the ship. This was, he said, a 'misunderstanding'. Peckover's habit of wandering alone on his trading missions was well known, and the woman's family had decided to exact revenge by attacking the most vulnerable member of the European party. Bligh's first concern was to make peace, and to this end he invited the woman onto the ship and arranged for Fryer to give back her property, which he did, though he must have resented this public humiliation.[25] Bligh's sentiments about the 'misunderstanding' are not recorded, but his scornful comments on Fryer's selfish and thoughtless action, when they were having enough trouble with thefts by the islanders, can be imagined.

In the final days of the *Bounty*'s stay, the main concern was to get the ship ready for its voyage and the men back into the ship's routine. All the men's spare time was spent with their friends, collecting local foods and curiosities. Such was the inflow of these goods that orders were given confining each man's collection to what he could store in his sea chest.[26] By the day of its departure, the *Bounty* had been transformed into a greenhouse-cum-

[25] *ibid.*, 25 March 1789.
[26] *ibid.*, 27 March 1789.

menagerie. Apart from the 1015 breadfruit plants and the numerous other plants collected by David Nelson, the deck itself and the ship's boats were loaded with fresh fruit and coconuts, and pens containing twenty-five hogs and seventeen goats.

The crew took their final farewells of their friends and of their women, with whom some had formed deep attachments. Bligh entertained the Chiefs and their families on the ship and made his parting presents to them. To Tinah he gave the most coveted of all gifts: two muskets and a thousand rounds of ammunition. Departure was delayed by the weather until 4 April; then, to the accompaniment of the noisy population on the shore, and with three cheers for Tinah from the mustered crew, the *Bounty* slipped out of the anchorage and headed for the open sea. Bligh wrote: 'We bad farewell to Otaheite, where for 23 Weeks we were treated with the greatest kindness: fed with the best of Meat and finest Fruits in the World.'[27]

I am not suggesting that at this stage any of the men had definite plans to stay in Tahiti. The three deserters had tried that and failed. If, however, the ship had run aground not many of the men, apart from Bligh, would have regretted it. The Tahitians had been kind to them, and they knew nothing of the other kind of islander who would soon have killed them as unwanted intruders. Bligh, Nelson and Peckover knew how unstable relationships with the islanders could be, but war, murder or maltreatment of seamen did not seem very real to the Pacific first-timers on the *Bounty*. For some, there was in effect no argument against staying at Tahiti other than the long arm of the Admiralty and the person of Bligh. Not everyone would have wanted to try a deserter's life, which meant cutting all ties with home and family. Some of the men – Bligh, Christian, Hayward, Heywood, Hallet, Stewart, Young and the petty officers – had careers waiting for them on their return. But for seamen like Smith, Churchill, Thompson, Martin, Millward, Musprat and Quintal the Royal Navy merely meant miserable treatment on foggy coasts off Britain by officers who were uninterested in them and in ships that seemed to have been designed to be uncomfortable. Events were now moving towards a climax when they would be given a choice between the two.

---

[27] *ibid.*, 5 April 1789.

12

Tahiti to Annamooka

What happened on the *Bounty* in the next three weeks has taken on a particular significance as authors have searched for clues that might explain what caused the mutiny and why Christian led it. The main problem is the triviality of the events that apparently prompted it. Having failed to find much that is convincing, critics have either assumed that there is no smoke without fire and that therefore Bligh must have been tyrannical; or, failing that, they have looked elsewhere into the psychological failings or sexual secrets of the protagonists of the drama. The motives behind Christian's demented actions will be discussed later; but the background to the mutiny, which I think fully explains the behaviour of the men and goes some way to explaining Christian's behaviour, should be summed up here.

As I have tried to show, the parsimony of the Admiralty, the small size of the ship, the inadequacies of the officers, the attractions of Tahiti, the remoteness of the Pacific from anything that could reinforce Bligh's authority, and the long train of incidents starting with Purcell's insolence in Tasmania, had created a situation where a spark could touch off an explosion. Aversion to duty had spread from the officers to the midshipmen and Bligh could do nothing to halt the trend. His attempts merely advertised his isolation as the only commissioned officer on board. His own competence only made matters worse; he was angrier, and his officers felt more resentful because they were at fault. His criticism and attempts at discipline appeared as merely the latest example of the Captain's bad temper, instead of asserting the hierarchical authority of the Navy over everybody on the ship. This situation cannot be blamed on Bligh; if anybody was to blame it was the Admiralty, as the mistakes of 1787 can be seen as the basic cause of the eventual loss of the ship.

Bligh's Log is a document of considerable weight as evidence about what led up to the mutiny; he could not doctor it to suit a post-mutiny rationalisation of his own role, though this was an option open to Morrison, Fryer, Heywood, Purcell and others, since they wrote after the event. Bligh was taken completely by surprise. In the Log there is no hint that he anticipated serious trouble. He slept with his cabin door open; he left his two pistols in charge of John Fryer, the man in whom he had least faith. As we shall see, the mutiny surprised other people on the ship as much as Bligh. The diet had improved; nobody had been excessively flogged, as on the *Hermione* under Captain Pigot; nobody had been given excessively arduous duty; nobody had had his wages stopped; nobody, at least of those who

5. Sketch by George Tobin of the Matavai River at Matavai Bay, Tahiti.

6. Sketch by George Tobin of Oparre in Tahiti.

mutinied, was in fear of legal retribution when the *Bounty* returned to England. Fryer and Purcell, the ones likely to get bad character reports from Bligh, did not join the mutiny. Only in retrospect was Bligh blamed. It was in the mutineers' interest to blame somebody, and so arose the picture of Bligh as a sadistic bully, a picture which is still powerful.[1] The events leading up to the mutiny have been recounted many times, with Bligh becoming a more monstrous tyrant each time, and more 'explanatory' details added at each retelling. But the events can also be seen as a continuation of the social situation I have described, with discipline breaking down and the souring relationships between Bligh and his officers; the mutiny is then easier to understand, even if some aspects, such as the motivation of Christian, remain obscure.

In the Log the daily business of the ship is recorded, in particular the food allowance.[2] The daily allowance to each man consisted of pork and plantain (later yams). Considerable quantities of the pork had been salted for the voyage, but for these early days of the return leg the live pigs on the deck were being killed. This was the diet that the men had got used to at Tahiti, with the difference that it was not issued improvidently. The men also had their own personal sea-stores accumulated from their island friendships. They were eating better than they had been on the first leg of the voyage from Britain to Tahiti. The only deprivation that they had had to put up with was the loss of the free atmosphere of the island and the free sexual relations with the women.

Additional food supplies were picked up from islands that they called at. For example, the *Bounty* passed close to Huaheine, where, with Captain Cook, Bligh had been present at the establishment of Omai in his home. Out of sentiment Bligh steered close to the island to see if he could see Omai's house, which had been built for him by the British seamen. Nothing remained of it. Some canoes came off from the island to the ship and an islander in one of them recognised Bligh and called him by name. Bligh was told that Omai was dead, his house burnt down, and only the mare remained of the animals left with him by Captain Cook. All his plants were destroyed except one, but the description was too vague for Bligh to recognise it. After a little trade the *Bounty* pulled away.

On 11 April 1789, the *Bounty* discovered a new island – unexpectedly, since this part of the ocean was fairly well known to European seamen. The island was called Aitutaki and was in the Cook group. Its position was noted but the ship did not stop. The next day John Sumner was punished with twelve lashes for some unspecified neglect of duty. It was the last flogging before the mutiny.[3]

During the next week the *Bounty* was beset with rain, storms and lightning.

---

[1] An example of more recent remarks in this vein is that by Peter Mathias, in 'When Britannia rules the waves', *Observer* Magazine, 28 July 1974, p. 24: 'Captain Bligh of the *Bounty* was promoted to flag-rank, and in no way censured for the monstrous cruelty that provoked the mutiny.'

[2] *Log of the Bounty*, 5 April to 27 April 1789.

[3] John Sumner was an active participant in the mutiny.

If it was not raining it was cloudy and overcast. Every morning the men were exercised with their small arms, and the only other work, beside sailing the ship, was done by the carpenter and his crew repairing the small boats. They passed Savage Island on 18 April and arrived at Annamooka on 23 April. The only other interesting thing in the Log at this point is that an unnamed seaman was on the sick list from 8 April. The Log mentions that he was suffering from a complaint that had begun with a fall in the ship at Cape Horn a year before. This was either Thomas Hall, the ship's Cook, or Charles Churchill, the Corporal. Both men had fallen at the Horn.[4]

Annamooka was the last stop before the mutiny. It was meant to be the last stop before the ship reached the Endeavour Straits, and once through the Strait there would be no returning to Tahiti. Bligh wanted wood and water from the island and after settling on an anchorage on 24 April he went ashore with David Nelson to find suitable places for the working parties to collect wood and water. While ashore, he met a man he recognised from his previous visit to the island with Cook in 1777. The man told him that the friendly Chiefs, Poulaho, Feenow and Tubow, were visiting another island, and he promised to send for them. However, Bligh reports that he did not see any canoe leave Annamooka while the ship was there, and he surmised that, in order to monopolise the trading with the Europeans, the local inhabitants had decided not to broadcast their arrival. This was to the disadvantage of the *Bounty*, because it meant that the islanders were less disciplined in the absence of the friendly Chiefs.

While the ship was being positioned and preparations were being made to go ashore, Elphinston, the Master's Mate, through 'want of a little exertions' according to Bligh, allowed the bower buoy to sink and it had to be replaced.[5]

Bligh decided to use Cook's wooding and watering places of 1777. This involved hauling the full water-casks 400 yards from a stream to the beach. Wood was obtainable about 200 yards along the beach from the loading point for the watering party. Eleven men were placed under Christian's command as a watering party, and four men formed the wooding party under Elphinston. In case of trouble arms were provided but these were ordered to be left in the boat as there were no men spare to act as sentries. Bligh notes:

> To those people I not only gave my Orders but my advice, that they were to keep themselves unconnected with the Natives, they however had not been an hour on shore before One Man had lost his Axe and another his Adz. The cause of this was, that the Officers, contrary to my direct orders, suffered the Indians to croud round them and amuse them, and by that means the Theft was commited. The Men cleared themselves of the Neglect as they could not comply with every part of their duty and keep their Tools in their Hands, and they therefore merit no punishment. As to

---

[4] *Log of the Bounty*, 8 April 1789 and 23 April 1789; another person on the sick list had VD.
[5] *ibid*., 24 April 1789.

the Officers I have no resource, or do I ever feel myself safe in the few instances I trust them.[6]

The axe had been stolen from Elphinston's group and the adze from Christian's. The thefts had occurred in the first hour. Neither officer had the excuse that he did not anticipate thefts by the local islanders. The enjoyable sojourn at Tahiti had lulled the two officers into a false sense of security, and they had forgotten the problems that could arise. Bligh added in his Log: 'These Islanders are clever dextrous set of People, and would ever take advantages if they saw People Negligent, even before the Centinels when the Resolution was here, if they ever caught them inattentive they took whatever they could lay hold of. We are therefore not to be surprized at those petty Violences as our Iron Utensils are Jewels of inestimable Value to them'.[7]

Morrison in his Journal tells the story slightly differently. He wrote that the islanders 'were very rude & attempted to take the Casks from the Waterers and the axes from the Wooding party; and if a Musquet was pointed at any of them [it] produced no other effect then a return of the Compliment, by poising their Club or Spear with a menacing look; and as it was Lieut. B.'s orders, that no person should affront them on any occasion, they were emboldend by Meeting no return to their Insolence, and became so troublesom that Mr. Christian who had the Command of the Watering party, found it difficult to carry on his duty, of this He informed Lt.[8] Bligh of this [sic], who dam'd him for a Cowardly rascal, asking him if He was afraid of a set of Naked Savages while He had arms; to which Mr. Christian answerd "the Arms are no use while your orders prevent them from being used".[9] The alleged exchange between the two men has since been accepted by most critics as of unquestionable veracity, and Morrison's version has been used to show that Bligh gave Christian an impossible task.

There are several questions raised by Morrison's version. According to him, Christian's men had muskets with them, although Bligh had ordered the weapons to be kept in the boat. If Christian had disobeyed the orders[10] and taken the arms to the watering place, and it was this that prevented further thefts after the first hour, then Morrison's point about the arms being useless does not hold. It seems more likely that the rest of the day passed without further thefts because Christian and Elphinston eventually obeyed the orders to resist being distracted by the islanders. There were not enough men to spare any as sentries. The exchange of 'menacing looks' and the mutual pointing of weapons could have occurred at the beach while the boat

---

[6] *ibid.*, 25 April 1789. This entry was written only three days before the mutiny.

[7] *ibid.*

[8] In Morrison's Journal (ML MS, Safe 1/42, p. 33) text the word 'Cpt' is crossed out and the word 'Lt' has been written in, which suggests that Morrison had slipped into referring to Bligh by his 1792 status instead of his 1790 rank, again supporting my belief that the Journal was written some time after the events it describes.

[9] Morrison, Journal, p. 34.

[10] *See* Hough, 1972, p. 136 for a claim that Christian did in fact disobey Bligh's orders. No evidence is given by Hough for this assertion.

was being loaded, and not at the watering place.

If we accept this then the exchange between Bligh and Christian makes more sense. Being an uncontrolled man, Christian had little patience with islanders, and when their attempted depredations threatened to get out of hand, he had wanted to resort to arms. From Bligh's point of view the matter was fairly straightforward. He wanted water, not violence. He expected his officers to be able to cope with curious and thieving islanders without resort to arms. When Christian reported to him about the progress of the watering and the loss of the adze, he would have been angry about the loss, and hardly sympathetic about the apparent inability of Christian and Elphinston to carry out his orders, let alone act on his advice. Christian had had no experience of hostile islanders; his only experience was of the tranquil population of Tahiti. His first encounter with aggressive behaviour from islanders may have surprised and perhaps also frightened him.

In these circumstances the alleged conversation might well have taken place, and is really far more damaging to Christian than to Bligh. There is no evidence that the islanders were using their spears and clubs and unless they were, there was no need to use firearms in reply. If Bligh's critics suggest that he should have authorised Christian's party to open fire on the islanders crowding round them – many of whom were women and children – they have a lot to answer for. The fact that this is what Christian wanted, and what Morrison hinted would deal with the 'insolence' of the crowd, hardly marks out Christian or Morrison for their humanity. There are other examples of Christian's inability to deal with situations where islanders were not behaving in a docile manner. In his first command of the mutineers in contact with islanders, several were killed and wounded; this was why Christian called his first post-mutiny landfall 'Bloody Bay'.

The next day Bligh sent John Fryer to help in the supervision of the watering party. There were two officers attending to the filling of the water casks. Elphinstone was still working away with his party collecting wood, apparently unarmed and without further trouble. The axe that had been stolen was returned by one of the chiefs and nothing else was stolen from the work parties. But two other thefts took place. David Nelson, who had gone ashore looking for plants, had his spade stolen. The islanders were also playing about near Fryer's boat which he had brought with him to the shore, and during the course of the day they managed to steal the grapnel. They got an opportunity because the men in the boat had used it to steady the boat in the water, a relief from the more tiresome activity of using their oars. Fryer claims in his Journal[11] that the men's use of the grapnel was against his orders; his story is that when he got to the beach he left his men (as he thought) at their oars and went inland to the watering place, immediately saw just how bad the situation was for Christian and his men under the incessant harrassment of the local population, and ordered Christian to quit

---

[11] John Fryer, Journal (Rutter, ed., 1934), p. 54; we note later how Fryer in his Journal exhibits a tendency to claim that almost every correct decision of any importance was either made by himself or suggested to Bligh by him (see p. 90n.).

the work and take the remaining casks, empty or full, to the boat. When they arrived at the beach through the crowds he was told about the stolen grapnel. Even if this is true, it does not say much for his control of his men; and he made matters much worse when, according to Morrison, he suggested that the loss of the grapnel was not very serious. Fryer reports Bligh as exclaiming: 'By God Sir, if it is not great to you it is great to me.'[12] Another interesting point is that an Acting Lieutenant would not usually take orders from a Master; it is conceivable that Christian had been demoted back to Master's Mate.

Bligh was furious at the latest loss and doubly furious that Fryer was once again responsible. Like Cook before him, Bligh was hastily driven to the stratagem of seizing chiefs as hostages, although he noted that several canoes had put to sea and it was possible that the thief was among these and no longer on the island. As this was the last stop before Timor, the ship was thrown open to trade on an all-comers basis. The crew could trade whatever they had for whatever they could get without having to go through Peckover. The men went at what little trade there was with alacrity, and then Bligh confined five of the lesser Chiefs on Board. The grapnel was not returned and he had to let them go, though he claims they parted on friendly terms. Morrison later claimed that Bligh insulted the chiefs by getting them to peel coconuts while they were below decks. Morrison's concern for the Chiefs' dignity does not fit well with his hint that Christian should have been allowed to open fire on the natives earlier. None of his supporters has noticed this double standard.

After this, the entire crew was paraded in arms and Bligh addressed them. According to Morrison's later account, he threatened them and told them what he thought of them. He said, claimed Morrison, that they were a 'parcel of lubberly rascals and that he would be one of five who would with good sticks would [sic] disarm the whole of them, and presenting a Pistol at Wm. McCoy threatend to shoot him for not paying attention'.[13] If this is anything near true, it shows that Bligh lost his head. His position was compromised; as we have seen, he despised and distrusted his officers, and the men obeyed neither them nor him. But this ineffective outburst could only have made matters worse. He had not, however, yet given Christian cause for mutiny.

The day before the mutiny, 27 April 1789, produced the final incident that has been identified as its possible cause – a row over a pile of coconuts. That men could mutiny over a pile of coconuts seems extraordinary; yet this is the incident that most writers, including Christian's family, have claimed as the cause of the mutiny. If this had been asserted by Bligh instead of by Bligh's critics, it would have been seen as a libel on Christian, for it makes his act of mutiny ridiculous if not insane. It is not surprising that the Hollywood scriptwriters have had to use their imagination to create an image for Bligh that would justify Christian's actions. Of all the mutinies in British naval

[12] Fryer, Journal, p. 55.
[13] Morrison, Journal, p. 38.

history the *Bounty*'s is the most laughable: no question of lashings, of terror, of the legalised murder of innocent seamen by a sadistic officer; just a thief in the night making off with some nuts!

There are four versions of what happened over the coconuts: Morrison's, Fryer's, Edward Christian's and Bligh's. It is worth examining them closely in the order in which I think they were written, to see how the incident was subtly transformed and added to in order to make it more convincing as the final insult which drove Christian to mutiny. I shall discuss in the next chapter the other theories of what his motivation might have been; here I will only say that while the incident might have helped to push him over the edge, and must have made some of the crew more ready to side with him, his actions cannot be understood without an examination of his character and of the other reasons why he was under stress.

First let us look at John Fryer's version, written in his Journal in 1790.[14]

In the morning when Mr Bligh came on deck he sent for me and said Mr Fryer dont you think those Cocoanuts are shrunk since last Night? I told him that they were not so high as they were last night, as I had them stowd up to the Rail but that the people might have put them Down in walking over them in the Night – he said no, that they had been taken away and that he would find out who had taken them and emmedially Ordered the Master at Arms to see every nut that was below on Deck. Every Body's he repeated several times – after all the nuts was on deck that was found below every Body was on Deck that ownd them – when Mr Bligh began, wḥo[se] are these; when the owner answer which was Mr Young – how many nuts did you bye. So many Sir. And how many did you eat? he did not know but there was the remainer which he had not counted – then all the other Gentlemen was call'd and likewise the People – when Mr Bligh had examined as far as he thought proper, he told the Master at Arms, that they might take there nuts down again, and told every Body that he allowed them a pound and a half of Yams which was more than their Allowance, but if he did not find out who took the Nuts that he would put them on 3/4 of a pound of Yams – & said I take care of you now for my own good, but when I get you thro the Straits you may all go to hell and if they did not look out sharp that he would do for one half of them – many times in the Voyage have he told his young Gentlemen that he would leave them at Jamaica – that they should not go home with him – ...'

Some points to be noted: first, there is no mention of Christian. Only Young is mentioned by name – almost the only mention of Edward Young in all the

[14] Fryer's Journal was written, he tells us, as a protest against Bligh's refusal to show him what had been written about his conduct in the official Log. Fryer felt he had a right to see this, in order, presumably, to prepare a defence for his expected court martial back in Britain. Internal evidence suggests that the bulk of the Journal was written in 1790; it may have been begun at Batavia, but there are references to Bligh's 1790 publication on the mutiny which show that it was written in part in Britain. *See* Rutter (ed.), 1934, pp. 55-6.

surviving documentary evidence from the *Bounty*.[15] Secondly, there is no mention of Bligh's being abusive except in the extraordinary threat about 'the Straits'.[16] Thirdly, he ordered the coconuts to be returned to the men and taken below, and Fryer specifically mentions the man ordered to do this, the Master at Arms, Charles Churchill. Fourth, Bligh threatened to cut the yam allowance to three-quarters of a pound if he did not find the thief by the next day. These are all important points for comparison with the other versions.

The next version was that of James Morrison, which I believe was written in late 1792, three years after the incident. He wrote:[17]

In the Afternoon of the 27th Mr. Bligh Came up, and taking a turn about the Quarter Deck when he missed some of the Cocoa Nuts which were piled up between the Guns upon which he said that they were stolen and Could not go without the knowledge of the Officers, who were all Calld and declared that they had not seen a Man toutch them, to which Mr. Bligh replied then you must have taken them yourselves, and orderd Mr. Elphinstone to go & fetch evry Cocoa Nut in the Ship aft, which He obeyd. He then questioned evry Officer in turn concerning the Number they had bought, & Coming to Mr. Christian askd Him, Mr. Christian answerd 'I do not know Sir, but I hope you don't think me so mean as to be Guilty of Stealing yours'. Mr. Bligh replied 'Yes you dam'd Hound I do – You must have stolen them from me or you could give a better account of them – God damn you you Scoundrels you are all thieves alike, and combine with the Men to rob me' – I suppose you'll Steal my Yams next, but I'll sweat you for it you rascals I'll make half of you Jump overboard before you get through Endeavour Streights – He then Calld Mr. Samuel and said 'Stop these Villians Grog, and Give them but Half a Pound of Yams tomorrow, and if they steal then, I'll reduce them to a quarter'. The Cocoa Nuts were Carried aft, & He Went below, the officers then got together and were heard to murmur much at such treatment, and it was talked among the Men that the Yams would be next seized, as Lieut. Bligh knew that they had purchased large quantitys of them and set about secreting as many as they Could.

Morrison dates the incident as the afternoon of the 27th, though Fryer reports it as the morning, which makes more sense of his suggestion that the men had trodden down the pile in the night. According to Morrison, William Elphinston, the Master's Mate, and not the Master at Arms, Charles Churchill, collected the nuts from below. If Morrison was right, Fryer had forgotten who was sent or did not know the difference between his own Mate and Churchill; this is unlikely and a small point in favour of Fryer's version.

---

[15] The almost total lack of mention in the surviving documents of Edward Young, the midshipman who went with Christian to Pitcairn, has excited considerable speculation recently. *See* Darby, 1965, 1966, for the argument that Young was the real power behind the mutiny.

[16] If half the crew were to be 'done for' at or after the Straits, the passage through those dangerous waters and the safe delivery of the plants would be at stake; it is unlikely that Bligh forgot his aims so far as to mean this. See p. 94 for my suggestions as to what he may really have said.

[17] Morrison, Journal, pp. 40-1.

But the most important difference between the two versions is the appearance of Christian in the story as a special target for Bligh's abuse. Fryer made no reference to Christian, which suggests that Morrison's introduction of his name was a post-mutiny rationalisation or afterthought. There is some documentary evidence for this too, if we compare Morrison's Journal with his earlier Memorandum, written in October 1792. In the Memorandum he wrote: 'In the afternoon of the 27th a Number of Cocoa Nuts were missd by Mr Bligh, from the Quarter Deck, upon which, all the Officers were called, and on their declaring, that they had not seen any person take them, he told them they were all thieves alike.' At the bottom of the manuscript page there is a footnote stating: 'He particularly called Christian a Thief and a Villain and challenged him with the Theft of the Nuts.'[18] The footnote in the Memorandum of October was moved up and turned into a major part of the rewritten Journal version of November or December 1792. This supports the view that Christian's involvement as one of the officers was given a personal importance long after the mutiny, when it was being suggested by Edward Christian and his friends that his brother had been driven to mutiny by Bligh's ungentlemanly aspersions on his character.

In 1794 Edward Christian published an attack on Bligh after conducting interviews with the crew, including Fryer, in 1793. In this, various details are changed, and Christian is moved right into the centre of the stage:

At this island [Annamooka] the Captain and the ship's company had bought quantities of cocoa nuts, at the rate of 20 for a nail; the Captain's heap lay upon the deck, and in the morning of the 27th, Captain Bligh fancied that the number was diminished, but the master, Mr. Fryer, told him he supposed they were pressed closer from being run over by the men in the night.[19] The Captain then ordered the Officer of the morning Watch; Mr. Christian, to be called; when he came, the Captain accosted him thus, 'Damn your blood, you have stolen my cocoa nuts;' Christian answered, 'I was dry, and I thought it of no consequence, I took one only, and I am sure no one touched another.' Captain Bligh then replied, 'You lie, you scoundrel, you have stolen one half.' Christian appeared much hurt and agitated, and said, 'Why do you treat me thus, Captain Bligh?' Captain Bligh then shook his hand in his face and said, 'No reply;' and called him a 'thief', and other abusive names. He then ordered the quarter masters to go down and bring all the cocoa nuts both from man and officer, and put them upon the quarter deck. They were brought. The Captain then called all hands upon deck, and desired 'the people to look after the officers and the officers to look after the people, for there never were such a set of damned thieving rascals under any man's command in the world before.' And he told the men, 'You are allowed a pound and a

---

[18] Morrison, 'Memorandum and Particulars respecting the Bounty and her crew', ML, Safe 1/33, pp. 32-3; to avoid confusion between Morrison's two journals, I refer to them as the Journal and the Memorandum. I discuss their origins in Chapter 19.

[19] This is almost verbatim from Fryer's Journal and suggests that he may have showed it to Edward Christian.

half of yams today, but tomorrow I shall reduce you to three quarters of a pound.'[20]

Compared with Fryer's 1790 account, this version reverses the sequence of events by having the officers abused before the coconuts were brought up on deck instead of after. There is also a change in the identity of the collector of the nuts. The mutineer, Charles Churchill, is replaced by the Quartermasters, John Norton, George Simpson and Peter Linkletter. This change may have been made to link the incident still further with the mutiny: all three Quartermasters were loyal to Bligh. If these small changes of detail are due to memory getting more unreliable with the passage of time, we have another point to consider; while the details become less reliable, there is a remarkable improvement in the reporting of the alleged exchanges between Bligh and Christian. From Fryer's 1790 memory which merely mentioned 'officers', we find Christian's brother claiming in 1794 to show that Fletcher, alone, got the worst abuse, and even reproducing the exact words.

Why should Edward Christian bend the facts? The answer is fairly clear. In order to show that the mutiny was over something serious rather than trivial, the coconut row had to be made into a major row between Bligh and Christian. Edward could not hope to exculpate his brother without an overwhelming attack on Bligh, and it had to be shown that the events of the day before the mutiny were so distressing that Christian could not contemplate another day with his commander. In Fryer's 1790 version the whole business was comparatively innocuous; by the time Edward Christian had finished with the incident in 1794 we have his brother being called a thief and a villain by his Captain, and being shouted at and humiliated in front of the whole crew.

The public had no access to the documents now available, and they would not have been aware of the changes in the successive versions, ranging from vagueness of detail to the introduction of specific personal attacks on Christian leaves out the reason for bringing the nuts on deck, and the reason present writer's knowledge these questions about this incident have not been asked up to now. Thus the rashness of an unhappy young man is covered up, and we are presented instead with a picture of Bligh as an incredible ogre. Other changes make Bligh's words and actions seem near insane; Edward Christian leaves out the reason for bringing the nuts on deck, and the reason for the threat to cut the yam allowance. He goes back to Fryer's version, that the cut was from a pound and a half to three-quarters of a pound, without mentioning that this was merely a threat made by Bligh to be carried out if the thief was not found – a point Fryer was unlikely to have made up, as he had no reason to soften his criticism of Bligh. Morrison's version, that the allowance was cut to half a pound immediately, found more favour with Bligh's critics when it was published by Heywood in the nineteenth century.[21]

[20] Edward Christian, Appendix, pp. 63-4.
[21] Apparently Edward Christian had not seen Morrison's Journal when he wrote his attack, and did not interview him in person. Morrison's version of the cuts was followed by Barrow, 1831, which set the pattern for the next 130 years.

I have gone into detail here in order to show how the charges against Bligh evolved within a few years of the mutiny into what has through constant repetition become established as the folklore of the *Bounty*.[22] There are a few other points to be made about the incident and about what was going on in Bligh's mind, once we accept that he was not an insane tyrant deliberately affronting Christian's honour in front of the crew. In all the versions, Bligh came up on deck on 27 April and thought the coconuts piled between the guns had been reduced in number. Fryer, according to himself and Morrison, agreed that this appeared to be so, but to avoid yet another row made the rather fatuous suggestion that they had been trodden down in the night watches. Fryer's apparent indifference, or his facile explanation, annoyed Bligh enough for him to make an issue of this latest theft. He would have sent for Christian as the officer of the previous watch. If Christian exhibited the same lack of concern (and, to read his brother's version, he was hardly bursting with indignation at the thefts) Bligh would be driven into deeper exasperation. When he ordered all the men up and all stores of coconuts to be brought on deck, his hope of forcing the thief into the open by identifying each man's pile was forlorn from the start; most probably several men were involved, through a casual act of a night's refreshment rather than by a deliberate theft. As shown by Fryer's report of Young's answer, Bligh's questions were parried by vagueness. Each man would have taken the hint from Young's answers, and the responses to Bligh's questions would become predictable, increasing his impotent rage. Without evidence he was yet again prevented from punishing anybody. The apparent laxity in the watch officers, or, worse, their collusion in letting the ship's stores be removed, may have led him into a blanket tirade against everybody and to the use of the epithets 'thieves' and 'villains'. The other threats could have been based on remarks by Bligh that though they had outsmarted him on this occasion, they would soon regret their actions – when the ship got to Endeavour Straits they would soon find out what useless sailors they really were: being lazy and incompetent they would need to rely on their captain's skills to get them through the straits safely, though he suspected (being sarcastic) that they were also cowards and that half of them would jump overboard with fright. He ended, according to Fryer, the most likely witness, with the hardly tyrannical threat that the yam allowance would be cut if the thieves did not own up.

Bligh did not write this incident into the Log, possibly because it was overshadowed by the excitement of recording the next morning's events. He had no reason to consider it particularly important until five years later when Edward Christian published his attack in London. Bligh's only known reference to the coconuts incident is found in his 1793 notes made for Sir Joseph Banks. He sets out his motives for acting as he did, even justifying the use of the words 'thieves' and 'villains', and also makes the valid point that

---

[22] The dialogue from these 'doctored' versions of the events leading to the mutiny is almost always repeated in modern books, as if what was said and by whom was not open to doubt.

these accusations, if he did make them, did not explain what happened the next day.

> When the ship sailed from Anamooka [...] A heap of Cocoa Nutts were between the guns under the charge of the officer of the Watch, with orders for no one to touch them untill the ship was clear of the land, when they would be issued equally and considered highly refreshing, without which caution some would have & waste one half, & others would have none. In one Night (the first) the Officers permitted the whole within a score to be taken away. As this was evidently done through design Captain Bligh ordered all Cocoa Nutts to be replaced – The officers of the Watch declared they were taken away by stelth – Here was publick theft, a contumacy, & direct disobedience of orders – the particular offenders could not be found out, any more than had been effected in private thefts which had been frequently committed; could therefore either the epithet Thief or Villain, had it been used, have justified their taking the Ship next day.[23]

Edward Christian quotes Purcell as saying that after another row between Fletcher and Bligh at 4 p.m. that afternoon, Christian's distress was so severe that he came away with 'tears running fast from his eyes in big drops'. Other witnesses (unidentified) are quoted by Edward as saying that Fletcher exclaimed: 'I would rather die ten thousand deaths, than bear this treatment: I always do my duty as an officer and as a man ought to do, yet I receive this scandalous usage', and 'That flesh and blood cannot bear this treatment'.[24] Edward has built up the picture to its black finale; Christian is now contemplating any drastic measure to rid himself of his burden. Yet at no time have we had any indication of a burden that warrants 'ten thousand deaths' or mutiny.

That evening, Bligh sent his servant, John Smith, to Christian with an invitation to join him as usual for dinner. If Bligh did not in fact pick on Christian individually over the coconuts, this invitation is not as odd as it has been made to appear. He had had an altercation with his officers and crew in the morning over a minor disciplinary matter and settled the issue to his satisfaction, at least if the coconuts were returned the next day or the thieves discovered. He would have held Christian responsible as the officer of the watch, but this did not prevent him from acting as usual. Christian excused himself from dinner, pleading that he was unwell, and Bligh believed him. Eventually Hayward accepted the invitation. Bligh was not alarmed by his friend's conduct; after dinner and his final rounds on deck he spoke to Fryer on his watch and went to bed, unarmed and unprepared. If the rows had

---

[23] Bligh, 'Remarks on Morrison's Journal', Bligh, Bounty Mutineers, ML, Safe 1/43, pp. 50-1.

[24] Edward Christian, Appendix, pp. 64-5. Fryer does not mention this row in his Journal. If Morrison wrote to Edward Christian when he was collecting his evidence, and repeated the assertion made in his Journal that the coconut row was in the afternoon, Purcell could have been talking about the coconut incident but made the timing consistent with Morrison's. Or, if the second row did take place, it could explain why Morrison placed the coconut row in the afternoon: he got the two confused.

been as serious as his critics make out, his conduct is completely inexplicable. But it is their own elaboration on events that make the situation unlikely – one man driven to the verge of suicide and his tormentor calmly issuing an invitation to dinner. If we assume that the impulse to mutiny came from stresses within Christian, and not from Bligh's treatment of him – though Bligh's touchiness could have helped to push him to a crisis, and Christian himself may have channelled his feelings into hatred of Bligh – then the invitation and Bligh's unalarmed behaviour make much better sense. It is the state of Christian's mind, and what it led to, which I shall examine in the next chapter.

13

The Mutiny

Attention must now focus on the man who led the mutiny, Fletcher Christian, at this time twenty-four years old. He was five feet nine inches tall, strongly made, with a dark brown complexion and dark brown hair, and was tattooed in the Tahitian fashion with a star on his left breast and another tattoo on his backside. Apparently he was a little bow-legged and sweated profusely, so that he 'soils any thing he handles'.[1] Though not wealthy, he was from a well-connected family in Cumberland.[2] He went to the local Grammar School in Cockermouth and was a contemporary of William Wordsworth. Apart from these scanty details little is known about him. He left no letters, journals, or memoirs for posterity to judge him by. Except for the eulogies of his friends there is little information to go on and eulogies are hardly acceptable as evidence. We can only judge him by his behaviour; though this too is a risky enterprise, for we do not have his own version of why he behaved as he did.

'I am in Hell', Christian is said to have cried during the mutiny. And so he probably was; but exactly what caused this breakdown has never been settled. The question is whether this was a hell created in Christian's mind by himself, or by Bligh. I am in favour of the first view, and there are various pressures we can point to which could have upset an unstable young man. One is his forced parting from his Tahitian woman, 'Isabella',[3] with whom he had passed such a pleasant time in the shore camp, away from the animosities of the *Bounty*. He could have been jealous, imagining what she would get up to once he was gone, with a Tahitian husband or other men. She may have been reason enough for him to try to get back to Tahiti; she may have come to symbolise for him the difference between the easy life there and the deprivations and discomfort of the routine on the ship. And we have to think of what he had come back to; a thickening atmosphere of distrust,

[1] These details come from Bligh's summary of the mutineers' descriptions, passed to the authorities when he reached Timor to assist in their apprehension in case they tried to take the *Bounty* to a European settlement. A copy of this summary in his handwriting is in the Mitchell Library, Bligh, Bounty Mutineers, Safe 1/43, p. 1; what appears to be the first draft, made in the open boat with the assistance of the other men, was rediscovered with the pocket notebook in 1976 (*see* p. 114n.), and is now in the National Library, Canberra.

[2] There is a brief account of his life in Wilkinson, 1953.

[3] Christian seems to have named his Tahitian wife after his cousin's first wife, Isabella Curwen, a rich and beautiful heiress in the Cumberland area. The cousin, John Christian, changed his name to Curwen in 1790 when the news of the mutiny reached Britain, and later became an influential Whig M.P.

arguments and breakdown of authority, and a changed Bligh who had lost faith in the promising young officer he had promoted. There must have been a contrast between the West Indian voyages where Bligh and Christian had liked and trusted each other, and the new scornful impatience which Bligh was showing with all his officers as his command structure fell apart. These stresses may have made him inefficient, and Bligh's tetchiness may have increased his mental torment; Bligh may even have tipped the balance. But to blame this on Bligh is unjust.

Some incidents before the mutiny and Christian's behaviour after it give us an idea of his character. At the time of the mutiny his apprenticeship was not yet complete, and he was immature and as yet unfit for command. This immaturity had surfaced, for example, in his frustration at not being permitted by Bligh to open fire on troublesome islanders. In berating him with the epithet 'cowardly rascal', Bligh may have shown more perception that he is credited with. With time and experience, Christian might have grown wiser; but in the next year or so of his life he showed an instinct to run from trouble and to resort to violence too soon, and also treated islanders appallingly and thoughtlessly, particularly the women. His relatives and friends remembered him as a model young gentleman, 'adorned with every virtue', but in his two-year absence from home a great deal had happened to change him. Removed from the restraints of home, encouraged by a small number of evil and dangerous men, and given the power of life and death over others, he did not live up to his apologists' view of him.

It is this book's hypothesis that the mutiny is best explained by the coincidence of the collapse in the authority of the commander and an emotional storm in an immature and possibly mentally unstable young man. The fact that Christian was the son of a gentleman farmer in Cumberland, with a bright future before him in the Navy, does not make this any less likely. History is littered with well-connected young men who threw it all away through some rash act for apparently trivial reasons. One of the best supports for this hypothesis is the public acceptance by his family that he was guilty of mutiny and therefore in forfeit of his life, from at least 1790, when Bligh returned to Britain with news of the mutiny, to 1792, when some mutineers were brought back as prisoners and in justifying themselves suggested another hypothesis his family might use to justify Christian's actions.

His act was a crime according to the laws of the country, and if he had been caught he would have hanged, whatever his defence.[4] This was all there was to the matter until his family and friends suggested to the world that there was more. One must suspect that if the mutineers had all been common seamen, with no connections, no articulate sponsors, no position of respectability to protect, the *Bounty* mutiny would have been forgotten within a decade; how many mutinies in the British Navy can the reader identify? Indeed, if Bligh and the men in the open boat with him had perished and the

---

[4] There was no defence that could justify leading a mutiny. One could only deny the charge. His family did not directly challenge the charge.

mutineers in the *Bounty* had foundered or been killed in the battle with islanders, the world would never have known that a mutiny had taken place. The vanishing of the *Bounty* would have been as mysterious as that of La Pérouse.[5] But men did survive on both sides of the mutiny and the campaign of recriminations has been going on ever since. In spite of decades of attempts to prove that the mutiny was momentous and mysterious, a concerted revolt against a monstrous commander, it was really no such thing. Christian's actions took almost everybody on board by surprise and forced them to make the terrible decision between going with Bligh in a open boat and staying on board to risk the hangman's rope. That so many went with Bligh, and others wanted to, speaks volumes for the so-called tyrant and little for Christian the 'liberator'.

Before describing the events of that night we should look briefly at one of the more recent explanations of Christian's actions – the theory that Bligh and Christian were lovers, who quarrelled when Christian indulged in heterosexual intercourse in his stay at the shore camp on Tahiti. According to this hypothesis, Bligh wanted to resume the relationship when the *Bounty* left Tahiti, but Christian refused and the resulting harrassment of Christian by Bligh drove Christian to mutiny. This particular explanation is more honestly put together than the traditional one in which Bligh behaved so tyrannically that the frenzied crew were driven to overthrow him. The people who have advanced it have, in the main, been forced to seek another explanation by reason of the inadequacy of the traditional view, and have attempted sympathetically to found the homosexuality theory on a study of what little factual evidence is available.[6] However, the problem with this argument is its meagre basis in fact. It relies virtually on a single ambiguous statement made by Peter Heywood in 1830,[7] a year before he died, about a 'secret' that only he knew, which was passed on to him by Fletcher Christian on the night when Christian finally took the *Bounty* away from Tahiti to go to Pitcairn. We shall see later that it is doubtful whether this meeting ever took place; nevertheless, Christian is alleged by Heywood to have given him a most private message for his family to justify his behaviour. This message was so dreadful that he could not confide it to anybody else, and it was up to Heywood (at the time, let us remember, Heywood was only seventeen) to decide whether he should eventually let the world know the truth. The theory of homosexual love has taken long enough to flower, seeing that the alleged 'secret message' has been known of since 1830: Bonner Smith in the 1930s concluded that the secret was that Christian had venereal disease.[8] Naturally in the enlightened 1970s venereal disease is not shocking enough to justify Heywood's mysterious handling of the secret, so it has to be something even

[5] The French maritime discoverer, La Pérouse, disappeared for ever in the Pacific in 1788 (the year the *Bounty* was in the area). *See* Allen, 1959.

[6] Darby, 1965; Hough, 1972.   [7] Quoted in Barrow, 1961, p. 72.

[8] The possibility that Christian had syphilis, and was either aware of this and severely upset by it, or was actually clinically mad, has not as far as I know been properly discussed in the literature of the subject. One possibility is that Heywood was prevented from publicising Christian's syphilitic condition because of the sensibilities of his step-daughter, Lady Belcher, who had been through a stormy court case against her husband, Captain Belcher, whom she accused of giving her VD (Friendly, 1977).

more scandalous than VD, and the only thing left is homosexuality.

The circumstantial support for the homosexuality theory is at least consistent. Bligh was extremely friendly with his young protégé; he wined and dined him in his cabin regularly on both *Britannia* and *Bounty*. Christian had a key to Bligh's private liquor store and had access to it whenever he wanted. Bligh went to great lengths to favour Christian; he made him Acting Lieutenant over Fryer, gave him the shore-camp command and protected him from criticism in his Log (this last point, which does support the homosexuality thesis, has so far been missed by its proponents; see p.75).

There are several obvious objections, however. It seems odd, if they were lovers, that Bligh should separate himself from Christian at Tahiti by posting him ashore. Hough has suggested that Bligh also had a homosexual interest in Heywood, as he was indulgent to him and careful of his needs as part of his obligation to his father-in-law. But Bligh also posted Heywood ashore; an odd thing to do if this hypothesis were correct. A more telling objection is that, if Bligh and Christian were lovers, the entire elaborate campaign against Bligh by the Heywoods, the Christians and the petty officers was totally unnecessary. Even the most circumspect of affairs could not be kept entirely private on a small ship the size of the Bounty. The one charge that would have finished him for good was the charge of sodomy. A person found guilty of that offence at a court martial had a mandatory death sentence,[9] and at a hint of it would have been cashiered on suspicion. But his opponents never even implied it in their writings. There is no suggestion of it in Morrison's Journal, or Fryer's Journal, which both lay dormant for decades. We might accept that Christian's family, suffering the ignominy of having their relative branded as a mutineer, would not be anxious to broadcast that he also had a homosexual relationship with his commander; but this argument does not hold with Morrison, Fryer, Purcell or Heywood. For these reasons, and in the light of a detailed examination of the Heywood case, the homosexuality theory must be rejected until written evidence from an original source comes to light, such as a hitherto unknown letter or memorandum by Heywood or Edward Christian.[10]

Our information of what happened on the night before the mutiny comes from a number of reports written by eye-witnesses and some private letters from Bligh to the Admiralty, Sir Joseph Banks, Mrs Bligh and Duncan Campbell. Bligh's letters naturally present his own point of view, and when Christian appears in them he does so only in enough detail to establish his conduct as a mutineer. Other eye-witness reports that have survived, such as Fryer's and Morrison's, are attempts to exculpate their authors from guilt rather than to establish the psychological state of Christian. Morrison's account gives the clearest statement on behalf of Christian, in that he claims to quote from a speech made by Christian after the mutiny to the two

[9] 'If any person in the fleet, shall commit the unnatural and detestable sin of buggery or sodomy, with man or beast, he shall be punished with death, by the sentence of a court martial.' *See* MacArthur, 1813, Vol. I, p. 335, Article XXIX.

[10] Such evidence may have existed but been destroyed. New material on the *Bounty* does, however, come to light occasionally.

midshipmen, Peter Heywood and George Stewart. Some part of this speech was confirmed in an important detail by the last survivor of the mutineers on Pitcairn in 1825. This suggests that Christian's speech may very well be accurately reported by Morrison.[11] There are also the reports of Christian's state of mind that were published by his brother in 1794. But altogether the evidence is sparse. After the mutiny the character and behaviour of Christian become even more unclear and witnesses' reports are inconsistent and vague.

Whichever version we rely on, his behaviour during the night exhibited characteristics of severe mental distress, becoming completely irrational and suicidal. He seems to have been trying to avoid a choice between growing up – coming to himself again – and going ahead with the mutiny. Eventually, his extraordinary behaviour made it impossible to go back, and he had to go on. From several reports, it appears that at some point during the evening he decided to quit the *Bounty* by jumping overboard with a makeshift raft and some food. His object, it is said, was to swim to the nearest island, Tofoa. What he intended to do there is not clear, though judging by Bligh's own experiences there soon afterwards he would probably have been killed by islanders. Bligh later dismissed this report on the grounds that it was ridiculous for a man in his senses to contemplate jumping into a shark-infested sea thirty or more miles from the nearest land.[12] But Christian may not have been in his senses.

Christian committed himself to this ridiculous scheme by involving others in it. He asked Purcell, the carpenter, for some planks, rope and nails out of which he intended to construct his crude raft.[13] According to Edward Christian, Fletcher also told George Stewart of his plan;[14] according to Morrison, he told George Stewart, William Cole the Boatswain, and the midshipman Thomas Hayward. The idea that Christian told Hayward of his plans passes belief. Hayward was disliked by Christian and many others on board, and seems to have been the kind of person who would have run to Bligh straight away with the astonishing news about the Acting Lieutenant. If he was told, we can only speculate why he did not do so on this occasion. He might have hoped to get back into Christian's favour, or simply not have cared what Christian did. A possible explanation of Christian's confiding in him could be that suicidal behaviour often includes a 'cry for help', some action taken to make the intention obvious and allow someone else to prevent it. Perhaps Christian was appealing to Bligh through Hayward to step in and stop him going any further. But whichever way one looks at it, this confidence seems unlikely.[15]

[11] James Morrison, Journal, p. 46; *see* also the account given to Captain Beechey by Alexander Smith (John Adams) in 1825; Beechey, 1831, Vol. I, Chapter 3.

[12] Bligh, 'Remarks on Morrison's Journal', Bounty Mutineers, ML, Safe 1/43, p. 51; *see* below, p. 209n.

[13] Purcell's admission that he had helped Christian was published in Edward Christian's Appendix in 1794, p. 65. This admission could have been damaging for Purcell if it had been known at his court martial in 1790; aiding a deserter was a serious offence.

[14] Appendix, p. 71.

[15] One of the purposes of Morrison's Journal was to discredit the evidence given by Hayward and Hallet at the court martial; the assertion that Christian confided in Hayward would help to do this. For another explanation, *see* p. 105, n.25.

As well as the planks, rope and nails to make a raft, Christian collected extra nails and some beads for barter with the islanders. He also stole a roasted pig from his mess and put this into a bag that he allegedly got from Hayward. A mess was a group of men who had rations issued for them which they then prepared jointly; in Christian's mess were Robert Tinkler, George Stewart and Peter Heywood. Thus in removing the roast pig he was taking rations from his messmates – odd behaviour, we might note, if one were to believe the story that he was running away because his Captain had called him a thief. Fryer tells us that his brother-in-law Robert Tinkler was feeling hungry and went down to the mess to get some of the roast pig. He found the pig had disappeared, and thought that somebody from another mess had hidden it for a lark. Later, according to Fryer, he found the bag with the pig in it hidden behind a sea-chest while looking for his hat, though he did nothing about it.[16]

Christian's attempt to leave the *Bounty* was certainly suicidal; it meant almost inevitable death from drowning, sharks, starvation or murder ashore. But he never actually left. Perhaps saner moments of reflection made him temporise, like a man sitting on a window-ledge far above the ground waiting for the moment to jump. Other explanations have been given; Hough, for instance, widens the circle of men who were in on his secret, implying that this prevented him from going: 'As the evening advanced, more rumours circulated through the decks ... that the second-in-command was contemplating suicide or desertion ... Word of Christian's despair, of his plan to desert ship, had reached a number of ears by sundown.'[17] But the presence of people in the know need not have inhibited him; he had already told four people and probably expected others to find out. Another explanation, given in the 'Appendix' of Edward Christian,[18] is that there were too many people on deck during the night who were not in his confidence, some because of the heat, others watching a volcano on the horizon. But jumping overboard would hardly pass unnoticed, however many or few were on deck. The watch would probably hear him, and anyway his absence would be noticed at the relief of the watches at 4 a.m.

There is also the possibility that he might have been engaged in a more serious conspiracy at this stage that we were led to believe by his brother's version. Morrison reports that he was seen with George Stewart 'several times up and down the Fore Cock pit where the Boatswain's and Carpenter's Cabbins were, and where Mr. C. seldom or ever went'.[19] Morrison also says he overheard the Boatswain, William Cole, saying to Purcell 'It won't do tonight', though this could have referred to something other than a possible mutiny. But taking the evidence as a whole, it seems likely that the idea of mutiny surprised Christian as much as most others on board.

---

[16] The bag and pig move about . the various accounts. Morrison reports that Tinkler found it in the clue of his hammock; Edward Christian states that he found it with some breadfruit in Christian's own cot.

[17] Hough, 1972, p. 145.

[18] p. 65.

[19] Morrison, Journal, p. 47.

The picture of the evening's events left us by the accounts is a strange one. We are told that Christian planned to swim from the *Bounty* at some time during the night, that he collected items to assist him, that he destroyed his letters and personal possessions, giving several of them away, and that his confidants were not only George Stewart and William Cole but also two men against whom he bore grudges, Purcell and Hayward. He did not tell his close friend Peter Heywood, according to Heywood himself. Apparently the men to whom he had confided his plan and who had helped him in his bizarre preparations did not attempt to dissuade him but went to bed, though one would have expected them to have the elementary curiosity of spectators at a suicide attempt. Their testimony at the court martial was that they were woken up by the mutiny in the morning. What happened, they swore on oath, was a surprise to them.

If Christian had spoken to several men, as he is alleged to have done, he now had the problem of avoiding looking silly in the morning by still being on the ship. The men on deck may not have been watching a volcano at all, but waiting to see what he would do; Fryer, who had one of the night watches, does not say so in his Journal, but he might have avoided saying it to exculpate himself further from any idea of mutiny or knowledge of what was going on. Christian may have regretted his ridiculous plan. Although he could not hope to escape unnoticed, the actual sight of people waiting and watching might have put him off. Yet he could not turn back without gross humiliation; the pressure of the dilemma he had created for himself must have been unbearable. He was to take over the watch at 4 a.m., and in some accounts he now went to bed and slept fitfully.

Some accounts claim that it was George Stewart who gave him a way out of the dilemma. Morrison's account states that 'he [Christian] went to sleep about half past three in the Morning. When Mr. Stuart calld him to relieve the Watch he had not Slept long, and was much out of order, when Stuart begd him not to attempt swimming away, saying "The people are ripe for any thing", this made a forcible impression on his mind ...'[20] Thirty-three years later (1825) much the same story was told to Captain Beechey by Alexander Smith (John Adams), the last of Christian's mutineers, on Pitcairn Island. Captain Beechey reported his conversations with Smith in his book published in 1831. He wrote of this episode, quoting Smith's version:

His [Christian's] plan, strange as it must appear for a young officer to adopt who was fairly advanced in an honourable profession, was to set himself adrift upon a raft, and make his way to the island (Tofoa) then in sight. As quick in the execution as in the design, the raft was soon constructed, various useful articles were got together, and he was on the point of launching it, when a young officer, who afterwards perished in the Pandora, to whom Christian communicated his intention, recommended him, rather than risk his life on so hazardous an expedition, to endeavour to take possession of the ship, which he thought would not be very

[20] Morrison, Journal, p. 46.

difficult, as many of the ship's company were not well-disposed towards the commander, and would all be very glad to return to Otaheite, and reside among their friends in that island. This daring proposition is even more extraordinary than the premeditated scheme of his companion, and, if true, certainly relieves Christian from part of the odium which has hitherto attached to him as the sole instigator of the mutiny.[21]

The only 'young officer' from the *Bounty* to perish in the *Pandora* was George Stewart. The fact that two reports, separated both in time and circumstance, make the same point is convincing evidence in its favour.

Doubt has been cast on the role of Stewart by Peter Heywood's denials that Stewart had anything to do with the mutiny. Heywood's defence at his court martial was that he was too young and inexperienced to know what was going on, and was completely innocent of involvement in the mutiny. He claimed that he was forcibly prevented by the mutineers from going in the boat with Bligh, and that he and his friend, George Stewart, were kept below by armed mutineers against their will. It was essential to his case to assert the innocence of Stewart; if Stewart helped push Christian to mutiny, it would be hard to believe that Christian ordered them both to be kept below, and if they were not kept below then Heywood should have made more strenuous attempts to join Bligh or at least to speak to him. If the story of Stewart's remark had come out at the trial Heywood might well not have been pardoned.

As it was, Morrison's Journal was held privately from 1792 to 1825, when some extracts edited by Heywood himself were published by Marshall in his *Royal Naval Biography*; in this extract he drops Morrison's reference to Stewart's advice about the people being 'ready for any thing', leaving the impression that Stewart only tried to dissuade Christian from going into the water.[22] When Beechey returned from his voyage and began to write his book, he noticed the difference between Smith's account and that in Marshall, and wrote to Heywood for an explanation. Heywood replied that the remark attributed to Stewart by Smith was 'entirely at variance with the whole character and conduct of [Stewart], both before and after the mutiny; as well as with the assurance of Christian himself, the very night he quitted Taheite, that the idea of attempting to take the ship had never entered his distracted mind, until he relieved the deck and found his mate and midshipman asleep.'[23] He did not inform Beechey that Smith's story had been corroborated by Morrison in 1792, or remind him that in Edward Christian's account of 1794 the very same words had been attributed to Stewart: 'It is agreed that Christian was the first to propose mutiny, and the project of turning the Captain on shore at Tofoa, to the people of the watch; but he declared afterwards in the ship, he never should have thought of it, if it

[21] Beechey, 1831, Vol. 1, pp. 71-2; quoted in Barrow, 1961, pp. 90-1.

[22] Marshall, 1823-30, Vol. 2, Part 2. Heywood wrote later that he gave the facts verbally to Marshall. Much the same material appeared in at least three other major *Bounty* sources, all of them anti-Bligh. *See* Tagart, 1832; Barrow, 1961; Lady Belcher, 1870.

[23] Quoted in Barrow, 1961, p. 91-2.

had not been suggested to his mind by an expression of Mr. Stewart, who knowing his intention of leaving the ship upon the raft, told him, "When you go, Christian, we are ripe for anything".[24] Heywood was party to the preparation of Edward Christian's Appendix and knew of this statement. He has three separate and identical accounts of Stewart's role against him, and I think it is reasonably certain that Stewart did make some remark to Christian during the change-over of the watch which promoted the idea of mutiny in his mind.

An interesting point about Morrison's and Heywood's accounts is that they do agree upon Christian's mental state. Heywood quotes Christian himself as having said he had a 'distracted mind' and Morrison calls him 'much out of order'. This supports the interpretation of his behaviour as that of a man suffering from intense emotional stress or a mental breakdown.

What did Christian do when he took over the watch at 4 a.m. in the morning, 28 April 1789? Morrison writes, supposedly repeating Christian's own explanation of what he had done: '[Christian] finding that Mr. Hayward the Mate of his Watch (with whom he refused to discourse)[25] soon went to sleep on the Arm Chest which stood between the Guns, and Mr. Hallet (the midshipman of his Watch) not making his appearance, He at once resolved to Seize the Ship'.[26] Much the same story was told to Beechey by Smith in 1825.[27] Having made this decision, his first job was to recruit help. This was the point of no return; the bare suggestion of mutiny to any member of the crew put his own life at risk, and also the life of his listener.[28] Once the suggestion was made, they had to succeed, to avoid the death sentence. The Articles of War were read out at Sunday musters and nobody went into a mutiny ignorant of the penalty of failure. Thus Christian's mutiny put him into alliance with men with whom he would never normally have associated. The Navy worked by separating gentlemen from seamen, but Christian's plan united them by turning both parties into criminals, locked out from their country and at each other's mercy.

[24] *See* Edward Christian, Appendix, p. 71.

[25] The statement by Morrison that Christian 'refused to discourse' with Hayward comes only a few lines below the statement that Christian informed him of his intention to desert. Morrison offers no explanation of this contradiction, nor do the authors who quote him. One possibility is that when describing Christian confiding in someone Morrison may have written 'Hayward' by mistake for 'Heywood'. In original documents relating to the *Bounty* the two names were often confused, or one was written, crossed out and replaced by the other, even by people who knew them both well, such as Bligh, Morrison and Captain Edwards. Or Morrison could have heard Christian describing the incident and misheard 'Heywood' as 'Hayward'. It would make more sense of the accounts of the evening's business if Christian had told his young friend, Peter Heywood, instead of Thomas Hayward, the man he despised, about his intentions, especially as Heywood was a close friend of Stewart and a member of Christian's mess. Of course this would destroy Heywood's plea of innocence entirely.

[26] Morrison, Journal, p. 46.

[27] Beechey, 1831, Chapter 3.

[28] MacArthur, 1813, Vol. I, Appendix 1, p. 332: 'If any person in or belonging to the fleet shall make, or endeavour to make, any mutinous assembly, upon any pretence whatsoever, every person offending herein, and being convicted thereof by the sentence of the court martial, shall suffer death ...' (Article XIX); 'If any person in the fleet shall conceal any traitorous or mutinous practice, or design, being convicted thereof by the sentence of a court martial, he shall suffer death, or other such punishment as a court martial shall think fit ...' (Article XX).

Christian's first choice of recruit was a near-disaster.[29] He spoke to Matthew Quintal and Isaac Martin, and the first one he spoke to refused to join in the mutiny. Several modern accounts have him approaching Martin first and being rebuffed by him; Beechey's report of Smith's story has this incident in the reverse order, with Quintal refusing to join and Martin accepting.[30] As Martin later changed sides during the course of the mutiny it seems more likely that it was he who at first refused Christian's request to help him seize the ship. Martin was an American from Philadelphia, aged about thirty-two, and he had little love for Bligh. He may have suggested to Christian that he try out his scheme on Matthew Quintal. Christian's manner was by now urgent and frenzied; he had tied a heavy weight round his neck and hidden it under his shirt, to bring a speedy end to his life if the mutiny failed and he had to jump over the side.[31] Martin might have been put off risking his life with a man who appeared to be out of his mind, or he may have thought that as an American his chances in a trial for mutiny in a British ship were even slimmer than those of anybody else on board.

Quintal undertook to recruit two more men, and he went below and brought back the two most violent and aggressive men on the *Bounty*, Charles Churchill and his friend Matthew Thompson. The mutineers now numbered four, and so far the security of the conspiracy had not been breached, although it might have been if Martin had run to Bligh's cabin. The hard-liners now began to join in. Alexander Smith, the man who told Beechey about the conspiracy on Pitcairn thirty-six years later, William McCoy and John Williams joined in the first half-hour or so. Christian now had a formidable force with which to seize the ship, if he could arm it. From this point, his madness and despair gave way to a more calculating organisation; the decision was made, there was no time to brood. The nonsensical plan of swimming to Tofoa, and the indecision of the early hours, were replaced by a determination to risk all on the dangerous criminal act of mutiny. Having started the mutiny Christian could not abandon it; he had nothing to gain by stepping back and everything to lose. It is also doubtful whether the seamen would have backed down, for they could expect no mercy from British justice.

In the Navy, arms were not just left lying about the deck for anybody to pick up at will. They were secured in chests and only issued on lawful authority. In this case, John Fryer was responsible for them and was supposed to keep the keys. The watch officers might want a musket to shoot a shark, and if this happened during the night Fryer had to wake in order to give the keys to the watch. He disliked being disturbed off watch so he made the informal, and fatal, arrangement with the armourer, Joseph Coleman,

---

[29] The exact sequence of Christian's approach to the men on his watch, and the exact disposition of every person during the mutiny, cannot be known for certain. Almost every eye-witness account differs from the others in some material particular. The events themselves are fairly well known and accepted, but the identity of each participant in every event cannot be established accurately.

[30] Beechey, 1831, pp. 72-3.

[31] Danielsson, 1962, p. 90.

that he should keep the keys and give them to the watch officer if he wanted them during the night. Thus, to get the keys, Christian had no need to disturb Fryer (whose cabin was opposite Bligh's); he only had to get them from Coleman. The intentions behind Fryer's delegation of responsibility were obvious to Coleman, who probably did not like being disturbed either; and when the Acting Lieutenant woke him and demanded the keys, whispering that he wanted to shoot a shark, Coleman gave them to him without the slightest hesitation and went back to sleep. He would need a good reason to refuse Christian such a request.

The mutiny now ran into its first problem. The two midshipmen who had turned out for the watch had chosen to sleep on the arms chests. These were stowed below the main hatchway and on the main grating. In the hot Pacific night they made excellent sleeping berths. It was, of course, typical of the kind of thing that Bligh had to put up with that two petty officers, instead of being on their watch, were sleeping through it. The punishment of Hayward for sleeping during the watch when the deserters slipped away had apparently had no effect. However, Christian was not going to be put off by two lazy midshipmen. He simply woke Hallet and ordered him on deck. Hallet jumped to it, believing that he would be in trouble with Bligh in the morning. In his concern for his own fate he did not question Christian's behaviour in waking him up accompanied by several men, not all of them in his watch. Hayward, sleeping on the other chest, was woken by Norman, one of the men on the watch not yet approached by Christian, apparently to tell him about a shark following the ship. They both returned to the deck.

Christian meanwhile had opened the arms chest on which Hallet had been sleeping and handed out arms to his party, now swelled with some more recruits. Thomas Burkitt and Robert Lamb joined the mutiny and were under arms with the others. Thompson was left to guard the chest and Christian took his armed party to the quarterdeck to arrest Hayward and Hallet. This was accomplished without trouble. In the near-total darkness of the morning, mutineers with muskets were a frightening sight and the characters of the two lazy midshipmen were no match in these circumstances for men who were now firmly committed to their cause. Christian posted his men about the deck to guard hatchways and the prisoners. Ellison, the young boy at the wheel, left his post to join the mutiny, picking up a cutlass in his hand. His unnecessary enthusiasm cost him his life.[32]

The *Bounty* was now under Christian's control. The only task that remained was to arrest the sleeping and unarmed Bligh. He had given his pocket pistols to Fryer who, with his usual dedication to incompetence, did not even have them loaded (or so he claimed later, but Bligh never believed him). Christian selected his arrest party and went to Bligh's cabin. This was the first Bligh knew of the mutiny.

Bligh's own account of what happened next is that Christian was accompanied by Charles Churchill, John Mills and Thomas Burkitt and that

[32] Ellison was hanged at Spithead for the mutiny; the evidence that he had picked up the cutlass destroyed his defence.

they seized hold of him, tied his arms behind his back and took him, minus his trousers, to the deck where he was held by the mizzen-mast.[33] Resistance, physically at least, was impossible. He was unarmed and could only shout, trying to rouse the ship's company. Nobody could come to his assistance because every approach was guarded by armed mutineers. Those of the ship's company not involved in the mutiny were unarmed, and remained passive.

John Sumner and Matthew Quintal arrested Fryer and kept him in his cabin. Churchill came down from the deck where Bligh was being kept under guard and looked into Fryer's cabin, saw Bligh's pistols and pocketed them. Apparently neither Fryer nor his guards had noticed them. Churchill took them away with him, leaving Fryer in his cabin and Sumner and Quintal standing outside. In this position they could also prevent David Nelson and William Peckover from leaving their cabins below, as they had to climb the ladder past Fryer's cabin to get to the main deck.

Neither Nelson nor Peckover was expecting a mutiny. It is reported that when Nelson told Peckover that the ship had been taken, Peckover's first reaction was to assume that he meant it had been taken by islanders in a surprise attack.[34] Others were just as surprised; the romantic idea that everyone was aware of an atmosphere of impending doom, as the reaction to Bligh's supposed cruelty came to a head, only developed later, partly to justify Christian's actions and partly to exculpate those who did not immediately declare their opposition to him. The indecision of certain people came from their surprise; they were not debating whether to side with the hated Captain, but stunned by the approach of a small group of armed and determined men.

When Bligh was brought on deck, daylight had arrived, quickly as it does in those latitudes. Everybody soon knew what had happened. The mutineers were armed, and Bligh, Fryer (according to his own Journal), Hayward and Hallet were prisoners. The rest of the crew was left wandering about. Men such as Purcell, Cole, Lebogue, Elphinston, Stewart, Heywood and Young came up on deck and for the main part watched the proceedings. It was during this time that Peter Heywood, as he admitted during his trial, picked up a cutlass, though for what reason is not clear. Edward Young, however, was less indecisive. He threw in his lot with the mutiny and eventually became Christian's most loyal and intelligent supporter. William Purcell, not unexpectedly, was gloating over Bligh's predicament, at least until he realised that the mutineers did not want him either.

Christian's original plan had been to put Bligh, Samuel, Hayward and Hallet into the jolly-boat and set them adrift. Orders were given to this effect, but first the boat had to be emptied of its contents. Men were set to work to this end, and the 'neutrals' who were standing about were ordered to help. James Morrison, the Boatswain's Mate and a self-styled loyalist, was one of the men working on clearing the boat.

---

[33] Bligh named them in his Log and in his 1792 *Voyage*.
[34] Edward Christian, Appendix, p. 67.

It soon became evident to Christian that his mutiny was not proclaimed as a blessing by everybody on board. True, George Stewart was 'dancing and clapping his hands in the Tahitian manner, and saying, "It was the happiest day of his life" ',[35] but this was hardly typical. Whatever wrongs Bligh had committed, few outside the hard-liners thought they justified his being set adrift in a tiny boat with three others, one of them a boy. That was a death sentence and everybody knew it. Murmurings among the unarmed watchers, the exchange of views between them and the mutineers, the raucous exhortations from Bligh to 'knock Christian down' and the increasing confusion on deck as the contents of the boat were spilled in the hurry to get it emptied, began to have their effect on the solidarity of the mutiny, such as it was. Once violence erupted, there was no telling which way the situation might go.

At the same time it became clear that the jolly-boat was useless. It was rotten through with worms and would certainly sink if put into the water. This meant that if Bligh was to be sent away he had to have a larger boat, and in that case more men could go with him. As there was no sense in retaining trouble-makers this provided a way of eliminating opposition to the mutiny. What degree of disappointment Christian felt at his not being regarded as a saviour we do not know, but this failure to carry the whole crew with him was bound to follow from the fact that he was righting a personal problem and not a collective wrong. The original four 'exiles' were now joined by Nelson, Peckover and John Smith (Bligh's servant), plus others, making about a dozen in all. Those declaring against mutiny were nearly half the crew by the time the second boat had been emptied. This situation deserves consideration, for a declaration for Bligh was not some ill-considered gesture. These men were committing themselves to an almost hopeless venture by going with the Captain. Being cast adrift in an open boat thousands of miles from the nearest settlement probably meant either an early death or complete isolation on an unknown island for the rest of their lives. Whatever the legal quibbles about the mutiny that were to come later, the stark fact remains that nearly half the crew preferred to take this risk with Bligh rather than stay with Christian.

As a morale-booster Christian ordered John Smith to issue rum out of Bligh's cabin to all men under arms. Meanwhile both those wanting to go with Bligh and those ordered to go (now including both Fryer and Purcell, suggesting that Christian had no illusions about these two, even if his brother was to rely on their evidence later to condemn Bligh), were sent to collect what possessions they could and prepare to go over the side. Byrne, the near-blind fiddle player, elected to go and in fact was first into the cutter when it was over the side. Now, however, the cutter was found to be unsuitable. It was not seaworthy and was too small for the numbers that wanted to go. Christian then agreed to give the loyalists the launch, which was put over the side. The deck was by this time a complete shambles of food

35 *ibid.*, p. 72. This public statement by Christian is another argument for rejecting Heywood's claim that Stewart was innocent.

and stores. Two boats were over the side and in one sat Michael Byrne, alone and unheeded, as the men got into the other.[36]

Personal possessions were grabbed in the rush to get away. The rush was motivated more by fear that things would become bloody than anything else. The rum was having its effect. Undiluted rum is potent, especially among men used to its weaker form as grog. Purcell managed to get his tool chest into the launch, against the protestations of some of the mutineers. Bligh's servant, Smith, and his clerk, Samuel, managed to get some of his papers for him. He was still tied at the mizzen-mast and had been there now for a couple of hours. Among these papers was his all-important Commission. If they reached a European settlement, it would identify him as a King's officer and ensure that any sums of money advanced to him for purposes of returning to Britain would be repaid by the Admiralty. Without it he had no certainty of credit or of proper treatment. They also managed to get the *Bounty*'s Logbooks, but they were forced to abandon his many charts and notes of this and earlier voyages.

Hayward and Hallet, amidst their protests, were ordered into the launch. Fryer also, after a protest and an appeal to Christian, joined them. Others went into it voluntarily and the number of men in the launch made it sink deeper into the water until it was only seven inches clear. Fortunately the sea was calm.

Among the men who went voluntarily into the launch were two of the mutineers, Isaac Martin and Robert Lamb. Churchill spotted Martin abandoning his weapon and getting into the boat and briskly ordered him out at gunpoint. This was the second time Martin had wavered in his loyalties; Bligh went so far as to mention that Martin, who at one point was acting as guard over him, 'had an inclination to assist me, and, as he fed me with shaddock, (my lips being quite parched with my endeavours to bring about a charge) we explained our wishes to each other by our looks'.[37] Bligh then goes on to list the other men who 'were also kept contrary to their inclinations', which suggests that he thought that Martin was not a mutineer. Joseph Coleman, McIntosh, Norman and Michael Byrne are the only others he lists as loyalists who were kept on board by force. He does not mention Stewart, Heywood or Morrison, which is not surprising in view of their behaviour. Stewart was dancing and clapping his hands, Heywood had a cutlass in his hand and was reported (at the court martial) to be laughing, and Morrison helped to empty all three boats. Heywood and Morrison claimed at their trial that they were opposed to the mutiny and wanted to go with Bligh; I shall examine their evidence in more detail later, though it is worth noting that for all their supposed loyalty they have done more to damage Bligh's reputation than anybody else on the *Bounty*. They became, in effect, apologists for Christian.

---

[36] After Bligh's party had dropped away Byrne was noticed in the cutter by the men left on the *Bounty* and was found to be crying. He remained with the *Bounty* and was later acquitted by the court martial.

[37] Bligh, 1790, p. 4.

After three hours at the mast Bligh was hoarse with shouting. Nobody was listening to him except Christian, who kept his bayonet pressed against him and ordered him to silence on pain of death. Bligh knew the boat voyage was almost certain to fail, and according to Morrison made frantic appeals to Christian, swearing friendship and forgiveness. But just as Christian could not pull back from his madness of the night before, so he could not reverse the tide that morning. The men he had recruited to crime were armed, drunk, excited and desperate. Churchill and Thompson were appearing everywhere and strengthening the resolve of the waverers, threatening where they had to and ordering men about wherever there was slackness or delay. They wanted Bligh off the ship. They intervened ruthlessly in every decision. They stopped the boat party from taking anything except the most meagre possessions, and they decided who came on deck and who went into the boat (or got out of it). Their intervention was without doubt crucial. With Young under arms, Christian's party was strengthened by the visible propensity to violence of Churchill, Thompson, Smith, McCoy and Brown. Bligh's group was divided, unarmed and disorganised.

Only when the men who might support him were in the boat and the deck was completely dominated by armed mutineers did Christian untie the cords binding Bligh's arms behind his back. Then, with muskets pressed into his back, cutlasses swinging within striking distance and a bayonet in his side, Christian ordered him into the boat. 'Come, captain Bligh, your officers and men are now in the boat, and you must go with them; if you attempt to make the least resistance you will instantly be put to death,' said Christian.[38] According to Bligh, 'notwithstanding the roughness with which I was treated, the remembrance of past kindnesses produced some signs of remorse in Christian. When they were forcing me out of the ship, I asked him, if this treatment was a proper return for the many instances he had received of my friendship? He appeared much disturbed at my question, and answered, with much emotion, "That, – Captain Bligh, – that is the thing; – I am in hell – I am in hell" '.[39] The boat was dangerously low in the water and Bligh, to prevent anybody else getting in and perhaps capsizing it, told some of those left, 'Never fear my lads you cant all go with me, but I'll do you justice if ever I reach England'.[40]

When Bligh was in the launch it was veered astern by paying out the rope holding it. Some food and other necessities were passed or thrown to the boat from the stern, but some of the pieces fell into the sea. Meanwhile on deck the mutineers were getting drunker and more violently disposed. The influence of the rum and the realisation that death or exile was their lot from then on sharpened their anger towards the man they had rebelled against. While Bligh lived he was a threat to them, and while the odds were decidedly against anybody in the boat surviving, they respected his seamanship and navigation enough to know that if the voyage could be done he might just be

[38] *ibid.*, p. 5.
[39] *ibid.*, p. 8.
[40] Mackaness, 1951, p. 105 (quoted from Morrison's Journal).

able to do it; Christian had given him some crude navigational implements. The shouting increased as people egged each other on to shoot Bligh. 'After having undergone a great deal of ridicule, and been kept some time to make sport for these unfeeling wretches, we were at length cast adrift in the open ocean.'[41]

The sound of the shouts and laughter from *Bounty* grew fainter and fainter and eventually the ship passed from view. None of the nineteen men in the launch was ever to see the *Bounty* again, and it was three years before some of them saw a few of their tormentors of that morning in the dock at a court martial. The boat, 23 feet by 7 by 3, was to be their home and refuge for over thirty-six days. This 3,900-mile journey was the severest test of Bligh's capabilities, and in many ways his finest voyage.

[41] Bligh, 1790, p. 6.

14

The Open Boat Voyage

As the *Bounty* sailed from view, the full extent of their plight must have become apparent to the men in the launch. They were alone in an open boat, with very little food and water, thirty miles from the nearest land, the inhabitants of which would probably be hostile towards unarmed Europeans, and they were a very long way from the nearest friendly settlement. If Endeavour Straits was a danger in a ship the size of the *Bounty* it would be perilous in a small boat. Botany Bay was only a dot on the map which for all the men knew might by that time have been abandoned as a British colony; they had left Britain before news returned from the first fleet that went out there.

The idea of sailing to Botany Bay or Timor in the launch was probably not uppermost in anybody's mind at that moment, though from Bligh's remarks about doing the men justice if he got back home it was clearly his intention to make the effort. His immediate plan was to get the launch to the island of Tofoa. If the inhabitants proved to be friendly they might get enough assistance to reach Tongatabu, an island further to the south; Bligh had been there with Captain Cook, who had made friends among the Chiefs. If the inhabitants of Tofoa were unfriendly they only had four cutlasses with which to defend themselves.

The mutineers later assuaged their consciences by blithely stating that Bligh's party was put ashore to await a visit by a European ship, as if visitations were a regular occurrence in the Pacific in the eighteenth century. The next Royal Navy ship to visit these waters was H.M.S. *Pandora*, looking for the mutineers, and this had only been sent out because Bligh returned with news of the mutiny. It reached Tofoa in 1791. If Bligh had not returned home it might not have got there until 1793-4, which would have been a long time for Bligh's party to survive on any island. While the criminal act of the mutineers has been whitewashed over the years, the basic truth remains that it was an act of attempted murder. That anybody survived at all was extraordinary.

The launch made for the smoke of the volcano visible above the horizon, and with the easterly wind on the sail they made good time. On nearing the island they could see that the shore was too rocky to attempt a landing before daybreak, so they spent the night huddled in the launch out in the open sea. Even after the *Bounty* this was a very uncomfortable situation. The launch had too many men in it for anybody to lie down, and with a light meal of a morsel of bread, washed down with some wine and grog, they had to make the best of it.[1] Their fare on the ship must have seemed sumptuous in comparison.

At dawn Bligh took the launch along the coast looking for a place to land. They found a small cove and Bligh sent Samuel with a small party to forage for food and water. The rest of the party waited in the boat off shore. In the afternoon the forage party returned with a little water and Bligh decided to try further along the coast. Eventually some coconut trees were spotted on a cliff. The surf was very rough and another party went into the water, swam ashore and then climbed the cliff. They brought back some nuts, using the ropes in the launch to haul them through the surf, and Bligh took the boat back to a small cove they had found that morning and issued a coconut to each man for his evening meal. Again they spent the night in the boat off shore.

On the next day they returned to the cliff where the coconuts were, and this time the shore party was led by Bligh, who intended to make a longer expedition into the countryside. After a few miles all they found were some wild plantains, but they collected nine gallons of water. At noon they returned to the boat. On the way down the cliff Bligh had an attack of vertigo and needed assistance to get down. The meal that day was a comparative feast – an ounce of pork, two plantains and a glass of wine – but it was clear that the island was not going to provide a comfortable living for them. In the afternoon Bligh sent another party out to forage in a different area but they returned with less than the morning's party. The only consolation was their temporary settlement in the cove, as it was sheltered by a cliff and had a small cave at its head. That night one group slept in the cave and the other in the boat, and the luxury of stretching out was welcome. Fryer was placed in command of the boat party with instructions to look out for a surprise attack.

On 1 May 1789, the first contact with the inhabitants was made. One of the foraging parties came across some islanders and brought them back to the cove. A little trade was attempted, and they went off to get some food and water, returning with some of their companions. Because Bligh was

[1] Bligh, 1790, pp. 11-12; Private Log, p. 22. Bligh kept up his Log for each day of the open boat voyage, and went to some trouble to ensure that a full account was preserved for the authorities, along with a full description of the mutineers. From Thomas Hayward he commandeered a small notebook (16 x 10 cms) into which he entered details of the boat's progress and preliminary rough sketches of the islands they passed, complete with navigational measurements; I shall refer to this book (recently rediscovered and now in the Australian National Library, Canberra) as the 'pocket notebook'. It is available on microfilm in the Mitchell Library, MLFM/4344, 'Memorandum on board H.M.S. Bounty's launch'. From the notebook, which he tells us in it he kept close to his bosom (presumably in case of an emergency in which the boat and his other documents might be lost), he wrote up his main Log, adding daily remarks about the journey and the crew's condition and behaviour. From this, which I call the private Log (now in the Mitchell Library, Bligh, 'Voyage in Bounty's Launch', Safe 1/37), he had the official version copied out for the Admiralty (PRO Adm. 55/151), taking out some of the more critical remarks he made, particularly about Fryer and Purcell. This version is available in Rutter's edition of the whole of the Log of the *Bounty* (1937). At Batavia Bligh wrote a despatch to the Admiralty giving the events of the mutiny and boat journey, and saying little about Purcell and Fryer. This is also available in an edition by Rutter (1934). In this chapter most of my quotations from the Log are from Rutter (1937), with references to the private Log and pocket notebook where necessary. When Bligh's *Narrative* of the mutiny and boat voyage was published in 1790 the editing was severe, and his 1792 account repeated the 1790 version almost word for word.

determined to keep the food stock in the launch intact in case of an emergency he issued a small share of the traded food for the day's allowance. Naturally the islanders wanted to know where his ship was, and Bligh ordered the men to say it had been sunk. It was a dangerous gamble: although food supplies were improving, without a ship and unarmed they were at the mercy of the inhabitants.

The next day canoes began to arrive at the cove from nearby islands. Among them were some from Annamooka where Christian had experienced trouble collecting water. Several faces that were known to the men from the mobs at Annamooka appeared in the growing crowds. Soon trouble began. Some of the islanders attempted to haul the launch onto the shore by its line and Bligh had to brandish his cutlass to make them desist. With his party split into two, some at the cove and others foraging inland, Bligh had cause for alarm; the number of islanders kept increasing and some of them were getting bolder and noisier. The problem was how to get away without provoking an attack.

When the forage party returned with some more water, Bligh told his men to get ready to leave the beach and get to sea; this was to be done at sunset so that the darkness would give them cover if they were pursued. The tiny cove was becoming very crowded and anxiety showed on the men's faces. Bligh and Peckover had seen this before. Memories of Kowrowa must have flooded back when some of the islanders began to knock stones together – the traditional Polynesian manner of calling for an attack.

Diplomatically, Bligh ate with the Chiefs. It was a tense meal. The islanders were eyeing the property of the seamen, the seamen the weapons of the islanders, and everybody the distance between the boat and the shore. The Chiefs invited Bligh to sit down with them but Nelson was on hand to warn that it might be a ruse, so he stood and ate with his cutlass in his hand. After eating Bligh ordered that the possessions be moved out to the boat but that it should be done unhurriedly to minimise suspicion. Peckover took Bligh's Log to the boat and had to fend off an attempt to snatch it away from him. Camp fires were lit around the cove and more visitors arrived, adding to the general excitement.

At sunset Bligh gave the order for a move to the boat. Every man picked up his belongings and walked down the shore towards the boat. Bligh ordered Purcell to remain by his side and be last off with him.[2] He cannot have expected Purcell to be the best rearguard fighter in the party; perhaps he thought he was going to die and vengefully decided he would not let the hated carpenter get away. Bligh walked slowly to the surf, with Purcell on one side and one of the Chiefs on the other. This man had been alternately showing friendship to the stranded seamen and cheering on the noisiest inhabitants. By now everybody was on his feet, more stones were clicking, and Bligh later described the tension as a 'silent kind of horror'. The Chiefs

---

[2] Fryer claimed in his Journal, p. 65, that Purcell had stayed by Bligh's side voluntarily. 'Mr Purcel stood by Captain Bligh longer than one man in twenty would have done in that situation, if Mr Bligh had thought of that he would not have tryed him by a court martial.'

came up to walk with him and asked him to stay the night on shore, but Bligh refused, telling them that they always slept in their boat and that they would come ashore next day and trade. The Chiefs' reply was ' "Mattie" – We will kill you'.[3] At this Bligh and Purcell leapt into the surf and made for the boat.

The boat was still held by the line to the shore as nobody had released it. With Bligh in the water the islanders charged, some at the boat and others towards their own canoes. Stones began to fly through the air; many of them weighed about two pounds. The seamen were scrabbling over the side into the launch and one of them, John Norton, fell back into the water and swam towards the shore to release the line. He was pounced on and knocked down when he reached the shore and his brains were bashed out with rocks by the jubilant islanders. He was the first victim of Christian's mutiny. The seamen in the boat had no illusions about their fate after this. Bligh was hauled aboard, cut the line quickly, and defended himself with his knife against some islanders who had followed him and were trying to get into the launch.

The launch was still held by the grapnel but for once their luck was good. It broke free, allowing the men to get their oars into action and pull for the open sea. Canoes were following and catching up, and stones were hailing down around the launch. Bligh quickly ordered the men to throw overboard their spare clothes and anything that would float. The islanders stopped to pick them up as early prizes from the fray, and this gave the launch a start. With darkness falling it managed to move out of range.

The experience had terrified everybody. Only Norton had been lost; once he went back there was nothing that could be done for him. His sacrifice was noble but pointless. Bligh was later to express his sorrow at losing him; he clearly regarded him as a loyal seaman.[4] Had things been a little different the entire party could have been wiped out and the mutineers' intentions would have been achieved in the first few days. While they took stock of their provisions and contemplated their situation they knew that the alternatives for them were limited. An attempt to go to Tongatabu and get help from Cook's friends was unattractive after Tofoa. They had to steer clear of contact with islanders. But they only had 150 lbs of ship's biscuit, 28 gallons of water, 20 lbs of pork, 5 quarts of rum, 3 bottles of wine, some coconuts and breadfruit.[5] At normal rations this was a few days' supply, and the distance they would have to travel would take several weeks. Fear and necessity are powerful persuaders, however. Bligh made each man individually swear in front of everybody else to accept rationing and enjoined them to agree that he was not to alter the ration under any circumstance whatsoever. Everybody swore and agreed to this; anything rather than what happened to Norton.

[3] Bligh, 1790, p. 20.

[4] In the *Narrative* (1790), p. 21: 'The poor man I lost was John Norton; this was his second voyage with me as a quarter-master, and his worthy character made me lament his loss very much.' Bligh's uncle, the Reverend James Bligh, made several comments on his copy of the *Narrative*, among which is: 'John Norton ... of this man I have heard Captain Bligh say it was, with respect to the boat's crew, a fortunate circumstance, for he was the stoutest man in the ship, which circumstance wd very materially have interfered with the boat's progress and the allowance of provisions.' Quoted in Mackaness, 1951, p. 141.

[5] Bligh, 1790, pp. 22-3.

7. Engraving (1790) by Robert Dodd of Bligh and his companions beginning their voyage in the *Bounty*'s launch after the mutiny.

8. Bligh's prayer, written in his pocket notebook on the voyage in the *Bounty*'s launch. A transcript is given on pp. 119–20.

and agreed to this; anything rather than what happened to Norton.

Bligh writes of the situation on 3 May just after they had escaped from Tofoa:[6]

> We were now sailing along the west side of the island Tofoa, and my mind was employed in considering what was best to be done, when I was solicited by all hands to take them towards home: and, when I told them that no hopes of relief for us remained, but what I might find at New Holland, untill I came to Timor, a distance of full 1200 leagues,[7] where was a Dutch settlement, but in what part of the island I knew not, they all agreed to live on one ounce of bread, and a quarter of a pint of water, per day. Therefore, after examining our stock of provisions, and recommending this as a sacred promise for ever to their memory, bore away across a sea, where the navigation is but little known, and in a small boat, twenty-three feet long from stem to stern, deep loaded with eighteen men; without a chart, and nothing but my own recollection and general knowledge of the situation of places, assisted by a book of latitudes and longitudes, to guide us. I was happy, however, to see every one better satisfied with our situation in this particular than myself.

A gale blew up, necessitating some reorganisation of their stores. The carpenter's chest and tool box were appropriated to store the ship's biscuit and keep it dry. The tools were put in the bottom of the boat. All extraneous clothes, some spare rope and sail were thrown over the side to lighten the boat and create more room. Bligh was 'determined to make what provisions I had last eight weeks, let the daily proportion be ever so small'.[8] But to start off the journey in the wet with a little comfort, a tot of rum was issued to everybody.

They passed some small islands the next day but did not attempt a landing for fear of treatment similar to that at Tofoa. The daily allowance was issued even though the bread was found to be rotten. It was too precious to throw away. By now they had been on their reduced diet for a week. 'Our wants,' wrote Bligh, 'are now beginning to have a dreadful aspect which nothing but a firm and determined resolution can fight against, a situation particularly miserable on a Commander.'[9] The misery was only just beginning. 'It may readily be supposed that our Lodgings are very miserable and confined and I have it only in my power to remedy the last defect by putting ourselves at Watch and Watch so that one half is sitting up while the other has no other Bed than the Bottom of the Boat or upon a Chest, and nothing to cover us but the Heavens. Our Limbs are dreadfully Cramped for we cannot Strech them out, and the Nights are so cold and being generally very wet, we can scarce move ourselves after a few hours Sleep.'[10] Characteristically, even

---

[6] *ibid.*, p. 22.

[7] Andrew David has calculated that the open boat journey was 3,900 sea miles in length, give or take 25 miles.

[8] Bligh, 1790, p. 24.

[9] *Log of the Bounty's Launch*, 5 May 1789.

[10] *ibid.*, 7 May 1789.

amidst these kind of conditions Bligh was still anxious to plot the location of the islands they were passing. He had arranged a make-shift Log-line to estimate the daily distance travelled by the ship, and he sketched the islands, but 'Being constantly wet it is with the utmost difficulty I can open a Book to write'.[11]

The islands they passed appeared 'fruitfull and hilly' but they did not dare land. On 7 May, among the Fiji islands, two sailing canoes were spotted chasing after them. After days without much food they were weaker physically and less able to defend themselves if their reception was hostile. In spite of hunger, they raced away from the canoes as fast as they could go. The chase went on most of the day until about 3 p.m. when the islanders gave up. The usual allowance of food, two ounces and a little water, was passed round after the chase.

On 9 May Bligh 'amused all hands with describing the Situation of New Guinea & New Holland' and to illustrate his little lecture he drew a map on a piece of paper and passed it round. This was meant as a morale-booster. For all the seamen knew they could be lost and going round in circles. He also made a pair of scales out of two coconuts to measure the food more accurately;[12] if arguments developed about the distribution of the rations this would be a danger to everybody.

On 11 May the sea was breaking over the boat and the situation was 'highly dangerous'. The rain brought fresh water which was eagerly collected, but it also soaked them through. The exercise of bailing out the rainwater from the boat was a welcome diversion, but also an onerous burden for hungry men in poor physical shape. It rained for several days; the sun broke through for a little while, but it was generally squally. 'The day showed to me a poor Miserable set of Beings full of Wants but nothing to relieve them. Some complained of a great pains in their Bowels and all of having but little use of their Limbs. What Sleep we got was scarce refreshing, being covered with Sea and Rain, and two persons were always obliged to keep bailing.'[13]

There was no way to dry clothes and Bligh therefore recommended a strange but apparently refreshing practice. The men stripped, wrung their clothes through with sea-water and then put them on again. By this means they 'received a Warmth', claimed Bligh, and avoided 'Catching Colds and violent Rheumatic complaints'. The extent of the rain during the boat voyage can be gauged from the Log which records twenty-one days of rain and gales out of the forty-three days spent in the open boat.

The effects of rain, cold and hunger began to tell on the men. An ounce of pork was issued but there were incessant demands for more, which Bligh with characteristic firmness refused. He considered it 'better to give it in ever so small quantities than use all at once or twice, which would be the case if I

[11] *ibid.*; by marking off a line in specific distances and then letting it run out behind the ship while a time check is made, it is possible to estimate the speed of travel.

[12] These implements are on display in the Maritime Museum, Greenwich, along with the pellets used as weights.

[13] *Log of the Bounty's Launch*, 12 May 1789.

would allow it'.[14] The next day the demands continued with 'some of them solliciting extra allowance'. The rain continued and the situation was 'truly miserable'. The pressure was on him to relent, for he 'could look no way but I caught the Eye of some one. Extreme hunger is now evident.'[15] Sleep was no comfort because the nights were bitterly cold. The voyage was in its worst phase since the attack at Tofoa. How long it would be before somebody succumbed to the deprivations, or the boat capsized from the sheer exhaustion of the bailers or of the person handling the tiller, was an ever-present anxiety for those with enough strength to think about it.

The day after Bligh wrote these lines in his main Log he wrote out a long prayer in his pocket notebook, presumably to be read out for the benefit of the demoralised crew. It is a revealing statement of Bligh's reactions to the difficult circumstances of the boat voyage. The prayer, while addressed to God, is also addressed to his men, urging them to have faith in their eventual survival and to pray for the relief of their dreadful sufferings.

O Lord our heavenly Father almighty and everlasting God. Receive us this Night into thy almighty protection, who has safely brought us to the beginning of this day; In and through the merits of our blessed Saviour through whom we are taught to ask all things, – we thy unworthy servants prostrate ourselves before thee & humbly ask thee forgiveness of our sins and transgressions.

We most devoughtly thank thee for our preservation & are truly conscious that only through thy Divine Mercy we have been saved – We supplicate thy glorious Majesty to accept our unfeigned Prayers and thanksgivings for thy Gracious Protection. – Thou has showed us wonders in the Deep, that we might see how powerfull gracious a God thou art; how able & ready to help those who trust in thee. – Thou has given us strength & fed us hast shown how both Winds & Seas obey thy command, that we may learn even from them to hereafter obey thy holy word and to do as Thou hast ordered.

We bless and glorify thy name for this thy Mercy in saving us from perishing, and we humbly beseeach thee to make us as truly sensible of such thy Almighty goodness that we may be always ready to express a thankfullness not only by our Words, but also by our lives in living more obedient to thy Holy Commandments.

Continue O Lord we beseech thee through the mediation of our blessed Saviour Jesus Christ, this thy goodness towards us, Strengthen my Mind & guide our Steps – Grant unto us health & strength to continue our Voyage, & so bless our miserable morsel of Bread, that it may be sufficient for our undertaking.

O Almighty God relieve us from our extreme distress, such as Men never felt, – conduct us through thy Mercy to a Safe Haven, and in the End restore us to our disconsolate Families and Friends. We promise O Lord with full & contrite hearts never to forget thy great Mercies vouchsafed unto us – We promise to renew our unfeigned thanks at thy Divine Altar & mend our lives according to thy holy Word. – and now

[14] *ibid.*, 16 May 1789.
[15] *ibid.*, 20 May 1789.

Almighty God as thou hast given us grace at this time to make our
common supplications unto thee & hast promised that to those who ask in
thy Son our Saviours name thou wilt grant their request; Fulfill O Lord we
beseech thee the desires & petitions of thy Servants as may be most
expedient for them granting us in this world a knowledge of thy truth & in
the World to come life everlasting through the Merits of our Lord
Mediator and Redeemer Jesus Christ Amen – Our Father. – [16]

On 25 May 1789 Bligh took stock of the remaining provisions and came to
the dreadful conclusion that the rations had to be cut still further to give
them a margin of safety. He wrote: 'I determined to proportion my Issues to
6 Weeks. I considered this would be ill received, it therefore demanded my
most determined resolution to inforce it provided I was Opposed, for small as
the quantity was I intended to take away for our future good, yet it appeared
like robbing them of life, and some who were particularly Voracious would
not like it.'[17] However, the men accepted the necessity of the action. The
'supper' bread allowance was accordingly cut out. Fortunately a noddy bird
was caught which, though providing only a minute ration at 1/18th per
person (with the blood directed to the weakest men), also reminded them of
the seaman's ancient principle that birds were never far from land. The next
day another bird was caught.

With the birds came the sun and the problem of heat exposure for the
weakened men. But after catching two more birds, they heard the sound of
the breakers on the Great Barrier Reef.[18] On 28 May the launch entered the
smooth water on the land side of the Reef.[19] Bligh had headed the boat
towards the Australian coast to get advantage of this smoother water, and of
the prevailing wind which would take them up towards the Dutch East
Indies; this course also provided them with a chance to land earlier than if
they had gone further to the north.

On 29 May, a month since the mutiny, when the boat had landed on the
coast of Australia, Bligh and Fryer clashed in the first of many incidents that
occurred in this second part of the voyage to Timor. In the journey so far
Bligh had hinted in his private Log at some dissent in the crew over his
decisions, and recorded the complaints they made about their condition,
without identifying the people concerned. But after landfall at Australia he
becomes specific and Fryer's name is mentioned several times. The first row
was over the recipe for oyster stew. In a copper pot, which somebody had
brought along in the boat, some oysters, ship's biscuit and pork were made
into a stew, and 'each person received a full pint'. Bligh continues: 'In the
distribution of it the Voraciousness of some and the moderation of others was

---

[16] Pocket notebook, 21 May. First published in Murray, 1853.

[17] *ibid.*, 25 May 1789.

[18] Fryer (Journal, p. 75) claims that it was while he was at the helm that he heard the sound of
breakers. Readers of Fryer's account of the voyage will be struck by the number of times the
critical events of the voyage find him in the decisive role; if this is true, he is one of the world's
unsung heroes, though perhaps it is more likely that he is one of its most consistent liars.

[19] Bligh went through the reef only a few miles from where Cook went through; Bligh's
position for his channel was 12° 51′ south and Cook's was 12° 34′ south.

very discernable to me. The Master [John Fryer] began to be disatisfyed the first, because it was not made into a larger quantity by the addition of Water, and showed a turbulent disposition untill I laid my commands on him to be Silent.'[20] The extremity of deprivation and discomfort during the earlier part of the boat voyage had been so severe that dissent had been a half-hearted affair; with landfall a psychological change occurred and the increasing possibility of survival revived the old habits of dissent.

The next day, parties were sent out to collect oysters for the day's stew, but this time Bligh decided not to add bread to it on the principle that the boat's supplies should not be used while the party was on land – a thoroughly sensible principle while alternative food was available. However, both Fryer and Purcell murmured against this decision, 'the former of whom wanted to prove a propriety of such an Expenditure, and was troublesomely ignorant, tending to create disorder among those, if any were weak enough to listen to him'.[21] From this point the men split into two more or less distinct parties: those 'weak enough to listen' to Fryer and Purcell, and those loyal to Bligh who gave him no 'uneasyness'. In the troublemakers' party there were Purcell and Fryer; Elphinston, the passed-over Master's Mate; Robert Lamb, the mutineer who had changed his mind; Tinkler, Fryer's young brother-in-law; and Linkletter and Simpson. In Bligh's party were Nelson, Samuel, Hayward, Ledward, Peckover, Hallet, Cole, Smith, Hall and Lebogue.[22] Fortunately Bligh's party was in a majority.

Bligh told the men to gather as many oysters as they could for a sea-store, as he intended to depart at noon on the Saturday. Just before this some 'inconsiderate persons' stole some pork from the store and Bligh decided to prevent any further theft of this article by permitting the consumption of the remainder – about 2 lb – in one go at dinner. Thus, 'our full Bellies made us forget the Necessity (of collecting oysters) and I had an Opposition to such a plan Alleging they were too Weak. I was told also that when they were from me there were several complaining of my Stay at this place and that it was much better to be going on. I [saw] that these unthankfull people were no sooner saved from perishing with want and fatigue than they had forgot the mercies they had received.'[23] Bligh does not mention who was complaining but from the context it was some of Fryer's 'party', and he reports that he reproved them for their conduct.[24]

After dinner they loaded the boat and pushed off, soon after seeing a large number of aborigines across the bay, some of them armed. In the interests of prudence Bligh decided to ignore them and carry on up the coast. They

[20] *Log of the Bounty's Launch*, 29 May 1789.
[21] *ibid.*, 30 May 1789.
[22] *ibid.*, 31 May 1789.
[23] *ibid.*, 30 May 1789.
[24] The stolen pork is referred to in the pocket notebook – the only reference it contains to dissent among the men. Bligh wrote: 'The little pork I had when we sailed we have found frequently to be stolen. I found it so now, but cannot discover the Wretch that did it – Kind providence protects us wonderfully but it is a most unhappy situation to be in a Boat among such discontented People who dont know what to be at or what is best for them' (pp. 60-1).

passed several interesting features on the coast but did not stop until he saw an island (Sunday Island) which he considered safe to land on.

It was here, on 31 May, that Bligh had his most serious altercation with Purcell and Fryer and, for the first time, lost his head with them. It is a tribute to his patience in the face of their combined provocation since Adventure Bay that he had not lost control before. Bligh's account of the incident is included here in full to illustrate both the problem Bligh had with these two men and the lengths to which they finally drove him by their exertions to undermine his authority.[25]

> I now sent two parties out, one to the Northward and the other to the Southward, to see what could be got, and others I ordered to Stay by the Boat. A muttering now began who had done the Most, and some declared they would rather go without their Dinner than go out. In short I found I had but little Command among a few if they had not feared I was yet able to enforce it by more than laying simply my Commands.
>
> The Carpenter [Purcell] began to be insolent to a high degree, and at last told me with a mutinous aspect he was as good a Man as I was. I did not just now see where this was to end, I therefore determined to strike a final blow at it, and either to preserve my Command or die in the attempt, and taking hold of a Cutlass I ordered the Rascal to take hold of another and defend himself, when he called out that I was going to kill him, and began to make concessions. I was now only assisted by Mr. Nelson, and the Master [Fryer] very deliberately called out to the Boatswain [Cole] to put me under an Arrest, and was stirring up a greater disturbance, when I declared if he interfered when I was in the execution of my duty to preserve Order and regularity, and that in consequence any tumult arose, I would certainly put him to death the first person. This had a proper effect on this Man, and he now assured me that on the Contrary I might rely on him to support my Orders and directions for the future.
>
> This is the outlines of a tumult which lasted about a quarter of an hour. I saw there was no carrying command with any certainty or Order but by power, for some had totally forgot every degree of obedience. I saw no one openly scouting the Offenders altho they were known, and I was told that the Master and Carpenter at the last place were endeavoring to produce altercations and were the principal Cause of the murmuring there.[26]

Bligh was anxious to avoid contact with any inhabitants in the area and for this reason preferred to hop along islands off the main coast rather than make night camp on the mainland. He also attempted to prevent the aborigines from approaching the camp by refraining from advertising the presence of his party and selecting spots to camp in that were difficult to reach undetected. His main concern was the security of his party, in view of

---

[25] *Log of the Bounty's Launch*, 31 May 1789.

[26] In his private Log Bligh added: 'I would do the other people the justice to say that they began to appear dissatisfied with these two men, and particularly the Master, who notwithstanding he held an ostensible place as the next officer in command, not a person but considered him a mean and ignorant fellow, ever disposed to be troublesome and then ready to beg pardon.' Quoted in Mackaness, 1951, pp. 153-4. See also Bligh, 1790, p. 55.

their weakened physical condition and their lack of arms. The local inhabitants had, of course, seen the boat party and could follow its progress along the shore. But they made no serious attempts to approach. The sight of the European mariners would have been strange, if not alarming, to them; this was probably the first sighting of Europeans by the aborigines in that part of Australia.

It was in consequence of this policy that Fryer got himself into trouble again. The party were camped on a little key at the extremity of an island on 2 June, and to avoid the possibility of any inhabitants spotting the camp from a distance orders had been given to keep the camp fire damped down. Peckover and Samuel had been placed in charge of the fire, and Bligh had gone along the beach to explore and to check how far away the camp fire could be seen. He had only just satisfied himself that it could not be seen very far away when 'on a sudden the Key appeared all on a blaze that might have been seen at a more considerable distance. I therefore ran to know the Cause of such an Open Violation of my orders when I found all the Grass set on fire owing to the Master [Fryer] while I was absent insisting on having a fire to himself, notwithstanding Mr. Peckover an[d] Samuel had remonstrated with him and told him the Consequence, and he knew [my] very particular Orders. This disobedience was of a very serious nature. I might have been seen by more Natives than at the last place as I past the Coast; and now being assured that we were on this Key it only rested with them to come after us and we must inevitably have fallen a sacrifice, for even when all were in health I had only 12 men that had either Spirit or resolution to Combat any difficulty.'[27] Bligh had written off five men as being without 'Spirit or resolution'; presumably these were among the seven I have listed as being in Fryer's party, and Bligh still had hopes of the two others. On the same day Robert Lamb, the ex-mutineer, was sent bird-catching with two companions but, separating himself from them, he went on a private expedition during which he caught nine birds and ate them raw on the spot. His personal endeavours meant less food for the group and moreover in chasing the birds he disturbed the remainder, reducing the catch of the other two men in the same area. Bligh was furious and reports in his Log how he gave him 'a good beating'.[28]

The party left the key at dawn and pushed on northwards along the coast. Bligh was not idle in this part of the voyage for in his Log he was entering details of the coast, the currents and the daily positions as well as he could fix them with his crude instruments. He was one of Australia's earliest cartographers and from his descriptions and map-making his voyage may be followed on a modern map. It was not long before the boat was in the open sea again, having left Australia behind. The men were once more on sea diet

[27] *Log of the Bounty's Launch*, 2 June 1789. Fryer, in his Journal (pp. 72-3), claims that he had fallen asleep when Bligh gave the order about the fire, and that he lit the fire in innocence and what happened was an accident. He also added that Bligh's shouting caused more disturbance than the fire.

[28] *Log of the Bounty's Launch*, 2 June 1789. The person who did this was not named in Bligh's Log, but in the reports made at Timor it came out that Lamb had done it.

and Bligh was remarkably pleased with their acceptance of the privations after the 'rest' along the coast of Australia. 'It seemed as if every one had only embarked with me to proceed to Timor, and were in a Vessel equally calculated for their Safety and convenience.'[29] The men's confidence in him was essential for survival. The fact that Fryer's party had no confidence in Bligh and was 'murmuring' on occasions when his resolve to stay the course was expressed presented the most dangerous threat to the lives of the survivors from within the boat. But Bligh's indomitable will, and the support of more than half of his seventeen companions, saved them from falling into the kind of small-boat madness that has engulfed more than one isolated life-boat and brought about the destruction of its occupants.

The days' events on the passage to Timor include the usual items of navigation, diet and the condition of the men. Fryer's party was 'murmuring' almost from the beginning of this stage of the voyage. On Friday, 5 June, they demanded more bread, but Bligh refused as he was not sure that the stores would last the passage. He identified the murmurers as Fryer, Purcell, Simpson and Linkletter.[30] Somebody stole some of the clams that were placed in the boat for sea-store but 'every one sacredly denied it'.[31] The next day the rate of progress of the boat was established with some certainty and therefore the bread ration which had been cut before sighting Australia was restored. This was none too soon, as on 8 June the condition of Ledward and of Lawrence Lebogue, 'an Old Hardy Seaman', was showing signs of becoming critical. The men generally were showing a 'common inclination to Sleep, a Symptom of Nature being almost reduced to its last effort'.[32] But the only medicine available was a little wine and this was given out to the sick men.

The next day Bligh himself was very ill and he knew that unless relief came quickly people would begin to succumb. 'People begin to appear very much on the decline. Law'ce Lebogue and the Surgeon [Ledward] cannot live a Week longer if I do not get relief. ... An extreme Weakness, Swelled legs, Hollow and Ghastly countenances, great propensity to sleep and an apparent debility of Understanding give me melancholy proofs of an approaching dissolution of some of my people. This is the 8th day from New Holland and from meeting with weed and gannet I hope to fall in with Timor every hour.'[33] Bligh kept the men's spirits up by telling them how near they were to Timor. His navigation led him to believe this, but what opinions the men held, half collapsed in what appeared to be an empty sea, we can only surmise.

On 12 June 1789 Timor was sighted. The great voyage was nearly over. The impossible had been achieved. 'Indeed, it is scarce within the scope of belief', wrote Bligh, 'that in 41 days I could be on the Coast of Timor in which time we have run by our Log 3623 miles which on a Medium is 90

[29] *ibid.*, 4 June 1789.
[30] *ibid.*, 5 June 1789.
[31] *ibid.*, 6 June 1789.
[32] *ibid.*, 8 June 1789.
[33] Private Log, 11 June 1789.

Miles a Day'.[34] As if to celebrate their arrival off Timor, Bligh decided they would have for dinner a booby bird that they had caught, but Fryer started muttering and demanded it for breakfast, 'for this ignorant Man conceived he was instantly to be in the midst of Plenty'.[35]

The next day, as they passed along the coast looking for the Dutch settlement, they saw several clearings and smoke rising in the hills. This suggested the presence of what Bligh called 'Malays'. Fryer and Purcell wanted to land and complained loudly when Bligh refused. He was determined to land only where there were Europeans. 'Therefore, after giving the master a severe reprimand and telling him that he would be dangerously troublesome if it was not for his ignorance and want of resolution; I assured them I would give an opportunity to land on the very place. For this purpose I stood back on a wind into a bay and came to a grapnel and gave the master and carpenter leave to land, but neither of these chose to venture out ... I would not suffer any others to go, who ever had been too obedient to disobey my orders.'[36] Having settled this matter, Bligh took the boat along the shore and a few hours later spotted a little settlement. He sent Peckover and Cole ashore to get information and they returned some time later with some local inhabitants who informed Bligh that the Dutch Governor lived a little way along the coast. One of the Malays agreed to conduct the boat the short distance to Coupang harbour after Bligh showed him 'a parcel of dollars'.[37] With safety in their grasp a double issue of bread and wine was made.

At daylight on 14 June 1789 the boat entered Coupang harbour and Bligh informed the Dutch authorities of his presence. The Governor, William Adrian Van Este, was seriously ill but received Bligh and ordered all assistance to be given to him and his men. The men were washed and their sores attended to by the Dutch, and the Acting Governor, Timotheus Wanjon (the Governor's son-in-law), took personal charge of the arrangements. The boat voyage ended with only eleven days' ration of bread left over. The men, though safe from the sea, were still in danger of death: the Dutch settlements in Indonesia were notoriously unhealthy places, even for fit men.

Notwithstanding the universal joy that their salvation had occasioned, the old quarrels were never far from the surface. Purcell refused point-blank to hand over some chalk which Bligh had offered to the Dutch Governor. He was sent in disgrace on board a Dutch ship in the harbour (Captain C. Spikerman) along with Peter Linkletter. It is not clear why he wanted the chalk, only that he claimed ownership of it, even though it was for the Dutch

[34] *Log of the Bounty's Launch*, 12 June 1789.

[35] *ibid.* Fryer implies that Bligh kept everybody at rations deliberately when it was no longer necessary. This is a typical example of his retrospective spite.

[36] Private Log, 13 June 1789. This entry exposes the short-sighted stupidity of the Fryer-Purcell faction. To go ashore at the first sight of smoke would have been an unacceptable risk for the party. Once the men started wandering around the forest they could easily got lost, or be attacked.

[37] Pocket notebook, 14 June 1789; this shows that Bligh did have some cash with him, probably Rix Dollars or Ducats.

Governor whose hospitality he was enjoying. There is no doubt that without the Dutch settlement on Timor there could have been no hope of the party's survival, and it was diplomatic to flatter their hosts with anything that their meagre possessions were capable of providing.

When he was fit enough Bligh made a formal statement to the Dutch authorities regarding the mutiny and the circumstances of his arrival. He provided them with detailed descriptions of the mutineers compiled from the reports of everybody in the boat party. He also used the authority of his Commission to purchase a small schooner and supplies for the voyage to Batavia, where passage could be taken in ships returning to Europe. The schooner, named H.M.S. *Resource* by Bligh, cost 1000 Rix Dollars (roughly £300); he would have paid for this by using his Commission as authority to sign a bill on the Admiralty (he may also have used some of his 'parcel of dollars').

As the men gradually recovered the troubles with Fryer and Purcell erupted again in a long series of squabbles and arguments. To their Dutch hosts this behaviour must have seemed undignified, to say the least. Bligh and Fryer were reduced to communicating with each other by letter only. Fryer later made serious charges against Bligh of financial mismanagement at Timor. The first fight was Bligh's fault, in the sense that he could have avoided it, though in formal terms Fryer's behaviour was inexcusable. Bligh suspected Purcell of slacking on the job of preparing the *Resource* and he directed Fryer to keep an eye on him and report anything that Purcell did contrary to his instructions. Fryer told Bligh that as he was not a carpenter he would not know whether Purcell was slacking, and that anyway he would not attend to Bligh's request without a written order. Bligh wrote: 'This man's insolence and contumacy joined with extreme ignorance is always giving me some trouble. I have no immediate resource but severe reprimands, which bring him to order for a few days when he meanly conducts himself to endeavour to make me forget his bad behaviour. His being the only responsible person next to myself on board, has been the only reason for his not being a prisoner for the greatest part of the voyage.'[38] In these circumstances Bligh should not have used Fryer to watch Purcell, especially as they were such obvious associates in disruption.

The next day, while Bligh was in the company of the Acting Governor, Mr Wanjon, Fryer was involved in a somewhat sinister explosion of bad temper between his brother-in-law, Robert Tinkler, and William Cole, the Boatswain. Tinkler had apparently been impertinent to Cole and had been 'chastised' in return. For a boy to be cheeky to a Boatswain was itself an extraordinary event in the eighteenth-century Navy but when Fryer intervened and told Tinkler to stab Cole with his knife the situation was bizarre. Cole told Bligh what had happened and Bligh was compelled to warn Fryer that he was criminally responsible if any violence was committed by Tinkler.[39]

[38] Private Log, 6 July 1789.
[39] *Log of the Bounty's Launch*, 7 July 1789.

David Nelson 'imprudently leaving off some Warm Cloathing caught cold and had an Attack of a Fever' on 8 July, and he died ten days later. Bligh was upset at losing this man: it 'bears very heavy on my mind, his duty and integrity went hand in hand, and he had accomplished through great care and dillegence the object he was sent for, always forwarding every plan I had for the good of the Service we were on. He was equally servicable in my Voyage here in the Course of which he always gave me pleasure by Conducting himself with Resolution and integrity'.[40] As Bligh was not normally given to expressing such sentiments we may be sure that they were sincerely meant, and that what he states in his Log he genuinely felt.

The attempts of Fryer and Purcell to disrupt Bligh's preparations to leave reached new lengths. They were staying on board Captain Spikerman's ship and were in close contact with the Captain and his wife, who was the sister of the Governor's wife. They apparently advised the Governor through this chain of social contacts to get another signature besides Bligh's on the bills he signed for his various purchases. The implication was that this would be the signature of the second-in-command, Fryer himself. Mr Van Este understood from this that there was some doubt of Bligh's authority to commit the Admiralty to expenditure, but Mr Wanjon stepped in and offered to provide the funds on Bligh's signature alone. Bligh had naturally refused to have the probity of his Commission diluted with Fryer's signature. This would have placed Fryer in a position to exert pressure on Bligh by sharing his authority and making his goodwill negotiable, perhaps in return for a guarantee of no action against him on return to Britain.

Bligh was keen to get away from Coupang before the monsoon rains came, and to this end he directed Fryer to take the *Resource* out into the roads to be ready to catch the tides. This meant Fryer stayed on board for a couple of days away from the shore. But 'by neglect he let the tide fall two feet and by that means I am detained'.[41] Two days later Bligh ordered Fryer to stay with the *Resource* and not to come ashore, but Fryer boldly told him: 'When I am commanding officer, I shall come ashore when I please.'[42] Whether Bligh was thwarted in his punishment of Fryer by these tactics we do not know, but it certainly did not reconcile him to Fryer, as we can see from the entries in the Log. The fact that Bligh was recording all these remarks and altercations in the Log suggests that he might have been considering building a court martial case against him. If he was, he did not proceed with it on return to Britain, though he did proceed against Purcell.

The *Resource* left Coupang on 20 August and arrived at Surabaya on 12 September. An incident occurred here which was not recorded in Bligh's published *Narrative*, though it was a virtual mutiny on the part of the Fryer party. Bligh only made a single reference to it and from his account it is not entirely clear what happened. That a fair number of the men had been drinking heavily and were not in control of themselves seems evident, but

[40] *ibid.*, 18-20 July 1789.
[41] *ibid.*, 12 August 1789.
[42] *ibid.*, 14 August 1789.

there was also present an underlying current of dissent.

Bligh, accompanied by Dutch officials, was taken out to the *Resource* in a boat belonging to the local Army commander. This compliment restored some of his dignity, and he was anxious to impress his hosts in return. He ordered his own boat to follow him to the *Resource*. But when he got on board he found that his men had not yet left the dock in his boat. This was acutely embarrassing for him. Eventually the boat came alongside and the boat crew came on board. The men in the boat were Purcell, Elphinston, Linkletter, Cole, Hallet, Peckover and Hayward. Of these Bligh mentions Hayward as being the only one who had insisted on following his orders. Cole, Hallet and Peckover had seemed to be in Bligh's party during the altercations on the journey to Timor.

Soon after, when the Dutch officials had departed, while getting ready to depart from Surabaya, the men complained that others had refused to work and were lying down below. When Bligh investigated he found Elphinston and Hallet 'beastly drunk'.[43] He immediately summoned Fryer and demanded to know why he had neglected to order these men on deck. Fryer replied he did not know why he had not done so, but added that as he was not a doctor he did not know whether the malingerers were drunk or ill. On further questioning by Bligh he was led to exclaim: 'You not only use me ill, but every man in the vessel, and every man will say the same.' Apparently this remark was taken up by some of the men on the deck. 'Yes, by God, we are used damned ill, nor have we any right to be used so.' This was mutinous. Purcell stepped forward to speak on behalf of what he thought was a crew united against Bligh, and 'with a daring and villainous look' and supported by the 'master's sneers and provocation' proceeded to abuse Bligh and his alleged behaviour towards himself and others. Bligh wasted no time in arguing with him. He seized a bayonet, marched Fryer and Purcell below and sent for the Dutch officials to come to his assistance.

When the Dutch returned on board Bligh was told that the men had been making statements ashore that he was to be hanged or blown from the mouth of a cannon when he got back to Britain. It so happened that one of the Dutch seamen who had been told this was with the Dutch officials. When ordered to point out the person who told him this he pointed to Purcell and other officers who had made up the boat party. Hayward was mortified at being accused along with Purcell and he went into a tearful rage, denying complicity and begging Bligh not to believe such a charge against him. Hayward claimed that he never 'but when he was obliged, had any conversation with anyone on board, for he believed that they had not good principals'. Bligh believed this public display of contrition, but he determined that the rumour must be quashed if he was to receive further assistance from the Dutch authorities. He therefore ordered everybody ashore who had been charged by the Dutch with making the remarks. Ledward, Hallet, Cole,

[43] Rutter (ed.), 1934, p. 82.

Fryer and Purcell were taken ashore to be examined by the Dutch Governor.[44]

The next day Cole, Hallet and Ledward were examined by a make-shift court of inquiry consisting of the Army Commander, a Captain and the Master Attendant of the Port. The only charges made against Bligh were one from Hallet that he had been beaten at Tahiti for some trivial offence, and another from Ledward that he had been refused permission to go ashore at Coupang until his Captain returned. Cole made no charges at all. Certified papers were made out containing the questions and their answers and with this done the men were ordered on the boat again.

The charges made by Fryer were much more serious. He was being held in confinement on shore with Purcell, and he showed the Army Commander a paper from Van Este in Coupang that, he claimed, proved that Bligh had been overcharging the Admiralty for the items he had purchased there; and he said that when they returned to Britain this paper would cause Bligh a lot of trouble. Bligh replied: 'I had nothing more to do to show the villainy of this man and the improper and unwarrantable conduct of Van Este in laying a plot with an inferior officer to trap his commander, than to show my papers, in which were receipts and vouchers for all my transactions in Timor, signed by the master and boatswain and witnessed by two respectable residanters.'[45] With this counter-evidence Fryer's charges collapsed. That night Fryer wrote Bligh a letter asking for forgiveness: 'Sir, I understand from what the Commandant says that matters can be settled. I wish to make every thing agreeable as far as lay in my power, that nothing might happen when we came home. As I have done every thing in my power, as far as I knows, to do my duty, and would still wish to do it, therefore, if matters can be made up, I beg you will forward it. [Signed] John Fryer.[46] Fryer was seeking forgiveness once again and attempting to bargain his way out of trouble back in Britain.

Bligh was in no hurry this time to forgive and forget. His honour had been impugned by Fryer once too often. This was the second attempt to bargain for a 'good conduct', and it was the second time that Bligh had responded to his bluff with a public refutation. The first time was his attempt in 1788 to get a certificate of good conduct by refusing to sign the books. Bligh wrote back and told Fryer he was too busy to see him. Fryer was put on board one of the local boats accompanying the *Resource* on its voyage to Batavia and Purcell was put on another one. The next day, accompanied by Samuel and Mr Bose, the Army Commander, Bligh visited Fryer, who 'like a villain who had done every mischief he could, and going to receive punnishment for it, he trembled, look'd pale and humbly asked to be forgiven, declaring he would make every concession and disavowal of the infamous reports that he spread'.[47] Bligh left him to contemplate his position and later that day the

[44] Private Log, 12 September 1789. 'Particular transactions at Sourabaya', quoted in Mackaness, 1951, pp. 164-8.

[45] Rutter (ed.), 1934, p. 83.

[46] *ibid.*, letter to Captain Bligh from John Fryer, 16 September 1789.

[47] 'Particular transactions at Sourabaya', quoted in Mackaness, 1951, pp. 164-8.

little convoy sailed for Batavia. They reached Samarang on 22 September and Batavia on 1 October 1789.

From Batavia ships were available to take the men back to Britain, but the party had to split up to get accommodation. Bligh was advised by the Dutch Surgeon-General, Mr Sparling, to leave as soon as he could because his condition, which had worsened on arrival, would not see him through the next months in that climate. To arrange passages for everybody and to provide them with funds Bligh sold the *Resource* and the *Bounty*'s launch in the town auctions, realising the dismal price of 295 Rix Dollars, compared with the 1000 Rix Dollars he paid at Timor.[48]

Thomas Hall, the ship's cook, died on 11 October. A few days later, Bligh, Samuel and Smith boarded the *Vlydte* for Europe. He had arranged for affidavits regarding the mutiny to be taken from everybody before the Dutch authorities,[49] and had left specific instructions to Fryer, who was to be in charge of the remaining men until their ships left in the next few weeks. But before they sailed, Elphinston and Linkletter died, and after them Robert Lamb during his passage. Ledward disappeared on his passage.[50] Fryer, Purcell, Hayward, Hallet, Peckover, Simpson, Cole, Lebogue and Tinkler returned safely to Britain. This made twelve survivors out of nineteen in the open boat voyage. Bligh arrived in Britain on 14 March 1790 after an uneventful passage from Batavia via the Cape. His time *en route* was spent in writing letters to his wife, Sir Joseph Banks, The Admiralty, and the Governors of New South Wales and India. Possibly the most moving of the letters he wrote on the journey is the one to his wife, written at Coupang on 19 August:

> My dear Betsy,
> I am now in a part of the world that I never expected, it is however, a place that has afforded me relief and saved my life, and I have the happiness to assure you I am now in perfect health. That the chance of this letter getting to you before others of a later date is so very small I shall only just give you a short account of the cause of my arrival here. What an emotion does my heart & soul feel that I have once more an opportunity of writing to you and my little Angels, and particularly as you have all been so near losing the best of friends – when you would have had no person to have regarded you as I do, and you must have spent the remainder of your days without knowing what was become of me, or what would have been still worse, to have known that I had been starved to Death at Sea or destroyed by Indians. – All these dreadful circumstances I have combated with success and in the most extraordinary manner that ever happened, never dispairing from the first moment of my disaster but that I should overcome

[48] Quoted in Mackaness, 1951, p. 170; Bligh was the victim of a 'Dutch auction'.
[49] These, with a Dutch translation, are in the Mitchell Library, Sydney; Bligh, Bounty Mutineers, Safe 1/43.
[50] The Reverend J. Bligh, on his copy of the *Narrative*, mentions that Ledward was lost with a Dutch vessel *en route* to the Cape. He may, however, have got off at the Cape or never left Batavia. A ship's Surgeon by the name of Ledward is recorded on George Vancouver's voyage to the North Pacific in 1790.

all my difficulties. Know then my own Dear Betsy, I have lost the *Bounty* ...[51]

Convincing his loyal wife of his integrity was one thing; protecting his reputation with the Admiralty was another. When he arrived home, almost eleven months after the mutiny, he set about his campaign to clear his name, amid enormous public interest in what had happened. One of his earliest tasks was to explain his failure to transport the breadfruit to Sir Joseph Banks. This was a crucial task, because though his leadership in bringing the survivors to safety at Timor was exceptional, it did not meet the interests of Sir Joseph Banks that the plants were still in the Pacific instead of in the West Indies. Bligh constructed a letter to Sir Joseph in which he attempted to look on the brighter side of his failure and above all to secure his interest with his patron:

> It is peculiarly distressing that I am to be the person to inform you of the failure of an expedition in which I had the honor to have your confidence and regard; but Sir I undertook it zealously and I trust you will find I have executed faithfully, securing every object but my return with the wonderful success I had acquired.
>
> If there is any one disposed to look unfavorably on the unhappy circumstance, I see with pleasure it can only be on the loss of the Ship; for the intention of the Voyage was completed – Your plants were secured in the highest perfection – every thing in that particular, even more than you could have imagined, and equal to that the world expected from your honoring the expedition with your countenance and direction, and in this rests the greatest satisfaction I am now possessed of. –
>
> As an Officer and a Navigator I have ever looked with horror on neglect and Indolence, and I have never yet crossed the Seas without that foresight which is necessary to the well doing of the voyage; but in the present instance I must have been more than a human being to have foreseen what has happened.
>
> It is with a View that you may readily understand the whole of my misfortune that I present to you the following Sheets, where you will find a series of distresses that are not made the most of; but simply a recital of facts as they happened, and which I hope will show you that to the last I never lost that presence of mind, or professional skill, which you have been pleased to allow was the first cause of my being honored me [sic] with your notice.[52]

Bligh's efforts to reconcile himself with Sir Joseph were successful and Banks was instrumental in getting Bligh appointed to command the Second Breadfruit expedition despatched in 1791.

Meanwhile, when he was fit enough, Bligh undertook some relief work for the Admiralty, and also wrote a best-selling account of the voyage which was

---

[51] Bligh to his wife, Coupang, 19 August 1789, ML, Bligh Family Correspondence, Safe 1/45.
[52] Bligh to Sir Joseph Banks, Address/Letter accompanying 'Voyage in the Bounty's launch', Safe 1/37.

published in late 1790 by the King's bookseller, George Nicol. He still had to face his court martial, but this was a formality in naval legal practice when a ship was lost for any reason. The court martial took place on H.M.S. *Royal William* at Spithead on 22 October 1790.[53] The legal formalities required that Bligh state if he had any complaints to make against any of the officers or men present respecting the seizure of the *Bounty*. The officers and men present being, of course, the survivors from the open boat voyage, finally arrived from Batavia, Bligh said he had no charges except against Purcell. He did not make charges against Fryer which, in view of his Log, is remarkable; but he may have felt that in the exchange of charge and counter-charge his reputation could be compromised, and indeed he may have been advised of this by Sir Joseph Banks, whose advice in the circumstances he would be anxious to follow. The rest of the court martial established the events of the mutiny and the fact that Bligh and the survivors had no knowledge of it before it occurred.[54]

Midshipman Hallet's contribution to the mutiny by sleeping during the watch was not disclosed to the Court, neither was Hayward's. There was no attempt to discover what had caused the mutiny – and given the evidence before them and the necessity for most of the witnesses to play down their own lack of effort to re-take the ship, it is unlikely that such a line of enquiry would have found much out. The Court without delay gave its verdict that Fletcher Christian and others had mutinously seized the ship, and Bligh and his party were acquitted of responsibility for loss of the *Bounty*.

The Court then tried Purcell on six charges that had been submitted to the Admiralty on 7 October 1790. The charges covered the incidents at Adventure Bay, his refusal to take the anti-scurvy medicine, his refusal to produce a grinding stone at Tahiti, his provocation of the 'duel' at Sunday Island, his refusal to give chalk to the Dutch Governor at Timor, and the general charges of disrespect during the voyage. After a short deliberation the Court found that the charges had in part been proven and they reprimanded him. But little effort seems to have been made to get a serious conviction. Perhaps in a spirit of goodwill Bligh was advised not to push hard against one of his fellow survivors in case it was misunderstood by the public. Whatever the truth, Bligh's magnanimity did not relieve him of the provocations of Fryer and Purcell, who returned to the controversy a couple of years later when Bligh was in the Pacific and unable to make effective answer to their charges.

After the acquittal Bligh was presented at Court to King George III by Sir Joseph Banks. The Admiralty responded by promoting Bligh from Lieutenant to Commander of the sloop *Falcon* and then a month later by awarding him the coveted prize of Post-Captain, assigned to the *Medea*, with the three years' service condition waived. He went on half pay on 8 January

---

[53] For details of the court martial I have relied on Mackaness, 1951, pp. 186-9.

[54] Fryer did not offer any evidence against Bligh to the Court, though he did three years later to Christian's enquiry.

9. Bligh's cup, gourd, bullet-weight and book, used in the *Bounty*'s launch. From Murray's *Pitcairn* (1853). The book depicted here is almost certainly the recently rediscovered pocket notebook, from which Murray quotes.

10. Bligh and his companions arriving at Timor after the voyage in the *Bounty*'s launch. Engraving from a watercolour by C. Benezach.

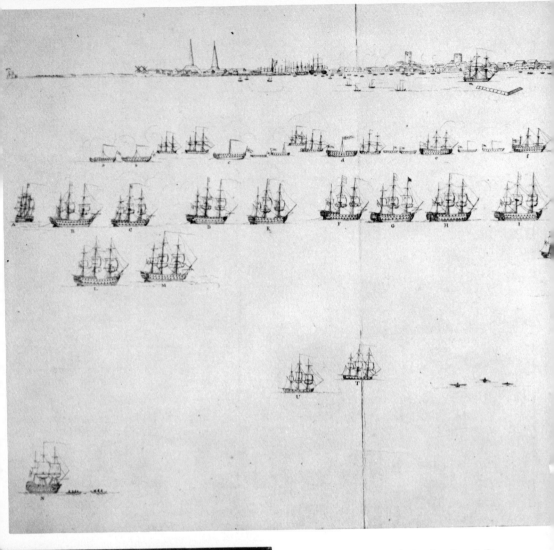

11. Bligh's plan of the battle of Copenhagen, 1801.

12. Portrait of John Fryer by Gaetano Calleyo.

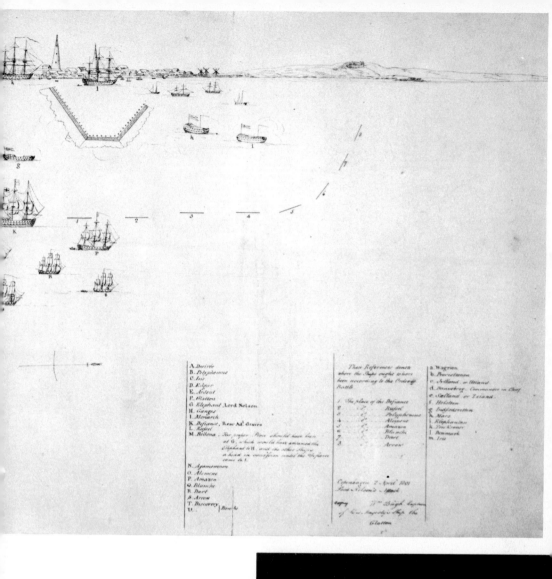

13. Portrait of Captain Peter Heywood
by J. Simpson.

14. Sketch by George Tobin of the *Providence* and *Assistant* firing on canoes in the Torres Straits.

1791, until on 16 April he was appointed Captain of H.M.S. *Providence* to undertake the second breadfruit expedition.

Captain Edward Edwards had on 10 August 1790 been appointed to H.M.S. *Pandora* to go to the Pacific in search of the mutineers, and bring them back for trial. He was to reach Tahiti before Bligh left Britain in the *Providence*, and what he was to find there is best approached by returning to events on the *Bounty*, which we left in the hands of Christian after Bligh had been set adrift in April 1789.

15

Huzza for Otaheite!

In the hours following the mutiny there was too much confusion on board for anybody to think about the future. But the magnitude of the problems that Christian had created for the men left on the ship would have dawned on everybody eventually. They were now fugitives from the British Navy. Bligh had his Commission, the ship's Logs and other papers, and this meant the mutineers had no proof of their mission, legitimacy or credibility. A captainless ship was difficult to explain, but one without papers was an impossibility in any European settlement. This effectively locked out the *Bounty* from Europe and its overseas settlements.

By steering clear of European settlements, however, they only postponed the hue and cry. If Bligh survived, they would be hanged if they were caught; even if he perished (at that moment a near-certainty) the failure of the *Bounty* to reappear at Portsmouth would prompt the Admiralty eventually to send a ship to look for it. Christian could calculate that he had three years at most before this happened, or not much more than a year if Bligh survived. The best policy for the mutineers was to 'disappear' into the Pacific and hope that Bligh got lost as well. Then it might be assumed that the *Bounty* had sunk without trace, and as long as nobody found the ship they could live out their lives in isolation. However, a number of problems made this best policy difficult to put into practice.

First, Christian's crew were not loyal to him; in fact some were distinctly hostile, such as Coleman, Norman, Byrne and McIntosh, the men mentioned by Bligh in his publication of 1790 as being kept on board against their will. There were also the men who later became known as 'neutrals', such as Heywood, Stewart and Morrison, and these might join the Bligh loyalists; even among his mutineers there was dissension, particularly from that troublesome pair, Churchill and Thompson. The idea of taking all these men into the Pacific to avoid contact with Europeans and live in peace and security for ever was clearly impracticable. The Bligh men might try to seize the ship, or leave it at the first opportunity. If they seized the ship they could sail it to Botany Bay and hand over the mutineers to the authorities, and in so doing clear themselves of complicity in the mutiny. Others might join them in this gambit; treachery promotes treachery. Contrary to the claims later made by his relatives, Christian had not got the personal authority to keep his mixed band together. Second, even if this plan had been practicable, they could hardly form a settlement without women and help from friendly islanders. As far as they knew, both were available only at Tahiti, but returning to Tahiti compromised the purpose of disappearing without trace, and disclosed their criminal act to the Tahitians and eventually to the world.

Although the mutineers could not have hoped to escape justice if they remained at Tahiti, Bligh thought that the prospect of returning there, especially the sensual attractions of the women, was the inspiration of the mutiny. He claimed in his *Narrative* that after the mutiny cries of 'Huzza for Otaheite' echoed round the ship.[1] This point was challenged by Christian's relatives after interviewing the survivors.[2] But the last survivor of the Pitcairn settlement, Alexander Smith, corroborated Bligh's account of the 'huzzaing' in his interview with Captain Beechey; as we saw, according to Edward Christian's account, George Stewart was dancing for joy in the Tahitian manner during the mutiny, and we know that he had a steady liaison with a Tahitian woman that eventually produced a daughter.[3] Another point in favour of Bligh here is that at their trial in 1792 Morrison and Heywood went to great lengths to establish their 'sorrowful countenances', and there would have been no point in doing this if they had not wanted to contrast themselves with the happy countenances of the mutineers – although Edward Christian later took the line that everybody who mutinied was driven to it in sorrow.

Again, in a recently discovered journal, Heywood reports a conversation he had with Charles Churchill during the mutiny: 'He [Churchill] told me that he [Bligh] and those who chose to accompany him were to take the launch and go on shore where they thought it proper after which the ship was to be taken back to Otaheite and those in her to settle there.'[4] On balance it seems reasonable to believe that most of the men left on the *Bounty* considered it certain that they were going back to Tahiti, even if one does not accept, as Bligh did, that they mutinied specifically for that purpose. Morrison reports that by 9 o'clock that morning the mutineers had agreed to steer for Tahiti.[5] This would have been cheerful news even for Bligh loyalists, who might hope to escape from the ship and await rescue by another vessel. The confusion has been caused by the later attempts to blame the mutiny on Bligh; in order to do this the Tahitian motive has been played down. Something has been made of the fact that the *Bounty* did not make directly for Tahiti. But because of the prevailing winds (easterlies) a sailing ship was forced to make a deep southern loop to get to Tahiti. The stop off at Tubuai, about 450 miles south of Tahiti, is entirely consistent with Morrison's assurance that Tahiti was

[1] Bligh, 1790, p. 7.

[2] 'Every one of those who came in the boat, as well as all who staid in the ship, declare, that they neither heard nor observed any huzzaing whatever in the ship'; Edward Christian, Appendix, p. 69.

[3] On Bligh's return to Tahiti he reported on the children left behind by the arrested *Bounty* seamen. Stewart's woman, Peggy, had a daughter and after the mother's death the child was brought up by the missionaries who arrived in the island about 1792. Bligh reports at least five children by his former crew's relationships with Tahitian women.

[4] Extracts from Heywood's Journal made by Captain Edward Edwards (H.M.S. *Pandora*), in Edwards' personal papers in the Admiralty Library, Fulham.

[5] Morrison, Journal, p. 47.

decided on in the first hours of Christian's captaincy.[6]

This is not to say that Christian, at least, had any illusions about remaining on Tahiti until the Navy turned up to arrest them. That clearly would have been madness. Others may not have looked so far ahead. But even if they realised that they had to find somewhere else to settle permanently, they insisted on returning to Tahiti to collect their womenfolk. Christian's alternatives were not abundant; his route back to Tahiti gave him time to think, and there is evidence from the witnesses that he was depressed for long periods.

Four weeks after the mutiny the *Bounty* arrived off the island of Tubuai.[7] Christian had decided on the way that Tubuai would make an ideal island for the mutineers' settlement. It had a pleasant climate, if slightly cooler than Tahiti, was away from the main shipping lines and had an anchorage inside the reef. The island had been visited and mapped by Captain Cook. In retrospect the choice was a strange one. Tubuai was one of the obvious places to look when the man-hunt began. Christian's view that it was too far from the normal routes to be accidentally visited was disproved even while he was there, when Captain Cox, in the *Mercury*, passed within two miles of it during the night and saw camp fires. Had he passed during the day he would have seen the *Bounty*. Morrison disagreed with Christian's choice: 'I cannot say that ever I agreed in Oppinion With Mr. Christian with respect to the plan he had formd nor did I ever form a favourable Idea of the Natives of Toobouai whose savage aspect & behaviour could not gain favour in the Eyes of any Man in his senses, but was fully capable of Creating a distaste in any one.'[8]

The 'savage aspect' of the inhabitants was demonstrated on the first day of arrival at the island. George Stewart was sent ahead in the ship's boat to survey the entrance through the reef and was attacked by some islanders in their canoe. He fired his pistols at them, wounding one man, and one of his men was wounded with a 'pointed stick'.[9] The islanders later attacked the *Bounty* in force and were driven off by the ship's guns at close range. Several were killed, and many others were wounded before they fled in terror. Christian named the anchorage 'Bloody Bay'. The violent relations that existed between Christian's party and the inhabitants of Tubuai from the beginning to the last day of the settlement are in marked contrast to the

---

[6] There is an outside possibility that on the previous visit to Tahiti at least Churchill and Thompson had already contemplated mutiny in order to return there. There is the incident with the paper and the three names on it during the desertions (p. 74); the fact that Churchill told Heywood in the opening moments of the mutiny that the plan was to return to live in Tahiti; and the fact that Churchill and Thompson consistently argued in favour of Tahiti as a settlement and voted against Christian at Tubuai on the issue.

[7] Some sources give the date of arrival at Tubuai as 28 May, following Morrison, who is unreliable on dates. Heywood and Stewart in their Journals are quoted as giving 25 May. On the principle that contemporary accounts are more likely to be accurate, I have adopted this calendar.

[8] Morrison, Journal, p. 56.

[9] Heywood, Journal, p. 2.

peaceful relationships that Bligh maintained with islanders while he was in command of the *Bounty*.

Another aspect of Christian's command that remains in stark contradiction to his family's defence of him is his relationship to the men under him. His defenders sought to show that Christian was held in high esteem by everybody and that, while guilty of mutiny, he still inspired the men to the highest levels of devotion and thus did not permit them to degenerate into a desperate bunch of criminals. Edward Christian includes the following testimony from an unidentified seaman: 'One of the seamen being asked, if they never mutinied afterwards in the ship, and told Christian, they had as good a right to the command as he had, said, 'No, no man would ever have mutinied against Mr Christian, no one ever thought of resisting his authority.'[10] As only two seamen were interviewed by Christian's brother, Michael Byrne and William Musprat, we can make a good guess as to which one made this absurd claim. Byrne was near-blind and not implicated in the mutiny. Musprat was one of the deserters and a mutineer, and therefore no friend of Bligh. We have three sources that show that this claim was not true: Morrison's Journal and the extracts from the hitherto unpublished Journals of Peter Heywood and George Stewart. Morrison's Journal was not written until after the return of the mutineers to Britain in 1792 (see p.202), but Heywood's and Stewart's Journals were written at the time that the events occurred, and were seized at Tahiti by Captain Edwards of the *Pandora*. He made the extracts which have survived in his private papers now held by the Admiralty. Neither Heywood nor Stewart was in a position to know the significance of his evidence in the defence of Fletcher Christian. These sources reveal that Christian was incapable of keeping control of his men, just as he could not control his passions, and his command was riddled with dissension, mutinous actions and outright refusal to comply with his orders.

First we can take Morrison's accounts of his efforts to lead a counter-mutiny. These efforts, he assures his readers, began soon after the mutiny, and indeed it was Morrison's defence at his trial that he remained on board precisely in order to overthrow Christian's command. He writes:

As I had reason to believe from the Countenance of Affairs that the Ship might yet be recovered if a party could be formd and as I knew that several on board were not at all pleased with their situation, I fixd on a Plan for that purpose and soon gaind several to back my opinion, when We purposed to take the Opportunity of the Night the ship should anchor at Taheite when we could easily get rid of those we did not like by putting them on shore, and that in all probability our design might be favoured by an extra allowance of Grog. These matters being settled I had no doubt but that evry one would stand to the test; and to prevent the others from knowing our design affected a shyness toward each other, but I soon found out to my unspeakable surprize that Mr. Christian was acquainted with our Intentions, some of his party overhearing some part of the Business –

[10] Edward Christian, Appendix, p. 75, footnote.

but as he was not positive how many were Conserned he took no further Notice then threatning Coleman that he should be left on shore at Toobouai till the Ship returnd from Taheite and Got the Arm Chest into the Cabbin taking the Keys from Coleman who had always kept them, they were now given to Churchill who made his bed on the Chest and each of Mr. Christians party were Armd with a Brace of Pistols Mr. Christian himself never going without a Pistol in his pocket the same which Lieut. Bligh formerly used, and a sharp look out was kept by his party one of which took care to make a third when they saw any two in Conversation.[11]

When we turn to Captain Edwards' extracts from Heywood's Journal we find this entry; '2 of the men were put in Irons by a Majority of Votes – and drunkenness fighting and threatening each others life was so common that those abaft were obliged to Arm themselves wth pistols.'[12] By 'those abaft' Heywood would normally have meant officers, but in the conditions of the *Bounty* under Christian he may have meant the mutineers' party as opposed to the loyalists. As we know that midshipman George Stewart was made second-in-command by Christian,[13] that some of the petty officers (Morrison and Coleman, for example) were also acting in responsible positions, and that these men were also neutrals or loyalists, it does not seem likely that they would have been issued with pistols unless their claims that they were plotting against Christian were untrue. Whichever way the puzzle is resolved, the fact must remain that the men 'abaft', whoever they were, had to arm themselves against threats to their lives from some people 'for'ard'.

In Captain Edwards' short extracts from Stewart's Journal we find an entry for 7 July, the day after the above entry appeared in Heywood's Journal, that shows the vain attempts made by Christian to abolish the atmosphere of crisis in the ship. He writes: 'Articles were drawn up by Christian & Churchill specifying a mutual forgiveness of all past grievances which every Man was obliged to Swear to and sign. Matthew Thompson excepted who refused to comply'.[14]

In spite of the bloody beginning to the settlement plan at Tubuai, Christian determined to go through with it. Having surveyed part of the island, he left, taking the *Bounty* back to Tahiti to collect women and the stocks he thought he would need. This was a tricky part of his plan. He had to think up some plausible reason for returning to Tahiti in the *Bounty* without Bligh and he also had to prevent knowledge of his eventual whereabouts getting out among the islanders, who would naturally pass this on to ships sent to look for them. Like Bligh before him he did not want his

---

[11] Morrison, Journal, p. 50a-1; this section is crossed through in the original manuscript.

[12] Heywood, Journal, p. 2.

[13] Edward Christian, Appendix, p. 72. 'After some persuasion from Christian, they [the mutineers] permitted Mr Stewart to be second in command, though they were desirous, from Stewart's former severity, or preferring Mr Heywood.'

[14] From the mention of Churchill's name here, and from the general impression gained from familiarity with the literature, I am fairly sure that the role of Charles Churchill in the mutiny has been underestimated in subsequent accounts. It is my opinion that Churchill, by his strong personality and aggression, was a major influence in the mutiny and its aftermath.

errand endangered by careless talk or desertions. Unlike Bligh, his purposes were criminal and his measures to preserve his security were considerably more extreme. He therefore 'Gave orders that no man should tell the name of the Island, or mention It to the Natives and if any person was found to mention the real name he would punish Him severely and declared if any Man diserted he would shoot him as soon as he was brought back, which promise evry one knew he had in his power to perform'.[15] In spite of the charisma attributed to Fletcher by his brother Edward, he had to threaten severe retribution to keep his plans and his party intact.

There is a typical piece of Morrison moaning at this point in his Journal. The possessions of the men who had been sent away in the boat were divided into lots for distribution among the crew. This, of course, was theft. However, Morrison was more concerned with the allocation of the lots. He complains: 'These were made out in lotts by Churchill, & were drawn for by ticketts, but it always happend that Mr. Christians party were always better served then these who were thought to be disaffected, however as they had diffrent views No Notice was taken of it at present.'[16]

The *Bounty* returned to Tahiti, and Christian told the Chiefs that Bligh had met Captain Cook and had gone off with him and that he had been sent back to get some stocks for a new settlement. The Chiefs' willingness to help Cook and Bligh exceeded their curiosity about the missing men and the plants. Just in case there was trouble, Christian had armed guards posted around the ship's deck. They also acted as a deterrent to potential deserters. In the short time the *Bounty* was at Matavai under Christian there were two shooting incidents; under Bligh during five months there were none. William McCoy fired at some islanders who 'did not get so fast out of His way as he thought proper' and Charles Churchill fired at a canoe that did not respond to his challenge.[17]

On 19 June 1789 the *Bounty* sailed again for Tubuai. (This was a few days after Bligh and his party arrived at Coupang in Timor.) They had on board 312 hogs, 38 goats, 96 fowls, nine Tahitian women, eight men and seven boys. 'Most went voluntarily',[18] so some must have gone otherwise. The men were taken along to smoothe relationships with the Tubuai islanders, but the use to which the women were to be put was discreetly evaded by Edward Christian's Appendix in an effort not to tarnish Christian's virtuous image. The *Bounty* returned to Bloody Bay on 26 June and through the Tahitian intermediaries Christian established more peaceful relationships with the inhabitants.

The trouble within the crew soon broke out again. John Sumner and Matthew Quintal went ashore without Christian's leave and they stayed away all night, presumably with local women. The *Bounty* had not brought with it a woman for each man, and it was necessary for those without women

[15] Morrison, Journal, p. 56.

[16] *ibid.*

[17] *ibid.*, p. 58. This entry is crossed out; presumably Heywood or somebody else found its candour embarrassing.

[18] Heywood, Journal, p. 2.

to find their amorous comforts ashore. When they returned in the morning Christian demanded to know on what authority they had gone ashore, to which they replied, according to Morrison: 'the Ship is Moord and we are now our own Masters.'[19] Christian went into a rage; clapping his pistol against the head of one of them, he declared: 'I'll let you know who is Master,' and ordered them into irons. Morrison considered that this 'resolute behaviour convinced them that He was not to be playd with, and when they were brought up next day, they beg'd Pardon and promised to behave better for the future on which they were released'.[20] The next person to fall foul of Christian was Tom Ellison. He was accused of stealing from Christian a red feather, which was an item of great value in trade with the islanders. Ellison was brought on deck and stripped, ready for a flogging, but after loudly protesting his innocence, in the absence of positive proof he was let off.[21]

Christian's plan for a settlement included the ambitious plan of building a large fort, to be known as Fort George. With the ship's guns mounted on it the mutineers would have protection from the local population and, perhaps, from a lightly armed naval search party. The plan was to build the fort and then fire the ship. Though this would cut off the mutineers from escape if their haven was discovered, it would reduce the chances of discovery by an accidental sighting of the *Bounty* at anchor. However, it is likely that a passing ship would investigate on sighting a large wooden construction such as a fort, especially one that flew a Union Jack.[22]

Morrison claims that the imminent removal of the *Bounty*'s masts for conveyance ashore prompted him to revive his plans of escape. This time he would sabotage the blocks and tackle to prevent the masts being put back in the ship and then steal one of the ship's boats for a voyage to Tahiti. 'I spoke to G. Stuart', says Morrison, 'on the Affair, who told me that He and P. Heywood had formed the same plan.'[23] But fortunately for Morrison and his friends the plan was made redundant by the new crisis over women that developed in the ranks of the mutineers.

As already mentioned, the men without women had to find them ashore, but as Christian would only allow two men ashore at a time this meant sexual company only about once a fortnight. Meanwhile, those who had Tahitian women had company every night. The plan for a settlement meant a permanent acceptance of this arrangement. Heywood's Journal reports:

On 1 August a party went on shore to get wives by force but they met with

[19] Morrison, Journal, p. 64.
[20] Morrison, Journal, p. 64. When Bligh in similar circumstances drew a pistol and pointed it at a seaman, William McCoy, this led to his being criticised by posterity – cf. Hough, 1972, p. 140: 'What had happened to their captain? He appeared to have lost all control of himself. They experienced a mixture of fear and resentment.' But in reference to Christian's loss of control of himself, Hough passes it off as nothing: 'The proceedings ... now assume a more unreal tone than ever' (p. 198).
[21] Morrison, Journal, p. 65.
[22] The fort was never finished. The remains were still recognisable in 1902; see Maude, 1958.
[23] Morrison, Journal, p. 72.

some opposition from the Natives, one of whom was shot and another run through with a Bayonet. The natives propos'd peace & requested that their goods might be restored that had been taken out of the house that was burnt, but Christian refused to accept it unless the Men were provided with Wives – however women were not got & on 24th those that were without them were heard to declare that the place wd not do & that the Masts shd not be got out until Women were procured & that the ship shd be carried where they could be had – on 30th the discontented party proposed to make slaves of the Otaheitians Men Women & boys and to cast lots for them or land & destroy the Natives to procure Women by force, but Christian wd not agree to either Scheeme & work at the fort was now discontinued.[24]

Heywood's account agrees in substance with that of Morrison on that crisis. Morrison states that the men in Christian's party 'began to Murmur, and Insisted that Mr. Christian would head them, and bring the Weomen in to live with them by force and refused to do any more work till evry man had a Wife'.[25] This again conflicts with the image developed in the Appendix that 'Every body under his command did their duty at a look from Mr Christian'.[26] Christian proposed that they hold a meeting to discuss the situation and this was agreed to, though some of the more difficult among them demanded grog while they debated the issue. Christian did not like the way things were developing, especially the proposal to put his Isabella into a lottery, and in an effort to restore his authority he refused to issue the grog. The men then broke into the spirit room and helped themselves. With his command in shreds, Christian changed tack and ordered a double allowance of grog for everybody.

The 'meeting' lasted three days and in the end it was decided to abandon the settlement and return to Tahiti. The proposal to end the settlement was resisted by Christian, but he was now in a minority. He accepted that he had to return to Tahiti to disembark his dissidents. The vote to return was carried by 16 votes to 8. The seven neutralists and loyalists would have wanted to return to Tahiti, namely Coleman, McIntosh, Byrne, Norman, Heywood, Stewart and Morrison. They were presumably joined by Churchill, Thompson, Hillbrant, Ellison, Sumner, Millward, Musprat, Skinner and Burkitt among the mutineers, as these were the men who stayed on Tahiti. The eight who voted to continue the settlement would have been Young, Mills, Brown, Martin, Smith, McCoy, Williams and Quintal, those who eventually went with Christian to Pitcairn. Christian apparently did not vote. Some of the men who voted against him in this crisis later made statements to his brother that they would 'wade up to the arm-pits in blood to serve him', 'go without wages in search of him' and 'go through fire and water for him'.[27]

[24] Heywood, Journal, p. 3.
[25] Morrison, Journal, p. 75.
[26] Edward Christian, Appendix, p. 76.
[27] *ibid.* Several of the interviews took place in the dining rooms of public houses. The interviewers were prominent gentlemen, several of them in the legal profession and all friends of Fletcher Christian. The circumstances did not assist objectivity.

After the vote the *Bounty* sprang to life again in the preparations to leave. But before leaving, Christian authorised and led a punitive expedition whose bloody consequences are inexcusable.[28] He had already killed a local inhabitant in an altercation – according to Heywood this was in a row over the man's coconuts – and beaten up islanders while searching for stolen property. It was consistent with his temper that Christian should vent his anger at losing his settlement on the islanders; he probably regarded them as responsible for all his troubles because they had not given up their women to the mutineers. In the battle that followed between fifty and sixty men and six women were killed and scores more wounded. Though the islanders' party numbered 700-800, gunfire is a great equaliser. This unnecessary bloodshed may have satisfied desires for revenge, and Christian may have been forced into it by some of his wild men, just as he was forced into issuing a double allowance of grog, but it is one of the burdens of command to resist such pressures and it is one of the symptoms of lack of leadership and immaturity to succumb to them.

The *Bounty* returned to Tahiti on 20 September 1789. It was of course no longer possible to continue the deception that they were working for Captain Cook. The islanders who had accompanied them to Tubuai would tell their families the truth. The disclosure had no serious repercussions, but Christian was not lulled into any false sense of security. His behaviour was not that of the prodigal returned; it suggested rather a distressed and demoralised man who had realised his own limitations and was frightened of the future. He had his Isabella, but how long would he be able to keep her before he was seized, either by some of his party, anxious to sail back to Britain, or by the eventual pursuers? On the other hand, in the short term he had at least two factors on his side. Fortunately the potential trouble-makers, such as Churchill and Thompson, were diverted by the prospect of their return to Tahiti and its women. Secondly, the loyalists and neutralists were leaderless and were anxious merely to get off the ship and away from their association with the mutiny. Thus the immediate interests of the men who had voted to return to Tahiti did not include plans for the ship, and for the moment there was no danger that they would try to seize it.

It is difficult to understand exactly what future prospects the hard-line mutineers who voted to return to Tahiti had in mind. It was abundantly obvious to everybody that Tahiti was the first place that the Navy would look for them and was therefore the last place to remain. To stay there meant hanging, unless Bligh and his men were dead and they had no witnesses against them in which case they could claim that they were innocent victims of Christian and the eight who wanted to remain with him. This gamble seems to be the only explanation of their wilful choice to remain at Tahiti and await their fate. Perhaps they preferred this gamble to Christian's plan, which was to 'Cruize for some Uninhabited Island where he would land his Stock ... and set fire to the Ship, and where he hoped to live the remainder of

[28] Heywood in his Journal (p. 4) states that it was 'brought on to avenge a quarrel Oediddo [one of the Tahitians with the mutineers] had with the natives a day or two before'.

His days without seeing the face of a European but those who were already with him'.[29]

When they arrived at Tahiti the possessions of the men who were staying and their share of the ship's stores were unloaded. This was completed by early evening and the shore party left for their friends' homes. The *Bounty* departed that night, though it appears that this was a surprise. Christian seems to have said that he would stay at Tahiti for a few days, and even asked the men ashore to help him load fresh water the next day. Morrison writes in 1792 that he was surprised at the abrupt departure of the *Bounty* during the night:

> In the night we found the Ship under way, standing out of the Bay, but it proving Calm in the morning She was not out of Sight till Noon ... We were all much surprized to find the Ship gone, as Mr. Christian had proposed staying a day or two to give us time to get on shore what things we might want or had forgot to take on Shore; this Gave us reason to suppose that He either was affraid of a Surprize or had done it to prevent His Companions from Changing their mind.'[30]

When Heywood was helping Edward Christian with his enquiries he told him a meeting had taken place between himself, Stewart and Christian just before Christian left, in which Christian declared his intention of leaving within the hour. He even gave details of the conversation, claiming that Christian 'desired them, if they ever got to England, to inform his friends and country what had been the cause of his committing so desperate an act'.[31] This is difficult to believe. In the extracts we have from Heywood's and Stewart's journals, written at the time, there is no mention of such a meeting. Further, between September 1789 and October 1792 when he wrote his Journal Morrison was in almost daily contact with Heywood, and we know that the two men often discussed the departure of the *Bounty*. Yet Morrison makes no exception in his statement that 'all' were surprised. However, by the time Lady Belcher, Heywood's stepdaughter, wrote her book the conversation had been elaborated; we find Christian saying to Heywood and Stewart 'You are both innocent, no harm can come to you, for you took no part in the mutiny' and adding that 'he alone was responsible for the act and exonerated all, even his adherents from so much as suggesting it'.[32] Many books on the *Bounty* uncritically accept Heywood's report of this last meeting. Thus are myths created.

Stewart drowned in the *Pandora*, so in his case we have only the negative evidence that the meeting is not mentioned in Captain Edwards' extracts from his Journal. I think it likely that Heywood invented it. It was a

---

[29] Morrison, Journal, p. 100.

[30] *ibid.*, p. 102.

[31] Edward Christian, Appendix, p. 74.

[32] Lady Belcher, 1870, pp. 50-1. Another example of her use of the Journal is her description of Christian's departure 'as the day began to dawn ...' (p. 50). Morrison originally wrote (Journal, p. 100-101a) that the *Bounty* left 'in the night'. Somebody – presumably Heywood – has amended this to read 'at daylight'. Her poetical phraseology stems from this amendment.

convenient way of exonerating himself from mutiny; in the context of Edward Christian's enquiry the 'cause' of Christian's 'committing so desperate an act' is Bligh's cruelty to him, so no-one else is to blame. It also helps Heywood's contention that Stewart was innocent – although as we have seen this was contradicted by other evidence collected by Edward Christian and also published in the Appendix. On the other hand, if Fletcher trusted Heywood at this point, Heywood's defence at the court martial, that he was too young to know what was going on, might have been compromised; this could explain why Heywood and Stewart kept the meeting secret, if it did take place. But for the moment it is more consistent to assume that no meeting took place – that Christian trusted nobody in the shore party, but left unexpectedly, abducting several of the inhabitants, before those who remained could change their minds about letting him have the ship.

16

The Long Arm of the Navy

The story of the mutineers' settlement at Tahiti, from the time that Christian sailed away in the *Bounty* in September 1789 until the arrival of Captain Edwards in the *Pandora* in March 1791, is not a happy one. It is a story of brutality, theft, rape and murder. It is not surprising that the Tahitians were glad to see the back of the *Bounty* men when Edwards came to collect them.

An interesting aspect of the settlement is the way the men divided into small groups to live with their island friends. There was no attempt to separate into mutineer and loyalist parties, which, in view of their precarious position, would have seemed prudent on the part of the loyalists, and even more so on the part of the 'neutralists'. Apparently this distinction between the two groups was less formal at the time than they claimed at the court martial. The mutineers Musprat and Hillbrant and the loyalists McIntosh, Byrne and Norman went to stay together at Oparre with Oreepiah, the brother of Tinah. Morrison, who later claimed to be a neutralist, lived with Millward, the mutineer, and Chief Poeeno at Matavai. Stewart and Heywood lived together, the former with his wife, 'Peggy'. The mutineer Thompson lived with the loyalist Coleman, the man warned off by Christian for plotting a mutiny against him. Sumner, Burkitt and Ellison, all three of them mutineers, lived together. Skinner and Churchill were the only men living separately.

According to Morrison's account, Churchill was a trouble-maker causing problems with the Tahitians, while he himself was a pillar of moderation and goodwill. Morrison's account implies that he was the 'leader' of the settlement, the one who made the decisions. Even if one allows for some hyperbole and a tendency to self-praise, Morrison does seem to have been at the centre of several incidents and he was also the only one to conceive of making a boat in order to escape from Tahiti. Both Morrison and Churchill, however, broke the most important rule for contact with the peoples of another culture – the avoidance of interference in domestic affairs. Bligh had understood this and so had Cook before him. Bligh adamantly refrained from intervention in local customs and local politics, insisted on complete neutrality and even punished Isaac Martin for using violence against a local inhabitant. By breaking this rule Churchill and Morrison brought death and misery to hundreds of islanders on an even larger scale than Christian at Tubuai. Heywood fully participated in these bloody excesses, though from later eulogies of this misguided man one would never guess that he could speak harshly to anyone, let alone spill their blood.

The *Mercury* under Captain Cox had called at Tahiti while the *Bounty* was at Tubuai, and a seaman called Brown had been put ashore after knifing a colleague.[1] He was still on the island when the *Bounty* returned for the last time, and he made himself known to the stranded mutineers, though it does not seem that he was universally liked. Brown, however, took part in all the mutineers' depredations on the Tahitians, and may have instigated some of them.

Morrison claims that he conceived the idea of building a boat to escape from Tahiti with the intention of returning to Britain. The fact that several of the hard-line mutineers participated in the heavy work of construction suggests that they may have had different ideas about their eventual destination. In the absence of any plan to escape the situation of the mutineers does not make much sense. Morrison explains their help by claiming that he told them that the boat was to be used for visiting other islands, which was also the story he told to the local chiefs. The boat-building was constantly interrupted by theft, and to deal with it Morrison introduced the summary punishment of flogging. Any islander caught in the act of theft received a smart flogging.[2] The boat was eventually built; it measured 33 feet by 9 feet. It was launched on 5 July 1790 and named the *Resolution*. It was first used to participate in local wars, and there was also an attempt to take it to Batavia, but Coleman changed his mind about Morrison's navigating ability and insisted on returning to Tahiti. Heywood reports that a second attempt was to be made after the rainy season.[3]

There is no mention by Morrison of any punishments meted out to Europeans for misdemeanours, which suggest that his shipboard talents as the official flogger were confined to retributions on the backs of the islanders. If individual seamen had been flogged much trouble might have been prevented, especially in the case of Thompson, whose treatment of the unfortunates who crossed his path threatened the lives of everybody else. He was set upon and beaten up by a party of Tahitians after he had raped one of the women in a local family. This must have been a particularly brutal act on his part, in view of the normally permissive sexual code of the islanders. Thompson was lucky that they were so restrained. However, being a man of violent disposition, he returned home bruised and 'vowing revenge on the first that Offended him'.[4]

It so happened that some islanders from another part of Tahiti were visiting the area at the time, and they were curious about the ways of the strangers in their midst. They paused to look at Thompson's house before returning home. Thompson, in a fierce temper, ordered them away from his

---

[1] When the *Pandora* arrived, Captain Edwards signed Brown on as a seaman and used him to get intelligence about the *Bounty* men on Tahiti and also the possible whereabouts of Christian and his party. Brown sailed with the *Pandora* but whether he survived the sinking and the journey back to Britain I cannot confirm.

[2] Morrison, Journal, p. 117. The punishment was 100 lashes in one case.

[3] Peter Heywood, Journal (extracts in Captain Edwards' Private Papers, Admiralty Library, Fulham), pp. 4-5. Renouard of the *Pandora* reported that the intention had been to sail 'to the NW coast of America', and that they had 'actually put to sea for that purpose'. *See* Renouard, 1842.

[4] Morrison, Journal, p. 119.

house, speaking in English. The Tahitians did not understand what he was saying, nor were they alarmed at his strange behaviour – after all, it was what they had come to see. Thompson produced his musket and fired at them. His shot killed a man and the child he was holding in his arms and also wounded a woman in the jaw and another man in the back. He fired at point-blank range, adding murder to his crimes of mutiny and rape.

It is incredible that the other seamen did nothing to restrain him even though a war of revenge might have been sparked off. Heywood magnanimously compensated the dead man's wife, mother of the dead baby, with a shirt. This side of Christian's allies was kept from the readers of the Appendix. That his mutiny made it possible for them to inflict their methods on defenceless islanders must weigh heavily against him. His own actions at Tubuai and his murder of the islander protecting his coconuts had set a standard for the likes of Thompson.

When Churchill heard about the two incidents involving Thompson, far from feeling shame at his friend's behaviour, he wanted to organise a punitive expedition to revenge him. Morrison's group refused to support such a reckless proposal, and in the recriminations that followed the seamen split into two parties. Churchill, Thompson and Brown went off to another part of Tahiti feeling 'betrayed' by their fellows and the rest were glad to be rid of them. The Churchill-Thompson proposal for a punitive attack suggests that they were the source of the earlier proposal, unfortunately aceeded to by Christian, to revenge the attack at Tubuai, and the proposal to kill in order to acquire local women.

The division of the European community did not lead to peace. Churchill shot two islanders 'for frightening away some ducks which he was about to fire at'. One of them died later from festering wounds.[5]

Churchill and Thompson quarrelled at their new residence and during the row Thompson threatened to shoot Churchill. To protect himself Churchill arranged with some islanders to have the muskets stolen. When Thompson discovered the theft he sought Churchill and, being weaponless, agreed to make up their differences. Brown was blamed for causing the row between them. Churchill, assured of Thompson's peaceful intentions, pretended to find the stolen muskets and returned them. Everything was amicable until one of the islanders who had stolen the weapons for Churchill had a row with him and in revenge informed Thompson of the truth. Thompson resolved to kill Churchill at the first opportunity, and this he did, shooting him in the back. Burkitt, who was staying nearby, rushed to the scene without a weapon and, seeing the enraged Thompson standing over the dead Churchill, promptly ran away. But Churchill's Tahitian friends were less discreet. They rushed Thompson and beat him to death in the Polynesian manner with stones, until his brains were splattered on the ground. None of the *Bounty* men was upset about this news; Morrison told the leader of the men that had killed Thompson that he 'looked on Him as an instrument in the Hand of

[5] *ibid.*, p. 125a.

Providence'.[6] With these murders two of the worst hard-line mutineers were dead just after Bligh and his party had got home to Britain.

In September 1790 the *Bounty* men joined in a civil war between two Tahitian kingdoms, and they must have used their weapons to effect, because the issue was resolved 'with a great slaughter'.[7] The help given to one chief antagonised the others. Inter-kingdom warfare was fairly common in Tahiti, but by introducing their fire-power into the disputes the Europeans ensured that the mutual destruction was on a far greater scale than before. Personal ambition and self-aggrandisement were the common ingredients of these civil wars, which had had an important demographic effect of keeping the population within the limits of the island's resources. But once the scale of the slaughter went beyond the culturally derived norms, the balance was upset, and the Tahitian social system was threatened. The population declined after this and their living standards collapsed; the mutiners must carry part of the responsibility for this process.

Having won this opening round, the local victors planned an even more spectacular victory over their rivals. They embarked on the stratagem of taking round the island the boy-king, Tu, accompanied by a Union Jack, and compelling the other chiefs and their subjects to show deference on pain of violence. That Morrison and company would have permitted the Union Jack to be used in this way says little for their sense of responsibility. By allowing the British symbol to be misused in a bloody fight between factions which had nothing to do with British interests, they put at severe risk future callers at the island who displayed the same symbol. Fortunately the planned tour was prevented by the arrival of the *Pandora* on 24 March 1791.

Before the *Pandora* arrived there was another noteworthy incident of violence, this time involving Coleman, Millward, McIntosh, Hillbrant and Morrison. Coleman was accused by a Tahitian of raping his wife and the Tahitian remonstrated with him. In the course of the altercation the man ran away, obviously frightened. Morrison confesses forming an armed party, not to arrest Coleman, but to hunt down the man. Morrison felt that the rape charge was merely a ruse to get compensation from Coleman in the form of iron goods, and unless these charges of rape were stopped the compensation would get out of control. In the man-hunt that followed, shots were fired and two islanders were wounded, 'one in the Thigh & body and the other in the Arm'.[8] Further violence was prevented by the arrest of the mutineers.

---

[6] *ibid.*, p. 133. Morrison gives an account of their deaths which he says he received from Burkitt and Brown, dating it 15 April 1790 (Journal, p. 127): 'This day we received a letter from Burkett informing us of the Death of Churchill & Thompson, also a letter from Brown to the same purpose ... Next morning the 16th Came Brown himself, Having been Sent by Matte to inform us by word of Mouth, as he thought that He could not explain it by letter; and He now gave us the following particulars ...' In giving Brown's report Morrison allows certain sentences to creep in that are critical of Brown's role in the affair, e.g. 'Churchill and Thompson found that Brown had been Active in promoting their Quarrel' (p. 129). This slip supports the contention that he was composing the report from memory and not from his own notes of Brown's verbal report, or direct from either of the letters.

[7] Morrison, Journal, p. 148. Danielsson, 1962, gives a helpful outline of the Island's political battles at the time when the mutineers were present.

[8] Morrison, Journal, p. 158.

The *Pandora* had left Britain in August 1790 and Captain Edwards had taken the Cape Horn route to Tahiti. He had passed within a few hours' sailing of Pitcairn Island on his way out and missed the chance to seize the leader of the mutiny. Captain Edwards was then forty-eight years old and an experienced Post Captain.[9] He had fought under Lord Howe and Sir Samuel Barrington and had the confidence of the Admiralty that he could accomplish the mission to seize the mutineers and bring them back for trial in Britain. His Lieutenants on the *Pandora* were Larkan, Corner and Thomas Hayward. When he got back to Britain Hayward had received his promotion to Lieutenant specifically to accompany the *Pandora*: he knew the mutineers and could recognise them and also knew the area, having been there in the *Bounty*. The *Pandora* reached Matavai Bay again on 23 March 1791 and the Captain set about arresting the *Bounty* crew. But before the *Pandora* had dropped anchor, Coleman swam out to it and surrendered himself. He was followed by Stewart and Heywood shortly afterwards. From them Edwards was able to get full details of who was on the island and what had happened to them. At the time Morrison had taken the *Resolution* on a voyage to another part of Tahiti.

Before I describe the arrest of the mutineers and the journey back to Britain, an important point must be made about Morrison's Journal. This document has been accepted since 1825 as a major part of the evidence against Bligh, as it makes charges against him such as theft of the *Bounty*'s provisions, falsification of the ship's accounts and general unsuitability as a commander. It has been widely assumed that Morrison either wrote the account day by day while the events he describes were happening or kept notes of the events on the *Bounty* and the *Pandora* which he later wrote up into a journal. Nobody has been able to explain how he preserved his journal or notes through his arrest and the shipwreck of the *Pandora*; Sir Basil Thomson wrote in 1915 that Morrison 'kept a journal, not only throughout the *Bounty*'s cruise, but during his sojourn with the mutineers in Tahiti, and, though it is not explained how he contrived to preserve it through the wreck of the *Pandora* and the boat voyage, there can be no doubt that it was a genuine document';[10] and even George Mackaness, the distinguished Australian historian, took this line: 'The truth of the whole matter appears to be that in some way or other – I cannot attempt to explain how – Morrison really did preserve a note-book or diary of some of his experience while on the *Bounty* ... Some time after the court martial, Morrison wrote up, in his own uncultured style, the complete story from his notes, the gaps being filled in as far as possible from his excellent memory.'[11] F.M. Bladen in 1908 and H.S. Montgomerie in 1937 seriously questioned the credibility of the journal,[12]

---

[9] He had been the object of a mutiny in his first year of command in 1782 on H.M.S. *Narcissus*. Twenty seamen went on trial for that mutiny; twelve were acquitted, six hanged, and two got 500 and 200 lashes respectively. See MacArthur, 1813, Appendix XXXIV.

[10] Thomson (ed.), 1915, p. 33n.

[11] Mackaness, 1951, p. 537.

[12] Bladen, 1908, p. 194: 'Nothing could be more absurd than to treat such a document seriously'; Montgomerie, 1937 and 1938.

but by the time Nordhoff and Hall had popularised the Morrison charges (and invented many others) in their ridiculous film scripts, the historical doubts about Morrison's writings had been swept under the carpet for the next forty years. It is time the record was put straight.

I shall examine in Chapter 19 the actual circumstances of Morrison's composition of the Memorandum and Journal, and his motives in writing them. Here we are simply concerned with whether he could have preserved a journal, or notes, through the events described in this chapter. The manuscript of Morrison's Journal in the Mitchell Library, Sydney, can be fairly conclusively proved not to have accompanied him on the journey. It consists of 378 folio pages written on one side only, measuring $17\frac{1}{2}$ inches by $13\frac{1}{2}$ inches. It could most certainly not have been hidden in even the most casual search of his person or possessions, and the evidence we have of the diligence with which Edwards and his first officer, Larkan, went about their searches suggests nothing remotely casual. The Journal shows no signs of having been in water; as at one point Morrison spent some considerable time in the water after the sinking of the *Pandora*, the Journal in the Mitchell Library could not have been with him during that episode. But the most telling argument against the proposition that Morrison had his Journal with him is the matter of the watermarks in the paper, which prove conclusively that this copy of the Journal was written after the mutineers were returned to Britain in 1792. The company that made the paper was John and Edward Gater, which traded from 1790 to 1816.[13] Morrison left Britain in the *Bounty* in 1787, three years before the earliest date that the paper could have been produced. He did not return until 1792. The *Pandora* left Britain in 1790 and could conceivably have had some of this paper on board, but as we shall see, it is implausible that Morrison got his paper from that source.

If we exclude the possibility that the manuscript Journal was written before October 1792, there remains the possibility that he 'somehow' preserved another journal or some notes through his experiences. I hope to show in the rest of this chapter that this is extremely unlikely. The point of the controversy is, of course, that if the Journal was composed in 1792 in the condemned cell and later, it is of absolutely no use as eye-witness evidence against Bligh. This does not prevent it from being a useful source of evidence about what happened on the *Bounty*, in Tahiti, and on the *Pandora*, as long as one takes into account the author's anti-Bligh motive, his desire to show himself in a good light, and the fact that he wrote after the event. He had a good memory and wrote vividly and in detail.

According to Morrison the *Resolution* was anchored near the shore on 23 March 1791, when his party received the news that a ship was at Matavai. We can take it that Morrison had his personal possessions with him in the boat; he would not have left anything behind to be stolen and if he had any notes they would have been with him. The Tahitians told Morrison and his companions that one of the officers who arrived in the *Pandora* was none other than Thomas Hayward. They knew therefore that any hope of concealing the

[13] Shorter, 1957, pp. 262, 308-9.

circumstances of the mutiny were gone and that they were fugitives. The mutineers in the party knew they were dead men, and the loyalists had only a slim hope that Bligh had survived to clear their names. Morrison claims that the group agreed to surrender voluntarily to the ship in the hope of 'better treatment', but they then indulged in behaviour which magnified any suspicions that Edwards had about them.

Burkitt, Sumner, Musprat, Hillbrant, Millward (all mutineers) and McIntosh (cleared of mutiny by Bligh, though he did not know it) went ashore, allegedly to chastise some islanders for some offence.[14] They did not return, but ran off into the mountains in a panic. This left Norman, Ellison and Morrison on the *Resolution*. Morrison writes: 'I went on shore to get some Cocoa Nuts & some provisions dressd, leaving Norman and Ellison on board, and as the surf run high on the Beach I took no arms with me when I left the vessel.'[15] If the surf was high enough to spoil a gun it would have spoilt papers; and he had no reason at that moment to expect that he would not be able to get back on board. However, contrary to his expectations, the islanders attacked the vessel while he was ashore and 'soon stripd her of evry thing that they could remove and brought the things on shore'.[16] If Morrison had had papers on the vessel these would have been removed along with everything else. Morrison, Norman and Ellison were made prisoners and confined in a local hut. The islanders wanted them to run away with the others into the mountains, and had 'arrested' them to prevent them going to Matavai. Their possessions were not returned. They were able to escape through a friendly Tahitian and the procurement by Brown (who was in the area) of a pistol, two hatchets, a knife and a canoe. They slipped away in the dark and made for the sea, taking none of their possessions.

The three men gave themselves up to a search party led by Lieutenant Corner, who later that morning handed them over to Lieutenant Hayward. Their hands were tied behind their backs and when they got aboard the *Pandora* they were put into irons with the men who had surrendered the previous day. All prisoners were searched and their possessions examined for evidence that might lead Edwards to Christian. Edwards reported that he had read some journals belonging to the prisoners which he had found in their sea chests.[17] From his private papers in the Admiralty Library at Fulham we know he saw journals by Heywood and Stewart and that he made notes from them. There is no mention of any journal or notes belonging to Morrison. This does not mean that there was no such item. As an officer he may have been prejudiced in favour of material written by midshipmen and against material written by a Boatswain's Mate, but given the extent and the detail of Morrison's journals, it would seem unlikely that he would exclude them on these grounds if he had seen them. One thing is certain,

[14] Another interesting version of this incident and of the return of the mutineers to London is in the 'Authentic History of the Mutineers of the *Bounty*' (1820), attributed by Rolf du Rietz to Samuel Greatheed. *See* Du Rietz's forthcoming edition of this article.
[15] Morrison, Journal, p. 175.
[16] *ibid.*, p. 176.
[17] Thomson (ed.), 1915, p. 34.

however; if Morrison had written anything and managed to keep it up to the time of the *Pandora*'s arrival, it was taken from him or from his chest by Edwards and that was the last he saw of it.

The captured mutineers were placed in leg irons in a roundhouse specially built on the poop deck, measuring 11 by 18 feet. It has been known ever since, inevitably, as 'Pandora's Box'. The entrance was a small scuttle eighteen or twenty inches square and there were two other smaller scuttles nine inches square for air. During the night the prisoners were also handcuffed, and they were under guard twenty-four hours a day. Edwards was very worried that the prisoners might make his crew mutinous and he was determined to prevent contact between them. The measures that he took have been criticised by everybody since.

In spite of his efforts, the prisoners seem to have managed to talk to the crew. Edwards noted in his papers that 'Lieutenant Corner reported that when the Prisoners went forward they could not be prevented from conversing with the Ships Company in defiance of the orders that had been given to prevent it'.[18] This entry is not dated but it was presumably in the early days of their imprisonment. The expression 'went forward' seems to suggest that the prisoners obeyed the calls of nature in the normal sea-going fashion. This would mean that they were taken out of the 'Box' and escorted to the forward 'head'. The crew were quartered in this area and the passages were cramped, making it difficult to prevent the prisoners whispering to the crew and exchanging messages. Lieutenant Corner either reported this circumstance to the Captain or explained it thus when the Captain complained about the breach of his orders. The result was that, since allowing the prisoners to use the ship's facilities also allowed them to talk to the crew, Edwards simply withdrew the facilities. Heywood when he wrote to his mother described 'being obliged to eat, drink, sleep and obey the calls of nature' in the 'Box'.[19] He does not mention the circumstance of Edwards' harsh decision.

Edwards' obsession with keeping the prisoners away from his crew dominated his thinking in the first days of their arrest. Lieutenant Corner also reported to him that 'he suspected that they carried on a correspondence with some of our people by letter'.[20] This is the only direct reference to the ability of the prisoners to write while under arrest during the early days of their confinement. It seems extraordinary that they had the facilities to do so. Seamen had no access to paper, and the Box was not provided with pen and ink. If they did manage to scribble a note, it would have been easy enough to pass it on to a friendly face in the crew in the visits forward, but these visits were stopped; and Corner's information to the Captain about the letters would provoke a search for the materials and their removal from the Box. The possibility that Morrison wrote notes in the Box and passed them to a

18 Edward Edwards, Private Papers, 'Memo made at Otaheite'.
19 Thomson (ed.), 1915, p. 9. Tagart, 1832, p. 34.
20 Edward Edwards, Private Papers, 'Memo made at Otaheite'.

friendly crew member would require a high degree of intimacy between Morrison and someone on the ship.

Heywood, in his memoirs, mentioned his contacts with Lieutenant Hayward on several occasions, indicating that Hayward's treatment of him, while hardly that of a friend, was not that of a tyrant. Heywood was informed that in his absence from Britain his father had died: 'Alas! I was informed of the death of the most indulgent of fathers, which I naturally supposed to have been hastened by Mr Bligh's ungenerous conduct. This thought made me truly wretched. I had certainly been overpowered by my grief had not Mr Hayward again assured me, that he had paid the debt of nature before news of the *Bounty*'s fate arrived in England, and that he had news by letter from my best-beloved Nessy, which made me somewhat easier and I endeavoured to bear it as I ought.'[21]

The islanders were kept well away from the prisoners while the ship was at Tahiti. This provoked many tears and emotional scenes from the women friends of the prisoners, some of them mothers and others visibly pregnant. Edwards noted that there were reports to him that 'the natives of Otaheite particularly those that had been connected with the Prisoners intended to cut our cables should the wind blow strong from the sea towards the shore'.[22] While these reports may have been exaggerated, the possibility was real that an attempt would be made to founder the *Pandora*, as was tried against the *Bounty*. Instead of its being merely the grievance of an individual (the Tahitian tyo of midshipman Thomas Hayward) that was involved, this time there were several dozen whole families concerned, some of whom were grievously upset at the removal of their friends. Edwards took the threat seriously and kept the Tahitians well away from the ship. Thus, the prisoners were denied even the little comfort of seeing or talking to their Tahitian friends and women.

Some of the prisoners, from their long stay on the island, were fairly conversant with the Tahitian language. This enabled them to speak to one another in a language unintelligible to a European listening from outside the 'Box'. Edwards suspected that he was threatened by a conspiracy. He ordered that the prisoners were to talk only in English on pain of being shot. Thus the guards could listen for plots and plans. This has given Edwards an odious reputation. But, considering the information he had, his conduct was nothing but elementary prudence. He had reports of Tahitian threats to wreck his ship, of the prisoners' talking to his crew, of their talking among themselves in a strange tongue, and he had the fact of the *Bounty* mutiny and what had happened to Captain Bligh. He also did not know where Christian and his party were or exactly what their relationship was to the captured mutineers.

The harsher the conditions in the Box, the more difficult it would have been for Morrison to write and preserve notes on the voyage. This is how Morrison described the conditions:

---

[21] Tagart, 1832, p. 36, quoting from a letter to his mother, 20 November 1791, Batavia.
[22] Edward Edwards, Private Papers, 'Memo made at Otaheite'.

The Heat of the place when it was calm was so intense that the Sweat frequently ran in Streams to the Scuppers, and produced Maggots in a short time; the Hammocks being dirty when we got them, we found stored with Vermin of another kind, which we had no Method of erradicating but by lying on the Plank; and tho our Freinds would have supplyd us with plenty of Cloth they were not permitted to do it, and our only remedy was to lay Naked, ... the roughness of the Work made our Habitation very leaky, and when any rain fell we were always wet. As the place was washd twice a week we were washd with it, there being no room to shift us from place to place and we had no other alternative but standing up till the Deck dried (which we could but very badly do when the ship had any motion), or lying down in the wet. ...[23]

The *Pandora* left Tahiti on 8 May, taking with it the *Resolution*, which had been commandeered by Edwards and had had proper sails fitted to it and a small crew assigned to it. They sailed for Wytootackee, which Edwards had heard was the island that Christian intended to aim for, though why he thought Christian would go to an island discovered by Bligh is not explained. Finding nothing there, he went on to Palmerston Island and arrived there on 21 May. Here some pieces of the *Bounty* were found – some spare masts and rigging lost by the mutineers at Tubuai, which had been taken there by the tides. Having found a part of the *Bounty*, the *Pandora* lost some of its crew. A midshipman, Mr Sivall, and four seamen were in the jolly-boat on an errand between the *Pandora* and the shore, when a storm blew up and they disappeared. They were never seen again and were presumably drowned or starved at sea. These were the first casualties on the *Pandora*.

The search was continued as the vessel went towards the west, each day taking it further and further from Pitcairn where Christian and his party were established. The prisoners were on full rations, including grog, though they were cramped in their Box. The islands that were visited were a relief to the *Pandora*'s crew but of nominal interest to the prisoners. Each day that took them from Tahiti also took them towards Britain.

On 22 June, the *Resolution* became separated from the *Pandora*. Edwards spent two days looking for it and then sailed for Annamooka. The *Resolution* was not seen again until the survivors of the *Pandora* arrived at Samarang in October. Its solitary voyage to the East Indies was an event in itself. It was a tribute to the solidity of the structure built by Morrison's party at Tahiti.[24]

Edwards continued to move from island to island, though apparently with less and less interest in the mission. He had now lost fourteen of his crew – five in the jollyboat and nine in the *Resolution* – and the immensity of the Pacific and the smallness of his quarry must have demoralised him as each day went by. There were literally hundreds of islands for the mutineers to hide in, and if they had burnt the *Bounty* they would be even more invisible. It was when in this mood that he passed an island on 13 August in which 'we

---

[23] Morrison, Journal, pp. 181-4.
[24] The reports that the *Resolution* was later used as a sailing vessel in the China Seas have been shown to be false by Andrew David, in his article in *Mariner's Mirror*, 1977a.

saw smoke very plain, from which it may be presumed that the island in inhabited'.[25] The real tragedy about this incident is that there is reason to believe that the inhabitants of this particular island were survivors of the La Pérouse expedition. The *Pandora's* surgeon, George Hamilton, had noted in his Journal how on 15 July 1791 they had visited an island (Otutuelah): 'Here we found some of the French navigator's cloathing and buttons; and there is little doubt but they have murdered them'.[26] Yet when Edwards saw smoke, perhaps frantic signals from the stranded survivors, on the island of Vanikoro (which he named Pitt Island), he did not investigate, but sailed on without stopping.

The *Pandora* headed for the Great Barrier Reef of Australia, having given up the search for Christian. This brought them to the most dangerous waters in the Pacific. Edwards proved incapable of taking his ship through the reef, and on 28 August the ship violently struck coral. It began to take in water – nine feet in fifteen minutes – and as the ship settled in the water it heeled over enough to cause a gun to break loose and crush a seaman to death. The ship's boats were loaded with provisions and sent astern. By early the next morning the end was near. The last men to be allowed off the sinking ship were the prisoners, though not all of them made it.

Captain Edwards has been accused of ignoring the prisoners while the ship was sinking and of taking no steps to ensure their safety. The prisoners were manacled in irons in the 'Box' with only a small exit to escape through, which was guarded until the last moment by an armed sentry. Three of the prisoners were let out to help man the pumps in a futile bid to keep the ship afloat. The others were left in the Box and ignored. Some of the prisoners broke their irons so as to save time when the scuttle roof exit was eventually opened for them; the Captain heard about this and sent the ship's Armourer into the Box with orders to re-iron the prisoners, and also gave orders that the Master at Arms was to shoot any prisoner who created a disturbance. When the scuttle was eventually opened the prisoners had only minutes to make good their escape, and one was too late and went down with the ship. Morrison clearly thought that Edwards delayed the release to a point where their lives were endangered. But we can explain, even if we cannot justify, Edwards' actions. In an overlooked sentence Morrison writes: 'We could hear the Officers busy getting their things into the boats which were hauld under the stern on purpose & heard some of the Men on Deck say "I'll be damnd if they shall go without us"'. According to him, at this the prisoners began to clank their irons and join in the shouting. Edwards may have thought he had a mutiny on his hands, and his order to the Master at Arms to 'fire upon the buggers' is more understandable if this was so. Another point is that there was not enough room in the boats for everybody, and occupancy was related to rank. Booms were cut loose to act as rafts for the seamen (in an accident during this operation a seaman was killed when a boom fell on the deck). It seems reasonable to assume that Edwards was

[25] Thomson (ed.), 1915, pp. 67-8.
[26] *ibid.*, p. 137.

delaying the release of the prisoners so that he and his officers could take their places in the boats. Edwards seems to have wanted an orderly release of the prisoners in threes, to keep them under control, but the lurching of the ship prevented this, as the Master at Arms who was supervising the operation went over the side, and Hodges, the Armourer's Mate, who was preparing the next lot of prisoners for release, was trapped in the Box with them. It seems probably that the final plunge of the *Pandora* came earlier than expected; the first Lieutenant was clinging to the roof of the Box when Morrison saw it float by with three of the prisoners on it, so he had not had time to get into the boat.[27]

Morrison's description of the sinking of the *Pandora* is a moving account of survival in adversity and a graphic example of his style, obviously written later and with the passion of an angry man. It also makes it clear how difficult it would have been for him to keep notes or a diary safe through the dreadful events he is writing about. The officers had got their belongings into the boats and were making preparations to leave. Morrison writes:

> Most of the Officers being aft on the top of the Box, we observed that they were armd, and preparing to go into the Boats by the Stern ladders – We Beggd that we might not be forgot, when by Captain Edwards's Order Joseph Hodges, the Armourers Mate of the Pandora, was sent down to take the Irons off Muspratt & Skinner & send them & Byrn (who was then out of Irons) up, but Skinner being too eager to get out got hauld up with his handcuffs on, and the other two following him Close, the Scuttle was shut and Bar'd before Hodges could get to it and he in the Mean time knockd off my hand Irons & Stuarts. I beg'd of the Master at Arms to leave the Scuttle open when he answerd "Never fear my boys we'll all go to Hell together". The words were scarcely out of his Mouth when the Ship took a Sally and a general cry of "there She Goes" was heard, the Master at Arms and Corp. with the other Centinals rolld overboard, and at the same instant we saw through the Stern Ports Captain Edwards astern swiming to the Pinnace which was some distance astern, as were all the Boats who had shoved off on the first Appearance of a Motion in the Ship. Burkett & Heildbrandt were yet handcuffd and the Ship under Water as far as the Main Mast and it was now begining to flow in upon us when the Devine providence directed Wm. Moulter (Boatsns Mate) to the place. He was scrambling up on the Box and hearing our Crys took out the Bolt and threw it and the Scuttle overboard, such was his presence of Mind tho He was forced to follow instantly himself on this. We all got out except Heildbrandt and were rejoiced even in this trying scene to think that we had escaped from our prison – tho It was full as much as I could do to clear my self of the Driver boom before the Ship Sunk.[28]

The men were in the water, though not yet saved. A sinking ship is a dangerous object both while it goes down and in the immediate period afterwards. Loose timbers and appurtenances sucked down in the initial

[27] Morrison, Journal, pp. 186-91.
[28] *ibid.*, pp. 189-90.

moments are likely to surface quickly and cause danger to men swimming in the vicinity. Morrison was almost dragged down by the driver boom (the boom on the aft mast); a gangway that 'came up' killed some of the survivors; planks and objects galore littered the surface where the ship had been. Morrison goes on to describe what happened to him in the water after the *Pandora* had gone down:

> The Boats were now so far off that we could not distinguish one from the other, however observing one of the Gangways Come up I swam to it and had scarcely reachd it before I perceived Muspratt on the other end of it having brought him up with it but it falling on the Heads of several others sent them to the Bottom,[29] here I began to get ready for Swimming and the top of our Prison having floated I observed on it Mr. P Heywood, Burket & Coleman & the First Lieut. of the Ship, and seeing Mr. Heywood take a Short plank and Set off to one of the Boats, I resolved to Follow him and throwing away my trowsers, bound my loins up in a Sash or Marro after the Taheite Manner, got a short plank & followed and after having been about an hour and a half in the water, I reachd the Blue Yaul and was taken up by Mr. Bowling, Mrs Mte, who had also taken up Mr. Haywood after taking up several others we were landed on a small sandy Key on the Reef about 2½ or 3 Miles from the Ship.

The point at issue is whether, after throwing away his trousers and being in the water for an hour and a half, Morrison could possibly have secreted papers on his person and kept them from damage in the sea. Lady Belcher, in a footnote to her description of the sinking of the *Pandora*, claims that Heywood saved his prayer book, a gift from his mother, by carrying it between his teeth, which in the circumstances was an extraordinary feat of concentration in the midst of near-disaster. Heywood, in his own account, states that he was 'stark-naked'.[30]

For nineteen days the survivors of the wreck stayed on a small key while the ship's boats were prepared for the long journey to Timor. Thirty-four men had drowned in the sinking, four of them prisoners. With the fourteen men lost earlier in the jolly-boat and *Resolution*, Edwards had lost a total of forty-eight crew and prisoners, and the journey was not half completed. These figures are a real measure of the competence of Edwards and his worth as a seaman and commander, and he is rightly criticised for his ship management.

His conduct during the rest of the long journey to Britain was to be as severe on the prisoners as it had been up to this point. He clearly blamed them for his predicament and the loss of his ship. While at the key near where the *Pandora* sank, the prisoners were kept apart from the main body of the survivors. They were given no shelter from the sun during the day nor covers during the night. They lay naked and got blistered in the daytime, and shivered in the cold nights. Any possessions that any of them might have had could not have been hidden in these circumstances.

---

[29] He names two of the men killed by the gangway as Stewart and Sumner; *ibid.*, p. 191.
[30] Peter Heywood, letter to his mother, quoted in Tagart, 1832, p. 36.

When the party eventually set off on the boat voyage, Morrison was put into Edwards's boat. The prisoners were separated in the boats, presumably to prevent them seizing command.[31] Morrison reports his treatment while in the boat: 'On the 9th as I was laying on the Oars talking to McIntosh Captain Edwards ordered me aft, and without assigning any Cause ordered me to be pinnioned with a Cord and lasshd down in the Boats Bottom, and Ellison, who was then asleep in the Boats Bottom, was ordered to the same punnishment.' One cannot help feeling that there was more to this than Morrison admits to. Morrison goes on: 'I attempted to reason and enquire what I had now done to be thus Cruelly treated, urging the Distress'd situation of the whole, but received for answer, "Silence you Murdering Villian are you not a Prisoner? You Piratical Dog what better treatment do you expect?" ' This expresses Edwards's view of Morrison in a credible way; to Edwards Morrison and his mates were pirates, due for a hanging, and the indirect cause of the deaths of over forty of his crew. Even though Morrison felt bitter about what had happened in the scuttle and regarded Edwards as a monster, he was asking for trouble. However, he did not leave it there, according to his own account; he persisted in arguing with Edwards, which is frankly unbelievable and could only have been included in his account to impress whom ever he was writing it for with his own importance. He writes: 'I then told him that it was a disgrace to the Captain of a British Man of War to treat a prisoner in such an inhuman Manner upon which he started up in a Violent Rage & snatching a Pistol which lay in the Stern sheets, threatened to shoot me. I still attempted to speak, when he swore "by God if you speak another Word I'll heave the Log with You" and finding that he would hear no reason & my mouth being Parchd so, that I could not move my tongue, I was forced to be silent & submit; and was tyed down so that I could not move'.[32]

Morrison claims he was kept in these conditions until the boats reached Timor; if he had argued back as he claims he did in a ship in the Channel

---

[31] According to Edwards (Thomson [ed.], 1915, p. 75n.), the crew and prisoners were divided up as follows:

Pinnace:	Capt. Edwards; Lieut. Hayward; Rickards, Master's Mate; Packer, Gunner; Edmonds, Captain's Clerk; 3 prisoners [we know these to be Morrison, McIntosh and Ellison]; 16 privates.
Red Yawl:	Lieut. Larkan; Surgeon Hamilton; Reynolds, Master's Mate; Matson, midshipman; 2 prisoners; 18 privates.
Launch:	Lieut. Corner; Bentham, Purser; Montgomery, Carpen[ter]; Bowling, Master's Mate; Mackendrick, midshipman, 2 prisoners; 24 privates.
Blue Yawl:	George Passmore, Master; Cunningham, Boatswain; Innes, Surgeon's Mate; Fenwick, midshipman; Pycroft, midshipman; 3 prisoners; 15 privates.

According to him 102 men were saved.

[32] Morrison, Journal, p. 197. In his Journal Hamilton, the Surgeon, describes an odd incident in Edwards' boat: 'In the Captain's boat, one of the prisoners took to praying, and they gathered round him with much attention and seeming devotion. But the Captain suspecting the purity of his doctrine, and unwilling he should make a monopoly of the business, gave the prayers himself' (ed. Thomson, 1915, p. 155; 1793 ed., p. 129). McIntosh could have been bewailing his fortunes after Morrison and Ellison were tied down; or this could be Morrison 'praying', and inserting thinly disguised criticism of Edwards. It may have been this incident that provoked Edwards to have Morrison secured.

fleet he would have been lucky to receive less than 500 lashes. By challenging the authority of Edwards, already brooding on his bad luck and the cause of his misfortunes, in a small boat in front of the crew, Morrison brought his difficulties on himself. This is not to say that Edwards was right, but simply that Morrison was on his own admission a loud-mouthed fool.

During the boat voyage to Timor Morrison was certainly unable to keep notes. He does not say much about the voyage in his Journal except how uncomfortable his situation was. At Timor the prisoners were put into a Dutch prison in stocks in a cell so disagreeable that the Dutch surgeon sent to look them over would not enter the cell until a slave had washed it out. When they were eventually ready to depart, Lieutenant Larkan, the *Pandora*'s First Officer, and the man whom Morrison and Heywood least liked among their captors, personally supervised the binding of the prisoners. He used a cord and 'setting his foot against our backs, and bracing our arms together so as almost to haul our arms out of their socketts; we were tyed two & two by the Elbows, & having our Irons knockd off were Conducted to the Beach and put on board a long Boat to proceed to the Ship but before we reachd her some of us had fainted owing to the Circulation of the Blood being stopd by the lasshings – When we got on board we were put both legs in Irons, and our lasshings taken off.'[33] Again, the worse the treatment, the more difficult it is to believe that Morrison had a diary with him.

The passage from Coupang in Timor to Batavia was not without incident. The ship carrying the survivors and prisoners (the *Rembang*, a Dutch ship) was struck by a storm during which even the prisoners were released to man the pumps. Morrison reports that when he remonstrated with Lieutenant Larkan about the prisoners' state of health and their inability to work a full shift on the pumps, Larkan replied: 'You dam'd Villain, you have brought it on yourself and I'll make you stand it; if it was not for you we should not have been here nor have met with this trouble.'[34] The Dutch crew were apparently so frightened that they were hiding below and the *Pandora*'s crew were effectively sailing the ship. Having survived one shipwreck and being in danger of another, this time without hope of survival if they went down, it is not surprising that Lieutenant Larkan was unsympathetic.

The *Rembang* survived and reached Batavia on 7 November 1791. *En route* they picked up the missing *Resolution* at Samarang and heard the crew's tales of how they had brought the little ship to the Dutch settlement after losing touch with the *Pandora* six months earlier (see above, p.154). At Batavia the crew was divided into groups to make the journey back to Europe in separate ships. The prisoners' treatment did not improve. ' ... our lodgings were none of the Best,' writes Morrison, 'as we lay on rough logs of Timber, some of which lay Some inches above the rest and which our small portion of Cloathing would not bring to a level, the Deck also over us was very leaky, by which means we were continually wet being alternately drenchd with Salt water, the Urine of the Hogs or the Rain which happend to fall.'[35]

---

[33] Morrison, Journal, p. 199. [35] *ibid.*, p. 204.
[34] *ibid.*, p. 200.

Before leaving Batavia, however, we know that some facilities were made available, at least to Peter Heywood, to write a letter to relatives in Britain. Heywood's long letter to 'My ever-honoured and dearest Mother' was dated: 'Batavia, November 20th, 1791.'[36] There was nothing necessarily unusual in this. Sea voyages being the gamble that they were, it was prudent to send written reports home at every opportunity, and Batavia presented that opportunity, as it was a Dutch shipping centre with regular sailings to Europe. Captain Edwards sent a report to the Admiralty of his misfortunes, and his officers almost certainly did likewise to their families. Whether Heywood wrote his letter with the approval of Edwards we can only surmise. Tagart, in his version of Heywood's life, states: 'At Batavia, Heywood availed himself of the first opportunity to write to his mother. The following letter was sent off by one of the *Pandora*'s men, who was to sail in the first ship.'[37] It would be interesting to identify the man. Judging by later friendships it could have been Lieutenant Corner. Whoever sent the letter for him, it was consistent with Heywood's status as the only officer of the *Bounty* among the prisoners, and in no way suggests the presence of such writing facilities among the prisoners as could establish the existence of Morrison's 'diary'.

When the party arrived at Cape Town they were transferred from the Dutch ship to H.M.S. *Gorgon*. Once on a British ship they came under its discipline, which had the singular advantage that they were not under the personal supervision of Captain Edwards and Lieutenant Larkan. They went onto regulation diets, and had daily exercise and only one leg in irons.

In several places in his Journal Morrison makes reference to the different treatment given to McIntosh, Coleman and Norman on the passage from Coupang to Batavia.[38] They were regularly let out of irons unlike the rest of the prisoners. This treatment was repeated on the passage from Batavia to the Cape and thence on the journey to Britain. Even earlier, these were the three prisoners let out to help with the pumps on the *Pandora*, though Morrison reports that several volunteered; and Edwards did not punish McIntosh in the boat voyage to Timor. Bligh in his published accounts of the mutiny specifically names these three men as having been kept on board the *Bounty* by force and against their inclinations.[39] When Edwards was sent out he had probably received these reports from the Admiralty and possibly from Bligh personally. At Timor, Edwards would have been able to see Bligh's original account of the mutiny left with the Dutch Governor, and this would have reinforced the reports made by Bligh, which would also have been supported by the statements of McIntosh, Coleman and Norman.[40]

---

[36] Tagart, 1832, p. 23.
[37] *ibid.*, p. 22.
[38] Morrison, Journal, pp. 200-5.
[39] Bligh, 1790, p. 4.
[40] This indirectly supports the idea that Edwards intended all the prisoners to escape safely when the Pandora sank. The first three prisoners let out were Musprat, Byrne and Skinner; if he was 'favouring' Coleman, Norman and MacIntosh, and did not care what happened to the others, he would have ordered these three to be let out first.

H.M.S. *Gorgon* reached Spithead on 18 June 1792 and the prisoners were transferred to H.M.S. *Hector* where they remained until soon after their trial. News of their arrest and the sinking of the *Pandora* had preceded them to Britain. The letters and papers of the Heywood family show that the months of waiting to find out who had survived the shipwreck, who had been captured, and who was guilty of mutiny, were productive of intense emotion. If Peter Heywood had survived and was being brought back to Britain to stand trial they were determined to devote all their resources to establishing his innocence, even to the point of indifference whether he was guilty or not. The family closed around 'young Peter' and set to work to save him from a hanging. Families of the survivors of lesser importance and wealth may have hoped to do the same, but lacking interest in the Admiralty and political power in the land, they had to be content with hoping. There were two exceptions to this: both men had cunning and confidence. Their names were Musprat and Morrison.

17

The Trial of the Captured Mutineers

The *Bounty* prisoners were transferred to H.M.S. *Hector* on their arrival at Spithead on 19 June 1792. Their court martial opened on H.M.S. *Duke* on 12 September and lasted until 18 September. Between the date of their arrival and their court martial they had a lot of spare time. In consideration of their privations as prisoners under Edwards they were to regard their treatment on the *Hector* as generous. These months were put to good use by at least one of the prisoners, Peter Heywood.

As we saw, when Bligh returned to Britain with his depleted crew and the story of the mutiny he had managed to convince his family, the Admiralty and Sir Joseph Banks of the perfidious nature of Christian and the mutineers. At the formal court martial he had been acquitted by the court with honour and resumed his naval career, being appointed to command H.M.S. *Providence* for a second expedition to Tahiti to transplant the breadfruit, and had left Britain on this voyage in August 1791. He was on his way to the Pacific when the *Pandora* sank off Australia, and had left the Cape *en route* for Adventure Bay, Tasmania, in December, long before the *Pandora*'s survivors and their prisoners passed there on the final lap of their journey home. When the prisoners landed at Spithead in June 1792, Bligh was anchored off Matavai Bay in Tahiti. He left Tahiti in July 1792 and was navigating the treacherous Torres Straits during the trial of the mutineers in Britain. I shall discuss this voyage and Bligh's return in the next chapter, and then go on to the subsequent campaigns against Bligh by the Christian and Heywood families. In this chapter I shall simply outline the events of the trial of the mutineers and show how, in the summer months of 1792, the Heywoods rallied round Peter and engineered his acquittal. Fortunately, a great deal of the correspondence about Heywood has been preserved, though in an edited form, in the eulogy published in 1832. The manipulation of interest is shown clearly in this correspondence; that it nearly failed to save his life shows how hard the lobbying had to be, even though the principal witness against him, William Bligh, was then out of the country and unable to lead for the prosecution.

First, we must look at two letters written by Bligh to Heywood's family on his return from the open boat voyage. Many have criticised him severely for the content of these letters.[1] I think that the criticism is less than fair.

---

[1] The letters from Bligh were first referred to by Sir John Barrow, 1831, pp. 129-130. Barrow wrote that 'The only way of accounting for this ferocity of sentiment towards a youth, who had

Heywood's mother wrote to Bligh asking for news of her son and for his opinion of his guilt on the charge of mutiny. No copy of her letter is extant, so we do not know in what terms it was phrased. Bligh's reply (only available as reported by Tagart) is apparently a cold-blooded refutation of a mother's faith in her son. Bligh wrote:

London, April 2, 1790.

MADAM,

I received your letter this day, and feel for you very much, being perfectly sensible of the extreme distress you must suffer from the conduct of your son Peter. His baseness is beyond all description, but I hope you will endeavour to prevent the loss of him, heavy as the misfortune is, from afflicting you too severely. I imagine he is, with the rest of the mutineers, returned to Otaheite.

I am, Madam,
[Signed] WM BLIGH.[2]

In my experience of Bligh's papers this is among the shortest letters he wrote, especially on the important subject of the mutiny, that is, assuming that we have the letter entire. Tagart, like many *Bounty* authors, is not to be trusted in his editing of evidence. Earlier, Bligh had received a similar request for information from an uncle of Heywood's, Colonel Holwell. His reply to this letter (again Tagart's is the only version we have) is as follows:

March 26, 1790.

SIR,

I have just this instant received your letter. With much concern I inform you that your nephew, Peter Heywood, is among the mutineers. His ingratitude to me is of the blackest dye, for I was a father to him in every respect, and he never once had an angry word from me through the whole course of the voyage, as his conduct always gave me much pleasure and satisfaction. I very much regret that so much baseness formed the character of a young man I had a real regard for, and it will give me much pleasure to hear his friends can bear the loss of him without much concern.

I am, Sir, &c.
[Signed] WM BLIGH

To my mind it is understandable that Bligh should write so harshly of Peter Heywood. The court martial agreed with his legalistic view of Heywood's guilt and even Heywood in his own testimony to the court stated that if he had betrayed Bligh's friendship he would have been a 'monster of depravity'.

in point of fact no concern in the mutiny, is by reference to certain points of evidence given by Hayward, Hallat [sic], and Purcell at the court martial, each point wholly unsupported'. Tagart, in his biography of Heywood, 1832, merely lifts this section out of Barrow. Mackaness, 1951, p. 227, says of these letters: 'It is impossible to excuse or even palliate the harshness of Bligh's reply.'

[2] Tagart, 1832, p. 7; Barrow, 1961, p. 129; Mackaness, 1951, p. 227.

Bligh thought that he had, since Heywood did not come to his assistance or show openly where he stood, and did not try to go with him in the boat. Heywood had failed Bligh at a moment when he needed all the help he could get.

In Bligh's letter to his wife, Elizabeth, written in August 1789, we see the view that he had taken of the roles of Heywood and Stewart in the affair. He pulled no punches in this personal letter, and he had no reason to believe that it would ever be published. He wrote:

> Besides this Villain see young Heywood, one of the ringleaders, & besides him see Stewart joined with him. – Christian had been assured of promotion when he came home, & with the other two I was every day rendering them some service. – It is incredible these very young Men I placed every confidence in, yet these great Villians joined with the most able Men in the Ship got possession of the Arms and took the *Bounty* from me, with huzzas for Otaheite. I have now reason to curse the day I ever knew a Christian or a Heywood ...[3]

These were his feelings seven months before Mrs Heywood wrote to him, and when his ordeal was not yet over (he had to survive the voyage home from Batavia, which some of his companions did not manage to do); they had not altered by the time the family wrote to him, full of concern about their offspring. That offspring in Bligh's view had contributed to the sufferings he had gone through, and to the deaths of his companions; beginning with Norton on the beach at Tofoa and continuing with Nelson, Hall, Ledward, Elphinston, Linkletter and Lamb at Coupang, Batavia and on the journey home.

At the time Bligh was not alone in his judgment, and even Heywood's family accepted the possibility that he was guilty of mutiny up to the time when he was brought back alive to stand trial. W.S. Stanhope wrote the following to Captain Shuttleworth, who had been making enquiries on behalf of the family:

> With respect to young Heywood in particular, I have been able to learn nothing further than that, as he was not one of those who were sent off with Captain Bligh, he is presumed to be among the mutineers. The consequence of such a mutiny is very alarming, of which his friends appear to be very sensible; – but, on the other hand, the particular circumstances of this mutiny are unknown, the possibility that young Heywood may have had little to do with it, but have been kept on board on account of his youth, the possibility also of escape, and in the case of the worst, there being, I believe, a senior officer to him on board in the same predicament, who is nearly related to a man in high office, are

[3] William Bligh, letter to Mrs Elizabeth Bligh, 19 August 1789, ML, Bligh Family Correspondence, Safe 1/45.

circumstances which may administer some little hope of comfort to his family in their present distressful state.[4]

Nessy Heywood, Peter's sister, wrote to her uncle, J.M. Heywood, a couple of weeks after Bligh's letter to Mrs Heywood, quoted above, was sent. He replied:

London, April 14, 1790

DEAR MADAM,

I should have given an earlier answer to the favour of your letter if I had not waited to see Lieut. Bligh. I yesterday had the good fortune to meet with him, when I obtained all the intelligence I could respecting your unfortunate brother. When I inquired what his behaviour and conduct had been previous to the arrival of the ship at Otaheite, he told me he had no reason to find any fault with him, but expressed his astonishment at his having been of the number of those who deserted, after having shewn him always great kindness and attention. I believe Mr. Bligh and the whole of the ship's crew, who came away with him, are unanimous in ascribing this horrid transaction to the attachments unfortunately formed to the women of Otaheite. He has no idea of any other, and believes that the plan of the mutiny had not been concerted many days before it was carried into execution. He particularly told me that your brother was not one of those who entered his cabin, – which circumstance gave me great satisfaction ... As the unfortunate and uncommon situation into which his strange conduct has thrown him, may prevent, for a length of time at least, his return to England, the only consolation I can hold out to you is, that when he does return, his general good conduct and character, previous to this unhappy business, may, with some allowance for the unbridled passions of youth, plead for his pardon. You must have the philosophy at present to consider him as lost for ever. But I trust that Providence will restore him to you, and enable him by his future good behaviour to make atonement to his country, and to those shipmates who have suffered such extreme hardships, and so narrowly escaped death.[5]

This was the situation in 1790, on the basis of Bligh's evidence and interpretation of Heywood's conduct. The family had to accept the possibility that Peter was a mutineer and had by his actions, forfeited his life, though there was a possibility that Peter was not as guilty as others, and that he might be pardoned by the court. Of course, if Heywood had been a hard-line mutineer and had gone off with Christian on that final journey, it would have been more difficult for his family to succeed in exculpating him.

With the return of the prisoners the campaign to save Heywood's reputation began. The difficulties they faced in this objective were real, but they were not insurmountable. The fact that the mutineers had split into two groups, one remaining at Tahiti and the other going off to some unknown

[4] Tagart, 1832, p. 9; the 'senior officer' mentioned is probably George Stewart, but it could be a mistake for Edward Young, who was related to Sir George Young. Stewart had no important relatives.

[5] Tagart, 1832, pp. 10-11.

island, was of great assistance. Heywood's presence in the Tahiti group certainly brought him within reach of the hangman, but it also brought him within range of a pardon. There was a grey area in which Heywood's conduct shaded in and out of the culpable. If testimony could be organised to narrow the area of his possible guilt and increase the area of doubt, he might be saved. This needed interest, energy and resources, and the Heywoods had all three in large measure. Thomas Hayward's father was contacted by the irrepressible Nessy, and he advised her thus:

> I will therefore take the liberty, my dear young lady, of requesting you to make all possible interest with all your friends, that application be made to his Majesty, so as to be prepared against the most fearful consequences of the impending trial, as I well know that Mr. Bligh's representations to the Admiralty are by no means favourable.[6]

It was clear to the Heywoods that the real source of danger in legal terms was the testimony of Bligh. At that moment Bligh was away in the Pacific and not likely to return for another eighteen months. Bligh's testimony therefore consisted of written evidence that he had handed over to the Admiralty. While this was damaging, it was not necessarily damning; without verbal evidence to answer qualifications, deal with quibbles, answer charges and so on, written evidence is as inflexible as it is specific. The legal case against Heywood could have been influenced very much by the presence of Captain Bligh in the court room, able to answer any points that arose in the defence testimony of the prisoners. Thus the strategy of the Heywood family was clear: to get the trial over before Bligh came back; to secure testimony in Heywood's favour from officers who came away with Bligh; to concentrate the defence on destroying the credibility of the specific charges against Heywood made by witnesses for the prosecution; and to undermine Bligh's credibility by the informal means open to them through their family connections. In all these aims they were successful.

The family view of Heywood's conduct is candidly presented by Nessy Heywood in a letter to Peter, sent on his return in H.M.S. *Hector*. She wrote:

> I will not ask you, my beloved brother, whether you are innocent of the dreadful crime of mutiny; if the transactions of that day were as Mr. Bligh has represented them, such is my conviction of your worth and honour, that I will, without hesitation, stake my life on your innocence. If, on the contrary, you were concerned in such a conspiracy against your commander, I shall be as firmly persuaded *his* conduct was the occasion of it. But alas! could any occasion justify so atrocious an attempt to destroy a number of our fellow-creatures? No, my ever dearest brother, nothing but conviction from your own mouth can possibly persuade me that you would commit an action in the smallest degree inconsistent with honour and duty; and the circu.. stance of your having swam off to the Pandora, on her arrival at Otaheite (which filled us with joy to which no words can

[6] *ibid.*, p. 38.

do justice), is sufficient to convince all who know you, that you certainly staid behind either by force or from views of preservation.[7]

We will see that this was one of the major lines of reasoning behind the Heywood family campaign. Miss Heywood went on in this letter to tell Peter that the family was pulling all possible strings on his behalf. She wrote: 'We are at present making all possible interest with every friend and connexion we have, to insure you a sufficient support and protection at your approaching trial; ... But, alas! while circumstances are against you, the generality of mankind will judge severely. Bligh's representations to the Admiralty are, I am told, very unfavourable, and hitherto the tide of public opinion had been greatly in his favour.'[8]

One of the instruments of family interest was Commodore Pasley, an uncle of Peter's, who at the time commanded the *Vengeance*, and was in a position to intervene on his behalf with his friend, Captain Montagu, captain of H.M.S. *Hector* where the prisoners were confined. He was under few illusions about young Heywood's predicament. He reported to Nessie: 'They have been most rigorously and closely confined since taken, and will continue so, I have no doubt, till Bligh's arrival ... I cannot conceal it from you, my dearest Nessy, neither is it proper I should – your brother appears by all accounts to be the greatest culprit of all, Christian alone excepted. Every exertion, you may rest assured, I shall use to save his life, but on trial I have no hope of his not being condemned. Three of the ten who are expected are mentioned in Bligh's narrative as men detained against their inclination. Would to God your brother had been one of that number!'[9]

Another correspondent quoted by Tagart was a 'J.C. Curwen'. His letter, according to Tagart, had the 'same or still darker views of Peter's connection with the mutiny'. It is a great pity that we do not have the original, because J.C. Curwen was in fact the head of the Christian family, John Christian Curwen. As we saw, he had changed his name from John Christian to Curwen, his wife's name, in 1790 when the news of the *Bounty* mutiny reached Britain. One passage of Curwen's letter is given by Tagart: 'His extreme youth,' wrote Curwen, 'is much in his favour, and I wish to God, for your sakes, it may extenuate a fault, the extent of which I dare say was not foreseen or considered. It would be cruel to flatter you; and however painful, I think it just to say, that unless some favourable circumstances should appear, any interest which can be made will be of little avail.'[10]

The former members of the *Bounty* crew who could be called in evidence at the trial were all approached by the Heywoods. Their replies to letters sent enquiring their views of Peter's part in the mutiny identified both friendly and hostile witnesses. It was the division of opinion among the witnesses that gave them hope. Hallet, for example, took a pro-Bligh line. 'I shall begin with

[7] *ibid.*, pp. 41-3.
[8] *ibid.*, pp. 46-7.
[9] *ibid.*
[10] Tagart, 1832, pp. 47-8; Edward Christian also made enquiries about Heywood on his return, *see* Edward Edwards, private papers, Admiralty Library, Fulham.

saying,' he wrote, 'that before the unfortunate period at which the mutiny in the Bounty took place, the conduct of your brother was such as to have procured him our universal esteem. But what were the unpropitious motives by which he was induced to side with the criminal party, I am totally ignorant of, nor can I (as you may readily conceive it was a time of great confusion among us) declare positively the part he acted in it.'[11] As Hallet was likely to be the most hostile of witnesses, the above letter confessing an inability to declare positively what part Heywood played in the mutiny was a message of even greater hope. While interested parties, such as the family and the head of the Christian family, were warning that the evidence on the table from Bligh was damaging to Heywood's case, the main witnesses for the prosecution were displaying a contrasting lack of certainty about what he actually did. This meant the court would have to decide rather on the legal merits of his presence on the *Bounty* while the mutiny was in progress than on direct evidence as to his actual role. In these circumstances, the defence could shift the whole case onto a judgment about Heywood's character and integrity, for which the friends of the family could campaign remorselessly outside the court.

When John Fryer, former Master of the *Bounty* and a personal enemy of Bligh, wrote to Heywood he was decidedly positive in his advice: 'Keep up your spirits, for I am of opinion, no one can say you had an active part in the mutiny, and be assured of my doing you justice when called upon.'[12] Commodore Pasley, a senior naval officer, used his office to effect. He personally interviewed John Fryer and William Cole (the *Bounty*'s Boatswain) and pronounced them 'favourable witnesses'. He travelled from Portsmouth to Woolwich and Deptford to see William Peckover, Gunner, and William Purcell, Carpenter. He declared them both 'favourable' witnesses. He went to the Admiralty, and 'read over all the depositions taken and sent home by Bligh and his officers from Batavia, likewise the court martial on himself; in none of which appears any thing against Peter'.[13] Everything pointed to the benefits of an early trial before Bligh returned.

Heywood's uncle, Pasley, sent a legal adviser to see Heywood on H.M.S. *Hector*. Heywood wrote to his elder sister, Mary Heywood, of the visit by Mr Delafons, 'who, after inquiring into the particulars relative to my situation, advised me to write a petition to the Lords Commissioners of the Admiralty to grant me a speedy trial, the form of which he was so good as to draw up and send me on Tuesday. I hope it may have the desired effect of speedily making my guilt or innocence known to the world, and of relieving me from the miserable state of anxiety and suspence I am now in.'[14] The petition was delivered to the Admiralty in July 1792. The inference from Heywood's

---

[11] Tagart, 1832, pp. 11-12.

[12] *ibid.*, p. 62.

[13] *ibid.*, p. 65; Pasley's conviction that Purcell was a friendly witness was wrong, in so far as Purcell testified that he had seen Heywood with a cutlass in his hand during the mutiny.

[14] *ibid.*, pp. 62-3; this letter was dated 5 July 1792. On 15 July Commodore Pasley was writing to Nessy Heywood: 'As soon as Lieut. Hayward arrives with the remainder of the Pandora's crew, the court martial is to take place', *ibid.*, p. 65.

action is that a delayed trial might have jeopardised his case, even though it might have helped the others.[15]

Commodore Pasley did not cease his efforts at this point; he in fact became more committed to Heywood's cause, somewhat encouraged, we must believe, by the realisation of the weaknesses in the case against him. After sending Mr Delafons to Heywood to draw up the petition for the early trial he sent Aaron Graham to act as legal counsel for Heywood in the approaching trial. Aaron Graham had been a secretary to various Admirals for twelve years on the Newfoundland station and had acted as judge-advocate in many court martials. 'He has a thorough knowledge of the service, uncommon abilities, and is a very good lawyer', wrote Pasley to Heywood. His attendance at the trial was of great significance for Heywood because it provided his defence with a first-class experienced naval lawyer.

Pasley was also active in other areas. Captain Albemarle Bertie was related to Heywood's family by marriage; he was also in command of a ship at Spithead. Pasley hoped to get a friend to supply Heywood with some money, and found that in fact Captain Bertie was already doing this. There is nothing untoward in a relative helping out in these circumstances, but the relative in question was to become one of the trial judges at the court martial. The powerful web of interest of the Heywood family was not merely pushing for an early trial befoore Bligh got back, but was also able to extend its goodwill into the court-room, with a top naval lawyer retained for the defence, a family member sitting in judgment, and witnesses for the prosecution who were 'very favourable indeed'. It is possible that the Heywood interest promised them good postings in return for their favourable evidence.

The court martial took place on H.M.S. *Duke* from Wednesday, 12 September to Tuesday, 18 September 1792, under the presidency of Lord Hood, Commander-in-Chief of the fleet at Spithead.[16] Eleven Post-Captains made up the court, namely: Sir Andrew Snape Hamond, John Colpoys, George Montagu, John Bazeley, John Thomas Duckworth, John Knight, Richard Goodwin Keats, Sir Roger Curtis, Sir Andrew Douglas, John Nicholson Inglefield and Albemarle Bertie.[17] The prisoners were charged with 'mutinously running away with the said armed vessel the "Bounty" and

[15] It has been suggested that Bligh was somehow responsible for the trial's taking place without him – that if he had been there he would have betrayed the real cause of the mutiny as being his own 'coarseness of nature, tyrannous conduct and base outrages upon Christian' (MacFarland, 1884, p. 75). This is absurd.

[16] Several authorities have dated the trial as 12-18 August instead of 12-18 September. The source of the error lies in the incorrect date on the original pamphlet describing the trial published in 1792 by Stephen Barney, which contained the Appendix written by Edward Christian. There is no doubt that the trial took place in September 1792; *see* Rutter (ed.), 1931. Wilkinson, 1953, possibly got the date wrong because his book used Edward Christian's Appendix for its source material.

[17] Besides Heywood's uncle by marriage among the Court members, he also had Captain George Montagu of H.M.S. *Hector* to whom Commodore Pasley referred in glowing terms in several letters to Heywood's relative: 'every attention and indulgence possible is granted him [Peter] by Captain Montagu of the Hector, who is my particular friend.' Letter to Miss Heywood, 15 July 1792, in Tagart, 1832, p. 64

deserting from His Majesty's Service'. The written evidence from Bligh was entered into the records. This consisted of his letter to Secretary Stephens of the Admiralty, dated 18 August 1789, which was his first official description of the circumstances of the mutiny, and an extract from his *Narrative* of 1790. A letter from Captain Edwards to the Admiralty written at Batavia, 25 November 1791, was also entered in the record. This presumably detailed his activities in capturing the mutineers and his knowledge, such as it was, of the whereabouts of the missing mutineers with Christian. It is normal procedure, according to Owen Rutter, for written depositions from persons who are alive not to be accepted as evidence because this prevented the court from cross-questioning their authors. Bligh's documents were, however, admissible as evidence, on the grounds that where a public official records facts for the information of the Crown there is a legal presumption that his record is true when so made.[18]

It suited Heywood's defence that these documents should be the ones accepted by court, because he was not mentioned in either. His defence was ready to take even further advantage of this situation, and attempted to get him tried separately from the others. The Court had received a request from Peter Heywood to be tried separately 'by the advice of my friends'. The association of Heywood with a trial in which the guilt of some of the prisoners was presumed weakened his case, and if he had succeeded in separating himself off from them he would have been in a good position to be found not guilty. The court rejected his request, deciding that the 'whole of the prisoners must be tried together'. This had two consequences: firstly it established at least, in the minds of the court, the individual claims of Peter Heywood; and secondly, it created the legal technicality which was to get Musprat a pardon.

Rather than present a verbatim account of the trial and the evidence for and against each of the ten prisoners, I have drawn on Owen Rutter's excellent summaries of the cases against the ten prisoners to present a rapid survey. In many ways what happened in the couple of months after the trial is more important than what took place during it, and it is the subsequent period on which I will concentrate rather than the trial itself.

The case against Peter Heywood was largely based on his neutrality during the mutiny. Neutrality was a crime, as Pasley told Nessy Heywood: 'our martial law is severe; by the tenour of it, the man who stands neuter is equally guilty with him who lifts his arm against his captain in such cases.'[19] The defence to that charge was to convince the court that he was not neutral, that through his extreme youth and confusion he did not know what to do, and that his intention was to leave the ship with his Captain but he was prevented from doing so by force.

The witnesses gave varying degrees of comfort to Heywood's defence. Fryer stated he had not seen Heywood during the mutiny; this was supported by Peckover, but then he slipped up and stated that he had

[18] Rutter (ed.), 1931, pp. 47-8.
[19] Tagart, 1832, p. 65.

supposed everybody who had remained on the ship, except those mentioned by Bligh (Coleman, Norman, McIntosh and Byrne), to be in Christian's party. He had to be given an opportunity to correct this by Heywood's defence on cross-examination. William Cole was more helpful in positively stating that he thought Heywood was on Bligh's side and that he did not see him armed. He was also able to corroborate indirectly Heywood's claim to have been held by force, by telling the court he heard Churchill shout out to somebody below to keep someone down there, but he did not know to whom this referred. When pressed he said it could have been Heywood. William Purcell, the Carpenter, while supporting the story that somebody had been held below by force, delivered a blow to Heywood's defence when he announced that he had seen him on deck armed with a cutlass. This was a specific instance of evidence that could hang Heywood, and though Purcell shifted under questioning on the implications of Heywood's action, he did not shift on the basic point that at some time on the deck the prisoner had held a cutlass.[20]

When Hayward and Hallet came to give evidence the case against Heywood took a further turn for the worse. Hayward told the court that he had told Heywood to get into the boat and that 'I should rather suppose after my having told him to go into the Boat, and he not joining us, to be on the side of the Mutineers'.[21] Hallet's evidence was even more damning for Heywood. He said: 'Captain Bligh said something to him, but what I did not hear, upon which he laughed, turned round and walked away'.[22] Even under strong pressure from the defence Hallet would not alter his story. Heywood's defence was in difficulties if the court believed these witnesses, even though they had nothing more specific against him than that he had held a cutlass for a little while, that he had not got into the boat and that he had laughed at something Captain Bligh had said to him.

In defence Heywood asked the court's leave, which was granted, to have a written statement read to the court by Mr Const, one of his advisers and probably author of the statement. It is a verbose treatment of the mutiny, somewhat flowery in expression. Mr Const must have read it with great effect. Heywood's defence was that he was asleep when the mutiny occurred and that he knew nothing of it. When he went up on deck and saw his Captain a prisoner he was 'benumbed' and 'did not recover the power of recollection until called to by somebody to take hold of the tackle fall and assist to get out the launch.' In this 'state of absolute stupor' he may have handled a cutlass, but innocently. He had not realised, owing to his 'extreme youth and inexperience', that he had to make a choice between the boat and the ship, and he was also influenced by the behaviour of his seniors, Hayward and Hallet, who when ordered to get into the boat by Christian entreated him not to send them away; Hayward even burst into tears at the prospect. He further went on to plead that if he had got into the boat it might

[20] *See* Rutter (ed.), 1931, pp. 100-12; Tagart, 1832, p. 96.
[21] Rutter (ed.), 1931, p. 121.
[22] *ibid.*, p. 126.

have sunk with his extra weight, so close was the gunwale to the water. He denied he had spoken with Captain Bligh, much less laughed at anything he said. He also categorically denied that he had ever engaged in activities inimical to Captain Bligh: 'Indeed,' Heywood's deposition stated,' from his attention to and very kind treatment of me personally, I should have been a Monster of depravity to have betray'd him – The Idea alone is sufficient to disturb a mind where humanity and gratitude have, I hope, ever been noticed as its Characteristic features'.[23]

His defence was credible in that, if the court believed that he had been detained on board by force, they could hardly convict him when they failed to convict Coleman, Norman and McIntosh, who were not detained by force but by Captain Bligh's orders. The court, however, did convict him, presumably on the grounds that he had made no public appeal to Christian or statement to Captain Bligh during the mutiny that would have made clear his affiliations. Once the court decided they had to convict him and on this score, they could only sentence him to death – mutiny allows no lesser penalty – but they could exercise their prerogative and recommend him for the King's mercy, which they did.

James Morrison, the Boatswain's Mate, was also in the grey area of culpability. His story was more dubious than Heywood's, and he had much less interest to call on. Fryer was able to testify that he had not seen Morrison under arms, and though Cole was able to corroborate this detail of Morrison's conduct, he also made the point to the court that he had not heard Morrison express any desire to get into the boat with Captain Bligh, nor to his knowledge did anybody stop him from doing so. Purcell's testimony supported Fryer's that he did not consider him to be one of the mutineers. Hayward came close to charging him with complicity with the mutiny, but this seemed to be based more on an interpretation of Morrison's 'countenance' in comparison to that of others, such as McIntosh, who were clearly innocent, than anything really substantial. Hallet, against the trend of the other witnesses, stated that Morrison had been under arms. This was said to have been at the time when the launch was astern of the *Bounty*, and he was alleged to have said to the men in the boat: 'If my friends enquire after me, tell them I am somewhere in the South Seas'.[24] Cole said he heard something like that said, but Fryer claimed he had not seen him at the taffrail at all.

Morrison, like Heywood, took advantage of the time during the preparations of the trial and the days of evidence to prepare a written statement in 'vindication of my conduct' which was read to the court by the judge-advocate. His written statement is familiar in style (and spelling) to

---

[23] *ibid.*, pp. 137-143. Another example will suffice to show the tone of the statement: 'Yet if I am found Guilty this day they will not construe it, I trust, as the least disrespect offered to their discernment and opinion if I solemnly declare that my Heart will rely with confidence in its own innocence until that awful period when my Spirit shall be about to be separated from my body to take its everlasting flight and be ushered into the presence of that unerring Judge, before whom all Hearts are open, and from whom no Secrets are hid' (p. 148).

[24] *ibid.*, p. 127.

anyone who has read his Journal and was clearly written unaided by legal counsel. Nevertheless, it displays a 'sea lawyer's' mind. On the charge of his countenance having been one of rejoicing he replies thus: 'My countenance has also been compared with that of another employ'd on the same business. This Honorable Court knows that all Men do not bear misfortunes with the same fortitude or equanimity of Mind, and that the face is too often a bad index to the Heart. If there were No sorrow mark'd in my Countenance, it was to deceive those whose Act I abhorred, that I might be at liberty to seize the first Opportunity that might appear favourable, to the retaking of the ship.'[25] This was ingenious, but hardly convincing. It all depended on how much notice the court took of the implications of his behaviour, for there was nothing specific stated against him in court or in Bligh's documents.

Morrison's next hurdle was to convince the court that his motive for not getting into the boat with Captain Bligh was a reasoned decision, rather than of his support of the mutiny. Morrison's style was certainly clever, probably a bit too clever. He wrote: 'Let the Members of this Honorable Court Suppose themselves in my then unfortunate situation, and it will appear doubtful even to them, Which alternative they would have taken. A Boat alongside already crowded, those who were in her Crying Out she would sink, and Captain Bligh desiring no more might go in, with a slender stock of Provisions; what hope could there be to reach any Friendly Shore, or withstand the boisterous attacks of Hostile Elements? The Perils those underwent who reached the Island of Timor, and whom Nothing but the Apparent Interference of Divine Providence could have saved, fully Justify my fears, and prove beyond a Doubt, that they rested on a solid foundation; for by staying in the Ship an opportunity might offer of escaping, but by going in the Boat nothing but Death appeared, either from the lingering torments of Thirst and Hunger, or from the Murderous Weapons of Cruel Savages, or being Swallowed up by the Deep.'[26] How the court would react to this plea would depend on their inclination towards the logic of his choice – staying on the ship was evidently the safest course, though it might have been the improper course for a loyal British seaman if it meant abandoning his Captain.

He denied the charge that he was under arms at the taffrail, pleading that in the press somebody next to him with a weapon could have been mistaken for him, and he made the same claim about the words that Hayward testified he heard Morrison say. Morrison asked the court to wonder why he should have taken up arms at the last moment when Bligh and the loyalists were already in the boat.

The court convicted him of mutiny, presumably on similar grounds to those on which they convicted Heywood, in that his positive opposition to the mutiny had not been made explicit enough to witnesses, even if his part in the mutiny had not been made explicit either. If Heywood could be recommended for a pardon – owing partly to the intense lobbying on his

[25] *ibid.*, p. 166.
[26] *ibid.*, pp. 166-7.

behalf outside the court – it was not unreasonable to expect that Morrison would also be recommended for pardon, as their plights and their pleas, with the exception of the 'extreme youth' gambit from the Heywood camp, were similar.

Norman, Coleman and McIntosh had been specifically mentioned by Bligh in his Coupang despatch as being 'detained against their inclination' and this meant that their trial was a formality. The court, having heard the formal evidence, none of which contradicted Bligh's, acquitted them. In a similar action, Michael Byrne, the near-blind seaman, was acquitted by the court. He was in no physical condition to participate in the mutiny and his affliction was good enough reason for not getting in the boat. The testimony of Fryer and others that Byrne had indeed got into one of the boats ready to leave with Captain Bligh, but had been left behind when the orders were changed, was compelling evidence in his favour.

This left the remaining four prisoners, for whom no real plea of innocence was tenable. Ellison was named by several witnesses as being under arms, acting as a sentry, and obeying instructions from Christian. He had no chance of avoiding conviction, and in spite of his 'extreme youth' he had little chance of a recommendation of mercy, especially as he had no powerful family to plead for him.

Thomas Burkitt was one of the men who entered Bligh's cabin under arms to arrest him and witnesses testified to this to the court. With that testimony and no denial from Burkitt he was a certainty for conviction. He pleaded that he was under arms because of threats of instant death from Christian, McCoy and Churchill. It did not convince the court, and he was sentenced to be hanged.[27] Millward's defence was even weaker than Burkitt's. He was seen under arms and had acted as a sentry. The court convicted him and sentenced him to death.

Musprat was in a slightly more secure position than Ellison, Burkitt or Millward: some of the main witnesses had not seen him under arms, and neither Fryer nor Hallet remembered seeing him at all. Hayward and Cole saw him with a musket but Musprat claimed that he was armed with the intention of assisting Fryer's retaking of the ship. This alleged plan of Fryer's to retake the ship had been mentioned several times in the evidence over the days, and Musprat hung his defence on it; as Fryer had not actually made a real move to retake the ship, Musprat was not required to prove his intentions by reference to deeds. But his defence was not entirely convincing. The court convicted him.

---

[27] Burkitt said in evidence after his written statement had been read out: 'The foregoing is a copy of a narrative that was written soon after I left the 'Bounty' and had got clear of Christian and his Party – foreseeing, that either, sooner or later, myself, as well as every other person on board, would be obliged to render an account of our Conduct and the Motives by which we were actuated.' (*ibid.*, p. 189). This is an intriguing piece of evidence about the existence of Journals among the *Bounty* crew at Tahiti. The fact that his statement was a 'copy' could mean it was a replacement for a lost journal, or the copy of an actual one. If the latter, one might ask, as with Morrison's Journals, where he preserved it through the wreck of the *Pandora*. Burkitt's testimony was a detailed description of the mutiny – the only testimony the Court heard of what happened from one of the mutineers.

However, Musprat had not finished, even with a death sentence over him. His lawyer, Stephen Barney, was resourceful and concocted a legal defence that worked. By trying all the men together and deciding their cases together the court had created a legal loophole through which Musprat was able to get free. He alleged that he wanted to call Norman and Byrne as witnesses for his defence. He asked the court to acquit Norman and Byrne so that he could call them, but the court declined to acquit them until it had heard the entire case against everybody. After the trial Musprat put in an immediate plea that he had been wrongly convicted by being prevented from calling witnesses not guilty of mutiny to testify for him (their evidence being as credible as that given by other witnesses for the defence who had not been charged) while in a civil court he would have been allowed to call them. On this technical appeal his hanging was postponed until the Judges on the King's Bench could rule. He had to wait in custody until 11 February before he heard that they had found in favour of his complaint and he was discharged a free man. In the meantime the other three had been hanged. It would have been interesting to test this ruling by having all the prisoners make a similar plea. Only Musprat's lawyer was clever enough to spot it. We may also note that if Heywood's plea to be tried separately had been accepted and each case had then been tried separately, Musprat might very well have hanged.[28]

The court's decision, given on Tuesday, 18 September 1792, was that 'the Charges had been proved against the said Peter Heywood, James Morrison, Thomas Ellison, Thomas Burkitt, John Millward and William Musprat', and it 'did adjudge them and each of them to suffer Death by being hanged by the Neck, on board such of His Majesty's Ship or Ships of War, at such Time or Times and at such Place or Places, as the Commissioners for executing the Office of Lord High Admiral of Great Britain and Ireland etc. or any three of them, for the Time being, should in Writing, under their Hands direct; but the Court, in Consideration of various Circumstances, did humbly and most earnestly recommend the said Peter Heywood and James Morrison to His Majesty's Royal Mercy – and the Court further agreed That the Charges had not been proved against the said Charles Norman, Joseph Coleman, Thomas McIntosh and Michael Byrn, and did adjudge them and each of them to be acquitted'.[29]

---

[28] For an account of the legal processes that took place on the basis of Musprat's petition *see* Smith, 1936, pp. 232-7.
[29] Rutter (ed.), 1931, pp. 198-9.

18

The Voyage in the *Providence*

Bligh's life from 1791 to 1793 was taken up with his voyage in the *Providence*. I shall deal in subsequent chapters with the events that took place after the trial of the mutineers, and what happened in London in the year before Bligh returned.[1] As we saw, the attempt to transplant breadfruit had not exhausted official interest in the venture and neither had Bligh's failure exhausted official interest in him. Due to the efforts of Sir Joseph Banks, in March 1791 the King authorised a second breadfruit expedition and the appointment of Captain William Bligh to command it. This time a great deal more notice was taken of Bligh's views as to what the expedition required. He had lamented at length to his superiors the inadequate provision of the *Bounty* expedition, in particular the smallness of the armed vessel, the absence of a party of marines, the thinness of the command structure, the quality of the men sent with him as petty officers, and the delay of the sailing instructions.

Bligh chose as his ship the newly built West Indiaman, the *Providence*, and to assist in the intricate navigation of the Torres Strait he was also given a small brig, the *Assistant*. He chose Nathaniel Portlock[2] to command her, who had sailed with him on Cook's third voyage. His own second-in-command on the *Providence* was Francis Godolphin Bond, a son of his half-sister, Catherine; he and Bligh had corresponded for years.[3] Bligh was recommended to take a young midshipman named Matthew Flinders,

[1] My account of this voyage is based on Lee, 1920 (which also contains the Journal of Nathaniel Portlock), and Bligh, *Log of H.M.S. Providence, 1791-3*, ML MS A564-1, A564-2. The Admiralty's copy of the Log (a transcription of which, made by Ida Lee, is in the Mitchell Library, MS 75/20-22) shows variations in style and minor details, made by Bligh, in George Mackaness' opinion, with a view to publication. Lieutenant George Tobin's Journal, a copy of his official Log deposited with the Admiralty at the conclusion of the voyage as was the custom, is also available in the Mitchell Library (Tobin A562). Lieutenant F.G. Bond's Log of the *Providence* is in the Public Record Office, London.

[2] Nathaniel Portlock entered the navy in 1772 and in 1776 was rated Master's Mate in the *Discovery* by Captain Clerke. He joined the *Resolution* in 1779 after the death of Cook. He became a Lieutenant in 1780, serving in a channel ship, H.M.S. *Firebrand*, and overtaking Bligh in the promotion ladder. In 1785 he commanded a voyage to the north-west coast of America in H.M.S. *King George* (a small vessel of 320 tons) and wrote an account of his voyage on his return. After the *Providence* voyage, 1791-3, he is listed as commanding the *Arrow* sloop and in an action in September of that year he captured a Dutch ship, the *Draack*. He died on 12 September 1817 after several years in Greenwich Hospital. In view of his undoubted abilities as a seaman and commander, shown particularly on the *Assistant*, his relative obscurity and confinement to small ship commands is remarkable. Like many other talented men in the Royal Navy, he may not have had the necessary interest or patronage to secure better commands.

[3] Bligh-Bond Correspondence, 1776-1811, *Australian Historical Monographs*, No. 19, Sydney, 1949, also ML MS Ab 60/11.

through the offices of none other than Captain Thomas Pasley, the uncle of Peter Heywood.[4] Bligh also took a small party of marines under the command of Lieutenant Thomas Pearce.

The expedition sailed from Spithead on 3 August 1791, almost four years after the *Bounty* had tried to leave Spithead on its last voyage. Bligh decided to sail the Cape of Good Hope route to the South Seas rather than the quicker route via Cape Horn, even though he was sailing at a time of year suitable for doubling the Horn. He was taking no chances. There is also the possibility that as he had not properly recovered from his ordeals he decided that he was not well enough to take the strain of the Cape Horn passage.

The Log of the *Providence* shows that Bligh immediately instituted a similar regime of management to the one he had established in the *Bounty*. He put the ship on three watches 'as an encouragement to the People to be alert in the execution of their duty as well as from considering it conducive to their health'. Instead of giving the Master the command of a watch, as he had done with John Fryer, he did not specify a watch for him but stated he was 'to be ready at all calls'. He ordered an officer from each watch to tend a fire to dry out the clothes of the watch and he also instituted the regular cleaning and drying below that is familiar from a reading of the *Bounty* Log.

At Tenerife Bligh became ill, and he remained on the sick list almost until the ships reached the Cape of Good Hope. His illness necessitated a temporary change in command: he brought Portlock across from the *Assistant* to command the expedition and sent Bond to replace him as Commander of the *Assistant*.[5] At Table Bay Bligh had the following recorded in the Log: 'I ordered the Ships Companies to be victualled with fresh Mutton, Greens, & soft Bread every day, and directed the Surgeon to send all such persons to Sick Quarters, who he thought would require the advantage of the land air. Perhaps no Ship's Company ever required less attention in this particular than our own; but a few of them having embarked with virulent venereal complaints, it was necessary to do every thing to eradicate the remains.'[6]

He was not fully recovered from his illness and had to get the ship's Surgeon, Edward Harwood, to write his correspondence, among which was the following letter to his wife, sent from Santiago on 13 September 1791:[7]

---

[4] It is clear from a letter Pasley wrote to Flinders (quoted in Mackaness, 1951, p. 235) that Pasley used his influence with Bligh to get Flinders a position on the *Providence*. Flinders was to become a talented cartographer and navigator; in later life he felt his own contribution to Bligh's work had not been fully acknowledged, and some biographers of Flinders have criticised Bligh for not specifically recommending Flinders for promotion after the voyage. *See* Flinders, 1814; Scott 1914. From papers in the Flinders collection, Public Library of Victoria, Melbourne, it seems that he kept in touch with Wiles, the botanist on the *Providence*, for many years; he remarks to him in a letter, 5 March 1812: 'Our old friend Bligh introduced me with my charts the other day to the Duke of Clarence. He is remarkably obliging and attentive to me: yet I have been very far from courting his friendship, but I believe he is proud to have had me for his disciple in surveying and nautical astronomy.'

[5] Bond was a senior man, connected with Nelson by marriage, and ambitious; Darby, 1966, suggests that he was disappointed at not getting command of the *Providence*.

[6] *Log of the Providence*, 7 November 1791.

[7] Bligh Family Correspondence, ML MS Safe 1/45. The letter is torn in some places and I have suggested possible words.

My Dear Betsy,

I beg you will not be alarmed at not seeing my own handwriting. Am vastly recovered since my [last letter to] you from Teneriffe – but as my [illness] is of a nervous kind, Mr Harwood thought it improper for me to attempt writing. I anchored here to day to procure a little fruit, and shall leave it by midnight, as I find it an unhealthy time of the year. I am now taking the bark, and feel considerably stronger; so that hope before we reach the cape to be perfectly re-established in my health: from thence shall give you a full account, how I have proceeded – I am confident it is ordained for us once more to meet, you may therefore cherish your dear little Girls in that happy hope.

My blessing to them all and with that affectionate esteem and regard you have ever known me, I remain, yr sincere & affecte. Husband Wm Bligh. God bless you my Dear Love & my little angles.

Mr Harwood has wrote the letter. God bless and preserve you. This letter goes by a Vessel to Boston.

Port. I have written to Sir J Banks but no one else. You will therefore remember me kindly to your Uncle and Family.

Bligh was not really fit enough for this voyage, but his failure to complete the original mission might have meant the end of his career or at least a block to all further promotion, so he had not been able to refuse the chance to redeem himself and to justify Sir Joseph Banks' confidence in him. However, his eagerness to prove himself almost killed him. Bad health plagued him throughout the entire voyage and he only picked up in the last lap. Even in the Log one gets the impression of a less exuberant, less confident man than the man who set out on *Bounty*.

A week before landfall at Table Bay the Log records the first flogging on either of the two vessels. John Letby, Quartermaster, refused orders from Mr Impey (one of the Mates) and in an altercation knocked down F. Barber, the Boatswain's Mate, for which he was awarded thirty lashes.[8]

At the Cape they met Captain John Hunter of the *Sirius*, which had sunk off Norfolk Island near Australia.[9] The ships stayed in the port for a couple of months, but on 20 December 1791 Bligh gave final orders to Portlock who was to return to command of the *Assistant*, stating at which places they would rendezvous. Before he left, Bligh wrote to Sir Joseph Banks, in one letter making several pertinent remarks about the new colony of New South Wales and the character of Captain John Hunter, at that time its Deputy Governor. He thought that the British Government should send out cattle to the new colony, which would help manure the poor soil there; 'untill it is done there will be eternal discontent and little returns'.[10] Bligh also suggested that a couple of sloops should be sent out to be used on coastal exploration, which was in line with his own interest in cartography and navigation. His midshipman, Matthew Flinders, may have been inspired by these suggestions, in that he later became one of Australia's map-makers, unfortunately on his

[8] Lee, 1920, p. 5. There were only twelve floggings in the two-year voyage; Rutter, 1936, p. 171.
[9] *See* Hunter, 1793.
[10] Bligh to Banks, 7 December 1791.

own responsibility and using vessels totally inadequate for the job. Of John
Hunter Bligh wrote perceptively: 'I may pronounce with some certainty that
the present second in command ... is not blessed with a moderate share of
good knowledge to give much stability to the new settlement.' As Bligh
remarks in his letter, he was about to chart the northern passage between
Australia and New Guinea.[11] Bligh would have been an excellent person to
complete a full survey of the coasts of Australia. In the absence of military duty
this would have been one way to climb in his naval career and in the public
esteem. Possibly his letter and interest in the colony were remembered by
Banks when the post of Governor came up in 1806; he encouraged Bligh to
accept nomination.

Just before the ships left Table Bay George Tobin recorded in his Journal
a comment on his commander. It is worth noting here, for it is one of the few
surviving comments on Bligh written in confidence by one of his officers with
no eye to publication. First he has a passage that is tantalising in its double
meaning: 'A few passing squalls had taken us, within board as well as without,
but by clewing up in time, without any serious mischief.'[12] He seems to be
referring not just to the weather but also to the atmosphere on the ship. A
sudden squall could have been an outburst from Bligh who, on the few
occasions when he felt fit enough to inspect the ship, might have noticed some
slackness or mistake being made about which he would naturally speak
bluntly. But presumably by snapping to it and removing the object of
displeasure the junior officers got through the inspection without too much
pain. Tobin goes on to write:[13]

> For myself James [his brother], I began to feel at home in the charge of a
> watch nor without considering my appointment to the *Providence* as a very
> flattering one particularly as she was the first ship in which I had made my
> debut as a commissioned Officer. In her Commander I had to encounter the
> quickest sailors eye, guided by a thorough knowledge of every branch of the
> profession necessary on such a voyage. He had been Master with the
> persevering Cook in his last voyage in 1776, and as has been already
> noticed, commanded the *Bounty* Armed Ship, when the first attempt was
> made to convey the Bread fruit Tree to the West Indies. It is easy of belief
> that on first joining a man of such experience, my own youth and inferiority
> were rather busy visitors. They were, but we had by this time crossed the
> equinoctial, and were about doubling the Cape together and I had courage
> to believe that, my Captain was not dissatisfied with me.

Tobin was a very talented artist and drew and painted dozens of pictures of
the voyage.[14] Owing to Bligh's illness, he had been able to get in a lot of

---

[11] Matthew Flinders, 1814, included 'with the permission of Captain Bligh' Bligh's charts of
the Torres Strait made in the *Providence*.

[12] Tobin, Journal, A562, p. 85. To clew is to haul on a line which shortens the sail. This is
done in a sudden gust to prevent the sails being split by the wind, or the rigging being put under
too great a strain.

[13] *ibid.*, pp. 85-6.

[14] He made a hundred or more water-colour sketches on the journey. Black and white
reproductions of these are available (ML PX A565), but they do not do them justice. Among

practice in charge of his watch before he had to deal with Bligh's style of command at first hand. His own view was that he had passed the initial critical test of Bligh's standards and indeed one can remark, reading the Logs and Journals and thinking of the *Bounty* and its sorry tales of incompetence, indifference and outright impudence on the part of its officers, that Bligh had with him on this voyage young men of an entirely different calibre.

The ships left Table Bay on 23 December 1791 and headed into the Indian Ocean for the passage to Adventure Bay. On the way Bligh surveyed St Paul Island and Amsterdam Island, which he had also passed in the *Bounty*. He noted that Mortimer did not mention these islands in his account of Captain Cox's voyage in the *Mercury*.[15] The Log shows that Bligh was conducting detailed surveys of everything within his reach that was of value to the Navy and continued this work throughout the entire voyage. This made for a leisurely pace, but speed was not very important to him. He knew that Edwards was ahead of him in the *Pandora*, searching for the mutineers, and he naturally assumed that, if they were found and taken home, they would be detained in Britain until his return before the inevitable trial. His intention was to carry through the voyage with his accustomed devotion to navigational and cartographic detail, complete the transplant of the breadfruit to the West Indies settlement, and return in triumph as a vindication of his abilities in command. He would then face the mutineers in court to ensure justice was done for his sufferings.

The ships reached Adventure Bay on 9 February 1792. The wooding and watering parties were sent ashore and they used the traditional places in both cases. The wooding party used the saw-pit that the *Bounty* had used, where Purcell had had his first public row with Bligh. George Tobin made some sketches of the Bay, including the wooding area, which are preserved in the Mitchell Library. These show the Bay as sheltered and tranquil, with tree-clothed hillsides coming down steeply to the water's edge. The *Providence* and the *Assistant* are shown from different angles with the ships' boats working to and fro. In a drawing of the wooding area, Tobin shows a marine standing guard under a tree while the men load the boat with the wood. Overhead there is a profusion of bird life including geese flying in formation. (See plate 4.)

It was Bligh's third visit to the Bay, and he took the opportunity to explore the area with a little more thoroughness than on his previous visits. This was made easier by the fact that he had reliable officers to whom he could delegate duties. Mackaness' account of Bligh's explorations notes the lack of official recognition for Bligh as one of Tasmania's early discoverers. Bligh made mistakes, in common with others at the time. It was many years before mariners realised that Tasmania was a separate island and not part of the Australian mainland. A few months after Bligh's third visit, Adventure Bay

---

them are many drawings of animals, birds and fish; in the same collection are several talented and sympathetic drawings and paintings by Bligh. See plates 4-6, 14 and 15.

[15] Lee, 1920, p. 14.

was discovered to be on a small island off the coast of Tasmania, not a part of Tasmania. This was discovered by D'Entrecasteaux while he was himself searching for La Pérouse.[16]

While Bligh was at Adventure Bay he and his officers took an interest in the flora and fauna, and their accounts go into considerable detail. Tobin's drawings are full of birds and fish and so are Bligh's. The expedition had two botanists among its establishment, a Mr Wiles and a Mr Smith. They set to work on reporting on the area. As on his previous visits, Bligh planted several fruit trees, and to commemorate his visit he had a message cut on a nearby tree: 'Near this tree Captain William Bligh planted seven fruit trees 1792: – Messrs. S. and W., botanists.'[17] When the Frenchman, Labillardière, visited the area in February 1793, he saw the inscriptions and remarked: 'Several inscriptions, engraved on the trunks of trees, acquainted us that Captain Bligh had anchored in this bay in the month of February 1792, when he was on his voyage to the Society Islands for bread-fruit trees'.[18] He went on to remark, bitterly, about the 'despotism which condemned men of science to initials and gave a sea captain a monopoly of fame'.[19] As a naturalist himself he was not entirely objective on this issue.

A few days before the ships sailed from the Bay a seaman by the name of Bennet went missing. Bligh had no intention of leaving him in Tasmania: his chances of survival without implements and supplies were minimal. There was no telling when the next ship would call. After a thorough search Bennet was found and returned to the *Assistant*.[20] On 24 February the ships sailed for the southern route round New Zealand. During this voyage Portlock came across from the *Assistant* to dine with Bligh, which suggests that his dining relationships had not deteriorated as they had done on the *Bounty* at this stage of the voyage. The ships were making the long sweep to the east to bring them into the prevailing winds for the run to Tahiti. A few days' sailing further east would have brought Bligh to Pitcairn Island where the settlement of Christian and his mutineers was going through its first troubled year. The fact that Edwards missed Pitcairn from the eastern approach to

[16] Mackaness, 1951, Chapter 14; *see* also Lord, 1922.

[17] Lee, 1920, p. 22n.

[18] Mackaness, 1951, pp. 241-2.

[19] Lee, 1920, p. 22; Labillardière, 1800.

[20] *Log of the Providence*, 20 February 1792; 'Search was made after him, & guns fired from the Ship, We could hear no tydings of him. – Fires were made about the shore for the Night, & I directed a light to be kept all Night at the Ships Masts heads, that the poor fellow might find his way to the Bay ... I directed two Parties to be ready to Set off in the Morning, each under the command of a Lieutenant, to search for the poor Man who was absent ... The Parties who were sent particularly after the Man, whose name is Bennet, missed him; but very fortunately Mr. Pearce, the Lieut. of Marines, and the Gardiners found him a little from the Beach, & brought him to me where I was observing. It is wonderful to relate that this unhappy creature has determined to Stay behind with a wish to perish & never return to his Native Country. I found that he was of creditable Parents, but had been a disgrace to them, therefore they had recommended him to go this Voyage, as the most elligible either to improve or send him to destruction. I had many of these impertinent or thoughtless recommendations. Our minds were now at ease – the Man was kindly taken care of, and I ordered the Ships to be towed further out of the Bay.' Bligh's remarks show his capacity to distinguish between criminal desertion and human folly; Bennet was not punished.

Tahiti, and Bligh from the southern, indicated the intelligence of Christian's choice of refuge: it was between the major shipping routes (which themselves were hardly bustling with activity) and was just far enough off other routes to remain in isolation.

It is interesting to note, in the rules of conduct which Bligh drew up and posted before landfall, what he had learnt from his last visit to Tahiti. They read:[21]

1.	No officer or seaman is to speak of the loss of the 'Bounty', or tell that Captain Cook was killed by Indians.
2.	No officer or seaman is to mention that we have come on purpose for the breadfruit plant.
3.	Every one is to study the goodwill of the natives and not to recover by violence any article that has been stolen.
4.	All care is to be taken that no arms or implements are stolen.
5.	No man is to offer for sale any part of the King's Stores.
6.	A proper person will be appointed to regulate trade and to barter.
7.	The mate of the watch will be answerable for all neglects of the sentinel.
8.	No canoe is to come on board after 8 o'clock.
9.	Everything is to be handed out of the boats at sundown.
10.	The awnings are to be set at sunrise and furled at sunset (except the after one).
11.	The officer of the watch is not on any pretence whatever to get into conversation with the Indians.
12.	All boats to be moored alongside.
13.	No curiosities are to be kept between decks.
14.	No person is to take fire-arms (without permission) on shore.

Any transgression of these rules will be punished with the utmost severity.

Bligh knew from Captain Cox that the *Bounty* had returned to Tahiti after the mutiny, and he believed the mutineers meant to go there, but he had no proof that the islanders knew the truth. In that case, there might have been an advantage in acting as if the voyage home had gone according to plan and that this was a return visit. He did not want gossip by his crew to compromise his position with the Chiefs. By these rules he was keeping his options open to enable him to take advantage of circumstances as they presented themselves. This is supported by his second rule about not disclosing the purpose of the visit, though he probably could not have hoped to re-use the former ruse of persuading the Chiefs to make a gift of the plants to King George.

The articles on theft and purloining ship's stores are similar to his previous rules; making use of an appointed person to conduct the trading had worked well in the past. In Rule 7 we see a stiffening of the direct responsibility of the ship's officers for security, especially as the officer of the watch was to be responsible for his sentinels' performance. This arose directly out of the experience on the *Bounty* and the general slackness exhibited by both

---

[21] Lee, 1920, pp. 36-7, footnote.

sentinels and officers. In conjunction with Rule 11 these directions to watch officers were specifically directed at increasing the ship's security.

Bligh's ships pulled into Matavai Bay where they were met by a ship's boat which, it transpired, had come from the wrecked *Matilda*.[22] The Captain, Matthew Weatherhead, had called at Tahiti on his way to Peru and the twenty-one survivors of the wreck were reasonably well received by the local inhabitants when they returned in their distressed state. Before Bligh got there the *Jenny*, from Bristol, had called at Matavai and Weatherhead had taken passage with her for America, leaving his crew to their own devices. Three of them had left the same day, 31 March 1792, for Port Jackson in one of the *Matilda's* whaleboats, which says much for their courage and something about the desperation of their plight stranded on Tahiti without much hope of raising funds for a passage home.[23]

Bligh was interested in the fortunes of the *Bounty* mutineers. He had heard nothing of them since 28 April 1789. His sole source of information about Tahiti since he had left it was the report from Captain Cox, who had no information on the mutineers because he had visited Tahiti between the visits of the *Bounty* under Christian's command. Cox had been unable to make sense of what the Tahitians had told him about Bligh, Christian and Cook. Bligh made inquiries and recorded his discoveries about the fate of the mutineers:

> I find that two months after I left Otaheite in the 'Bounty', Christian returned in her to the great astonishment of the natives. Doubting that things had gone well with me the first questions they asked were: 'Where is Bry?' 'He is gone', he replied, 'to England.' 'In what ship?' asked the natives. 'In Toote's ship'.[24] 'How came you to meet Toote, and where is he?' 'We met him at Wytootackee where he is going to live ... and he wants the bull and cow and as many hogs as you will send him.' 'What has become of the breadfruit?' 'He has sent it home to England with Bligh.' Everything was given him, and in eight or ten days he left Matavai with ten men, two boys, nine women and one girl. In one month after Captain Cox had left this place, Christian again arrived, and having landed sixteen of his villains, he sailed in the course of a day, but I cannot find that any person was acquainted with the route he intended to take. It may readily be believed that I found great satisfaction to hear of these men all being taken by Captain Edwards except two who were killed by the Indians.[25]

Bligh heard about the families left behind by the mutineers who had been taken away by Edwards. 'George Stewart, Thos. McIntosh, and Richard

---

[22] The *Matilda* was a small vessel of 460 tons, first a convict transporter to Sydney, then a whaler, which had left Sydney Cove for Peru on 28 December 1791 and been wrecked on a reef at Mururoa on 25 February 1792. Whaling ships from as far afield as Britain and the east coast of America were becoming active in the Pacific at this time.

[23] Captain Weatherhead met George Vancouver at Nootka Sound in December 1792 when the *Jenny* reached the American coast. I have been unable to find out if the three men in the boat ever arrived at Sydney; it would have been remarkable if they did. *See* Lee, 1920, p. 42n.

[24] 'Toote' was the local pronunciation of 'Cook'.

[25] Lee, 1920, p. 43.

Skinner each left a daughter by women here. Thos. Birkitt and John Millward each had a son. I have seen none of them and some are said to be dead. The man whom Captain Cox left here called Brown had a son. He sailed with Captain Edwards four months before Vancouver arrived. The anchor which Christian left behind the natives got and delivered to Captain Edwards. Captain Vancouver with Lieutenant Broughton arrived here after the 'Pandora' and stayed five weeks. After he sailed on January 12th, 1792, a disease afflicted the natives and they declare it was caught on board.'[26]

George Vancouver had been a midshipman on the *Resolution* with Bligh on Captain Cook's last voyage. He had been sent on an expedition to chart the north-west coast of America and had called at Tahiti on his route there, before going on to Hawaii. His geographical exploits and his cartographic work gained him a place in the history of north America. In his account of his voyage he wrote of the *Bounty*:

It is natural to suppose we should be very solicitous to become acquainted with the circumstances that had attended the vessel and the unfortunate persons belonging to the Bounty ... Whatever particulars could be collected from the natives, respecting this no less criminal, than melancholy event, I thought it an incumbent duty to procure and transmit to England, lest any accident should befall the Pandora. But as a legal investigation has since taken place, I trust I shall neither incur the displeasure of the humane, nor the reproach of the curious, by declining any further digression on this sad subject: the former will readily find an apology for me in their own bosoms; and the latter may resort to the publications of the day, for any other particulars with which they may be desirous of becoming acquainted.[27]

It is tantalising that a witness who visited Tahiti after the mutineers were arrested, and talked to the islanders about their impressions of the affair, apparently about to reveal some interesting information, for some reason he drops the digression and refers readers to the 'publications of the day'. Either Vancouver did not find out anything of interest, or discretion overcame him. His book was edited by his brother, and it may be the brother's discretion which is being exercised.

In contrast to the behaviour of Morrison and his party, Bligh studiously avoided getting involved in the local wars that were in progress when he arrived. He recorded what was going on in his journals but made no attempt to interfere, instead concentrating on accomplishing his task. Intervention in a local war required a political judgment as to British interests, and this was not a task that was within Bligh's mandate; he endeavoured only to preserve

---

[26] *ibid.*, p. 44. In reference to the possibility that Vancouver's men introduced venereal disease, we can note a passage in his book: '... and lest in the voluptuous gratifications of Otaheite, we might forget our friends in old England, all hands were served a double allowance of grog to drink the healths of their sweethearts and friends at home. It is somewhat singular that the gunner of the Discovery was the only married man of the whole party' (Vancouver, 1798, Vol. 1, p. 102).

[27] Vancouver, 1798, Vol. 1, p. 104.

goodwill towards Britain on the part of the local Chiefs. It was the goodwill created by Cook, and later Bligh, that ensured the safety of the British seamen who arrived at Tahiti after shipwrecks, without the protection of their vessels.

Not that the arrival of British sailors, in or out of their vessels, was an unmixed blessing for the Tahitians. Bligh on this third visit to Tahiti was gloomy about the influence of the British seamen on the manners and customs of the islanders. He wrote: 'Our friends here have benefited little from their intercourse with Europeans. Our countrymen have taught them such vile expressions as are in the mouth of every Otaheitan, and I declare that I would rather forfeit anything than to have been in the list of ships that have touched here since April, 1789.'[28] Their dress had deteriorated. 'The quantity of old clothes left among these people is considerable; they wear such rags as truly disgust us. It is rare to see a person dressed in a neat piece of cloth which formerly they had in abundance and wore with much elegance. Their general habiliments are now a dirty shirt and an old coat and waistcoat; they are no longer clean Otaheitans, but in appearance a set of ragamuffins with whom it is necessary to observe great caution.' Paradise was degenerating into an island slum.[29] Bligh disclaimed any responsibility for the actions of Europeans since his previous visit in the *Bounty*. He was indirectly commenting on the long residence of the *Bounty* mutineers (1789-1791) and the visits of various ships since then, including George Vancouver in the *Discovery*, Cox in the *Mercury* and the crew of the *Matilda*.

It was about this time that Bligh heard reports that Captain Weatherhead had suffered a certain loss of money when he had called there, and he set out to recover it from the chief who had taken it. He sent Mr Norris, the *Matilda*'s Surgeon, to recover it but he was not successful, though he did get an assurance through intermediaries that the money would be returned. He doubted their sincerity, 'but I dare not involve myself in trouble with these people although I will do my utmost to regain it'.[30] Captain Weatherhead had left details of his loss in a letter which was shown to Bligh. This showed that 407 dollars, $17\frac{1}{2}$ guineas and 3 to 4 lbs of English silver had been taken from him. Eventually Mr Norris was able to get back 172 dollars and three half-crown pieces only.[31] Bligh had to be satisfied with this token achievement. His interest in recovering stolen property was revived some weeks later when he heard that Chief Tomaree had some of his own books, taken by the mutineers on the *Bounty*. Bligh naturally wanted to recover these, probably hoping that some of his charts had survived. But his haul was meagre. After much canvassing among his island friends, he rescued a few volumes of his books, but nothing significant. One of these volumes was *Dampier's Voyage*: 'some remarks I had written on it with a pencil in the blank pages at the end of the book were perfectly distinct.'[32] Tomaree had offered to trade Bligh's

[28] Lee, 1920, p. 74.
[29] Quoted in Mackaness, 1951, p. 253.
[30] Lee, 1920, p. 76, 14 April 1792; p. 89, 26 April 1792.
[31] *ibid.*, p. 100, 9 May 1792.
[32] *ibid.*, p. 121, 7 July 1792.

papers for cartridge paper for his muskets, saying that otherwise he would use Bligh's personal papers instead. A large proportion of the papers had probably ended up as cartridge paper over the months since the *Bounty* men had been taken away.

While at Tahiti among the people of Matavai Bay and the surrounding districts, Bligh often came across memories of the men of the *Bounty*. He noted these in his Journal and, though the notes are infrequent, we can get an idea of his sensibilities over this matter. He notes on 12 May: 'Not far from this spot was the residence of Peter Heywood, the villain who assisted in taking the 'Bounty' from me – the house was on the foot of a hill, the top of which gave him a fine lookout. He had regulated the garden and avenue to his house with some taste.'[33] In an earlier entry in his Log he had gone into some detail about the information received from a visitor:[34]

A woman with a child in her arms eighteen months old, called herself wife of McIntosh, late of the 'Bounty', and gone home in the 'Pandora', came to see me to-day. This woman with several others had been with Christian to Tobooi: she related that they had stayed there two months with the 'Bounty'. Christian's intentions were to settle in that island, and he had begun to build houses and a battery there to defend himself – with the ship's guns. Two principal chiefs on the island on seeing these proceedings objected to his staying longer. Altercations ensued and war was declared. Many of the islanders lost their lives. Christian did not find it safe to remain among them and embarked with all his party and arrived two days later at Otaheite ... the principal chiefs here treated Christian with so much coolness that he determined to part with those of his men who were discontented, and immediately to set sail: it took place in the course of sixteen hours. The 'Bounty' then left Matavai with some natives on board, never to return again. The only knowledge of his future proceedings was that he openly declared his intentions to look for some land where he could make a settlement and then to haul the ship on shore and break her up. The woman calls herself Mary and her child Elizabeth, and says all wives of the men had English names. She constantly remarked that McIntosh, Coleman, Hillbrant, Newman,[35] Byrne, and Ellison scarce ever spoke of me without crying. Stewart and Heywood were perfectly satisfied with their situation, and so were the rest of them. 'They deserved to be killed', she said, but she 'hoped those who cried for me would not be hurt'. She agreed with Tabyroo's account that Coleman had to swim from the ship by stealth when the 'Bounty' left, as he was detained, being a blacksmith and a useful man. So perfectly had this woman learned the whole story that she told me names of all the men who came into my cabin at the time of the mutiny, and assisted to tie my hands, and said that no person beside myself was tied.

[33] *ibid.*, pp. 101-2, 12 May 1792. According to one of Vancouver's officers, Heywood had a Tahitian wife with him. See Bell, 1794, 'Journal of a Voyage in *HMS Chatham*, 1791-4', Turnbull Library MS, Wellington, New Zealand.

[34] *ibid.*, pp. 95-7, 2 May 1792.

[35] A mis-spelling for Norman.

In his letter to his wife written after the mutiny at Batavia, Bligh had implicated Ellison in the mutiny, and evidence at the court martial condemned him. McIntosh's 'wife' claimed he was not guilty, or at least was very sorry for his actions. Bligh merely records what she said without comment and probably had an open mind on the matter. His presence at the court martial might just have got young Ellison a pardon, though it would have hanged Heywood. The other interesting aspect of Mary's story is her reference to Coleman, who was one of the loyalists left on the ship at the mutiny. He had also swum out to the *Pandora* before it anchored to surrender to Edwards, somewhat naïvely believing that he would be treated differently from the outright mutineers. Mary tells us that Coleman had been kept on the *Bounty* on its last visit to Tahiti and implies that Christian intended him to be taken away with the ship because of his general usefulness as a handyman. Apparently this was also the story Bligh heard from Tabyroo, but it is not reported in other accounts of the last moments of the *Bounty* at Matavai. If the islanders knew the story it is a wonder that Morrison, or Heywood, did not report it. Again Bligh simply records it without comment.

The acquisition of the breadfruit plants was a minor matter this time, swiftly arranged, not subtly finessed. The Tahitian social system was rapidly declining; the respectful diplomatic negotiations with a stable Chief which were carried out on the previous visit were not needed this time. Thieves were whipped and put in irons, with a lesser concern for the sensibilities of their rulers. Bligh records the thefts and who the victim was – Lieutenant Bond lost a sheet from his cabin, etc. – and was most concerned in case a serious incident arose from a sentinel shooting a suspect: 'These people have become so troublesome on dark nights that it requires all our exertions to prevent them taking all we have. I fear some one will be shot for I have been under the necessity to give orders to deter them. One vicious fellow may destroy our plants and cut our ship adrift! Every one knows they must not come near the Post after dark.'[36]

Bligh's relations with his officers appears to have been good, unlike those with the officers of the *Bounty*. After being taken ill while making observations, he wrote a rare entry in his Log of his appreciation of Lieutenant Portlock: 'I left the rest to be done by Lieutenant Portlock whose alertness and attention to duty makes me at all times think of him with regard and esteem.'[37] From Bligh that was indeed a recommendation. He was sparing in his praise and therefore when he gave it it was genuine.

The time for departure came, and with 2,634 plants on board (of which 2,126 were breadfruit) the ships left Matavai Bay. They also had on board thirteen stranded crew members of the *Matilda*, though the other five

---

[36] Lee, 1920, p. 113, 11 June 1792. In an earlier entry Bligh reports: 'Another complaint was made to me of a native beating one of the seamen and giving him a black eye. The parties happened to be on board, so I could hear both sides of the story, which went so against the native that I told the seaman to take his own satisfaction. A few strong blows made his antagonist jump into the sea. In general I forbid officer or man to strike a native on any pretence whatever' (Lee, 1920, p. 104, 20 May).

[37] Lee, 1920, pp. 115-6, 20 June 1792.

expressed a desire to stay at Tahiti, which Bligh ungraciously conceded, accusing them of 'desertion'. A couple of Tahitians joined the voyage home, one officially and the other as a stowaway. Neither returned to Tahiti. The ships left Matavai Bay on 20 July 1792, and set off on a navigational and cartographic exploration of the islands and channels between Tahiti and Timor. Bligh had sailed through these waters in the *Bounty*'s launch, making many new discoveries and filling in gaps in the naval charts. He sometimes went long distances out of his way to pursue these discoveries and to verify the ones he had made in the launch. His charts show a meandering course, especially for a man with a specific mission and with an interest in returning as soon as possible for the trial of the mutineers. On the other hand, he had no idea whether he would ever return to these waters, and his well-established inclination to explore and chart was enough to ensure his attention to any opportunities that arose.

The description of his journey through the islands is highly technical, and by his Log books and charts he establishes his claim to the discovery of hundreds of islands, including many in the Fiji Group. The *Assistant*, under Portlock, went ahead to guide the much larger *Providence* through the reef-studded seas. His working partnership with Portlock was an outstanding success; their skills blended superbly. It may be surmised that if Bligh had taken Portlock instead of Christian on the *Bounty* his career would certainly have been entirely different, possibly ranking with Cook's. For proof that Bligh was able to get the best out of his subordinates one has only to refer to his relationship with Portlock.

The ships visited Wytootackee, the last island discovered by Bligh in the *Bounty*, partly out of curiosity and partly seeking news of the *Pandora* and the *Bounty*. They also kept a sharp eye out for anything that might solve the mystery of La Pérouse. On 29 August 1792 (incidentally a fortnight before the trial of the mutineers in London) Portlock records in his Log the following incident:[38]

About this time the master reported to me that during the forenoon he had seen pass a stick that appeared very much like a white studding-sail boom. It was great neglect of his duty his not mentioning the matter to me, as I had given orders that when leaves, rock-weed, or anything drifting was seen I might be acquainted of it. If I had known or had any idea that it really was a studding-sail boom or any other ship's spar I most certainly would have hoist a boat out and picked it up, judging it must have belonged to a ship lost at sea hereabouts or cast on shore or some coast not far distant. My alarm would have certainly been for Mr Perouse who is missing, and I understand had orders to visit these seas and explore the coasts of these islands.

In 1793 the survivors were, in fact, on an island about 1,400 miles from the *Providence* and the *Assistant*.

There were two violent exchanges between the ships and local inhabitants

---

[38] Quoted in Mackaness, 1951, p. 277; Lee, 1920, p. 243.

on this voyage. The first was between some manned canoes and a boat party under the command of Lieutenant Tobin. Tobin was exploring near Darnley Island when several canoes appeared on course to intercept his boat. He was five miles from the ships and his signal for assistance was not noticed, even by one of his boats which was on its way back to the *Providence*. He could not outsail the canoes and had to decide whether to row on, trusting the islanders, or stand and fight them. Sensibly he continued to row towards the ships, while preparing his men to repel any aggressive actions by the islanders, who were bearing down on him fast. When the canoes drew abreast one of the men in the leading canoe held up a coconut and gesticulated towards Tobin's men. Tobin declined to accept the coconut, trying to indicate that it should be taken to the ships; but in 'a moment the whole crew were busy about the enclosure furnishing themselves with bows and arrows, which had hitherto been concealed from view'. Moreover, it appeared that some men in the canoes had been hiding and with the turn in the situation displayed themselves for the first time.

Two of them now took a deliberate aim at the stern sheets of the boat, about twenty yards distant, while the rest were stringing and preparing their bows with great expedition. As it appeared that they only waited to be ready for a general discharge of arrows, and as any misfortune or loss on our part must inevitably have placed us in the power of the other canoes, which were closing fast, self preservation prompted me to fire a volley of musketry among them, and to which I have little doubt, from what occurred by a few days afterwards near the islands of O and P we were indebted for our safety; yet, had they rallied and attacked the boat in conjunction, our opposing efforts perhaps, would have been but impotent, against such numbers, with weapons nearly as destructive as fire arms ... They soon withdrew from their retreat, but after viewing us some minutes, seemingly undetermined how to act, made sail for Island A the other canoes soon taking the same direction.[39]

For Bligh, Tobin's account was a disappointment: 'This was the most melancholy account I have received. All my hopes to have a friendly intercourse with the natives were now lost.'[40] However, in view of other events it was probably a forlorn hope of Bligh's that anything 'friendly' could be achieved with these people at that time. For some years, mariners shipwrecked in these parts continued to be murdered by the natives.[41]

Eight days later, after some friendly contacts had been made with a different group of inhabitants, there was another violent exchange with

[39] Tobin, quoted in Mackaness, 1951, p. 282. The *Providence* passed so many islands that Bligh took to giving them letters, and later numbers, instead of names.

[40] Mackaness, 1951, p. 283.

[41] *ibid*., p. 282n. Mackaness mentions an incident in July 1793 when a small party of eight in a ship's boat was separated by accident from the *Chesterfield* and the *Hormuzear*, *en route* between Sydney and India. Five of the stranded party were killed by islanders and the other three escaped in their open boat and sailed it to Timor. This incident occurred in the area where Tobin was attacked. Mackaness quotes another incident of a similar nature as late as May 1814.

islanders, this time involving the use of the ships' guns. Lieutenant Portlock describes the entire incident, which began when he was at the masthead of the *Assistant* preparing for a survey of the channel ahead:[42]

> I was at the masthead for the purpose of hauling out, and at that instant saw some of the Indians in one of the canoes (that had separated from the rest) seize their bows, and without the smallest provocation on our part, discharge several arrows at the people in our cutter which was alongside preparing to put off for the purpose of sounding, and at those most exposed on deck.
>
> I called out to the men to arm and fire on them, which order was complied with, but their first arrows had wounded two men in the boat and one on deck. The wounds, though painful, the surgeon did not think dangerous.
>
> I came down at once from the masthead ... and kept up a smart fire of small arms on the canoes which attacked us, which made them all jump overboard, and at once shelter under their canoes. I made the signal for assistance to the Commodore ... and he understood my meaning. Just at that instant the savages in the large canoe under his starboard bow were observed firing a number of arrows at his ship.
>
> A smart fire of small arms and now and then from a four-pounder began from the 'Providence', which very soon drove them all off except one large canoe near the 'Providence' and the one which had attacked us, these two being disabled, having many shot holes through them, the people belonging to them being killed or wounded or had taken to the water. On the 'Providence' boats coming on board, they told me that they had seen the natives firing at us some time before we fired, and by the height they were aiming, apprehended that they were firing at me when at the masthead ...

Portlock's description of the casualties on his ship as light was not borne out by subsequent reports in the Logs. William Terry, a Quartermaster, died on 24 September from his arrow wound and one of the others wounded did not recover the use of his arm.[43]

The passage through the Torres Strait from the Pacific to the Indian Ocean took nineteen days. Flinders was to write of this passage: 'Perhaps no space of $3\frac{1}{2}°$ in length, presents more dangers; but, with caution and perseverance, the Captains Bligh and Portlock proved them to be surmountable.'[44] The passage was made possible by the exceptional blending of skills between Portlock and Bligh. There was a constant need for peak performance, but the intangible understanding between the sounding boats of the *Assistant* and the *Providence*, and the quick responses to warnings and directions, made it a fairly safe passage. A lack of standards in the

[42] Portlock, Journal (Lee, 1920, pp. 264-5), quoted in Mackaness, 1951, pp. 289-90.

[43] Lee, 1920, p. 200. Other seamen died after Timor: Thomas Lickman, marine, died 'from illness he caught at Timor' on 6 November 1792; John Thompson, of the *Matilda*, deserted at St Vincent; Henry Smith drowned; and Mydiddhee, the Tahitian, died at Deptford on 9 August 1793. Bligh himself was extremely ill at Coupang.

[44] Flinders, 1814, p.xxix.

Pandora had led to a tragedy, and even in the *Providence* only a lightning reaction to dangers on Bligh's part prevented a similar tragedy on more than one occasion. For instance, he writes in his Log for 17 September 1792: 'I furled all sails and also came to anchor. To my horror when the half cable came out it had the dogstopper on, which although I cut it immediately and let go a second anchor I only had it just in my power to save the ship from the rocks. The men who had done this were no more faulty than the officer who was in command so I did not punish them.'[45]

While the passage was a triumph for Bligh and Portlock it was a trying time for the crew. For some weeks there was a scarcity of water. The breadfruit plants needed water, and as they were the object of the mission they had to receive priority. This made life difficult for the crew, who, tired and stretched by the difficult voyage, and probably bored by the fastidious navigational work of Bligh the cartographer, went without water while the plants were fed. Even so 224 plants died. According to Flinders the absence of sufficient water caused discontent and led the thirsty men to lick water drops that fell from the plants.[46] Flinders does not suggest anything Bligh could have done about it, but he could have abandoned his explorations so that they left the drought zone sooner; some probably thought he should have done. But the discontent did not lead to mutiny. If Bligh had been aware of the criticism he might well have reminded the critic of how he and his companions had sailed roughly the same track with only a mouthful of water and a morsel of bread a day.

On arrival at the Dutch settlement at Coupang, Bligh was delighted to meet the new governor, Mr Timotheus Wanjon, who, as the previous governor's assistant, had been such a help to him when he had arrived in 1789 in the *Bounty*'s boat. Four of the other Dutch residents whom Bligh had met on his last visit were dead, which is some indication of the inhospitable character of the place.[47] Mr Wanjon had some papers which he showed to Bligh. One of these was a copy of Bligh's original representation to the Dutch authorities about the mutiny on the *Bounty*. Unfortunately, Wanjon had mislaid the account given him by Captain Edwards of the loss of the *Pandora*. This must have been agonising for Bligh who had a close interest in the fortunes of the *Pandora* and its prisoners.

Bligh's letter from Coupang to his wife Elizabeth is representative of his private correspondence and I include it here in full.[48]

---

[45] Lee, 1920, p. 197.

[46] In one of the film versions of the mutiny on the *Bounty*, this incident from the second voyage is included as one of the factors provoking the mutiny. In the film Bligh makes anybody who wants a drink of water climb the mast to get the ladle. In such a climb a crew member falls to his death; when Christian remonstrates with Bligh they come to blows and this provokes the mutiny! The imagination of the script writer actually helps the case for Bligh. He could not find sufficient cause for the mutiny in real-life accounts of Bligh's actions so he had to make one up.

[47] It must ever remain a wonder that the Dutch chose to stay in places like Timor when just to the south there was an entire empty continent. They made no attempt to colonise Australia though they had an open door to it before the arrival of the British. 'New Holland' lapsed by default (or lethargy or ignorance) into New South Wales.

[48] Bligh Family Correspondence, Safe 1/45.

Coupang in Timor
Octr. 2nd, 1792

My Ever Dear Love and my Dear Children,

I am happily arrived here – I anchored this day & found a Country Ship bound to Batavia, by which I have this opportunity to tell you I am well, except a low nervous disease which I have had more or less since I left Tenariffe – I have gone through the most extreme dangers, but after all a gracious God has restored me to this place of safety.

I left Otaheite 19th July wth 2634 Plants on board, & came through Endeavour Streights surrounded by Reefs, Dangers & treacherous inhabitants, with the loss of only one Man, who was shot wth an arrow. – I shall leave letters for you when I sail & I hope my Dear Betsy, a week will be the utmost of my stay – to fill up my water & get Fuel – Portlock has been of great service to me & behaved very well, indeed every person has come up to my expectations. This is the last voyage I will ever make if it pleases God to restore me safe to you. I hope I shall live to see you & my Dear little Girls. Success I hope will crown my endeavors – & that we shall at last be truly happy. – I only wait to wood & water wch will not detain above a Week, for I am anxious not only to be with you, but the Westerly Monsoon is at hand. My Voyage through the Straits is Wonderful – there is an end of all conjectures respecting it, for the Pass between New Holland & New Guinea is covered with Reefs and dangerous Sholes.

There is nothing to be had here – it is a poorer place than when I last left it – Wanjon is made Governor & C. Edwards has been here, having lost his Ship, but I know not the particulars.

I sent to you feathers & Valuable papers from the Cape of Good Hope, which I hope you have received.

My plants, except 200 which are dead, are in fine order, & I think it not likely for 200 more to die in the remainder of my Voyage.

I have left letters for you, the Admiralty, & Sir Joseph Banks at Otaheite, but that – Edwards left me not a word how he had proceeded, altho I learnt by the Natives he had taken some of the Villains.

I have written to Sir Jos. Banks (& the Admiralty) recommending you & my Dear little Girls to him. I hope he has shown some kindness since I left you – Next June, my Dear Dear Betsy, I hope you will have me home to protect you myself – I love you dearer than ever a Woman was loved – You are, nor have not been a moment out of mind – Every joy and blessing attend you my Life, and bless my Dear Harriet, My Dear Mary, My Dear Betsy, My Dear Fanny, My Dear Jenny & my Dear little Ann. I send you all many Kisses on this paper & ever pray to God to bless you – I will not say farewell to you now my Dear Betsy because I am homeward bound – I shall lose no time every happyness attend you My Dearest Life and ever remember me your best of Friends & most affectionate Husband.

Wm Bligh.

Kindly remember me to your Uncle & family. I am sure he will excuse my not writing to him – My Eyes are now ready to start out of my head &, I am tortured with the heat – Complts. to Mr. Keate & all Friends – God bless you my Dear Betsy.

The voyage to the Cape of Good Hope was through well-charted seas. Bligh arrived at St Helena in the South Atlantic on 17 December and deposited some of the plants there in accordance with his instructions. He remained at the island for ten days and then resumed his voyage to the West Indies. The ships anchored at St Vincent on 23 January 1793. They received a civic welcome and about 500 plants were deposited in the care of the botanical gardens. Bligh was feted as a dignitary and presented with a hundred guineas' worth of plate by the island's government. They then set sail for Jamaica to deposit the last of the plants. Bligh received a thousand guineas from the Jamaican government and Portlock received five hundred. In spite of all the congratulations, breadfruit was never found palatable by the slaves and never fulfilled the purpose intended by the King's advisers; though it took to its new habitat and still thrives there.[49]

The two ships were delayed at Jamaica from 5 February to 15 June by news of the outbreak of war with France. The local naval commodore refused permission for the ships to leave while his port was so badly defended. The *Providence* and *Assistant* joined the line of battle. While this prevented an early return home, it did bring with it the prospect of a share in prize money, if any French vessels were captured. But eventually help arrived and the ships sailed for Britain. They arrived home on 7 August 1793 and delivered a cargo of plants from the West Indies for Kew Gardens.

Bligh completed his Log with the following entry. 'This voyage has terminated with success, without accident or a moment's separation of the two ships. It gives the first and only satisfactory accounts of the pass between New Guinea and New Holland, if I except some vague accounts of Torres in 1606; other interesting discoveries will be found in it.'[50] But the Torres Strait had nothing positive to contribute either to the war with France or the development of trade with the East. If Bligh had discovered an easy passage through the Torres Strait, one useable by captains without his special skills, he might have enjoyed a warmer reception in the Admiralty. But well-drawn charts of the almost impassable seas of an inhospitable and inaccessible part of the earth thousands of miles from the French were unlikely to excite rapturous applause among men who were already prejudiced in their opinions of the discoverer. By the time of his return Bligh was out of favour, both with the public and with the Admiralty. The trial of the mutineers, and the subsequent spreading of rumour and gossip by the Heywood and Christian families, had tarnished his reputation. Even his success in transplanting the breadfruit was regarded by the scientific world as a triumph for Sir Joseph Banks, who had sponsored the expedition, rather than for Bligh. The honour went to the botanists, not to the crew of the ship.

The expected promotions for the officers did not materialise. Tobin wrote to his brother James: 'Save the regret occasioned by quitting our friends and country, we were full of hope and spirits. Our *calculations* on the Admiralty, in

---

[49] The mangoes Bligh brought, on the other hand, the West Indians found very acceptable. He transported a great many other fruits and vegetables; *see* Lee, 1920, pp. 220-1.

[50] *Log of the Providence*, 6 September 1793; Lee, 1920, p. 220. Bligh prepared a manuscript of an account of the voyage of the *Providence* for publication in two volumes. These were to include all his surveys and drawings made on the voyage. See *Manuscript Surveys by William Bligh*, Dixson Collection, Sydney. Quoted in David, 1976.

the event of accomplishing the expedition, were rather sanguine – We calculated erroneously.'[51] Tobin candidly expresses the motivation of young officers who participated in long expeditions which took them away from sight of the Admiralty for a couple of years. It was a calculated gamble. By being away they missed the chance of promotion in the event of war or opportunity at home; but if they survived the voyage and it was successful, and their commanding officer remained in favour, they could count on promotion. In 1790, when Bligh was promoted to Post Captain, attended Court and was feted by the establishment, he had been a promising sponsor for a young naval officer. But in this case the gamble had not come off. Tobin hinted at the reasons for the change:[52]

> I fear that the popularity which attended the equipment of the expedition was considerably diminished towards its completion. You are perhaps unacquainted that, about a short twelvemonth previously to our return, a Court Martial had been held on the mutineers of the *Bounty*. It does not belong to me to judge of the necessity of such a measure while Captain Bligh was absent. It was thought proper – and it was not difficult to discover on our arrival that impressions had been received by many in the service, by no means favourable to him. It is hard of belief that this could have extended to the officers of the *succeeding* voyage – Yet we certainly thought ourselves rather in the 'back ground' – but enough at present of this truly melancholy subject.

'Many in the service' had gained the impression from the court martial that Bligh was not a reputable commander. As we shall see, 'impressions' had also been 'received' from the informal actions of those hostile to Bligh. Their hostility seems to have extended even to his associates on the *Providence* voyage; he was being isolated from potential supporters.

Before the full implications of Bligh's disgrace had sunk home among the officers, a final touching scene took place between the crews of the ships and the commander, on the occasion of the termination of the ship's commissions. The *Kentish Register* for 6 September 1793 reported: 'His Majesty's ship *Providence* ... was paid off at Woolwich. It was a scene highly gratifying to observe the cordial unanimity which prevailed amongst the officers; the decency of conduct and the healthy and respectable appearance of the seamen, after so long and perilous a voyage, not one of whom but evinced that good order and discipline had been invariably observed. The high estimation in which Captain Bligh was deservedly held by the whole crew, was conspicuous to all present. He was cheered on quitting the ship to attend the Commissioner; and at the dock-gates the men drew up and repeated the parting acclamation.'[53]

---

[51] Tobin, Journal, ML A562, p. 9.
[52] *ibid.*, p. 10.
[53] Quoted in Mackaness, 1951, p. 301.

19

Morrison's 'Journal' and 'Memorandum'

The attack on Bligh's reputation was made up of separate elements, connected with each other, though sometimes tenuously. Of these, the most effective was not to surface publicly until 1825; I refer to the charges against Bligh in Morrison's 'Journal', which appeared in a biography of Peter Heywood published in Marshall's *Naval Biography*.[1] Morrison's active role in the campaign was confined to the months between October 1792 and about February 1793, when he was confined on H.M.S. *Hector* and shortly after his release. After writing his Memorandum and Journal he dropped out of the campaign, until his accusations appeared posthumously.[2]

Peter Heywood contributed to Edward Christian's campaign by initiating it, but then dropped into the background and eventually out of it altogether. At this point he was not connected with Morrison's activities, and as far as we can tell was either unaware of them, or regarded them as confidential. He does not appear to have told Christian about them. Thirty-three years later he revived the Morrison campaign and joined it with his own. Edward Christian's campaign, started by Heywood, gained momentum and became a separate attack in 1792-5. I propose to deal with Morrison's efforts first; I shall deal with Edward Christian's separate campaign last, and also with Fryer's efforts against Bligh in 1790-4, as it was through Christian that Fryer found expression. A great deal of Bligh's behaviour after 1793 makes much more sense when the campaigns are presented in this way.

In previous chapters I have criticised the view of some authors that Morrison kept a dairy while on the *Bounty* and recorded things as they happened. If the latter had been true it would give his 'diaries' (as he himself entitled his Journal) some substance as evidence against Bligh. For reasons given earlier (in Chapter 16) I do not accept that Morrison could have preserved any notes or diaries though his experiences. I have already mentioned the fact that the Journal in the Mitchell Library is on paper to which Morrison could only have had access after his return. There is also internal evidence that he was not writing his Journal at the time or from a diary. He got dates wrong, sometimes by weeks, and for the most part does not give dates. In the main Journal only months are given in the margin.

---

[1] Marshall, 1823-35; Heywood's entry was published in the volume for 1825.
[2] Morrison perished in the sinking of H.M.S. *Blenheim* off the African coast in 1807. He was rated Gunner. The distinguished commander, Sir Thomas Troubridge, returning from India, was also on board.

Occasionally an accurate date is given, but these are exceptions.[3] A more spectacular bit of evidence is that in his Journal he refers to Bligh's *Narrative*, which was published in 1790 in London when Morrison was at Tahiti. The book was only available to him when he returned in 1792 – it was admitted as evidence for the prosecution at the court martial.[4]

In the Mitchell Library, Sydney, there are two Journals ascribed to James Morrison. The larger of the two, and the more prolific in detail, is 378 pages long and incomplete, ending abruptly before the end of the text. It was donated to the Mitchell Library from the estate of the Rev. A.G. L'Estrange, who was a family friend of Lady Belcher, Peter Heywood's stepdaughter.[5] How he came to possess the document we can only speculate, for it was not mentioned in Lady Belcher's will. She probably gave it to him. He passed it to the Mitchell Library during the First World War. We know that Lady Belcher had the document because she quoted from it in her book on the *Bounty*; presumably she acquired it from Peter Heywood when he died in 1832. How Heywood acquired it is a little mystery at which I shall look in a moment. The main point is that the Morrison document, known as the Journal, presumably in his own handwriting, with many scorings out and emendations (not to mention corrections of style by other hands), can be traced back as far as Peter Heywood.

The other Morrison document in the Mitchell Library is entitled 'Memorandum and Particulars Respecting the Bounty and Her Crew'. It was given to the Library by a descendant of Bligh's, W.R. Bligh, of Parramatta, Sydney. Unlike the Journal part of it is precisely dated, the part where Morrison had written a letter to explain his views. The date is 10 October 1792 and the place given is H.M.S. *Hector*. Morrison was on the *Hector* as a prisoner at the time. The Memorandum is not in the same handwriting as the Journal; the Mitchell Library has a note on their files stating that it was copied from the original by Captain Bligh, but from a rough comparison with Bligh's handwriting in his letters, he does not seem to have copied it himself. The Memorandum is only 50 pages long and strictly limits itself in the first part to charges against Bligh and in the second part to charges against Edwards of ill-treatment of his prisoners.[6]

---

[3] *See* p. 215 for an accurate date which has been taken as proof that Morrison kept notes; *see* Montgomerie, 1938, for a full discussion of the inaccuracies in Morrison's dates.

[4] Morrison, Journal, p. 48b: 'By this statement it appears that the Party who remained on board was stronger than the one that went in the Boat if however we consult Capt Blighs narrative we shall find by his own account that several of those who continued in the Ship were averse to it and called to him after he was in the Launch to take notice that they had no hand in the mutiny.' This comment is written on the back of p. 48; in his text on p. 49 he simply says Bligh 'must, and has already acknowleged' that some of those in the ship were innocent.

[5] He wrote a book about her (L'Estrange, 1891); in it we learn of several connections between the Belchers and the *Bounty* story. To mention one, Lady Belcher's mother – who became Captain Peter Heywood's wife – was connected with Aaron Graham, the naval lawyer who defended Heywood at the court martial. It was through Aaron Graham that Heywood was introduced to his future wife. Captain Belcher, Lady Belcher's husband, visited Pitcairn Island and the mutineers' settlement.

[6] As Sir Joseph Banks had the original Memorandum sent to him in 1792 (*see* p. 203), and as presumably it went from him to Bligh, who had it copied, it was probably returned to Banks by Bligh and may be among Banks's papers somewhere. They are scattered in several libraries in

The Memorandum has some interesting features indicating that it was written for a particular purpose, separately from the major effort put into the Journal. Its title page is comparatively elaborate. Under the title there is a quotation from 'Faulkiner Shipwreck': 'Say Memory for 'tis thou alone can tell / What dire mishaps a fated Ship befell.' The copier has also transcribed the flourishes in the headings, including the motto 'Vidi et scio' (I have seen and know). In the Journal there are no attempts to embroider the headings, no mottoes, no poetical quotations; just a straightforward account of the voyage. After this somewhat pretentious beginning the Memorandum also gets down to a simple account, almost identical to the one in the Journal. The small differences between the texts enable us to tell from which version subsequent quotations were made. At no time in either document does Morrison make a direct claim that he was writing other than from memory. In the quotation 'Memory' is invoked. The claims that the documents are, or are based on, eye-witness accounts, written at the time the events took place, originated in Marshall's publication of 1825, and have been supported by modern authorities who should have checked the original material.

Even George Mackaness made a remark which did not help sort out the confusion: 'The third and most important document is "Captain Bligh's remarks on Morrison's Journal". From the context there is not a shadow of doubt that Bligh accepted Morrison's Journal as an authentic document. In his "remarks" he answers most explicitly every charge made by Morrison' (1951, p.538). Quite apart from the fact that Bligh was referring to the charges in the Memorandum, not the Journal (see p.209n.), Mackaness' considerable and deserved authority lent support to the extreme claims of others that because the document was authentic, that is to say, written by Morrison – the sense meant by Mackaness – its contents were also authentic, i.e. a true account of what happened.

To understand the origin and purpose of these documents we must go back to Morrison as a prisoner on the *Hector* in June 1792. Unlike Heywood he had no interested supporters. In the depositions to the court it appears that at one time he was a midshipman on H.M.S. *Termagant*, a sloop of war.[7] This was in 1782, five years before the *Bounty* voyage. He did not continue his

---

London, San Francisco, Chicago and Sydney; a thorough search of these collections might produce it. A comparison between different people's quotations from Morrison's Journal and Memorandum suggests that there may have been other versions or copies in circulation. We have two versions: (a) the Journal, written 1792-3, in Morrison's handwriting, 378 pages, incomplete, ML MS Safe 1/42; (b) the 'Memorandum and Particulars respecting the Bounty and her Crew' and letter to Rev. Wm. Howell, October 1792, copy in Bligh's possession, ML MS Safe 1/33; and a third is known to have existed – (c), Morrison's original of (b). There are five main references to Morrison's account: (1) Greatheed's reference to 'papers referring to Capt. Bligh' (1797) and 'MS statement by one of the mutineers' (1820); (2) Peter Heywood's quotations from Morrison's Journal, 'long in our possession', in Marshall, 1825; (3) Barrow's quotations from Morrison's Journal in 1831, which differ from both (a) and (b), suggesting a different version or heavy editing; (4) Lady Belcher's quotations from Morrison's Journal in 1870, with even wider discrepancies from (a), though it is believed to have been in her possession; and (5) Fletcher's quotations in 1877, which again vary from (a) considerably, though he states that Lady Belcher loaned him her copy of the Journal.

[7] Rutter (ed.), 1931, p. 169.

career as a midshipman, probably because he did not have the requisite interest in the navy and the corridors of power. Nobody sponsored him and he knew nobody who was likely to. His choice, then, had been between the hopeless quest for a commission – some men had to wait until their forties for a Lieutenancy through lack of interest or lack of ability – and settling for a petty-officer non-commissioned rank. His station on the *Bounty* – Boatswain's Mate, a junior petty officer rating – indicates which course he had chosen.

A prisoner charged with mutiny is vulnerable to a court's mercy. Morrison was smart enough to know that there was little direct evidence against him and certainly none that pointed to his active support for Christian. His lack of support for his captain could, however, be enough to hang him. He had therefore, besides clearing himself from association with the mutiny, to persuade the judges that an attempt to save Bligh would have been hopeless. The former he could do by emphasising the lack of proof against him, and the latter by showing that he made efforts to assist Bligh but nobody would raise an arm in defence of the Captain. To explain and justify this lack of effort on the part of others he had to show that Bligh's command was so poor, divisive and harsh that even the loyalists were unwilling to stand by their duty, so that he, Morrison, could not have expected help in a rescue attempt. This would explain why he went to great lengths to identify every possible cause of friction between Bligh and others on board, and showed as best he could that during the mutiny, while James Morrison was willing to have a go at the mutineers, nobody would back him, least of all his superior officers. For instance, in a much quoted passage he remarks that 'the behaviour of the Officers on this Occasion was dastardly beyond description none of them ever making the least attempt to rescue the ship which would have been effected had any attempt been made by one of them ...'.[8]

If we keep this intention of Morrison's in mind, the Memorandum, which is concise and specific about the inadequacies of Bligh's command, his foul tempers and also his financial irregularities in stealing from the navy, can be seen as in effect a charge-sheet to show the Admiralty and the King's advisers that while the mutiny was criminal on the part of those who supported it (which of course excluded Morrison) it was only possible because Bligh had destroyed the support of the loyalist seamen (which of course included Morrison). While in confinement on the *Hector* before the court martial he had also prepared the 'Statement' which was read out in court and to which we have already referred (p.173). This had concentrated on proving that he was not involved in the mutiny, and had made no mention of Bligh's character; to accuse Bligh in open court would have hanged him. His views on Bligh's failings as a commander had to be circulated informally.

Included in the Memorandum is the letter about his treatment as a prisoner, dated 10 October 1792. It is addressed to the Reverend William Howell. The court martial had sentenced Morrison to death on 18 September 1792, but 'in consideration of various circumstances' (not specified) he had been recommended to the King for a pardon. This was

---

[8] Morrison, Journal, p. 45. This passage is crossed out in the manuscript.

delivered on 24 October 1792. Thus Morrison's letter to Howell was sent while he was awaiting the result of his recommendation for a pardon. Two questions are raised by this information: who was Howell, and why was Morrison writing to him about the treatment he received on the *Pandora*? The answers go some way to explaining why Morrison wrote his Memorandum, which in my view pre-dated the letter to Howell.

William Howell was born in Portsea on 18 April 1764, son of John Howell, Gent.[9] He was ordained on 25 May 1788 from Magdalen Hall, Oxford and took up his first and only appointment as minister of St John's Chapel, Portsea, in July 1789. This ministry brought him into close contact with seafarers from Spithead and the main naval port of Portsmouth. It was to Spithead that the prisoners were brought in 1792. Howell probably came into contact with the prisoners in the summer of 1792. He may have been conducting divine service on the *Hector*, or he may have been invited to meet the prisoners to take care of their spiritual needs. I believe that in Howell he found the person he wanted to circulate the charges in the Memorandum. The local clergy of any seaport mixed with the officers and local officials, as well as with the ranks. They were in a position at least to know what doors might open to a special plea or the threat of a scandal. Howell was fairly young at the time – 28 years old – and probably less cynical than many about port sinners. The message in the Memorandum is fairly clear: 'Do me justice or I will press these charges'. Morrison was too much awake to the realities of life in the navy not to know that this was only a gamble. The implied blackmail could have hanged him, but if his instrument was a respectable man of the cloth, the implications of blackmail were mitigated by the appeal to morality and fairness. Howell did not have to canvass for a repentant sinner; he was canvassing for an 'innocent' man who had been sadly wronged. It is fairly easy to see how Howell could have argued: Morrison had wanted to participate in resistance to the mutiny but had been prevented by the lethargy and reluctance of the very men called to condemn him at the trial. Of course, Howell would not be entirely pliable, nor would he be entirely efficient at this job. But the Memorandum gave him ammunition for argument with those he came across in the naval base, on the ships he visited and in the town circles in which he moved. He could spread Morrison's charges without having the contacts that Heywood had. The navy was a relatively small closed society in which rumour and gossip were always rife. The vast correspondence between officers on all kinds of tittle-tattle ensured a quick circulation of rumours regarding the trial. Given that Heywood's friends and family were pushing his interest, it was more likely that news of Howell's version of Morrison's case would be able to penetrate through informal channels to the ears of the establishment.

The court eventually decided 'in consideration of various circumstances' to recommend Heywood and Morrison for a pardon, although they found them both guilty, as they had to do on the evidence. They must have taken their

[9] Information about William Howell (1764-1822) was obtained from the Portsmouth City Archivist, M.J.W. Willis-Fear, and the Hampshire County Assistant Archivist, S.J. Berry.

decision in the light of special pressures on their judgment from outside the court-room. Heywood had his uncle by marriage among the judges, he had Captain Pasley pushing his case from inside and outside the court, and he had the finest naval court martial experts defending him; Morrison had none of these advantages yet he received the same sympathy from the court. I can only conclude that Morrison's Memorandum, circulated and quoted from by Howell in the background, contributed to the court's finding 'various circumstances' in his favour.

The charges against Bligh, explaining the lethargy of his officers, might not have been enough to save Morrison. To help his plea he needed something more. His treatment by Edwards as a captured mutineer would cause no surprise, but as a wrongly arrested man, innocent of the charges and only in the dock because his superiors betrayed his captain, Edwards's treatment of him could be seen as an affront on the rights of a loyal citizen.[10] Thus, on 10 October 1792 we find Morrison writing what was in effect an open letter to Howell. The letter is a detailed account of the *Pandora* voyage and the events subsequent to the shipwreck. It is simply addressed to Howell from H.M.S. *Hector* and goes straight into details. Howell could circulate the letter on Morrison's behalf, and it could be one of the 'various circumstances' to be considered when the King asked for advice on what to do about the sentences.

In the eighteenth century it was not unusual for charges and counter-charges to be made in regard to a mutiny. Records show several cases of multiple cross-charges being made at the subsequent enquiries. For example, in 1775, the Gunner of H.M.S. *Glasgow* was court-martialled by his Captain for contempt and disobedience of orders, for which he was found guilty and reprimanded. The next day the Captain was court-martialled on charges of cruelty and oppression at the instigation of the Gunner. He was found guilty and dismissed from his command. Again, in 1777 a mutual court martial took place between the Gunner and the Captain of H.M.S. *Thunder* and in 1778 there was another mutual court martial, this time between the Master and the Captain. Indeed, in 1778 there was a confused mutual court martial in which a Captain charged his Lieutenants and his Master and the Master charged the Captain. In the event everybody was satisfied; they were all found guilty and all dismissed from the service.[11] From Bligh's Log we can extract a whole series of possible charges that he might have pressed on his return, some of which were breaches of the Articles of War. Morrison's charges in the Memorandum were serious enough to warrant a court martial. If any of them had been proved to the court Bligh could have been dismissed from the service and his career ruined. Likewise Morrison's charges against Edwards could have been pressed in a court martial on the grounds of malicious cruelty and oppression. I do not think it is too fanciful

[10] Morrison's claim to have told Captain Edwards that his conduct was an affront to the Navy (*see* p. 158) makes more sense if we accept this motivation. It is unlikely that he would speak so to a Captain, especially while a prisoner, but likely that in his letter to Howell he would insert a speech expressing this view for current consumption.

[11] MacArthur, 1813, Appendix XXXIV.

to suppose that Morrison was considering playing this hand in his defence if he was found guilty without a recommendation for a pardon.

If the court convicted him without recommending a pardon, he could demand a court martial of Bligh, who at that time was in the Pacific; he had already detailed the specific breaches of naval discipline indulged in by Bligh and could lay them before the court straight away. Any sentence against him would have to wait until Bligh returned and answered the charges. Once these charges were made in open court, the tables would be turned, and Morrison would seek to show that Bligh was responsible for the failure of the officers to lead a counter-mutiny against Christian, and that this cleared Morrison of the charge of complicity in the mutiny. One of the 'various circumstances' considered by the court in their verdict may have been the implications for naval discipline of a confused trial of the officers, crew and Captain of the insignificant 'floating greenhouse', the *Bounty*, at a time when war with France was imminent. The King would have been embarrassed, as he had appointed Bligh to the Post-Captains' list on the recommendation of the Admiralty; the Admiralty would have been embarrassed, as they had made the recommendation. The whole affair was an embarrassment, and this made Bligh a nuisance, a black spot, a conflict-prone commander to be marked down for the future as not worth further trouble. He had failed to keep his ship in order and had created an impossible position for the navy. If it came out, as it surely would, that officers had not resisted mutiny, that a small band of determined men could take one of His Majesty's ships away from its lawful command, and that they had promoted the culprit to the coveted list of Post Captains, it would do intolerable damage to the confidence of the country. It is my view that these were some of the 'circumstances' which got Morrison his pardon. This explanation fits the known facts better than some of the explanations with which scholars have so far been satisfied.

There is some indirect evidence on the progress of Morrison's Memorandum and the dating of the Journal that is relevant to the above explanation. First, consider the following letter from the Rev. W. Howell to Captain Molesworth Phillips, dated 25 November 1792, from Portsea:

Dear Phillips,
I should have taken much pleasure in complying with your request had not Morrisons narrative been at present in the Isle of Wight – I shall have it in the course of a few days and will send it to any place you may wish – It is very natural of Sir Joseph Banks not to think so unfavourably of Bligh as you or I may – there was a time when no one could have an higher opinion of an officer that I had of him – so many circumstances however have arrisen up against him attended with, such, striking marks of veracity That I have been compelled to change that idea of him into one of a very contrarry nature – Morrison is getting very forward with his publication which will be ready for the press in about six or seven Weeks – nothing however will be mentioned that may tend to any disturbance or reflect on any characters. It will consist of a very particular & diffuse account of the proceeding of Christian & party after the mutiny – with a very accurate discription of

Taheite under the enclosed arrangement. If Sir Joseph would like to
[... *torn* ...] materials before it goes to Press [... *torn* ...] take care he shall
have a sight of [... *torn* ...] I am glad to hear Norbrey is well tell him his two
companions got forward very fast – Believe me Dr sir,
yours Sincere Friend,
W. Howell
I cannot at present put my hand on the arrangement and am fearful of not
being in time for the Post. I will send it with the narrative. W.H.[12]

This letter assists in the dating of the two documents written by Morrison.
The first was the Memorandum, which according to this letter was in the Isle
of Wight in November 1792. The second was a 'publication', with details of
what happened to Christian after the mutiny and describing Tahiti. This is
undoubtedly the Journal. The Memorandum does not mention the fate of
Christian's party after the mutiny, nor does it describe Tahiti with anything
like the detail of the Journal.

The letter also establishes other things of importance about Morrison's
campaign against Bligh. Howell states that Morrison was working on his
publication with a view to getting it to press in 'six or seven weeks'. This
means that Morrison, who had been released from the *Hector* on 25 October
1792, was still in the Portsmouth area working on his Journal on 25
November 1792 with a work programme that would take him, on Howell's
estimation, until January 1793. This dates the Journal almost exactly.
Howell also had an outline of the Journal in the form of an 'arrangement', or
contents.

Of even greater significance is the name of the person to whom Howell sent
his letter: Captain Molesworth Phillips. Howell's letter is addressed to Soho
Square, the home of Sir Joseph Banks. Phillips was working for Banks at the
time. Phillips's father-in-law, Charles Burney, the famous historian of music
and the father of James and Fanny Burney, in the hope of persuading Banks
to use his influence to get Phillips the post of Agent of Marines, had written
to Banks informing him that Phillips had served on Cook's last voyage; 'his
services were then recognized by promotion and he has a good reputation
with his Commander and officers'.[13] Banks had not managed this but had
given Phillips a job. He was, of course, the same Molesworth Phillips who
had accompanied Captain Cook ashore on the fatal morning of his death and
had, in Bligh's opinion, behaved with a lack of resolve. Phillips, according to
Bligh, was a crony of Lieutenant King's, and 'was never of any real service
the whole voyage'.[14] By 1792 Phillips still thought 'unfavourably' of Bligh,
according to Howell's letter.

Phillips was certainly not averse to blackening Bligh's name in the mind of
Sir Joseph Banks. Without Banks Bligh would be isolated, and Phillips could
use (or misuse) his position to discredit Bligh. Hence his interest in acquiring

[12] Banks Papers, Brabourne Collection, ML MS A78-4.
[13] Dawson (ed.), 1958, p. 189.
[14] *See* Bligh's comments on King's *Voyage of Captain Cook*, Vol. 3, in the Admiralty copy (*see*
p. 9 above).

the Memorandum. We do not know how he discovered its existence, but from Howell's letter of 25 November it is obvious that Phillips had knowledge of the existence of the Memorandum by at least early in November. This supports the argument that the Memorandum was in circulation and that reports of its contents were also being spread about. At the time that Phillips wrote somebody else was reading the Memorandum in the Isle of Wight. Howell was prepared to send it to London for Banks to see, and could have sent copies to other people.

There is further evidence supporting the Phillips-Howell connection in a letter from Phillips to Banks, dated 12 December 1792, from Portsea. Phillips was visiting Portsmouth to report for Banks on a meeting called to declare the town's loyalty to the King and its opposition to republicanism – a small insight into the simmering passions of the time that were to boil over in the Revolutionary Wars. Phillips writes: 'I am at length able to procure for you the narrative I had the honour of mentioning to you, there is an account to be published amplified and corrected by a clergyman. I imagined you would prefer the genuine unsophisticated story so I have sent you this in the man's own writing.'[15] Here is direct proof that Banks received a copy of the Memorandum, and from Phillips's letter it is clear he received a copy written by Morrison himself. It is also clear that the Journal was still under production at the time. The most interesting piece of information is the fact that Howell was apparently going to 'amplify and correct' the Journal. This is important because it helps to dispose of the claim made by Lady Belcher that Morrison gave his Journal directly to Heywood when they parted after the pardon. They parted in October, yet the Journal was still being written in December and was to be edited later by Howell.

What happened to the promised publication of Morrison's Journal? According to Phillips and Howell, publication was imminent. Phillips had mentioned to Sir Joseph Banks the existence of Morrison's narrative, and had eventually been able to procure him 'the genuine unsophisticated story', presumably the Memorandum, in Morrison's own hand. The Memorandum would interest Banks; of that we can be sure. He would appreciate the seriousness of the charges against his protégé Bligh, and the likely consequences if publication went ahead in February 1793 before Bligh returned home. Did he intervene? He had enough political weight to do so, and it may be that he did, either through the local political establishment of Portsmouth, his Admiralty contacts, the influential people of the area, or even through the Church of England. Not much pressure would have been needed to convince young Howell of the indiscretion of publishing a damaging attack on a senior naval officer who was serving his country at the other end of the earth. Howell believed that he could publish an account written by Morrison which would not 'tend to any disturbance or reflect on any character'; reading the manuscripts of the Memorandum and the Journal does not support that belief. The Memorandum makes specific

[15] Molesworth Phillips to Sir Joseph Banks, BM Add. MS 33.9.79; noted in Dawson (ed.), 1958, p. 188, though he attributes the 'narrative' in question to Cook.

charges of malpractice against Bligh; the Journal repeats most of them. Friendly advice to Howell would have made him aware of the legal complications in publishing either of these documents. Moreover, the political mood of the country regarding subversion and dissent was swinging towards the right. It was not a good time to publish books describing the activities of mutineers, especially those not yet brought to justice. We cannot be sure what prevented publication, but something did. Morrison's Journal was not published in its entirety until 1936; and extracts were published for the first time only in 1825.

There are some hints as to where the Journal was after 1792, at least for part of the time. Unfortunately, these hints create more problems. Let us go back for a moment to the prisoners on H.M.S. *Hector*, in particular to Peter Heywood. That writing materials were available to the prisoners on the *Hector* we know from Heywood's voluminous correspondence with his family from June to October 1792. In the latter month, James, Peter's brother, visited him and composed the following letter to the family: 'While I write this, Peter is sitting by me making an Otaheitan Vocabulary, and so happy and intent upon it, that I have scarcely an opportunity of saying a word to him.'[16] Apparently there were enough writing materials for two. According to Tagart, the Vocabulary consisted of 'one hundred full-written folio pages, the words alphabetically arranged, and all the syllables accented'. In all comments since, the vocabulary has been credited to Heywood, but there are some doubts about this claim.

The Heywood entry in Marshall's *Naval Biography* contained the following quotation from the records of the London Missionary Society:

> An ingenious clergyman of Portsmouth kindly furnished Dr. Haweis and Mr. Greatheed with a manuscript vocabulary of the Otaheitean language, and an account of the country, which providentially he had preserved from the mutineers who were seized by the Pandora, and brought to Portsmouth for their trial, which was of unspeakable service to the missionaries, both for the help which it afforded them to learn before their arrival much of this unknown tongue, and also as giving the most inviting and encouraging description of the natives, and the cordial reception which they might expect.[17]

Thomas Haweis and Samuel Greatheed were the founders of the London Missionary Society which sent out missionaries to the Pacific islands, including Tahiti, from 1795.[18] Haweis had persuaded Bligh to take a couple of missionaries on the *Providence* voyage, after successfully lobbying Bligh

---

[16] James Heywood to Nessy Heywood, quoted in Tagart, 1832, p. 142.

[17] Quoted in Tagart, 1832, p. 142n. The passage comes from William Wilson, 1799.

[18] Wood, 1957, p. 178; it is of interest that this study refers to 'Mr Howell, the clergyman of St John's, who has been so friendly in communicating his papers' (p. 120). It is possible that at some time Howell loaned his papers, including Morrison's Journal, to Haweis (who, as seen below, may have been in discussion with Greatheed about an edited version of some of Howell's papers) and that after Haweis' death they were sent to Heywood. The date of Haweis' death, 1820, would fit in with Heywood's use of the papers in 1825.

directly and putting pressure on the navy through Sir Charles Middleton and William Wilberforce. The two men chosen as missionaries backed out at the last moment; after all, Tahiti was a long way from Britain. But of most interest to us here is the reference to the vocabulary as being a product of the 'mutineers' and not just of one of them in particular.

There is a reference in the Haweis Papers that again refers to 'mutineers' as the authors: 'It pleased God after returning to Spithead again to favour us with a more full and complete specimen of the Otaheitan language than that found in Captain Cook's *Voyages*. The original manuscript was compiled in Alphabetical order by some of the mutineers of H.M.S. *Bounty* ... the original was left in England.'[19]

The last sentence of the Mitchell Library ms. of Morrison's Journal is as follows: 'Such is the best account that I have been able to Collect of these Islands and their Inhabitants who are without doubt the Happiest on the Face of the Globe and Shall now proceed to give such a Vocabulary of their language as we were able to obtain during our Stay among These islands.' Morrison apparently also prepared a vocabulary but it is missing from his Journal manuscript. It could be that the vocabulary that Heywood was writing – 100 pages long – was a joint effort by him and Morrison, and perhaps by others as well. Morrison gives the impression of a joint effort by using the plural: 'As we were able to obtain'. The Haweis papers and the London Missionary Society records refer to a vocabulary from 'mutineers'. The quotation above (n.17) describes the vocabulary as containing a description of Tahiti and its people, which fits the last part of Morrison's Journal.[20]

It seems certain that Howell provided the description and vocabulary for the missionaries when they called at Spithead before their voyages of 1794-7. If he had the vocabulary, and it was Morrison's, he almost certainly still had the Journal, which he had intended to edit and publish, but for some reason (possibly pressure from Sir Joseph Banks) had not. His interest in Tahiti, fired by his contact with the mutineers – he may have been the first Bounty scholar! – and his access to the Journal would have given him an excellent opportunity to produce his own version of the vocabulary plus a description of Tahiti for the missionaries. He could have amalgamated a vocabulary by Heywood with the one by Morrison, or used the one in Morrison's Journal alone, if it was a joint effort; in either case it could be described as coming from the 'mutineers'.

Howell seems likely to have had the Journal in 1797, as shown by the following letter from Greatheed to Haweis, dated 7 February 1797: 'I think if you write to Mr Howel it will be more proper, and more effectual than if I wrote. If he retains his objections to the publication of the general Substance of the papers he perhaps may assent to the insertion of such leading facts as have no reference to Captain Bligh in my memoir on which I have made a beginning.'[21] It seems that Greatheed had had a sight of papers relating to

[19] Haweis Papers, A1963, No. 23, 12 September 1796.
[20] Morrison's descriptions may not have been entirely his own. He had Bligh's *Voyage* of 1792 and Cook's *Voyages* to draw on.
[21] Haweis Papers, Vol. 5, ML MS A3024, p. 115.

Bligh which in some way might be damaging, presumably Morrison's. If so, why did Howell not want the Journal published and in particular not want reference made to Bligh? We know very little of Howell's life and a possible explanation could have been lost. Whatever prevented him from editing and publishing the Journal in 1793 might still have weighed with him.

In 1825 Marshall's *Naval Biography*, which consisted of brief biographies of all naval officers on the lists, contained an unusual entry under Captain Peter Heywood. It was unusual for three reasons: first, it was over fifty pages long, when almost all others were a few pages at the most and many less than a page long; second, it largely consisted of a vigorous personal attack on another officer, Vice-Admiral Bligh, who had been dead since 1817; third, the basis for the attack was almost exclusively the writings of an obscure non-commissioned officer who had been dead since 1807 and who was a pardoned mutineer, namely, James Morrison. Heywood had decided to use the format of a service publication (largely purchased by fellow officers and their families, who supplied the entries and probably paid for them too) to open up the *Bounty* controversy again. He had not publicly commented on the *Bounty* since 1793.

In one of the most enigmatic passages associated with Morrison's Journal, we find it introduced into Heywood's biography in the following way: 'A private journal, long in our possession, the publication of which was only prevented by the death of its original owner, the late Mr James Morrison, Gunner of H.M.S. *Blenheim*, who had the misfortune to witness all that he has related, enables us at length to withdraw the veil by which the world has been so long blinded.' Why was publication 'only prevented by the death of its original owner'? If by 'original owner' Heywood meant James Morrison, which is what the passage suggests he means, why should Morrison's death in 1807 have prevented publication until 1825? And Morrison died fifteen years after writing the Journal, specifically, according to Howell, for publication. To assert that Morrison's death prevented publication is absurd. It follows that there must be something missing in this passage, either something edited out or something which, if known, gives meaning to the passage.

I confess I have spent a not inconsiderable amount of time thinking about this passage. It still baffles me, even after trying a dozen scenarios. If Heywood had the Journal at the time he parted from Morrison after the trial in 1792, which is asserted by Heywood's family, then it was not Morrison's death in 1807 that 'only prevented' publication but his own insistence on its not being published. Heywood might have got the Journal just before Morrison's death, without having time to get permission to publish it, or he might have got it as a result of Morrison's death in a will which bound him not to publish it.[22] But it seems unlikely that Morrison changed his mind and did

[22] It is possible that Heywood and Morrison met in 1805. Morrison was in the *Blenheim*, which left Britain for India in April under the command of Admiral Troubridge. Heywood was en route to Britain after retiring on health grounds from the East Indies fleet in January 1805. They could have met at the Cape. Morrison might have loaned his old shipmate the Journal on condition that it was not made public. The *Blenheim* was lost in January 1807; Heywood was back at the Cape in December 1806.

not want it published. It is possible that Howell and Morrison had agreed in 1793 not to publish the Journal for a 'consideration', and they were abiding by the deal, but this is rather far-fetched and is completely unsupported by evidence. Morrison might, though it seems improbable after he had taken the trouble to write it, have been frightened of what would happen to his career as a Gunner if he offended the Admiralty by bringing out the dirty linen of the *Bounty*. But this assumes that he had the Journal in his possession, when the evidence suggests the contrary.

He could have left the Journal with Howell, perhaps with instructions about its use and future. This last, though it does not answer all the questions, seems to me more plausible than the alternatives that Heywood or Morrison had it. Howell might have left it to Heywood when he died. The exact date of Howell's death is not known. I have, however, found an approximate date for it.[23] The Reverend William Stevens Dusautoy was appointed to St John's Parish, Portsea, on 12 January 1822, 'the Reverend William Howell having departed this life'. This places his death some time before January 1822. So if he left the Morrison manuscript Journal to Heywood, Heywood would have had time to incorporate it into his biographical entry in the volume of Marshall's publication which appeared in 1825. Howell's reason for leaving the Journal to Heywood could have been that he knew Heywood from the vocabulary that he contributed to at the time of the trial and knew him to be sympathetic to its point of view. It is also possible that the approach came from the other side: Heywood, contemplating writing something on the mutiny, remembered Howell as the local minister during the trial and wrote to him asking him if he still had his documents (i.e. Heywood's vocabulary and notes) and if he would loan them to him while he wrote out his biographical details. From this contact Howell might have passed on the Morrison documents as well.

This explanation does not throw much light on the enigmatic passage in Marshall's *Biography*; the Journal would not have been 'long' in Heywood's possession and the death of the 'original owner' would have made possible, rather than preventing, the publication of the Journal, even if one assumes that something might have gone wrong with the grammar of the sentence and the 'original owner' was not Morrison.[24] But I think it fits best with the other evidence, particularly the letters quoted earlier in this chapter and the

---

[23] His successor to the ministry of St John's, Portsea, was licensed on February 13, 1822, but the Hampshire Records Office has been unable to find a trace of Howell's burial in the Portsea Bishop's Transcriptions for 1821 to February 1822; nor does he appear in the burial registers in the parishes of Portsea or Portsmouth, nor in the neighbouring parishes of Wymering, Widley or Farlington. He must have moved further away by then. Some support for this view comes from an exchange of correspondence between Howell, his Parish, and the Church Authorities over complaints that he was not living in his parish but some distance away and had let out the Church House privately on his own account. This gives Howell's removal from the parish, while retaining his ministry, as about 1799.

[24] If Heywood obtained the Journal from Howell (or from Haweis, *see* note 18; or Greatheed, *see* p. 205) in about 1820, and intended to consult Howell about its publication (as he had originally meant to edit it), he could be said to have been 'prevented' from publishing it by Howell's death in 1820-2.

probability that Morrison was using Howell as a channel for the publication of his grievances.

This somewhat complicated discussion about the two documents has been necessary because their charges have been included in so many books about the *Bounty*, while the many questions concerning them have been totally ignored. To sum up, there were two Morrison documents; they were separated at the time of composition; one went to Sir Joseph Banks via Captain Phillips from William Howell; the other probably also went to Howell, and remained out of circulation until 1822, reappearing in Heywood's hands in time for his own anti-Bligh campaign. We can thus distinguish the impact of the first document (1793) on Bligh's career from the impact of the second document (1825) on his reputation. The fact that many of the charges made against him in Morrison's first account were repeated in his second account makes it convenient to discuss the charges in one section, and this I shall do in the next chapter.

20

Morrison's Charges Against Bligh

The best way to approach Morrison's charges is to examine them in the context of the time that they were made (1792) and answered (1793).[1] I have not included them in the chapters on the voyage of the *Bounty* because they do not belong there, but to an account of the actions of James Morrison, prisoner, on trial for mutiny, and later after his release following the Royal Pardon. It is not possible within the confines of this book to develop every nuance of difference between the Memorandum and the Journal. Neither would it be appropriate, because I am concentrating on Bligh's replies to the charges which appeared in the Memorandum, sent to him by Sir Joseph Banks. Bligh did not see the Journal.[2] This is not altogether surprising, as hardly anybody was aware of the Journal's existence between Howell's correspondence with Phillips in November-December 1792 and Peter Heywood's biographical entry in 1825. It may be that Sir Joseph Banks was introduced to the Journal after he had seen the Memorandum – Phillips mentions its existence in his letter to Banks of December 1792. The manuscript now known as the Journal was probably too rough a version to be sent to Banks and it is unlikely that he saw it. Even if he was responsible for suppressing its publication, he would have been able to act on what he saw in the Memorandum. Banks was fiercely

---

[1] In the Mitchell Library there is a series of notes in Bligh's handwriting, answering the charges made by Morrison and others. Presumably these formed the basis of letters to Sir Joseph Banks, who must have sent Bligh letters he had received from Edward Christian, and the Memorandum, and asked for his comments. The notes on the Morrison charges are entitled 'Captain Bligh's Remarks on Morrison's Journal'; the words 'Captain Bligh's' have been added in pencil. In the Remarks Bligh speaks of himself in the third person; Bligh, Bounty Mutineers, ML MS Safe 1/43.

[2] George Mackaness, who managed to avoid most of the pitfalls of former (and recent) *Bounty* scholars, slipped up when he attributed Bligh's remarks to criticism of the Journal, when in fact Bligh was referring to the Memorandum (Mackaness, 1951, p. 538; quoted above, p. 197). Bligh obligingly makes several direct quotations which we can compare with both texts. I will give one example out of many available.

Journal (p. 46): '[Christian] also made fast some Staves to a Stout Plank which lay on the larboard Gangway.'

Memorandum (p. 35): '... together with a roasted Pig, he put into a Bag, and prepared two Staves for Paddles, intending to take a large fir Plank which lay on the starboard Hog Stye.'

Bligh's Remarks: 'That Christian ... intended to go on shore 10 legs. from the land on a fir Plank with two Staves for Paddles with a roasted pig is too ridiculous.'

We may also note that in the Memorandum, but not in the Journal, Morrison charges Bligh with financial irregularities at the Cape of Good Hope. Bligh answers this charge in his Remarks: if he had been quoting from the Journal he would not have done so. H.S. Montgomerie (1937, 1938) noted the discrepancy between Bligh's Remarks as quoted by Mackaness (1931) and the published version of Morrison's Journal (1935), but, with no access to the Mitchell Library, could not solve the mystery.

loyal to Bligh throughout his life and he may have acted on his behalf until he returned home.[3]

Morrison's charges vary from the maliciously trivial to the criminal. Both kinds eventually did irreparable damage to Bligh's reputation. The charges I discuss here are in the main the most famous ones. It is necessary to remember the broad strategy that Morrison was following from his prison cell. He had to convince the court and later the King's advisers that he had not participated in the mutiny; that he had wanted actively to oppose it; that he was prevented from doing so by the failure of his superior officers to resist Christian; and that the cause of that failure was Bligh's peculiar manner, personality and mode of management of the ship and its crew. In the Memorandum, he did a masterly literary job in support of his strategy. He told the *Bounty* story as a narrative, from the day the ship left Spithead up to the morning of the mutiny. In the Journal he continues the story up to the arrest by H.M.S. *Pandora*.

The tenor of Morrison's charges can be seen in the first, and possibly most famous one: that of the missing cheese. 'Some few days after' leaving Tenerife (note the typical absence of a date), he says,

> the weather being fine, the cheese was got up to the Air, when on opening the Casks, two Cheeses were declared to be stolen, the Cooper affirmed, that the Cask had been opened by Mr. Samuels order, and the Cheese sent to Mr. Bligh's House, while the Ship was in the river. Mr. Bleigh without enquiring any farther into the affairs, ordered the Allowance of Cheese to be stoped from the Officers & men, till the dificiency was made good, and at the same time told the Cooper he would give him a damned good flogging, if he heard him say any more.
>
> These orders were punctually obeyed by Mr. Samuel who was both clerk & steward, and on the next serving, Butter only was issued, this the Seamen refused to take, alledging that their acceptance of it would be a tacit confession of the supposed Theft, and John Williams said, that he had carried the Cheese to Mr. Bligh's house, with some other things and a Cask of vinegar which were sent in the Boat.[4]

To understand Morrison's allegation we should note the standard naval practice of the day regarding the opening of casks of food. On a long sea voyage food was a matter of great contention. Not only was the food bad in itself but its distribution was miserly. Arguments about food were common among men dependent on unknown suppliers for its quality, on superior officers for its fair distribution and on their mates for its security once allocated. To prevent some of the arguments it was customary to open the food casks before distribution to the messes and to count out the contents in public. If there was short measure, this was noted in the Log by the Captain and the men were compensated for it in their wages.

---

[3] There is no direct evidence that I know of connecting Banks with the suppression of the Journal, but something deterred Howell and Morrison from publishing, and he is the most likely explanation. They had intended to publish in February 1793 and Banks received the Memorandum in December 1792.

[4] Morrison, 'Memorandum and Particulars Respecting the Bounty and her Crew', ML MS, Safe 1/33, p. 7. Differences between the Memorandum and the Journal are minimal.

On the *Bounty*, because of its smallness, Bligh had been made both Commander and Purser – a dual role that was vulnerable to the kind of charge that Morrison was preferring.[5] Pursers were commonly dishonest. They made their income by squeezing the already reduced rations of the seamen to create 'savings' on the voyage (for which they received a bonus from the Admiralty) and by buying food from unscrupulous merchants or by conniving at cheating the ship of its due quantities. Thus the Admiralty, in making Bligh his own purser, certainly made it possible for him to abuse his position. It was definitely not in order for Bligh to direct naval supplies to his personal use.

While Bligh had the opportunity to cheat, he had the incentive not to, especially at this point. He had received his first command only a few months previously; yet here he is stealing naval stores, inviting his clerk, Mr Samuel, to give orders for the theft, involving the Cooper in opening the casks, and ordering a seaman, John Williams, to carry the stolen goods to his house, thus providing three witnesses of a criminal act which, if brought to trial, would cost him his commission. This seems incredible.[6] Morrison's charge goes beyond the actual theft, however; he claims that Bligh tried to put the blame on the crew for stealing the cheese. The result, according to Morrison, was that the men refused to take the butter ration, to avoid being implicated in the theft. With the entire ship in rebellion in this way we are asked to believe that Bligh was willing to continue his bluff and also to threaten the Cooper with a flogging if he said 'another word'.

Bligh writes in his Remarks: 'Captain Bligh declares that a cask of cheese having signs of getting into a bad state was brought up on deck and when opened was found full and counted out. In the interval of dinner time two of the cheeses were stolen. Captain Bligh considered this an audacious theft and could not be committed without the knowledge of most of the ship's company – he therefore in preference to charging the value of the cheese against their wages, ordered it to be stopped from each person until the whole was repaid.' This is a plausible explanation. Another possible explanation of the second part of Morrison's story is that after a month or so at sea butter was usually 'condemned as putrid' and handed over to the Boatswain for use on the ropes.[7] The incident occurred in February or March, after two months at sea and as the *Bounty* was nearing the equator. The men's refusal of butter in their ration

[5] On the *Providence* Bligh had once again been both Commander and Purser. After the voyage he found his pay as Commander had been docked by a quarter because it was assumed that he would make a profit from the pursery. He wrote to the Admiralty on 16 January 1794 to complain that, on the contrary, 'of those profits I shall not receive sufficient to clear my expenses which have been occasioned in contributing to the comfort of every individual under my command and what were necessary for the outfit of such a voyage'; he argued that he had saved the Government the expense of a Purser and a Purser's servant, and that since a Lieutenant who took on the job of Purser received the profits 'without any deduction of pay', he had been unfairly treated (PRO Admiralty 1/509 B 165). Eventually he received an extra allowance of eight shillings a day for the voyage. This precedent was used to justify a similar payment to George Vancouver in 1797 (Godwin, 1930, p. 164).

[6] Even Barrow, a critic of Bligh and a friend of the Heywoods, wrote (1831, p. 79): 'It can hardly be supposed that a man of Bligh's shrewdness, if disposed to play the rogue, would have placed himself so completely in the hands of the cooper, in a transaction which, if revealed, must have cost him his commission.'

[7] *See* Masefield, 1971, p. 67.

may have had more to do with its condition than any moral reasons. It might be that Bligh had sent some food to his home, and that Morrison is mixing up a garbled version of the incident with rationalisations about the butter. In passing we should also note that two of his witnesses to the incident, Hillbrant and Williams, were not available for comment; Hillbrant had drowned in the *Pandora* and Williams was with Christian in the Pacific. Bligh on the other hand could call Mr Samuel as a witness if legal charges were made. Bligh was not slow to point this out in his notes, which would carry weight with Banks. It should also be remarked that Fryer did not mention this incident in his criticism of Bligh and in the circumstances it is hardly credible that he would not have known about it.

Morrison was not finished with the subject of food; it is constantly raised by him in the first leg of the voyage from Britain to Cape Horn, but does not re-appear again until his descriptions of the return journey home from Tahiti. This cannot pass without some comment because it implies either that Morrison had become weary of inventing stories about food and turned to other subjects, or that Bligh's management of the food supply altered dramatically after Cape Horn, which defies explanation. Morrison wrote:

> As the Ship approached the Equator, the Pumpions began to spoil, and being in General too large for Cabbin Use, they were Issued to the Ships Company in lieu of bread. The People being desirous to know at what rate the exchange was to be, enquired of Mr Samuel who informd them that they were to have one pound of pumpion in lieu of two pounds of bread this they refused, and on Mr. Blighs being informed of it He came up in a violent passion, and Calld all hands telling Mr Samuel to Call the first Man of every Mess and let him see Who would dare refuse it or any thing else that He should order to be served, saying 'You dam'd Infernal scoundrels, I'll make you eat Grass or any thing you catch before I have done with you'.[8]

This is one of the most unsatisfactory of Morrison's charges. It is unsupported by witnesses. Bligh's reply is as follows:

> Captain Bligh declares that as in the course of the Voyage the ship's company would be at 2/3 allowance of Bread, He directed Twenty three Pumpkins bought at Teneriffe to be issued to those who liked them, and the amount of what each person took up, was to be deducted out of whatever bread might become due to him, at the Rate of two lbs of Pumpkin for one lb of Bread.
>   Captain Bligh knowing what difficulties he had to encounter off Cape Horn, & the length of time he was to be without fresh supplies, had directed these Pumpkins to be bought (as the only fruit kind that would keep) & likewise two large dripstones to give his People pure water – These were certainly acts of kindness, & not oppression.[9]

Bligh claims that the rate of exchange was the opposite to that claimed by Morrison. We have no way of knowing which is correct. But behind this story

[8] Morrison, Journal, pp. 3-4.   [9] Bligh, Remarks, p. 43.

is a possible truth, namely that the seamen did not like the change from ship's biscuit to pumpkin and complained about it. Ship's 'bread', or biscuit, came in thick, round, browned 4-oz pieces. The centre, which was the last piece eaten, was compressed and consequently far tougher than the edges. Biscuit was made of mixed wheat and pea-flour and sometimes had ground bone-dust added. It quickly became hard and uneatable or riddled with maggots. The maggots could be killed by re-baking, and hard biscuit could be broken up and cooked with other foods or pounded back into flour. If the sight, smell or taste was too much, the seamen could eat his biscuit in the dark 'when the eye saw not, and the tender heart was spared'.[10] In spite of all this, seamen were attached to their biscuit as it was a food that they were used to and expected. Cook had flogged two seamen for refusing fresh food and concoctions to prevent scurvy. For Bligh the pumpkins were part of his anti-scurvy sea-diet to promote good health; for the seamen they were new-fangled rubbish. At no time in his Journal does Morrison exhibit the slightest awareness of the relationship between good food and health; food to him was an aspect of life at sea conditioned by thieving merchants and cheating pursers.

Morrison's complaints about the food in this part of the voyage did not end with this incident. The crew members' 'private stock began to decreace and the Beef and the Pork to appear very light, and as there had never yet been any weighd when opend, it was supposed that the Casks ran short of their weight, for Which reason the people applyd to the Master, and beggd that he would examine the business and procure them redress'.[11]

> As soon as Lieut. Bligh was informed of the Complaint, he ordered all hands aft, and informed them, that every thing relative to the Provisions, was transacted by his orders, and it was therefore needless to complain, as they would get no redress and further added, that he would flog the first severely who should attempt to make any Complaint – The Seamen seeing that no redress could be had, before the End of the voyage, resolved to bear it with patience, and no complaint was ever offered after.[12]

This charge was one that might have been made to stick against Bligh. If it was true that he threatened to flog anybody who complained, then he was in breach of the Admiralty's regulations. Article 21 of the Articles of War stated: 'If any person in the fleet shall find cause of complaint of the unwholesomeness of the victual, or upon other just grounds, he shall quietly make the same known to his superior, or captain, or commander in chief, as the occasion may deserve, that such present remedy may be had, as the matter may require; and the said superior, captain or commander in chief, shall as far as he is able, cause the same to be presently remedied.'[13] Morrison makes Fryer a witness to this charge, and if Fryer had confirmed the evidence as the *Bounty*'s Master, the court would be bound to take notice, though the charge would probably have

[10] Masefield, 1971, pp. 64-5.
[11] Morrison, Journal, p. 4.
[12] Morrison, Memorandum, p. 11.
[13] MacArthur, 1813, Appendix I, Article XXI.

warranted only a reprimand, if proven. Fryer, however, did not mention this incident in his own complaints against Bligh.

Bligh took Morrison's charge to be one of falsifying the weights in his own interest, and wrote: 'It is a well known thing – that an officer attends the opening of all casks of Beef & Pork & sees the whole weighed and divided according to the Navy Rules of 4lbs to a Piece of Beef, & 2lbs to a Piece of Pork – it is done publickly before the Ship's Company, & it cannot be to the interest of any one to go contrary to the Rules laid down.'[14] This was clearly a direct matter of evidence and, if pushed by Morrison in a court martial, it would simply be a matter of establishing who had the most witnesses. In Bligh's Log of the *Bounty* there are numerous references to the opening of casks of meat and the number of pieces of meat missing; these were recorded so as to report to the Admiralty on the ship's return. Bligh's point that 'it cannot be to the interest of any one to go contrary to the Rules laid down' carries weight. To arrange the distribution differently would have invited considerable dissent and it would have been remarkable in the *Bounty*'s case if it had not been raised afterwards in view of what happened. I have found no other reference to this charge in Fryer, Purcell, Heywood or the combined evidence of the men collected together by Edward Christian.

Referring to Morrison's claim that the seamen gave up complaining, seeing that they would get no redress, Bligh writes: 'Nothing can mark the Villainy of this Morrison more, than the reason he gives for the People never afterwards complaining, by this at once to shew that the Peoples good behaviour was not a proof of my commanding equitably.'[15] This was obviously what Morrison was trying to do. In his Journal he added a similar passage about the officers who, he claimed, 'were not so easily satisfied and made frequent Murmurings among themselves about the Smallness of their Allowance and could not reconcile themselves to such unfair proceedings; but they made no complaint seeing that the Men had drop'd it, and did not appear either in publick or private to take any notice of it'.[16] He is trying with difficulty to establish two points at the same time: he wants to show widespread dissent among both officers and men and also to explain why there was no manifestation of it. This leads to further inconsistencies. A few lines later he mentions a new circumstance which 'served to increase their distress' and 'to draw forth heavy Curses on the Author of it in private': 'When a Cask was broached they saw with regret all the prime pieces taken out, for the Cabbin table, while they were forced to take their Chance in Common with the men of what remaind without the satisfaction of knowing whether they had their weight or Not.' Bligh's denial of this charge as it appeared in the Memorandum is forthright: 'As to chosing particular pieces of Meat I deny it – it stands on record in my general orders that such a thing is forbidden on any pretence whatever.'[17] This is somewhat naïve: it is natural for servants of commanders to seek out the best in everything, irrespective of rules or of the wishes of the commanders. It may be

[14] Bligh, Remarks, p. 44.
[15] *ibid.*, p. 45.
[16] Morrison, Journal, p. 5.
[17] Bligh, Remarks, p. 45.

that Bligh's servant and clerk did select the better pieces of meat (which were of a uniformly poor quality to begin with). It is possible that this was exaggerated in significance by Morrison. It certainly could not be proved either way. If the choice pieces did go to the cabin table then this was not just for Bligh's benefit. He messed with Fryer and Huggan and also invited other officers to dine with him, particularly Christian. Morrison does not mention this point here but it is worth remembering in judging the significance of his charges.

Lack of consistency does not deter a man who is writing for his life. Morrison was no exception. He complained about everything at one time or another, including the fact that the ship's hogs 'must have starved but for bread & the Indian Corn purchased for the Poultry'.[18] His complaints about the food provoked Bligh to respond: 'On investigation, these low charges would strongly mark the character of Morrison – they are convenient at a remote period. – Captain Bligh declares every person had as much as was necessary; and what was never known in any Ship before, & perhaps in none but his own since, they had hot breakfasts every day of boiled Wheat sweetned with sugar, or Burgoo enriched with Portable soup.' Then, with an exasperated air of unreality, Bligh delivers the following passage: 'So happily did every person with him feel themselves, that letters from the People and Warrant officers from the Cape of Good Hope were particular in remarking how happy they were under Captain Bligh's Command – His treatment to them was such that songs were made on him extolling his kindness.'[19] A more modest presentation would have carried more weight. But Bligh, it should be remembered, was writing his remarks on the Memorandum for Sir Joseph Banks in a private communication and not for the public. Bligh's point that the charges 'on investigation' would be likely to expose Morrison as a sea-lawyer and purveyor of malicious gossip is not unfounded. Strip Morrison's Memorandum and Journal down to provable charges, i.e. those that could be backed by evidence and witnesses, and they dwindle to a few areas of greyish doubt. It may have been this kind of consideration that stopped Morrison and Howell proceeding with their publication plans. Banks, who was probably connected with the prevention of publication in some way, would have appreciated Bligh's point about the remoteness of the events, the lack of credible witnesses, and the outright contradiction of the charges in Bligh's denials.

The *Bounty* had carried some live animals, which was a common practice for preserving edible meat at sea. The disposal of at least two of these animals became a matter of controversy with Morrison. He gave the date of the first incident as 23 March 1788. 'One of the sheep dying,' Morrison writes, 'this morning Lieut. Bligh orderd it to be Issued in lieu of the Days allowance of Pork & Pease; declaring that it would make a delicous Meal and that it weighd upwards of fifty pounds, it was devided and most part of it thrown overboard, and some dried shark supplyd its place for a Sundays dinner, for it was no other than Skin & Bone.'[20] The second incident occurred on 18 April, when 'A

[18] Morrison, Journal, p. 5.
[19] Bligh, Remarks, pp. 45-6.
[20] Morrison, Journal, p. 7.

hog was now killd & served out in lieu of the days Allowance, which tho scarce anything else but skin and bone was greedily devoured.'[21] Bligh represents these incidents in an entirely different light: 'It is a general rule on board of Ship, not to suffer any thing that died to be used by the Seamen, because they would always find means to kill any animal if they knew this Rule was not observed.'[22] This is a highly credible piece of reasoning. It is more than likely that he would have kept the dead sheep from the crew for this reason; the fact that both he and Morrison agree that the crew managed to get a share of the sheep before it was thrown overboard suggests that it was in fact killed by one of the crew. He continued:

> But Captain Bligh declares on his honor he never did or could permit his people to eat any thing that was improper – If Captain Bligh thought proper to shorten any allowance, he lived on the same himself, and it is known to the lowest seamen in the King's Service, that if he has not his *full allowance* he is paid for it by Government in money, & the Captain can draw Bills to pay such account, when he is employed abroad: if on his return, such a payment due to the Ship's Company has not been made, the Captain is obliged to pass on account for the same, & every man & officer will be paid all short allowance Money that is due for the Voyage, at the time they receive their Wages – For this reason it would be extremely vicious in a Captain to put his men at less than full allowance unless from a prospect of being in want of Supplies. The men who came home with Captain Bligh received their short allowance Money.[23]

This is a reasoned reply to the charges. Bligh had no interest in the prolonging of misery for its own sake. His view was that he gave as full rations as possible, and his entire mode of management was directed to proper and regular (and hot) food.

Morrison makes another complaint about food to which Bligh does not reply in his notes. The gist of the complaint was the quantity of food in the hot breakfasts allowance:

> The quantity was so Small, that it was no uncommon thing for four Men in a mess to draw lots for the Breakfast, and to divide their bread by the well-known method of 'Who shall have this', nor was the Officers a hair behind the Men at it ... The division of this scanty allowance Caused frequent broils in the Gally, and in the present bad Weather was often like to be attended with bad consequences and in one of these disputes the Cook, Thos. Hall, got two of his ribbs broke, & at another time Churchill got his Hand Scalded and it became necessary to have the Master's Mate of the watch to superintend the division of it.[24]

Bligh did record in his Log something that might refer to the same incidents. For 13 April 1788 the Log reads: 'My Gunner who has had charge of a Watch

[21] *ibid.*, p. 10.
[22] Bligh, Remarks, p. 46.
[23] *ibid.*, pp. 46-7.
[24] Morrison, Journal, p. 8.

is now laid up, and my Carpenters Mate, and from the violent motion of the ship the Cook fell and received a severe bruize and broke one of his Ribs and One Man Dislocated his shoulder.' The very next day the Log records that the surgeon, Thomas Huggan (probably contributing to his fall by drink), fell 'from a heavy lurch and dislocated his shoulder ... but happily it was soon put in again'. The *Bounty* at the time was in heavy seas off Cape Horn and, being a small ship, was tossed around wildly. The Log was written at the time; the charges five years later. Morrison at least concedes that the 'present bad weather' contributed to the accidents, which weakens his story. In a court in 1793 he could not produce the men he named, Hall and Churchill, as they were both dead by then; Hall died in Batavia after the boat voyage in 1789 and Churchill was murdered by Thompson in 1790. We know that Churchill was a trouble-maker and aggressive and he may indeed have been rowing about his share of the food. He was also the ship's Corporal and was meant to be assisting in keeping order and discipline. He might have had an argument which had nothing to do with food and somehow got his hand scalded. If he did, the altercation was unofficial; no action was taken to punish the man who scalded him. The officer of the watch may have sympathised with the other man.

As we saw, after Cape Horn Morrison does not complain about Bligh until the *Bounty* is at Tahiti, but in the Memorandum he makes a charge about financial deals at the Cape of Good Hope, more or less as an afterthought at the end of the text. Morrison introduces the subject of false book-keeping by alleging that the officers 'had in the former parts of their Voyage been base enough to sign false *Survey Books* and papers to the prejudice of his Majesty & Government'. The almost legal phraseology supports the suggestion that the Memorandum could have been the basis for a possible legal confrontation with Bligh. He goes on: 'That it may not be supposed, that this account has no foundation the Bills drawn at the Cape of Good Hope, will prove, that Wm. Muspratt and Thos. Hayward, both belonging to the *Bounty* have signed as respectable merchants of that place.'[25] Musprat was not an officer, he was an ordinary seaman, and Hayward was a midshipman, so they were not 'officers', a small detail perhaps but not one that would escape a legal enquiry. In the first quotation Morrison must be referring to something else, probably the well-known incident of Fryer refusing to sign the books. Bligh recorded that incident (discussed in Chapter 7) in his Log, which made it an official matter of record: the Admiralty could enquire further into the matter, calling Fryer and others as witnesses.

The second point, that Musprat and Hayward posed as 'merchants' to make false claims off the Admiralty, was answered by Bligh as follows:

> Surely if any thing will confute this assertion, & show this Morrison, (who was the worst of the Mutineers next to Christian & Churchill, if not their adviser,) in the light he ought to be held, it is this – Musprat & Hayward signed only as witnesses in C. Bligh's behalf that He payed the Money to

[25] Morrison, Memorandum, p. 39.

Mr C. Brandt due to him on an account with Capt. Bligh to prevent by any accident his calling on Capt. Bligh for a second payment – These Papers are now to be seen at the Publick Boards.[26]

This transaction is mentioned by Bligh in a letter from the Cape to Duncan Campbell, for whom he had spent four years in the merchant service as agent and Captain: 'My transactions here have enabled me to realise a little Cash, for which I beg leave to transmit to you an indorsed Bill to you by Christoffel Brand, Esqr. on the Victualling Board for 1236 Rix Dollars.'[27] Duncan Campbell was no doubt acting as agent for Bligh's affairs while he was away. Captains of Royal Navy ships signed bills on the Admiralty for their provisions and in due course the merchant presented them on the Admiralty in London for payment. False Bay is a long way from London, and no doubt the practice was to sell the bills to visiting captains, the local merchant selling the bill at a discount, i.e. accepting less than its face value, and the captain pocketing the difference when the bill was paid in London. Once the bill was endorsed, the Admiralty would pay the holder the face value. This arrangement made victualling at a long distance possible in an age when international money markets were comparatively primitive. Bligh would make a small commission – perhaps £30, as the sum involved is about £300 – which he would probably split with Campbell. This was the sort of 'profit' the Admiralty expected him to make on the victualling to supplement the low pay for doing both jobs (see note 5 above). When we remember that he had given up his job with Campbell at £500 a year to work for the King at about £70 a year, the need for this kind of supplement to his income becomes obvious.

Bligh's explanation of Musprat's and Hayward's signatures could be checked by an examination of the books. Hayward and Musprat were both available for questioning, and if Bligh had involved them in a fraud he would have been risking his neck on their goodwill. Their signatures on any paper in which they purported to be 'merchants' would get Bligh dismissed from the service, or worse. In view of Banks' continuing support for Bligh after this, it seems that he was satisfied with Bligh's explanation. Morrison himself dropped the charge in his Journal; something made him less sure of himself between October and December 1792.

A claim calculated to rouse Bligh was that just before landfall at Tahiti some men fell ill with scurvy. I have discussed in an earlier chapter the Surgeon's feud with Bligh and the way the scurvy question was used as a counter in the game. He replied to Banks: 'Captain Bligh never had a symptom of scurvy on any ship he commanded.' Once at Tahiti, the first complaint was again over food: 'The Market for Hogs beginning now to slacken Mr Bligh seized on all that came to the Ship big & small Dead or alive, taking them as his property, and serving them as the Ships Allowance at one pound pr man pr Day.'[28] The trade in hogs was carried on through Mr Peckover, the officially appointed trader, and islanders could also trade privately with their friends among the

[26] Bligh, Remarks, p. 52.
[27] Bligh to Duncan Campbell, 28 June 1788; Bligh Correspondence, MS Safe 1/40.
[28] Morrison, Journal, p. 19.

seamen (though this was forbidden by the ship's rules), or make them presents. When Morrison says the market had 'slackened' he presumably means that the demand from the ship exceeded the supply offered to the trading post. This could have been because the price in nails and so forth offered by Peckover was less than the price offered by unofficial dealings on the black market, or because there had been a diminution in stocks or in the amount the Tahitians were prepared to sell. We know that Peckover was having to roam further afield to get supplies (see p.82). In these circumstances it does not seem unreasonable that Bligh should requisition the hogs; as a result every man on board would get a pound of pork a day, instead of only some men having pork, while others less fortunate in their local friends got none. It is unlikely that a court would have convicted Bligh on this charge. Bligh, according to Morrison, 'also seized those belonging to the master and killed them for the ship's use'. Considering the state of affairs existing at that time between Bligh and Fryer, it is no wonder he made no exception regarding his pigs and it would be a cause for criticism if he had.

As any study of non-market allocation of goods, especially by legislative rationing, would show, the very act of trying to circumvent the market promotes increasingly sophisticated counter-measures:

> The Natives observing that the Hogs were seized as soon as they Came on board, and not knowing but they would be seized from them, as well as the People, became very shy of bringing a hog in sight of Lieut. Bligh either on board or on Shore, and watchd all opportunity when he was on Shore to bring provisions to their friends, but as Mr. Bligh observed this, and saw that his diligence was like to be evaded, he ordered a Book to be kept in the Binacle wherein the Mate of the Watch was to insert the Number of Hogs or Pigs with the Weight of each that came into the Ship to remedy this, the Natives took another Method which was Cutting the Pigs up and wraping them in leaves and covering the Meat with Breadfruit in the Baskets, and sometimes with peeld Cocoa Nuts, by Which means, as the Bread was never seized, they were match for all his industry; and he never suspected their artifice.[29]

The alternative would have been to raise the price of pigs at Peckover's trading post, by giving more nails per pig than before. But the iron 'money' in circulation was increasing, officially and unofficially; women got nails for sexual accommodation of the seamen, for instance, which not surprisingly was a brisk market; and it may be that a new official price for pigs was too high in Bligh's and Peckover's view. But by attempting to curb the unofficial dealings, Bligh only encouraged the most determined of his crew to engage in counter-measures in collusion with their friends. The problem, however, died down after a while; there is scant mention of it over the next four months up to the departure of the *Bounty* from the island.

The final paragraphs of the Memorandum are candid about Morrison's motive for writing, and support my point that he was trying to explain his own

[29] *ibid.*, p. 20.

lack of resistance to the mutiny by the failings of the officers, and explain these failures in turn by Bligh's own failings: 'It will no doubt be wondered at, that a Ship with 44 Men on board, should be taken by so small a Number as 10 or 11 which were the whole that ever appeared in Arms; on that Day 10 muskets, 2 Cutlasses and 2 Pistols were all that appeared to have been in use, when the Boat put off – But no resistance was made. It will here be asked why? It may be answered, that the Officers were not on such good terms with their Commander, as to risk their Lives in his service, and the Service of their Country was not at their Hearts.'[30] The entire Memorandum and Journal are dedicated to proving that proposition because on it depended Morrison's plea of innocence. The Memorandum and charges, circulated during the trial and afterwards while he was under appeal for King's mercy, established the special circumstances that gained him the pardon. The Admiralty establishment was cool to Bligh on his return from the voyage of the *Providence*. It was only by being able to answer each charge that he regained his state of grace, though it took him eighteen months to do so. His success in 1793, which was a private one between him, Sir Joseph Banks and the Admiralty establishment – his 'Remarks on Morrison's Journal' were never published – did not help in the aftermath of Heywood's biography. His detailed answers to the charges were 'lost' in the papers of Sir Joseph Banks, the Admiralty and his own family. Morrison had a monopoly for the next hundred years. A one-sided broadside into a person's reputation can hardly be less than damaging: in Bligh's case it was irreparable.

Bligh could justly point out to Sir Joseph Banks the most outstanding fact of all, namely that 'Among all these charges there is not one of cruelty or oppression'. I think this is the most significant aspect of the entire Morrison campaign against Bligh. He was unable to document, or invent, any action that could be regarded as a justification for mutiny. All his charges are aimed at showing why there was so little resistance to the mutiny once it started. Those who defended Christian were forced to invent cruelty and oppression where none could be found, and later authors have misused Morrison's testimony to support this view.

Did Morrison succeed in his aims of discrediting Bligh? The answer must be both yes and no. Bligh's unofficial answers to the individual charges stood up to examination, and still do. All the charges on food are weak, unsubstantiated and malicious. They are in complete conflict with the official record in the Log. To accept them is to suggest a major literary fraud on Bligh's part. The three most serious charges, those of the theft of ship's property, falsification of the books, and financial malpractice at the Cape, required documentary evidence to support them, and Bligh was confident this did not exist, even though Fryer, Coleman, Purcell, Musprat and Hayward were all available for questioning by the authorities. The fact that Morrison withdrew the charges relating to the books at the Cape of Good Hope, that he was not specific about what was going on in the refusal-to-sign incident when he compiled his Journal soon after the Memorandum was in circulation, and that the story of the theft of the

---

[30] Morrison, Memorandum, pp. 37-8.

cheeses depended on the testimony of two men implicated in the mutiny, neither being available for questioning, casts further doubt on these points. But many of the charges were later accepted, when in 1825 Heywood took the Journal, a special plea written by a condemned mutineer as a basis for possible charges against Bligh in a court martial, and presented it as a neutral documentary record of the voyage, an objective piece of independent testimony written by one who 'had the misfortune to witness all he has related'. As such, Morrison has had an enormous success.

21

Edward Christian's 'Appendix'

In the weeks after the trial, while awaiting the result of the court's recommendation to mercy, Heywood and his family remained optimistic that in due course he would be free. The news that he had been condemned was mitigated by informal assurances from relatives. One of these, Mrs Bertie, wife of one of the judges of the trial and a relative of the Heywoods, wrote to Mrs Heywood on 18 September 1792: 'I think your son's life is more safe now than it was before his trial. As there was not sufficient proof of his innocence, the Court could not avoid condemning him; but he is so strongly recommended to mercy, that I am desired to assure you by those who are judges, that his life is safe.'[1] Captain Albemarle Bertie was telling Mrs Heywood, through his wife, what the judges in the court had done to preserve his life while keeping the decencies of the service intact.

Heywood was in much the same predicament as Morrison. Like Morrison, his defence had been that he had not participated in the mutiny, and that as there had been no resistance to Christian by his superiors in rank and age he could not have been expected to initiate a resistance on his own. He argued in court that it was his inexperience and youth that caused him to be confused initially and that when he realised what was happening he was prevented from leaving the ship, or even from coming up on deck, by armed mutineers. Morrison had a different defence on this last point, as he was on the deck during the mutiny and was also at the aft rail while the boat was being set adrift. Also Heywood's defence did not, like Morrison's, try to make the conduct of Bligh a contributory factor to the success of the mutiny; this would have made Heywood more sophisticated than his defence allowed. Innocent youths cannot also appear to be perceptive analysts.

The contrite attitude Heywood displayed in court vanished, however, in the time it took him to get from H.M.S. *Hector* to London. He had been put through a lot of misery and uncertainty because Bligh had not cleared his name; he had come close to a hanging and his family had been driven to extremes of anxiety over his safety. From Aaron Graham's house in Great Russell Street he wrote the following letter to Edward Christian, brother of Fletcher Christian, and Professor of Law at Cambridge University:

Sir, I am sorry to say that I have been informed you were inclined to judge too harshly of your truly unfortunate brothre, and to think of him in such a

[1] Quoted in Tagart, 1832, p. 127.

manner, as I am conscious from the knowledge I had of his most worthy disposition and character, (both public and private) he merits not in the slightest degree: therefore, I think it my duty, Sir, to endeavour to undeceive you, and to re-kindle the flame of brotherly love (or pity now) towards him, which I fear the false reports of slander and vile suspicion may have nearly extinguished. Excuse my freedom, Sir: if it would not be disagreeable to you, I will myself have the pleasure of waiting upon you, and endeavour to prove that your brother was not the vile wretch void of all gratitude, which the world had the unkindness to think him: but, on the contrary, a most worthy character; ruined only by having the misfortune, if it can be so called, of being a young man of strict honour, adorned with every virtue, and beloved by all (except one, whose ill report is his greatest praise) who had the pleasure of his acquaintance.[2]

What a transformation from Heywood's public statements during the trial! If he had exhibited these sentiments there he would undoubtedly have hanged. Indeed, it was somewhat rash of him to commit them to paper so soon after his pardon. Taken at face value, the letter is an admission of his personal leanings during the mutiny and makes nonsense of his claim to have been young and confused. If this is an expression of his real views then we can take it as plausible that he did pick up a cutlass, that he did laugh at Bligh's predicament and that he had no intention of getting into the launch with his commander; that his pose at the trial was a contrived and rehearsed one designed to make it easy for the court to acquit him.

Heywood had arrived at Aaron Graham's house in London on Monday 29 October 1792 and he dated his letter to Edward Christian 'Saturday November 5'. During the intervening week, while recovering from his ordeal as a prisoner, he must have been informed by somebody of the state of opinion in Christian's family about their relative. Bligh's accounts of the mutiny and the voyage of the *Bounty* had been published in 1790 and 1792; both accounts exonerated Bligh and his conduct, and by virtue of the epic voyage in the *Bounty*'s launch made him into a hero of the times. Fletcher Christian was in public disgrace. The verdicts of the trial regarding the men who were hanged – they were executed the very morning that Heywood arrived at Great Russell Street to meet his sisters and brother – were an ominous portent of Christian's fate should he be captured and returned to Britain. Clearly, the person who informed Heywood of the Christian family's distress must have known both of them; and it may have been this person who persuaded Heywood to write a letter of comfort to Edward Christian.[3] Heywood did this with unrestrained enthusiasm. He resolutely attacked Bligh's version of the mutiny – 'false reports of slander and vile suspicion'[4] – and of Bligh's ill regard of Fletcher he declared that his 'ill report is his

[2] There are two sources for this letter: *Cumberland Packet*, 20 November 1792, of which an original cutting is in the Banks Papers, Brabourne Collection, ML MS A78-4, p. 2; and Bligh, 1794.

[3] This could have been Aaron Graham.

[4] This clearly refers to the *Narrative*, and its assumption that the cause of the mutiny was the mutineers' interest in getting back to Tahiti and the women they had left there.

greatest praise'. This was a direct encouragement to Edward Christian to alter his views on his brother's behaviour.

I am assuming that this letter was not a contrived piece of public propaganda. That, of course, is a distinct possibility. It could be that the Christian family were not so inwardly convinced of Fletcher's guilt as the letter suggests, or that, even if they were, they had already considered possible ways of clearing his name. They had not raised their colours before or during the trial because they did not want to jeopardise any trial he might have to face if he was caught. But once the trial was over and Heywood was released to them as a hostile witness against Bligh, the possibilities materialised of laying the ground for an eventual defence of their relative.

Edward Christian had made enquiries about Peter Heywood from Captain Edwards in July 1792. There is a copy of a letter to Edward Christian in Captain Edwards's papers[5] which reads as follows:

I am exceedingly sorry that I was prevented answering your very kind & obliging letter sooner by its not coming to my hand till this moment. The unfortunate young man Peter Heywood whom you mention in your letter I understand is at present on board a Guardship at Portsmouth and is to take his trial with the other men that are involved in the same affair with himself – I apprehend he did not take an active part against Mr. Bligh – how far he may be reprehensible for not taking an active & decided part in his favour in the early part of the business will depend on the construction the court may put on the evidence given, & the allowance that may be made in consideration of his youth – shd. that also be made to appear – I have had some conversation on the subject w. Comt. Pasley with whose family the Young man has some connection he like you says that he has been informed that the Young Man was only sixteen years old at the time of the mutiny – I have only to observe that he appeared to me to be much older and I understand that he passed for, and was considered to be so onboard the Bounty – whatever might be his conduct in the affair when on bd. the Bounty he certainly came onbd. the Pandora of his own accord almost immediately after she came to an Anchor at Otaheito. I believe he has abilities & am informed that he made himself master of the Otaheetian Language whilst on that Island which may be of public utility – it is greatly to be lamented that Youth through their own indiscretion or bad example shd. be involved in such dificulties and bring ignominy on themselves & distress to their friends.

It is interesting that Edward Christian wrote to Edwards asking about the fate of Peter Heywood and not, apparently, about Christian or anybody else. This suggests he was collecting information about Heywood to pass on to Heywood's family. The Christians and the Heywoods knew each other from their connections in the Isle of Man and in Cumberland. The indefatigable Nessy was writing to everybody, including the Admiralty, and it would have been surprising if she had missed writing to the Christians.

---

[5] Captain Edward Edwards, Private Papers, Admiralty Library, Fulham; letter from him to Edward Christian, 17 July, 1792.

Whether it was contrived or genuine, Heywood's letter certainly had a dramatic effect upon the Christians. They moved swiftly to take up the chase for Bligh's reputation. Heywood must have met Edward Christian in the week or so after he sent his letter. On 20 November the *Cumberland Packet and Whitehaven Advertiser* carried the following report:

The world will be astonished at the information, which will shortly be communicated by a gentleman who attended the trial as an advocate: the public will then be enabled to correct the erroneous opinions, which from a false narrative[6] they have long entertained, and to distinguish between audacious and hardened depravity of the heart which no suffering can soften and the desperation of an ingenious mind torn and agonised by unprovoked and incorrect abuse and disgrace.

Though there can be certain actions, which even the torture of extremity of provocation cannot justify, yet a sudden act of frenzy so circumstanced, is far removed in reason and mercy from the final deliberate contempt of every religious and virtuous sentiment and obligation. For the honour of this county we are happy to assure our readers, that one of its natives, Fletcher Christian, is not the detestable and horrid monster of wickedness which with extreme and perhaps unequalled injustice and barbarity to him and his relatives he has long been represented, but a character for whom every feeling heart must now fiercely grieve and lament.

Along with this statement Heywood's letter to Edward Christian was published. His name was not mentioned; he was billed simply as a 'late officer of the *Bounty*'.

That Edward Christian had been busy in the short time between Heywood's letter and the appearance of the news item in the local county paper can be seen from the statement that 'a gentleman who attended the trial as an advocate' was shortly to produce a communication which would expose Bligh's *Narrative*.[7] Stephen Barney had been at the trial representing Musprat and he had arranged for his assistants to take minutes of the proceedings, presumably to assist in the defence. Musprat owed his life to Barney's legal skill. In his own Introduction to the minutes, eventually published in 1794, Barney writes the following:[8]

[6] Bligh's 1790 *Narrative*, then fairly well known in the country.

[7] I have assumed that this referred to Stephen Barney, Musprat's advocate, in view of his later connection with Christian's efforts to get the Appendix published; it may, however, refer to Aaron Graham. After Heywood's apparent withdrawal from the campaign fairly early on, taking Graham with him, Christian would have needed to find someone else and might then have turned to Barney.

[8] Barney, 1794. Quoted in Rutter (ed.), 1931, p. 56. He writes (p. 55): 'A comparison between [Barney's *Minutes*] and the official minutes shows that the former contains a great deal of free paraphrase on the part of those responsible for its publication. It also contains numerous errors, the most serious of which is that the trial is stated to have begun on 12 April 1792 – whereas in reality the date was 12 September. Nor is this all; for at the end of the work there is printed the correction: 'Page 1, line 1, for *April* read August'. The evidence does not go beyond that given by Lieut. Corner, and none of the defence is printed, but Bligh's Coupang letter, of which no copy is attached to the original minutes, is given.' Christian's Appendix to the *Minutes* is reproduced in full in Smith, 1937.

The following Minutes of the Trial of the Mutineers of the Bounty were taken by myself and my clerks, being employed to give Assistance before the Court-Martial, to William Musprat, one of the Prisoners. They were not continued beyond the Evidence for the Prosecution, nor do they comprize the whole of the Evidence respecting the Capture of all the different Prisoners at Otaheite. They were not intended for Publication. Repeated Assurances have been given, that an impartial State of all the Circumstances attending that unhappy Mutiny, as well as a complete Trial of the Prisoners, would be published. The anxious Relations of the unfortunate Parties in that Mutiny, worn out with Expectation of that Publication, have repeatedly solicited my consent to publish my Minutes, and as such Publication may in some Degree alleviate their Distress, I cannot think myself justified in witholding such Consent, and hope this will be a sufficient Apology for my Conduct. I affirm, that as far as those Minutes go, they contain a just State of the Evidence given at the Court-Martial.

The *Minutes* as they stood were of little use to the campaign against Bligh. They only put the prosecution evidence and were in any case confined to a discussion of the role played by the prisoners during the mutiny. The cause of the mutiny was not discussed, on the sound legal grounds that mutiny is not justifiable under any circumstances. Edward Christian needed to turn the discussion to the cause of the mutiny without appearing to countenance mutiny itself. He was a resourceful and intelligent advocate and he set to work to achieve this difficult task. The delay in the publication of the *Minutes* was to give him time to prepare his Appendix.

The method he adopted was brilliant. He decided to organise a 'court of enquiry' that would hear 'evidence' from the men of the *Bounty* and sit in 'judgment' as to the causes of the mutiny. Whether Fletcher was guilty of mutiny was not in question – his guilt was conceded in advance. The Appendix was designed to help protect him if he was caught. The 1792 trial, while making probable a conviction against Fletcher, also raised the possibility of mitigation 'in consideration of various circumstances'. The longer the period of time that Fletcher was free, the greater were his chances of surviving a court martial. The *Pandora* had failed to find him and other ships might also miss him. There was the possibility of accidental discovery – Bligh, for example, was in the Pacific at that moment in the *Providence* – which added some urgency to the campaign. The purpose of the campaign was to discredit Bligh by damaging his integrity and weakening his credibility, which would make possible an inconclusive trial. If the witnesses for the prosecution testified in favour of Christian as Heywood was volunteering to do, the chances of Fletcher's escaping the gallows increased. It was not a strategy guaranteed to succeed. The court could just as easily move a formal verdict of Guilty and remain ummoved by a plea of mitigation. But three men found guilty of mutiny had escaped legal retribution and a gentleman with strong connections might do likewise.

Edward Christian's public attack on Bligh opened with the publication of Stephen Barney's *Minutes* in 1794, with an Appendix written by Edward

Christian. In a letter to Barney, Christian made the following observations on his publication:

> Sir, I assure you I regard the publication of your Minutes of the Court-martial as a very great favour done to myself, and I am the more sensible of the obligation from being convinced that they were not originally taken with an intent to publish. But they appear to be so full and satisfactory; that, from your further kindness in permitting the extraordinary information which I have collected to be annexed as an Appendix, the Public, I trust, will at length be possessed of a complete knowledge of the real causes and circumstances of that most melancholy event, the Mutiny on board the Bounty. It is unnecessary for me to add, that I alone am responsible for the authenticity, or rather accuracy, of the information contained in the Appendix, as far at least as it has been obtained by me, in the manner and from the persons described therein.[9]

What was left out of the Appendix, and has been left out of much of the comment on it since, is an account of the 'real causes and circumstances' of how the 'extraordinary information' was collected. This is a defect that I hope to rectify.

To appreciate the full significance of Edward's actions we must go back to Fletcher's boyhood in Cockermouth, Cumberland. Fletcher was born at the family farm, Moorland Close, near Cockermouth in 1764.[10] Among his contemporaries were William and Dorothy Wordsworth, whose home still stands at the junction of the road from Moorland Close to Cockermouth.[11] William Wordsworth went to the local grammar school and later had Edward Christian as one of his headmasters. He was eight years younger than Fletcher and went on to St John's College, Cambridge, in 1787, not long before the *Bounty* left Sp   ad for Tahiti. Edward Christian had preceded Wordsworth at St John's,   had Wordsworth's uncle, the Rev. Mr Cookson, and William Wilberforce. Wordsworth's tutor at St John's was a Rev. Dr Frewen. The Wordsworth family knew Christian and, as we shall see shortly, all the gentlemen mentioned above turn up in Edward Christian's campaign in 1792-4.

Among Fletcher's distinguished relatives was his cousin, John Christian, who as we have seen changed his name to John Curwen.[12] Fletcher had been named after his mother's family, the Fletchers, who were prominent local people with distant connections to the Earl of Annandale, the Earl of Westmorland and the Marquesses of Cleveland. The political connections of the Christians were extensive. John Curwen was a whig Member of

---

[9] Appendix, p. 60.

[10] The original house still stands and is occupied (1974). On the wall in the yard is a plaque identifying the house as the birthplace of Fletcher Christian, 'Leader of the Mutiny on the Bounty'.

[11] The Wordsworths' house is now a museum; the local school, now used as a kindergarten, has a plaque commemorating the fact that Wordsworth and Fletcher Christian were once students there.

[12] The Curwens resided in Workington Hall, Cockermouth, which had been visited by Mary, Queen of Scots. In 1973 the hall was demolished to make way for a car park.

Parliament and became a national figure in politics. He was closely identified with the interest of the Duke of Portland (later Prime Minister). In fact, the family was well enough connected to be able to draw on a wide range of influential people, and some measure of Edward's abilities can be gained from the number of such family contacts he persuaded to participate in his 'enquiry'.[13] Naturally, there was no overt reference in his Appendix to the relationships between the enquiry's members and the Christian family. This might not have been necessary in the smaller public society of the time where the political and personal affiliations of people were known by those interested; the men named in the Appendix might have provoked wry smiles in several quarters among people who knew the true extent of their 'independence'. But in the wider public the mere appearance of respectable gentlemen in the list carried weight. Certainly in later years the Christian enquiry came to be accepted as what it purported to be, an informal, unbiased and independent group of gentlemen, including several from the Church, who simply reported what they were told by the seamen and officers of the *Bounty*.

The men listed in the Appendix were:

John Farhill, No.38, Mortimer-street;
Samuel Romilly, Esq. Lincoln's Inn;
Mr. Gilpin, No.432, Strand;
the Rev. Dr. Fisher, Canon of Windsor;
the Rev. Mr. Cookson, Canon of Windsor;
Captain Wordsworth, of the *Abergavenny* East Indiaman;
Rev. Mr. Antrobus, Chaplain to the Bishop of London;
John France, Esq., Temple;
James Losh, Esq., Temple;
Rev. Dr. Frewen, Colchester;
John Atkinson, Esq. Somerset Herald.[14]

The striking fact is that all but two are known to have had strong connections with the Christians before the enquiry. Interestingly, there are among them a number of connections with William Wordsworth, who was at the time in his early and unrestrained passion for the French Revolution. Young, energetic, idealist and available, William Wordsworth came into the campaign some time after his return from France in late 1792. Some of the gentlemen drawn into the enquiry may have come in as a result of canvassing by the young Wordsworth.

The Reverend Mr Antrobus came from Cockermouth and therefore knew Fletcher and Edward Christian; he also went to St John's College, Cambridge, of which college Edward was a Fellow and William Wordsworth a student. The Reverend Doctor Frewen, already noted as a tutor of William Wordsworth at St John's College, was also a friend of Edward Christian. The Reverend Mr Cookson, listed as 'Canon of Windsor', was the uncle of

[13] The information in this chapter on the Christian family background is based on Wilkinson, 1953.
[14] Appendix, pp. 62-3.

William Wordsworth, and during the months of the enquiry in 1793 he was giving William and Dorothy hospitality at his house at Forncett in Norfolk. Another Wordsworth relative, Captain John Wordsworth, was also related by marriage to Isabella Curwen. Apart from this reason for participating in Christian's inquiry, he was also employed by the East India Company, which brought him within the reach of Christian's relative Sir Harry Fletcher M.P. and Dr Fisher, both involved at high level in that company's affairs.

The Reverend Dr Fisher had several connections with both Christian and Wordsworth. He was an intimate friend of Edward Law, a first cousin of Fletcher Christian. Edward Law was a brilliant advocate, who had defended Warren Hastings at his trial, and rose to be Lord Chief Justice and a member of the Cabinet. Dr Fisher became Rector of Nether Stowey, in Somerset, and in 1795-6 we find the Wordsworths and Coleridges also living there.

James Losh, a legal contemporary of Edward Christian, knew Fletcher Christian and both himself and his brother were also close friends of the Wordsworths. He was by all accounts an extraordinary personality. He was deeply sympathetic to the French Revolution and counted Marat among his friends. He was a member of the Society of Friends of the People, which even John Curwen had joined. The possible parallel between the 1789 mutiny on the *Bounty* and the storming of the Bastille probably did not escape him in the attempt to re-write Christian's actions as a struggle against tyranny. Losh was unlikely to be objective about the affair.

Samuel Romilly was also a legal contemporary, though older and much more experienced. He was a close friend of Edward Christian and of Wilberforce, the anti-slavery campaigner, and also an honorary member of the French Revolutionary Convention. The fact that the *Bounty* was on a mission to transplant a cheap food for black slaves would help to turn him against Bligh. Both Mr Gilpin and John Atkinson were neighbours of the Christians in Cockermouth (thereby also knowing the Wordsworths), and would be keen to restore the honour of the county. I have not been able to fit John Farhill and John France into any similar category, but given the weight of connection between the others and the Christians it seems more than likely that they were also connected in some way.

Having drawn up the personnel with such meticulous care to protect the family interests, he arranged the panel's working arrangements in the way best calculated to minimise the risk of legal redress. The Appendix asserted the following: 'Each of these gentlemen has heard the declarations of one at the least of the persons before mentioned; some have had an interview with five or six of them at different times, together with the writer of this Appendix, who is confident that every one of these gentlemen will bear testimony that what he has heard is not here exaggerated or misrepresented. There is no contradiction or variance whatever, in the account given by the gentlemen and people of the *Bounty* though they could not upon every occasion, be all present together, and therefore cannot all relate exactly the same circumstances.'[15]

[15] *ibid.*, p. 63.

This tells us a great deal about the working arrangements of the panel. Only Edward Christian was present at all meetings of the gentlemen in the panel. He kept notes and from them drew up the Appendix. His authority for the accuracy of his account was that members of the panel were present on each occasion. Everything was witnessed, but individual gentlemen could testify only to the sessions that they attended. They did not meet as a complete group. Some met the *Bounty* men several times and others only once. When they were assembled, often in a local hotel after a dinner, individual members of the *Bounty* crew were brought before them and those present questioned, or listened to Edward Christian questioning, the 'witness' for his version of life on the *Bounty* before the mutiny. This procedure made it impossible to know which of the panel of gentlemen were witnesses to which part of the evidence. As Edward only rarely attributed a statement to a particular *Bounty* man, we do not know who said what; and as we do not know who witnessed the evidence, we cannot comment on the partiality of Edward's interpretation or reportage.

As the intention of the enquiry was the defamation of Bligh's character, the presentation of the Appendix had to protect Edward and his associates from prosecution. The procedures of the enquiry ensured this brilliantly. Edward was so confident that he agreed to indemnify Stephen Barney for any action that Bligh might take over its publication. Should Bligh wish to sue for libel, whom would he sue? He could not identify who said what. With a professor of law, several distinguished lawyers of formidable intellect, and men of the Church forming the panel, Bligh would have been hard pressed to get a clear-cut verdict. It would have been a confused and expensive case. The Appendix appeared to be a statement of the views of the *Bounty*'s crew, and the witnesses needed by Bligh to clear his name could all be compromised by allegations about the testimony made by them to the gentlemen.

It would not be worthwhile here to examine every part of the Appendix line by line, but it is necessary to look at what it said, its consistency as evidence, its effects on Bligh and the Admiralty, and Bligh's answers, both published and unpublished, to the charges.

Altogether twelve of the survivors of the *Bounty* mutiny were named in the Appendix as in contact with the panel at unspecified dates in 1793. These were John Fryer; Thomas Hayward; William Peckover; William Purcell; John Smith; Lawrence Lebogue; Joseph Coleman; Thomas McIntosh; Michael Byrne; Peter Heywood; William Musprat; James Morrison. Not all of them were interviewed face to face. James Morrison, for example, was in contact with the panel only by letter, which is one of the major mysteries of the episode, in view of the Journal with which he was busy during the early part of the Christian campaign. Other members of the *Bounty* who were available were not identified as being interviewed, or even contacted, which does not mean that they were not in fact brought before the gentlemen; their evidence may not have been of use to the campaign. Among the people not listed as interviewed were John Samuel, Bligh's loyal Clerk; George Simpson, Quartermaster's Mate; John Hallet, the junior midshipman, who gave the damaging testimony against Heywood in the trial; Robert Tinkler, brother-in-law of John Fryer, and surely a safe Christian man; and Morrison's boss, William Cole the Boatswain. The Appendix simply states that 'the following circumstances have been collected from many interviews and conversations' without specifying whether or not some interviews and conversations were excluded.

The striking thing about the Appendix is that only two men are directly identified with their statements, namely, John Fryer and William Purcell. This is highly significant, first, for Christian's motives in identifying them and secondly, for their motives for allowing him to do so. Of Christian's motives, we have evidence that with the Appendix he hoped actually to provoke Bligh into a libel suit. In a subsequent exchange of pamphlets between Christian and Bligh, Christian confesses the following: 'Many gentlemen, besides myself, suppose that if any answer could be given, it would be attempted in a court of justice by some judicial proceeding.'[16] It did not take him long to realise that he had cast-iron witnesses against Bligh in the persons of Fryer and Purcell; they hated Bligh too deeply to lose their nerve before a court. Fryer and Purcell were themselves willing tools in Christian's campaign. Their records on the *Bounty* were nothing to be proud of and they were so unpopular that even Fletcher Christian had not wanted them to stay on board. This should have created an awkward situation with Edward, but a common enemy helped them overcome natural hostility. Their own role in the breakdown of discipline on the *Bounty* hardly marks them out as competent witnesses, and the fact that Christian had to use them extensively says much about the paucity of evidence against Bligh. In all there are six references to Fryer and six to Purcell in the Appendix. Bligh had not mentioned the impossible conduct of these two individuals in his *Narrative* and therefore the general public was unaware of the reasons behind their testimony. In the Appendix they were simply listed as officers of the *Bounty*, with the implication that they were responsible witnesses against Bligh. Purcell had been court-martialled by Bligh on their return, to escape with a reprimand which only served to encourage his impudence and insubordination. Fryer had also received evidence of Bligh's continuing hostility to him when Bligh refused him a character reference as Master on the request of Captain Riou.[17]

Edward used Fryer's testimony to establish that Fletcher had planned to get away on some planks the night before the mutiny and the references in the Appendix are identical to those in Fryer's private Journal. Fryer is also quoted as testifying that two of the mutineers told him that Christian and the mutineers had agreed not to commit murder. This gratuitous mention of their humanitarianism is in contrast to the facts. The food allowed to the loyalists by the mutineers more or less sentenced them to death by starvation. Fryer's statement is used to discredit Hayward and Hallet: 'This

[16] Edward Christian, 1795.
[17] Bligh, Bounty Mutineers, ML MS Safe 1/43, p. 49, 'Remarks of Captain Bligh on the Court Martial': 'Riou applied for Fryer, & I refused to give any a good Character, Capt. Burney present.'

statement cannot be reconciled with the testimony of Mr. Hayward and Mr. Hallet', the implication being that these two witnesses for the prosecution were liars. The Appendix also permits Fryer to repeat his claim at the trial that he was put in the boat with Bligh 'in consequence of his design to retake the ship being overheard', a proposition singularly lacking credibility.

To assist in the destruction of Bligh the Appendix notes that Fryer and Bligh had not been dining together since some time before the mutiny. The readers of the Appendix are left in ignorance as to what had passed between these two men, and were directed implicitly to conclude that Bligh's behaviour was so intolerable that his Master had found it more congenial to eat alone. Fryer is also used to bring out Fletcher's self-torment and distress at the 'hell' he was suffering from Bligh, again without reference to what had been going on since leaving Matavai Bay. Fryer's subjection to the needs of the Appendix is completed by associating him with the joint opinion 'of all those who came in the boat' that in spite of their 'sufferings and losses' on Fletcher's account, they nevertheless speak of him 'without resentment and with forgiveness', and, indeed, 'with a degree of rapture and enthusiasm'. This is really the most extraordinary testimony in the entire Appendix. Fryer and the others in the boat with Bligh went through great deprivation and danger and in spite of it all they speak 'with rapture and enthusiasm' of the perpetrator of their misfortunes, and transfer all their hatred to Bligh, whose seamanship saved their lives.

William Purcell proves as reliable a witness as Fryer, giving a vivid and emotional description of Fletcher's state of mind before the mutiny. Purcell told the panel that 'tears were running fast from his eyes in big drops'. He also reports an alleged conversation between himself and Fletcher, unlikely when one considers that Fletcher sent him away in the boat. 'Do not I receive as bad as you do?' says Purcell to Christian, and is told that 'you have something to protect you, and can speak again; but if I should speak to him as you do, he would probably break me, turn me before the mast, and perhaps flog me; and if he did, it would be the death of us both, for I am sure I should take him in my arms, and jump overboard with him.' We can believe that Purcell told the panel this; it fits his independent character and his way with Bligh on the *Bounty*. Whether Fletcher said anything like it to him is another matter. How much more Purcell said which is excluded from the Appendix on the grounds that it would expose him as an unreliable witness we do not know, but public disclosure of his behaviour on the *Bounty* would not have helped his testimony. The suggestion that Bligh had any idea of breaking Christian – the man he made Acting Lieutenant – or of flogging him is absurd. To soften the public impact of the mutineers' action in sending nineteen men away in an overcrowded boat in the middle of the ocean – an act more serious from a humanitarian point of view than the mutiny – Purcell is quoted to show that those who went in the launch 'were sure of getting to shore, where they expected to live, until an European ship arrived, or until they could raise their boat or build a greater'. The folly of such a belief is shown by the fate of the survivors of the La Pérouse expedition.

Other remarks are almost laughable. In the passage quoted a mutineer states of Purcell: 'You might as well give him the ship as his tool chest', a remark also noted by Bligh in his *Narrative*. To excuse Christian's attempted murder of nineteen of his crew mates on the grounds that he sent along the ever-willing Purcell to build a boat for them to go home in makes Edward Christian both gullible and mischievous. Purcell's unique contribution to the open voyage – a continuation of his disgraceful behaviour in the *Bounty* – is not mentioned in the Appendix. What is mentioned instead is the charge that the difficulties which the men met with on their landfall at Tofoa were the result of Bligh's treatment of the chiefs at Annamooka. In a final blast at Bligh, Purcell is quoted in a fine example of his usual clever impudence against his commander. 'In a misunderstanding about some oysters, between the Captain and the carpenter, Captain Bligh told him: 'If I had not taken so much pains with you, you would never have been here'; the Carpenter replied, 'Yes, if you had not taken so much pains with us, we should never have been here'.[18] It is not surprising that Bligh lost his temper with the man.

Edward wanted to assure the public that he was not relying on the testimony of men who were pardoned mutineers. He wrote: 'The writer of this Appendix thinks it necessary to assure the reader that no material fact here stated stands in need of their testimony or confirmation.' Thus Heywood, Morrison and Musprat are apparently only used in conjunction with other witnesses untainted by association with the mutiny. A closer study of the Appendix shows Edward to have been less than candid about this. The Appendix mentions the now famous incident between Heywood and Fletcher when the *Bounty* was about to sail on its final voyage from Tahiti, although the sole witness for this transaction was Peter Heywood. George Stewart, the other person supposed to have been present, was dead. Therefore Edward Christian had to rely on the testimony of Heywood for this information. That it was important is evidenced by the inclusion of the following in the Appendix: 'Christian took leave to Mr Stewart and Mr Heywood, and told them he should sail that evening; and desired them, if they ever got to England, to inform his friends and country what had been the cause of his committing so desperate an act; but to guard against any obstruction, he concealed the time of his sailing from the rest.'[19] I have argued (p.143) that this 'meeting' probably never took place. Some years later, however, it took on an even more mysterious character. In an exchange of correspondence between Heywood and Captain Beechey in 1830, Heywood wrote: 'At that last interview with Christian he also communicated to me, for the satisfaction of his relations, other circumstances connected with that unfortunate disaster, which, after their deaths, may or may not be laid before the public. And although they can implicate none but himself, either living or dead, they may extenuate but will contain not a word of his in defence of the crime he committed against the laws of his country.'[20] This is good stuff for a

[18] Appendix, p. 68.
[19] *ibid.*, p. 74.
[20] Peter Heywood to Captain Beechey, 5 April 1830; quoted in Barrow, 1961, pp. 91-2.

mystery, but makes little sense. The letter implies that he had passed on these 'other circumstances' to the Christian family but he gives no clue as to what they were. His only suggestion was that he might tell the public at large after the deaths of the relatives. But who could Heywood have been protecting in 1830? Edward Christian had died in 1823, John Curwen in 1828. Was he waiting for the entire family to die out? He was dead himself by 1831. The assurance that the 'other circumstances' would implicate none but Christian weighs against the theory that they were a confession of Christian's homosexual relationship with Bligh.[21] If they referred entirely to himself they could either have been something physical (venereal disease has been suggested)[22] or an acknowledgment of his disturbed mental state – that is, assuming that they were not a figment of Heywood's resourceful imagination.

The other incidents in the Appendix which involve Peter Heywood also involve William Peckover. We can establish this by knowledge of where both men were during the first visit of the *Bounty* to Tahiti. Fletcher had the command of the shore party, assisted by Heywood and Peckover. The two botanists, Nelson and Brown, were also on shore, but in 1793 Nelson was dead and Brown was in the Pacific with Fletcher. The incidents mentioned in the Appendix could only have come from Heywood or Peckover. The most interesting, if historically futile, claim made by the Appendix in regard to the shore-party was that Fletcher had no particular female friend at Tahiti. Besides restoring his public virtue this claim could serve also as a rebuttal of Bligh's charge that the mutiny was occasioned by a desire to return to the women of Tahiti. The Appendix says: 'The officers who were with Christian upon the same duty declare, that he never had a female favourite at Otaheite, nor any attachment or particular connection among the women.' This was not true; he did have a female companion and he took her to Pitcairn.

The Appendix makes several statements which are hypocritical. For example, it alleges reasons for Christian's taking Tahitian men and women to Tubuai which totally contradict their real function – to be servants and concubines. 'It was thought that the Otaheite men would be useful in introducing them to the friendship and good offices of the natives.' What use the women were to be put to is not, of course, mentioned and cannot be without conceding something to Bligh's charges. The presentation of the voyage to Tubuai as a friendly jaunt across the ocean hides the bloody truth of Christian's first visit, and naturally there is not a word about the man whom Christian murdered there for his coconuts, and the terrible retribution exacted on the innocent in the final bloody massacre. But the purpose of the Appendix was not to bring out the truth; it was to present Fletcher Christian as the clean-living gentleman, beloved by all.

According to the Appendix Bligh denigrated Fletcher in front of the Tahitian chiefs. Edward quotes some speeches here which could have come from either Peckover or Heywood, who both spoke the language. There is no

[21] *See* Darby, 1965; and *see* Chapter 13 above for a fuller discussion of the homosexuality theory.
[22] Smith, 1936.

mention of the provocative incident at the tents with the blatant breaking of the local taboo, no mention of Christian's incompetent seamanship in the launch while negotiating the tricky entrance to the harbour at Oparre, no mention of the beating Peckover was threatened with by the behaviour of the star witness of the Appendix, John Fryer, no mention of the murders, assaults and rapes of the *Bounty* mutineers at Tahiti, nothing in fact that' could possibly sully the reputation of anyone except Captain Bligh.

Even the dead Nelson is brought forward as a witness against Bligh. 'It ought to be known,' writes Edward Christian, 'that Mr Nelson, in conversation afterwards with an officer at Timor, who was speaking of returning with Captain Bligh if he got another ship, observed, 'I am surprised that you should think of going a second time with one (using a term of abuse) who has been the occasion of all our losses'. Who gave Christian this information? It could not have been Nelson, because he died shortly after reaching Batavia. It must have been the officer to whom Nelson was speaking, probably William Peckover. It certainly could not have been Fryer or Purcell, because Bligh would never have let either of them near a ship of his again, and both knew it. If it had been Thomas Hayward there was no need to hide his identity because he was one of the witnesses for the prosecution. John Hallet was not listed as having been called before the panel, Linkletter and Elphinston had died in Batavia, and Ledward, the Surgeon, had disappeared *en route* to the Cape of Good Hope. Among the 'officers' this leaves William Cole, who apparently did not testify before the panel, and possibly Lawrence Lebogue and John Smith. Lebogue, the sailmaker, was with Bligh in the *Pandora* and was loyal to him; John Smith was the ship's cook. It would have been stretching the use of the term 'officer' to use it to refer to either of them.

If it was Peckover who provided the information, this fits the fact that Nelson and Peckover knew each other well. They had spent five months on shore-duties and had been on one of Cook's voyages together. In a letter from Bligh to Sir Joseph Banks, written nearly two years before Christian wrote his Appendix, we find confirmation that it was Peckover, and also a reason for Peckover's disliking Bligh:[23]

> Should Peckover my late Gunner ever trouble you to render him further services I shall esteem it a favor if you will tell him I informed you he was a viscious and worthless fellow – He applied to me to render him service & wanted to be appointed Gunner of the *Providence* but as I had determined never to suffer an officer who was with me in the *Bounty* to sail with again, it was for that cause I did not apply for him.

Clearly the motive of his testimony was in return for Bligh's refusing to have him with him again. Peckover was fascinated by the Pacific and the *Providence* was another chance to go there. Of course, it was Bligh's own doing that he turned all his officers against him by his break with them on the return of the

---

[23] William Bligh to Sir Joseph Banks, 17 July 1791; Hough, 1972, p. 286, incorrectly describes Peckover as 'a steady and reliable Bligh man'.

survivors of the boat voyage in 1790. In this way he created hostages against his good name, open to exploitation by the Christian family.

One piece of evidence brought into the open by the Appendix concerns the role of George Stewart, midshipman, in instigating the mutiny. The Appendix published this account of Stewart's role: 'It is agreed that Christian was the first to propose the mutiny, and the project of turning the Captain on shore at Tofoa, to the people of his watch; but he declared afterwards in the ship, he never should have thought of it, if it had not been suggested to his mind by an expression of Mr Stewart, who knowing of his intention of leaving the ship upon the raft, told him, "When you go, Christian, we are ripe for any thing". '[24] This was published in 1794, only two years after the trial in which Heywood's defence had been that he and his friend, George Stewart, were both innocent of the affair, knew nothing about it until they were woken by the shouting, and were too inexperienced to know what to do. Heywood must have been worried by this evidence because it was contrary to his own sworn testimony. He rejected it, we can be sure, and the associated disagreement may have ruptured his relations with Edward Christian. He may have realised that the Christian family in pursuit of their family interests were a threat to himself. Certainly he seems to have dropped out of contact with Christian soon after the Appendix was under way. As we saw in an earlier chapter, not only was Morrison's Journal against him, but new testimony supporting Morrison turned up when Captain Beechey was able to question John Adams, the last survivor on Pitcairn; Beechey wrote to Heywood in 1830 to point out the discrepancy between what Adams told him and what Heywood had written in his biography in 1825. Even at this late stage, however, Heywood continued to protest Stewart's innocence (see pp. 103-4).

The last aspect of the Appendix that I want to deal with is the special contribution of Edward Christian himself to his plea for his brother's reputation. Denying that he wanted to be an accomplice to the crime of mutiny or to be vindictive against Bligh, Edward claimed to have 'studiously forborn to make more comments than were absolutely necessary upon any statement which he has been obliged to bring forward'. This disarmingly innocent plea comes at the end of three long, well-written paragraphs of unattributed praise for Fletcher's character and career. Edward knew his profession well. The ending is powerful polemic: 'The sufferings of Captain Bligh and his companions in the boat, however severe they may have been, are perhaps but a small portion of the torments occasioned by this dreadful event: and whilst these prove the melancholy and extensive consequences of the crime of Mutiny, the crime itself in this instance may afford an awful lesson to the Navy, and to mankind, that there is a degree of pressure, beyond which the best formed and principled mind must either break or recoil. And though public justice and the public safety can allow no vindication of any species of Mutiny, yet reason and humanity will distinguish the sudden unpremeditated act of desperation and phrenzy,

[24] Appendix, p. 71.

from the foul deliberate contempt of every religious duty and honourable sentiment; and will deplore the uncertainty of human prospects, when they reflect that a young man is condemned to perpetual infamy, who, if he had served on board any other ship, or had perhaps been absent from the Bounty a single day, or one ill-fated hour, might still have been an honour to his country, and a glory and comfort to his friends.'[25] The Appendix meets the promise of the announcement in the *Cumberland Packet* – they were written of course by the same person. Edward manages to condemn mutiny in general but make an exception of one in particular by the clever stratagem of showing the Admiralty, and the general public, that in this case a young man, 'adorned with every virtue', had suffered such a 'degree of pressure' in the hands of Bligh that he had snapped.

The Appendix appeared in the first half of 1794. Bligh was at the time in London at home with his family. He had been on half-pay since he signed off the *Providence*, and, as we have noted, he had felt a little out in the cold with the Admiralty establishment. His hopes of letting the *Bounty* mutiny die a natural death – as most mutinies tended to after a while – were completely dashed by the appearance of the Appendix. London society buzzed with speculation and gossip; sympathies were broadly in favour of Fletcher Christian and the earlier post-mutiny glory accorded to Bligh became distinctly tarnished. Bligh was in a dilemma. He could take legal advice and eventually action against the publisher and author of the Appendix, but faced the risk of a long legal haggle about the truth or falsity of the assertions. A civilian court would naturally have a different viewpoint from a naval court on important elements of testimony and military conduct. It was ground best suited to Edward Christian and his battery of legal advisers. On the other hand he could ignore the Appendix and wait for it to die down. In the end he chose a difficult road between the two, and not unexpectedly failed miserably. He chose to answer the Appendix with his own pamphlet.

Bligh's *An Answer to Certain Assertions contained in the Appendix to a Pamphlet ...* appeared in 1794. It was not really a proper answer to the Appendix; it merely presented some material that formed the basis of an answer. It is simply a short introduction and fifteen items of evidence, not all of them obviously germane to the Appendix, all presented without comment. It may be that these items were originally collected as the basis of a legal response, and he was advised instead to issue them as they were, which from the point of view of his case was a great pity. The Appendix is a brilliant polemic; *An Answer* ... a mere skeleton of a legal brief, completely inadequate to destroy the credibility of the Christian's campaign.

Among the items is a letter from Peter Heywood to Mrs Elizabeth Bligh, written 14 July 1792, not long after his return as a prisoner. It speaks highly of Bligh and is in marked contrast to the sentiments expressed in his letter to Edward Christian after his pardon. Heywood is shown to lack consistency, or integrity, in the juxtaposition of these letters, but not many readers of the Appendix would grasp this point unaided. Another item is a letter praising

[25] Appendix, p. 79.

Bligh from Edward Harwood, Surgeon of the *Providence*, published in *The Times* of 16 July 1794. Testimony from one's Surgeon is hardly a weighty defence. It would have been far better if Bligh had gone to the expense of having the Log of the *Providence* published. This would have been cheaper than a legal case but better than the most optimistic construction that could be placed on his *Answer*. An account of this voyage, with the absence of strife and gossip, and the evident success of the mission, plus its many discoveries and new charts, would have been an excellent testimony to Bligh's fitness for command. The *Providence* was the complete answer to the Appendix; Fletcher's behaviour would have been seen to have been the isolated madness of a young man rather than the product of his commander's tyranny.

Bligh also included affidavits from Coleman, Smith and Lebogue, taken in August 1794, denying assertions traced to them in the *Appendix*. But there was not enough; if this line is to be followed it requires at least a majority of the men involved. The testimony of Fryer and Purcell could only have been destroyed by a detailed account of their misdemeanours taken from his Logs, which would have meant going over to the offensive. Bligh's last item in his *Answer* is of historical interest, though hardly of great help to his predicament in 1794. He published a letter from Edward Lamb, a former officer of the ship in which Fletcher first sailed with Bligh, which purported to show that Fletcher was 'foolish' with the opposite sex and that he owed Bligh a great deal.

The only bright spark in the entire reply is the Introduction. A few more pages in the same style would have wiped the floor with the Appendix much more effectively than his fifteen 'proofs' did. He attacks the credibility of the Appendix in these words:[26]

> The information which furnished Mr Edward Christian with materials for his Appendix, he states to 'have been collected from many interviews and conversations, in the presence and hearing of several respectable gentlemen'. He then mentions the names of all the persons with whom these conversations were held, without distinguishing the particular information given by any individual. The mixing together the names of men, whose assertions merit very different degrees of credit, and blending their evidence into one mass, is liable to two objections: 1st, the impossibility of tracing the author of any particular assertion; and 2dly, the danger, which to a reader is unavoidable, of supposing, that the statements made by those who were actually accomplices in the Mutiny, came from men of respectable character, with whom he has thus associated them.
>
> One of the hardest cases that can befall any man, is to be reduced to the necessity of defending his character by his own assertions only. As such, fortunately, is not my situation, I have rested my defence on the testimony of others; adding only, such of the written orders issued by me in the course of the voyage, as are connected with the matter in question; which orders being issued publicly in writing, may be offered as evidence of unquestionable credit.

[26] Bligh, 1794, pp. 1-2.

These testimonials, without further remark from me, I trust will be sufficient to do away any evil impression which the public may have imbibed, from reading Mr. Edward Christian's Defence of his brother.

The only result of Bligh's efforts to answer Edward Christian was that Edward promptly issued *A Short Reply to Capt. W. Bligh's Answer* (1795). This is an extremely rare pamphlet today. It continues the polemics of the Appendix and rebuts some of the implications of Bligh's answers. In doing so it gives more details about how the Appendix was written. For instance, we find that when Thomas Hayward was interviewed the only person present was Edward Christian; also, that John Fryer had first communicated with Joseph Christian (10, The Strand), a distant relative of Edward's, about the situation on the *Bounty*. Edward reserved his most barbed remarks for Lawrence Lebogue for his 'most wicked and perjured affidavit that ever was sworn before a magistrate, or published to the world; and it is perhaps a defect in the law that these voluntary affidavits are permitted to be made; or that, when they are false, the authors of them are subject to no punishment'. Lebogue had denied that he had made statements to Edward Christian, who called John Atkinson and James Losh as his witnesses. We also find that Edward wrote a letter of introduction for William Purcell to present to Sir Joseph Banks.

Among Bligh's papers, now in the Mitchell Library, is an interesting manuscript which is a draft of a reply to the charges made by Edward Christian, though from the format they are answers to letters written by Edward to Sir Joseph Banks rather than to the Appendix itself.[27] The letters have dates in December; one is dated 1792, and from their contents they could easily double for the broad charges made in the published Appendix. This suggests that Edward Christian was writing to the authorities in late 1792 in an attempt to get an official enquiry into the *Bounty* affair, if possible before his brother could be brought back to Britain. These letters were passed on to Bligh for comment in much the same way as the Morrison Memorandum was sent to him on his return in August 1793. It is a great pity that this entire correspondence has not been traced and published. Bligh should have used his notes to construct a written reply to the Appendix, as his defence in them is sound, and much of it has not been made public before. For instance, 'Mr Christian asserts that his Brother has been driven to desperation would have been a Glory to his Friends, had he not sailed with Captain Bligh'.[28] In reply, Bligh refers to Fletcher's three years' previous experience with him in the merchant service and how he was his only support during these years:

To render him still further help, Captain Bligh took him with him into the *Bounty* where he made him Acting Lieutenant, & he would have received his

[27] William Bligh, Bounty Mutineers, ML MS Safe 1/43, pp. 19-24. The three letters are bound in this order: 1. Letter dated 16 December – pp. 19-20; 2. '3rd letter' 17th December, pp. 21-2; letter dated 16 December 1792, pp. 23-4.

[28] The phrase 'glory to his friends' is used by Edward Christian in the Appendix, suggesting that parts of the Appendix were written within six weeks of Heywood's letter to Edward of 5 November; it may be that Sir Joseph Banks, who received Edward's letters, persuaded him not to publish them until he had given Bligh a chance to reply to them on his return in the *Providence*.

Commission on his return to England. – He occupied the same place of confidence & trust to the moment of his Horrid act of ingratitude. –

The Facts made publick in the *Narrative* are not of a nature to be concealed or altered, and as Mr Christian observes; it, & Captain Bligh's private communication to himself & Mr Curwen have agreed. – Captain Bligh declares every thing in his *Narrative* to be sacred truths, & defies the utmost Malice to pervert them. – Captain Bligh makes allowance for Mr Christian wishing to do away the stain which he may feel his Brother's conduct has thrown upon his Family; provided he does nothing inconsistent with the Character of a Man of Honor or (to use his own expression) with eternal Justice.[29]

How different from the feeble replies of the *Answer*! It is the kind of stuff upon which a defence can be built, especially against the attacks of the *Appendix*. In reply to another letter[30] Bligh makes a good point about the letter that Peter Heywood wrote to Edward on his pardon: 'That Peter Heywood the Mutineer would write to Mr Christian a favorable account of His Brother, cannot be doubted; for by endeavouring to prove the Ringleader of the Mutiny not guilty; the rest of the party must in case he succeeded be surely free of any blame.' He makes several other good points:

Mr Christian acknowledges that Captain Bligh declared pointedly the Villainy of His Brother, both to him, and Mr. Curwen on his arrival in England. – Captain Bligh appears by this to have acted with candor. Mr Christian had the same Men (*Viz all those except the Mutineers who were brought home as Prisoners*) to have come forward against Capt Bligh, – Fryer was in disgrace with Captain Bligh, and Purcell he tried by a Court Martial. Yet these men knew at this time of no charge to bring against Capt. Bligh, & not untill the Mutineers were arrived was any thing suggested; *when their Friends formed connections with the others, to save the Mutineers from being hung.*

As all the Men & Officers who came home with Captain Bligh declare, that four Men were deserving of Mercy, & as such were recommended & acquitted; can a Mind open to conviction be more perfectly satisfied that it was their opinion that all else who remained on board were guilty. –

As to Mr Heywood's letter to Mr Christian, let him read the Court Martial, & he will there find that Heywood criminates his Brother in the fullest Manner, and justifies the remark of tampered evidence, which is also clear in many other instances, & can almost be brought to certain Proof.[31]

The last note in the papers is headed: 'Rem[ark]s on Mr Christian's Letters The 1st dated December 16, 1792, Purcell, Fryer, Peckover, Hayward, Smith.' It reads:

These People had an opportunity at the Court Martial held on the loss of the *Bounty*, & for many months after it, (before Captn Bligh left England,) of declaring every thing they knew; it is therefore extraordinary there should

[29] Safe 1/43, pp. 19-20.
[30] '3rd letter', 17th December.
[31] Safe 1/43, pp. 21-2.

be any new assertions at this time. – It appears that these People have been tampered with, for Captain Bligh tried Purcell by Courtmartial immediately after the Tryal for the loss of the Ship, – Fryer (the Master) was particularly under his displeasure, & Peckover received some proofs of his disapprobation, yet the latter applied to Captain Bligh to accompany him again in the *Providence* & received a refusal. – They would therefore surely have brought forward, any thing they knew against Captain Bligh before the arrival of the Mutineers, if there had been just grounds.

Mr Purcell's Credit & Veracity are much to be doubted. He has a bad character amongst his own Class and Captain Bligh had a bad opinion of him while under his command. As to the others who Mr Christian has named in his Letter to Sir Joseph Banks, they can never speak of Captain Bligh but with respect and gratitude.

The Mutineers, Heywood, Morrison & Musprat who were condemned & afterwards pardoned are now turned out upon the World & to paliate their own conduct they may think it the most effective way to plead their temptation arose from having been ill used.[32]

The public controversy between the two camps died out in 1795. The public image of Bligh was never to be so high as it was on his hero's welcome of 1790 and he spent, in all, eighteen months on half-pay following his return in the *Providence* in 1793. This was an expensive time for him to be idle, as the war with France was taking place. There does not seem to be a trace of his activities during this period, other than the proofs of his literary efforts to combat the letter-writing of the Christians and their pamphlets. How much his shore duty was condign punishment for the mutiny and the attendant publicity, or whether it was the result of his exhaustion and illness while on board the *Providence*, we do not know. Some say he was deliberately kept without a command by the Admiralty.[33] The fact that up until then he had been a specialist in long voyages, not in home-water combat duty, might also suggest that he was not used because nothing suitable was available. Whatever the reason, he remained on shore until 29 April 1795. On 13 April he was given a Commission, as Captain of H.M.S. *Warley*, and its name was quickly changed to H.M.S. *Calcutta* on 30 April. The *Calcutta* was to become a 24-gun ship, under Admiral Duncan in the North Sea. He held this command until 7 January 1796 when he took over H.M.S. *Director*, a 64-gun ship with a crew of 491 men. Bligh's naval career had resumed its onward progress. The real test was to come in one of the most dramatic episodes in the history of the Royal Navy, namely the Great Mutinies of 1797 and the two major naval engagements of Camperdown and Copenhagen. How Bligh came through these turbulent episodes we shall see in later chapters. It is necessary here to divert the story once again, this time to inquire what had happened to Fletcher Christian and his fellows on the *Bounty* since 1791 and to look at some of the mysteries associated with that island hell, Pitcairn.

[32] *ibid.*, pp. 23-4.

[33] For example, this is the view of Hough, 1972, pp. 286-7. However, Bligh had promised his wife in his letter from the *Providence* at Coupang that if it pleased God to restore him to her, he would not make another voyage; and the 1000 guineas from the Jamaican government may have induced him not to seek work for a while.

22

Pitcairn and the End of Fletcher Christian

From the night of 21 September 1789, when Fletcher Christian sailed away from Tahiti, his fate was a mystery for nineteen years. He was not heard of again until the Captain of an American whaler out of Nantucket sent a message to the British Government about what he had found when he had called at an obscure and remote island, known on the charts as Pitcairn Island. The mariner who found the island haven of the mutineers was Captain Mayhew Folger of the *Topaz*, and the date was February 1808. In the small colony he found only one European alive, eight middle-aged Polynesian women and twenty-six boys and girls of various ages. The sole European survivor was Alexander Smith, seaman. The story of what happened to the other men of the *Bounty* was a dreadful catalogue of betrayal, murder and massacre.

The *Bounty* had left Tahiti with Fletcher Christian and the final eight hard-line mutineers, William Brown, Matthew Quintal, William McCoy, Alexander Smith, John Mills, Edward Young, John Williams and Isaac Martin, together with six male islanders and nineteen females, plus a baby girl. One woman leapt overboard and swam ashore as the ship left Tahiti, and six women who were 'rather ancient' were put off the next day at the island of Eimeo.[1] The mutineers had voted to divide the ship's property, leaving the ship and about half the stores to Christian. The departure was hurried and secret; Christian probably wanted to get away before any of the other men, such as Churchill and Thompson, changed their minds about being abandoned on Tahiti to the inevitable mercies of the ships sent to look for them. Such was Christian's hurry that he 'slipped his cable' – instead of hauling in his anchors he simply let them go. An anchor was afterwards collected by Captain Edwards and lost in the *Pandora*.

Christian did not know where he and the mutineers were headed in the first months out from Tahiti. We know that the *Bounty* went westwards searching for an island that would meet their needs. It had to be fertile, uninhabited and remote. The thousands of islands scattered across the Pacific should have given them every possibility of success in their quest. But in these early weeks they were to meet continual disappointment and with disappointment came the risk of defection or mutiny. The *Bounty* was also

---

[1] *See United Service Journal*, 1829, Part ii, pp. 589f.; *Sydney Gazette*, 17 July 1819. From their point of view, they might have done better to keep the 'ancient' women on board, as it might have reduced the sexual pressures of the island prison. Abduction of people against their will was, of course, not a trivial offence even in the eighteenth century.

grossly undermanned, having only nine experienced men on board. Christian did all the navigation, assisted by the excellent charts he had acquired from Bligh's personal possessions. The *Bounty* went to within a hundred miles of Tofoa, the scene of the mutiny, before Christian's research among Bligh's books and charts produced the solution that he was looking for. He found it in Hawkesworth's *Voyages*, in a description of Carteret's discovery of Pitcairn's Island.[2] The *Bounty* was swung round and began a long southern detour of 1,000 miles to find it. Christian was not helped in this search by the fact that the charts had located Pitcairn Island about three degrees out of its true position.[3] The descriptions of Pitcairn that he had were confirmed by the rugged appearance of the island when it appeared before them; there was no obvious place for a landing, but though this made it difficult for them, it also made the island an unlikely place for a casual visit from a passing ship. For the purposes of the escaping mutineers the island appeared ideal. It was fertile, it did not appear to be inhabited and it was certainly remote. Its mis-charting would also help them.

The story of what happened on Pitcairn in its first bloody years has been pieced together from the contradictory accounts given by Alexander Smith to various captains who visited the island between 1808 and 1828. Another source was one of the Tahitian women, Jenny, who left the island in a visiting whaler in 1818 after twenty-nine years there, and told her story to Captain Peter Dillon.[4] Finally, there are the written accounts of the island's history, in particular the 'Pitcairn Register' which was indifferently kept in the early years, and a journal attributed to Edward Young. There was an oral tradition of story-telling on Pitcairn which unfortunately produced as many versions as Smith's. To add to these rather inadequate accounts there has been plenty of rumour and romance.[5] While the details differ, the broad fact, common to all the versions, remains: the Europeans died in bloody massacres a few years after the settlement.

The basic problem of Pitcairn was its isolation. For the mutineers it was sanctuary from a hanging, but for the islanders it was a prison. There was an unequal balance between the sexes, with each European having his own wife but the male islanders having to share theirs. In the early months of building the community this did not matter too much. They landed on 21 January

---

[2] Captain Philip Carteret, 'An Account of a Voyage round the World, in the Years MDCCLXVI, MDCCLXVII, MDCCLXVII, and MDCCLXIX', in Hawkesworth (ed.), 1773, p. 561. Carteret discovered Pitcairn in H.M.S. *Swallow* in 1767. He named it after one of his midshipmen who was the son of Major Pitcairn of the marines. Major Pitcairn was killed at the battle of Bunker Hill.

[3] Captain Folger placed Pitcairn at 130°W, while Carteret had it at 133° 30′W.

[4] She was interviewed by Captain Peter Dillon, of the *Research*, who later (1826-8) solved the mystery of the disappearance of La Perouse (Dillon, 1829); his account of Jenny can be found in 'Jenny', 1819.

[5] See *Pitcairn Island Register Book*; Young, 1894 (by Edward Young's daughter); Nicolson, 1966; Silverman, 1967; Wilson, 1958; anon., 1815; anon., 1826; Brodie, 1851; Chauvel, 1933; McFarland, 1884; Murray, 1853, Shillibeer, 1817. This is only a small selection. I am using the version of events told by Smith to Captain Beechey in 1825 (Beechey, 1831); as this is the last known version told by Smith, and the most detailed, it seems best to use it as the definitive version, although it should still be treated with scepticism, as I shall show.

1790. The *Bounty* was stripped of everything movable. It was no mean task in the heavy surf to manhandle stores ashore and then up the cliff face to the tiny settlement area where the Europeans built their small houses. The intention was to break the *Bounty* up and salvage its valuable timbers, but before this could be accomplished Matthew Quintal set it on fire. Why he did so is not known for certain. It may have been a precaution to prevent anybody changing his mind and leaving the island. Their security depended on there being no leakage as to their whereabouts. The wreck sank in what is today known as Bounty Bay and with it sank all hope of escape. The only boats left were the small cutters and these were hardly seaworthy. Christian divided the land, leaving nothing for the islanders except the role of heavy-duty labourers for the Europeans. In this Fletcher was a man of his times, if out of step with his anti-slavery supporters back in Britain. The Europeans' treatment of the islanders, male and female, was the root of the civil strife on Pitcairn.

Within a few months, John Williams's Tahitian wife slipped and fell to her death on the cliffs while looking for birds' eggs. He managed for a while as a widower but eventually grew restless. When the European men turned down what seemed to him a reasonable request, namely, that they should support his taking one of the women from the six islanders, he was resentful. He even threatened to leave the island in the ship's cutter. In the end Fletcher Christian, 'adorned with every virtue', agreed to Williams's requests and organised an armed party that went to the islanders and took one of the women away, handing her over to Williams. It was the worst decision he could have taken.

The six islanders now had only two women between them. The inevitable soon appeared: a conspiracy to kill the Europeans led by the islander whose wife had been taken from him. The conspiracy did not get very far because the men let their plans become known to their women who passed on warnings to the Europeans. Women were here supporting the dominant male party. The result was the arming of the seamen and a march on the islanders, chasing the two ringleaders off into the hills. The other islanders were spared their lives on the promise that they would seek out their companions and kill them. This they managed to do in the usual brutal way. The Europeans thought there would now be peace; in fact their action showed the remaining four islanders the way to a redistribution of the benefits of the island. They were forced into murder by the Europeans and they learned their lesson well.

The peace lasted from 1791 to 1793. During that period the mutineers had been tried and sentenced and Bligh had revisited Tahiti and returned to Britain. While Edward Christian was rallying his family and friends to defend his brother's honour, Fletcher was facing his final test. The treatment of the remaining islanders, men or women, did not improve. It was not the best of communities in which to bring up children and inter-family tensions, jealousies and hostilities were becoming a major feature of life. The men who had been turned into murderers turned on their masters.

The conspiracy was aided by the training in the use of arms that they

15. Sketch by William Bligh of a heron in Van Diemen's Land (Tasmania). Made on the voyage of the *Providence*.

16. John Adams (Alexander Smith), the last surviving mutineer and the possible instigator of the massacres on Pitcairn. From Murray's *Pitcairn* (1853). Engraved by Adlard from a sketch by R. Beechey.

17. The residence of John Adams on Pitcairn. From Barrow, 1831.
From a sketch by Lt. Smith of H.M.S. *Blossom*.

received from the ever-lazy Europeans, who taught them to shoot and hunt for them. The Europeans were dispersed over the island tending their fields. The islanders met, checked their arms and set out to kill the seamen one by one. Surprise and speed were the deciding factors. The first man to die was Williams, the original cause of the first outbreak of violence. The next man to die was Fletcher Christian; according to most versions, he died among his yams.[6] McCoy and Quintal heard the shots and, stumbling upon one of the attacks, took off into the woods. Mills fell next and after him Martin and Brown. With all this shooting it is a wonder that the Europeans had not been roused into some form of retaliation or defence, but for most of the time the shooting was a one-way affair. Cold-blooded too: the islanders just went up to their victims and shot them at close range, finishing them off with a good battering around the skull. Smith at first got away and then returned, only to get wounded in the neck by a musket shot. He escaped again but in an extraordinary deal between himself and the attackers he agreed to return with them in exchange for their doing him no harm.

There is something very strange about this deal. It does not make sense. Nor does the apparent inviolability of Edward Young, who was never attacked. The darkest construction that can be placed on this immunity is that Edward Young masterminded the entire massacre. It certainly has the hallmark of an intelligent mind behind it. But the clever choice of time and method ought not to be assumed to have been beyond the abilities of the islanders. It certainly suited the promiscuous Young, a favourite of the women, that five of his companions died: this released their women into the pool. Smith was a close crony of Young's and shared his tastes in women. It must also be remembered that the accepted version of the massacre on Pitcairn is based almost entirely on the statements of Alexander Smith, who is at least suspect. His role may have been somewhat different from what he claimed. Smith proved to be a wily witness over the years. The reports on Pitcairn sent back to Britain by various ships showed remarkable contradictions in his statements.

After their victory over the white men, the islanders fell out. The dispute could have been about anything, perhaps the division of the widows among them. In a shoot-out one islander was killed by another, Menalee; he then ran off into the hills to meet Quintal and McCoy who were still hiding there. Alexander Smith alleges that he, Smith, was sent from the settlement to find the two men and tell them to kill Menalee and then return in safety to the village. If Young, Smith and the islanders were living together in the village and Smith was sent on this mission, it seems even more likely that Young and Smith masterminded the massacre. They would not have been too worried at first about McCoy and Quintal; they could smoke them out eventually. In the heady days immediately after the massacre the victors would be busy

---

[6] Becke and Jeffery, 'The Mutineer' (MS in Mitchell Library, A1391) retell an oral tradition in which Christian was not killed in the 1793 massacre, but survived until 1800, when he saw a ship off the island and, intending to sail to it in the ship's boat, was accidentally shot by Smith, who was trying to prevent him from putting to sea. Another, more unlikely (but more interesting) story is told later in this chapter.

enjoying the fruits of their conquest, namely, the company of the women. They were armed, they had food and they had women, traditionally ingredients for festivity after the battle. Menalee, who ran away after killing his companion (or after discovering a plan to kill himself, perhaps by seeing Young or Smith kill the unwary Temua) had apparently played a major role in the massacre of Christian and the others, and was also one of the leaders in the first killings of the two Tahitians. He was therefore in a position to disclose the full story to Quintal and McCoy about Young and Smith's role in the massacre. Instead of two frightened men in the bush there would be two men determined on revenge. It would have been essential that Menalee was killed before he talked too much to McCoy and Quintal.

It is unexplained why Menalee should seek refuge with McCoy and Quintal, whom, after all, he had tried to kill during the massacre. Smith's mission may simply have been to get McCoy and Quintal to hunt down Menalee in return for a safe-conduct back to the village. According to Smith, the two fugitives agreed to kill Menalee and did so, but they refused to return to the village until the two remaining islanders were killed. This story could be a clever cover-up for Smith and Young; it places the deaths of the remaining islanders on the shoulders of McCoy and Quintal instead of on themselves.[7] Or the truth may be that Smith chased Menalee into the bush, tracked him down and killed him, and then contacted McCoy and Quintal, telling them that with Young he hoped to revenge the murders within a day or so, whereupon it would be safe for them to come back. Menalee was killed before he could tell them the full story of the murders.

The next step was to get rid of the two islanders left alive. One of them was killed by the widows, who used an axe to dispatch him, and the other was shot at close range by Young. Smith apparently had no part in this transaction. (We may note in the whole story so far that Smith manages to keep himself out of all the violent incidents.) This left Young, McCoy, Quintal and Smith, with ten women and some children. Thus, by October 1793, Pitcairn was under the command of four men, of whom two were survivors of a massacre which the other two had probably played some part in planning. This did not make for peace.

The major problem appears to have been the dissatisfaction of the women. With no men left to be servants to the whites, the women had to take on this role. The relatively settled life of small family groups had been destroyed in the bloodshed and the new large extended family commune altered their status completely. Some of them had lost husbands and they now had to share four men. McCoy and Quintal were rough seamen, already with a reputation for harsh treatment of their women, and they now extended their behaviour to all the women. Everybody lived together promiscuously. The women apparently decided to build a boat in which to escape from the island. According to Young and Smith, they helped them in this scheme, but the boat was not seaworthy and sank in the rough waters of Bounty Bay. This did not end the troubles; according to Smith, the women then turned to

[7] According to Smith, he had to send them the hands cut from their bodies before McCoy and Quintal agreed to leave their sanctuary.

a more immediate solution of their problems, and entered into a conspiracy to kill the Europeans. By vigilance and judicious intervention the seamen managed to break up these conspiracies, but life can hardly have been relaxed in these circumstances.

McCoy was the first of the quartet to die. He had been making a form of alcohol since he arrived on the island, using his knowledge of the distillation of Scotch whisky, and in one of his drunken bouts he apparently fell off a cliff and was killed. It is not impossible that he was pushed. Certainly Quintal was murdered, in 1799. In his only recorded confession of violence, Smith declared that Quintal became a threat to the community after he demanded the women belonging to himself and Young. His violence may have made the women less willing to have anything to do with him and perhaps they sought out Young and Smith for protection. The upshot was that these two killed him with an axe while he was sleeping. This left the island under the command of the two conspirators of the 1793 massacre. Young only lived another year after Quintal's murder. He is alleged to have died a natural death from an asthmatic complaint. In 1800 Alexander Smith was the only survivor of the *Bounty* left on Pitcairn.

The history of the island as handed down to us is that, from the death of Quintal, the small community began a process of moral regeneration that was to transform it from its bloody genesis into a model· Christian community which impressed its early visitors with its sincere piety. This moral transformation was credited in great measure to Alexander Smith. When Royal Naval captains visited the island in 1814 they decided that their best course was to leave the wanted mutineer on the island instead of arresting him and taking him back for trial, as the community was dependent on his leadership and authority for its continuation.

The colony was not discovered until February 1808. Captain Folger was the first person to visit Pitcairn and make contact with the community.[8] Smith was afraid of being arrested and refused to meet Folger on his ship; Folger was invited ashore to meet the Englishman – being somewhat astonished that the brown islander boys who came out to the *Topaz* in their canoes spoke English – but was likewise frightened that he would be detained to prevent news of the colony reaching the Admiralty. Eventually these fears were overcome and he went ashore and met Smith, staying for a few hours. He reported to the British authorities what he had found, offering as proof of his report two important pieces of evidence. The first was the name of Alexander Smith, which could be checked against the *Bounty*'s muster roll. The second was the fact that when he left the island Smith had given him a chronometer made by Kendall which had been taken by the *Bounty* on its voyage.[9] Unfortunately Folger had been deprived of it by the Governor of

[8] Several ships are recorded as appearing off the island before the *Topaz*. The first appeared on 27 December 1795 but did not stop; another appeared 'sometime later' and a third came close enough to be able to see the settlement. One ship is known to have managed to land a boat on the island but did not attempt to explore: it simply cut some plants and left again. Other sightings may have taken place but not been seen or recorded by the early inhabitants.

[9] However, both items of information could have been gleaned from Bligh's *Narrative* of 1792. For an account of Folger's visit *see Log of the Topaz*, reprinted in Stackpole, 1953, pp. 237-53.

Juan Fernández in a dispute over money. The first official report, sent by Sir Sydney Smith from Rio de Janeiro to the Admiralty who received it on 14 May 1809, reads as follows:[10]

> Captain Folger, of the American ship Topaz, of Boston, relates that, upon landing on Pitcairn's Island, in lat. 25° 2'S., long. 130° 0°W. he found there an Englishman of the name of Alexander Smith, the only person remaining of nine that escaped in his Majesty's late ship Bounty, Captain W. Bligh. Smith relates that, after putting Captain Bligh in the boat, Christian, the leader of the mutiny, took command of the ship and went to Otaheite, where great part of the crew left her, except Christian, Smith, and seven others, who each took wives and six Otaheitean men servants, and shortly after arrived at the said island (Pitcairn), where they ran the ship on shore, and broke her up; this event took place in the year 1790.
>
> About four years after their arrival (a great jealousy existing), the Otaheiteans secretly revolted and killed every Englishman except himself, whom they severely wounded in the neck with a pistol ball. The same night, the widows of the deceased Englishmen arose and put to death the whole of the Otaheiteans, leaving Smith the only man alivé upon the island, with eight or nine women and several small children. On his recovery he applied himself to tilling the ground, so that it now produces plenty of yams, cocoanuts, bananas and plantains; hogs and poultry in abundance. There are now some grown up men and women, children of the mutineers, on the island, the whole population amounting to about thirty-five, who acknowledge Smith as father and commander of them all; they all speak English and have been educated by him (Captain Folger represents) in a religious and moral way.
>
> The second mate of the *Topaz* asserts that Christian the ringleader became insane shortly after their arrival on the island, and threw himself off the rocks into the sea; another died of a fever before the massacre of the remaining six took place. The island is badly supplied with water, sufficient only for the present inhabitants, and no anchorage.

Captain Folger wrote directly to the Admiralty on 1 March 1813, enclosing with his letter an azimuth compass which Smith had given to him.[11] His letter confirms the points he made in his Log about the fate of the mutineers as related to him by Smith in 1808. These points were that after about six years (1796) all the English except Smith were killed by the Tahitians and that same night the widows killed the Tahitians.[12] We should note the

[10] Anon., 1810; quoted in Barrow, 1961, pp. 256-7.

[11] Mayhew Folger, Letter to Admiralty, Nantucket, 1 March 1813, in *Quarterly Review*, April 1815, pp. 376-7; see also Smith, 1936.

[12] Folger also wrote to his friend, Amasa Delano, Letter in *Quarterly Journal of Science and Arts*, 1819, Vol. 1, p. 265; Captain Delano writes that 'Captain Folger was very explicit in his statement that Alex Smith told him Christian got sick and died a natural death' (Delano, 1817, p. 140), which only complicates the story further. Delano also claimed that Smith changed his name to John Adams on hearing from Folger that the United States had a new Federal Constitution in 1808; and there is a correspondence in the *Gentleman's Magazine*, 1818, Part 2, p. 37, purporting to show that John Adams was his real name, and that he came from Hackney and had a married sister living in Derby.

content of Smith's first version of the fate of the community. There is not enough detail to give other than the impression that everybody had died in a single massacre and that since then Smith had brought the community into respectability. The implication was that he should be left alone, as the guilty men had paid their debt to society in the blood-bath and the survivor had atoned for his sins by regeneration. This was Smith's intention, and it shows a man who had more than the average appreciation of the effect of apparent rectitude on men in authority.

In 1814 two British frigates were searching the Pacific for the American ship *Essex* which was attacking unarmed British whalers. The ships were H.M.S. *Briton*, Captain Sir Thomas Staines, and H.M.S. *Tagus*, Captain Pipon. They visited Pitcairn, met Smith and sent reports back to the Admiralty. In them there is a shift in the details of Smith's story. The most obvious is that he had changed his name to John Adams. Captain Staines's letter from Valparaiso reads:[13]

Sir,
I have the honour to inform you, that, on my passage from the Marquesas Islands to this port, on the morning of the 17th Sep., I fell in with an island where none is laid down in the Admiralty or other charts, according to the several chronometers of the *Briton* and *Tagus*. I therefore hove to until day-light, and then closed to ascertain whether it was inhabited, which I soon discovered it to be, and, to my great astonishment, found that every individual on the island (forty in number) spoke very good English, as well as Otaheitan. They prove to be descendents of the deluded crew of the *Bounty*, which from Otaheite, proceeded to the above-mentioned island, where the ship was burnt.

Christian appears to have been the leader and sole cause of the mutiny in that ship. A venerable old man, named John Adams, is the only surviving Englishman of those who (then) left Otaheite in her; and whose exemplary conduct and fatherly care of the whole of the little colony cannot but command admiration. The pious manner in which all those born on the island have been reared, the correct sense of religion which has been instilled into their young minds by this old man, has given him the pre-eminence over the whole of them, to whom they look up as the father of the whole and one family.

A son of Christian was the first born on the island, now about twenty-five years of age, named Thursday October Christian; the elder Christian fell a sacrifice to the jealousy of an Otaheitan man, within three or four years after their arrival on the island. The mutineers were accompanied thither by six Otaheitan men and twelve women: the former were all swept away by desperate contentions between them and the Englishmen, and five of the latter died at different periods, leaving at present only one man (Adams) and seven women of the original settlers.

The island must, undoubtedly, be that called 'Pitcairn', although erroneously laid down in the charts. We had the meridian sun, close to it, which gave us 25° 4' S. latitude and 130° 25' W. longitude by chronometer of the *Briton* and *Tagus*.

[13] *Quarterly Review*, April 1815, pp. 377-8. Extracts appear in Mackaness, 1951, pp. 215-16.

It is abundant in yams, plantains, hogs, goats, and fowls, but affords no shelter for a ship or vessel or any description; neither could a ship water there without great difficulty.

I cannot, however, refrain from offering my opinion that it is well worthy of the attention of our laudable religious societies, particularly that for propagating the Christian religion, the whole of the inhabitants speaking the Otaheitan tongue as well as English.

During the whole time they (Christian and his comrades) have been on the island, only one ship has ever communicated with them, which took place about six years since, and this was the American ship *Topaz*, of Boston, Mayhew Folger, Master. The island is completely iron-bound, with rocky shore, and landing in boats at all times difficult, although safe to approach within a short distance in a ship.

Smith had not only changed his name to Adams; he had also changed some details of the death of Christian. In particular the date of his death has moved from six years after the arrival, or 1796, to three or four years, or 1793-4. The cause of his death is alleged to be the 'jealousy of an Otaheitan man' presumably over some sexual irregularity with a woman. Also, the sequence of events in the massacres has been altered. Instead of all of the white men dying at one go and then the widows murdering the Tahitians, it is the Tahitians who were 'swept away' in one go and the five white men who die at various dates afterwards. The deaths of three Europeans are left unaccounted for in this version. We cannot help but be struck by the differences in the two accounts, one given in 1808 and the other in 1814. It may be that Smith, an ordinary seaman, was a little overawed by the presence of two senior Royal Navy Captains; whereas Folger in the *Topaz* was merely a whaling master from a foreign country, Staines and Pipon were British commanders with full authority to apprehend Smith as a mutineer and deserter. He apparently convinced them beyond doubt of his sincerity and piety, and gained their unqualified praise for his manifold virtues.

Captain Pipon wrote an account of Smith's community in a private Journal which is kept in the Mitchell Library.[14] It differs in some material respects from Staines's account though it gives much greater detail regarding the alleged fate of Fletcher Christian, including a different version of his death. It is worth making an extract from this remarkable Journal, which gives some views on Christian's behaviour after the mutiny. Pipon writes:

I next come to the interesting narrative of Fletcher Christian. It appears that this unfortunate & ill fated young Man, was never happy after the rash & inconsiderate step he had taken, but always sullen & morose, a circumstance which will not surprise any one, this moroseness however led him to many acts of cruelty & inhumanity, which soon was the cause of his incurring the hatred & detestation of his Companions here: One cannot avoid expressing astonishment, when you consider that the very

[14] P. Pipon, 'Interesting Report of the only remaining mutineers of His Majesty's Ship "Bounty"', Banks Papers, Brabourne Collection, ML MS A77. Quoted in Mackaness, 1951, pp. 217-19.

crime he was then guilty of towards his Companions (who assisted him in the Mutiny) was the very same they so loudly accused their Captain B— of. It is indeed very singular this circumstance should not have been a serious lesson to him, for his guidance in his future treatment of his Ship-mates in error. This miserable young man after having left Otaheite the last time, (for he has visited Anamooka one of the Friendly Islands, after his desertion from his duty & disobedience to his Captain, not finding the reception he expected there, or rather that his Plans could not be carried into execution without fear of detection) returnd to Otaheite with a feigned Story, which the Islanders readily gave ear to; of having met *Captain Cook*, who had sent him (Fletcher) for a supply of Provisions; his wishes were readily complied with, Capt. Cook being a great favourite there; & having filléd the Bounty with Hogs, & such other Articles as he thought necessary, he sailed away suddenly in the night, on or about the 22nd Sept. 1789 & never since been heard of: this was the period when 16 of his crew left him & went on shore: his object was to find an uninhabited Island, where he could establish a settlement, & hither he at last arrivd, tho with a very reduced Crew, & finding no Anchorage round the Island, & that the operation of landing the stores of the Bounty as well as his live stock, &c., was tedious & laborious, he ran the ship against the Rocks, a little to the southward of the place we landed at, & having cleared her of everything he thought necessary, set her on fire: this certainly was a wise plan on his part to avoid detection, for as Pitcairn is mentioned in the Charts & in all the accounts I have seen of it, as uninhabited, it is not probable that any one would seek refreshments there: whereas had the wreck *ever* been observed by any vessel passing that way, humanity if not curiosity would have led them to enquire, if some fellow creature in distress, might not have been cast away here: again, had the ship been preserved, there might have been a possibility that some of the dissatisfied would sale away in her & give information of the retreat of the Mutineers of the Bounty. It is therefore an extraordinary circumstance, that chance & meer accident should have led us hither, for had we been aware that Pitcairn Island was near us, we should have avoided it. We considered ourselves nearly 200 miles from it, when Land was discovered, & we verily believd that in Sight was some new discovery. To the error therefore, in which it is laid down is to be chiefly attributed this unexpected visit of ours to it; happy however that it is in our power to communicate the fate of the wretched people who composed the Crew of the Bounty, after their shameful Mutiny against their Captain. It is impossible to describe the surprize we all felt when we heard the Natives the descendants of Fletcher Christian speak the English language uncommonly well, & that this should be the general language among them: the old women who are from Otaheite, retain the Mother tongue, tho as has been mentioned before, they have pickd up many English words & understand the English language tolerably. The fate of Fletcher Christian himself was such as one might have expected from his cruelty & extraordinary unfeeling behaviour: from what we could learn he was shot by a black man whilst digging in his field & almost instantaneously expired: this happened about eleven months after they were settled in the Island, but the exact dates I could not learn: the black or Otaheite man that thus murderd him was himself immediately assassinated: the cause of these disturbances &

violence is thus accounted for by John Adams; that as he has before related, Fletcher Christian behavd with such cruelty & oppression towards the people, as soon alienated them from him & in consequence they divided into parties which ran very high, seeking every opportunity on both sides to put each other to death: old John Adams himself was not without his enemies, having been shot through the neck; as however the ball enterd the fleshy part, he was enabled to make his escape, & avoid the fury of his pursuers, who sought his life. Another circumstance had arisen which gave particularly the Otaheite men still more discontent & roused their fury to a degree not to be pacified: Christian's wife had paid the debt of nature, & as we have every reason to suppose sensuality & a passion for the females of Otaheite chiefly instigated him to the rash step he had taken, so it is readily to be believed he would not live long on the Island without a female companion, consequently after the demise of his wife, he forcibly seized on one belonging to one of the Otaheitan men & took her to live with him: this exasperated them to a degree of madness, open war was declared & every opportunity sought to take away his life, & it was effected *whilst digging in his own field.* It is surprizing he should not have been more upon his guard, for he was well aware of the hatred & enmity of all the blacks or Otaheitan men. Thus terminated the miserable existence of this deluded young man, whose connexions in Westmorland were extremely respectable & who did not want talents & capacity to have become an ornament to his profession had he adopted another line of conduct. We could not learn precisely the exact number of Blacks or Whites who were killed whilst this kind of warfare continued, certainly however, many must have perished by the hands of each other & only old John Adams remains of the Men that landed on the island with Christian.

On one thing Smith was fairly consistent in these early accounts. This is the alleged conduct of Christian. There had to be some explanation for Christian's early death. It is consistent with suspicion as to the credibility of Smith and his probable role in the massacres that he would attempt to blacken the name of Christian as a prelude to the conclusion that he fell a victim to his own tyranny. That Christian was morose, bad-tempered and moody is also consistent with the view that his mutiny was a rash, ill-considered act motivated by some form of mental instability. Yet when Smith told his story to Captain Beechey in 1825 the entire character of Christian had changed; he was now a model of cheerfulness and virtue, and an inspiration to the settlement.[15] Smith gave no explanation for this change in his assessment. Remorse at his own role in Christian's death, and the growing security of his own position, may have induced him to be more generous to Christian's memory. It was now thirty-three years since the massacre and Smith's world was bounded by the six miles of Pitcairn Island with only very occasional visits from ships. His own end was near and he may have thought the community would be better prepared to face its isolation and continued life if it had some comforting myths about its genesis. The

[15] Beechey, 1831, pp. 68-9.

guilt of the conspirators and the murders could be left as general rather than identified with names.

Smith tended to be vague about what happened and who died at which time. The life of the colony began for him in 1800, not 1790. The previous decade is fogged over with vagueness and contradiction and no doubt he thought it best to leave it like that. Some measure of his credibility can be seen in his own version of his role in the mutiny; in one of his accounts he says he was ill in bed at the time of the mutiny and only became an active mutineer with great reluctance after almost everything had been settled. The fact is that Smith was one of the early men to join the mutiny – some accounts make him the third recruit to Christian's cause – and was also one of the most determined and militant of mutineers. He was trusted enough by Christian to be set as armed guard over Bligh at the mizzen-mast. As he redrafted his own role in the mutiny so conspicuously, it is not improbable that he also redrafted his role in the first ten years of the colony.

This leaves one final mystery of Pitcairn – the real fate of Fletcher Christian. The case for believing that the whole truth about Fletcher Christian was never told is circumstantial. It must be said at once that so far there is no shred of direct evidence to support the view that he died elsewhere than on Pitcairn in the 1793 massacre. But the romantic possibility exists that somehow he escaped from Pitcairn and got back to Cumberland. I will take up the rest of this chapter in exploring this possibility.

Sir John Barrow published his book on the *Bounty* in 1831. He modestly describes his role as that of an 'editor', and he published the first edition anonymously, as was fitting for a senior civil servant, Secretary to the Admiralty. His discretion extended to publication of the following footnote:

As the manner of Christian's death has been differently reported to each different visitor, by Adams, the only evidence in existence, with the exception of three or four Otaheitan women, and a few infants, some singular circumstances may here be mentioned that happened at home, just at the time of Folger's visit, and which might render his death on Pitcairn's Island almost a matter of doubt.

About the years 1808 and 1809, a very general opinion was prevalent in the neighbourhood of the lakes of Cumberland and Westmoreland, that Christian was in that part of the country, and made frequent private visits to an aunt who was living there. Being the near relative of Mr. Christian Curwen, long member of Parliament for Carlisle, and himself a native, he was well known in the neighbourhood. This, however, might be passed over as mere gossip, had not another circumstance happened just about the same time, for the truth of which the Editor does not hesitate to avouch.

In Fore Street, Plymouth Dock, Captain Heywood found himself one day walking behind a man, whose shape had so much the appearance of Christian's, that he involuntarily quickened his pace. Both were walking very fast, and the rapid steps behind him having roused the stranger's attention, he suddenly turned his face, looked at Heywood, and immediately ran off. But the face was as much like Christian's as the back, and Heywood, exceedingly excited, ran also. Both ran as fast as they were able, but the stranger had the advantage, and, after making several short turns, disappeared.

That Christian should be in England, Heywood considered as highly improbable, though not out of the scope of possibility; for at this time no account of him whatsoever had been received since they parted at Otaheite; at any rate the resemblance, the agitation, and the efforts of the stranger to elude him were circumstances too strong not to make a deep impression on his mind. At the moment, his first thought was to set about making some further inquiries, but on recollection of the pain and trouble such a discovery must occasion him, he considered it more prudent to let the matter drop; but the circumstance was frequently called to his memory for the remainder of his life.[16]

In Tagart's biography of Heywood there is no mention of this incident and Barrow appears to be the only source for the story. In view of Barrow's avowal of the 'truth' of the 'circumstance', we must accept that Heywood did relate the incident as having taken place. It is not entirely clear whether Barrow is vouching for the truth of Heywood's story or merely the fact that Heywood related it to him; I assume he means the latter. Dating the incident is not easy. According to Tagart, Heywood arrived in Britain in January 1808 and was occupied ashore from May 1808 to 3 November 1808, preparing navigation charts of the Indian seas for a book written by a friend, James Horsburgh. He joined the *Donegal* on 4 November 1808, as relief Captain and was engaged in blockade actions off the French coast until he returned to London on 11 March 1809. He was at the Admiralty on 18 March 1809, received command of a frigate in May 1809 and some time in June joined the Mediterranean fleet, where he was employed until March 1810. Thus, Heywood was in Britain from January to November 1808 and from March to June 1809.[17] The incident in Fore Street, Plymouth, could have occurred during either of these times up to May 1809.

The report from Captain Folger reached the Admiralty on 14 May 1809 and it was in May of that year that Heywood received from the Admiralty the command of the *Nereus*, after 'having expressed his readiness and desire for immediate employment again'. There is a possibility that Heywood was told about the discovery of Pitcairn as the haven of the *Bounty* mutineers while he was visiting the Admiralty in May 1809; it would have been a natural item of conversation between him and one of the clerks or the senior officers.[18] If the Fore Street incident occurred before May 1809, Heywood may have kept quiet because he feared that by opening the issue he might raise doubts as to his suitability for command. Barrow tells the story as if Heywood did not know at the time that Christian was dead. There is always the possibility that he made a mistake, and the man ran off merely because he was frightened by the spectacle of someone running after him.

There are various indirect and mysterious pieces of evidence that can be

[16] Barrow, 1961, p. 279n.
[17] *See* Tagart, 1832, pp. 186-92.

used to support Heywood's story. One of these is the intervention of William Wordsworth over a book published in London in 1796 and supposed to be by Christian: *Letters from Mr Fletcher Christian, containing a narrative of the transactions on board His Majesty's Ship Bounty, Before and After the mutiny, with his subsequent voyages and travels in South America.*[19] This volume is generally accepted to be a clever forgery; it does not fit any of the known activities of the mutineers after setting Bligh adrift and leaving Tahiti for the last time. It is, however, an extremely well written tale, showing that the author, or authors, had considerable detailed knowledge of the west coast of South America and the culture and customs of the people there. It also presents an interesting opinion on the mutiny, especially in view of the public debate that had taken place the year before. In the letters, written allegedly from Cadiz, Fletcher Christian praises Captain Bligh and apologises for the mutiny. This presentation supports the view that public opinion about the mutiny was not all one-sided in favour of the Christian family.

There are two interesting comments on the so-called Fletcher *Letters*. The first is Bligh's. He had heard nothing of Fletcher Christian or the mutiny since the exchange of pamphlets with Edward in 1795. He wrote to Sir Joseph Banks in 1796: 'Mr Nicol has been so good as to send me down a Pamphlet called Christian's Letters – is it possible that Wretch can be at Cadiz and that he has had intercourse with his Brother, that sixpenny Professor, who has more Law about him than honor. – My Dear Sir, I can only say that I heartily dispise the praise of any of the family of Christian and I hope & trust yet that the Mutineer will meet with his deserts.'[20] This response disposes of any idea that the forgeries originated from Bligh's camp.

The second response was from William Wordsworth. In 1796 the Wordsworths were at Racedown in Dorsetshire and in receipt of the *Weekly Entertainer*,[21] which carried in one of its issues a report of the publication of the so-called Christian *Letters*. The following was published in the issue dated 7 November 1796:

Sir,
There having appeared in your *Entertainer* (vide the 255th page of the present volume) an extract from a work purporting to be the production of Fletcher Christian, who headed the mutiny on board the *Bounty*, I think it proper to inform you, that I have the best authority for saying that this

[18] The matter first became public when a report was published in the *Quarterly Review*, February, 1810, pp. 23-4. This inspired at least one major poetic effort: Mary Russell Mitford, *Christine, The Maid of the South Seas; A Poem*, London, 1811.

[19] This pamphlet is now extremely rare, and so is the one that followed it in 1798. *See* Rutter, 1932, for a discussion of the pamphlets.

[20] Bligh to Sir Joseph Banks, Letter, H.M.S. *Director*, Yarmouth Roads, 16 September 1796; Bligh Letters, ML MS C218, p. 31. Mr Nicol was Bligh's publisher.

[21] *The Weekly Entertainer: or Agreeable and Instructive Repository, Containing A Collection of Select Pieces, Both in Prose and Verse; Curious Anecdotes, Instructive Tales, and Ingenious Essays on Different Subjects*, published at Sherborne, Dorset. Wordsworth had a poem, 'Address to the Ocean', published in a subsequent issue.

publication is spurious. Your regard for the truth will induce you to
apprize your readers of this circumstance.
I am, sir,
Your humble servant
William Wordsworth.

For believers in the escape of Fletcher Christian from Pitcairn this is a most
tantalising letter. Could Wordsworth's authority for repudiating the *Letters*
have been Fletcher Christian himself? If it was – and surely this would
indeed have been 'the best authority' – then the poetic events of the following
year take on a new meaning. In 1797 William and Dorothy Wordsworth
went on a walking tour with Samuel Taylor Coleridge, during which
Coleridge wrote his *Rime of the Ancient Mariner*. More than one author has
seen in this poem a reflection of the *Bounty* story and the return of Fletcher
Christian to England.[22] The Argument of the poem, published in the 1798
edition, is as follows: How a Ship having passed the Line was driven by storms
to the cold Country towards the South Pole; and how from thence she made
her course to the tropical Latitude of the Great Pacific Ocean; and of the
strange things that befell; and in what manner the Ancyent Marinere came
back to his own Country.'[23] Though somewhat far-fetched, the suggestion is
worth looking at in detail.

An old man stops a wedding guest on his way to the wedding and insists
on telling his story. He describes the ship's voyage:

> The sun came up upon the left,
>   Out of the Sea came he:
> And he shone bright, and on the right
>   Went down into the Sea.
> Higher and higher every day,
>   Till over the mast at noon –
> The wedding-guest here beat his breast,
>   For he heard the loud bassoon.

The ship is sailing southwards towards the equator. It reaches the colder
reaches of the south Atlantic:

> Listen, Stranger! Storm and Wind,
>   A Wind and Tempest strong!
> For days and weeks it play'd us freaks –
>   Like Chaff we drove along.

---

[22] Houston, 1965-6; Squire, 1953; Wilkinson, 1953.
[23] I have used the first version of the poem published in *Lyrical Ballads*, 1798. The poem has
gone through many editions; Coleridge later altered parts of it, and added marginal glosses
which gave it a more mystical framework. *See* E.H. Coleridge (ed.), *Poetical Works of Samuel Taylor
Coleridge*, London, 1969. For the view that the poem is an allegory of Captain Cook's second
voyage, *see* Smith, Bernard, 1956.

Listen, Stranger, Mist and Snow,
   And it grew wond'rous cauld:
And Ice mast-high came floating by
   As green as Emerauld.

And thro' the drifts the snowy clifts
   Did send a dismal sheen;
Ne shapes of men ne beasts we ken –
   The Ice was all between.

The Ice was here, the Ice was there,
   The Ice was all around:
It crack'd and growl'd, and roar'd and howl'd –
   Like noises of a swound.

The *Bounty*'s experiences in the ice and snow off Cape Horn were horrific and beyond comparison with anything the men had experienced before. These lines vividly evoke the same atmosphere as permeates Bligh's Log about the conditions he and his men suffered at this time. The ship eventually turns north again:

The Sun came up upon the right,
   Out of the Sea came he;
And broad as a weft upon the left
   Went down into the Sea.

While the ship is at Cape Horn the Mariner kills an albatross – an apparently motiveless crime which causes him to feel desperately guilty.[24] This has been interpreted in many ways, but could be seen as an allegory of the mutiny and the events that followed it, although it comes earlier on in the voyage than the mutiny did. The voyage continues:

The breezes blew, the white foam flew,
   The furrow follow'd free:
We were the first that ever burst
   Into that silent Sea.

The *Bounty* sailed into new unexplored seas and made several new discoveries. As it approached Tofoa the winds slackened until on the night of the mutiny the ship was hardly moving and tempers were short from the fierce heat of the day.

---

[24] Wordsworth claimed many years later that he had suggested this symbol: 'I had been reading in Shelvocke's Voyages a day or two before that while doubling Cape Horn they frequently saw Albatrosses in that latitude ... "Suppose," said I, "you represent him as having killed one of these birds on entering the South Sea, and that the tutelary Spirits of those regions take it upon them to avenge the crime" ' (*The Poetical Works of William Wordsworth*, 2nd ed. (1952-4), ed. Helen Darbyshire, Vol. 1, pp. 360-1).

> All in a hot and copper sky
>   The bloody sun at noon,
> Right up above the mast did stand,
>   No bigger than the moon.
>
> Day after day, day after day,
>   We stuck, ne breath ne motion,
> As idle as a painted Ship
>   Upon a painted Ocean.
>
> Water, water, every where,
>   And all the boards did shrink;
> Water, water, every where,
>   Ne any drop to drink.

The poem goes into some obscure and powerful imagery here, and this section finishes with:

> Ah wel-a-day! what evil looks
>   Had I from old and young;
> Instead of the Cross the Albatross
>   About my neck was hung.

As I have argued, Christian's mutiny was not supported by the majority of men on the *Bounty*, and the private hell he was in did not justify his act in their minds. His guilt was personal; he was not righting any wrongs but externalising his own torments.

The mariner then goes through a horrific experience; a skeletal ship comes alongside containing Death and his beautiful but diseased mate:

> The western wave was all a flame,
>   The day was well nigh done!
> Almost upon the western wave
>   Rested the broad bright Sun;
> When that strange shape drove suddenly
>   Betwixt us and the Sun.

This incident could be seen as the *Bounty*'s first visit to Tubuai, which Christian approached on a southern tack to catch the prevailing winds. This would put the sun behind it as he approached. The island became identified with death after the slaughter of the islanders by Christian's party:

> Four times fifty living men,
>   With never a sigh or groan,
> With heavy thump, a lifeless lump
>   They dropp'd down one by one.

> Their souls did from their bodies fly –
>   They fled to bliss or woe;
> And every soul it pass'd me by,
>   Like the whiz of my Cross-bow.

The slaughter is linked to his use of the cross-bow to kill the albatross, just as the mutiny led to the Tubuai massacre. The mariner implies that he takes full responsibility for the killings.

There are two interesting verses at this point:

> Alone, alone, all all alone
>   Alone on the wide wide Sea;
> And Christ would take no pity on
>   My soul in agony.
>
> The many men so beautiful,
>   And they all dead did lie!
> And a million million slimy things
>   Liv'd on – and so did I.

Although in the poem the 'many men' are presumably those killed in the previous massacre, this could be a switch to the massacre at Pitcairn, in which Christian, though delirious with his wounds, had managed to escape and survive, haunted by the memories of the dead men left behind.

> An orphan's curse would drag to Hell
>   A spirit from on high:
> But O! more horrible than that
>   Is the curse in a dead man's eye!
> Seven days, seven nights I saw that curse,
>   And yet I could not die.

Christian might have lain in his hiding place for a week, recovering slowly from his wounds, but still delirious. Somehow he got away out to sea where he was 'all alone'. A ship could have picked him up: 'The Albatross fell off, and sank/Like lead into the sea'. He was safe, in some way freed of guilt, and able to forget the corpses on Pitcairn.

> O sleep, it is a gentle thing,
>   Belov'd from pole to pole!
> To Mary-queen the praise be yeven
>   She sent the gentle sleep from heaven
> That slid into my soul.[25]

[25] At the risk of being over-literal, I have searched through various records of the time to see if there were any ships, British or American, called the *Mary Queen* or something similar, but without success. I am grateful to Edouard Stackpole of the Folger Museum, Nantucket for assistance in these enquiries. The nearest I got to a similar name was *Mary Ann*, which was in the Pacific in 1792.

He was given water to drink which slaked his feverish thirst:

> My lips were wet, my throat was cold,
>   My garments all were dank;
> Sure I had drunken in my dreams
>   And still my body drank.

The ship sails on; the mariner watches the crew working the ropes and describes the effect of a storm on the ship. There is a shipwreck; the mariner survives and reaches his home country. But he is not at peace:

> Since then at an uncertain hour,
>   Now oftimes and now fewer,
> That anguish comes and makes me tell
>   My ghastly aventure.

> I pass, like night, from land to land;
>   I have strange power of speech;
> The moment that his face I see
> I know the man that must hear me;
>   To him my tale I teach.

Many sources have been traced for *The Ancient Mariner*, including a dream of a skeletal ship experienced by a friend of Coleridge's, travel books of the time, various literary traditions and the depths of Coleridge's own psyche; we can only speculate on how much Coleridge could have been influenced by a possible real-life adventure narrated by Fletcher Christian. Wordsworth was capable of keeping a secret – his illegitimate child from his visit to France is one secret he managed to keep during his lifetime – and he was passionately loyal to Fletcher's memory and to the interests of the Christian family.[26] If Fletcher had come back, he would have found a close friend and reliable collaborator in Wordsworth, and the Wordsworth family would have assisted in hiding him from the authorities.[27] Wordsworth made a large contribution to the plot of the poem (see note 24) and certainly wrote some lines of it. The connection remains unprovable; the similarity may be coincidental between Coleridge's ancient mariner, struggling with a terrible and causeless guilt, and Fletcher Christian's apparently causeless mental torment, as he first tried to cure it by mutiny and then found the mutiny an albatross round his neck.

Edward Christian appears to have dropped all references to his brother's

---

[26] As late as 1830 he was writing to Sir Walter Scott to defend the Christian family name. In *Peveril of the Peak* Scott had dramatised an episode in the Isle of Man's history which concerned the judicial murder of William Christian in the seventeenth century. Wordsworth acted as intermediary between the Christian family and his friend Scott, who was somewhat surprised at the intensity of feeling displayed by the Christians, but agreed to add an Appendix to the novel pointing out that his treatment of the incident was fictional.

[27] His aunt Isabella owned the estate at Belle Isle, a sheltered refuge if Fletcher needed one; it is a small island in Lake Windermere and contains a large family house.

case after 1795 and to have been circumspect about raising the issue at subsequent dates when he had the opportunity to do so. For instance, from 1814 to 1818 when he was Professor of Law at Cambridge one of his students was John Macarthur's son. Macarthur at the time was in exile in Britain from his adopted home country of Australia, and the source of his misfortunes was William Bligh, who had been Governor of New South Wales from 1806 to 1810. Macarthur had been prominent in Bligh's overthrow as Governor and had left the colony to avoid trial. Yet though Edward Christian and young John Macarthur were together in Cambridge for those years I have found no reference in the Macarthur papers to this fact or to any exchange of views about Bligh.[28] I find this the most extraordinary aspect of the Christian family's campaign against Bligh. Could the Christians have refrained from raising the issue in case it compromised their preservation of Fletcher in hiding, by provoking the authorities to look closer at the source of the rumours about Fletcher's re-appearance in Cumberland?

There is another possible instance of Edward's reticence about the *Bounty* after 1795. This concerns the Morrison Journal. On page 115 there is an initialled note by someone other than Morrison which reads: 'Note it shd be explained when Brown got the letter from Paono – as text now stands it seems contradictory.' This refers to a letter that Brown had with him from Captain Cox of the *Mercury* that explained his presence on Tahiti. The initials beside this note appear to be 'E.C.' The note is intended as advice to the editor of the Journal, presumably with a view to tidying it up before publication. If Edward Christian made the note this indicates that he at some time read Morrison's Journal. If so, when? Here we are again in a difficulty. There is no evidence that Edward saw Morrison's Journal during the time he was writing his polemical attacks on Bligh, 1793-5. He only refers to correspondence he had with Morrison during 1793, by which time Morrison had completed his writing. If we exclude this period – during which time, anyway, a decision had been made by Howell and Morrison not to publish, making E.C.'s advice redundant – Edward Christian could only have looked at the Journal when Heywood had possession of it. This would place it, at the earliest, in the years after 1807; Morrison died in 1807, and as we saw (Chapter 19) one possibility is that he left the Journal to Heywood. In Marshall's *Naval Biography* Heywood spoke of publication of the Morrison journal being delayed only by the death of its 'original owner'; Heywood states unambiguously that Morrison was the original owner, though I have suggested some other possibilities (see pp. 204-8). If Morrison *was* the original owner, Heywood could have intended to publish it on Morrison's death but been held up by representations from Edward Christian who did not want the matter raised again. Heywood might have passed the Journal to Edward Christian for a comment and for advice. There are one or two other notes, in the same handwriting as E.C.'s note but not initialled, dealing with similarly trivial points on other pages; Edward might have gone through and

[28] A detailed and intensive search of the MacArthur and Christian papers might throw more light on this mysterious silence.

commented on the Journal but finally decided against publication. This decision might not have been unconnected with Heywood's sighting of Fletcher in Portsmouth in 1808-9.

Let us accept for a moment that Fletcher did return to Britain. It is then necessary to explain how he got away from Pitcairn. This was not physically impossible; there are some circumstantial factors that support such a view. When Captain Beechey visited the island in 1825 he wrote a detailed account of its terrain. One interesting item concerned Christian's cave. Beechey described it thus:[29]

> At the northern extremity of this ridge is a cave of some interest, as being the intended retreat of Christian, in the event of a landing being effected by any ship sent in pursuit of him, and where he resolved to sell his life as dearly as he could. In this recess he always kept a store of provisions, and near it erected a small hut, well concealed by trees, which served the purpose of a watchhouse. So difficult was the approach to this cave, that even if the party were successful in crossing the ridge, as long as his ammunition lasted, he might have bid defiance to any force. An unfrequented and dangerous path leads from this place to a peak which commands a view of the western and southern coasts.

From later accounts it appears that Christian visited his cave regularly, disappearing for days on end into solitude. This behaviour fits in with a man who was moody, depressed and mentally ill. His command of the settlement had long ended and his authority over the seamen was only a memory. That Edward Young and Alexander Smith could have set out to murder him for the womenfolk is proof enough of their regard for him.

We can introduce the day of the massacre into this speculative picture. The islanders shoot Christian down and leave him for dead.[30] In another incident one of the attackers tried to save the life of William Brown by telling him to fall down and pretend to be dead; the ruse almost working but Brown moved too soon and Menalee is credited with finishing him off. If a prostrate body could fool them, then surely a body with a bloody wound on it could easily pass muster as a corpse. Christian, however, is not dead but is able to crawl away across the fields and up the difficult paths to his cave. McCoy and Quintal have already run off unpursued, and there are other bodies lying about neglected while the victors celebrate their grisly triumphs and share out the women. There is no reason for them to believe that Christian is alive; the only person ever credited with seeing Christian's body is McCoy and he was hiding in the bush for several weeks.

Christian, badly wounded and delirious with pain and shock, lies up in his

[29] Beechey, 1831, Vol. I, p. 80.

[30] There is no known marked grave for Christian on Pitcairn, though Beechey mentions that a grave was pointed out to him when he visited the island in 1825. According to Edward Young's account he saw 'Jenny' with five skulls in March, 1794 but he would have had no way of knowing whether they were the skulls of seamen or islanders. The rest of the remains were buried on 16 August 1794 but no mark was made on the place. This is not entirely conclusive proof that Christian died in the massacre.

cave. He is left alone in his misery. He knows that, if found, he will be killed and if he stays in the cave it is only a matter of time before they find him. He has to get away even at the risk of death at sea. The only means of escape is by the *Bounty*'s boat. (This is a possibility; after 1793 it is not mentioned on Pitcairn again. It was either destroyed or lost.) He gathers his stock of provisions and makes the dreadfully difficult journey to the bay, hiding and resting alternately. Somehow he makes it, clambers aboard and under cover of darkness steers the boat out through the rough waters of Bounty Bay. He has done this many times while out fishing. Once out to sea he collapses in the boat and lets it drift under the prevailing westerly winds.

His chances of success in this venture are minimal, but so long as food and water last and he does not succumb to his wounds, he has a chance with somewhat shorter odds of survival than if he stayed on the island. The seas around Pitcairn were becoming well known as whaling waters, and he could have drifted until picked up by a whaler. His condition, his appearance and his manner would have been shocking at first sight but it would still have been obvious that he was European. The *Bounty*'s boat would have shown that he was from a European ship. The days at sea in the open boat would have made him too ill to explain his presence for several weeks, by which time the whaler might have been nearer its home port.

If something like this happened – and it is by no means impossible – the physical survival of Fletcher Christian and his return could be accounted for. But we do not know for sure. The balance of probabilities is enticing in its evenness, leaning one way, then another. The romantic view must be that he got back to Britain, probably around 1796, and that he died some time after 1818. The realistic view, on the contrary, must be that he was killed in October 1793 in the massacre manipulated by Young and Smith. As there is a little of the romantic in every realist, and vice versa, and no concrete evidence (as yet) either way, it must be left to each reader to believe whatever suits his or her mood. The present writer confesses to being agnostic.

23

The Nore Mutiny

We left Bligh at the time when he was appointed commander of the *Calcutta* on 30 April 1795. The relatively small 24-gun ship was assigned to the North Sea command of Admiral Duncan, whose major task was blockading the Dutch coast. He had orders to engage the Dutch fleet if it left harbour at the Texel. Blockade was monotonous, unpopular work. It meant long shifts waiting at sea, boredom and bad weather – wind, rain and sleet were common. Blockade ships were relieved after several weeks, and sometimes months, and returned to Britain for a refitting or victualling. Small ships like the *Calcutta* made regular return trips carrying messages, or seeking them, and patrolled sea lanes to inspect commercial shipping. Neutral traders were a source of information as to what was happening in the ports and occasionally, if their behaviour was suspicious, they were boarded. For Bligh this was an active military command, rather than a geographical one, and marked his entry into the fighting navy. Whatever 'difficulties' he had suffered during the public controversy of 1793-5, these were overcome by virtue of his appointment to the *Calcutta*.

While on the *Calcutta* Bligh distinguished himself by attracting no attention; in his personal circumstances this was an achievement. It is clear from correspondence between Sir Joseph Banks and the Admiralty that Banks strongly supported Bligh's being given another command. The *Calcutta* was a kind of probation; not that the *Providence* had been anything but a credit to his abilities, but the damaging attacks on his command of the *Bounty* had gained credibility from the persistence with which the Christian family persued their quarry. The other thing that helped Bligh was the war with revolutionary France. If some of Christian's friends – particularly on the Wordsworth side – had encouraged the image of the 1789 *Bounty* mutiny as a smaller version of the storming of the Bastille, the reactionary forces in public life simply turned the image upside down and made Bligh into a hero who had defied unreason, rebellion, republicanism and sedition. The revolutionary image credited to Christian probably helped Bligh's case with the authorities. If Bligh kept out of trouble in the *Calcutta*, and won the support of Admiral Duncan by attention to duty, he could hope for a more substantial command than a 24-gun transporter. Attention to duty Bligh never found difficult; it was probably his strongest characteristic. Meticulous in seamanship and navigation, he had no trouble passing probation.

In October 1795 Bligh was involved in a revealing incident which hitherto has not been noted by his biographers.[1] His ship, the *Calcutta*, was in Leith (Edinburgh) and due to sail when a mutiny broke out in H.M.S. *Defiance*, Captain Sir Greig Horne. In a long letter to Sir Joseph Banks Bligh describes the mutiny and what was done to put it down.[2] 'Yesterday there were several messages sent the mutineers from Admiral Pringle, which they received in their barricaded appartments with no trifling arrogance', writes Bligh:

> The grievances they wanted to have redressed were:– a New Captain, – a new Lieutenant, – liberty to go on shore – and their Grog to be mixed with less than five waters – they were talked to on these subjects by Captain Leckmore and Mr Donal who were sent by the Admiral for this purpose to assist Captain Horne, and soon after some of the Men, (about seven or eight), were seized & put in Irons by the Officers of the Ship – quietness was established untill towards Night, when the Mutineers thought proper to insist on their companions being released, – as they would have effected it themselves and the Captain had no marines, he thought it best to comply, at which they gave him three cheers.

The mutineers' demands were a foretaste of the mutinies that were to take place a couple of years later at Spithead, Plymouth and the Nore. These grievances are almost identical to the ones put forward by the fleet mutineers of 1797, with the exception that in the latter case a demand for a pay rise was also advanced. Oppressive treatment by the officers produced a demand for their removal. The refusal of shore leave to the seamen, in case they deserted, was in contrast to the shore leave allowed to the officers. Sometimes seamen were kept on board even in their home port. Watering down the grog, while unpopular, was also necessary to combat drunkenness; but harsh conditions, and little hope of relief, produced a need for a 'groggy' escape, if only momentarily and at risk of punishment (or accident) while 'under the influence'. The technique of barricading the crew's quarters and refusing duty was about all that was open to unarmed seamen, especially in a home port. Bligh's comments on the attempts to end the mutiny without marines to enforce the Captain's orders suggest that he was somewhat critical of Captain Horne.

Bligh continues his letter to Banks with a description of the measures taken to recover command of the *Defiance*. He appears to have played an active part in the operation of placing troops on the *Defiance* but he is also critical of the lack of resolution in the commanders (and, by implication, in the person of the Admiral) and the lack of support to the loyalist seamen who resisted the mutineers. It is an interesting expression of his own views on how to deal with mutiny and also reveals him to be reasonably objective about such incidents and their causes. We shall see later how he reacted to the Nore

---

[1] For instance Mackaness, 1951, p. 305, writes of the period on the *Calcutta*: 'There are a few other Bligh letters at the Admiralty from the *Calcutta*, but they relate merely to routine matters, such as reporting his arrival at the Nore, requesting a draft of marines "sufficient as centinels", and recommending "Francis Williams as one of his lieutenants". Of matter biographical there is a total dearth.' This is quite untrue.

[2] Bligh to Sir Joseph Banks, *Calcutta*, Leith, 19 October 1795, ML MS C218, p. 7.

mutiny and its aftermath. 'This morning the Admiral sent again by the same Captains to them to order them to return to their Duty, and that as some one had refused to stand Centinel, he had to insist on a party of Soldiers being sent on board for that purpose, – from whatever way this message was delivered, or whatever cause it arose from, the Mutineers said they would receive the soldiers. Soon afterwards they declared they would not admit them.' Whether or not this was a ruse to get soldiers on the *Defiance* it was certainly taken that way, and Bligh implies, not too directly, that a more tactful handling of the message might have saved the proposition from being rejected.

Bligh continues: 'Many plans were mentioned, & the best way discussed, how to subdue this mutiny, & I did not hesitate to declare that a party of Troops embarked on board of another Ship & laid alongside, was the most effectual manner that I knew of, because they would be protected, which by any other means they would not, if resistance was made.' From this it is clear that Bligh was drawn into the discussions between the Admiral and the naval Captains present. As a commander of a relatively small ship he was not endowed with enough authority to convince the commanders in the discussion, though his experience of the *Bounty* mutiny would have made his views worth listening to. It appears that the Admiral agreed at first to Bligh's plan, and the *Jupiter* and *Edgar* (two 74-gun main battle ships) were ordered to be got ready and two hundred soldiers ordered to embark. The plan was, presumably, to place the ships along each side of the 74-gun *Defiance* and send the soldiers over the sides onto its decks. Suddenly, however, the plan was changed. Bligh does not say why but, reading between the lines, it may seem that he was not pleased with the decision, especially as he was given command of a much smaller boarding party and ordered to place these troops on the *Defiance* from ship's boats, a much more hazardous operation if the mutineers resisted. The fact that Bligh was given command of this operation probably arose from his putting forward clear opinions on what could be done, while the more senior captains present merely raised objections to the involvement of their own men and ships. Bligh, a junior captain, could not, and would not, refuse such a duty though it is clear that he was not happy at the role in which he was cast by officers who he thought should have shown more leadership. The officers concerned may have been prompted for cynical reasons to use Bligh for this operation; if anything went wrong and there was violence Bligh's reputation would allow them to escape blame in the subsequent enquiry.

Bligh tells Banks:

Suddenly the Plan was changed, and I was pitched upon to take all these Troops directly on Board of the *Defiance*. From this moment I heard no more of what was to be done; but set off to take command of the Boats wch were filled with eighty men – With these Boats I proceeded in two Divisions untill close to the Ship, when from the orders I had given to the respective officers, the Divisions opened and rowed to each Gangway preceded by myself & a Major, the commanding officer of the Soldiers, in a separate Boat. Instantly was the cry of one & all – 'clear away the Guns – sink them' & we cheered the Troops not to mind this, but to come on, wch they did, and got up the side in a better manner than I expected & were formed on the Poop[3] without any hurt but a slight Bruise or two & a boat stove with the shot that were thrown out of the ports.[4] We had now the remaining soldiers to get on board, which I effected very speedily, and without any resistance which it was expected I should have met with, both in going out & coming in; but I had only a few fellows who pointed at me & said there *he* goes.

No doubt there were mutterings about the 'Bounty Bastard' among the seamen of the *Defiance* when they saw Bligh leading this operation; Bligh was tolerably well known in the fleet.

The presence of the soldiers on the *Defiance* broke the mutiny and according to Bligh the mutineers sent a letter to the Admiral offering to return to duty if the soldiers and the 'Royalists' were removed.[5] This ends Bligh's role in the affair and he spends the rest of his letter attacking the decision of the Admiral to seek further instructions before proceeding to accept or reject the mutineers' demands. 'I now left the Ship', writes Bligh, 'as did the other captains, as our presence was no longer necessary, since wch I have heard nothing of them, but that the Admiral has written to Ad[miral]ty to know he is to proceed. – I trust that all the offenders may be brought to condign punishment, or else I fear the Royalists will have had but a poor prospect ...'

With the ending of the mutiny on the *Defiance* Bligh's probation was over. In the course of his command he recommended Lieutenant Francis Williams to the Admiralty for his conduct, but complained about the conduct of three other Lieutenants. One Lieutenant Thomas Russell deserted the *Calcutta* in August 1795, removing with him £21 2s. 6d. Another Lieutenant, David McDowall did not appear for duty, and Lieutenant Thomas Gillespie was delayed in joining his command owing to some pecuniary difficulties.

Meanwhile, Mrs Elizabeth Bligh was lobbying for her husband to be appointed to a shore post as Captain of Greenwich Hospital.[6] It is not clear why Bligh should have wanted this establishment, unless he was tired of sea duty and did not think much of his chances of promotion. Mrs Bligh had an interest in getting her husband this post as it would mean she and the family would see a lot more of him, and she may have been anxious for him after hearing about the mutiny on the *Defiance*. She wrote to Sir Joseph Banks on

[3] The poop deck was the highest and aftermost part of the hull, forming a cabin above the quarter deck.

[4] The mutineers who threw shot out of the ports onto the crowded boats would have done considerable damage; if enough had been thrown they could have sunk the boats.

[5] 'Royalists' referred to the seamen who had refused to join the mutiny, and perhaps indicates the political sentiments of the mutineers. At the time, and after, many political prisoners were sent to the fleet, especially Irishmen, and the example of the Republican triumph in France was available to encourage the disaffected. At least one Royalist from the *Defiance*, Benjamin Cocks, was transferred to Bligh's command.

[6] Bligh later wrote to Sir Joseph Banks regarding Mrs Bligh's 'intrusion on your friendship' over the Greenwich Hospital appointment: Bligh to Banks, 7 January 1796, Mitchell Library MS C218, p. 17.

her husband's behalf and asked him to use his offices to get Bligh the appointment. Banks obliged with a letter to the Lords of the Admiralty in the form of a memorial, the standard procedure for making a request in these matters. Some extracts from the memorial will show its style:[7]

> The service he [Bligh] since did by saving the part of the Crew of the *Bounty* that did not Mutiny was meretorious in the extreme – the reward he met with an attack upon his Character unfounded & illiberal which I trust he compleatly answerd by the exhibition of documents only, without the necessity of urging a single argument – ... His health has by the Voyage from the *Bounty* to Timor been utterly ruind, his head achs in the hot climates nearly killd him in his second Bread Fruit Voyage, & he now suffers much from Rheumatisms in the North Sea.
>
>   Active & indefatigible in the service however he never either complains or sollicits.
>
>   I have not heard from him for some weeks & nothing in his Letter tended to express a wish for retirement it is not by his desire that I sollicit it. I take that liberty merely because I know that his Constitution requires rest now or will soon require it.

Banks's solicitations were not successful on this occasion, but he was not a man who could be absolutely refused when he took up a case. The Admiralty Lords replied to him and while declining to appoint Bligh to the command of Greenwich Hospital informed Banks that Bligh was soon to be promoted from the *Calcutta* to a larger ship.

Neither Banks nor Bligh attempted to play down the *Bounty* mutiny; instead they used the attacks on Bligh's character as an argument for his advancement:[8]

> Capt. Bligh can feel no disapointment in hearing that Capt. Hunt's station is filld up as he had no idea of his having any hopes of succeeding him & I am confident he will hear with infinite pleasure that he is to be removed into a larger ship as every degree of notice he has the honor to receive from your Lordship will assist greatly towards healing the wound his spirit has received by the illiberal & unjust treatment his Character has met with from the Relatives of the Mutineers of the *Bounty*.

Bligh was transferred from the *Calcutta* to H.M.S. *Director*, a 64-gun ship with a complement of 491 men, on 7 January 1796.[9] This was his first major sea command. He was forty-two years old and had served in the Royal Navy for twenty-six years. The transition from geographer and explorer to combat

[7] Banks to Lords Commissioners of the Admiralty, Memorial addressed to Lord Spenser, 20 December 1795, C218, p. 15.

[8] Banks to Lords Commissioners of the Admiralty, Copy of Letter, December 1795, C218, p. 16. These letters were drafts by Banks's clerk. See also Bligh's letters to the Admiralty, 10 May and 21 May 1796, on behalf of the widow of a Dutch surgeon who had ministered to the *Bounty* survivors at Timor, and whose papers had been taken by the Royal Navy from a Dutch ship in the current hostilities.

[9] Bligh took 27 of his crew from the *Calcutta* with him to the *Director*.

command was an important step, and showed that in the eyes of the Admiralty his conduct was acceptable. They needed experienced commanders in the naval wars, men they could rely on to carry out the difficult and sometimes hazardous military tasks that were the 'sharp edge' of Britain's foreign policy. The Christian family must have received this news of Bligh's promotion with sadness; it showed that their campaign had been unsuccessful. It could be that this was the reason why Edward Christian gave up his interest in blackening Bligh from this moment; we know that he did not engage in public attacks on Bligh again in his lifetime. Bligh and his wife had much to be pleased about. His arrested career again went forward, as it had done after the shabby treatment he had received following the voyage with Cook. At that time Bligh had felt his conduct merited advancement, but the men who replaced Cook made sure that he received nothing that was his due. After the *Bounty*, Bligh's letters and actions suggest that he was absolutely convinced of his creditable role in the mutiny, and certainly he believed that the *Providence* had proved this point. Once on the *Director*, he had every reason to feel completely vindicated, even if he still felt somewhat bitter about the interruptions to his career.

During 1796 Bligh commanded the *Director*, but he did not see action, as the apparently interminable blockade of the Dutch at the Texel went on. He was in constant correspondence with Sir Joseph Banks, informing him of every development and commenting on the conduct of the war. In July he writes to Banks about the arrival in Yarmouth of H.M.S. *Glatton*, a ship with which Bligh was to command in the 1801 Battle of Copenhagen.[10] Bligh writes: 'This morning arrived the *Glatton*, Captain Trollop, who was sent out last week on a cruize ... The *Glatton* has only one Man wounded by Musquet Ball, the Officer of Marines. – We have every reason to suppose the Carronade 68 and 32 pounders did great execution, and think much praise is due to Captain Trollop.' The carronades Bligh refers to were an attempt at a heavier weapon for naval vessels than the traditional guns. The *Glatton* had been selected for the experiment and Bligh was to use them to devastating effect at Copenhagen.

In September 1796 Bligh was at the Texel again in the *Director* but he had returned to Yarmouth by 16 September. In his letter to Banks he discusses the health of the crew: 'One of the Russian Ships has a number of Sick, and I understand the Squadron in general have some in the scurvy. I am fortunate that our Sick list contains only six & only one with scurvy, but I consider a ship healthy that has not more than five Men ill to every hundred.'[11] On the *Director* that would give 20 sick men before he considered the ship unhealthy. His own health was none too good. The North Sea winter was causing him problems 'but a hot climate would kill me in a month'.[12] The routine work of the naval blockade, reflected in Bligh's correspondence from the *Director* throughout 1796, was a lull before the storm; in the British

[10] Bligh to Banks, *Director* at Yarmouth, 21 July 1796, C218, p. 29.
[11] Bligh to Banks, *Director* at Yarmouth, 16 September 1796, C218, p. 31.
[12] *ibid.*

fleets the universally down-trodden common seamen – many of them conscripts and political dissenters – were reaching the end of their tether.

In 1797 there was a general mutiny in the fleets of the British navy. The seamen mutinied for a multitude of motives: some in revolt against conditions, both general and particular; others for a mixture of political beliefs, to some extent polarised by the upheavals of the times. France, the American secession, the ideas of Tom Paine and the Irish national question provided a wide range of potential revolutionary sentiments among the seamen. The British elite was not monolithic, especially in the midst of uncertainties, and the official measures of domestic repression – the campaign against the London Corresponding Society[13] and the adoption of laws against combinations of work people – reflected fears about the message coming across the Channel from Revolutionary France. Criticism of the authorities, combined with advice from within the elite, provided plenty of material for public debate, as any examination of the pamphleteering activities of the day would show.

The wars with France were dragging on and peace was no nearer. The cost of the wars was increasing, though not just from the direct cost of fielding and supplying the armed forces. Britain was obliged to bribe its 'allies' to stay in the war or remain hostile to France. In 1795 £4½ millions went to Austria and another £1 million to Russia; then another £1½ millions to Austria in 1796, and £75,000 a month to the Czar. In all, Britain paid out £52 millions between 1793 and 1815.[14] Not all of this was good value; some of the 'allies' became enemies, switching their allegiances to suit the squalid deals in the diplomatic rounds of bribery and betrayal that was continental Europe at its most corrupt. At home the profligate Prince of Wales had his private debts of £630,000 covered out of state revenue and Prime Minister Pitt was at his eloquent best in persuading Parliament to pay the Prince £125,000 a year as well as footing the bill of £77,000 for the royal wedding. In contrast, the arrears of pay owed to British seamen reached the staggering sum (in view of their abysmal earnings) of £1,408,720 7s. 11d.[15]

This was the age of the notorious pressment system. In 1795 the courts were empowered to send those found guilty of offences, trivial or otherwise, and the vagrant, to the fleets. As a source of manpower this was hardly in the interests of the fighting capabilities of the navy. The men drafted into the ships as common seamen were not the normal port riff-raff; many of them were articulate and angry. Political malcontents, Irish Republicans by the score, rebels of all kinds, nutcases and cranks spread in the ships of the fighting fleets. The conditions they found there were a natural source of complaint which, once combined with their doctrines of dissent, became a dangerous combination for sedition. The Establishment was obviously satisfied that traditional naval discipline would restrain, if not break, the rebels. It was a foolish mistake and almost cost Britain the war.

---

[13] Interestingly it was the Duke of Portland, John Curwen's political sponsor, who, while he was Home Secretary, initiated the civil trial against John Binns, the society's secretary.

[14] Pope, 1963, p. 77.

[15] Dugan, 1966, pp. 28, 33; I have used this book for background in much of this chapter.

The first outbreak began in February, 1797 in the *Queen Charlotte* and the *Royal Sovereign*. The men demanded a wage increase. They drew attention to the last wage increase the navy had received – under Charles II over 100 years previously. The men circulated a petition in the Channel Fleet, signed by men on thirty-eight ships, and sent it to Lord Howe, the fleet commander, in early March 1797. There was no reply from Lord Howe by the end of the month when the fleet was back in Spithead. Howe retired from command, having been ill for sometime, and on 13 April the mutiny broke out.[16]

The first response of the Admiralty was to order the ships to sea but the men refused to carry out the sailing orders from their officers. They elected delegates instead and held a meeting to decide what to do next. Once it was clear to the Admiralty that the men meant business they offered a pay increase of 5s. 6d. per month for Petty Officers, 4s. 6d. for ordinary seamen and 3s. 6d. for landsmen. The delegates mistrusted the sincerity of the offer. They recalled the mutiny on the *Culloden* in 1794 when the Admiralty had not kept its promises.[17] A King's pardon was demanded to protect the lives of the prominent mutineers once the officers were in control of the ships again; this was offered by the Admiralty, but not all the ships were persuaded by it to put to sea. The basic problem remained: while the Admiralty had agreed to the pay rise and the King had been persuaded to offer a pardon, Parliament had agreed to neither, and without Parliament's agreement neither was of lasting value. The Prime Minister, Pitt, sought an early opportunity to persuade Parliament to approve the measures taken to end the mutiny, but was delayed by the political problems his party was having with the notoriously difficult assembly. The delay was fatal; as ships returned home and heard about the Spithead mutiny they became infected by the demands. The men were not aware of the delicate political balancing act that was a Prime Minister's burden in a Georgian Parliament, and naturally suspected that Pitt, the Admiralty and the King were equivocating in order to betray their promises. As a result the mutiny spread to Plymouth. Twenty-six ships there declared solidarity with the Spithead ships, some of them being ships that had been moved from Spithead under the first terms of the settlement.

News of the mutiny spread round the home fleets and naturally their crews wanted to know when they were to get the new pay rises. Admiral Duncan, Commander of the North Sea Fleet, had a forewarning of trouble on his flagship, *Venerable*, on 30 April 1797, when there was an illegal muster of his crew to discuss their pay. The Government acted on 1 May by sending a general order to all the fleet commanders asking them to pay attention to formal discipline – parades, uniforms, marines, and the Articles of War – and at the same time to avoid provocative behaviour. If the news about the

---

[16] *ibid.*, pp. 89-90.

[17] *Culloden* had mutinied against Captain (later Sir) Thomas Troubridge. After several days the men were persuaded to return to duty and Troubridge seized ten of the leaders, court-martialled them and had five hanged. It was believed among the seamen of the time that the men had been promised no retribution if they returned to duty, and they never forgave the officers for what they regarded as a breach of faith. It was on Troubridge's ship *Blenheim* that James Morrison drowned in 1807.

mutiny reached France or the Netherlands it was possible that the enemy would take advantage of Britain's weakness and engage in hostilities. Thus, the officers should ensure that the code of discipline was enforced and that provocative acts such as cheating on the provisions or conspicuous long shore leaves for officers should be stopped. The hope was to get the Channel fleet to sea again before the mutiny spread. This was partly achieved: the Channel fleet returned to duty – after personal intervention by Lord Howe and a reconciliation dinner for the officers and the leaders of the mutiny, itself a unique event in the history of the Royal Navy – but the mutiny spread to the North Sea fleet.

Captain William Bligh was commanding the *Director* in Admiral Duncan's fleet. The *Director* was not a small ship; it had 491 men on board. The Captain was supported by four Lieutenants and a party of marines. In March 1797 the *Director* was on a tour of duty at the Texel. There were incidents of insubordination that led to punishments by flogging. One man received eighteen lashes, four others twelve lashes and one other eight lashes. It is significant that these punishments arose from incidents during the running out of the ship's guns in a practice session. The crew must have participated in practices countless times; they were already disturbed by the reports coming from Spithead and incessant practice to achieve perfection was likely to become an irritation. They had been on blockade duty for nearly three years, never seeing the enemy and never firing their guns in anger.

It does not follow, and it would be most unlikely, that it was Bligh who found fault with the men directly. In a ship as large as the *Director*, the Lieutenants had direct charge of their crews and it was their reports to the Captain that procured punishment orders. The Captain of a 64-gun ship was a remote figure, removed from direct contact with the crew by several layers of authority. Even midshipmen could report a seaman for a flogging. The Captain was obliged in almost all circumstances to order punishment after a report from a Lieutenant. Bligh's record shows that he resorted to the lash with leniency and regret.

The punishments ordered on 10 April 1797 did not stem the insubordination, which suggests that the incidents ran deeper than mere aberration. Between 12 and 17 April a further five seamen were ordered to punishment and received twelve to twenty-four lashes for 'neglect'.[18] The *Director* returned to Yarmouth on 25 April, and Bligh read out the official notice of the wage increases agreed by the Government. This concession did not quell the dissent. The Spithead mutineers had called for a general stand-down of the entire home navy for 18 April, but the *Director* had put to sea on 27 March and the Texel fleet remained on station an extra ten days, contrary to intentions and orders, which probably exacerbated the trouble with the ships' crews. It is possible that the trouble on the *Director* (and on other

---

[18] *Log of the Director*, Captains' Logs, PRO 51/1195. In 1796, the *Director* had 41 men flogged (including one marine who got two lashes) and in 1797, up to May, 20 men were flogged. The average was a dozen lashes each.

ships) was caused by the excitement of the challenge to the authorities, which manifested itself in the unusual frequency of incidents of insubordination and 'neglect' in early April.[19]

Altogether there were 119 ships in a state of mutiny in 1797. The Spithead mutiny was not settled until Lord Howe acted as the conciliatory intermediary between the seamen and the Government. He used his moral authority over the seamen to get a settlement that they would trust. Meanwhile the Government was looking at the political implications of the mutiny. The Duke of Portland was engaged in the less prominent activity of collecting evidence of political subversion among the seamen. Among the agents provocateurs recruited and sent to collect evidence was Aaron Graham, the man Admiral Pasley had persuaded to act as defence counsel for Peter Heywood during the trial of the *Bounty* mutineers in 1792.[20] His role this time was to find evidence to convict men of mutiny and sedition. He quickly adapted himself to the role of police spy and informer and began sending reports to the Duke of Portland and the Government, which at the time believed itself to be surrounded by a Jacobin conspiracy. In fact it was facing a rebellion of hungry seamen. Graham shows himself by this activity to be merely the client advocate of the rich and powerful.

Lord Howe managed to get a settlement agreed by 14 May. Part of that settlement involved the removal from command of 114 officers, including an Admiral (Colpoys), four Captains (Griffith, Nicholls, Campbell and Cook), 20 lieutenants, 8 marine commanders, 3 masters, 4 surgeons, a chaplain, 17 master's mates, 25 midshipmen, 7 gunners, boatswains and carpenters, 5 marine N.C.O.s and 3 masters at arms. With the acceptance of the seamen's demands for a pay increase and the removal of tyrannical officers, the Channel fleet sailed on 17 May and got back into the war. Aaron Graham failed to turn up evidence of a conspiracy and the Government, showing considerable sense for once, allowed the agreement to go through. But as the Spithead and Plymouth mutinies ended, the Nore mutiny broke out.

The Nore ships sent a delegation to Spithead consisting of Charles McCarthy, Thomas Atkinson (*Sandwich*), Hinds (*Clyde*) and Matthew Hollister (*Director*). The wage offer had whetted their appetites. While there is no hope, men tend to live under the burden of precedent and contribute to their fate by a resignation to it. But once hope is kindled, it is not an easy emotion to control. The Spithead mutinies had shown the powerful leverage the seamen could exert. The pay increase and the extraordinary concession of the removal of the hated officers had been won because of the threat to Britain of a navy in mutiny in the midst of a war with France. The Yarmouth fleet had just returned from a blockade tour and had not yet experienced the emotional strains of confrontation with the Establishment; what seemed a generous settlement to those who had fought for it was of minimal significance to those who had returned to benefit from it.

---

[19] Gill, 1913, quotes a Lieutenant Irwin who ordered a seaman 36 lashes for 'silent contempt' after a previous flogging (p. 270); Captain Henry Nicholls of the *Marlborough* had a seaman flogged to death and this helped to spark off the Spithead mutiny (*see* Dugan, 1966, p. 89).

[20] For a fuller account of Graham's police work *see* Dugan, 1966, Chapters 8 and 9.

That the situation was not quiescent in Admiral Duncan's fleet can be seen from Bligh's Log of the *Director*. Thomas Norton was given twenty-four lashes for drunkenness – not an exceptional charge nor an exceptional punishment – but the next day William McDougall was given twelve lashes for insolence to a superior officer on the *Venerable*, Admiral Duncan's flagship. Presumably McDougall had been in a boat party sent to the *Venerable* on a message under a Lieutenant or Midshipman, or one of the officers of the *Venerable* had visited the *Director*. That the offence was against somebody on the Admiral's flagship is a measure of the mood in the fleet. William Roland on the same day received twelve lashes for insolence to a sentry on the *Director* and Bligh sent ashore 'one Emanuel Castulo' for refusing duty. Castulo claimed to be a French citizen, which shows the sweepings that the pressment system brought into the ships.

Floggings may excite the more liberal sentiments of our age but before we conclude that floggings were a cause of the mutiny it might be as well to put them in perspective. In the eighteenth century flogging as a punishment was a normal aspect of service life. The seamen's attitude to flogging can best be seen by the measures the mutineers took to enforce discipline in the ships that they took over in 1797. Any person in breach of the mutineers' discipline was given thirty-six lashes. The only difference was that the mutineers voted in a meeting to punish a recalcitrant seamen whereas on the King's ships it was at the discretion of the commanding officer. The mutineers of Spithead and the Nore were not driven to mutiny by floggings – though unjust floggings were always contentious – but by a general demand for better wages and conditions.[21]

Admiral Duncan ordered Bligh to take the *Director* to the Nore for a refit on 6 May 1796. At this time the ships anchored at the Nore were in a state of ferment. On 12 May Bligh was on board H.M.S. *Inflexible* attending a court martial under Admiral Buckner with several other captains from ships at the anchorage. This was a standard port duty for captains. Thus many captains were not on their ships at the moment when the mutinies broke out. As soon as the news reached the *Inflexible* the courts martial were adjourned and the captains hurried back to their ships.

When Bligh returned on board the *Director* he was presented with a number of demands from the crew. These included the immediate removal from the ship of three of his officers accused of ill-using the men. These were Lieutenants Ireland and Church and the Master, Mr Birch. The crew were hoping to get Lord Howe's settlement extended to the North Sea fleet. It is important to note that there were no complaints of Bligh in the matter of 'ill-use'; the complaints that arose against Bligh later were primarily and exclusively concentrated on his political role in undermining the mutiny. The crew had very little to do with their Captain and they would feel the oppression only of those with direct command over them.

Bligh refused to send the three men ashore but relieved them from duty

---

[21] I have not found a single complaint against Bligh for his flogging any of his men, except among his critics in the literary field.

and confined them to their cabins. He remained in command of the *Director* and the crew carried out his routine orders, but these did not amount to much as the ship was at anchor. The mutineers did not stop with the demand for the removal of the officers. They wanted Bligh to issue them with the ship's small arms, but he firmly refused. From this point the leaders were at odds with Bligh. The mutineers on the *Sandwich* had got hold of the ship's small arms and the fact that the *Director* was still under the captain's command to this extent was an affront to the credibility of the militants on board. Thomas McCann from the *Sandwich* clashed verbally with Bligh on a visit to the *Director* when he tried to incite the crew to seize the ship's arsenal. By his actions Bligh drew attention to himself as a militant anti-mutineer, and when the Nore delegates met aboard the *Sandwich* opinion was easily swung against him by references to his refusal to send ashore the oppressive officers and his refusal to issue small arms. No doubt his 'below decks' reputation as the 'Bounty Bastard' was used in the harangues calling for his removal. 'President' Richard Parker, the leader of the Nore delegates, was opposed to Bligh remaining even in *de facto* command; this meant that the delegates from the *Director* must either do something about his presence or forfeit the respect of the rest of the fleet leaders. Even so it took another week for them to work up sufficient resolve among the crew to get Bligh ashore.

The Nore delegates met in a kind of 'parliament' (or, in modern revolutionary terminology, a 'soviet') which was made up of two delegates from each ship. This parliament issued the demands of the mutiny to the Admiralty. It also passed the disciplinary code for dealing with offenders. A certain amount of brutality entered into the code when mutineers re-introduced ducking from the yard arm as a punishment. While less injurious than keel-hauling of the kind practised several decades previously, it was nevertheless an extremely unpleasant experience.[22]

At this stage the Admiralty encouraged Admiral Buckner to respond in a low key to the Nore mutiny in the expectation that Howe's settlement would defuse the situation at the Nore. As anticipated, Howe got the Channel fleet to sea, but matters took a turn for the worse at the Nore. For this the Admiralty and the Government were entirely to blame. At Spithead, Lord Howe personally met and negotiated with the leaders of the mutiny – he even dined with them with Lady Howe present. The pay increases were made public and the other main aspect of the seamen's demands, the removal of oppressive officers, was carried out, even if it was not exhibited for public scrutiny. But the men at the Nore were ignored; they received no personal visits from Lord Howe[23] or other representatives of the Admiralty, there were no written offers, no wining and dining, no friendly socials with the

[22] The yard-arm was a long cylindrical timber, having a rounded taper towards each end, slung from its centre to the mast; it was used for spreading the square sails and had a block on each end for ropes. Keel-hauling was punishment by hauling the victim down one side of the ship, under the water and up the other side.

[23] Lord Howe did meet a deputation of the mutineers at Yarmouth (one of whom was Hollister of the Director) but he was unable to negotiate with them and advised them to return to duty.

Admirals' ladies, and no offer, private or public, to remove the oppressive
officers. The Nore men were simply snubbed. Their mutiny was treated as a
mere sideshow to the Spithead mutiny. The result was that the Howe
settlement became a minimum basis for a Nore settlement, and the ships'
delegates presented to the Admiralty a far more ambitious programme of
demands.

It is by no means a coincidence that the heightened mood of militancy
among the Nore delegates was accompanied by a fleet decision to have Bligh
removed from the *Director*. McCarthy of the *Sandwich*, who had gone to
Spithead as leader of the Nore delegates, was superseded by others of a more
militant persuasion McCarthy's fall from grace – accompanied by many
personal indignities – was a prelude to Hollister's rise to prominence. His
reports from Spithead hardened the resolve of the Nore delegates. They
passed the following programme of demands:[24]

> Article 1. That every indulgence granted to the fleet at Portsmouth, be
> granted to his Majesty's subjects serving in the Fleet at the Nore, and
> places adjacent.
> 2. That every man, upon a ship's coming into harbour, shall have
> liberty (a certain number at a time, so as not to injure the ship's duty) to
> go and see their friends and families; a convenient time to be allowed to
> each man.
> 3. That all ships before they go to sea shall be paid all arrears of wages
> down to six months, according to the old rules.
> 4. That no officer that has been turned out of any of his Majesty's ships
> shall be employed in the same ship again, without consent of the ship's
> company.
> 5. That when any of his Majesty's ships shall be paid, that may have
> been some time in commission, if there are any pressed men on board,
> that may not be in the regular course of payment, they shall receive two
> months advance to furnish them with necessaries.
> 6. That an indemnification be made any men who have run, and may
> now be in his Majesty's naval service, and that they shall not be liable to
> be taken up as deserters.
> 7. That a more equal distribution be made of prize-money to the crews
> of his Majesty's ships and vessels of war.
> 8. That the Articles of war, as now enforced, require various alterations,
> several of which to be expunged therefrom; and if more moderate ones
> were held forth to seamen in general, it would be the means of taking off
> that terror and prejudice against his Majesty's service, on that account too
> frequently imbibed by seamen from entering voluntarily into the service.
> The Committee of delegates of the whole Fleet assembled in council on
> board his Majesty's ship *Sandwich*, have unanimously agreed that they will
> not deliver up their charge until the appearance of some of the Lords
> Commissioners of the Admiralty to ratify the same.
> Given on board his Majesty's ship *Sandwich*, by the Delegates of the
> Fleet, 20th May, 1797.

None of these demands could really be regarded as extreme; 'radical' would

[24] Quoted in Dugan, 1966, pp. 201-2.

18. George Young (son of the mutineer Edward Young) and his wife Hannah Adams (daughter of John Adams) on Pitcairn. From Barrow, 1831. Engraved by Lt.-Col. Batty from a sketch by Lt. Smith of H.M.S. *Blossom*.

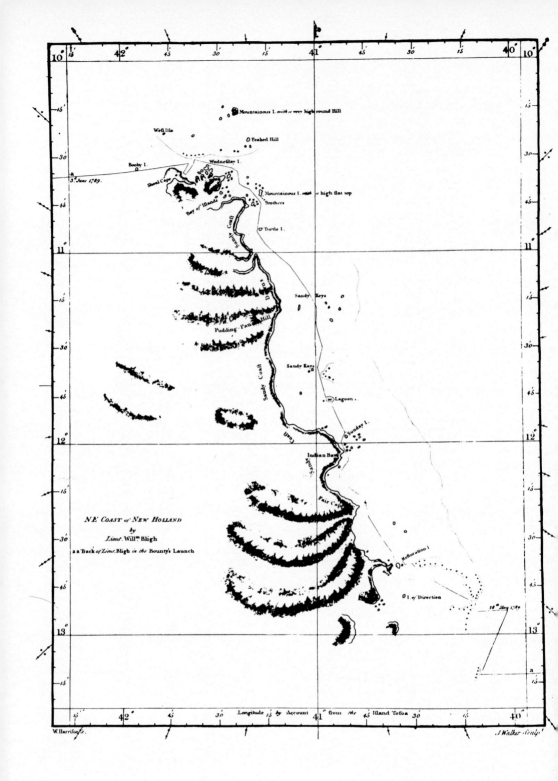

19. Bligh's chart of the north-east coast of Australia, made on the voyage of the *Bounty*'s launch. From his *Narrative* of 1790.

be about the strongest adjective for them, but then this would only be true in the context of the social structure of eighteenth-century Britain. Many of the demands made sense from the point of view of an Admiralty that wanted manpower for its ships. Voluntary recruitment was better than the pressment system, which threatened the workability of the ships. Lack of shore leave encouraged desertion by seamen anxious to see their wives and families even though the punishment was extreme. It could be that Articles 4, 7 and 8 threatened the interests of officers. If the crews had the right to remove an officer this would create yet another barrier between the officer and promotion, though it would only intimidate the kind of officer the navy could do without. Prize money was a contentious subject for all ranks; redistributing it downwards might or might not benefit officers, depending on their position in the hierarchy. Certainly those highest in the hierarchy would lose if there were changes. The list of demands did not specify which of the Articles of War they wanted moderated, but any dilution in the powers of the officers would undermine their absolute authority. The Admiralty and the Treasury would not be overjoyed to accept Articles 3 and 5 in view of the King's financial problems. They would raise the cost of the war which was already the most expensive in British history.

The demands, while just, were contrary to the custom and practice of the navy of the day. The use of force to fill the ship's establishments at least almost guaranteed a crew, whereas reliance on the economic instincts of potential seamen might not. The habit of paying crews in arrears suited the convenience of the King's finances and presented the additional benefit that some seamen died before they were paid. In the political circumstances of a monarchy that had lost the American colonies and had witnessed the execution of a King across the Channel it was unlikely that any moderation of the authoritarian rules of conduct would be acceptable. There was, in fact, little chance that any of these demands would be met. The Establishment was acting in its own interests in resisting the Nore demands, even if it was its own stupidity that made the confrontation inevitable. The 'reformers' in the Establishment were battered by the 'reactionaries' with the argument that giving an inch – the Howe settlement – only encouraged sedition and more arrogant demands – the Nore Articles. Moreover, the Georgian regime had little practice in treating with social 'inferiors'. The economic and organisational demands of the Nore mutineers were seen as a rebellion and the Georgian Establishment had plenty of practice in dealing with that kind of problem, though its track record was only remarkable for its pig-headedness (America and Ireland). Aaron Graham's role indicates the Government's view of the real implications of the mutinies.

Hollister returned to the *Director* and set about having Bligh removed. On 19 May 1797 Bligh wrote to Nepean at the Admiralty announcing his involuntary removal from command of his ship for the second time in his carrer:[25]

---

[25] Bligh to Evan Nepean, Sheerness, 19 May 1797, PRO Admiralty 1/1516, Captain 'B', also quoted in Dugan, 1966, p. 206. Lieutenants Ireland and Church, and Mr Birch, had been sent on shore by Bligh the previous Sunday.

Sheerness, May 19, 1797

Sir,

You will please to inform my Lords Commissioners of the Admiralty that this morning about nine o'clock, soon after the return of the delegates from Spithead, they came on board and declared to me they had seen Earl Howe, who had told them all officers were to be removed from their ships who they disapproved of; they were in consequence to inform me in the name of the ship's company that I was to quit the command of the ship & for it to devolve on the first Lieutenant, who they in the same breath ordered to supercede me. Being without any resource I was obliged to quit the ship. I have stated the whole transaction to Admiral Buckner, and now await their Lordships' directions, being ready to meet any charge that can be brought against me or such investigation as they may think proper to direct. I have reason to believe the whole has originated with the *Sandwich*'s crew – hitherto never did a ship's company behave better or did ever a ship bear more marks of content and correctness.

Mr Purdue, Mr Blaguire, and Mr Eldridge, Midm. are also turned on shore for being too much noticed by their Captain & Mr Purdue particularly because he did his duty like a spirited young officer – I know of nothing dishonourable they can be accused of.

With this second seizure of command by a crew, Bligh's reputation took another knock. Historians have not been kind to him over this; some of them have been malicious. An example of the latter is the following comment: 'In the French Revolutionary War, Bligh commanded a ship in the line, but again exciting the disaffection of his men by his harshness, they mutinied and ran the ship into a French harbour.'[26] This is, of course, nonsense. None of William Bligh's ships was run into a French port. There were, however, two other Captain Blighs on the lists at the time. Captain Rodney Bligh, while in command of the *Alexandria*, was captured by the French in November 1794 and taken to the French port of Brest. He was later released in a prisoner exchange, court-martialled and honourably acquitted. He later became an Admiral and his portrait is sometimes wrongly identified as William Bligh. Captain John Bligh was appointed to command the *Latona* which had been sent to Spithead during the 1797 mutiny. The crew sent him ashore in the first batch of officers on 12 May after only eighteen days' experience of him.

Howe's acceptance of the removal of officers, while necessary to get the Spithead ships to sea, was now seen as a dangerous precedent, as it had spread to the Nore ships. The situation between the two sides hardened in the days after 19 May. The delegates elected Richard Parker as their leader and settled down to what they knew would be a tough battle. Parker was an interesting leader. He was about thirty years old in 1797. His personality bears resemblances to Christian's – he had the same impetuousness, the same intelligence, the same instability. The major difference between them was that he was not well-connected. His father was a grain merchant and baker – a tradesman – not a landowner or farmer. He had been educated at

[26] *Chambers' Encyclopaedia*, 1861 edition, p. 155, quoted in Mackaness, 1951, p. 323; *see* also Lloyd, 1963, pp. 110-11.

Exeter Grammar School and had run away to sea. Because of his education he became a midshipman and had a promising career ahead of him. He served during the American War of Independence, at one time under Edward Riou, Bligh's former shipmate from the *Resolution*. He claimed to have been a petty officer on H.M.S. *Mediator* in 1783 and in peace time to have been a Master's Mate in the merchant service. At the time of the *Bounty*'s voyage he held the same rating as Fletcher Christian. It is believed that on the merchant ship he led a mutiny over bad food.

In the French wars Parker continued his naval career and joined H.M.S. *Assurance* as a junior officer in the Channel Fleet. However, he was court-martialled for disobeying an officer and in consequence disrated to ordinary seaman. He was transferred to H.M.S. *Glebe* as a foremast hand. Much the same fate might have befallen Fletcher if the *Bounty* had been on patrol in home waters instead of in the Pacific. In 1794 Parker was discharged from the navy on medical grounds – rheumatism was the official reason. He returned to his wife's family in Braemar, Scotland. In 1797 he was in Perth debtor's prison and took the option of a £30 bounty for rejoining the navy. He was posted to H.M.S. *Sandwich* on 9 April; this brought an articulate ex-officer and an imaginative leader into a ship with ready-made grievances and the example of Spithead to emulate. Parker had just enough arrogance – he once challenged Riou to a duel over a difference of opinion while serving as a midshipman – and the right amount of style to be different from the simpler and more straightforward leader of the Spithead mutiny, Valentine Joyce. He pushed the Nore men to the ultimate challenge to authority and also kept the mutineers under control – no mean achievement.

The Government had from the start contemplated the use of force against the Nore mutineers. Their only problem was that the advantages in a military engagement lay with the anchored ships, rather than with the Sheerness battery. Local army units might be unreliable. The only other possible form of attack was by sea, and this meant finding reliable ships. The Channel fleet was at sea and had only just recovered from its own mutiny; bringing it to the Nore was too risky, and the transfer of the fleet to this duty would leave the way open to the French to invade Ireland. The only other available fleet was under Admiral Duncan. The Government had to be sure that the North Sea fleet would carry out its orders and not defect to the mutineers.

Nepean wrote to Duncan on 22 May 1797: 'You know the state of your fleet, I believe, as well as anyone can do, and what use could be made of it. Do you think that you could depend upon any of the ships if you were to bring them up to the Nore, if it should be necessary to employ them in bringing the two or three ships of the line over there to reason?'[27] The vagueness of Duncan's reply said as much about the true situation as if he had spelled it out. He did not say yes or no. He even offered what was in fact a silly suggestion: 'As to the 'Sandwich', you should get her cast adrift in the night and let her go on the sands, that the scoundrels may drown; for until

---

[27] Nepean to Duncan, 22 May 1797, PRO Admiralty 2/1352.

some example is made this will not stop.'[28]

The need for action became more obvious each day as the situation deteriorated. It was essential to find out the real state of Duncan's fleet. Incredibily, the King and the Admiralty spent much time deciding on a ship to carry the Prince on his honeymoon. On 26 May the Admiralty decided a special envoy should be sent to Duncan's fleet to report on the true state of affairs. For this mission they chose William Bligh, itself a testimony to their regard for his reliability. Bligh took with him the following letter:[29]

> Private.
> We send you Captain Bligh on a very delicate business on which the Government is extremely anxious to have your opinion. The welfare and almost the existence of the country may depend upon what is the event of this very important crisis. But till we know what we can look to from your squadron it will be very difficult for us to know how to act.
> EVAN NEPEAN

By the time Bligh got to Yarmouth Duncan had demonstrated the true situation. He had tried to get his fleet to sail for the Texel, but was unsuccessful. The *Agamemnon, Repulse, Ardent, Isis, Glatton* and his sloops and frigates refused to sail. Only the flagship, *Venerable*, and the *Adamant* were prepared to fight the Dutch. If the ships would not fight the Dutch they would certainly not fight their comrades at the Nore.

Bligh spent a few days visiting as many ships as would let him on board and he talked to dozens of the ships' crews. On 30 May the following report was sent to the Admiralty:

> Secret
> Memorandum by Captain Bligh for the Board of Admiralty. Arrived at Yarmouth, Saturday 28th May. Admiral sailed at 5 am with 12 sails. The *Standard* and *Lion* refused to obey the Admiral's orders, but afterwards complied and sailed. *Nassau* refused to obey the sailing order on account of pay due to the people. The ship's company observed, on being questioned whether they would resist mutiny in other ships, that every Captain should keep his own ship quiet. *Montagu* claims pay although but a month due. The ship's company went to their quarters and shotted their guns when the *Venerable* got under weigh. The ships in the road will only permit their own boats to come alongside, and no strangers. The Captain of the Marines of the *Standard* turned on shore and a Lieutenant of the *Repulse* put into the Admiral's ship by command of the people. The *Glatton*'s Company have a remarkable loyal and good character. The delegates arrived from the Nore, but Admiral Duncan was informed of eighteen coming round in the *Cygnet* cutter, and he had given orders to prevent their communicating with any of the ships (dated 26th May).
> It appeared to me very doubtful and hazardous what would be the conduct of the favourable party of seamen, if employed against the other.

---

[28] Duncan to Nepean, *Venerable*, Yarmouth, 23 May 1797; quoted in Dugan, 1966, p. 209.
[29] Quoted in Mackaness, 1951, p. 309.

The *Standard* and *Lion* wanted to send delegates to the other ships, but they were refused admittance.

When I received Admiral Duncan's letters for their Lordships, I thought it advisable to return without a moment's loss of time. *Montagu* and *Nassau* only in the road.

Wm. Bligh.[30]

The Admiralty knew from this report and the refusal of duty of some of Duncan's ships that an attack on the Nore mutineers from the sea was not practicable. By sailing for the Texel Duncan had brought the mutiny in his fleet to the surface. The Admiralty at least knew where it stood. So did the Nore mutineers. The party of delegates from the Nore in the *Cygnet*'s cutter also found out what the state of affairs was at Yarmouth. Duncan had ordered that the Nore delegates be refused admission to his ships and had sent a Lieutenant Reddy to intercept the *Cygnet* and arrest the delegates. Reddy found the *Cygnet* but the delegates were by then ashore meeting their comrades. They eventually returned and fooled Reddy with a ruse that he ought to have seen through. Hollister told him that they had discovered that the fleet was against the mutiny and that when they reported this to the Nore the mutiny there would collapse. Incredibly, he believed this even though he must have known that it was not a true picture of the state of affairs in Yarmouth. The result was that he let Hollister go. When Hollister returned to the Nore he was able to tell Parker and the delegates that they had nothing to fear from the Yarmouth fleet. This strengthened their hand. If Reddy had arrested Hollister this would have kept the Nore delegates in ignorance of the true state of affairs (uncertainty can cause paralysis in decision-making) and it would have also removed one of the most intelligent of the leading mutineers.

The Cabinet, on the basis of Bligh's report, tried a new initiative. It suggested to the Admiralty that they send someone down to Sheerness to meet the leaders of the mutiny and offer them the King's pardon if they would return to duty. This was not the same mission as had been given to Lord Howe; he had had some freedom to negotiate a return to duty. The mutineers were told that they could meet the Lords Commissioners to accept the King's pardon but could not discuss any grievances. This was unacceptable to the delegates, who knew the real balance of forces at the time. Thus, although the delegates and the Lords Commissioners were in the same building they did not meet. The Lords Commissioners returned from Sheerness empty-handed and the Cabinet had no new ideas. If Lord Howe had been sent down to talk to the mutineers – without preconditions – something constructive might have been done. The Admiralty did not send him, largely, it seems, because they did not agree to the removal of officers which they knew he would have to accept.

But if the Cabinet had no new ideas, neither had the mutineers. There was

---

[30] Bligh to Admiralty, Memorandum, PRO Admiralty 1/524, F149. Bligh's remarks about the *Glatton* and its loyal crew are interesting in view of his later command of the ship. This was the second time he had praised them in his correspondence with the Admiralty.

no one to treat with, and they had nothing to do, unless they attacked the capital or sailed to France. As they did neither, it was only a matter of time before the mutiny disintegrated, unless the French or Dutch attacked. They tried to blockade the Thames and they received a boost to their morale when some ships from Yarmouth arrived to join the mutiny. Eight 64-gun ships strengthened the mutineers' power, but they had little to exercise it against. Unwilling to use their military power, the Nore mutineers became people living in floating cages off the shore, and as such they became vulnerable to psychological measures taken against them.

Admiral Buckner ordered all officers ashore to isolate the seamen. Supplies were cut off to impose hardship on the mutineers. Further, to make any intended escape to sea too risky, he also ordered the Thames marker buoys to be removed. These simple measures and the lack of any signs of a settlement weakened the resolve of some of the crews in the mutiny. It became obvious that some ships were ready to return to normal duty but were prevented by the militant minority. Some ships, including the *Director*, were 'completely under the influence of terror' from *Sandwich* and *Inflexible*.[31]

Buckner was told that the *Director* 'was wavering' and this was confirmed by an attempted seizure of the ship from the mutineers on 30 May. A bitter fight took place on deck which the mutineers eventually won. The signals that had been raised proclaiming an end to the mutiny were pulled down and red flags raised in their place. That this was not an isolated incident is shown from another attempted seizure of the ship on 6 June; Lieutenant Roscoe read the assembled crew the meaning of the King's pardon which had been sent up from London. Parker himself came across to debate the issue and persuade the men to remain in the mutiny. The fact that Parker found it necessary to make this tour of the ships indicates the fragility of the mutiny. In some ships the mutineers introduced flogging by up to thirty-six lashes for waverers (in a later age they would have been called 'defeatists'). Other ships experienced deck brawls such as took place on the *Director*. Even on the *Sandwich* trouble broke out. The men were on short rations and water was scarce. A plan to take the ships down the Thames to the sea was defeated because of the unmarked channels. In a last bid to compromise the mutineers offered to settle for an agreement to end the mutiny in exchange for the removal of some officers. The Admiralty refused.

The anti-mutineers in the *Leopard* succeeded in seizing their ship and they removed it to Gravesend under Lieutenant Robb. The *Repulse* also changed hands, but a similar move in the *Standard* failed. Parker ordered the *Director* to chase the *Repulse* and fire on her but the men refused to obey the command and the militants had to be satisfied with firing a single gun at the escaping ship. Parker also went to the *Monmouth* with a similar order but again only managed to get some guns fired. This exposed the weakness of the mutiny, especially to the men of the *Standard*, and they took another vote and decided

---

[31] Quoted in Dugan, 1966, p. 230; this may have been the source of the statement made by Ellis, 1955, pp. 256-7, that the 'terror' in the *Director* originated from Bligh, which is contrary to Buckner's report.

to re-instate the Captain to command of the ship. The *Ardent* was the next to change sides and it steered from the Nore. In the course of the next twenty-four hours more ships surrendered. The *Agamemnon*, the *Isis* and the *Vestal* moved away from the Nore. Parker became a virtual prisoner on the *Sandwich*. The *Monmouth*, which had failed to act with determination against the escaping *Repulse*, placed itself under Lieutenant Buller's command and surrendered.

The mutiny was almost over. Lord Keith, accompanied by Sir Thomas Pasley (Peter Heywood's uncle), went round the remaining ships persuading the men to surrender. The flagship of the mutiny, H.M.S. *Sandwich*, surrendered and handed over Richard Parker, who was taken in irons to Gravesend. Without support on the ship, and restrained from leaving, Parker calmly accepted his fate. Six ships, including the *Director*, remained under red flags. Lord Keith visited each in turn and the men hauled down the red flag. The *Director* was the last ship that he approached and without further resistance the militants gave in.

There has been some attempt[32] to make capital out of the fact that the *Director* was the last ship to surrender. This was in fact a coincidence. Lord Keith visited ships flying red flags but not in any apparent order of increasing militancy. The fact that he went to the *Sandwich* and the *Inflexible* before going to the *Director* shows that if there was a rank order in his visits the most militant ships came first. The Admiralty's own estimations of militancy in the ships was that the *Sandwich* and *Inflexible* were the source of the mutiny and were exerting 'terror' on the other ships, including the *Director*. The loyalists on the *Director* had tried twice to restore normality during the mutiny. The Admiralty had no reason to believe that the *Director* was especially militant, other than the fact that Hollister was on board. The implication drawn by Bligh's critics from Lord Keith's action has been that the *Director* was the last to surrender because it was Bligh's ship and that the men were terrified of his coming back to command. As we shall see, nothing could be further from the truth, since it was Bligh's personal intervention that prevented twenty-one of his men from being punished for mutiny. Lord Keith might just as easily have gone in a different order round the ships, though the fact that Pasley was with him suggests that if any influence was exerted to reach the *Director* last and embarrass Bligh, it was exerted by Pasley's prejudices against him.

With the end of the mutiny the retributions began. In theory the entire crew of every ship that had mutinied was guilty unless they could establish their active role against the mutineers. But to have punished the guilty would have depleted the ships of men at a time when the prime urgency was to get them back into the war. To lose thousands of men in this way – apart from the difficulty of dealing with them all judicially – would have struck as great a blow against the war effort as if they had been lost at sea.

Lord Keith had been sent down as nominal second-in-command to Admiral Buckner. He nevertheless directed the entire operation as if he was

[32] By Ellis, 1955.

in command of the station. He decided to deal with a representative number of men from each ship rather than with everybody who had participated. He chose ten as the representative number of guilty in a rough and ready way; rough because the tenth guilty man on some ships was not as guilty as the thirtieth or fortieth on some other ships. Admiral Buckner, resuming his command, decided to re-assert his authority in a different way. Naturally, he felt personally disgraced by the mutiny in his command and he took a less tolerant view of the presence of mutineers in his ships than the man who had gained the laurels from ending the mutiny. Magnanimity and failure are not happy companions. He demanded that the officers on the ships hand over all the guilty men, no matter how many.

Buckner's orders demanded 'a minute state of the crews of the ships and vessels under their respective commands, as far as possible the different degree of guilt that may be imputed to particular men, and stating the good conduct of such men as have in any particular manner evinced the same'.[33]

Bligh was not on his ship when Buckner's order arrived. McTaggart, his first lieutenant, dealt with both orders. He sent ten men ashore under guard as Lord Keith requested and a further nineteen men were named who fell under Buckner's orders. By the time Bligh got back on board his ship there were twenty-nine men from the *Director* under suspicion of mutiny plus another two who had been arrested while they were ashore.[34]

The mix-up in orders was not sorted out quickly. When Bligh resumed command on 16 June 1797 he acknowledged the orders from Lord Keith and Admiral Buckner. But he did not act on the latter's orders to send a detailed account of the guilt of each man. This produced some correspondence between Bligh and the Admirals. Bligh wrote to Admiral Buckner: 'I beg leave to state to you that Lord Keith having been on board and particularized with the opinion of the officers ten men who were sent on shore and are now in prison, I conceive the intent of your order is fully answered, except that part respecting good men, whom I shall with much zeal particularise as soon as I can with consistency discover them and consider myself free of error in my representation.'[35] Lord Keith took up Buckner's request to Bligh for confirmation of the nineteen names given by McTaggart. Bligh no doubt had words with McTaggart for getting him into this mess in the first place. On 22 June, Lord Keith wrote enquiring of the 'situation of the 29 men represented to have been the most violent and the proceedings of each person respectively to be particularly stated, that a certain number of the worst of them may be brought to trial by a court martial.'[36] Keith's intention to satisfy both his own and Buckner's orders can be seen here. He accepted the twenty-nine names (meeting Buckner's request) and wanted particulars of each from Bligh so that he could make a

[33] PRO Admiralty 1/728.

[34] The two delegates ashore, Hulme and MacLaurin, were captured by Aaron Graham, who was travelling about the area looking for evidence of sedition and republicanism among the seamen.

[35] PRO Admiralty 1/728, F485.

[36] Mackaness, 1951, p. 312.

selection of the worst among them for trial. Bligh, however, had no intentions of placing in jeopardy any more than the ten names asked for in Keith's orders.

He wrote back to Lord Keith: 'I considered from the moment you went on board in my absence, and pointed out from the opinion of the officers ten men who had been most active in the Mutiny, that the remaining persons were to expect a pardon and when I was afterwards sent to take command again of the *Director*, Adml Buckner told me of what your Lordship had done and that a pardon would be sent, but it could not be said positively what day – In consequence, I conceived any report from me would be like a desire to counteract your Lordship's humanity in considering ten great offenders to be a sufficient example when brought to punishment – The pardon is expected by the remaining men on board, and I conceive it is not meant for me to make out a list of any of them, as the order particularly alludes to the persons represented by the Lieutenants.'[37]

Bligh had told the remainder of the crew when he returned to the *Director* that they would receive the King's pardon. If he carried out the orders of Buckner, and the follow-up enquiry of Lord Keith, he would be in breach of faith with his men. This is hardly the image of the 'Bounty Bastard' eager to damn mutineers to their deserts. He was in fact arguing on very thin legal grounds to avoid compromising his word to his crew. It was a commendable stance for him to take, especially in view of the special circumstances of his own career and what being sent off the *Director* meant to him. The pardons that were issued in July omitted the names of thirty-one men from the *Director*, who by this were in legal jeopardy of court martial for mutiny. Bligh protested to Vice-Admiral Skeffington Lutwidge who in turn wrote to the Admiralty for instructions. Lutwidge told the Admiralty that because of the different instructions Bligh had received he 'had led the remainder of the ship's company fully to depend that there would be a pardon for all the rest, and that he was apprehensive the confinement of a further number (meaning those also excepted in the pardon) would cause a very serious dissatisfaction in the crew'.[38]

The Admiralty also received a letter from Bligh, accompanied by copies of the orders that he had received and his replies that set out the complicated circumstances of the case. It was like a legal brief: Bligh had learned something from his public controversy with Christian. He showed that the difficulty had arisen from the conflicting orders from Keith and Buckner and that he had been told by Buckner before taking command of the *Director* again that his instructions had been carried out by the sending ashore of the ten most guilty men. He added at the end: 'I, nevertheless, do not mean to plead in favor of them [i.e., those arrested ashore] as they are certainly a very dangerous set of men.'[39]

The Admiralty accepted Bligh's arguments and he was ordered to muster

[37] *ibid.*, p. 313.
[38] PRO Admiralty, 1/728, F486.
[39] Mackaness, 1951, p. 314.

his men and 'obtain from them individually a solemn promise to persevere in future in a regular and orderly discharge of their duty and obedience to their officers, and that they will not engage in future in any mutinous assemblies, nor take an oath of any kind whatever excepting such as may be administered to them by persons legally authorised so to do'. This compromise satisfied everybody and the nineteen men joined their comrades in celebrating their pardons. In the courts martial that followed none of the twelve prisoners from the *Director* was among the thirty-six mutineers hanged.[40] Richard Parker was hanged, of course, but Hollister, who turned up a witness for the prosecution, was not. Many of them were imprisoned, several dozen were deported to New South Wales (where Bligh was to meet some of them again when he became Governor), others were flogged and yet more were kept in hulks until after the victory of Admiral Duncan at Camperdown, which induced a free pardon from a happy Government.

The Nore ships returned to their postings and several of them, including the *Director*, joined Admiral Duncan off the Texel and fought the long-awaited sea battle with the Dutch. If the Dutch had come out during the Nore mutiny they could have defeated the British navy by sheer weight of numbers, let alone naval skill. That they chose to come out after the mutiny to fight ships many of whose crews were anxious to prove their loyalty, was, by one of those quirks of history, an unfortunate decision for the Dutch. What happened at Camperdown, and Bligh's role in the battle, are the subjects of the next chapter.

---

[40] Dugan, 1966, p. 396; there were thirty-eight ships involved in the Nore mutiny (including some ships that remained at Yarmouth). At ten men per ship the total in legal jeopardy should have been 380. In fact 560 men were arrested which shows that not all Captains were as assiduous as Bligh in defending their men from Buckner's orders. The number of men held for trial was 412; of these at least fifty-nine were sentenced to death and about thirty-six executed. Only about 200 actually went through a trial and sentence.

24

The Battle of Camperdown

The ending of the mutiny did not resolve the problems of Admiral Duncan and his fleet off the Texel. Blockade duty was still unpleasant, frustrating and unrewarding. By 1797 Duncan had been engaged in this activity for two years with a motley collection of old ships, including, for part of the time, eighteen ships from the Russian navy. The North Sea fleet was never able to develop into a strike-force like other British fleets, such as the Mediterranean fleet under Jervis (later Lord St Vincent). It hardly ever practised in fleet manoeuvres and was fortunate when it had more than a token force together. From Bligh's letters we can see how frequently his ship was back in home port, and with all the traffic to and from the Texel, plus numerous search and detain missions over a wide area of the North Sea; it is obvious why Duncan was unable to mould his fleet, such as it was, into a well-trained fighting machine of the kind that Nelson eventually put together. Individual discipline on his ships was taut; gunnery practice was at the inclination of the individual captains (we know that Bligh was attentive to this detail) but all-fleet manoeuvres were few. The Russian ships, though some of them officered by Scotsmen, were as good as useless to Duncan. They did not recognise his command, were indifferent in accepting his signals – largely because they did not understand them – and were often away without notice. When the battle finally took place the Russians were on one of their unilateral absences, though this did not prevent them putting in a claim years later for a share of the prize money.[1] It was by signals at sea that a fleet commander kept order among his ships and directed them in the crucial stages of the beginning of a battle. Individual captains had to know what the signals meant and to log them, with the response given. As we will see, Bligh's Log throughout the battle is by far the most detailed.

Jervis's victory at St. Vincent in February 1797 was in the traditional pre-Nelsonian style; it also had the usual measure of success: four enemy ships captured.[2] Duncan was a less spectacular man than Jervis. He was sixty-five years old at Camperdown and was a son of the Provost of Dundee.[3] His naval record was sound but his health was poor. Though he reached Post Captain at thirty he took another twenty-six years to reach flag rank and another ten

[1] Lloyd, 1963, p. 121; in common with many others I have benefited immensely from reading Professor Lloyd's accounts. Much of the information in this chapter comes from his book.
[2] *See* Lloyd, 1963, Chapter 4; also Oman, 1947, Chapter VII; for an account of Lord St Vincent, *see* Berckman, 1962.
[3] Lloyd, 1963, p. 118; a Provost in Scotland is the same as a Lord Mayor in England.

years before he got a fleet command. In 1795 he was offered the Mediterranean command but declined in favour of Jervis; instead, he took command of the North Sea. In 1797, after two gruelling years in blockade duty, plus the Nore mutiny, he was still awaiting his chance for battle honours. He had been given the oldest ships, the most disaffected of crews and enjoyed almost complete lack of support from the Admiralty, though reinforcements were often promised.

Duncan had just brought his ship back to Yarmouth after nineteen weeks at sea when news arrived in the lugger *Speculator* that the Dutch fleet had left the Texel and were at sea. Immediate orders were given to prepare the entire North Sea fleet for sea and within hours Duncan led his ships out from Yarmouth. The *Russell*, the *Ardent* and the *Circe* were on station off the Dutch coast but naturally did not offer battle to the Dutch under De Winter, the Dutch Admiral. De Winter had with him sixteen ships of the line, five frigates and five brigs. Captain Trollope, the British commander of the small token force, kept out of range of the enemy but within sight, with the intention of following them and being in a position to send messages in his small cutters to Duncan who, he knew, would be racing across the North Sea at the first news of the Dutch movements.

The reason for the Dutch move to sea is not easy to follow. There did not appear to be any proper purpose attached to their voyage. Their original purpose was to support an invasion fleet under the inspiration of Wolf Tone, the Irish revolutionary, but these plans had been dropped by October 1797.[4] Without apparent purpose the business was foolhardy, unless the Dutch could beat Duncan. If they had sailed in May they would have had the freedom of the seas because most of the fleet mutinied. But by October the men were in a different mood; now they had to prove their loyalties to wipe out the mutiny on their records. Even with poor ships, the British crews and their officers were geared to extra effort. On the Dutch side the situation was not conducive to victory. Although the British were worn down with boring blockade work, at least they had been able to get sea-practice, while the Dutch had been confined to port. All the same, they had a distinguished naval record and might prove hard to defeat.

There was also another factor in the person of Admiral Duncan. Duncan was a sound, solid commander. He had not shown on his past performance – mainly, in retrospect, from lack of opportunity – that imaginative spark of leadership that distinguishes one competent commander from another. At Camperdown he rose to the occasion.

The Dutch commander took his fleet down the Dutch coast for about forty miles and then changed his mind: he decided to return to port. De Winter knew that Duncan's fleet would intercept him before he got back to safety, unless bad weather or the mercies of incompetence intervened, and he chose a battle plan designed to give him the advantage of the lee shore.[5] The Dutch ships were of shallower draft than the British, which meant that if Duncan

[4] For an account of these plans for military adventures *see* James Dugan, 1966, pp. 72-5.
[5] A lee shore is one towards which the wind is blowing.

attacked the Dutch in the shallow waters there was the chance that the British ships would overrun into shoals or fail to press hard in case they were shipwrecked. Similar attempts to use shallow waters as protection from British ships failed at/the Nile in 1798 and at Copenhagen in 1801.

According to the charts the Dutch were sailing in nine fathoms (54 feet) of water, about five miles off shore. Duncan's original plan was to form a line of attack, place each of his ships alongside a rival and let the exchange of broadsides decide the issue. The Dutch expected the British to use this tactic and formed themselves accordingly.

Duncan's first plan had to be abandoned because of the nature of the contest. The Dutch were sailing for their home port and continued to do so when the two fleets came in sight of each other. De Winter was not refusing battle; he was offering it 'on the run', which forced the British to attack on the move rather than go through the difficult and time-consuming task of bringing all the ships into a line with the sailing pace decided by the speed of the slowest ships. By the time the British had formed into battle order and brought their guns to' bear, the Dutch would be miles up the coast. The threat of grounding on the shallows might inhibit reckless moves. From the Dutch point of view this was the best tactic to pursue.

The British force was divided into two, one part headed by Duncan in the *Venerable* and the other by Admiral Onslow in the *Monarch*. They approached the Dutch line in two somewhat disorganised groups. The signals that were made do not seem to have had much effect. Some part of this lapse is explained by ships either not seeing the signals owing to distance or not understanding them; another part of the explanation lies in the inapplicability of the signals in the situation. However, Duncan's signal for close action was understood and acted upon. Like two packs of wolves the British ships fell on the Dutch line, seizing the initiative and bringing the greatest pressure to bear on a small number of points. A line defence is not the best response to this tactic. Duncan had discovered something about naval engagements that Nelson had been developing, and which he was to put to brilliant use up to Trafalgar. Once engagement commenced, the smoke and confusion made it almost impossible to direct all but the most immediate ships and they could be disabled in the fighting. De Winter's plan held him to a fixed course of action. If his ships could weather the British attack they could continue their progress along the coast; if his ships were broken up by the two attacking packs they would be at the mercy of events. This latter is what happened. The Dutch had no response to Duncan's attack, other than standing and fighting, and once they were forced into that option the advantages of fighting on the run evaporated. Duncan's brilliant improvisation gave him victory. The almost unanimous response of his captains to his dash for the enemy turned the battle into one of the most successful for British ships up to Trafalgar. In terms of enemy ships destroyed and captured it was magnificent by contemporary standards (Nelson began to set new standards of victory at the Nile in 1798).

The Log of the *Director*, written by William Bligh, is generally agreed to be the best and most consistent account of the battle and one which enables us to piece together the separate and often confusing accounts of other single ships. This was occasioned by two factors, one being Bligh's normal meticulous standards of reporting and the other the nature of the *Director*'s contribution to the fighting. The *Director* engaged enemy ships in the southernmost pack; when victory was assured, Bligh took his ship along the Dutch line to the northernmost group and joined in the fighting there. In the process, not unexpectedly, he both saw a lot of action and was also in a position to claim some credit for the afternoon's victory, even if in the case of the surrender of the Dutch Flagship, *Vrijheid* (*Liberty*), he appears to have claimed rather more than his share of credit. It is worth quoting the relevant parts of his Log to illustrate his version of the course of the battle. The account begins:

> At 7.45 ... *Russell* showed her double pennants and made the signal for an enemy being in sight, consisting of 16 line-of-battle ships, 4 frigates and 2 brigs. At 8.30, bore up. At 9, the *Russell* made the signal for 16 sail of the line. At 9.10, signal for sternmost ships to make more sail. At 9.15, signal to prepare for battle. Saw a fleet to southward. Cleared ship for action. At 11. 18, *Director*'s signal to lead no 95 Vice. At 11. 25, Signal for ships to enagage their opponents. At 11. 30 bore up for the enemy per signal. At 11. 36, signal for the lee division to engage the centre of the enemy. At 11. 38, signal for the lee division to engage the rear of the enemy. At 11. 47, signal – the Admiral means to pass through the enemy's line.[6]

The signals were coming thick and fast and Bligh records them as he saw them. Other captains were having difficulty getting into position and were not aware of the developing situation in which Duncan abandoned his plan of attack. Confusion on the ships was considerable. In the *Belliqueux*, Captain Inglis is reported to have reacted to the confusion about the signals and the plan with characteristic language. He threw the signal book onto the deck and shouted: 'Damn ... Up wi' the hel-lem and gang into the middle o' it.'[7] This was the fighting spirit that Duncan was relying on when he saw the opportunity presented him by the Dutch position. In another of his ships, The *Agincourt*, Captain John Williamson was displaying an altogether different reaction to the confusion and the opportunity. This is the same John Williamson who was in command of one of the boat parties on the morning of Captain Cook's death and who 'misread' Cook's signal for help as an order to pull further off the beach; at Camperdown he floundered about in his ship without attempting to engage the enemy.

Bligh's Log continues:

> At noon, Camperdown ESE 4 or 5 leagues. Our fleet standing down in two divisions for Action. The *Monarch*, *Russell*, *Director* and *Montagu* the headmost ships. The *Monarch* on our larboard beam, standing towards the

---

[6] Bligh, *Log of the Director*, 1 January-31 December 1797, PRO Adm. 1/195; the Log is reproduced in Jackson (ed.), 1899, Vol 1, pp. 282-8.
[7] Quoted in Lloyd, 1963, p. 141.

Dutch Vice-Admiral. Admiral Duncan nobly leading his Division towards the Dutch Commander-in-Chief. The enemy's line formed on a wind on the larboard tack about NE b E. At 12. 40, the *Monarch* (Vice-Admiral Onslow) began to engage the Dutch Vice-Admiral in a most spirited manner. At 12. 45, we began with the second ship in the rear, the *Russell* having just began before us with the sternmost ship, the rest of our Division came on and on all sides there was a general firing. The Dutch gave way, and the ships became mixed, so that it required sometimes great caution to prevent firing into one another.

The break-up of the Dutch line was of great advantage to the rear division. This brought two or three British ships to bear on a single Dutch ship; odds that in the circumstances were overwhelming. By 1 o'clock the Dutch rear were in grave difficulties. The *Russell* and the *Montagu* were either side of the *Delft*, the *Director* and the *Monmouth* were either side of the *Alkmaar*, the *Powerful* and the *Adamant* attacked the *Haarlem* (which the *Director* also moved up and attacked from the starboard side) and the *Monarch* and the *Veteran* attacked the *Jupiter*. At this time only *Beaulieu*, the frigate, and *Agincourt* had not got alongside any Dutch ships.

The Dutch began to strike, and particularly one to us, but we engaged different ships, indeed, believe most all of the enemy's rear received shot from different ships of ours. The *Director* was now advancing towards Vice-Admiral Onslow's ship, when we found the ship she was engaging had struck,[8] and the rear of the enemy done up. It appeared to me now that some force was wanted in the van, as we saw five ships unengaged and apparently not hurt, and also the Dutch Commander-in-Chief without any ships of ours engaged with him. There was no time to be lost, as night was approaching and as th... were enough ships in our lee division about the rear of the enemy to take possession of them, I made sail (and passed the *Monarch*) engaging some of the centre ships, for I considered now the capture of the Dutch Commander-in-Chief's ship as likely to produce the capture of those ahead of him, and I desired my first lieutenant to inform the officers and men I was determined to be alongside the Dutch Admiral.

Bligh was mistaken if he believed that the *Vrijheid* had not been attacked. It may be that at the time that he approached nobody was firing into her but from 1 o'clock several ships were engaging her, including the *Venerable* and the *Ardent*. For some hour or more the *Venerable* was surrounded by enemy ships which were also engaged with other British ships. The *Ardent* received appalling casualties in its engagement with the *Vrijheid*. Its captain was killed in the first exchange of broadsides, the master minutes later, and two Lieutenants received serious wounds. As Bligh sped the *Director* towards the *Vrijheid*, the *Ardent* was forced off with forty men dead and nearly a hundred

---

[8] A ship was said to have struck when it lowered its colours; at this its opponent was to cease firing and send a boarding party over to arrest the ship's officers and take over command. In the confusion, smoke and destruction of a battle, colours could be shot away and this might lead a commander to think the enemy had surrendered.

wounded.[9] As a 64-gun ship it was outgunned by the Dutch flagship and its crew's courage in going alongside and staying for so long undoubtedly weakened the *Vrijheid*.

It is to Bligh's credit that he saw the opportunity to move up to the forward fighting in the Dutch line and that he took his ship up there. He could just as well have remained in the rear division and taken a prize. Williamson in the *Agincourt* did neither. He too could have gone to the assistance of Duncan's division and he would have been a great help there, especially to the *Ardent* and perhaps also to the *Venerable*.

Bligh approached the *Vrijheid*.

> At 3.5, we began the action with him, lying on his larboard quarter within 20 yards, by degrees we advanced alongside, firing tremendously at him, and then across his bows almost touching, when we carried away his foremast, topmast, topgallant mast and soon after his main mast, topmast and topgallant mast, together with his mizen mast, and left him nothing standing. The wreck lying all over his starboard side, most of his guns were of no use, I therefore hauled up along his starboard side and there we finished him for at 3.55 he struck and the action ended.

De Winter on the *Vrijheid* was to deny later that he struck his flag at all and claimed that his colours were hoisted and re-hoisted as they were shot down until he ran out of flags and lines. That Bligh did not destroy the *Vrijheid* single-handed is fairly obvious from his description of his engagement. As he was only twenty yards distant at the opening of the engagement and almost touching by the time he had slid his ship alongside it is unlikely that his own casualties and damage would have been so light compared to the devastation on the enemy's masts and rigging. By the time he was emptying broadsides into the stricken *Vrijheid* the latter's guns were almost ineffective under the

[9] The nature of close action naval combat is described graphically in Dugan, 1966, pp. 409-10: 'In this high century of naval sail, an uncompromising sea battle was a horror unsurpassed by modern machine warfare. The compulsion of commanders was to bring the big wooden vessels physically together, forming a compact butcher's shop. The grappling of two matched warships was like a collision of over-crowded poor-houses, whose lousy, half-starved and choking inmates fired cannon point-blank through the windows at each other. Men literally shot each other to pieces, and saw the pieces. The carnage did not occur miles away, but where you stood: a messmate suddenly fell headless or a powder boy spun in uncomprehending annoyance on one leg while an iron ball splattered his other leg along the deck.' In a boy's journal of 1811 the following horrific account has survived: 'The whole scene grew indescribably confused and horrible. I was busily supplying my gun with powder, when I saw blood suddenly fly from the arm of a man stationed at our gun. I saw nothing strike him; the effect alone was visible ... the third lieutenant tied his handkerchief round the wounded arm, and sent the groaning wretch below to the surgeon. The cries of the wounded rang through all parts of the ship ... those more fortunate men who were killed outright were immediately thrown overboard ... Two of the boys stationed on the quarter-deck were killed. A man, who saw one of them killed, afterwards told me that his powder caught fire and burnt the flesh almost off his face. In this pitiable situation, the agonised boy lifted up both hands, as if imploring relief, when a passing shot instantly cut him in two ... A man named Aldrich had one of his hands cut off by a shot, and almost at the same moment he received another shot, which tore open his bowels in a terrible manner. As he fell, two or three men caught him in their arms and, as he could not live, threw him overboard ... Our men kept cheering with all their might. I cheered with them, though I confess I scarcely knew for what.' Quoted in Masefield, 1971, p. 82.

pounding they had received from the *Ardent* and the *Venerable*. Certainly the carnage in the *Vrijheid* was appalling. It had fifty-eight dead and ninety-eight wounded. But in the confusion of battle, and the euphoria of survival, Bligh's Log records the events as he saw them and as he believed them to be.

When the *Vrijheid* 'struck' Bligh took the *Director* over to the *Venerable* which was about half a mile away at this time. 'I therefore bore up to speak to him, when he hailed me to take possession of the *Vrijheid*, the ship we had just beaten, and I sent my first Lieutenant on board in consequence.' The Dutch Admiral was sent on board the *Venerable* (as protocol demanded) and Bligh received the second-in-command. The captain was mortally wounded and could not be moved, hence the next-in-command had to be sent. 'As soon as the action ceased, my officers came to congratulate me, and to say there was not a man killed who they knew of, and of such good fortune I had no idea, for it passed belief. We had only seven men wounded. Before we got up with the Dutch Admiral we had a share with the *Veteran* in making a Dutch ship strike, and we passed close to leeward of a Dutch ship of the line on fire.'

Duncan had achieved a significant victory. He had managed to capture or destroy eleven enemy ships in a single action. This was something of a record at the time. With victory followed the honours. Duncan was made a baronet (Viscount Duncan of Camperdown and Baron Duncan of Lundie), his second-in-command, Admiral Onslow, also became a baronet, and Captain's Trollope and Fairfax were knighted. Gold medals were issued to all the captains. The casualties were heavy: 228 dead and 812 wounded. The Dutch lost 540 dead and 620 wounded. But as with the conclusion of every battle where prizes were taken, after the honours and the celebrations the Admirals and Captains got down to the usual undignified business of squabbling over the prize-money.[10] Bligh, through his agents, fought long and hard for what he considered his fair share for capturing the *Vrijheid*. While persistent he was also unsuccessful and like many other officers of the day had to accept the share he was allotted with as much grace as he could muster.

Bligh was ordered to take back to Yarmouth the Dutch ship *Gelijkheid* (*Egalité*) and when he arrived on 18 October he sent the following letter to Evan Nepean:[11]

Director, Yarmouth Roads,
18th October 1797

Sir,
My Commander in Chief not being here, I have the honour to inform you for the information of my Lords Commissioners of the Admiralty that I anchored here last night with His Majesty's ship *Director* and *Egalité*, sixty-four, a prize to the Fleet.

I took charge of her by order of Admiral Duncan from whom, owing to

[10] The sum at stake was reputed to have been £150,000; Lloyd, 1963, p. 159.
[11] 1/1516, Captain 'B', PRO Admiralty. The reference to a Dutch ship *Liberty* is a translation by Bligh of *Vrijheid*.

the badness of the weather, and having the ship in tow, we unavoidably parted company.

Two ships are observed at the back of the Sand and I have reason to hope that one of them is the *Liberty*, Admiral De Winter's ship, as Admiral Duncan, from my having been alongside of her allowed me to take possession and I sent my first Lieutenant, Mr MacTaggart, to command her.

The *Director* had only seven men at all touched with the shot or splinter, three of whom only are now in the doctor's list.

Wm Bligh

It will be of no surprise to readers that criticism of Bligh's part in the battle was expressed, albeit anonymously and almost forty years afterwards. The bitterness of the controversy that surrounded Bligh may have accounted for this though it is not easy in the circumstances to understand why the criticisms or, more correctly, imputations waited so long to be voiced. From their context it appears that they were based on some account of the battle either written at the time or later by somebody on board the *Director*. But as the account is anonymous and the source not stated it is difficult to accept them as evidence. Certainly naval historians have not come to anything like the same conclusions as the unknown critic.

Captain E.P. Brenton published a two-volume history of the Royal Navy in 1837. Among other things, when describing the battle of Camperdown, he does not include the *Director* among the ships 'which bore the brunt of the action'.[12] Brenton was referring to the number of casualties suffered by the *Director* compared to some other ships, such as the *Ardent*. But neither did the *Russell* have any casualties to speak of, nor the *Adamant* (naturally the *Agincourt* had none either but this ship was not fighting). The *Montagu* had one more casualty than the *Director* and there were twenty-one wounded on the *Lancaster*. Some of the ships suffered severely and the abysmally low standards of surgery contributed to the death roll. A fractured leg or badly splintered body could result in a painful death.[13]

A reviewer of Brenton's book used the opportunity to attack Bligh.[14] Brenton had remarked that the conduct of one or two of the captains had 'elicited the severest censure' from Admiral Duncan. One of these men was Williamson and he was court-martialled for his conduct. Who the other was it is impossible to say. It might have been the *Montagu*, Captain Knight, but this is circumstantial. The *Montagu* was the rearmost ship and attacked the *Delft* from astern. It then passed on into open water, crossing the *Agincourt*'s bow, and sailed for Duncan's squadron, but did not arrive in time to engage

---

[12] Brenton, 1837, Vol. 1, p. 355.

[13] The Surgeon on the *Ardent*, Robert Young, recorded his ordeal that day and night: 'I was employed in operating and dressing till near 4.0 in the morning, the action beginning about 1.0 in the afternoon. So great was my fatigue that I began several amputations under a dread of sinking before I had secured the blood vessels. Ninety wounded were brought down during the action ... So that for a time they were laid on each other at the foot of the ladder where they were brought down ...' Quoted in Lloyd, 1963, p. 146.

[14] *United Service Journal*, 1837, Part ii, pp. 147-9; it was in this same journal (1831) that Bligh was attacked in Peter Heywood's death notice.

anybody. To appreciate the point that the reviewer makes we must quote his opinion of the course of the battle:

> We grieve to add that he might have said four or five, without fear of contradiction; and we repeat, that if all the officers had done their duty, every enemy's ship must have been taken or sunk. Indeed there never was a finer opportunity than the battle of Camperdown afforded for each commander in the British fleet to have distinguished himself had he been inclined so to do. The Dutch were lying-to directly to leeward, the breeze was fine and commanding, and every ship was able to steer for her opponent, independently of each other, and bring on an action as close as she chose. But from the backwardness of some who could not and would not understand the signals, nor the sight before them, five of the enemy's line – viz. the *Brutus*, *Leyden*, *Cerberus*, *Batavia* and *Mars* – were unoccupied.

This statement expresses a different tactical view of the battle from that of the commanders of the day, and most interpretations since. There was no time to line up ship for ship; and if the British had lined up in this manner the crippling losses would have been even greater. Those British ships that ended up in a ship-to-ship close-action exchange were extremely badly damaged and took heavy casualties, since the Dutch guns were as devastating at close quarters as the British. As it was, the success of the attack on the Dutch rear – most of the enemy striking their colours between 1pm and 2.30pm – released ships to join the attack by Duncan on the Dutch vanguard. Even so, Duncan's attack was a close thing, several of his ships taking enormous risks and casualties to match. At one stage the *Venerable*, the flagship, was within gunnery range of several Dutch ships and could have been captured or sunk if the Dutch had been able to direct their attention to her. That the fight was furious is seen from the battering that the *Vrijheid* took from several of the British ships, including the close-range raking from the *Director*, before it was made incapable of further action. The critic might have had something to complain about if the unoccupied Dutch ships had gone into their own vanguard to assist their Admiral; they most certainly would have turned the tables, but they merely fired as they passed on the lee-side of the Dutch vanguard and deserted the battle. As it was impossible for the British to attack every ship, in the circumstances this was an unavoidable risk.

After criticising the *Montagu*, the critic says:

> The *Agincourt*, instead of following the *Triumph* through the hostile line, in obedience to signal no 34, brought-to more than a mile to windward, where she afforded her captain an opportunity of 'looking on'. But the most modest of the shy ships was certainly the *Director*, of 64 guns, because in her Log book, in an article concocted under the express superintendence of her Commander, it is recorded that she got alongside of him [i.e. the *Vrijheid*] at five minutes past three, and after lying on his larboard-quarter and side with a heavy fire, working about him it appears like a cooper round a cask, 'at four he struck to us'.

The clear implication is that in the circumstances of the court martial on Williamson Bligh should have been court martialled. But this is a strange testimony to bring against Bligh. No mention is made of the action between the *Director* and the ships in the Dutch rear, which is also in the Log book and which we have discussed above. More, the critic quotes Bligh's Log incorrectly: Bligh claimed that the *Vrijheid* struck at 3.55 not 'at four'. This critic does, however, seem to have uncovered an important contradiction in the records between Duncan's two versions of the capture of the *Vrijheid*. Duncan's first note to the Admiralty is dated '12 October by Log 3 pm' and contains the words 'The Admiral's ship is dismasted and has struck, as have several others'. The critic makes the most of the apparent difference in times: 'Now in Duncan's letter, and in the Log of the flagship, it is stated that the *Venerable* commenced action at half-past twelve, and ceased firing at three, making two hours and a half that the *Vrijheid* and the *Venerable* were engaged when the former struck; and De Winter says, in his letter, that his masts were all shot away at two o'clock'. The critic is implying that Bligh falsified the time in his own account.

In Duncan's considered despatch, written after the battle, which the critic does not mention, we can find a refutation of this charge against Bligh. In his official despatch, Duncan gives the following details: 'The action commenced about Forty Minutes past Twelve o'clock. The *Venerable* soon got through the Enemy's Line, and I began a close Action, with my Division on their Van, which lasted near Two Hours and a Half, when I observed all the Masts of the Dutch Admiral's Ship to go by the Board; she was, however, defended for some Time in a most gallant Manner; but being overpressed by Numbers, her Colours were struck, and Admiral De Winter was soon brought on Board the *Venerable*.'[15] Duncan's squadron got to the Dutch line a little after the time that Onslow's attacked the rear; this would add some minutes on to the commencing time of 12.40 p.m. The *Venerable* had to pass through the Dutch line to begin its action against the *Vrijheid*, and it may be that actual close action between these two ships commenced at something like 12.45 p.m. According to Duncan's despatch his action lasted two and a half hours, which takes the time to 3.10 p.m. or 3.15, if time is allowed for the delays mentioned above. It was at this time that he 'observed' the masts on the *Vrijheid* to be shot away. This corresponds with the time scale that Bligh notes in his Log. Bligh says that he commenced his action against the *Vrijheid* at 3.5 p.m. and he reports that in his first pass from stern to bows at twenty yards he carried all the masts of the Dutch ship away. There is more support for Bligh in a close reading of Duncan's despatch. Duncan implies that the time of the dismasting was about 3.10-3.15, but he does not state that the *Vrijheid* surrendered at this time. He writes: 'She was, however, defended for some Time in a most gallant Manner; but being overpressed by Number, her Colours were struck.' This confirms Bligh's own timings, although De Winter claimed he never surrendered at all but said he was captured by Bligh's

---

[15] The entire despatch is quoted in Lloyd, 1963, pp. 169-71. Bligh's Log stated that the action commenced at 12.40 p.m.

boarding party under Lieutenant McTaggart. Bligh claimed it was 3.55 p.m. when the action ceased and when he went over to the *Venerable* to get his orders to board the flagship. Duncan has left the times a little vague in his despatch, to make it more consistent with his earlier note, written at 3 p.m. when he thought the action was over and was obviously in a state of euphoria. Bligh was meticulously detailed about things nautical; not only does his Log state that the *Vrijheid* struck at 3.55 p.m., but he repeated that time in the Memorandum about the battle which he wrote afterwards, which is preserved in his papers accompanied by several drawings. He writes there that the action 'ended precisely at 55 minutes past 3 o'clock'. I think it is unlikely that he was wrong.

The last part of the critic's attack on Bligh continues to imply that he had kept out of the battle as much as possible.

But had we no such high evidence on the part of the Commander in Chief, we have the irrefragable testimony of eye-witnesses as to the conduct of the *Director*, who, though ordered by signal to lead, made no additional sail. This is corroborated by information obtained from her second and third lieutenants, S. Birch and W.W. Foote, who repeatedly urged their Captain to carry on and close with the enemy, more especially when the *Russell* – who had been called within hail of the Admiral, and was returning to her station – passed them with top-gallant studding sails set. On those officers directing their Commander's attention to this, he ordered them to be silent, desiring Mr Birch to go to his quarters on the lower deck and on no account to return. He then directed the first Lieutenant to see the tarpaulins spread over the gratings,[16] and be careful that no other officer should leave his quarters. At length she dropped into the scene of action, but the ships which the *Director* fired into had all been engaged and disabled before she got near them. In the course of the night, Lieutenant Brodie, in the *Rose* cutter, was sent round the fleet to inquire the state of each ship, the number killed and wounded, and the condition for renewing action. On making known the purport of his orders to the officer of the watch on the *Director*'s quarter deck, that gentleman, knowing that the ship had not sustained the slightest damage,[17] immediately replied, 'Yes, quite as ready as when the battle commenced!' and reporting the message to his Captain, together with the answer he had given, Bounty B, boiled with rage. 'How dare you, sir,' roared he, 'give such an answer without my authority? Tell Lieutenant Brodie that the ship is not ready.' The Officer then remarked that Brodie wished to know the number of killed and wounded. 'Tell him,' answered the man of wrath, 'the surgeon has not yet made out his report,' he knowing well that there were only three men slightly hurt to report on.

---

[16] This was to prevent objects falling through to the gundecks, especially lighted objects.

[17] According to the *Log of the Director* the following damage was reported: 'Our defects are, our fore yard shot away, topsail yard badly wounded, bowsprit shot through, the fore topmast shot through the head, booms and boats shot through, stays, running rigging, and sails much cut – ten men after the report had been made to the Admiral were found to be wounded making in all seventeen.' Next day repairs were carried out: 'Employed refitting the rigging and getting the ship ready for service. Lowered the fore topgallant mast half way down and fished the fore topmast with it.'

There are several dubious points in this account. The 'irrefragible' witnesses are not named and although Lieutenants Birch and Foote are discribed as giving 'information', it is not clear to whom and in what circumstances they gave it. The *Russell*, a 74-gun heavyweight under Captain Trollope, later knighted for his action, attacked the rearmost Dutch ship and then moved along the line, firing into the ships it passed (which with its heavy broadsides was a great help to the British ships engaging their opponents), and joined Admiral Onslow off the Dutch flagship in the rear division. It remained close to Onslow in the *Monarch* and helped to capture the *Jupiter* and the *Wassenaer*. The fact that Trollope was ordered to use his large ship in this way is no discredit to Bligh in the older, slower and smaller *Director*. Bligh's log records the signals from *Russell* for the 'sternmost ships to make more sail' but this could not have referred to the *Director* as it was then line-abreast of the *Monarch*, the *Powerful*, the *Monmouth*, the *Russell* and the *Montagu*. The sternmost ships were the *Agincourt*, the *Adamant*, and the *Veteran*. All the signals were recorded in the Log. Knowing Bligh's temper, it is believable that if Lieutenant Birch told him what to do on his own quarter-deck when he should have been at his post below Bligh spoke sharply to him, and also to the First Lieutenant, whose responsibility it was to see that officers and men remained at their posts. This incident, and the fact that the article at no time mentions the name of the First Lieutenant, suggests that the 'irrefragible' eye-witness may have been McTaggart, the First Lieutenant. He displeased Bligh by sending a list of nineteen mutineers to the Admiralty at the end of the Nore mutiny; he may have borne a grudge, though against this view we have Bligh's repeated mentions in his reports that he sent McTaggart to take command of the *Vrijheid* – a strong recommendation for promotion.

There is an important error of detail in this part of the article. It mentions that after the battle Lieutenant Brodie in the *Rose* cutter 'was sent round the fleet' in 'the course of the night', and that he spoke to the officer of the watch. But Admiral Duncan in his letter to the Admiralty writes: 'Be pleased to acquaint the Lords Commissioners of the Admiralty, that, judging it of Consequence their Lordships should have as early Information as possible of the Defeat of the Dutch fleet under the command of Admiral De Winter, I despatched the *Rose* cutter at three p.m. on the 12th instant, with a short Letter to you, immediately after the Action was ended.'[18] The *Rose* could not possibly have gone to Yarmouth and back in a few hours, and could not therefore have been on the particular service to which the article alludes. I am not suggesting that such a service was not undertaken after the battle during that night: it would have been strange if it was not; but this critic's inattention to detail casts doubt on the rest of his argument.

While Bligh received the congratulations of Admiral Duncan and the coveted gold medal from the mint, Captain John Williamson of the *Agincourt* was tried and convicted after the battle. The court martial took place on

---

[18] Admiral Duncan, *Camperdown Despatch*, quoted in Lloyd, 1963. Rawson, 1930, p. 59, writes: 'At six o'clock H.M.s hired cutter *Rose* parted company and sped across the North Sea.' According to Oman, 1947, pp. 263-4, Brodie arrived in the *Rose* in the Thames at dawn on 13 October.

H.M.S. *Circe*, the attendant frigate to Duncan's squadron at Camperdown. There were two charges: disobedience to signals and not going into action; cowardice and disaffection.[19] The trial opened on 4 December 1797 and lasted until New Year's Day 1798. It was prolonged because of the complications of the evidence, which turned it into an inquiry into the battle itself. Such was the confusion about what had happened that dozens of witnesses were closely questioned for hours, with their Log books as evidence, as to who was where and who saw what. Bligh's appearance and evidence were brief.[20]

Bligh might have been expected to be a hostile witness against Williamson, judging by his views on those he thought responsible for Cook's death.[21] But Bligh's testimony was far from unhelpful to Williamson, though it was by no means central to the prosecution's case. The main charge from their side was that Captain Williamson had held his ship back during the conflict contrary to the order for close action from his Admiral. It followed that they had to prove this by the evidence of the other Captains; once this was proved as a deliberate act they could then make headway with the far more serious (and potentially fatal) charge of cowardice and disaffection. If that was proven Williamson was in danger of his life.

Bligh's evidence was as follows:

> *Q.* Did you make any observation on that day, on the *Agincourt*'s conduct, in making full sail during the action, so far as you were in a situation to observe her?
> *A.* No; I made no observations on the *Agincourt*, making sail. I don't recollect taking notice of the *Agincourt* but once and that merely momentary during the action, when the ships were engaged, and I fancied at that time the whole of the rear division was engaging. They seemed much crowded.
> *Q.* (By Captain Williamson). If the *Agincourt* had lain to a mile and a half to windward of the fleet for half-an-hour, under her topsails and her main topsail aback, after the Vice-Admiral had commenced the action, would you not have seen her?
> *A.* I did not see her in that situation.[22]

The Court's verdict was that:

> having heard the witnesses produced in support of the charges, and having heard what he had to allege in his defence, and having maturely

---

[19] 'That the said John Williamson did not upon that day, upon signal and order of fight and upon sight of several of the enemy's ships which it was his duty to engage, do his duty, and obey such signal, and also for that he did, on the said eleventh day of October last during the time of action, through cowardice, negligence or disaffection, keep back and did not come into the fight or engagement, and did not do his utmost to take or destroy such of the enemy's ships as it was his duty to engage, and to assist and relieve such of His Majesty's ships as it was his duty to assist and relieve', quoted in Lloyd, 1963, p. 161.
[20] For an account of the trial *see* Jackson, 1899, Vol. 1, pp. 309–42.
[21] *See* p. 9 n.12.
[22] *The Times*, 16 December, 1797, quoted in Mackaness, 1951, p. 319.

and deliberately weighed and considered the whole: the Court is of the opinion that the charges of cowardice and disaffection have not been proved, that the other parts of the charge have been proved in part. Therefore, in consideration of the case and the nature and degree of the offence, the Court doth adjudge the said Captain John Williamson to be placed at the bottom of the captain's list and rendered incapable of ever serving on board any of His Majesty's ships or vessels in the Royal Navy, and he is hereby sentenced accordingly.[23]

Williamson was lucky; if the engagement had not been so dramatically successful he might have suffered worse. Nelson considered the sentence deplorably light. He is reported to have said of it: '... if a man does not do his utmost in time of Action, I think but one punishment ought to be inflicted ... I would have every man believe, I shall only take my chance of being shot by the Enemy, but if I do not take that chance, I am certain of being shot by my friends.'[24]

Williamson's career was ended; Bligh's continued. For the next three years Bligh was to be engaged on hydrographic work for the Admiralty, producing charts and drawings. During these years he continued to write to Sir Joseph Banks, commenting on what he was doing and also on the conduct of operations. He was particularly critical of the plans to attack Tenerife by a landing operation (he advocated a blockade and bombardment instead) and the attempt to take Cadiz from the sea.[25]

There is one curious reference in a letter to Sir Joseph. From it we can see that Bligh was in the habit of closely consulting his sponsor on all matters affecting his career: 'I trust you are assured I would have taken nothing in hand, that I could possibly have avoided without first informing you of it. – In the present instance it was on His Majesty's Service, and I was in honor bound to secrecy.' There is no explanation of what this mission was. It is possible that it was for surveying purposes, but since he was bound to secrecy, the errand may have had something to do with secretly surveying on the south coast the defensive capabilities of the local harbours. Bligh undertook several similar missions for the Admiralty and during one such, in 1803, he was actually arrested as a 'French Spy'.[26]

In October 1798, Bligh told Banks he had heard from Admiral Duncan. The *Director* at the time was at the Nore, presumably on a refit, and Duncan wanted Bligh to rejoin the North Sea Fleet. Bligh quotes him a letter from Duncan: 'I have mentioned to the Admiralty that if your ship is paid off I hope they will immediately give you another as I have always observed her conducted like a Man of War.'[27] In the same letter Bligh told Banks that he was sitting in a court martial on 'a fellow' who had declared himself to be a

[23] Quoted in Lloyd, 1963, pp. 161-2.
[24] Quoted in Hattersley, 1974, p. 76.
[25] William Bligh to Sir Joseph Banks, *Director*, Texel, 12 September 1797, MS C218, p. 45. St Vincent had been trying to force Cadiz from the sea for months in 1797 without success; and the Tenerife affair was led by Nelson, who lost his arm there.
[26] Bligh to Banks, Lambeth, 27 September 1798, C218, p. 57. See also Polwhele, 1831.
[27] Bligh to Banks, *Director*, Nore, 9 October 1798, C218, p. 59.

'United Irishman' and that there were fifteen other seamen on the same charge, who had planned to take the *Diomede* into the Texel. This was part of a widespread Irish rebellion, both in Ireland and in some of the navy's ships. The suppression of the rebellion in Ireland was vigorous and brutal. Hundreds were killed. Lord Cornwallis, who had experienced rebellion in the American colonies, ordered the massacre of about four hundred Irishmen who had been captured in the only serious military engagement of the rising.[28]

The arrests and trials on the navy's ships went on through the autumn of 1798. Compared to the Great Mutiny trials of 1797, the verdicts were savage: four seamen on the *Caesar* were hanged, another twenty on the *Defiance*, eight on the *Glory*, four on the *St. George* and several more on the *Marlborough*. The trial of the men from *Diomede* resulted in one being hanged and another flogged round the fleet.[29] It was a savage few months even for the eighteenth-century navy.

One of the other matters Bligh was attending to at the end of 1798 was an attempt to help his former Lieutenant from the *Providence*, Francis Godolphin Bond. A letter to Banks shows something of how the interest and promotion system worked in the eighteenth century; it also shows how Bligh felt about the informal obligations that carreer-minded men entered into in the navy. He writes:

My Dear Sir when I went out in the *Providence* I took with me as my first Lieutenant, a relation Mr. Fras. Bond, who was made a Lieut. in 1782. He had seen a great deal of Service but as I had promised Mr. Portlock when he was a mate with me in the *Resolution*, to assist him when I had the opportunity, I did not forget my promise and applied for him to command the *Assistant*. I thought Mr. Bond would have had an equal promotion with him, because his services were equal as one of my Officers, besides his assistance to me in watching the covering and uncovering of the Plants, which was the most material thing & required hourly attendance Night & Day. I had a hope when I found Mr Portlock refused going to Botany Bay, that his service might have been accepted; but Portlock declined me there, & privitly prepared Captn. Hunter to get a Mr. Waterhouse out & he was appointed before I was aware of it, which was a very ungratifying act, for he was bound to Mr Bond as well as to me to have given him the chance of an application. Mr Bond has been in constant service. He was a very fine youth when he was blown up in the last war in a Prize belonging to the *Crescent*, Captain T. Pakenham. – He was cast away this war in the Active Frigate, Captain Leveson Gower upon the Isld of Anticosti, and he is now commanding the *Netty* Gun Vessel, in which under the command of Sir Richd Strachan on the Coast of France in last August he was badly wounded. – He continues a very active and Zealous officer and is much

---

[28] For an account of the rebellions of 1798 *see* Dugan, 1966, Chapter 23.

[29] The sentence to death of twenty in H.M.S. *Defiance* was something of a record from one ship. The two men dealt with at the Nore were George Tomms and John Wright, both marines. Tomms was sentenced to death and Wright got 500 lashes which, if it did not kill him, would have crippled him for life.

liked by every person who knows him. I have never had the resolution untill
this moment to mention him to you, & I am induced to say if you ever have
the opportunity to name him it will be gratefully remembered. I beg you
will pardon my asking this favor – I could not have said so much, but I hear
there is a great promotion preparing and I think Mr Bond a very deserving
and zealous officer & I see his old shipmates and the officers of other
voyages promoted.[30]

Bligh remained in the *Director* throughout 1799. The ship was mainly in the
North Sea with Admiral Duncan's fleet, though little happened in a military
sense. In June, Joseph Ramsey, Master of the *Director*, was court-martialled
for impertinence to Bligh and was found guilty. He was dismissed as Master.[31]
Later in the year Bligh took the *Director* on a cruise to St. Helena in the south
Atlantic. The main purpose in the long trip was to escort a convoy of East
Indiamen and collect some botanical specimens for Kew. Bligh took the
opportunity to draw a detailed chart of the cruise which was published in 1800
by Arrowsmith.

His periods of shore-leave were spent at his home in Durham Place. His
family was growing up and his steady employment in the navy on home water
duty brought him home regularly. Little is known about his home life at the
time. From his correspondence we know he visited Sir Joseph Banks regularly,
and we know that the Blighs entertained a little. He was a modestly successful
naval officer, comfortable if not affluent; he had been on active service during
the long wars against the French, at a time when the naval exploits of the
nation were capturing the imagination of the public, and were to reach new
heights as the full genius of Nelson began to flower. Nelson's career showed
that a little bit of notoriety was not as socially disadvantageous as it was to
become in the sterner Victorian era.

The voyage to St Helena was followed in 1800 by detailed surveys of Dublin.
His work at Dublin was much praised by the authorities. They said it 'would
be of infinite importance to their navigation, it being so correct and of such
authority'.[32] Bligh sought, and was given, permission by the Admiralty to have
his surveys published which always had the side-effect, apart from the

[30] Bligh to Banks, *Director*, Yarmouth, 6 December 1798, C218, p. 63; the letter suggests that
Bligh was not pleased with Portlock.
[31] PRO Admiralty 1/5349; Ramsey had a difference of opinion with Bligh about something
and is alleged to have said: 'If I am not able to work the ship, it is better to have some person else
here.' In another court martial that took place 'early in October' John Heugh was brought to
trial 'for endeavouring to excite mutiny and for disobeying the lawful commands of his officers
when at sea', PRO Admiralty 1/524, F227, quoted in Mackaness, 1951, p. 316.
[32] Bligh to Evan Nepean, 23 February 1801, PRO Admiralty 1/1525. This was the only
regular survey Bligh ever had the opportunity to make – a regular survey being one which the
surveyor has ample time to carry out, based on a triangulation either carried out by the surveyor
or done previously. Normally Bligh's were sketch surveys – done with limited time, rudimentary
triangulation and fewer soundings – or running surveys, rough surveys done from the ship as the
surveyor passes along an unknown coast. Bligh was an above average amateur surveyor of the
period. I am indebted to Andrew David for this assessment. His manuscript accounts of Bligh's
Heywood's and Hayward's surveys are lodged in the Library of the Hydrographic Department,
Taunton under the title *The Surveyors of the Bounty: A preliminary study of the hydrographic surveys of
William Bligh, Thomas Hayward and Peter Heywood and the charts published from them*, 1976.

prestige, of providing income. He also made a sketch survey of Holyhead harbour with a view to its suitability for use by Irish packet boats. He was in correspondence for payment of expenses in May 1801.[33] But in between this work and the correspondence, Bligh was assigned to a new command, H.M.S. *Glatton*, in which he was to fight the bloodiest battle of his carrer.

[33] Bligh's surveys of Dublin are at British Library Add. MS 35931, ff, 15, 18, 19. See also PRO Adm. 1/3523, Hurd to Poole, 14 September 1808. For Bligh's remarks on his survey of Holyhead Harbour, see MSS D.4, Taunton, David, 1976.

25

The Battle of Copenhagen

The Battle of Copenhagen, in which Bligh played a not insignificant role, was the bloodiest naval battle of Nelson's career and has been described as 'the great gamble'.[1] It came about through the political machinations of the mad Russian Tsar, Paul I, who persuaded three equally deranged kings and another who was of no consequence to declare the Baltic out of bounds to British commercial shipping. Britain was then at the height of her sea-power, and it was left to the amiable Danes to stand up against her in defence of the declaration. The Russian Court decided to end the blockade before it embroiled the country in a war with Britain, and Paul I was strangled in his bed; but this took weeks to become known to the rest of Europe. Meanwhile the British and Danish fleets met, and bled, outside Copenhagen harbour.

The determination with which Nelson set to the 'warm work' of war was not matched by the manner in which the fleet was despatched, commanded and instructed in its purpose. The British governments of the time dithered and manoeuvred through the various ministries formed during the crisis, with little understanding of its nature or of what should be done about it. Delay was dangerous; the ice-bound Baltic kept the fleets apart and gave time for the British to deal with the members of the Armed Neutrality agreement one at a time, but as the temperature rose the passage for ships would be cleared. The Admiralty ordered twenty ships of the line to form a fleet for action in the Baltic. This was a larger fleet than those that had fought at St Vincent, the Nile or Camperdown. They appointed Admiral Sir Hyde Parker to command the fleet; but Parker, then approaching his mid-sixties, had just married an eighteen-year-old bride, the daughter of Admiral Sir Richard Onslow, and was determined not to leave his wife until he had attended a ball in her honour fixed for Friday 13 March.

The Admiralty sent Nelson and his squadron, then lying at Spithead, to join Parker. Nelson was designated second-in-command of the Fleet. What he found when he got to Yarmouth was not at all to his liking. There was no sense of urgency about the fleet; everything seemed to be paralysed by the attentions of the Commander-in-Chief towards his new wife. Nelson wrote to his friend, Troubridge, on the Board of Admiralty, a frank letter of disgust: 'If a Lord of the Admiralty – and such a Lord – had not told me the Baltic fleet had order to put to sea, I would not have believed it, and forgive me, I

---

[1] Pope, 1972. Details of the battle have been taken from this book and from Oman, 1974, Bligh's Logs, and Jackson (ed.), 1899.

even think seriously that, by some accident, they have not arrived, for there is not the least appearance of going … I know, my dear Troubridge, how angry the Earl [St Vincent] would be if he knew I, as second-in-command, was to venture to give an opinion for I know his opinion of officers writing to the Admiralty. But what I say is in the mouth of the old market women at Yarmouth … Consider how nice it must be laying in bed with a young wife, compared to a damned cold raw wind.'[2]

St Vincent, a fighting commander, had recently replaced Spenser as First Lord of the Admiralty. One of his early acts had been to assure Admiral Lord Keith of the Mediterranean fleet that he would 'support Commanders-in-Chief upon all occasions, and prohibit any intrigue against them in this office'.[3] But he learned informally of what was going on, and wrote to Parker warning him of the 'irreparable injury' his career would suffer if he delayed sailing any longer.[4] Parker cancelled the ball and stood by for the next wind out of port. From his relations with Nelson for the next part of the voyage we might surmise that he heard of what Nelson had done; for some time he treated his second-in-command as if he did not exist. Up to the eve of the battle he did not disclose his orders to Nelson.[5] Nelson had arrived at Yarmouth on 4 March 1801; he had been in London for a few days about two weeks earlier at the same time as Parker, but they had not met. During the week at Yarmouth, and for some days after the expedition finally sailed, the Commander-in-Chief and the second-in-command did not have a single meeting to decide on the expedition or anything connected with it. They communicated by letter, with Parker ignoring or rejecting Nelson's written recommendations. Further, Nelson and St Vincent were not on close terms at that moment, as their legal wrangles over prize money were coming to the boil.

The composition of the Baltic fleet had been discussed as early as 12 February 1801. Of the nineteen ships chosen fourteen were ready for sea or at sea and two ships were 'doubtful'. Among those ready for sea was H.M.S. *Glatton*,[6] a 54-gun converted East Indiaman, armed with carronades.[7] The Admiralty was appointing the ship's commanders right up to the eve of the departure of the fleet. We know that Bligh was at home in London on 23 February and he may have been lobbying the Admiralty for another command. He had been working on surveying for the Admiralty for some years and wanted a change. On 13 March Bligh took over command of the

[2] Quoted in Hattersley, 1974, pp. 128-9.

[3] Earl St Vincent to Admiral Lord Keith, 21 February 1801, quoted in Tucker, 1844, Vol. 2, p. 175.

[4] Smith (ed.), 1922 and 1927, p. 86; letter dated 11 March 1801.

[5] *See* Oman, 1947, pp. 430-1.

[6] Nelson thought the *Glatton* unwieldy and difficult to sail; *see* Nelson to Evan Nepean, 23 May 1801, in Nicolas (ed.), 1844-6, Vol. 4, pp. 383-4.

[7] Carronades were designed to fire a larger round with a smaller charge by virtue of the close fit of the bore. The Admiralty adopted them after 1780, but they had passed the height of their popularity in 1800. For the smaller length and weight a much greater amount of shot could be fired, with a consequent increase in damage to an enemy; but the closer range necessary meant more possibility of damage to the ship firing, and another disadvantage was the fire-risk. *See* Padfield, 1973, Chapter 18.

Glatton by relieving Captain Stephen. This was a last-minute appointment. Bligh only had time to dash to Yarmouth by road and take command as the fleet was leaving port. If Parker had carried out his orders to sail on time, Bligh would not have taken part in the Battle of Copenhagen. He was told by Captain Stephen that the fleet 'were astonished to hear I was to command' the *Glatton*.[8] Bligh set about his task with his customary thoroughness. With no time wasted, the *Glatton* was at sea and with the main fleet.

Some of the other ships were not ready and had not yet joined the fleet, and Parker set out without them, leaving orders for them to catch up with the main body as soon as they could. If he had sent these orders to London, the ships at the Nore would have been able to sail straight across the North Sea instead of going first to Yarmouth. This lapse caused unnecessary loss of life: H.M.S. *Invincible*, which sailed for Yarmouth unaware that the fleet was then to the east of it, struck a sand-bar in the treacherous waters outside Yarmouth and sank, taking with it 400 seamen.[9] Parker's conservative management of the navigation and sailing orders led to a painfully slow progress of the fleet across the North Sea; they sometimes lost as much ground as they gained in a day's sailing.

On 19 March the Baltic fleet anchored off the Danish coast while diplomatic moves were made to get a peaceful settlement. Vansittart, a British diplomat, was sent to the capital to persuade the Danes to treat with the British. Nelson would have preferred the talks to be conducted within sight of the British fleet; in his opinion, 'A fleet of British men-of-war are the best negotiators in Europe'. He was not officially informed of the diplomatic moves and had to guess that a 'pen and ink' man had been sent by Parker to treat with the Danes.

Vansittart brought back the news that the Danes would not give up their membership of the Federation of Armed Neutrality and that they were constructing formidable defences at Copenhagen. This did little to encourage Parker's already flagging fighting spirit, and it forced Nelson to conduct a strenuous, almost insubordinate, campaign within the British command for militant action. Parker, a cautious man, had been hoping that the diplomatic part of his instructions would save him from the necessity of a battle. Nelson, in contrast, the audacious fighting man, wanted immediate action. He was under no illusion as to how to deal with countries that opposed Britain: overpower them with British naval might. He would have preferred to fight the Russians, on the grounds that they had instigated the Armed Neutrality Federation; he did not believe that barriers to British trade would last long once the Russians were dealt with. But he was not fussy about which part of the Baltic was tackled first.[10]

Copenhagen is situated on the east side of an island off the east coast of Denmark. The channel that runs between the mainland and the west side of the island was known as the Great Belt. To approach Copenhagen by this

---

[8] Bligh to Banks, 12 March 1801, *Glatton*, off Yarmouth, Mitchell Library MS C218.
[9] *See* Pope, 1972, pp. 238-9.
[10] *See* Nelson to Sir Hyde Parker, *St George*, at sea, quoted in Oman, 1947, pp. 435-7.

channel the fleet would sail south down the Great Belt, east between the island and the Prussian shore, then northwards along the east coast of the island towards Copenhagen. The alternative was to approach Copenhagen from the north. This would mean sailing through the narrow straits between Saelland and the Swedish coast. The first, longer route to Copenhagen would also put them in a good position for attacking the Russians, which meant that they could postpone the decision on which to attack; this attracted the indecisive Parker. Reports of the Danish and Swedish batteries commanding the narrow channel also dissuaded Parker from attempting it, and he decided to go through the Great Belt. But there was some confusion as to what the orders were; Captains Domett and Otway queried them, and in the course of doing so put it to Parker that the route through the narrow channel was the better one. The Admiral changed his mind. He signalled the fleet and brought it to rest, and new orders were issued to go through the narrow channel. Meanwhile, the pilots, who were against this approach on account of its dangerous shallows and shoals, tried to change Parker's mind yet again.

Exasperated by this dilatoriness, Nelson made a characteristic attempt to resolve the leadership crisis in the Baltic fleet. He sought permission to take a squadron through the narrow channel past Copenhagen and through the Baltic to meet the Russian fleet. His intention was primarily to force the pace of the campaign. A Nelsonian victory against the Russians, which was almost certain, would stop the Armed Neutrality compact at a stroke. Parker could sit it out at the entrance to the Baltic while Nelson got on with the war. The sooner the war was brought to a conclusion, the sooner Nelson could get back home to Emma Hamilton; his correspondence at the time shows how obsessed he was with Emma's faithfulness and love for him. Given a choice between attacking Copenhagen and waiting for new orders from London, Nelson chose the former. On 26 March, he finally won the approval of Parker for a single squadron attack on Copenhagen. Parker was assured of approval in London; he had not been ordered to attack himself, and as he could not permanently restrain his younger deputy from fighting or eventually complaining to London about the delays, it was better to let him get on with it. Nelson had powerful friends in the Admiralty and even critics of his personal life could not fault his fighting style.

The dithering and delays had affected the entire fleet by the time Nelson got his way. When he met the captains of the ships assigned to the squadron, they were far from enthusiastic. Some of them – it is not known which – expressed doubts about the ability of the squadron to silence the Danish guns. The delays in mounting the attack had given the Danes valuable time to strengthen their defences further even than when Vansittart had seen them some days before, particularly the menacing island forts specially built around the entrance to the harbour, such as the Trekroner (Three Crowns) Fort. Moreover, the inexperienced Danish recruits had used their borrowed time to get practice in operating the unfamiliar weapons, and the very delay in the mighty British fleet's attack gave them an unsought boost for morale. It is not surprising that Nelson had to spend a day discussing, persuading, and leading the group into a renewal of self-confidence. The positive result of this exercise was that every captain knew the plan of attack in minute detail by the end of the session, thus permitting improvisation if circumstances warranted it. This preparation also gave several captains, who had not worked with Nelson before, a personal loyalty to him which was to be a decisive factor in the conduct of the battle.[11]

Nelson remarked of the Danish defences: 'It only looks formidable to those who are children at War, but to my judgment, with ten sail-of-the-line I think I can annihilate them; at all events, I hope to be allowed to try.'[12] The entrance to the harbour was a narrow channel dominated by the great Trekroner Fort. To make things more difficult the Danes had removed the channel buoys; attacking Captains would require to have one eye on the battle and one on the leadline. True, they had pilots with them from the merchant service, but they had already shown that they were of little military use. Between the Danish line of defence and the main channel there was a shallow known as the Middle Ground. The channels either side of it were known as the King's Deep and the Holland Deep. Nelson's plan was to pass down the Holland Deep and then swing up into the King's Deep to get at the Danish defences from the south. They could not cross the Middle Ground with their·large ships. Another disadvantage was that the Danish ships were anchored close to shore and the waters were far too shallow to permit Nelson's ships to get behind them and use the tactics of the Nile.[13] Unlike the French at that battle, the Danes were in home waters, and they placed their ships with care. The British ships therefore had to pass along the Danish line firing broadsides from one side only. This was favourable for the Danes because it meant they could spread their experienced men along one side of their ships. If they had had to fight in open water British superiority in experience would have told quickly. Moreover, the island forts of Trekroner and Lynetten were unsinkable and provided their ships with good covering fire; this weighed the balance in favour of the defenders in any sea attack from the north into the King's Deep.

Having accepted the necessity of an attack from the south, Nelson had to take his ships through the Holland Deep under the Swedish and Danish guns. On several occasions when sounding the Holland Deep the pilots disagreed about where the channel lay. Eventually Nelson organised a night-time sounding of the channels and had them marked with temporary buoys. While the sounding parties were working through the night marking the channel in the Holland Deep, Parker and Nelson met on board H.M.S. *London*. The squadron of ten ships was barely sufficient even if all went well; Parker insisted that the *Ganges* and the *Edgar* join the squadron to strengthen

---

[11] Pope, 1972, pp. 278-9.

[12] Quoted in Oman, op cit, p. 437.

[13] At the Battle of the Nile, when Nelson destroyed and captured the French fleet which had taken Napoleon to Egypt, his ships had broken through the French line and sailed into the shallow water in a risky but brilliant stroke that surprised the French and eventually overwhelmed them because Nelson was able to attack the French ships from both beams.

it.[14] The next day, by keeping over to the Swedish side out of range of the Danes' gunfire, Nelson got through without injury. He then took the *Amazon* frigate to look at the Danish defences and got acquainted with its commander, Captain Riou. The two men took an instant liking to each other and Nelson worked closely with Riou during the preparations for the battle. If Riou had survived Copenhagen he would undoubtedly have been promoted to command in Nelson's squadron.[15]

Once the squadron was at the south end of the Middle Ground, they had to survey the King's Deep, again in the dark. The width of the King's Deep channel and the slope of the seabed were of great importance to the deployment of the British ships. For Nelson's plan to succeed, the channel had to be wide enough for ships to pass each other. The idea was that the leading British ship would drop anchor opposite the first Danish ship and engage it, and that the second British ship would leap-frog the first and anchor opposite the next Danish ship, and so on along the line of the Danish defences. Otherwise, the line of British ships would have to pass in order along the entire Danish line, exchanging broadsides, until each reached its opponent and the whole line was engaged.

The Danes had seen that a squadron had detached itself from the main British fleet and had passed along the Holland Deep. From the disposition of their defences, it seems they had been expecting the British attack to come from the north in a frontal assault on the entrance to Copenhagen harbour. The breakaway British squadron did not change their minds on this point. They could have drawn several conclusions from it. The squadron might have been on its way to attack the Russians, or it might have been a diversionary assault on the southern defences while the main attack came from the north. The idea that it was to be the sole attack on their defences never crossed their minds; after all, the defences were formidable even against the whole British fleet, let alone a mere twelve ships. The main danger from their point of view came from the possible deployment of British 'bombs' about 2,000 yards off the shore, protected by a British squadron of men of war, able to bombard the town with relative impunity.[16] The fixed anchorage positions of the Danish ships, floating batteries and dismasted hulks made them vulnerable to this long-range action. If the Danes had been more adventurous they could have made it more difficult for the British to carry out even that plan. They could have attacked the survey boats sent by the British into the King's Deep, they could have chased the *Amazon*, they could have cut loose the marker buoys, or even have sunk some hulks across the entrance. What Nelson was planning to do was a gamble; but it was

[14] Among the ships in the squadron was H.M.S. *Isis*, whose First Lieutenant was Robert Tinkler, formerly of the *Bounty*. He was 31 years old. John Fryer was also in the fleet.

[15] Riou and Bligh knew each other from Cook's voyage in the *Resolution* and they had recently met again at the court martials following the Nore mutiny where Riou was an officer of the court and Bligh a witness.

[16] A 'bomb' was a warship specially fitted to fire heavy mortars. The decks had to be strengthened to withstand the recoil and shocks.

made a little easier by the concentration of the Danish commanders on the northern approaches.

Nelson held a final conference with his captains on board H.M.S. *Elephant* during the night before the battle. Having explained his plans in detail and to each captain specifically, Nelson shook each captain's hand in turn, and they returned to their ships. Throughout the night and well into the next morning Nelson dictated instructions to his clerks and had them sent to each captain.[17] In the morning the wind turned, as if to order, and blew northwards – just what he needed to approach the Danish line.

William Bligh, in the *Glatton*, received his orders and prepared for the battle. Because of the nature of the waters Nelson had ordered every ship in his squadron to have its sheet and spare anchors over the side 'ready to let go at a moment's notice' because 'great precision is necessary in the placing the ships'. Bligh was at his best in placing a ship with precision exactly where it was wanted. Other Captains were not so fortunate and Nelson's plan almost collapsed from the start. The *Agamemnon* ran aground on the Holland Deep side of the Middle Ground and was completely out of the action for the duration. The *Agamemnon*'s target was to have been the 58-gun *Provesteenen*, which was now uncovered and able to fire at every British ship that passed it. The incapacity of the *Agamemnon* forced an immediate change in the attacking order. Nelson signalled the *Polyphemus* to attack the *Provesteenen* (its original target had been the last ship in the Danish line). The *Edgar* (74), Captain George Murray, was the first ship to open fire on the Danes, which it did as it passed them on the way to its target, the *Jylland* (54). The *Isis* (50), Captain James Walker, the *Russell* (74), Captain Cumming, the *Ardent* (64), Captain Thomas Bertie and the *Glatton* (54), Captain Bligh, followed next. Bligh fired carronades into the *Provesteenen*, doing much damage, and then re-loaded to fire into the *Wagrien*. He brought the *Glatton* up until he reached his target, the Danish flagship *Dannebroge*, then he let go the anchors and pulled up at about 200 yards' distance, and began to pour broadsides into the Dane with devastating effect. Bligh's Log is once again a useful source: 'At 9.45, prepare to weigh. At the same time *Edgar, Ardent* and *Glatton* to weigh, and the other ships in succession. After engaging from the south end of the enemy's line we anchored precisely in our station abreast of the Danish Commodore. At 10.26 the action began.'[18]

The other ships were settling abreast of their opponents. The *Isis* took on the *Wagrien* and the *Polyphemus* replaced the *Agamemnon*. Then the *Bellona*, in the smoke from the gunfire, which was billowing all round the channel, went too far to the right of the *Isis* and ran onto a spur running out from the Middle Ground. This left a gap ahead of the *Glatton*. The *Bellona* was grounded opposite the *Wagrien* and the *Rendsborg*. This accident was partly the fault of the pilots. They had insisted at Nelson's last meeting that the

[17] Nelson's orders to Bligh are among his papers at the Mitchell Library, along with a pen-and-ink drawing by Bligh of the disposition of the ships in the battle; Bligh Papers, Battles of Copenhagen and Camperdown, Safe 1/39.

[18] *Log of the Glatton*, Captains' Journals, PRO Admiralty 9750, reproduced in Jackson (ed.), 1899, Vol. II.

slope of the King's Deep went from left to right, with the deepest part against the Middle Ground. Captain Hardy's survey suggested that it was the other way round; in fact he was right, but because their advice was rejected, the pilots refused to take the ships into the channel. The Master of the *Bellona* volunteered to lead the fleet into the channel and he was removed into the Edgar to do this. His absence from the *Bellona* cannot have helped the sailing of the ship in the smoke-filled channel, and must have contributed to its grounding.[19]

The *Russell*, following behind the *Bellona*, went to the right of it and grounded on the same shallows. This took another ship out of the battle, making three in all. Instead of twelve fighting ships Nelson now had nine. He was in the *Elephant* following behind the *Russell*, but instead of repeating the *Russell*'s error he swung his ship to the left back into deeper water. Fortunately other ships followed him. By now the plan was completely hopeless in its original form, and Nelson had to improvise. He took the *Elephant* to the vacant space beyond the *Glatton*, anchored and opened up with broadsides. But his quarrels with the pilots were not over yet. He wanted to get his ship a little closer to the Danes, which suited his particular type of guns and also his style of warfare. He had said once that a 'Captain could not go wrong if he placed his ship alongside an enemy'. Incredibly, the pilots insisted that the ship would ground if it went any nearer the Danes, even though the Danish ships themselves marked the western edge of the King's Deep two hundred yards away. With other things on his mind, Nelson did not argue with them, and the *Elephant* anchored where it was.

The *Ganges* (74) was the next up and stood opposite Nelson's original target, the *Saelland* (74), followed by the *Monarch* (74) and the *Defiance*. This brought the fleet's third-in-command, Rear-Admiral Thomas Graves, ahead of Nelson and between him and Parker, who was then some miles to the north.

All the British ships were now opposite the Danish ships and floating batteries. At the northern end of the line, the mighty fortresses of Trekroner and Lynetten were being attacked by the frigates under Captain Riou, instead of by line-of-battle ships. The match was grossly uneven, but Riou had no choice in the circumstances. He had been infected so much by the Nelson style that he flung his fragile ships into action against the superior armaments of the forts and for the next few hours stood his ground through some of the heaviest gunfire of the battle.

After the first few exchanges the entire battle area was blanketed by smoke and neither side could see the other. As they were anchored, this did not matter too much; they simply kept firing through the smoke in the direction in which they were aimed. The stand-up contest was one of the severest

---

[19] Nelson wrote that he had 'experienced in the Sound the misery of having the honour of our Country intrusted to Pilots, who have no other thought than to keep the Ship clear of danger, and their own silly heads clear of shot ... Everybody knows what I must have suffered; and if any merit attaches itself to me, it was in combating the dangers of the shallows in defiance of the Pilots.' Nelson to St Vincent, Letter, September [about the 29th] 1801, in Nicolas (ed.), 1844-6, Vol. 4, p. 499.

many of the veterans had experienced. The best chance of survival lay in firing as accurately and as often as possible at the enemy to reduce the ability of his guns to fire back. Discipline and training were the ingredients of survival and British ships excelled in these. The Danes made up for their small experience of war with patriotic enthusiasm. Their enthusiasm caused bitterness among the British crews, as the Danes were apparently untroubled by the 'rules' of naval combat. If a Danish ship was smashed into a pulp they did not abandon it; as the British boat parties set off to board what they considered to be a surrendered enemy the Danes on the shore sent out a relief crew to re-open the contest. Exhausted British seamen found silenced battered wrecks opening up on them again with a fresh Danish crew. Because the British could not replace their casualties and because they were having to deal with an enemy that did not strike colours, they had to respond with murderous fire aimed at crippling the enemy ships and burning them into submission.

Bligh noted in his Log, after two hours of the battle: 'At noon, the action continuing very hot, ourselves much cut up. Our opponent, the Danish Commodore, struck to us, but his seconds ahead and astern still keep up a strong fire.' These were the Danish ships *Elven* and *Aggershuus*. The battle continued for the next two hours in like manner. Neither side could give up; the British could not withdraw to the north through the narrow channel without going past the forts nor could they manoeuvre back to the south without massive damage from collisions, grounding and gunfire. By the nature of the battle each side simply stood and blasted away, causing enormous damage and many casualties. From a distance the situation must have looked desperate and so it did to Parker, standing off with the main fleet a few miles to the north.

In fact the situation was beginning to turn slowly in favour of the British ships. The *Provensteenen* and the *Wagrien* were shot into submission and boarded, though the boarders only found dead and wounded. The *Rendsborg* was hit below the water line and driven out of its position; it moved out of one action and, in Danish fashion, back into another action further up the line, though it was badly crippled. The *Nyeborg* was blasted out of the line by the *Edgar* and drifted shorewards. The *Hylland* fought until it was exhausted and had to cease firing for lack of working guns and ammunition. The *Ardent* took on three Danish ships, the *Cronborg*, the *Hayen* and the *Elven*, firing at all three (a manoeuvre in which British gunnery supremacy was at a premium) until they were silenced after 2 p.m. The *Glatton* was firing its carronades at the *Dannebroge* and also at the floating batteries around it. The carronades were not successful against the low-lying batteries which were able to do considerable damage to the *Glatton*.

The *Svædfisken* was in a terrible state by noon but kept firing to the end of the battle. The *Sælland* lost a third of its crew from the gunfire of the *Ganges*, and when its cables were cut by shot it drifted out of the battle. The *Monarch* received the highest casualties on the British side. Its captain was killed in the first minutes and command passed to Lieutenant Yelland. He worked hard and courageously against the *Charlotte Amalia* (26), the *Sohesten* floating battery and the *Holsteen* (60) as well as being under fire from Trekroner. The Danish Commander, Admiral Fischer, was driven off his flagship, *Dannebroge*, when it was silenced by the *Glatton* and the *Elephant*, and he took his command to the *Holsteen*, opposite the *Monarch*. He was eventually driven off that ship as well and he went to the Trekroner Fort, but by then the Danish situation was critical. The *Hiælperen* surrendered right in front of the Trekroner and Admiral Fischer.

Admiral Parker, approaching the battle from the north, could not see what was going on; he could not advance into the King's Deep from the north without blocking off the escape route for Nelson's ships if they decided to pull out. But his very appearance with a fresh fleet was of concern to the Danes. They were taking a hammering from the King's Deep squadron and faced the prospect of a fresh fleet moving into the battle. The British 'bombs' were now in position to bombard the capital and the action showed no signs of ceasing. Incredibly, at this moment, Parker's caution overcame him. He decided not to await the report of Captain Otway whom he had sent to Nelson to get his view of the battle. He ordered Signal No.39 to be shown from his Flagship. This was the signal to 'discontinue the action'. If the Danes had been able to read the British signals they would have been amazed and encouraged.

A signal from the Commander-in-Chief was not discretionary; Nelson was under an obligation to obey. But Parker was four miles away from the battle and without information, Nelson was in the middle of it and in full command of what was happening. If he broke off at that moment, apart from the difficulty of extricating his ships under fire in the narrow unmarked channel, he would lose whatever initiative he had gained by attacking. If he did not break off he would have to countermand the Admiral's signal in some way to keep his ships where they were. Their signal officers might see Signal No.39 on the Admiral's ship and would be obliged to Log it. This could lead to a disorderly break-off and confusion at a critical moment in the action.

Nelson already had a reputation for the unorthodox. At the battle of St Vincent he had disobeyed precise instructions at a crucial point in the battle to inflict casualties on the enemy; fortunately for him his action was endorsed by success, and later by Admiral Lord St Vincent, as he became. Here again Nelson acted characteristically: he ignored the signal from the Admiral. He is reported to have said when told of the Admiral's signal: 'Leave off Action! Now damn me if I do!'' and to have pretended to look through the telescope with his blinded eye, saying 'I really do not see the signal.' But not everybody had the self-confidence of Nelson, nor was everybody positioned so as to be able to see both the Admiral's and Nelson's signal flags. The dense smoke from guns and fires which was drifting over the battle area precluded a clear view of anything.

Captain Riou continued firing at the forts from his frigate, *Amazon*, after the Admiral's signal at 1.15 p.m. But just astern of his frigate squadron there was H.M.S. *Defiance* with the fleet's third-in-command, Admiral Graves, on board. Graves was acutely embarrassed by Parker's signal and responded to it by showing a No.39 to the north, facing the Admiral, and keeping Nelson's No.16 (Close Action) flying to the south, while continuing to fire himself. He flew the two flags in such a way that neither Parker nor Nelson could see them both. However, Riou and his ships were ahead of him to the north, and saw the No.39. The captains of the *Dart* and the *Arrow* naturally acknowledged Graves's signal. Riou then had little option. Although he was completely imbued with the Nelson spirit and correctly surmised that Nelson would continue fighting, he now had signals from Parker and Graves instructing him to cease the action and two of his squadron were repeating the signal. He is reported to have declared, as he gave the orders to cease firing, 'What will Nelson think of us?' Even if this is apocryphal it is telling. He had spent the night with Nelson planning the battle and probably knew better than anybody what Nelson thought of the situation and of Parker. Wounded and bitter, he ordered the *Amazon* to swing round and leave the battle scene. As the smoke cleared round the ship, the Trekroner guns were given an easy target. They fired across the gap, and Captain Riou was cut in two by the full force of a shot and killed outright.

The loss of the frigates at the north of the line was not crucial to the outcome of the battle elsewhere. It lessened the fire on the forts and freed the attention of the Danes to some extent, but the battle was already turning slowly in favour of Nelson's squadron. The crucial decision lay with Nelson and the ships astern of him. If they dropped out of the fighting in the confusion of signals, the Danes might interpret this as victory. Nelson had to maintain the action until the possibility of a victory by the enemy was eliminated. Immediately astern of Nelson was Bligh in the *Glatton*. We know that Bligh was meticulous in the keeping of his Log; yet his Log of this part of the action is curiously vague for once. He writes: 'PM the action continuing very hot. At 2.45 it may be said to have ended.' He does not mention the signal from Parker. Of course, he may not have seen it. It may also be that he chose, like Nelson, to ignore it. He was immediately astern of Nelson and would be inclined to follow what Nelson did rather than act independently. If Nelson kept signal No.16 flying, Bligh would have been obliged in the circumstances to obey his immediate commander. As long as the *Elephant* kept in the action Bligh was 'covered' in the sense of being accountable to the Admiralty. Just as Nelson could be 'blind' for once, Bligh could for once be diplomatically vague in his Log. But the *Glatton*'s role as second to Nelson had a bearing on the behaviour of the ships astern. If the *Glatton* had pulled away this would have caused confusion in Nelson's squadron astern. By flying No.16 and remaining in action, Bligh ensured that Nelson's decision was transmitted all along the line. None of the ships astern of *Glatton* ceased firing in response to signal No.39.

By 2 p.m. the situation was clearly in Nelson's favour. None of his ships was seriously disabled or in distress. Some, including the *Glatton*, were badly damaged. Three of them were grounded (through their own actions) and some of the smaller ships had obeyed Parker's signal, but the main body was keeping up a rapid fire on the Danes. Five of the eight Danish ships were out of action, except for the occasional maverick gun fired by enthusiastic volunteers, and three of the four floating batteries were also silenced. Many of the smaller Danish ships were also no longer firing. Only the three forts, Trekronner, Lynette and Sixtus, were still firing for effect. To reduce these forts would require a landing of marines; but the space between the forts and the British ships was crowded with floating wrecks and disabled ships. Nelson also had the problem that he had been ignoring his Commander's direct orders for over an hour. Parker had sent Captain Otway to find out what was going on and once Otway had seen signal No.39 it was impossible for Nelson to argue, if it ever came to an inquiry, that he was unaware of Parker's wishes.

To preserve the fruits of his victory and comply with his duty as an officer, Nelson decided to offer the Danish Crown Prince a truce. He wrote out the following note and despatched it to the shore under flag of truce:

> 'To the Brothers of Englishmen, The Danes.
> Lord Nelson has directions to spare Denmark, when no longer resisting; but if the firing is continued on the part of Denmark, Lord Nelson will be obliged to set on fire all the Floating-batteries he has taken, without having the power of saving the brave Danes who have defended them.
> 'Dated on board His Britannic Majesty's ship *Elephant*, Copenhagen Roads, April 2nd, 1801.
> 'Nelson and Brontë, Vice-Admiral,
> under the command of Admiral Sir Hyde Parker.'[20]

Nelson was, in effect, trading the wounded Danes lying unattended in the ships and batteries in the King's Deep for a truce. The threat to fire them, and thereby immolate the wounded, was conditional upon the Danes ceasing fire. By signing the note in his own name (a name rightly considered by him to carry prestige in the Danish court), but associating his name with that of Parker, Nelson met all the problems of protocol that could arise. He also implicated Parker in his gamble.

The action continued while the message was passed to the shore and the Crown Prince, and also while the Prince's emissary went aboard the *Elephant* to find out what the offer of a truce meant. For instance, did the truce call for a surrender by either side or did it leave open the conclusions of the engagement to future negotiations? Nelson consulted his officers and even proposed a contingency plan to take some ships along the line and engage the Danish fort. To convince the Crown Prince of his intentions he sent a second note ashore: 'Lord Nelson's object in sending on shore a flag of truce is humanity, therefore, consents that hostilities shall cease till Lord Nelson can take his prisoners out of the Prizes; and he consents to land all the wounded Danes, and to burn or remove his prizes. Lord Nelson, with humble duty to His Royal Highness, begs leave to say that he will ever esteem it the greatest Victory he ever has gain'd if this flag of truce may be the happy forerunner of a lasting and happy Union between my most Gracious Sovereign and His

[20] Quoted in Oman, 1947, p. 443.

Majesty the King of Denmark.' These terms proved acceptable and firing ceased shortly after on both sides.[21]

Not long after this, Nelson signalled Admiral Graves to come aboard the *Elephant* and thanked him personally for his support during the battle. He also signalled Captain Bligh to come aboard. Bligh ever remembered what for him was the supreme honour, that Admiral Nelson personally thanked him on the quarter-deck of the *Elephant* for his support in the *Glatton*. His Log records the incident: 'Lord Nelson in the *Elephant*, our second ahead, did me the honour to hail me to come aboard, and thank me for the conduct of the *Glatton*.'

With the temporary truce the immediate problem was to remove the fleet from the King's Deep. Graves took the *Defiance* out first. Some of the ships grounded, including the *Elephant*, but Bligh got the *Glatton* clear and anchored with Parker's squadron about 4 p.m. During the evacuation, the *Dannebroge*, which had been blazing from fires started by the *Glatton*'s 'carcases', exploded.[22] The rest of the squadron sailed out and away from what could have been a trap for them, taking with them their prisoners. While the Danes worked to clear their ships of wounded the British anchored their 'bombs' just out of range of the shore batteries but within range for a bombardment of the city in case the truce broke down and further pressure was needed to conclude negotiations.

Over the next few days the negotiations were continued by Nelson, but the details are not of importance here. The news of the death of the Tsar eventually arrived, making the differences between Denmark and Britain redundant. Nelson's gamble over the truce came off; he secured a peaceful settlement to the dispute and opened the Baltic once again to British shipping. The Armed Neutrality collapsed from attrition at Copenhagen and the death of the Russian Tsar.

After the battle the melancholy task of clearing the ships of the dead had to be faced. The 'good and gallant Captain Riou' was committed to the deep with many others.[23] As always, promotions followed. Unnecessary bitterness was caused by Admiral Parker's taking it upon himself to draw up the promotions, instead of tactfully assigning this task to Nelson who had commanded the action. Parker promoted some of his own Lieutenants, who had watched the battle at a distance, to vacancies among the Captains

---

[21] *ibid.*, p. 445.

[22] 'Carcases' were incendiary devices fired out of guns and reputedly as dangerous to the ship firing them as to the target.

[23] The casualties in the British ships were as follows (Pope, 1972):

	Killed	Wounded		Killed	Wounded
Monarch	56	164	Elephant	9	13
Ardent	30	60	Blanche	7	9
Isis	28	84	Ganges	6	1
Defiance	26	64	Polyphemus	6	25
Edgar	28	104	Alcmene	5	14
Glatton	17	34	Dart	2	1
Amazon	14	23	Desiree	0	3
Bellona	11	58	Zephyr	1	1

instead of promoting the Lieutenants who had fought in the action. As a result of Parker's ineptitude and insensitivity, Bligh met difficulties when he was transferred from the *Glatton* to the *Monarch* over a week after the battle. Thus, once again, what ought to have been an unblemished honour for William Bligh was soured by events outside his control. Inevitably, his critics have taken advantage of the incident.

In view of Bligh's role in the battle, his promotion to the *Monarch*, a 74-gun, was legitimate. It was also a direct consequence of the bad feeling caused by Parker's promotion of one of his own Lieutenants to command the *Monarch* in the immediate aftermath of the battle.[24] The *Monarch* had lost its Captain in the opening minutes of the action and the First Lieutenant, Yelland, had assumed command and directed the ship for the duration until the cease-fire. Presumably if Nelson had been permitted to make the battle promotions he would have promoted Lieutenant Yelland. Yelland could not have expected to command the *Monarch*, in view of its prestige as a 74-gun, but he would have been happy to receive command of one of the frigates, almost certainly bringing him to the Post Captains' list on return to Britain. To have a Lieutenant appointed commander who had not been in the action was a cruel blow to hope and morale. The hostility aroused by this act must have whispered its way around the fleet because Parker changed his mind and on 13 April appointed Captain Bligh to command the *Monarch* and take her back to Britain, along with the *Isis* and the Danish prize, *Holsteen*. (Other Danish prizes were burned on Parker's orders, much to the consternation of officers and men, including Nelson, who knew the value of prize money and its cost in human life.)

Before leaving Copenhagen Bligh asked Nelson for a written testimonial regarding his conduct during the battle. This has sparked off considerable discussion among Bligh's critics. It is suggested that it was in bad taste and an embarrassment to Nelson. But if Bligh's role in the battle is taken into account, his request seems reasonable. The contradictory signals were sufficient grounds for Bligh to be worried about what might happen in the future as a result of his action in following Nelson's orders rather than Parker's. Mutual recriminations and intrigue were common in the Admiralty. The bitterness of these internal political struggles was not always in proportion to their importance. Sometimes the most trivial affront could lead to years of faction fighting. Nelson himself was not too sure about what would happen to him when he met Parker after the cease-fire. He is reported to have said: 'Well, I have fought contrary to orders, and perhaps I shall be hanged. Never mind; let them!'[25] If Nelson was killed in battle, Bligh's protection from reprisal would be removed. He had already found once, after the death of Cook, that the loss of a friendly and obliging commander could mean difficulties later; he might have felt more vulnerable than others in this situation. In response to his request Nelson wrote the following brief testimonial:

[24] Parker also upset feelings in the fleet by sending his Flag Captain, Captain Otway, to London with the news of the battle instead of letting Nelson pick the man for this honour.
[25] Oman, 1947, p. 446.

'To Admiral the Earl of St. Vincent, K.B.   14th April, 1801
Captain Bligh [of the Glatton, who had commanded the Director at
Camperdown] has desired my testimony to his good conduct, which
although perfectly unnecessary, I cannot refuse: his behaviour on this
occasion can reap no additional credit from my testimony. He was my
second, and the moment the Action ceased, I sent for him, on board the
Elephant, to thank him for his support ... I am, &c., NELSON AND
BRONTE.'[26]

When Nelson heard that Bligh was returning to Britain in the *Monarch* he
met him and discussed with him not only the above letter, which he
despatched to St Vincent, but also a personal matter. Having done Bligh a
favour, he asked Bligh to return the favour. This Bligh readily agreed to. The
favour was to deliver a complete set of Copenhagen porcelain to an address in
London, 23, Piccadilly, the home of Sir William Hamilton. Enclosed with the
gift was a letter to the Hamiltons saying: 'It will bring to your recollection
that here your attached friend Nelson fought and conquered.'[27]

On 10 April 1801, an incident occurred between the Captain of the *Glatton*
and a Danish Lieutenant, Johan Uldall, over a sword belonging to one of the
Danish prisoners. It has been assumed that the Captain in question was
William Bligh.[28] The terms of the armistice agreed on 9 April included
a return of the Danish prisoners to the shore and the Danish set about
organising this return immediately. The *Glatton*, in common with other ships,
had several Danish officers held on board and it was in pursuit of these men
that Lieutenant Uldall boarded the *Glatton* and assembled the prisoners. One
of these was a Lieutenant Winkler, who apparently paraded without his
sword, and he was ordered to explain its absence. He replied that the
Captain of the *Glatton* had taken it from him and asked Lieutenant Uldall to
get it back for him. When Uldall asked the British captain for the sword he
was told that another Danish officer, Lieutenant Ditler Lorentzen, had sold
it to him as a memento of war for one English pound. Lieutenant Lorentzen
was called out and when confronted with the report he confirmed that he had
indeed sold the sword to the Captain. Lorentzen was a reserve officer and
was apparently engaged in some private trading, much to the
embarrassment of Uldall. Military protocol was at stake in this relatively

[26] Nicolas (ed.), 1844-6, Vol. 4, p. 343; Mackaness, 1951, p. 328, states that Bligh wrote to
Nelson on his return to Britain and that the above letter was Nelson's response. This cannot be
correct because the date shows it was written before Bligh left Copenhagen.
[27] Oman, 1947, p. 453: in the letter accompanying the gifts Nelson referred to Bligh as 'one of
my seconds on the 2nd' and commended him as a 'good and brave man'. Nelson's private letter
echoes the public one to St Vincent and confirms the view that Bligh was not imposing himself
on the Admiral.
[28] The incident is described by Pope, pp. 477-8. The quoted reports do not refer to Bligh by
name. Pope makes the incident reflect badly on Bligh, but if there was any disgrace involved it
was in the conduct of the Danish officer who sold a fellow officer's sword. (How did he acquire it
in the first place?) The implication that only Bligh would get involved in such a business is
absurd. We have no way of knowing how many 'incidents' like this took place, whether they
were all reported and how important each was. We do know that the affair did not alter Nelson's
opinion of Bligh (assuming Bligh was the officer concerned), because the incident took place on
10 April and Bligh was praised by Nelson on 13 April.

minor issue, and Lieutenant Uldall sought to satisfy his code of military honour by having Lieutenant Winkler formally present the sword as a gift to the British captain. In response the British captain, to preserve his honour in the transaction, insisted that Lieutenant Lorentzen keep the pound note, but Lorentzen, no doubt regretting he had got involved, refused to take the pound with him, much to the satisfaction of Uldall, who terminated the interview by ordering everybody into his boats and off the *Glatton*.

On shore the Danish Commander, Admiral Fischer, was involved in rows with the British forces over the conduct of the battle. He was trying to justify his own role and to embarrass the Danish Crown Prince about his relations with Nelson and the conduct and terms of the armistice. Not everybody in the Danish Court appreciated the new agreement with the British, especially as it gave them the power to stop and search neutral merchant vessels entering and leaving the Baltic. Fischer was collecting material to use against the British, and among other complaints he was made aware of the incident on the *Glatton*. This may have blown it up out of proportion to its real importance. The incident on the *Glatton*, and the many other misunderstandings that occured during this time, were inevitable results of the disengagement of two proud military forces. Some misunderstandings led to cases where not all the Danish officers were released immediately, and this caused considerable strains between the two nations.

Bligh took the *Monarch* back to Britain on 15 April. For the reasons mentioned previously, he had not been welcomed on board, and probably nobody else, excepting Nelson, would have been either. Lieutenant Yelland was still the First Lieutenant, having refused a transfer to another ship, and because he no doubt felt he had been treated badly, he could hardly have been expected to regard the appointment of Bligh to replace Parker's Lieutenant as a cause for joy. He had been robbed of his promotion by Fleet politics and everybody on the *Monarch* knew it.

From one of the Midshipmen's journals we can get an idea of the atmosphere on board the *Monarch*. Midshipman Millard wrote: 'Captain Bligh was an excellent navigator, and I believe in every respect a good seaman, but his manners and disposition were not pleasant, and his appointment to the *Monarch* gave very general disgust to the officers.'[29] When Millard is specific about Bligh's manners and disposition, the shallowness of the criticism is exposed. Apparently Bligh did not think much of the competence of the pilots: 'Captain Bligh having had time to turn himself round in his new ship began to make himself known among us. Finding our pilots were not so scientific as himself, he liberally bestowed upon them the appellation of 'dolt' and 'blockhead', and pretending that the ship was not safe in their hands, he took charge of her himself. This was as unnecessary as it was unusual. These men had been accustomed to the Baltic trade the greater part of their lives, and were certainly well able to conduct the ship from the Naze of Norway to Lowestoft as Captain Bligh.'

[29] Millard discusses Bligh's role in the *Bounty* in his journal, showing that the issue was still alive. *See* ML MS Ab 60/15.

Millard clearly knew little of Bligh's mode of management of his ship, and nothing about the incompetence of the fleet's pilots during the preparation for the attack on Copenhagen. Bligh always took command of his ships, not just the nominal rank of commander. There is no record of any of his ships ever fouling its lines or grounding after the experiences of the *Bounty* in Matavai Bay, where he relied on Fletcher Christian and John Fryer. The fact that he relied on nobody, especially the pilots, made him unpopular with them, and with those others whom he made more attentive to their normal duties. This was just his way of doing things. Midshipman Millard may have been confident in the pilots, but he did not carry the responsibility for anything that went wrong. Bligh was on an errand for Nelson as much as for the Admiralty, and he was unlikely to take risks. Nelson five months after the battle referred to the Baltic pilots as having no other idea than to keep 'their silly heads clear of shot'; their conduct during the action was no recommendation for treating them with respect. If Bligh had placed his trust in them there might have been grounds for criticism.

The final point in Millard's complaint is worth a comment. Bligh decided to take the *Monarch* to Yarmouth and transfer the wounded in boats to the *Holsteen*, which would take them into harbour, and then to press on to the Nore with his own ship. This meant transferring the wounded during the night which undoubtedly caused additional discomfort and some distress among them. But Millard's main complaint is that Bligh inconvenienced the officers who wanted to go ashore at Yarmouth and visit their connections there. The sentence from Millard's journal quoted above, about his appointment to command the *Monarch* which 'gave very general disgust to the officers', continues: 'This they expressed to themselves without reserve, and even in his presence, behaved but with distant civility.'[30] One can forgive them this reaction, because of their resentment that Yelland had not been rewarded and Bligh had; but it is also not unreasonable of Bligh to react to this treatment by considering his own interests rather than theirs. There were also the broader interests of command for Bligh to consider. He had no idea when the fleet would return behind him to Yarmouth, and the *Monarch* and the *Isis* needed a refit which meant that they had to be transferred to the Nore. To stop at Yarmouth and accommodate the officers and their connections would only delay the work on the ships.

Bligh arrived with the *Monarch* and the *Isis* at the Nore on 7 May 1801. He reported to the Admiralty and the *Monarch* was paid off. The officers dispersed at their own convenience and Bligh was promoted to command H.M.S. *Irresistible*, a 74-gun ship of the line and formerly Nelson's flagship at the battle of St Vincent. This promotion was a fine reward for his role in the battle and shows that his credit in the Admiralty stood high. Nelson's letter may have helped in this. He was to hold this command for twelve months. Thus ended Bligh's part in the battle of Copenhagen. He had stood the stringent test of command under fire for the second time and under the watchful eye of Lord Nelson. This was his last naval action and it was also his most creditable.

[30] *See* Weate and Chapman, 1972, p. 117.

26

The *Warrior* Court Martial

Bligh's command of H.M.S. *Irresistible* lasted until May 1802, when, following the Peace of Amiens, the navy stood many of its ships down and placed their officers on half-pay. Bligh was fully conscious of his post-Copenhagen status as a combat officer. In a letter to Banks he writes: 'I can only say I shall continue to serve as Zealously as ever until I am paid off and be ready to serve again whenever it is required as I must hereafter command ships which will be of great consequence in the battles our fleets will be subject to.'[1]

Not long after his appointment to *Irresistible*, on 21 May 1801, the Royal Society elected him a Fellow 'in consideration of his distinguished services in navigation'. This was a considerable professional honour of which Bligh was proud for the rest of his life. On his tombstone, he appears as 'William Bligh Esquire, F.R.S.'. With Sir Joseph Banks as the President of the Royal Society at the time Bligh had a ready sponsor for the honour.

Half-pay meant shore-leave, and Bligh spent mucn of the time at home at Durham Place with his wife Elizabeth and his family of six daughters. In 1802, the eldest, Harriet, married a Henry Barker of Gloucester, and a son, William Bligh Barker, was born later in the year. The grandchild unfortunately died at three years of age, in 1805.[2] How Bligh spent his year's vacation is not known. There is a gap in the written record until he wrote to the Admiralty on 9 March 1803 asking for employment.[3] In the autumn of 1803 Bligh was employed by the Admiralty in surveying and charting of the kind which he had undertaken in the *Director*. He carried out surveys of Dungeness, the coast of Flushing and Fowey harbour.[4] This work was well within Bligh's competence but hardly the kind of employment that he was looking for. On 2 May 1804, the opportunity that he wanted was offered and he took it: he was appointed to command H.M.S. *Warrior*, a 74-gun ship of the line. This brought him into the centre of one of the British fleets, and if action occurred he could be sure to be of 'great consequence'. His Commander-in-Chief was Lord Cornwallis.

Bligh's major problem in his new command was to get enough men to sail

[1] Bligh to Banks, Letter, *Irresistible*, Yarmouth, 12 November 1801, ML MS.
[2] He was buried in the family vault at Lambeth Cemetery.
[3] PRO Admiralty, 1/529.
[4] *ibid.*, folios 382, 383 and 385. In early 1804, Bligh was working in the Hydrographic Department at the Admiralty. See David, 1976; Robinson, 1952. From material in PRO Adm. 1/3522, it seems that Bligh was responsible for several position fixes of places along the east coast of the British Isles. L.N. Pascoe, formerly of the Hydrographic Dept. has suggested that Bligh was probably responsible for getting Dalrymple to publish Heywood's surveys of 1804-5 (Andrew David to author, December 1976).

the ship after it was fitted out at Plymouth. In a letter to Mrs Bligh he discusses his difficulties:[5]

> The very great deal there is to do to Ships coming in and sailing to the Grand Fleet has delayed the Shipwrights work with me and my equipment, but with respect to our rigging we are nearly complete but I have not yet above 241 Men and only 40 of them Seamen. – Mr Johnston has been ill but is now getting about again.[6]   I continue to like my Surgeon, Mr Cinnamond, very well[7]... It is deplorable to hear the accounts of the Grand Fleet, every ship is 80 or 100 short of complement, & not one half of their Marines something must have been radically bad to have produced all this ... I wish I could get a Cook and a Baker for neither can I pick up here, the latter who I had with me in the *Director* Smith told me would like to go with me again, if my Dear you will tell Smith to send him I will receive him. Betsy knows where Smith lives. – I wish Senhouse was with me as he would be of real service, but I cannot ask him to come as he is so well off in the Frigate,[8] particularly with respect to serving his time. – Buchanan has not yet joined me or have I but two young Men who do duty as Mids that can be trusted – I have 5 or 6 but all came from the *Salvador del Mundo*, Old Dilkes[9] where nothing is fit & proper ... You may recommend any good youths to me that offer for Mids.

The fact that Bligh is asking his wife to arrange for his former baker out of the *Director* to join him, as well as any likely-looking midshipmen, shows how bad the manpower situation really was. The quality of the men sent to the fleet in these conditions cannot have been high. The long war of attrition with the French, the expansion of the naval force occasioned by the war and the seemingly endless need to keep a military force in being, combined to lower the standards of recruitment. The gallant youthful naïveté natural at the beginning of a war had been superseded by meanness and bitterness at all levels, again a normal product of difficult contests of national pride.

In such a situation, Captain William Bligh clashed verbally and persistently with one Lieutenant John Frazier over the issue of whether Frazier's sprained ankle prevented him from standing his watch – a trivial issue, but one of the innumerable court martials of the fleet resulted from it. During his time at Plymouth waiting for the *Warrior* to be fitted out, Bligh had complained to his wife about the time taken up by these court martials, where he was a member of the court. 'This is the first day I have been free of Court Martials,' he wrote, 'the confinement from which is very irksome & prevents us from having a day to ourselves to go anywhere from our Ships.'[10]

[5] Bligh to Mrs Elizabeth Bligh, *Warrior*, Plymouth, 16 June 1804, Bligh Family Correspondence, ML MS Safe 1/45.

[6] Lieutenant George Johnston, the First Lieutenant.

[7] He changed his opinion of the Surgeon after the court martial.

[8] Senhouse would have had to come as junior lieutenant and presumably he was a First Lieutenant on the frigate or in a position to win prize money.

[9] Captain John Dilkes had been at Copenhagen and later became an Admiral, but was apparently not highly regarded by Bligh for his seamanship.

[10] Bligh to Mrs Elizabeth Bligh, 16 June 1804.

Bligh set out the circumstances of the quarrel with Frazier in a letter to Vice-Admiral Collingwood and requested a court martial. His letter reads:[11]

Warrior, off Rochfort
October 27 1804

Sir,

Lieutenant John Frazier from his application as being fit to serve was appointed 2nd Lieutenant of the *Warrior* under my command. On his joining the ship he had an habitual lameness in his ankle, which had been occasioned by the bones being broken by accident in the Merchant Service, with which he, however, asserted he was capable of doing his duty, and did so to the 18th instant, when by our shortness of water and provisions and being out nearly 14 weeks, it was to be expected we were soon to return to port. On this evening he wrote to me requesting I would apply to you for a survey on him,[12] which I did on the 21st by enclosing his letter and remarking I thought he was the same as he had hitherto been. In consequence you directed that as he, Lieutenant Frazier was represented to be very much in the same state as he had been for some time past, and the *Warrior* would probably go soon into port, it would be an accommodation to him to wait until then. Lieutenant Frazier conceiving this application of his exempted him from further service, and that keeping watch would militate against his being discharged by survey on his arrival in port and thereby he would be obliged to return and experience a winter's cruizing did refuse to do any further duty, altho he had my assurance of every indulgence. The Surgeon put him one day, the 20th instant, in his sick-list, but the next day, finding no inflamation in his ancle, and that the appearances were no other than it must at all times have been subject to, he no longer continued him under his care and in consequence I ordered him to keep watch, but he refused. On the 22nd I directed Lieutenant Johnson (1st Lieutenant) to tell him it was my orders he was to take his watch. He came on deck in consequence, but on Lieutenant Boyack asking him if he was come to relieve him, he replied 'no, I am only come up to take the air.' – would not relieve him and went below soon after. At 8 next morning, the 23rd, he was again called on to relieve Lieutenant Russell and I sent him word by Mr Cosnaham, midshipman, it was my orders he should relieve him, to which he returned me an answer he was too lame. I again sent and repeated the orders to him and gave him til 9 o'clock to comply, but he refused to obey me inasmuch that he would not come on deck to keep his watch. And for which contumacy and disobedience on the 22nd and 23rd I ordered him under arrest and request he may be tried by Court martial.

I am Sir &c
Wm. Bligh

From Bligh's point of view this was a clear case of refusal of duty. He did not want to lose the Lieutenant, having had enough trouble getting his establishment before leaving port. The winter sailing was about to begin and

---

[11] Bligh to Vice-Admiral Collingwood, *Warrior*, off Rochfort, 27 October 1804, *Minutes of the Court Martial*, PRO Admiralty 1/5367.
[12] The survey would decide whether he was medically fit for duty or not and could get him a spell ashore to convalesce.

this unpleasant duty would be more unpleasant if they were a Lieutenant short. Frazier had come on board lame from his previous accident, and the fact that a 74-gun ship accepted a man in this condition as Second Lieutenant indicates the desperate manpower situation. There was also an element of sharing the misery, and not letting one whom Bligh considered to be a malingerer spend the winter in the comfort of port on sick leave.

However, Bligh's case had a flaw in it. In the evidence to the court martial from the Surgeon, Mr Cinnamon, Frazier was able to show that he was on the sick-list up to the time when Captain Bligh ordered Mr Cinnamon to strike him off the list. The Surgeon testified that in his opinion Frazier was not yet fit for duty and that he had taken him off the list 'because of the order written on the sick book and signed by Captain Bligh'. The order in question was to the effect that the Surgeon was to keep only those men on his list whom he could treat. The ambiguity of the evidence leaves open the possibility that Bligh had exceeded his authority in telling the Surgeon who to take off the sick list. The Court regarded this evidence as sufficient grounds to dismiss the charges against Frazier. To be guilty of a refusal of duty the person in question had to be fit for duty; Frazier in this case had the protection of the sick-list and the testimony of the Surgeon. The record states: 'As the charges had not been proved against Lieutenant Frazier he was acquitted by the Court.'[13] It seems that Bligh, thinking that Frazier was trying it on, may have bent the rules in an attempt to stop Frazier's scheme to spend winter ashore.

Bligh's intentions had been thwarted by his junior Lieutenant, but the trouble did not end there. Frazier decided to bring Bligh to a court martial, which was within his rights. He applied before he was court-martialled on 23 November. His letter reads:[14]

H.M.S. *Warrior*, Cowsand Bay,
November 13, 1804

Sir,
I beg to state to you that William Bligh, Esq., Captain His Majesty's Ship *Warrior*, did on the ninth October last, publicly on the quarter deck on his Majesty's Ship *Warrior* grossly insult and ill treat me being in the execution of my office by calling me rascal, scoundrel and shaking his fist in my face and that at various other times between the ninth of July and the thirtieth Day of October, 1804, he behaved himself towards me and other commissioned, warrant and petty officers in the said ship in a tyrannical and oppressive and unofficerlike behaviour contrary to the rules and discipline of the Navy and in open violation of the Articles of War. I have, therefore, to request that you will be pleased to order a Court Martial to be assembled to try William Bligh, Esq., Captain of his Majesty's Ship *Warrior*.
I am etc.,
John Frazier, Lieutenant

[13] *ibid.*
[14] *ibid.*, and PRO Admiralty 1/5368.

Frazier was making a wider charge against Bligh than that of personal tyranny against himself; he included 'other commissioned, warrant and petty officers' in his indictment. Either he was foolhardy, or he had some reason to expect that they would back him up in court. This may well have been another occasion when Bligh did not have the support of his officers. He may have lost that support because he told them that they did not match up to his high standards.

Bligh was in a difficult position once the court martial on Frazier acquitted him of 'refusal of duty'. This encouraged Frazier to pursue his own charges against Bligh. Nothing was heard for several weeks but the court martial could not be delayed indefinitely. As soon as the *Warrior* was back in port it would be listed along with the many others. Bligh wrote to his Commander-in-Chief, Admiral Cornwallis, stating his side of the affair, and received a letter back:[15]

Ville de Paris, Torbay
17th January 1805

Sir,
I have received your letter of yesterday's date; and never had heard of the intended Court Martial you mention. But I will send your letter to the Admiralty by this day's post – unless you signify a desire to the contrary.

What you state of your situation from this circumstance on board the *Warrior* is a very improper one for an officer of your rank to be in – Your conduct since you have been under my orders has always been perfectly to my satisfaction.

I am Sir, etc.,
W. Cornwallis

Cornwallis, like the Admiralty, would hardly have regarded the affair as serious. Bligh, however, may have been concerned about the effect the impending court martial was having on discipline aboard *Warrior*. He knew that some of his officers were going to testify against him and this undermined his authority. He set about asking his officers in turn whether they were joining the prosecution or the defence.

The court martial duly assembled on board H.M.S. *San Josef* in Torbay, over two days, 25 and 26 February 1805. The Court's President was Vice-Admiral Sir Charles Cotton. The charges were read out. The witnesses for the prosecution were brought in and gave their testimony. Bligh was permitted to question them and occasionally the court asked questions as well. The evidence, as reported in the minutes, is a confusing tale of personal interpretations of the relationship between Bligh and Frazier. Often the witness supports one aspect of the prosecution's case and then in questioning gives a contrary impression. The experience of appearing as a witness against a senior captain and before other fleet captains may have influenced their conduct.

---

[15] *ibid.*

Henry Cock, Master's Mate, was the first witness and he recounted an incident on 9 October 1804 in which Frazier and he were discussing Cock's report that the wardroom steward was playing cards again after having had his cards taken away from him. The sound of their voices carried to Bligh, who came out on deck. He demanded to know why Frazier was neglecting attention to his duty. Frazier replied: 'I beg your pardon, Sir, I am not, I am answerable for the occurrences of my watch.' Bligh retorted: 'What, Sir, you damned rascal, you damned scoundrel, never was a man troubled with such a set of blackards as I am. Take care, Sir, I am looking out for you.' Later in Frazier's watch, according to Cock, Bligh came out on deck, presumably to supervise and check the sailing of the ship. Lieutenant Frazier apparently began to give an order to set the main staysail. Bligh is alleged by Cock to have told Frazier that if he ever set a sail or gave an order while he, Bligh, was on deck, he would confine him and make him rue it. Bligh was never loath to remind his officers that he was in command, and it is consistent with his character and understanding of his duty that he would insist on having the command of the ship when he was on the quarter deck. A lieutenant in these circumstances would be expected to show deference to his captain and, if necessary, seek permission to 'carry on'. Cock's cross-examination extracted from him the fact that he would not have taken note of the incidents except that Frazier instructed him to make a note of them. Was Frazier already planning to entrap his captain as early as 9 October? Cock stood by his story under questioning, though he did concede that he had stated to several people, including officers, that he had never sailed with a better captain than Captain Bligh.

Midshipman Samuel Knowles testified that in July or August he was a mate of Mr Frazier's watch and that the captain had questioned him and Mr Frazier about the firing of the fog-signal guns. This happened twice, and on the second occasion Bligh had called him a liar and said that he and Frazier were 'a parcel of villains and scoundrels from Lieutenants to the midshipmen … to the quarter masters'. From his letter to his wife we know that Bligh was not pleased with his officers and midshipmen, so this outburst a few weeks later is not surprising. The exact nature of the incident that provoked the row is lost now. Knowles did not support Frazier's assertions that Bligh had behaved tyrannically and oppressively towards the officers on the *Warrior*.

Another witness, John Amplet, a marine, did not help the case for the prosecution, because he was extremely diffident about testifying in support of the charge that Bligh had called Frazier a 'rascal and a villain'. However, his testimony, such as it was, tells us something about the *Warrior* at the time. Bligh maintained a constant sentry outside his cabin, which was not unusual in the navy. Amplet denied that he had heard any of the crew say Bligh was tyrannical or oppressive. His only recollection of trouble was when Bligh came out and found the ship off station and that he was in a 'passion' about this. Amplet also confessed to having been approached by both Bligh and Frazier about whether he was to give testimony. Amplet told the court that Frazier had told him that if he gave evidence against Bligh he would be respected by every officer on the ship. He had decided to tell the truth. He had never 'heard of any grievance sustained by any person ... which had not immediately been redressed with strict impartiallity and justice'. He also mentioned that he had heard Bligh 'call the quarter master a damn rascal'.

Lieutenant Alexander Boyack took his turn and testified against Bligh. This was the first really credible testimony and it produced a long list of incidents in which Bligh called various people 'rascals and scoundrels'. But Boyack denied that he had heard Frazier abused in this way. His own opinion was that Bligh's 'expressions to his officers before the ship's company lessened their dignity as officers and was degrading in the extreme'.

The Surgeon, Robert Cinnamon, the man whom Bligh 'continued to like' back in June 1804, testified against him, mainly in support of Frazier over the injury to his leg. He told the court he had heard Bligh call Frazier 'either a damnation or a damned impertinent fellow' and 'either an imposition on the service or an imposter'.[16] His real damaging evidence, which had told against Bligh when he had court-martialled Frazier in November, was about the ankle injury. He stated that his medical opinion was that Frazier could not do duty in October. When Bligh had told him he was wrong and that Frazier was pretending, Cinnamon had become so agitated that he could not recall exactly what Bligh had said. It looks as though Bligh tried to browbeat Cinnamon into unprofessional behaviour and in this act lost his respect, friendship and support. Cinnamon was able to confirm that Bligh had abused the Master, Mr Keltie. He did not remember any other incidents in which Bligh abused his officers.

The Surgeon's Mate, Charles Queade, supported the medical testimony and also brought up an incident with Mr Jewell, the Boatswain. Bligh had called Jewell a 'rascal' and had shaken him physically because he did not believe Jewell was attending to some matter of seamanship with alacrity. This testimony was supported by Captain George Mortimer of the Marines.[17] He said he had seen Jewell pushed by Bligh and also that Bligh had abused Mr Waller, the Carpenter. He agreed with Frazier that Bligh's conduct was 'tyrannical and unofficerlike' to his officers but, strangely, that Bligh was 'polite and attentive' to the Marine officers.

The junior Lieutenant, Robert Russell, testified on Frazier's behalf and supported the charges that Bligh had abused Frazier, Johnston, Keltie and Jewell, calling the latter a 'damned vagrant'. But John Honeybone, a seaman, was not a good witness for Frazier. He declared that he had seen Frazier jostle Bligh while he was taking a sextant reading. Samuel Jewell was

[16] If the word was 'impostor', I wonder how close to the truth this charge of Bligh's was about John Frazier. Bligh had not faced similar resistance to his authority since the *Bounty* fifteen years earlier. Frazier arrived on the *Warrior* in July, and he dates his charges from 9 July 1804. It is strange that a single man brought all the worst features of Bligh's character to the surface so quickly, and persistently ruffled him over the next few months. It is as if Frazier had tormented Bligh and provoked him into rash acts. Frazier having refused duty, Bligh had no alternative but to court martial him and this gave Frazier the opportunity he wanted. Is it possible that Frazier was in some way connected with the *Bounty* affair or the campaigns against Bligh by the Christians? He disappeared after the court martial.

[17] Mortimer had been with Captain Cox in the *Mercury* on its voyage to the South Sea in 1789, and had written a book of the voyage (Mortimer, 1791). He died with the rank of Major in 1834.

called next and confirmed what had been said previously about Bligh abusing him, and also said that he had threatened to get him 'in a dark corner', presumably to assault him. He said that he did not take the matter seriously because Bligh was 'hot and hasty', and that he would sail with Bligh again.

Lieutenant William Pascoe supported the evidence that Bligh had called various people 'rascals and vagabonds' but said that he did not believe that Bligh was 'tyrannical, unofficerlike or oppressive'. James Keltie, the Master, told the court that Bligh had called him a 'rascal' and a 'Jesuit'. He thought the actions of Bligh in trying to force Frazier to do his watch were cruel, and mentioned another act of cruelty; Bligh had made Waller, the Carpenter, come on deck when ill to supervise the fishing of a yard.[18] He had thought of 'seeking public redress' for this conduct. The point about the Carpenter was taken up immediately and Cinnamon was recalled. He said the man's medical condition was not good at the time and he was very old. He did not think it was an 'act of tyranny or even of severity', because the Carpenter had been able to leave his cabin and walk on deck. This was supported by the Carpenter's Mate, Samuel Meggs, who said that the Carpenter had volunteered to go on deck for about ten minutes to supervise the fishing of the yard. He had not heard him complain afterwards.

The next day it was the turn for the defence. Bligh's first witness was his First Lieutenant, George Johnston, who had been with him for several years, including in the *Director*. Johnston did not think Frazier had been cruelly treated, in fact he thought that Bligh had been 'indulgent' by giving orders that Frazier was to be allowed to sleep in on 18 October and that he could do his watch while sitting down on the quarter deck. He had not heard Bligh call Frazier a 'rascal and a scoundrel', nor seen him shake his fist at him or behave in a tyrannical manner. He declared that Frazier had told him that he would not have brought Bligh to court martial if he had not been charged by Bligh. He said he had never heard of any complaints about Captain Bligh from the officers, and while not 'in the habit of courting the opinion of seamen' he believed they had a good opinion of Bligh. He rejected the idea that the Carpenter was badly treated and claimed that he had expressed the highest praise for Bligh before he was invalided off the ship. Johnston was candid about Bligh's manner of directing people to work. If Bligh wanted something done that needed doing quickly he acted energetically, 'frequently swearing at the quarter masters or men of that description who were standing round, with a considerable motion of the hand, which was not only used to persons of that description, but generally in giving orders, when the service had been neglected for want of proper attention in the officers, but I never conceived it done with the intention of personally insulting any officer'.[19]

Midshipman Peter Mills supported Johnston's evidence. He had been on Frazier's watch when the refusal of duty took place. He had never heard

[18] To 'fish' the yard meant to repair or strengthen it by bolting a piece of hard wood across the weakness. By the time of the court martial in February 1805, the Carpenter had died.
[19] PRO Adm. 1/5368.

Bligh call the Lieutenant a 'rascal' or a 'scoundrel' nor did he 'shake his fist in his face'. Mills also told the Court that Frazier had tried to force him to testify for him by producing a 'play-bill' or gambling debt with his name on it but that he had refused to assist him. He claimed that Frazier had said words to the effect that if Bligh tried him he would try Bligh, and that 'Captain Bligh intends to take my commission from me, but I dont care a fig for it, I will lose it, but I will have satisfaction of him'. On Bligh's general conduct towards the officers Mills stated that Bligh was attentive and also took time to teach navigation to the petty officers.[20]

The Master's Mate, William Ranwell, came forward next to support Bligh. He regarded Bligh 'more as a friend' and knew he was always ready to help those 'who deserved it'. When Bligh scolded somebody it was because the ship's duty was not being attended to properly but he never held this against the person concerned. He denied he had been promised promotion if he said nothing prejudicial to Captain Bligh.

The Gunner of the *Warrior*, William Simmons, denied he had heard Bligh abuse him. He thought Bligh sometimes 'passionate and sometimes cool' and said that he would as soon sail with Bligh as anybody else. He did not know of any instance when Bligh had acted improperly. The ship's Clerk, Mr Joseph Strephon, also denied that the Captain had behaved in the manner of the charges. He had on one occasion heard Bligh reprimand the Boatswain but Mr Jewell had been intoxicated at the time. Apparently Strephon and Frazier had been together on the *Spartiate* and Frazier attempted to get him to confirm that he had criticised Bligh in a conversation they had had on the *Warrior* when Bligh had been giving orders directly to the officer of the watch. The gist of the conversation was that this did not happen on the *Spartiate*. Strephon denied the construction placed on the matter; he asserted that he had merely referred to the fact that on the *Spartiate* the Captain did not give orders when the officer of the watch was on deck, and that he had not thought Bligh was abusing anybody.

Bligh's defence was quite humble. He pointed out that Frazier had delayed months before charging him, which itself was unfair. He then gave a candid and illuminating portrayal of his own character and way of acting, which is worth quoting in full.[21]

> I candidly and without reserve avow that I am not a tame & indifferent observer of the manner in which Officers placed under my orders conducted themselves in the performance of their several duties; a signal or any communication from a commanding officer have ever been to me an indication for exertion & alacrity to carry into effect the purport thereof & peradventure I may occasionally have appeared to some of those officers as unnecessarily anxious for its execution by exhibiting any action or gesture peculiar to myself to such: Gentlemen, [I now] appeal to you, Mr President & the members of this honourable Court, who know

[20] Subsequently, Mills was appointed by Bligh to a position with him when he became Governor of New South Wales.

[21] PRO Adm. 1/5368.

& have experienced the arduous task of responsibility and that of the magnitude of one of His Majesty's seventy-four gun ships, which will, I am persuaded acquit me of any apparent impetuosity & would plead in extenuation for my imputed charges: attributing the warmth of temper, which I may at intervals have discovered, to my zeal for that service in which I have been employed without an imaginary blemish on my character for upwards of thirty five years and not with a premeditated view of any personal insult to my Prosecutor or reducing the rank which he holds in it concerning an incumbent duty in our relative situations to render that rank mutual support which its dignity indispensably requires, as without such impression, dicipline could not ensure obedience in ships of war.

The Court did not take very long to come to its verdict. They 'were of the opinion that the charges were in part proved, and did therefore adjudge Captain William Bligh of His Majesty's Ship *Warrior* to be reprimanded and to be admonished to be in future more correct in his language'.

Bligh was immediately restored to his command of the *Warrior* and had to face the problem of working with men who had testified against him. He set to work through Sir Joseph Banks and the Admiralty to get them 'turned over' and posted elsewhere. He writes to Banks:[22]

Except my First Lieutenant they are a very bad set of men as I ever heard of, and I have begged Mr Marsden to assist or direct me how I can get them turned over. Robert Cinnamon our Surgeon, I really believe is the most designing wicked man ever came into the ship, and most highly perjured – perhaps you may know some of the Sick Hurt Board and be able to get him removed from me, which would give me great satisfaction. My Master, whose name is Keltie was with Hunter in the *Waaksamheid* when he lost himself in coming from Port Jackson to Cape Good Hope. The Captain of Marines is Mortimer who made that foolish voyage to the South Sea – as soon as his year of duty is up I shall write to get rid of him, and the Master shall likewise leave the ship as soon as possible – he cannot find his latitude to ten miles and he knows nothing about the variation of the compass or how to conduct a ship.

The situation was not a happy one on the ship. In a letter to Sir Joseph thanking him for his sympathy and support over the trial he wrote: '... altho I keep up my situation as high as possible sending for [the Lieutenants] to dinner and sitting at my Table in turns yet you will see it is not a very pleasant party altho I conduct myself as if nothing had happened.' Later in the same letter (parts are torn): 'I have this instant received a letter from Mr Marsden saying he had obtained the consent of the Board that my two Lieuts. shall be rem[oved]. I beg My Dear Sir you will tha[nk] him for me as I consider it not only a publick benefit but a very friendly act.'[23] The two Lieutenants in

[22] Mitchell MS.
[23] Bligh to Banks, *Warrior*, Torbay, 7 March 1805. Alexander Turnbull Library, Wellington, New Zealand. In the same letter Bligh writes: 'We have such a set of low Men crept into the service that to govern a Ship is now not an easy matter altho a Captain's responsibility is as great or greater than ever.'

question were Pascoe and Boyack. Lieutenant Frazier is not heard of again and according to subsequent notes was dismissed from the service. It may have been that he was invalided out over his ankle, which would have been a convenience to everybody.

Why did Bligh get himself into this situation? To be court-martialled by a junior Lieutenant, especially one of so little distinction, was something of a humiliation. A little light can be thrown on Frazier's motivation if we remember that although the controversy of the *Bounty* had died down by 1805, it was still common knowledge, and Bligh's nickname among seamen was 'Bounty Bastard'. Reading Frazier's evidence alongside the statements in Christian's Appendix one cannot help but be struck by the similarity of the broad case against Bligh. This is not, however, to say that I accept the veracity of the two sources nor the construction placed on them. It is as if Frazier had seen what sort of attack he could make to get his own back.

It is difficult to get a picture of what really happened from the minutes of the Court. There is plenty in Bligh's favour. The Court had many witnesses both for the prosecution and the defence who painted a picture of him that would have struck a sympathetic note among the Captains hearing the evidence. Bligh comes across as a person with a quick temper, who exploded whenever he thought something was not being done correctly and with alacrity. Both Master's Mates, Cock and Ranwell, even though they appeared for the prosecution and the defence respectively, said they would serve again with Bligh: Cock said he had not sailed with a better captain and Ranwell that he regarded him as a 'friend'. Midshipman Knowles and Marine Amplet, two witnesses for the prosecution, affirmed that they did not believe Bligh to be guilty of 'tyranny, oppression and unofficerlike' behaviour. This was supported by another witness for the prosecution, Lieutenant Pascoe.

The exact nature of Bligh's 'abuse' and 'tyranny' is difficult to see from the minutes. There is a long list of actual abusive sentences such as 'rascal and villain', 'rascal and scoundrel', 'Oh, you are a disgrace to the service, damn you', 'you lubber', 'you Jesuit', 'God damn you, Sir', 'what are you about?', 'infamous scoundrel', 'audacious rascal', 'vagrant', 'dastardly villain', 'God damn me', 'God damn you, you old thief, you are so great a liar, I would rather believe the quarter master or any other man in the ship', 'God damn you, why do you not hoist your sail?', 'damn your blood', 'he was a damn long pelt of a bitch' and so on. What the Court thought of all this language it is hard to say, but they were surely not horrified or shocked. The Navy had heard worse before and has since. Bligh is shown to be a rather articulate abuser. He would wave his hands about in an excited passion. Lieutenant Boyack for the prosecution testified that this was a common mannerism of the captain. Jewell, the Boatswain, who had been pushed along the deck by Bligh to attend to something forward, thought Bligh 'hot and hasty', but affirmed he would sail with Bligh again. Boyack testified that Bligh had made threats: one of these was that 'he would rule the *Warrior* with a rod of iron' and that if ever an officer did not perform, 'woe, be to them! mercy, no by God, he would show them none'. Another threat was to do over the

Boatswain in a 'dark corner'. Lieutenant Russell reported a threat to place the Boatswain in irons. Jewell, the man in question, stated he had not taken these threats seriously. Frazier made the best he could of them, and of Bligh's other outbursts and gestures.

The evidence suggests that the *Warrior* was an uncomfortable place for those that did not run their watches to Bligh's standards. He may have gone too far. But the other side of his nature also appears: he took considerable time out to teach the midshipmen and warrant officers, including the Master, the principles and practice of navigation. He took a pride in his work and tried to encourage others to improve themselves in this respect. He dined regularly with his Lieutenants and the other petty officers, except apparently the Boatswain, whom he regarded as a drunk, and he as readily entertained those he had quarrelled with as the others. We know that even after the court martial he continued this habit, dining with Pascoe, Boyack and Russell who had all testified against him. Ideally, a man of war would be run with the utmost decorum, hardly a whisper being necessary to get orders obeyed. But after a long and exhausting war and an expansion of the fleets it was not always possible to get the most co-operative and skilled officers together into one ship. The Court obviously took this into consideration.

The verdict, embarrassing rather than damaging, exposed the Achilles' heel in Bligh's personality. The Admiralty could have sent him with his ship to an area where military action was likely; he had proved himself at Camperdown and Copenhagen, and was perhaps chafing at being relegated to patrol duties when action was possible elsewhere. The battle of Trafalgar was in the offing and Bligh would have been useful there.[24] But his friends in the Admiralty and Government were already moving to place him as Governor of New South Wales. He was going to have to deal there with people far more resourceful and capable than Frazier, and he headed for collision with them from the start.

---

[24] Sir Joseph Banks remarked in a letter to Bligh, clearly repeating what he had heard: '& Ld. Nelson not only knows how you conducted your ship when it lay alongside of his Lordship's at Copenhagen, but will not omit any opportunity of giving you Credit' (Banks to Bligh, 17 September 1805, ML MS A78-5). Bligh was in Admiral Collingwood's fleet; it was Collingwood's appreciation of Bligh's fighting qualities, and character references from such as Lord Nelson, that gave Bligh the benefit of the doubt at the court martial. Nelson knew the value in close action of stubborn men who were not afraid of getting their heads shot off; Bligh was a man of this type.

27

New South Wales

The colony at Botany Bay had been established in 1788 when Captain
Phillip had taken a small fleet of transports carrying convicted persons, and
soldiers to guard them, and a small band of civilians, to settle in the new
lands.[1] By 1805 the colony had grown a little, but was not much more than a
foothold on the vast continent of Australia. Governor Phillip returned to
Britain in 1792 and was superseded in 1795 by Governor Hunter. In the
intervening three years the penal colony was run by the military, and in
particular was under the influence of a young officer in the New South Wales
Corps, Lieutenant John MacArthur.[2] The emergence of MacArthur at the
centre of the military government was one of the most important factors in
the formative years of the colony. His dominant influence in the colony's
affairs culminated in the 'Rum Rebellion' of 1808 against Governor Bligh,
which I shall look at in the next chapter.[3] First we need a little background
knowledge of the colony and of MacArthur himself.

When Captain Phillip, R.N. had been sent out to form the penal colony he
had taken with him a detachment of marines who were to act as a military
force for the colonist's protection from native inhabitants or foreign powers.
They had the ancillary job, which in the event became their major activity, of
guarding the convicted persons. Their posting had not been regarded as
permanent, and in due course the Government authorised the mustering of a
new force, specifically designated for the colony, to be known as the New
South Wales Corps. In common with naval careerism, the opportunities
presented to officers by such a corps were calculable; a young officer, such as
MacArthur, could wait three years for promotion elsewhere unless a
battlefield commission was in the offing; an older career soldier could see his
time out in a rank that he might have difficulty holding in a more active or
strenuous unit. Unless war was imminent, prospects for soldiers and naval
officers were not good; in 1789 the signs looked favourable for several years of
peace, which in retrospect says much for the fallibility of human perception.
MacArthur enlisted and rose from Ensign to Lieutenant on transfer. He also
became eligible for a share in the enlistment bonus distributed to officers on

---

[1] Phillip, 1789.
[2] John MacArthur was born in England on 3 September 1767. For an account of his life *see*
Onslow (ed.), 1914; Ellis, 1955. MacArthur came of Scottish stock and the family had left
Scotland at the time of the Culloden war, which enabled them to claim, justifiably or otherwise,
that they had fled from retribution for their part on the side of the Pretender.
[3] *See* also Evatt, 1938.

the number of men they recruited. That MacArthur's motives were material rather than patriotic can be seen in a comment of his wife's to her mother written at the time. 'In my last letter I informed you, my dear Mother, of my husband's exchange into a Corps destined for New South Wales, from which we have every reasonable expectation of reaping the most material advantages.'[4]

The MacArthurs boarded the *Neptune*, one of the ships in the fleet allocated to take the corps and a large party of convicted people to their new home, in November 1789. This was the year of the mutiny on the *Bounty*; by this time Bligh was on his way home to Britain in a Dutch ship with his survivors and Christian had left some of his fellow mutineers on Tahiti and had struck out for an island refuge somewhere in the Pacific. MacArthur and Bligh passed each other on their respective journeys, Bligh on his way to rehabilitate himself with the Admiralty and MacArthur to establish himself in the government of New South Wales.

MacArthur was not an easy man to deal with; he was touchy, obstinate and aggressive. In the *Neptune* he clashed strongly with its Captain, a Mr Gilbert from the merchant service. At first their relations were strained enough for MacArthur to refuse to speak to the Captain; later they deteriorated to the point at which MacArthur felt obliged to challenge Captain Gilbert to a duel, which duly took place when the ships docked at Plymouth after their journey from London. Fortunately neither was hurt.[5] MacArthur had other altercations with the equally irascible Captain Trail, who replaced Gilbert on the voyage. In the end, for the sake of peace all round, MacArthur was transferred at sea from the *Neptune* to the *Scarborough* at his own request. Under Captain Marshall he and his family found a little peace, but when the ships stopped at the Cape of Good Hope, he fell dangerously ill. He was nursed back to life by his wife, Elizabeth, but it is believed that he never really recovered from the illness, which culminated in his seclusion in the latter years of his life and his final collapse into lunacy.

Life in the tiny settlement was not encouraging when they arrived there in June 1790. Out of 1,024 who set out, 280 had died on the voyage. Port Jackson was a messy shanty town and many of its inhabitants were ill or starving.[6] The influx of unhealthy and demoralised new transportees did not help the general picture of decay. Thus things remained for the MacArthurs until Major Grose, commander of the New South Wales Corps, arrived in February 1792. He brought with him the remainder of the Corps and also, as senior commanding officer in the colony after the return to Britain of Captain

[4] Elizabeth MacArthur to Mrs Veale, 8 October 1789, MacArthur Papers, ML MS A2908; also in Onslow (ed.), 1914, pp. 2-3. A2908, headed 'Mrs John Macarthur – extracts from letters', consists of copies made by her son Edward.

[5] MacArthur never had to face military action – his units were not engaged in action. The practice of duelling was common in the British army and was probably a displacement of unexercised military aggressiveness; many of the duels were over absurd disputes and few were lethal. *See Historical Records of New South Wales* (*HRNSW*) Vol. 2, pp. 427-31, for an account of the quarrel; Ellis, 1955, Chapter 2; Onslow (ed.), 1914, p. 5.

[6] According to Onslow (ed.), 1914, p. 20, the colony was in a state of famine, being on rations of 2½ lb of flour, 2 lb of rice and 2 lb of salt pork per person a week.

Phillip, the authority to act as the colony's *de facto* Governor. This gave MacArthur the chance he needed. Grose was a veteran of the American War of Independence. He had fought at Bunker Hill, Fort Montgomery and Monmouth Court House. He was invalided home from wounds and then placed on half-pay until the post as commander of the N.S.W.C. came along. He saw the posting as a comfortable sinecure until retirement and was not looking for heroic action, or, for that matter, for the burden of administration. Phillip's illness and 'temporary' return to Britain thrust the day-to-day administration of the colony onto his shoulders, and he as quickly handed it on to the bright, energetic and ambitious young officer whom he had found on his first day in Sydney Cove, Lieutenant John MacArthur.

MacArthur was a thoroughly good choice from Grose's point of view. He was reliable and moderately honest; he was one of the few family men in the colony, legally married to a respectable lady. He was also enterprising and businesslike. An instance of his entrepreneurship was the chartering of the *Britannia* whaler with subscriptions from regimental officers for the purpose of a round trip to the Cape of Good Hope to fetch comestibles, livestock and stores. MacArthur's position as personal assistant to Major Grose gave him control of the Regimental Funds and the Regimental Store.[7] This was the real source of his leverage on the colony. As military commander at Port Jackson he was left with a free hand to run the colony's affairs, particularly those pertaining to the arrival and departure of ships. The main administrative centre of the colony was at Parramatta, some miles inland. MacArthur therefore supervised the arrival and disposal of goods for the entire colony and inevitably influenced the terms on which they reached their users. In this capacity he had one of his early difficulties with people who stood in his way. This time it concerned the landing of rum. It brought him into a clash with the civil powers. The regimental officers were allocated 25-gallon kegs for their rations and Colonel George Johnston (later to play a central role in the struggle with Bligh) had been prevented by civilian constables from removing the rum from the dockside. The military got their way in the end, but with typical sullenness MacArthur refused to meet Phillip socially for the rest of his time in the colony.[8] The incident itself was trivial; but it was a foretaste of the issues that were to divide the civilian and military powers in the colony until Governor Macquarie replaced Bligh in 1810.

Major Grose became acting Lieutenant-Governor from Phillip's departure in November 1792 until Governor Hunter arrived in September 1795. Grose dispensed with the civilian magistrates. Thenceforward all law, order and justice was held firmly in the hands of serving officers. This gave them a tremendous power over commerce and its twin, labour. Because much of the labour was forced, the opportunities for abuse of power on the side of personal gain were obvious. When MacArthur was appointed the Inspector of Public Works he became virtual controller of the entire life of the colony.

---

[7] *See* Collins, *An Account of the English Colony of New South Wales*, 2 vols, London, 1798, 1802.
[8] *Historical Records of Australia* (*HRA*). First Series, Vol. 6, pp. 239-40.

Agricultural resettlement, for example, was undertaken as an arm of the development policy of the government; it was, in effect, under the label of Public Works. This gave MacArthur the deciding voice in who went where and on what terms. But the most important source of power was accorded to the officers by Grose, in the shape of land grants.

MacArthur acquired land in this way from Grose, as did the other officers.[9] The legality of the grants was confirmed by London in a subsequent order and the arguments in favour of them were plausible. Retired marines and convicted persons who had completed their sentences received lands up to 25 acres, and private citizens or free settlers received more. It was not intended that officers who took on the burdens of serving the colony should receive any grant. This anomaly appears less glaring when the commercial trading habits of the Regiment are taken into account. Their early ventures in the rum business for regimental tippling passed into a monopoly of distribution ashore and of purchase at the docks. During the military government they simply acquired the right to all spirits placed in the colony from any ship. By controlling commerce, in particular the rum trade, the N.S.W.C. were in a position to enrich themselves, though the cash side of the economy was limited by the poverty of the mass of the people. Those who were granted land could complete the circle of commercial transactions; they used their power as military commanders to get convicted persons to labour on their land for wages in the shape of rum, and the rum acted as a medium of exchange among the labourers for their necessities. The military already had London permission for two convicted persons to be used on each farm, and they now used the rum monopoly as a means of enlarging the number of labourers per farm. The labour of the convicts was inefficient and indolent; they had little ambition to work long hours to enrich their jailers. Money was of little value as an incentive, as there was little to spend it upon. A successful money market presumes a market for goods. Rum provided the ideal incentive for work: men would work to acquire rum either for personal consumption or for trade. With the demand for alcoholic escapism at a premium, there was a ready-market for barter wages. It was also a wasting asset as a consumer good; enough would always be drunk by thirsty or tormented souls to ensure a steady requirement for more.

This, then, was the economics of the rum trade. By the accident of history the command of this trade passed to the military. With the unforeseen absence of Captain Phillip, the first Governor, and the delay in his replacement (there was a possibility he would return), the military contrived, partly by accident, partly by design, to entrench themselves at the head of the colony. There was no counter-balancing civil power to prevent them

[9] Onslow (ed.), 1914, p. 21, suggests that the acquisition of land by the officers was part of the colony's effort to increase food production. MacArthur's farm was an instant success. He received his first land grant in 1793 and within a year his farm was 200 acres, with 100 acres under cultivation. He sold some of his first year's crop for £400 (about four times his annual salary) and he stored 1,800 bushels of corn in his granaries, presumably for speculation. He had 2 mares, 2 cows, 130 goats, 100 hogs and poultry in the 'greatest abundance'. His table was 'constantly supplied'. *See* MacArthur Papers, John MacArthur to James MacArthur, 23 August 1794.

assuming this position. The Governors who went out to New South Wales up to 1810 were naval commanders; it was considered a naval posting. This did not lend itself to integration: inter-service rivalry has never been a modest competition of the mild and mannered. The other possible force that could reduce the power of the military – in an economic sense – was that of the so-called free settlers. But these were not a distinct grouping with political power sufficient to put the military in its place. They had no political rights and no institution that could represent those rights. The only alternative to regimental power was civil power exercised through the Governor. Once the officers and soldiers had acquired land they also acquired the basis of civil power, but in antagonism to free settlers.

The British Government in London continued to look for a Governor who could stand up to the *de facto* military power, restore civil power, and above all, resolve the local squabbles and arguments without constant recourse to the opinions of London. This last objective was qualified by an insistence that nothing took place in the administration of the colony that had not been provided for by London. Reconciling this last with the former was impossible, of course. Whenever a Governor resolved a problem by the use of his own initiative the aggrieved party appealed to London. The colony, judging by the official documents, was a difficult place to govern and a source of much petitioning. The points at issue were often petty and were almost always impossible to decide upon at a distance of twelve thousand miles and with a time lag (each way) of ten months to a year. London civil servants and politicians, faced with more pressing problems in Europe, had little time for the streams of letters, reports and petitions emanating from the tiny settlement at the other side of the earth.

The arrival of Captain John Hunter as Governor in 1795 did not reverse the trends in the colony. His administration smashed itself in impotence against the military-business monopoly. What formal powers the Governor had were diverted into the factional battles in the elite of the colony; the issues in dispute were intensely fought, though many were trivial. One incident was fairly serious: some soldiers (one an ex-convict) attacked a civilian, smashed up his house and then formed up and marched off.[10] This incident led to an intense personal feud between MacArthur, for the military, and another civilian who had made the mistake of offending MacArthur by advising the unfortunate victim to insist on his full rights of restitution.[11]

MacArthur, as one of the leading officers of the military regime that had ended with Hunter's arrival, was at the fore in most of the incidents

[10] *HRA*, First Series, Vol. 1, Proceedings, December 3-30, 1795, p. 575. Hunter was unrestrained in his condemnation of this action. He declared that the Corps contained within it many men who would 'have been considered disgraceful to every other Regiment in His Majesty's Service'. *See* Ellis, 1955, pp. 86-7.

[11] MacArthur made abject apologies on behalf of the Corps to the Governor, *see HRA*, First Series, Vol. 1, Proceedings, December 3-30, 1795, p. 579; these were accepted by Hunter who abandoned his intention to court martial the guilty. MacArthur by his apology had won the support of his mess-mates, deprived Hunter of a court martial and the victim of a public redress, and had also gained Hunter the disapproval of the Duke of Portland, who thought the soldiers should have been court-martialled: a typical example of MacArthur's skill as a troublemaker.

associated with the military during Governor Hunter's term of office. Hunter did not get on well with MacArthur, and they did not continue the relationship established under Grose when MacArthur acted as administrator. This did not bother MacArthur, who had made substantial property gains by this time; in fact, it freed him for work on his own behalf. He did not give up his military command after his resignation as aide to the Governor; he continued to exercise this position, with a flair for in-fighting against critics of the N.S.W.C. that would not have disgraced a papal court in sixteenth-century Italy. He fought a long battle with Richard Atkins, a close confidant of Hunter, which naturally embroiled him in conflict with the Governor.[12] His method of factional fighting was to make charges, usually over financial integrity, and then to take his opponent's response as an assault on his honour. In two other cases this behaviour led MacArthur to duelling with his adversaries. In Atkins's case it led to long rambling exchanges of correspondence, mostly Georgian invective and expressions of wounded dignity. The correspondence and various documents were even sent to London for perusal by Ministers; the Duke of Portland was drawn into the business, though he attempted to keep a sense of proportion.

In common with other officers, MacArthur grew more prosperous. By 1798 his land holding had grown to 500 acres of good farmland, well supplied with water, and he had a work force of forty men to do the chores. He had fifty head of cattle, a dozen horses and one thousand sheep. None of this was a discredit to his energy in pursuit of his own interests, but nevertheless it was no mean achievement for somebody on military pay of under £100 a year. The stock alone was worth about £5,000. No wonder Mrs MacArthur could report to her friend in Britain: 'You see how bountifully Providence has dealt with us.'[13] Mrs MacArthur explained the system of profit-taking: 'The officers in the Colony with a few others possessed of money or credit in England unite together & purchase the Cargoes of such Vessels as repair to this Country from various Quarters. Two or more are chosen from the number to bargain for the Cargo offered for sale which is then divided amongst them, in proportion to the amount of their subscription.'[14] The cartel-like effect of this agreement is underlined in the second part of it, not disclosed by Mrs MacArthur, that the members of the purchasing co-operative bound themselves under penalty of £1000 not to purchase goods from ships that did not sell their cargoes through the two agents. As the co-operative involved the majority of the richest persons in the colony, a ship's master arriving there faced the choice of a deal with the co-operative or no deal at all. Because there was always the possibility that an individual might break away from the buying agreement and offer a price to a captain above the cartel price, the

[12] The quarrel arose because MacArthur was alleged by Atkins to purchase grain for the government stores from the military only, leaving civilian farmers with excess stocks and low prices, and giving the officers a guaranteed income at high government prices; *see HRA*, First Series, Vol. 2, 1795, pp. 96-7; MacArthur to Hunter, 27 February 1796; *see also* Ellis, 1955, Chapter 9. Hunter believed Atkins and appointed him to replace MacArthur as official purchaser for the military.

[13] Elizabeth MacArthur to Miss Kingdon, quoted in Onslow (ed.), 1914, p. 52.

[14] Elizabeth MacArthur to Miss Kingdon, 1 September 1795, MacArthur Papers, ML A2908.

partners in this enterprise agreed to 'avoid the company' of any person who tried to go it alone.[15] The consequence of this arrangement was that instead of competition among the merchants and traders which would force the buying price up, they were able to keep the buying price down while setting a high selling price for the citizens, the difference constituting their profits.

Portland, and the British Government, were always appalled at the misuse of regimental time and resources on trade. Constant instructions were issued to end officer participation in commerce, without any effect.[16] Hunter was recalled by London in 1800 and Governor Captain Philip Gidley King appointed to succeed him.[17] Portland wanted somebody to clear up the mess and set the colony on the road to commercial prosperity; he did not make a good choice. He also demanded evidence and the names of officers who were engaged in the trading. Colonel George Johnston was the only man specifically charged with improper trading, though every officer in the Corps was involved. MacArthur was left alone. He had made a timely change by resigning as aide to the Governor; this had brought other men, such as Johnston, into Hunter's entourage, and involved them more publicly with the colony's management. MacArthur was able, by virtue of his wealth and financial credit, to participate in the trading without advertising his presence.

The arrival of Captain King heralded a change in policy in the colony. It was believed that the officers were to be deprived of their commercial interests, and the more perceptive of them decided that it was a good moment to quit gracefully. Governor Hunter, Captain Kent (R.N.), Major Foveaux and MacArthur made early offers to Governor King to sell the Government their livestock. MacArthur offered to sell his interests for the sume of £4000.[18] This was well below any reasonable valuation of his property. MacArthur's offer was made after Hunter had sailed for Britain. He also expressed a desire to return to Britain. King wrote to London asking for permission to make the purchases. After Hunter's rather 'profligate administration King had been warned to correct financial imprudence. If he had bought MacArthur out the colony's history might have been changed. Portland was not impressed with the bargain and remarked sardonically: 'Considering Captain MacArthur in the capacity of an officer on duty with his regiment, I can by no means account for his being a farmer to the extent

[15] *HRA*, First Series, Vol. 2, p. 169.

[16] *ibid.*, p. 38, Portland to Hunter, 5 November 1799; Portland regarded the agreement as 'a sanction to officers engaging in traffic' which 'may be found to have disgraced his Majesty's service in the persons of several of the officers of the New South Wales Corps'. It was the ordinary people who suffered, as they had to buy from the traders. *See ibid.*, pp. 445-6, 'Petition of Hawkesbury settlers to Governor Hunter', 1 February 1800: 'When ships arrive, the officers, civil and military, are exclusively admitted on board ... they there forestall the whole of the cargo, and then retail it to the colony at the most extortionate rates. Also *ibid.*, p. 443, 'Settlers' Appeal to Secretary of State' (Duke of Portland), quotes increases in prices from ship to shore under the officers' monopoly of 500 to 1,000 per cent.

[17] King had been with Phillip on the First Fleet voyage and had been recommended by Phillip as his successor.

[18] *HRA*, First Series, Vol. 1, pp. 524-6.

he appears to be, and I must highly disapprove of the Commanding Officer of the Corps to which he belongs allowing him or any other officer to continue in such contradictory situations and characters.'[19]

MacArthur's interest in returning to Britain may have been connected with the development of sheep in the colony. Several of the landowners were developing an interest in sheep with a view to the future export of wool. MacArthur had been doing so on a small scale aimed more at improving the quality of the wool by selective cross-breeding. When he offered his stock for sale King had sent some samples of the wool he had produced by his selective breeding to Sir Joseph Banks. If Banks knew good quality wool so did others, and MacArthur must have been convinced he was on to something worthy of a gamble. To sell his farm and stocks and return to Britain was not a permanent abandonment of the colony; far from it. MacArthur was merely hoping to finance a visit home in order to acquire major land grants and good quality sheep for breeding within New South Wales.. His subsequent behaviour confirms this. MacArthur was astute enough to know that the rum trade and the purchasing monopoly were not assured means to future wealth. Sooner or later they would end. The real future lay in the wool trade, worth millions of pounds, instead of a few thousand in rum and cargoes. By valuing his property at £4,000 MacArthur also ensured he had some alibi that represented his wealth at a more acceptable figure than the £20,000 which gossip claimed he had acquired since he arrived.[20]

MacArthur's return to Britain took place in a less respectable fashion than he had anticipated. He was sent back under arrest for court martial. It was his habit of getting involved in duelling that occasioned this mode of transportation. The immediate cause of his arrest was a duel he had fought with his commanding officer, Lieutenant-Colonel Paterson, in which Paterson had been hit in the shoulder by MacArthur's bullet.[21] This was in September 1801. He went home at the Government's expense this way, taking with him two of his children, a file on the case, and some samples of his wool. When he arrived in Britain his children went to an English school, his case was considered and the charges dismissed, and he provoked a sensation in Government circles about the quality of his wool at a time when the Spanish Peninsula was disrupted by Napoleon's armies and the wool trade was therefore in a supply crisis. Everything went so smoothly that one

---

[19] *ibid.*, Vol. 3, p. 101, Portland to King, 19 June 1801.

[20] Governor King wrote of him: 'He came here in 1790 more than £500 in debt, and is now worth at least £20,000. His fortune, and thro' accumulating gains in this colony, by the great quantity of stock and land he possesses, enables him to boast of his indifference of whatever change happens to him. His employment during the eleven years he has been here has been that of making a large fortune, helping his brother officers to make small ones (mostly at the publick expense) and sowing discord and strife. The points I have brought home to him are such that, if properly investigated, must certainly occasion his quitting the New South Wales Corps and the Army. But come out here again he certainly must, as a very large part of his immense fortune is vested here in numerous herds, flocks and vast domains.' *HRA*, First Series, Vol. 3, pp. 321-2, Letter, Governor King to Under Secretary King, 8 November 1801.

[21] *ibid.*, p. 280, Letter, King to Portland, 5 November 1801; Paterson is thought to have written to Sir Joseph Banks in terms which prejudiced Banks against MacArthur.

20. John MacArthur.

21. Mrs John MacArthur.

22. Cartoon: Arrest of Governor Bligh (26 January 1808).

may wonder whether he had deliberately engineered the situation to suit himself.

King had ordered MacArthur and the papers of the case to be sent to Britain in an attempt to clear himself. Instead of doing him good, as King had hoped, it only poisoned his own standing with the home Government. They were of the opinion that King should have administered any discipline himself in the colony,[22] and they probably dispaired of ever finding anybody to keep this unruly place in order. Thousands of Irish rebels were pressed into naval service at this time by London and hundreds of the most resolute in their rejection of British rule were shipped to New South Wales. Governor King's government relied on the military to protect it from Fenian plots and, unable to control the military, he directed his anger at the Irish, which meant that many unfortunates who came before his court got sentences of one thousand lashes or a hanging.

MacArthur set about his major mission as soon as his interviews with the War Office were completed. The Government, through the Privy Council, enquired into the possibilities of establishing a wool industry in New South Wales. After much deliberation it recommended that steps be taken to do just this. MacArthur was a star performer at the enquiry, and impressed them enough for a recommendation to be made that he be given extensive land grants and labour to develop his enterprise. The acreage offered was 5,000 acres and another 5,000 acres if his scheme was a success, ten times the acreage of his Parramatta farm. It was a triumph for MacArthur and marked his transition from the Rum Corps to civilian life as a major landowner and sheep farmer. He had official backing from Government and a generous land grant in his pocket. His return to the colony in this new situation was a turning point. Governor King had been shown to be lacking in judgement and the colony to be still lacking in order and discipline – yet another Irish rebellion had broken out and had been put down at some cost in the broken bodies of Irish patriots. The Government saw in MacArthur the means to raise the penal colony to a flourishing part of the Empire, providing Britain with good quality Spanish wool and, from its rising incomes and prosperity, a market for British manufacturers. That Governor King should be retired was not doubted; the question was when, and by whom he should be replaced. MacArthur and Sir Joseph Banks had fallen out, which meant that MacArthur had an enemy close to the Government and the King. Because Banks would have a major say in who was sent out to replace King, it followed that whoever Banks selected was bound to regard MacArthur in an unfriendly light. Given that Banks chose Bligh, the 'unfriendly' view was likely to prevail unremittingly, and so it did.

A public clash between Banks and MacArthur came about when the latter tried to purchase from the Royal Merino stock at Kew in August 1804.[23]

---

[22] *ibid.*, Vol. 4, pp. 37-8, Letter, Hobart to King, 24 February 1803. The argument against King's bringing MacArthur before a court martial in New South Wales was that the Court would consist of officers of the Corps, all beholden to MacArthur for pecuniary reasons, let alone their regimental solidarity.

[23] *HRA*, First Series, Vol. 5, pp. 834-5; Onslow (ed.), 1914, pp. 99ff.

Banks attempted to thwart MacArthur's plans by raising an ancient Act of Parliament against the export of sheep. His move was unsuccessful because MacArthur appealed to Lord Camden, who was in support of the wool industry venture. Banks's next move was to get Camden to reduce the land grant from 10,000 to 5,000 acres, presumably emphasising the sheer vastness of such a single grant to a person who only yesterday, so to speak, was a penniless Lieutenant in His Majesty's army and was also widely believed to have misused his position while in the colony to enrich himself, if not directly, then certainly indirectly, at the public expense.[24] Sir Joseph made several attempts to discredit MacArthur's schemes for wool production in New South Wales. His view that the sheep would not prosper in Australia was not a considered scientific opinion but part of his efforts to prevent MacArthur getting support from the Government. Banks was persuaded to his opinion by information about the colony and his knowledge of MacArthur's activities over the years. He simply did not consider him a fit person to be made into a rich man by courtesy of the government.

In March 1805 Lord Camden invited Sir Joseph to consider possible names for nomination as the new Governor of New South Wales. This was a short time after the *Warrior* court martial and four months after MacArthur had sailed from Portsmouth for Sydney on his return voyage. Banks had no doubt who should go out to Sydney and bring the colony to order. He immediately wrote to Bligh:[25]

My Dear Sir,
An opportunity has occurred this day which seems to me to lay open an opportunity of being of service to you; and as I hope I never omit any chance of being useful to a friend whom I esteem, as I do you, I lose not a minute in apprising you of it.

I have always, since the first institution of the new colony in New South Wales, taken a deep interest in its success, and have been constantly consulted by His Majesty's Ministers, through all the changes there have been in the department which directs it, relative to the more important concerns of the colonists.

At present, King, the Governor, is tired of his station; and well he may be so. He has carried into effect a reform of great extent, which militated much with the interests of the soldiers and settlers there. He is, consequently, disliked and much opposed, and has asked leave to return. In conversation I was this day asked if I knew a man proper to be sent out in his stead – one who had integrity unimpeached, a mind capable of providing its own resources in difficulties without leaning on others for advice, firm in discipline, civil in deportment and not subject to whimper and whine when severity of discipline is wanted to meet emergencies. I immediately answered: As this man must be chosen from among the post

---

[24] *See* Onslow (ed.), 1916, p. 101: 'My father was about to quit England', writes James MacArthur, 'when Lord Camden sent for him, and said that Sir Joseph Banks had been pointing out that 10,000 acres seemed an enormous grant. "Would you, Mr. MacArthur, object to take 5,000 at first, with the understanding that the other 5,000 shall be given on the completion of your undertaking?" To this, my father at once acquiesced.'

[25] *HRNSW*, Vol. 6, Part 35; Quoted in Mackaness, 1951, p. 352-3.

captains, I know of no one but Captain Bligh who will suit, but whether it will meet his views is another question.

I can, therefore, if you chuse it, place you in the government of the new colony, with an income of £2,000 a year, and with the whole of the Government power and stores at your disposal so that I do not see how it is possible for you to spend £1,000; in truth, King, who is now there, receives only £1,000 with some deductions, and yet lives like a prince, and, I believe, saves some money; but I could not undertake to recommend any one unless £2,000 clear was given, as I think that a man who undertakes so great a trust as the management of an important colony should be certain of living well and laying up a provision for his family. I apprehend that you are about 55 years old; if so, you have by the tables an expectation of 15 years' life, and in a climate like that, which is the best that I know, a still better expectation; but in 15 years, £1,000 a year will, at compound interest of 5 per cent, have produced more than £30,000, and in case you do not like to spend your life there, you will have a fair claim on your return to a pension of £1,000 a year. Besides if your family goes out with you, as I conclude they would, your daughters will have a better chance of marrying suitably there than they can have here; for as the colony grows richer every year, and something of trade seems to improve, I can have no doubt but that in a few years there will be men there very capable of supporting wives in a creditable manner; and very desirous of taking them from a respectable and good family.

Tell me, dear Sir, when you have consulted your pillow, what you think of this. To me, I confess, it appears a promising place for a man who has entered late into the status of a post-captain, and the more so as your rank will go on, for Phillip, the first governor, is now an admiral, holding a pension for his services in the country.

Joseph Banks

Banks was putting considerable pressure on Bligh to accept the offer. He makes explicit how much he has done for Bligh over the years and how much he has secured for him in the offer of the Governorship of the colony. There was scarcely anything he did not use: flattery about Bligh's character, increased pay (double, in fact), a proper pension, continuation of his rank in the Navy which ensured his Admiral's flag, and even marriage prospects for his several daughters. What was Banks up to? Was he calculating that if anyone could stop MacArthur's plans it was Bligh? It is hard to say now what was the intention behind the recommendation. Bligh was unlikely to tread carefully when faced with the problems of discipline and public order presented by the unruly colony. Nor was he likely to give MacArthur an easy time once Sir Joseph made it clear that he would receive with approbation details of how Bligh had interfered with MacArthur's grandiose schemes for enriching himself still further at the public expense.

Whatever may have been in Banks's mind in nominating Bligh, the fact is that Bligh accepted the offer of the Governorship, subject to certain minor conditions. This meant his leaving active sea duty as a Post Captain. With military action developing against the French, he had some hopes of engaging in a sea-battle, but this prospect was uncertain. In fact Nelson's

victory at Trafalgar in 1805 was to reduce the possibility of a major sea battle
on the Camperdown or Copenhagen scale. Banks's offer looked tempting;
the financial inducement was persuasive to a family man with six daughters.
This, plus the personal appeal of Sir Joseph, tipped the scale decisively
towards acceptance. Bligh decided to exchange the quarter-deck of the
Warrior for the Governor's House at Parramatta.

This meant a difficult domestic decision. Elizabeth Bligh was against
leaving Britain. They had been married since 1781. She was fifty-two years
old and apparently had an 'extreme horror' of the sea and would not
consider the long voyage to Australia. She had been ill quite a lot recently
and Bligh thought the voyage 'would be her death'.[26] He too was beginning
to show his age and the accumulated ravages of his experiences at sea: his
illness from the long open boat voyage, the fevers he caught at Batavia, the
headaches from the *Providence*, and the rheumatics from the North Sea. We do
not know what domestic conferences took place nor what pressures were put
on Bligh by his wife on the one hand and his sponsor on the other. Bligh was
devoted to both, but in the end Elizabeth had to make the best of the
inevitable, as she had done so often in the past.

In April 1805, Lord Camden, having received Bligh's agreement to accept
the Governorship, recommended his appointment to the King. On 29 April
1805 Bligh was superseded as commander of the *Warrior* and his half-salary
as Governor of New South Wales commenced from that date. There were
several administrative details to be sorted out, including his salary, which
appears to have got mixed up for a while with the old rate of £1,000 a year.
The agreement was substantially the same as originally offered by Banks,
with the points raised by Bligh added. He was to get £2,000 a year with no
deductions, a good chance of a pension of half-pay, his rank in the navy to
continue and his son-in-law, Lieutenant Putland, to accompany him as his
aide. He was to go to Botany Bay in the transport *Lady Madeleine Sinclair*
under escort of H.M.S. *Porpoise*. The command of the convoy was given to
Captain Joseph Short.[27]

Bligh left Britain for New South Wales in February 1806, nearly a year
after he was appointed Governor. His voyage out was marked by a furious
row between him and Captain Short, the commander of the small fleet of
transports. When MacArthur first went out to New South Wales he too had
quarrelled furiously with the ship's captains, duelling with one of them, and
Bligh's row probably stemmed from a similar cause: excessive personal
determination not to be slighted by anybody. Bligh was senior to Short on
the Post Captains' list; and Short was dependent on the goodwill of the new
Governor. He had decided to emigrate to New South Wales and settle there
as a landowner. He had been promised a grant of 600 acres which was to be
conferred by the Governor.[28] He had sold his own property in Britain and
had invested (he claimed) considerable sums of money in farming

[26] Bligh to Banks, 25 April 1805, 28 September 1805; Banks to Bligh, 31 April 1805. Banks
Papers, Brabourne Collection, ML MS A84.
[27] Colonial Office Papers, 201/39 15, PRO, London.
[28] Colonial Office Papers 201/38. Short to Cooke, 24 July 1805, PRO, London.

implements and stocks. He was also a married man with seven children, all of whom accompanied him on the voyage. It is remarkable in these circumstances that he persisted in trying to thwart a man who never hesitated to make life difficult for those who opposed him.

The row seems to have been about who was in overall command of the convoy. Short's instructions were to take command of the convoy and bring it to New South Wales, and there place himself under the command of Governor Bligh, who was to command all naval vessels in Australian waters.[29] Being the senior man, Bligh was made nominal First Captain of H.M.S. *Porpoise* but he made the journey in the more comfortable transport ship, *Lady Madeleine Sinclair*. Captain Short was captain of the *Porpoise*. From an operational point of view Short was in command, but this was not incompatible with due deference to Bligh's status. Somehow Short offended Bligh's conception of his status, and Short's recognisable general slackness as a commander did nothing to smoothe over the differences. Travelling as a passenger must have irked Bligh on the long months of the voyage, particularly as he had made the journey thrice before during his career.[30] He was the kind of person who always compared his ideas of performance with what he witnessed in others. These matters were not entirely academic, given the safety record of ships at the time. It is hardly conceivable that Bligh would have refrained from interfering in matters of navigation and seamanship, especially where he disagreed with the way they were being carried out. For Short the voyage to Australia was likely to be his last command; he wanted control all the way, and saw no valid reason why he should defer to Governor Bligh who, while senior on the list, was in his view, retired from naval duty.

Rather than try to disentangle the rights and wrongs of this unnecessary quarrel, for once I intend to present only one side of the question, and from an admittedly biased witness at that, namely, Bligh's daughter Mary. Mary was travelling out to Australia with her father in the company of her husband, Lieutenant Putland. She wrote an extremely long letter to her mother,[31] probably to occupy her time during the voyage, and it gives a vivid

---

[29] The confusion arose because Short's instructions specified he was to command 'the *Porpoise* on all occasions in the absence of Captain Bligh'. As Bligh was travelling in the other ship, Short interpreted this as 'absence' from the *Porpoise* and acted accordingly. Bligh told Short he was 'subject to my control and guidance'. *See* Banks Papers, Brabourne Collection, Mitchell Library MS A84, p. 127.

[30] Bligh had sailed most of the convoy route with Cook in the *Resolution*, 1777; in the *Bounty*, 1788; and the *Providence*, 1791; he had also made a voyage to St Helena in the *Director*, 1799.

[31] Mary Putland (née Bligh) to Mrs Elizabeth Bligh, 26 February etc., 1806, Bligh Correspondence, ML MS Safe 1/45. The letter is twenty three pages long. Additional contemporary evidence about this quarrel is found in Friendly, 1977, which quotes the opinion of Captain (later Admiral) Francis Beaufort. He was in command of H.M.S. *Woolwich* which arrived at the Cape two days after Bligh's convoy. On the dispute and its course Beaufort was extremely critical: 'they were both wrong, both had acted intemperately and foolishly, both had laid themselves open to censure, which both will probably meet with, and both were equally resolved to stick to what they had already done and not to retract a single expression.' Beaufort goes on to judge between the two men, as he must acknowledge one or the other as the senior officer: 'I immediately pronounced for Capt. Bligh ... and whatever I thought of their mutual conduct, I perceived that one was a man of talents and the other an ass.' Beaufort's papers are in the Henry E. Huntington Library, San Marino, California.

account of the increasing tension, and the passionate feelings that were aroused over such a trivial cause.

Mrs Putland writes:

...I fear I shall never be able to forgive Captn. Short, for keeping Putland at that time, when it would have been the greatest comfort to me, could I have had him to speak to at nights, as I could never sleep; if his duty was requisite I should not feel angry, but we have it under his own hand (Captn. Shorts) that it is not, his gunner being very competent to take charge of a watch.[32]

Feb. 27. This Morning Captn. Short sent Putland on board with a copy of his secret orders, I suppose not knowing that Papa had received a copy from the Admiralty.[33] He also sent a letter from himself, saying, he wished to consult with my Father upon different subjects; as, whether he thought it advisable to touch at Rio (his orders only mentioning the Cape) being fearful the convict ships would be in distress for water, &c., &c., Putland returned with 'Captn. Blighs' compliments to Captn. Short and expects to see him on board; not being able to discuss those subjects properly upon paper.' Captn. S. sent back his comps to my Father & could not think of waiting upon him untill he had received an answer to his letter. Papa, then wrote to him, exactly the same message he had just before sent verbally, and the *gentleman* then thought proper to come on board; & strange to relate, behaved in the most polite, and condescending manner; said he should now consider my Father his superior, & Commanding Officer; should obey his signals, (which had before refused to do) and as to Mr Putland, if Papa would give him a letter to that effect, he had not the least objection to his remaining in the *Lady Sinclair*. It is difficult to account for this odd behaviour. I hope Papa will not have any farther trouble with him, that he choses to be amicable, makes me quite happy; as I much feared some of his impertinent messages, would have obliged my Father, to take command of the *Porpoise*. I know it will give you pleasure to hear, that every body admires his conduct, in treating them with the proper contempt they deserve, nor appearing to take notice of any of them.

March 2. You will be astonished to find, that Papa has this Morning, received fresh insults from Captn. Short.

Upon my Father's going on board to seal his commission which was necessary after leaving the Kings Dominions, Captn. S. broke out into the most insulting language which Papa, bore with the greatest mildness, not answering to any of it. This increased the insolence of the others; and at last he told Papa, that he assumed a title which he had no right to, untill he arrived at the colony, and had sealed his comission. On leaving the ship, Papa said to the first Lieutenant, he hoped soon to have the pleasure of seeing him; when Captn. Short immediately answered 'I shall not allow any officers to quit the ship I shall keep Lieunt Putland on board, & make

[32] Lieutenant Putland was serving under Captain Short on H.M.S. *Porpoise* during the voyage, and was therefore separated from his wife.

[33] It was a common practice for the Admiralty to give Commanders secret orders to be opened at sea; we can recollect that Bligh waited until the *Bounty* was in the Atlantic before he opened his on that occasion. Short's orders came from Admirals Patton, Graves and Gambier, and were dated 15 November 1805, some months before the convoy left Britain. *See* Colonial Office Papers, 201/39, PRO, London.

him attend strictly to his duty!' ... It is strange he should behave so, knowing, that on his arrival at Port Jackson, he is ordered to put himself under my Fathers command.

March 4. At 10 o'clock this Morning, Papa, went on board the *Alexander* to see the state of the ship, and convicts; they poor unfortunate creatures, were delighted to see him and upon his telling them, that if Captn. Brooks[34] reported their behaviour to be such, during the voyage, as deserved it, he should do all in his power, to ameliorate their situation, they appeared quite happy ...

March 7. To day Putland got leave to dine with us, which was more than I expected from the late expressions of his Captain ... He tells us all the Officers remark the very ungentlemanlike conduct of Captn. Short and the very cool and contrary behaviour of Papa's ...

March 9. We were given to understand, that, Mr G. was commissioned by Captn. Short to try and conciliate matters; knowing that the *Justiana* leaves us in a day or two, he is much afraid, my Father will write to the Secretary of State concerning him: and he is not mistaking; the insults being so public, Papa, is obliged to do it in hopes of getting him superseded ...

March 15. The day before yesterday, in the evening, I went upon deck with Papa for a little walk; during which time, Captn. Short made the signal, for our ship to steer more to windward, and immediately fired a shot at us, and in about ten minutes repeated it: I assure you I did not much like it and it was considered a very insulting thing to my Father.[35] The bad conduct of Captn. Short has taken up Papa's whole time for this week past, nor has he yet finished. I cannot describe how much it has vexed him on account of its interference with his private letters. 3 o'clock, p.m. [Putland took a message from Short to Bligh]: [Putland] can scarcely speak from agitation, upon the subject of the Shot which were fired at us, the day before yesterday, Captn. S. had the brutality, to make him fire them; [that is he was Officer of the Watch] and told him, to prepare a third, for if we did not bear down immediately, he was to fire right into us. I think such an inhuman thing, as making a man fire at his Father, and Wife, was never done before.

Captain Short began to think more prudently about his position during the voyage and made attempts to reach a reconciliation. But Bligh would be satisfied only with total submission; failing that, he would wait until the convoy reached Sydney to prepare his vengeance, which was ruthless. On arrival of the convoy at Port Jackson Bligh began his public humiliation of Short. He left the *Lady Madeleine Sinclair* for the *Porpoise* and, once on board, hoisted his flag and claimed the command. Then he visited every ship in the convoy, receiving the appropriate salute from the guns and the manned yards, and then landed to a formal welcome becoming the status of a new Governor.

Short had arrested his ship's Master, Daniel Lyle, on the voyage for a breach of discipline. He had also quarrelled with his First Lieutenant, J.S. Tetley (the one invited by Bligh to supper on the *Lady Madeleine Sinclair*). Bligh

[34] Captain Brooks later became a friend of the Blighs.
[35] These shots may have been signal guns which Mrs Putland misunderstood; but if Putland is to be believed, Short was committing an incredibly foolish act.

used this quarrel to undermine Short instead of charging him himself. A Court of Enquiry was set up to sort out the rights and wrongs of the row between Short and his officers. The Court adjudged Short to be guilty and the charges against Lyle and Tetley (made by Short) were found not proven, presumably on the grounds that Short was the only witness. This placed Short in a difficulty in that *prima facie* he was liable to a court martial for the breaches of naval discipline he had been charged with. Short then tried unsuccessfully to make formal counter-charges against Lyle and Tetley in a second Court of Enquiry. This only weakened his position still further and cleared the way for a court martial, which meant he would have to return to Britain.

Having made a judicial case against Short by using the charges of others against him, Bligh accompanied these measures with official procrastination in awarding Short his land grant. Lord Camden had promised Short 600 acres but had not taken the necessary official steps to inform Bligh of his decision. Without a written instruction from Camden, Bligh was able to argue, he had no authority to issue a grant to Short. The only evidence Short had regarding his land grant was a letter from Camden's Secretary, Mr Cooke, stating clearly what Lord Camden intended to do about the grant.[36] Bligh informed Short that until he had official instructions he could not make a grant and he wrote to London asking for instructions, knowing full well that by the time these instructions were carried back Short would either be in desperate financial straits (with his investments tied up in agricultural equipment he could not use) or on his way back to Britain for his court martial. To avoid this last, Short had to clear himself of the Lyle and Tetley charges and to make the charges against them stick. He achieved neither.

The charges between Short and his officers were trivial and less substantial than the charges that Bligh could have brought (firing on the Governor's ship was serious enough).[37] But Bligh had no wish to return home as a major witness to a court martial on Short and neither did he wish to send Lieutenant Putland home as a witness. Putland was dying of consumption and probably would not survive the journey. The first Court of Enquiry, hearing the mutual charges of Short, Lyle and Tetley, concluded, probably justly, that the personal relations of the officers of the *Porpoise* were 'full of personal rancour, prejudice and partiality'.[38] In other circumstances that would have been the end of it, but Bligh was not interested in a proper perspective on this matter; his intentions were to destroy Short.

Using the decisions of the Courts of Enquiry, Bligh ordered Short home to be tried on those charges. He ordered Lyle and Tetley home as the main witnesses. Short had no choice but to go, though he attempted to exercise his rights by refusing to leave H.M.S. *Porpoise*. He would have to take his family with him, as without the land grant he would not leave them any means of support; his wife was one again pregnant and also, unfortunately, ill. His

[36] *See HRNSW*, Vol. 6, p. 174, note 2.

[37] It was alleged that Bligh persuaded Short's officers to proffer charges; this may or may not be true. Tetley later (1808) made an affidavit to the effect that he had not been influenced by Governor Bligh in making his charges.

[38] Quoted in Mackaness, 1951, p. 358.

action only got him deeper into trouble and Bligh ordered his arrest and forcible removal from the *Porpoise* and his detention in H.M.S. *Buffalo*.

On the way home Short's wife died, and also one of his children. He claimed that he had lost his savings by having to sell his agricultural equipment at a substantial loss. These blows were made even more painful by the verdict of the court martial that he be honourably acquitted. The Court also made a representation to the Admiralty that Short be compensated in some way for his treatment. He was not sent back to Australia but posted to the Sea Fencibles and eventually the Marines, seeing service in Canada. The court had some hard things to say about the conduct of Lyle and Tetley, whom it believed to have been influenced by Governor Bligh in pursuing the charges.[39] Opinion was not entirely one-sided in the Admiralty and the Colonial office on the issue. Bligh wrote in great detail his complaints about Short's conduct on the voyage in letters to Sir Joseph Banks. His daughter's letters to Mrs Bligh, and her account of the discomforts caused by Short, assured him of Mrs Bligh's support in their circle of friends. But the President of the court martial of Short, Sir Isaac Coffin, was able to use the Court's verdict, properly laced with his own indignation, as a means by which to press the claims of his friend, Captain William Kent, for appointment as Governor in Bligh's place.[40]

If Coffin was adamantly anti-Bligh, Sir Joseph Banks was as adamantly understanding as he always was when Bligh's affairs were in dispute. He wrote to Bligh regarding the conduct of Short: 'I have never met with such a series of misconduct & misrepresentation as has occurd in the case of Lieut. Short. I am confident that it is a matter of study with him how he can most effectually offend & irritate those Superiors with whom he is to act in order to extort from them Severities in return for his Crimes, which he may afterwards complain of as oppressions & cruelties which render him deserving of compassion and recompence.' He went on to describe the situation in Government regarding Bligh's good name: 'All I hear in Lord Castlereaghs Office however is in your favor, your Talents your perseverance & your spirited conduct are spoken of in terms of praise which flatter me, you may be sure as much as they can do you.'[41]

Political in-fighting over the Governorship went on throughout 1808 in London; everybody was ignorant of the fact that in January Bligh had been deposed by an insurrection of the New South Wales Corps. While those in London sought authority to remove him as Governor, others in the colony had taken the dangerous step of removing him without authority. The aims and ends of the London faction and the Sydney factions did not coincide, except that they both wanted to remove Bligh as Governor. To his London enemies he was in the way of their own appointees to the now lucrative post of Governor of

---

[39] *Proceedings of a Court Martial on Captain Joseph Short* (Copy), Banks Papers, Brabourne Collection, ML MS A85.

[40] For Admiral Coffin's correspondence with the Admiralty regarding Short see *HRNSW*, Vol. 6, p. 388, Coffin to W. Pole, 13 December 1807; Captain Kent had been in the Colony during the Grose military administration and had acquired considerable property, including an interest in sheep-rearing and the wool trade. He was thus well acquainted with the financial possibilities of the Governorship.

[41] Banks to Bligh, 25 August 1808, Banks Papers, Brabourne Collection, ML MS A78-5.

the unruly colony; for those in Australia, he stood in the way of their privileged trading positions, and, in the case of John MacArthur, he was in the way of the great Australian dream of a million sheep and riches from the wool trade.

Mrs Bligh was acting as a formidable political campaigner on her husband's behalf. She wrote to him in February 1808 (while he was already under 'arrest'):[42]

You will now see my love that the alarm I felt when I wrote to you by the *Sinclair* was not without foundation – but thank God your enemies have not gained their ends – their only wish was to have you recalled, they did not care upon what footing; if to answer charges, or to come home to defend yourself they cared not – so they made you leave N. S. Wales ... I have done every thing in my power to interest your friends – and had Sir Joseph not been in the Gout I think the Admiralty would not have gone the length of sending Sir Isaacs letter to the Secretary of States Office – but there they had the mortification to be told that a quarrel between a Capt. and Lieut. was not thought a sufficient reason to recall a Governor. This has made them all very desperate – Kent will never venture to N. S. Wales while you are there – General Grosse had some hopes but he also looks forward.[43] King had applied to the Duke of Clarence[44] for his interest to succeed you – the Duke told Fanny this when she was lately at Bushy – King told the Duke that the Government of N. S. Wales as you now had it was good £3000 pr Anm, and that he should like much to go back; but poor wretch, he has been laid up for a length of time in the gout and unable to move hand or foot and is going to Bath to try to prolong his worthless life which must have been a chain of fraud and deceit – I am told that he has lately tried to go out as Naval Officer – but Mr Cooke knows him too well.

The only thing your friends are anxious about is to remove any Record that may remain against you at the Admiralty which might be a pretence hereafter to prevent you getting your Flag should it come to you before you return, and this I make no doubt Sir Joseph will accomplish – The malice and cruelty of the people who were engaged in this bussiness exceeds everything I ever thought men capable of. Kent went down to Ports[mouth] in the same Chaise with King, and at Hunter's Lodgings with Short planned the bussiness – Foveaux was very active against you.[45] Sir Isaac Coffin who was President of the C. Martial of Tetley against Short, went the greatest

[42] Letter from Mrs Bligh to Bligh, Bligh Family Correspondence, Safe 1/45, pp. 123-5.

[43] It is of interest that each of the named aspirant Governors had been in Australia in one capacity or another, including, in King's case, that of Governor. None of them was motivated by altruism in soliciting for Bligh's recall: they simply wanted to get back to the Colony and make money.

[44] The Duke of Clarence was heir apparent to the throne and also a friend of William Bligh – they had met socially on several occasions, and Bligh as late as 1812 introduced Mathhew Flinders to the Royal Court through his contact with the Duke of Clarence.

[45] Mrs Bligh's allegations of a faction containing these men places an entirely different gloss on the allegations arising out of the Short court martial. If Short was advised by Kent, King and Hunter (all experienced and senior naval commanders – two of them ex-Governors) on how to proceed with the court martial, the Chairman of which, in the person of Admiral Coffin, was pushing Captain Kent for the Governor's post which required the recall of Governor Bligh, this destroys attempts by some authors to condemn Bligh with the Court's verdict as if the Court was making an objective assessment of the dispute. For an example of reasoning along these lines *see* Ellis, 1955, pp. 259-60; there is no mention in his book of the relationships between Short, Coffin, Kent and King.

lengths against you, but these you will have learnt from Captn. Jackson &c. He even went so far as to report against you at the Admiralty that during the scarcity in the Colony you had supplied the merchant ships for your own emolument. Mr Marsden[46] says he knows the transactions they allude to and he thinks King must have given them their information ... Mr Daysh desires me to beg you to be extremely cautious and not push things to extremities with any one, for you have a great many enemies.[47] I believe I told you that Sir Joseph said this gave him the higher opinion of your abilities ... I went through a great deal of anxiety about this wicked bussiness, but am now highly pleased at the train we have got it in – had I been absent all their scheme would have been kept secret – and Kent might have been sent out upon you and received without your knowing what an enemy he had been. I am told that they are all highly enraged against us but I have dropped all connection with them ... you must be much on your guard with them, they will give all the assistance in their power to your enemies here, by information &c. Mr Marsden is going on well, he will write to you himself – I look upon him as a friend in whom I place every confidence. He says the way to mortify your enemies is to take no notice of what has been going on, unless you hear something officially, and even then to make no complaint that may give them a pretence to send for you home to make your grievances heard – Lord Mulgrave is the intimate friend of Grosse and had promised him his interest if you were recalled – Oxley told me that a motion was to be made in the House of Lords by Lord Holland to put your Colony under the control of the East India Company as Ceylon &c – but Marsden laughs at this – I wish the troops could be changed. Fouveaux is very ill disposed to you and I hope you will send him to Norfolk Island. Mr Marsden thinks you will have a great deal to encounter if you oppose the barter of Spirits by which every body about you were making rich.

Now my Dear Mr Bligh I hope I have given you every information you could wish relating to this bussiness and that you approve of what I have done. Gatty was a little uncivil to me and presumed to take me to task for having told you that Tetley had conspired with Short but as I believe it to be the case at the time I wrote to you, I defended myself with spirit. He read one part of his letter to you ... and I think he made a little free with your Excellency in lecturing you about keeping your temper, but he appears our friend, and I shall forgive him – he appeared to fancy he had been of great use to us, but I told him the plot was all over before he knew any thing about it, and that he was like a man who had come in at the last act of a play and did not know the characters &c.

Mrs Bligh had the advantage of powerful friends to assist her lobbying. If the only source of dissension against Bligh had been located in London he would have survived his tenure as Governor. But in Sydney he faced other implacable enemies of a more immediate sort and he faced them alone, if one discounts the motley collection of unreliable hangers-on he drew to himself. His enemies knew that if they could get Bligh recalled – on any grounds – they would never see him again.

[46] Marsden was a secretary to the Admiralty. Mrs Bligh discloses that it was Marsden who provided her with the details of the plot to recall Bligh.
[47] If only Bligh had acted on this advice from the beginning!

28

The Rum Rebellion

It is no easy task to cover in a single chapter the stirring and deeply controversial events of the Rum Rebellion of 1808. To do it justice would require an entire book; for this reason only a sketch can be given here, though I hope to elucidate the main events and issues, so as to show what Bligh faced in his term of office and how he reacted to the challenge of MacArthur.

Bligh began his Governorship with some private land granting. This was not the best start to a campaign directed at those who made personal gain out of the trade in liquor; the only thing that can be said in favour of Bligh's actions was that at the time there was little that was unusual in what he did. The greatest fuss has been made by more recent commentators.

What happened was clever if irregular (though strictly legal). Governor King remained in office for a few days after Bligh's arrival. In his capacity as Governor he made land grants to Bligh. These consisted of 240 acres near Sydney, which Bligh named 'Camperdown', 105 acres near Parramatta, known as 'Mount Betham', and 1,000 acres off the Hawkesbury River named 'Copenhagen'. This brought William Bligh into the landowning class at a stroke. When Bligh assumed the Governorship in January 1807 he assigned 790 acres at Evan to Mrs King who, perhaps impudently, named her holding 'Thanks'. Bligh went too far in another land grant, this time to his daughter, Mrs Putland, by giving her 600 acres but carelessly dating the grant some time after Governor King had left the colony in the *Buffalo*. This made the transaction illegal, and in due course the legal processes caught up with Bligh's descendants.[1]

The new Governor set about his official mission with his usual zeal. It was, it must be remembered, his first official post ashore in his career.[2] It remained to be seen how a quarterdeck and a colony compared. The colony was in a poor state at the end of Governor King's tenure. Natural disaster had been added to personal mismanagement and weakness. The Hawkesbury River had flooded in March 1806, destroying a considerable

---

[1] The grants were the subject of a legal dispute in the 1840s when Bligh's descendants eventually made a deal with the Crown surrendering this grant in favour of the others. *See HRA*, First Series, Vols. 6 and 8. When Bligh's widowed daughter, Mary Putland, married Lieutenant-Colonel O'Connell in 1810, they received 2,500 acres as a wedding gift from the Government of Lachlan Macquarie. *See* Ellis, 1955, pp. 55-9, note 18.

[2] I am excluding his tenure as Duncan Campbell's agent in the West Indies in 1783 and also his five months ashore as Captain of the *Bounty* at Tahiti.

acreage of grain-producing farmland.[3] It was along the Hawkesbury River that the majority of the settlers had set up their farms; the officers had found drier parts. Food prices rose and grain reached a premium, being pushed up by speculation and the inevitable demands of the illicit stills that turned the seed-corn into liquid hope.[4] Meat was scarce as well. The floods had swept away animals and homes. Again the vast sheep-breeding flocks, such as those of John MacArthur and other officers and ex-officers, became a source of envy; the settlers complained of speculation and the withholding of stock, while the officers protested their innocence and claimed they were keeping their flocks to raise wool. Wandering sheep, assisted by wandering thieves, tended to disappear into hungry bellies.

Bligh's introduction to the conflicting sentiments of the different groups in the colony came in the modest gesture of loyalty accorded to him by the three uncrowned heads of the ruling elite, George Johnston 'for the Military', Richard Atkins 'for the Civil', and John MacArthur 'for the Free Inhabitants'. These gentlemen, though themselves bitterly divided by the jealousies of the past, sent Bligh a memorial which was published in the *Sydney Gazette* on 24 August 1806. It read:

The Officers Civil and Military, with the Free Inhabitants of this Colony, beg leave respectfully to offer their sincere congratulations to your Excellency, upon your appointment to this Government, and to express their happiness at your safe arrival.

They trust that your Excellency will not entertain unfavourable opinions of the fertility and natural resources of the country, from the unfortunate scarcity which the late inundations have occasioned; to be assured, Sir, you will find the country, under the ordinary dispensations of providence, neither wanting in fertility, nor barren of resources; but on the contrary capable of maintaining its inhabitants in plenty, and of becoming, with moderate encouragement, a Colony of considerable importance to Great Britain.

We have an undoubting confidence, that your Excellency by a just, moderate, firm, and wise Government, will promote the happiness of all who deserve it: and we feel animated by a pleasing hope, that under your Excellency's auspices, agriculture will flourish and commerce increase; while enjoying as far as circumstances will admit the Constitutional Rights of British Subjects, we shall in due time rise above our present comparative state of insignificance, and by our example prove to the World what great exertions Mankind will make when properly incited to exercise their natural powers.

We entreat your Excellency to believe, that anxious as we are for the improvement of agriculture and the extension of commerce (the two great

---

[3] A full account of the damage done by the floods is reported in *The Sydney Gazette and New South Wales Advertiser*, 30 March 1806.

[4] Characteristically, MacArthur, while expressing condolences to the people who had lost everything in the flood, was also concerned about the arrival of 400 tons of Bengal rice, which 'can produce no other effect than that of lessening of the value of our own produce'. MacArthur to Captain John Piper, undated but probably July 1806, in Piper Papers, Mitchell Library MS A256, pp. 477-9.

sources of population, civilisation and morality), we are perfectly sensible they alone are not sufficient to secure the welfare of our infant Establishment; but that it is the indispensible duty of us all to combine with our endeavours to accomplish these objects, a reverential regard to the Law, and a cheerful acquiescence in such measures as your Excellency may adopt, to improve the true interests of the colony.

Convinced that our prosperity and happiness will be the great object of your Excellency's care, we earnestly hope your Excellency will find your Administration productive of real and permanent satisfaction and honour to yourself.

Such protestations of loyalty were welcome but the hypocrisy of these men on this occasion was extreme. Being public, their declaration provoked comment. Within a few weeks Bligh was petitioned by an address from the independent settlers who had, to their minds, much to complain about. In particular they dissociated themselves and their class from John MacArthur, the self-appointed spokesman of the free inhabitants. They stated that he had no authority to speak for them and was actually acting against their interests by indulging in speculation to enrich himself during the scarcity to which he alluded in the address.[5]

That Bligh was prejudiced against MacArthur before he got to Australia is certain. MacArthur had offended Sir Joseph Banks and Bligh was never lax in promoting the interests of his sponsor. The unofficial address from the settlers (379 of them signed the repudiation of MacArthur) would have struck Bligh as confirming Sir Joseph's criticisms. The address by the settlers exposed MacArthur's unpopularity. Bligh believed he could act against MacArthur without fear of trouble. In this he was completely mistaken.

MacArthur had arrived back in the colony flushed with his successful petitioning of the Government in favour of his plans to develop a wool industry. It was not that he was the first of the sheep-rearers (though family and local myths persisted for years that he was, contrary to the evidence) but he was the first to think of scaling up wool production into something worthwhile. He thought in terms of ten thousand acres and vast flocks of thousands of sheep. He wanted to fill ships with his wool, not just export the occasional bundle. Unfortunately for his patience, he spent much of 1805-6 trying to realise the promises made to him by London, first through Governor King, who stalled with the time-honoured stratagem of sending to London for clarification and instructions, and then with Bligh, who promptly reopened the settled questions once again with London.

King's motives in thwarting MacArthur had been entirely personal. In 1788, when the first fleet landed, some of the cattle had wandered off and were not discovered again for some years. They had grazed their way to a perfect sanctuary, about twenty miles outside Sydney, which became known appropriately as the Cowpastures. Some of the original cattle had belonged to Governor Phillip, and when the herd was discovered again by accident King had inherited the title to them. Access to the Cowpastures was not easy

[5] *HRNSW*, Vol. 6, pp. 188-91.

or convenient, and the longer the cattle remained unmolested the greater their numbers became. Poachers were inhibited by the usual frightful punishments. King did not suffer a real loss, because he allocated to himself cattle from the Government stock by means of an 'equivalent estimate' of numbers on the basis that 200 cattle in the hand were worth 1,300 in the bush. MacArthur had visited the Cowpastures and wanted to locate his 5,000-acre land grant there. King did not want a settlement near his cattle. He therefore wrote to London asking for directions, but meanwhile made an arrangement which MacArthur to locate his 5,000 acres 'or a greater quantity' on the opposite bank of the Nepean River.[6]

Bligh, when he arrived, raised the issue again and naturally came into conflict with MacArthur.[7] But it was not just over sheep that Bligh fell foul of the Colony's most successful wealth-creator and political in-fighter.[8] His interventions were aimed at the entire structure of grasping dealers and manipulators that had battened on the colony in the first twenty years of its existence. If Bligh succeeded in breaking them he might very well break MacArthur, who felt himself on the edge of his greatest success. MacArthur was closely identified with the monopolists and merchants who dominated the elite of the colony – he was the most successful of them all – and this identification had a double edge to it. He had enough prestige among the monopolists to be their leader, but enough sense to know that wealth creation through the sheep industry and merchant shipping did not need the shadier commercial practices with which he, and the others, had made their initial gains. The officers of the Corps never thought in big enough terms to realise that their trading monopolies could not last for ever and that sooner or later London would act decisively to stop them. Indeed, through Bligh London had acted to end the abuses of the monopolists, and if he failed somebody else would be sent out to finish off the work. It was MacArthur's good fortune that, at the moment when he was being thwarted by the last obstacle in his road to riches, he had just enough leverage over the men who were also being threatened with ruin by Bligh to use them to help himself.

By the end of King's governorship the New South Wales Corps was a corrupt military force, possibly operationally incapable. Its officers were closely involved in the importing of spirits and their distribution.[9] Any attempts to end that traffic would mean financial ruin and loss of privilege for

---

[6] King to Camden, 20 July 1805, reprinted in Onslow (ed.), 1914, pp. 105-9; *see also HRA*, First Series, Vol. 5, pp. 530-1, 576-7.

[7] *See* Bligh to Banks, 7 February 1807, Banks Papers, Brabourne Collection, ML MS A85, p. 227; Bligh to Windham, same date, *HRA*, First Series, Vol. 6, p. 122.

[8] In a much quoted remark that Bligh is alleged to have made to MacArthur early in their relationship, he said: 'What have I to do with your sheep, Sir? What have I to do with your cattle? Are you to have such flocks of sheep and such herds of cattle as no man ever heard of before? No, Sir, I have heard of your concerns, Sir, you have got 5,000 acres of land, Sir, in the finest situation in the country, but by God you shan't keep it.' He also went on, it is alleged, to assert his independence of the law of Britain: 'Damn the Privy Council, and damn the Secretary of State, too; he commands at home, I command here.' *See* Onslow (ed.), 1914, pp. 137-8.

[9] Many others besides the officers were active in the rum trade, including some members of Bligh's own entourage. The profits were so great that nobody with any commercial sense and some capital could resist the temptation. Robert Campbell, Bligh's close friend and confidant during the difficult months of the governorship, was prominent in trading in rum. Andrew

them. Bligh took his time to move against the rum trade (possibly a mistake) but he made no bones about his intentions and the justice of his plans. He wrote home a scathing indictment of the state of the Corps in 1807: '... about seventy of the privates were originally convicts, and the whole are so very much ingrafted with that order of persons as in many instances have had a very evil tendency, and is to be feared may lead to serious consequences ... Considering this to be the case, there is no remedy but by a change of military duty, a circumstance which can only prevent a fixed corps becomming a dangerous militia; while by removal of both officers and men, it would be a valuable corps for immediate service.'[10] The idea of simply recalling the officers and men of the Corps to Britain, or India, was obviously sensible; the Government would have been saved considerable trouble if it had heeded the suggestion. But this would have meant replacing them with other troops, and at the time this was inconvenient. In London it appeared far easier than in fact it was to curtail the extra-military duties of the Corps. In Chelsea an order would have been sufficient, but the same order shouted from Chelsea towards New South Wales had about as much effect on what happened as sending written orders to Governors.

Because Bligh's actions were directed against the military he lost their support. In spite of the petty accusations from all sides during this period – and they fill volumes of notes – the real basis of Bligh's isolation was the inability of the force, ostensibly there to protect and enforce his writ, to separate their public service from their private interests. For example, one of the most pernicious habits of the corrupted officers was to insist on paying the privates' wages in kind instead of in currency. With a shortage of actual currency there may once have been some excuse for this practice; but by this time they were brutally exploiting their men, threatening to thrash into submission those that objected.[11] Bligh was stating the obvious when he wrote to London: 'I am aware that prohibiting the barter of spirits will meet with the marked opposition of those few who have so materially enriched themselves by it.'[12]

However, Bligh's measures against the trade in spirits were not successful.[13] His orders were easily flouted by clever persons with half their wits about them. The unruly consumers of spirits, whether it was imported or of domestic manufacture from the many illicit stills operating in the territory, adjusted their behaviour under the new regulations. With greater penalties came greater risks and in consequence higher prices. The punishments[14] did

---

Thompson, Bligh's farm bailiff, speculated in rum and was fined for illegal trading. Unlike Campbell, Thompson was very small fry in the colony. *See* Mackaness, 1951, p. 373.

[10] Bligh to Windham, 31 October 1807. *HRNSW*, Vol. 6, p. 354.

[11] *See* Holt, 1838.

[12] *HRNSW*, Vol. 6, p. 251.

[13] *See* Holt, 1838, Vol. 2, p. 273.

[14] Convicts offending the rum regulations received one hundred lashes and/or twelve months' hard labour; emancipists (persons who had completed their sentences) were liable to a fine of £20 or three months and the free inhabitants were liable to a fine of £50 and loss of the Crown's indulgences.

not stop the trade; they merely reorganised its distribution. As one monopolist was driven out of business a new one appeared. The rum economy of the colony had grown out of the vacuum created by an insufficiency of stable currency and a need for crude bartering to supply basic necessities. The plight of the desperate had made some substitute necessary and, until the colony prospered, edict was not enough to restore commercial orthodoxy. But there could be no real economic progress until the Rum Corps was removed and its activities stopped. Until the scores of farm settlers could be assured of proper financial reward for their labours, in the form of products that they wanted at reasonable prices, the commercial prosperity from working in the colony would be confined to a few. The real per capita income of the middle classes had to rise in order to lift the income levels of the labouring classes. The fact that Australia was a penal colony inhibited the economic development of the territory; people without a stake in a society make poor colonists.

Bligh had shown, in his early measures to relieve the distress of the Hawkesbury settlers, that he was conscious of the need to make a wider number of people economically secure if the colony was to break out of its stagnation. His personal visitation to the flooded settlement did much to assure him of the support of these people against the ruling elite. Unfortunately, when the confrontation with MacArthur came he was a long way from the Hawkesbury, and his support there was cowed by the military and by years of submission to the monopolists. In our more restrained age, where the vigour of capitalist entrepreneurs is mainly tempered by the power of the state and the many informal institutions of a democratic community, we might not appreciate the extent to which in the early nineteenth century independent men of means could lord it over everybody else. Hardness was a recognised virtue in a man seeking after profit and wealth, a point that John MacArthur never forgot.[15]

The road to the rebellion is marked by the struggles between MacArthur and Bligh. With each incident, MacArthur moved a step nearer to outright opposition to the Governor. His perceptive and fertile mind noted deteriorating relations between Bligh and the military, and he was not slow to appreciate the significance of that development. In October 1807 he noted: 'The Corps is galloping into a state of warfare with the Governor. And in my opinion they are most wretchedly circumstanced among themselves.'[16]

Bligh's first official clash with MacArthur began with his Proclamation on 1 November 1806 on the question of currency. In the colony the little amount of local currency available was supplemented by promissory notes issued by

---

[15] MacArthur wrote, with reference to his sons: 'I am endeavouring to break James and William in by degrees to oversee and manage my affairs. They appear to be contented with their lot, but I by no means think them well calculated for it. They have not sufficient hardness of character to manage the people placed under their control, and they set too little value upon money, for the profession of agriculture which as you know requires that not a penny should be expended without good reason. Whatever may be the result there is no alternative for them. Here their lot is cast.' MacArthur to Walter Davidson, 3 September 1818, in Onslow (ed.), 1914, p. 318.

[16] MacArthur to Piper, 11 October 1807, Piper Papers, ML MS A256, pp. 481-3.

individuals and bills endorsed by funds held in London. The trade between the colony and London ensured a steady stream of credit deposited with agents that could be used to pay for goods and services needed in the colony. Transactions in bills, notes and credit lines were an important feature of commercial life in New South Wales at this time, and the system went smoothly, except when a bill was returned unpaid.[17]   The main cause of trouble with this system was that the lack of money in the form of currency led inevitably to trading by barter and eventually to notes denominated in goods instead of currency. Debtors would agree to pay back in goods such as corn, so many bushels by such a date. The rate of the note was determined by the conversion factor of cash and wheat. If he owed ten pounds sterling and wheat sold at one pound a bushel, the debtor owed ten bushels of wheat. But what happened if the price of wheat rose (or fell for that matter)? Did the debtor owe the same amount of wheat? If wheat rose to three pounds a bushel because of extreme scarcity, such as in the Hawkesbury floods in 1806, then ten bushels of wheat were now worth £30, and if the debtor was obliged to pay back his debt in kind at the old rate he was paying back £30 for a £10 debt. The reverse was also implied. If the price of wheat fell to 10s. a bushel the money value of the debt would fall from £10 to £5.

Bligh had been in New South Wales only a few weeks when he issued his Proclamation on Currency. It should be remembered that he was experienced in the manipulation of bills and the funding of commerce. His opinions were formed from a personal visit to the distressed farmers and in consideration of their plight. He declared in favour of setting the money value of a debt as the prime instrument of the debt and through which the debt could be liquidated. In other words he declared that the movements in the price of barter goods raised or lowered the value of these goods but did not imply windfall gains or losses to creditors. His Proclamation read:

> WHEREAS the term *Currency*, made use of in this Colony, seems not to have carried its proper Signification in the small Notes generally circulated; It is hereby declared, that its meaning is only applicable to Money, and not *Barter* in Goods: so that if any Note is made payable in *Copper Coin* or the *Currency* of this Colony, it is to be inferred that *Money only* is the means by which it is to be liquidated.[18]

This made him most popular with hard-pressed and penurious debtors, of which there were many after the Hawkesbury floods, but brought him opposition from creditors. The windfall profits expected by creditors holding notes denominated in barter goods were liquidated at a stroke; but not without resistance. Inevitably, John MacArthur was one of the creditors who held barter notes on some of the small farmers. In particular he held a note on Andrew Thompson, employed by Bligh as a farm bailiff, denominated in wheat. At the time of the debt wheat was 7s. 6d. a bushel and when the note

---

[17] In the *Sydney Gazette* for 1806-9 there are regular advertisements from individuals regarding lost, or stolen, bills and notes.
[18] Published in the *Sydney Gazette*, 2 November 1806 (Vol. IV, No. 180).

was due it had risen to 30s. a bushel. Thompson refused to pay the debt on the basis of the new price of wheat, and insisted on paying at the old rate. MacArthur was enraged and took him to court. Under Bligh's guidance and following the proclamation of November 1806 the plea was lost; the note was declared to be valued at the old price of wheat.

The legal wrangles over Thompson's note occurred in July 1807. MacArthur was, not surprisingly, under the impression that Bligh's intervention was a personal attack on himself in favour of one of his own employees. He felt justice had been partial in this case, more so when the *Sydney Gazette* carried a statement of principle regarding the case that was somewhat intemperate in its language. The unsigned piece read:

> The extraordinary fluctuations that have taken place in the price of wheat since the flood in March 1806 have given rise to many litigations, which a little sincerity might have superceded. It is generally known, that when grain was plentiful nearly all bargains made at the agricultural settlements were for the produce of the ground at the store prices; the amount in cash was divided into bushels, and notes issued, rating wheat at its then present *maximum*, which seldom exceeded 7s. 6d. per bushel, though now at 28 to 30s. Losing sight, then, of the value of the commodity in exchange for which the notes had been exacted, the specific terms of the contract are conscientiously demanded, without any consideration of the excessive loss which must evidently fall upon an unfortunate debtor, who to cover an original demand of 50£ must necessarily expend 200£. How conscience can reconcile the requisition must be referred to those who are interested in the event of such transactions.
>
> It is a happy reflexion, however, that disputes of this nature are no longer permitted to arise from an indiscretion in the mode of granting notes of hand. By referring to His Excellency's General Order of November 1, 1806, and the Proclamation published on the 3 of January last we find a remedy to an evil which many have to lament the pressure of ... It is not only the duty, but the interest of every well meaning man to pay strict obedience to a Regulation, the design of which is to abolish the chicanery to which the inaccuracy of these instruments gave rise. Grain was once considered as a legal tender for a debt contracted, and was therefore one species of colonial currency. It is evidently dangerous, however, for an individual to bind himself in the payment of any specific number of bushels of an article to which unforeseen events may give even a ten fold value, and *Shylock* still insist upon his bond. The Orders admit not of misconstruction – the sterling value of the note when drawn in justice should be demanded, whatever be the mode of payment, and any excess upon that just demand is unquestionably an invasion of another's right.'[19]

By referring to litigation of the sort contemplated by MacArthur as an 'evil' and contrary to the Proclamation – thus prejudging the Court's decision – and making innuendoes about 'Shylock' insisting on his bond, the publisher was trying to intimidate MacArthur into dropping his resort to the law.[20] But

[19] *Sydney Gazette*, 5 July 1807, Vol. V, No. 219.
[20] Robert Howe was editor and publisher of the *Sydney Gazette*.

MacArthur was made of stern stuff, especially in regard to the exercise of his legal rights. That he persisted in his appeal to the courts and received the expected rebuff when he appeared before Bligh in a final appeal demonstrates the methods of the man in protecting his interests. He was not going to be intimidated by a Governor – he had already stood up to the previous three successfully – and neither was he going to be denied his day in court. The court's decision and the Governor's actions gave him cause and opportunity to complain to London.[21] The peculiar aspects of the currency question in the colony did not excite much interest in Britain, but the actions of the Governor were ever of interest to Government.

MacArthur did not leave the decision of the court uncontested in Sydney. He wrote, under a pseudonym, 'An Occulist', a short reply to the arguments of the court in rejecting his case:

> Every lover of truth must be pleased at the impartiality of your excellent publication, but much as I admire your luminous style of reasoning, and the logical precision of your arguments in general, I confess they failed of their usual effect in the lecture you favoured us with in your last paper on ABC. Permit me to continue the case you have assumed, and to suppose C. holds an obligation, drawn by a A when wheat was at 8s. per bushel, to deliver a certain quantity to B. or Bearer and that before the obligation is discharged it falls to 5s. could C demand either from A or B the difference in value occasioned by such a depression of the price? If not, it appears that the literal tenor of every engagement ought to be fulfilled, and that specific contracts must be sacred and binding; as it surely will not be denied that if the holder of an obligation is to bear the loss when the commodity he has bargained for falls in its value, he ought not to be deprived of the benefit of its rise. Your constant Reader, AN OCCULIST.
>
> P.S. – I think your honest zeal has animated you rather too much in your paper of the 5th instant, and the interest I feel for the success of your useful labours, induces me to recommend you to abstain as much as possible from calling names: – for although well informed liberal people are sensible of the powerful effect of that practice, there are many narrow minds with whom it may do you injury.[22]

The publisher of the *Gazette* replied to MacArthur's letter in the same issue. In doing so he brought out the main points of the case in question. 'The Publisher ... considered it a well known fact, that the notes floating about the different settlements were made payable in grain, because it was, with little exception, the only mode of payment which the settler had, and ought therefore rather to be considered as a security for the payment of a specific sum, than as a specific contract for furnishing the number of bushels expressed. In the one case the holder of a note for 20 bushels, granted to him

---

[21] *HRA*, First Series, Vol. 6, pp. 323-8.

[22] *Sydney Gazette*, 26 July 1807, Vol. V, No. 222; there is no direct evidence that MacArthur was in fact the author, but the style and the issue fitted him too well to leave doubts in the minds of the public as to the identity of the writer. In a further reply to the views of the *Gazette*, 'An Occulist' wrote another, sharper letter which was published in the issue of 2 August 1807. 17.

under a presumption that 8s. per bushel would be the market price when due, upon the recept of 8£. in money could not be a loser, since that was in the first instance the very extent of his demand.'[23]

MacArthur also reacted with his characteristic sense of pride. As with Governor Phillip, who had offended him and his interests, he refused to call on Governor Bligh at his official residence. It must be noted, however, that it was not at this stage that Bligh took his dispute with MacArthur to a personal level; indeed, some time after MacArthur withdrew social contact, Bligh, hearing that he was ill, visited MacArthur at his farm, only to find that he was fit and well. The calculated snub offended Bligh not a little.[24]

While the dispute over Thompson's debt was being pursued another source of dispute between MacArthur and the Government was festering in the background. This concerned two spirit stills which MacArthur and Abbott had attempted to import into the colony from Britain. They had arrived on the *Dart* in March 1807. As distillation of spirit was inimical to Bligh's plans to eliminate the dependence of the colony on the rum traffic, the stills were confiscated and ordered to be placed in the Government's stores until their shipment back to London. Because the stills contained various packages for their owners the order was complied with to the extent of confiscating the head and worm of the stills, but the bodies were left to be emptied out into MacArthur's private store.[25] The dispute between MacArthur and Government remained at rest until orders were received to place the stills in the *Duke of Portland* for shipment to London. At this point MacArthur became obstructive, and used proper legal process to entrap the officers of the Governor's administration into either compromising Bligh or provoking him into a rash act. He was waiting for his chance to revenge himself over the treatment of the court respecting the debt due to him from Thompson.

Dr John Harris,[26] the naval customs officer, in letting MacArthur take the body of the still away, ostensibly to empty it, instead of confiscating and emptying it for him, played into MacArthur's hands. MacArthur took the line that without the still-head and worm the copper body was no longer a still but a 'container'. As a still he now intended to ship it to India or China and sell it there; if he could he had no intention of sending it back to

---

[23] *Sydney Gazette*, 26 July 1807.

[24] *HRA*, First Series, Vol. 6, p. 323.

[25] The stills were owned by MacArthur and Captain Edward Abbott but both appear to have been taken to MacArthur's warehouse for emptying, suggesting some collusion. The fact that Captain Abbott was prepared to import a 60-gallon still as a private commercial venture shows how far the officers of the Corps (he was second-in-command to Johnston) were involved in rum trade speculation. Details of the dispute over the stills are given in *HRNSW*, Vol. 6, and *HRA*, First Series, Vol. 6.

[26] John Harris had gone to New South Wales with the Corps but resigned after he was granted land by Hunter; he was Naval Officer of the Port when Bligh arrived but Bligh dismissed him and Harris compared him to Caligula. Harris was hostile to Bligh from mid-1807 and was to participate in the insurrection in January 1808. He fell out with MacArthur in later developments of the revolutionary regime. *See HRNSW*, Vol. 6, Letter, Harris to King, 25 October 1807 and after.

London.[27] He therefore refused to hand it over. He was compromised to some extent because he protested that he had not ordered his London agents to send him a still and that they had done so of their own accord. If this was true, then he could have no objections to sending it back to London; but as always MacArthur had seen the prospect of a profit from selling the still. The determination with which he set about thwarting Bligh on this occasion was aided by the incredible stupidity of the new customs officer, Robert Campbell, in sending his nephew, who had no legal or official standing, to remove the stills from MacArthur's warehouse. This was a blunder that enabled MacArthur to sue the nephew for unauthorised removal of his property. The local court agreed with MacArthur and found against Campbell for illegally removing private property.[28] This was MacArthur's first success against Bligh and it encouraged him to believe that he was getting the measure of the 'Cornishman'.

Matters now raced to collision between Bligh and MacArthur. Again it was over a matter that had been pending for some time, namely the question of MacArthur's responsibility in allowing a prisoner to escape from one of his ships to Tahiti. The facts are, briefly, that the *Parramatta* trading vessel, in which MacArthur had an interest, left Sydney for Tahiti in June 1807.[29] As usual the ship had been searched for escapers before sailing, but the search was not thorough enough. A stowaway was found in a pile of wood after some days at sea. He was an escaped prisoner, John Hoare, and when the vessel arrived at Tahiti he jumped ship.[30] When the *Parramatta* returned to Sydney on 15 November 1807, the ship was arrested and refused permission to land its cargo. It was ordered to be moored alongside H.M.S. *Porpoise* and armed men were placed on board with the authority to act as constables.

In order to prevent traders from permitting convicted persons to escape from the colony, a special bond was imposed on them which became forfeit if their vessels were used by such people to effect their unauthorised journeys to freedom. This bond was sufficiently high – in the case of the *Parramatta* it was £900 – to ensure that determined searches were made for stowaways by owners and by the authorities. In a small vessel such as the *Parramatta* (120 tons) a person could only hide in collusion with the crew or through the utmost laxity in the searchers. When the authorities examined Captain Glen and his crew on their return they came to the conclusion that either collusion or carelessness had enabled Hoare to make his successful bid for freedom.

---

[27] MacArthur wrote to Campbell, 19 October 1807, that 'he intended to dispose of it [the still] to the master of some ship going to India or China. If that should be objected to, His Excellency could do what he liked with the head and worm, and he would appropriate the copper to some domestic use.' Details of this dispute are in *A Letter ... Addressed to the Right Honourable The Viscount Castlereagh, His Majesty's Principal Secretary of State for Colonial Affairs*, London, 1808, ML MS C475.

[28] The case is covered in *HRA*, Vol. 6, pp. 174-8.

[29] MacArthur's view of the *Parramatta* incident is given in Onslow (ed.), 1914, pp. 139-42; *Sydney Gazette*, 28 June 1807; *HRNSW*, Vol. 6, pp. 307-47.

[30] It was alleged that the *Parramatta*'s captain made no attempt to stop Hoare making his escape at Tahiti and there were unsubstantiated rumours that Hoare was assisted in his escape plans.

Bligh decided (not that he needed much persuasion) that the owners of the *Parramatta* were liable and the court ordered them to forfeit their £900. MacArthur refused to pay the £900, and in the altercations that followed took the extreme course of declaring that he had abandoned the schooner and was no longer responsible for it, its contents or its crew.[31] The crew were forced ashore by this action, although this was contrary to port regulations; they had no choice, because they were no longer being supplied either with wages or victuals. If they helped themselves to the ship's stores they would be acting illegally, offending either the court which was in possession of the vessel, or the owners, John Macarthur and Garnham Blaxcell.

The crew fruitlessly tramped back and forth between the Government and MacArthur, attempting to get official or private recognition of their distress. But they were pawns in the game now being played between Bligh and MacArthur through intermediaries and messengers, as each tried to trap the other into an impetuous action. The main character on the Government side was Richard Atkins, the colony's Judge-Advocate. He was one of MacArthur's mortal enemies in the colony, but MacArthur's antipathy to Atkins did him no discredit.[32] By all accounts Atkins was one of the colony's disgraces, all the more so for the fact that he held the position he did. Bligh had this to say of him, a couple of months before this latest row with MacArthur:[33]

> The most material thing to be done is to make every one confident he will enjoy a just and upright Government – remove without delay the very unfit & very disgraceful Judge Advocate ... The Judge Advocate is a disgrace to human Jurisprudence. The Criminal & Civil Courts should be changed & regulated by Rules approximating to those of England. – The Officers of the Crown should be honorable Men & at least we should have an Attorney General as well as a Judge besides some respectable Lawyer as a Solliciter. Let this be done and all will be well – at present justice is not duly administered in its first Stages, and my decision in the last does not relieve the subject altogether for what he has suffered in the course of the Trial.

Bligh was more specific in a letter written at the same time to London: Atkins '... has been accustomed to inebriety; he has been the ridicule of the community; sentences of Death have been pronounced in moments of intoxication; his determination is weak; his opinion floating and infirm; his knowledge of the Law insignificant and subservient to private inclination; and confidential cases of the Crown, where due secrecy is required, he is not

---

[31] Bligh ordered that the ship's papers be handed over to the Court; this effectively immobilised it and its contents because the owners could not prove possession without their papers.

[32] Richard Atkins was a 'remittance man', i.e., he was sent to Australia with an allowance by his wealthy and influential family to get him out of the way. Australia received more than its fair share of remittance men from Britain during the first 150 years. For an account of his long feud with MacArthur, *see* Ellis, 1955, in particular Chapter 9; also Mackaness, 1951, pp. 397-8.

[33] Bligh to Banks, Letter, 10 October 1807, Mitchell ML MS A85.

to be trusted with.'[34] Bligh was severely handicapped in the judicial battle over the *Parramatta* by Atkins's incompetence.

Atkins sent a written note to MacArthur 'requiring' his attendance before him 'to show cause of such your conduct'. The note claimed that Atkins had written it at the 'command' of 'his Excellency the Governor'.[35] MacArthur was not slow to realise that Atkins had not sent him a proper legal summons, and he used this to force the next move. It is arguable in law whether a letter from an official in Atkins' position requiring attendance to explain conduct that had led others (the crew) to break the law was a private communication, requiring a private reply, or a summons requiring attendance. MacArthur merely wrote a reply, which stated his side of the dispute, and served, as it was meant to do, to annoy the Government. He told Atkins:[36]

I have only in reply to say that you were many days ago informed I had declined any further interference with the schooner, in consequence of the illegal conduct of the naval officer in refusing to enter the vessel, and retaining her papers, notwithstanding I had made repeated applications that they might be restored. So circumstanced, I could no longer think of submitting to the expense of paying and victualling the officers and crew of a vessel over which I had no control; but previously to my declining to do so, my intentions were officially made known to the naval officer. What steps he has since taken respecting the schooner and her people I am yet to learn, but as he has had two police officers on board in charge of her, it is reasonable to suppose they are directed to prevent irregularities, and thereof I beg leave to refer you to the naval officer for what further information you may require on the subject.

MacArthur, by disclaiming ownership of the *Parramatta*, had managed to change the dispute from that of non-payment of the bond to that of the legality of the summons. To appreciate the audacity of this step, consider the relative cost to him of the bond and the ship: the bond was £900; the ship was valued at £10,000. He had thrown the ship away to draw the Judge-Advocate into an ill-considered move.[37] A far better move, from Bligh's point of view, would have been to declare the 'ownerless' *Parramatta* an abandoned vessel and promptly auction it and its contents for what they would raise. This would have touched MacArthur where it hurt him most. But Bligh was not able to manipulate Atkins in such a style because of Atkins' sense of his own regal importance, and also because Atkins leapt at the opportunity to pursue his private vendetta against MacArthur.

However, events proceeded to their conclusion in the way ordained by Atkins. He responded to the reply from MacArthur with a warrant for his arrest.[38] The validity of this move is in doubt. MacArthur had not received a

[34] Bligh to Windham, Letter, 31 October 1807, *HRA*, Vol. 6, p. 150.

[35] Atkins to MacArthur, Letter, 14 December 1807, in Onslow (ed.), 1914, pp. 139-41.

[36] MacArthur to Atkins, Letter, 14 December 1807, *ibid.*, pp. 141-2.

[37] MacArthur later claimed to be suing Robert Campbell for illegal possession of his ship and the estimated loss of £10,000, showing that his action in disclaiming responsibility was a gamble and a ruse.

[38] *HRA*, Vol. 6, p. 307; Onslow (ed.), 1914, pp. 142-3.

legal summons to appear before him and therefore it is doubtful whether a warrant was legal to force him to do so. The warrant was delivered by the Chief Constable of Parramatta to MacArthur at Elizabeth Farm. MacArthur was beside himself with rage. He wrote a quickly composed note, which shows his mood of defiance and which in calmer moments he surely regretted: 'Mr Oakes, You will inform the persons who sent you here with the warrant you have now shown me and given me a copy of that I never will submit to the horrid tyranny that is attempted, until I am forced; that I consider it with scorn and contempt, as I do the persons who have directed it to be executed.'[39] With this declaration it was open warfare, since no civil power could permit a subject publicly and specifically to declare his contempt for its proceedings, instruments and officers in the manner adopted by MacArthur. In his parting words to Mr Oakes as he left Elizabeth Farm without a prisoner, MacArthur said of his tormentors: 'Let them alone; they will soon make a rope to hang themselves.'[40] His son rode after Oakes and tried to persuade him to hand back the hurriedly scribbled note, but Oakes refused; the note would explain his own conduct in not returning with a prisoner.[41]

Atkins took Oakes and the defiant note to Bligh and from this moment Bligh personally directed the moves against MacArthur. If letting Atkins handle the early stages was Bligh's mistake, in that he was compromised by a barely legal summons, sending Oakes back with the note was MacArthur's mistake; it was seen as a general challenge to the integrity of the King's officers. The magistrates were convened and decided on action to restore the dignity of their office. Atkins, Major Johnston of the New South Wales Corps, Robert Campbell, and John Palmer voted to arrest MacArthur and to use force if necessary. Oakes was commissioned to take a body of armed men and bring MacArthur before the court without delay.[42]

Soon after Oakes had left him, MacArthur calmed down and began to think of ways to turn the tables on Bligh. He had always had a supreme gift for survival; he knew how to fight on legal territory, and how to bend the law and, above all, people towards his own ends. In this case he was of course helped by the complicated legal issues in dispute. Who was right depended on which part of the case was being argued. In these conditions he knew that either the matter would drag on into oblivion with the possibility that as a last resort London would recall Bligh to sort out the mess or his enemies would step just a little too far and he could crush them by recourse to legal writ. With renewed self-confidence, MacArthur hastened to Sydney, but not to present himself to court. Instead he went to friends in the town, making his presence known and forcing Atkins to make the next move. This was 16 December. The armed party led by Oakes looked for MacArthur in various places in the town and eventually caught up with him, calmly and characteristically conversing with friends a few steps away from the

[39] *HRA*, Vol. 6, MacArthur to Oakes, Note, 15 December 1807.
[40] Evidence of Oakes in *HRA*, Vol. 6, p. 349 and *HRNSW*, Vol. 6, p. 506.
[41] Ellis, 1955, p. 310.
[42] *HRNSW*, Vol. 6, p. 476.

Governor's residence. He was arrested and taken before the court but released on bail of £1,000 – hardly an imposition on a man who could afford to disown £10,000 worth of property.[43]

The next day, 17 December 1807, he was brought before the magistrates again, this time with two senior officers from the Corps on the bench, Major George Johnston and Captain Edward Abbott. Atkins wanted to find MacArthur guilty of refusing to obey a summons and warrant. He was pursuing his own personal vendetta against MacArthur and was not too concerned with the broader issues. The integrity of the Court would have been protected if he had taken the case, found MacArthur guilty and imposed a fine. But this was no longer a battle between Atkins and MacArthur; it was a fight between MacArthur and Bligh. Bligh had MacArthur's note to Oakes and he wanted a case against him with the prospect of banishment from the colony or substantial disgrace. It was a gamble, and a more cautious governor would have thought through the risks. Whereas MacArthur was in the wrong in committing contemptuous thoughts about civil magistrates to paper, Bligh was moving into dangerous grounds in stretching those thoughts to declarations of 'treason'.

In an extraordinary move, Bligh sent a message to Atkins while the Court was in session questioning an objection made by MacArthur against appearing before Robert Campbell. MacArthur cited his intended suit for £10,000 damages from Campbell. In Bligh's view the case before the Court was not a dispute about the *Parramatta* but one of civil obedience. Atkins supported by the other magistrates, decided to commit MacArthur to the criminal court.[44] This played straight into MacArthur's hands; once the Governor's intervention became public, it was no trouble to cry 'Tyranny'. Given bail again, MacArthur got to work to make his case.

The Court did not specify what charges were to be brought against him when the Criminal Court sat on 25 January; MacArthur was thereby able to pose as the victim of tyranny because it was an Englishman's right to know what he was charged with. Furthermore, he went to work to draw the Governor into actions calculated to cause concern among wide sections of the community. He found a perfect issue in the case of his lease to land in the town. Back in October, when Bligh had been getting together his campaign against MacArthur, he had noted that MacArthur had a lease given to him by Governor King on some land next to the church. This was in conflict with a memorandum made up by Governor Phillip that the centre of Sydney should not be leased away but should remain Crown land. This attempt at town planning was aimed at preventing private speculation from making profitable use of the best and most desirable commercial property. Bligh regarded the leases given by King as contravening Phillip's desires, which naturally he thought were admirable. He wrote to London, detailing his objections to each plot given by lease and in particular drew attention to MacArthur's lease on the plot next to the church 'which was too much

---

[43] For an account of the arrest of MacArthur, *see* Bartrum, 1811, p. 92.
[44] *HRA*, Vol. 6, Proceedings of the Magistrates, 17 December 1807.

confined' and which 'if he holds will deprive the inhabitants of a great convenience as well as the public place of worship;.[45]

Bligh's town planning motives may have been impeccable but his actions in rushing this matter raise doubts as to his good sense. As the home Government had not commented on his October letter – it had still to reach Britain – he could only raise the matter in January with a view to irritating an already irritated man. He ordered the Surveyor-General[46] to write to MacArthur telling him in effect that he could not build on his plot next to the church and that he should either pick another spot in the town acceptable to both sides or appeal to London and await a decision. MacArthur played along with this gambit by nominating several sites in the town, none of which was likely to be acceptable to the Government. He may have been assisted in this by his friend the Surveyor-General. With each request Bligh refused to make a lease. Therefore, MacArthur decided to erect a fence round the plot next to the church to demonstrate his ownership, though up to then he had shown no inclination to build upon it; it was a speculative lease. This was another confrontation of some gravity. The Governor had expressly forbidden him to erect anything on the land pending advice from London. By erecting a fence, and using soldier labour to do so, MacArthur was once again challenging the Governor's authority.[47]

MacArthur had earlier, with some cunning, tried to discredit Atkins and possibly force a breach between Atkins and the Governor. This time it was over a dispute about a bill for £26 6s. which, with interest over fourteen years, MacArthur claimed was now worth £82 9s. 5d. He demanded payment and when Atkins refused he petitioned Bligh to intervene. Bligh, suggested that MacArthur take the issue to court. MacArthur replied that if he took Atkins to court it would mean taking him to appear before himself and asking him to issue a writ for payment naming himself as the debtor. He asked for an impartial judge. On 12 January 1808 he made a third and final plea to Bligh, getting, as he had hoped, the same refusal to act. He was able to claim that Bligh was refusing him normal rights of settlement. If Bligh had sent the case before another magistrate he would have undermined Atkins' credibility in the case yet to be heard about MacArthur's competence to disobey a warrant from him. The merits of these cases and counter-cases were getting lost in the innuendoes and gossip between the two camps. That MacArthur had waited fourteen years to make use of this unpaid bill on London exposes his motivation, though it did not lessen its point-scoring value in the battle.[48]

On 20 January 1808, Bligh ordered a party of workmen to take down the

---

[45] *HRNSW*, Vol. 6, p. 359, Bligh to Windham, October 31 1807.

[46] Charles Grimes was Surveyor-General under Bligh and was a firm member of the MacArthur faction; it was in his house that MacArthur was arrested by Oakes and he played an important role in the insurrection. He was forced to resign his post because of his role in MacArthur's conspiracy, and remained in Britain after the trial of Johnston.

[47] Details of this dispute from MacArthur's point of view are given in *Letter to Castlereagh ...* ML MS C475, pp. 96-9; for Bligh's version *see* Bartrum, 1811, pp. 56-7 and 182; *see also HRNSW*, Vol. 6, pp. 413.

[48] MacArthur sent Bligh a Memorial stating his case, *see HRNSW*, Vol. 6, p. 395: Bligh's reply to the request to change the magistrate, conveyed by his Secretary Edmund Griffin, *ibid.*, p. 420.

fence around MacArthur's property next to the church. This was done in the presence of MacArthur and several officers of the Corps, including Captain Edward Abbott.[49] This public demonstration of affability between MacArthur and the Corps had more significance than the satisfaction the Governor might have received at the news that his orders to take down the posts had been carried out. The fact that a party of soldiers had erected them was itself an omen of where sympathies lay among the Corps. Some measure of sympathy for MacArthur may also have been occasioned by his promise to Sergeant-Major Whittle that he was prepared to sell a quantity of rum to the soldiery at the bargain price of 5s. per gallon.[50] The normal price off the ships was 8s. per gallon and it sold for around 30s. a gallon. It is hard to think of a more powerful inducement to disaffection in that thirsty colony.

Some time during early January MacArthur formed an alliance with the military leaders to thwart the Governor's intentions. Whether a military *putsch* was planned from the beginning is not known; but it is certain that defiance of the civil power, and in particular its prime instrument, Richard Atkins, was deliberately embarked upon. The incident of the fence around the open disused plot of land on 14 January was the first public declaration of sentiment by the army in favour of MacArthur; there are other incidents that have significance.

The most brazen was the request on 22 January by Major George Johnston for permission to hold a mess-dinner for the Corps on a regular basis on the 24th of each month. MacArthur's trial was to take place on 25 January. The construction we can place on this request, with the benefit of hindsight, ought to have been imaginable to a Governor in Bligh's position. But Bligh does not appear to have been aware of people's motives. He was so innocent about the matter that he even donated a large quantity of wine for the festivities. This gathering of all the officers of the Corps and many other prominent citizens of Sydney could not have avoided discussing the trial next day and what they stood to lose, or believed they stood to lose, from Bligh's continuation as Governor.[51] The men who attended the dinner were to number almost to a man the signatories of the petition produced to justify the arrest of Bligh a few days later. John MacArthur, out on bail, former Captain in the Corps, was just outside the mess room, walking up and down, listening to the music and 'amusing' himself.[52] His son Edward and his nephew Hannibal were inside, joining in the songs and merriment of the people who were plotting the 'final solution'.

Next day, 25 January 1808, the court met. Atkins was joined by Captain Anthony Fenn Kemp (who had stood bail for MacArthur), Lieutenant John Brabyn, William Moore, Thomas Laycock, William Minchin and William

[49] MacArthur was staying at Captain Abbott's residence in Sydney during January, a fact of some significance.
[50] Evidence to this effect was given by Whittle at Johnston's trial in 1811; *see* Bartrum, 1811, p. 371.
[51] At his trial Johnston strenuously denied that there were discussions of this nature during the mess-dinner. Bartrum, 1811, p. 149.
[52] *ibid.*, p. 198.

Lawson. MacArthur was assured of a safe passage by the military members of the bench, who were bound to be in a majority, and he knew he could take considerable liberties. He launched into a protest at being tried by Atkins, with a long indictment which if true showed Atkins to be incompetent, vindictive and unsuitable to try him.[53] His intervention was not intended to make a fair trial possible. His purpose was more daring than that; he wanted to discredit Atkins and make any trial impossible as a prelude to forcing Bligh out of the Governorship. His attack on Atkins was an attack on Bligh's weakest point, because not even Bligh could defend Atkins from most of the charges made against him in public, and as we have noted he had himself made a few pointed remarks about Atkins only the previous October. By inviting Bligh before the trial to remove Atkins as Judge-Advocate on grounds of personal interest MacArthur had prepared his ground well, because once Bligh had refused this request MacArthur was able to wax indignant that he could not get a fair trial with Atkins prosecuting.[54]

MacArthur's violent attack on Atkins could only lead to a collapse of the proceedings. By objecting before Atkins was sworn in, MacArthur ensured that everybody in the Court had status except Atkins. When Atkins tried to bluster his way out of the predicament by telling MacArthur he would send him to jail for contempt Captain Kemp told him loudly that *he* would send *him* to jail, making clear in the process where he stood in the matter.[55] Under the circumstances Atkins left the *Court* declaring that without him there was 'no Court'. Kemp replied: 'We are the Court', which in other times and other places would have been taken as sedition.[56] In this case, in the quieter atmosphere of a later trial, the officers asserted that they had thought that because they were sworn in they were in fact a Court, and that nothing rebellious had been meant.

Atkins repaired to the Governor, who by all accounts went wild with anger that a Court had been treated that way. MacArthur was triumphant and was cheered in the crowded Court. The next move was up to Bligh. MacArthur left the Court with an escort provided by the military against 'ruffians' that MacArthur alleged were sent to murder him.[57] This was in fact a declaration of support for MacArthur by the body sent to the colony to defend the King's

[53] The complete document is in *HRNSW*, Vol. 6, p. 554; Mackaness, 1951, pp. 405-6; Onslow (ed.), 1914, pp. 145-50.

[54] In the legal view of Judge-Advocate-General Manners-Sutton, 'It was perfectly incompetent, to any person brought before that Court, to offer a challenge against the Judge Advocate sitting upon it; he might as well offer a challenge against a judge in this country sitting at the assizes ... The Governor has no more right to change the Judge Advocate who sits upon that Court, than he has to change a judge in England, or any where else.' Quoted in Mackaness, 1951, p. 402; Bartrum, 1811, pp. 36-7.

[55] *HRA*, Vol. 6, p. 227.

[56] *ibid.*, p. 239.

[57] William Gore, the Provost-Marshal, interpreted MacArthur's armed escort from the Court as an absconding from bail and reported this to Bligh. It was for this reason that a warrant was issued to arrest MacArthur. The officers had released MacArthur on bail, though their status in Court without the Judge-Advocate did not allow them to do so. In the later administration revenge was exacted on Gore; he was imprisoned for perjury, which is the way his statements on that day were interpreted. He testified for Bligh at Johnston's trial in Britain and returned to New South Wales.

writ and its local representative, the Governor. To clear themselves, the
officers sent a note to Bligh informing him that they had accepted
MacArthur's request for a person other than Atkins to prosecute him.[58] Bligh
replied with a refusal to replace Atkins.[59] This was possibly a mistake, since
to comply would have called MacArthur's bluff though it made his acquittal
inevitable as much as if Atkins was present. From a tactical point of view
Bligh was defeated and he must have known it. There was simply no way in
which he could get a conviction against MacArthur with the Court composed
as it was. MacArthur had turned the fine of £900 imposed in the naval Court
into a victory over the Governor. Bligh was once again fighting for survival.
MacArthur was determined to destroy Bligh's Governorship, and his success
in Court pushed him on. Bligh had to deal with an open defiance of his
Government with hardly any cards to play.

He sent a message to the officers and instructed them to return to him the
papers of the trial including the notes of the Judge-Advocate.[60] The officers
refused to comply but offered to send copies. Naturally MacArthur and his
friends had the opportunity to peruse the official papers meanwhile. Bligh sent
another letter instructing them to obey and again they refused.[61] A
Government rests on its legitimacy in the eyes of its subjects or on force of
arms. Bligh's Government could not get the instruments of its power, the
army, to obey it. That afternoon, for all intents and purposes, his Government
ended.

Bligh tried in a last effort to bring the army into line. He wrote to Major
Johnston, Commander of the New South Wales Corps, who was at his farm
at Annandale outside Sydney during the momentous day. He claimed that
he was too ill to come to Sydney.[62] His 'illness' and absence from Sydney
were diplomatic. It was also a declaration of his commitment. January 25
closed with the two camps facing each other but with the Government resting
on the mercies of MacArthur and the officers of the Corps. Mercy was a
quality in which MacArthur was never judged to be abundant.

Perhaps, if Bligh had sat it out and waited for common sense and fear of
the consequences to prevail, he would have survived long enough to get
assistance from London. But he can never be accused of shirking
difficulties, though he can legitimately be accused of making them. On the
next day he sent the Provost-Marshal, William Gore, to arrest MacArthur,
which he accomplished without trouble. MacArthur had hoped for this; he
knew that Bligh would never be able to make his arrest stick. The six officers
of the criminal Court met that morning and, discovering that MacArthur
was in jail in spite of their bail for him, sent messages to the Governor
repeating their request for somebody other than Atkins to act as Judge-
Advocate and also asking for MacArthur to be released on bail.[63] Bligh did

[58] *HRA*, Vol. 6, p. 221, Members of the Court to Governor Bligh.
[59] *ibid.*, p. 222.
[60] *NRNSW*, Vol. 6, p. 426.
[61] *ibid.*, p. 427.
[62] *ibid.*
[63] *ibid.*, p. 224.

not reply to their requests as such but sent them individual summonses to appear before him the next morning to explain themselves.[64] He also informed Johnston of his actions.

This step of Bligh's was another mistake. The six officers who made up the Court were already a closed group by virtue of their profession and companionship in the Corps. By summoning them he placed them under some unknown threat, made more threatening by the unusual nature of their predicament. The officers had until 9 o'clock the next day to prepare themselves for interview by the Governor and were at liberty to make other plans up until then. Bligh would have done better to see them immediately, thus forcing them to act without consulting Johnston. Johnston, recovering from his illness, travelled to Sydney late that afternoon and went to the barracks. His intervention set the wheels of the military coup turning. The fact that he went to the barracks, not to Government House, must imply that his journey was not that of a peace-maker but that of a person who had already made his mind up about what he was going to do.

Much is made by some authors of the alleged state of the colony on the night of the coup.[65] Certainly it was Johnston's claim at his trial that he had acted to stop a bloody insurrection. In all the charges and counter-charges, it is not clear what party was supposed to be likely to rebel if Bligh was not removed. Various parties have been named: the 'respectable inhabitants', the soldiery, the Irish, the convicts, even the Government. The truth appears to be that the only force likely to take to arms was the army. That there was excitement in the town is beyond doubt. The performances of the six officers in the Court had seen to that. It was not every day that a Governor's instruction was disobeyed and in a penal colony such behaviour had implications beyond that of the 'wrongful arrest' of the colony's richest inhabitant. Men who had felt the lash of MacArthur's agents, or lost their property to his avarice, would not be uninterested in such goings-on. But that the mass of people were so excited by events that they were ready to take up arms on MacArthur's behalf is nonsense. The soldiers were, because he had made himself their champion, though their causes were no longer linked.

When Johnston arrived at the barracks he closeted himself with his fellow officers and some of MacArthur's friends. He was persuaded to order MacArthur's release and call out the Corps.[66] He claimed later that when MacArthur was brought to him he had already decided to take action against Bligh and did not need MacArthur's advice to that effect.[67] When he

[64] He had before him a Memorial from Atkins stating, *inter alia*, that the crimes committed 'amount to an usurpation of His Majesty's Government and tend to incite or create rebellion or other outrageous treason'. This was strong stuff, and it is highly doubtful whether it convinced Bligh that severe measures should be taken against the six officers. Atkins had got carried away by his humiliation.

[65] e.g. Ellis, 1955, pp. 345-7.

[66] *HRA*, Vol. 6, pp. 212, 429; Bartrum, 1811, pp. 151-2.

[67] At his trial Johnston made a vague statement about the events at the barracks. He tried to give the impression that he was under enormous pressure from various people. He makes the point (Bartrum, 1811, p. 152) that when MacArthur was brought from the jail to the barracks: 'He observed to me, that if I resolved to adopt such a measure (the arrest of Bligh) I should not

wrote an order for MacArthur's release, and signed it as self-appointed 'Lieutenant Governor', this was itself an act of rebellion; but the only armed force available to arrest him was under his own command. London was a long way over the horizon.

MacArthur was never without a sense of history and he quickly wrote a petition: 'Sir, The present alarming state of this Colony, in which every man's property, liberty, and life is endangered, induces us most earnestly to implore you instantly to place Governor Bligh under an arrest and to assume the command of the colony. We pledge ourselves, at a moment of less agitation to come forward to support the measure with our fortunes and our lives.'[68] He signed, followed by John Blaxland, James Mileham, S. Lord, Gregory Blaxland, James Badgery, Nicholas Bayly, George Blaxcell and Thomas Jamison. Within a day a further hundred signatures appeared on it. For some time the fiction persisted that the signatories had been present and clamouring for Johnston to arrest Bligh before he did so, when in fact all but ten (perhaps even more) had signed after Bligh was under arrest. Whatever the response to Johnston's rebellion after the event, there is no doubt now that he acted on the request of less than a dozen friends of MacArthur and his officers. The coup was the culmination of a conspiracy by MacArthur and a few merchants working in concert with the Rum Corps. It was not a popular revolt of the down-trodden masses, the small farmers or even the 'respectable citizens' of Sydney; it was a tussle between one factious group in an unruly penal colony and the Governor, in which the military force adjudicated in favour of the conspirators for their own ends.[69]

Bligh was arrested by Major Johnston accompanied by the entire Corps who marched in military order to Government House. They carried fixed bayonets. When the force arrived at the Governor's house a small party went inside to arrest him. This took some time – over an hour – because at first they could not find him. In the accusations and counter-accusations that have been reported since, perhaps the most pathetic and trivial is the charge that Bligh was a coward because he did not immediately appear before the usurpers of his authority and submit to their will.[70] It seems he hid himself in the house and was not found until an armed party looked more closely in a room and found him behind, or under, a bed. Much has been made of this, too much in my view. Major Johnston did not conduct the search himself, preferring to stay downstairs with the ladies in case they were harmed; this

do it without a requisition in writing. He drew up a paper to that effect, which as soon as laid on the table was filled with as many signatures as it could contain ...' (Mackaness, 1951, pp. 414-19, claims that it only had four or five names on it at this dramatic moment). 'This strong requisition, and the evident state of the public mind, determined my proceedings.' This is in conflict with his final statement at the trial: 'This representation, made by all persons present, before Mr. M'Arthur came, alone influenced my conduct ... but the written paper which has been laid before the Court had no share in deciding the resolution I had adopted, nor did I, at the time, consider who signed it, or, in fact, give myself any concern about it', *ibid.*, pp. 383-4.

[68] *HRNSW*, Vol. 6, p. 434.

[69] For a contrary view, *see* Ellis, 1955, Chapters 20-25.

[70] Mackaness, 1951, Chapter 42, deals in detail with the arguments and testimony regarding this aspect of the affair. *See also* Rutter, 1936a; Evatt, 1938.

23. Miniature portrait of Bligh's daughter Mary (Mrs Putland, later Lady O'Connell).

24. Portrait of Lt.-Col. George Johnstone by Henry Robinson Smith.

25. Bligh's house at 3, Durham Place (now 100, Lambeth Road), London.

26. Bligh's family tomb at St Mary's, Lambeth, showing his wife's epitaph.

throws light on the situation. A sergeant and party of privates did the searching, no doubt taking their time in an inspection of how a gentleman lived. The accusation of cowardice is particularly cynical coming from a military force that had one of the cushiest postings in the British army. Occasional brushes with individual Irish rebels, or small groups of them, and the arrest of Governor Bligh exhausted the military experience of the Corps. True, individual soldiers had served in other countries and in military engagements of some substance; but so had Bligh. His credibility in this regard stretches back to the *Resolution* and passes through the bloody battles of Camperdown and Copenhagen. He may have been shocked, indecisive or desperately trying to think of a way of avoiding defeat, but he was not a coward.

When found, Bligh was presented with a demand that he resign his Commission and that he agree to Major Johnston's taking over the command of the colony. In the circumstances he could hardly do otherwise than accept the situation, though he denied later that he ever relinquished the King's Commission. In the other camp that day there was jubilation. MacArthur wrote to his wife, Elizabeth: 'My Dearest Love, I have been deeply engaged all this day in contending for the liberties of this unhappy Colony, and I am happy to say I have succeeded beyond what I expected. I am too much exhausted to attempt giving you the particulars, therefore I must refer you to Edward, who knows enough to give you a general idea of what has been done. The Tyrant is now no doubt gnashing his Teeth with vexation at his overthrow. May he often have cause to do the like!'[71]

As I hope I have shown, the insurrection against Bligh in New South Wales should, I think, be looked at from the point of view of the conflicts in the colony first, and of the character of Bligh second. It is facile to argue that the Rum Rebellion occurred because Bligh was a 'tyrant' with a record of provoking mutiny that went back to the *Bounty*. Some of the participants took this point of view – it suited their interests – and expressed it loudly at the time. In October 1807, for example, an anonymous author penned the lines: '*Oh tempora! Oh mores!* Is there no CHRISTIAN in New South Wales to put a stop to the tyranny of Governor Bligh?'[72] Even before Bligh got to Australia, his past was well known among the factions awaiting his arrival.[73] The *Warrior* court martial in 1805, while not creating much of a stir, also had potential as a subject for gossip.

It is my view that Bligh's past, especially the mutiny on the *Bounty*, undoubtedly contributed to the decision of the MacArthur faction to risk their necks in an insurrection. If Bligh had been a controversial figure in one mutiny, he might more easily be argued to have caused another. From this point of view the appointment of Bligh was suspect, which is a criticism of the London government rather than of Bligh. Bligh's character is revealed in this

---

[71] Onslow (ed.), 1914, p. 153. The letter is not dated.
[72] *HRNSW*, Vol. 6, p. 339.
[73] 'Governor Bligh (formerly Captain of the *Bounty*) is daily expected to assume the command of this blessed Colony', MacArthur to Piper, undated letter, Piper Papers, ML MS A256, p. 477.

episode, as in the rest of his career; he was too stubborn and too proud to be intimidated by difficulties, utterly loyal to the King, and attached to his duty whatever personal stresses arose. These characteristics appear again in the difficult circumstances of the next two years in Australia. He refused to abandon his post until ordered to by London. He was advised by friends to return home and make his case against the rebels, but he could not take this easy way out. It was more than pride; it was something like adherence to the naval tradition that you did not leave your watch until relieved.

29

Interregnum

After the military coup Bligh was a Governor with a commission but no authority. Johnston assumed command of the Colony as 'Lieutenant-Governor'. He issued a 'General Order' which dismissed all the officers of Bligh's Government, including Atkins. Friends and associates of MacArthur were appointed in their place. MacArthur was technically still a prisoner on bail, but a court was arranged which formally cleared him of all charges. It consisted of the six officers of the original court plus the new Judge-Advocate, Surveyor-General Grimes. Its legality was in doubt from the start and its processes even moved Captain Abbott to complain to Johnston.[1] But the verdict, not surprisingly, was unanimous.

With the rebels in complete command of the colony, and in control of the only military force available to challenge their writs, they set about building a colony in the image of their ambitions. Bligh's 'tyranny' was overthrown to be replaced with a tyranny as heavy as it was illegal. Gore, the former Provost-Marshal, was sentenced to seven years' transportation, a savage sentence on a public servant for doing his duty under lawful authority.[2] Crossley, an adviser to the Governor, also received seven years' transportation.[3] When Macquarie arrived in the colony he carried with him an order from London that all legal proceedings following on Bligh's removal were null and void and all sentences were set aside. His arrival came too late, of course, for the poor wretches who were sentenced to be hanged in the rebels' courts and the others ruined by the soldiers' rough justice.[4]

Johnston had a difficult task. He had to satisfy the numerous competing factions which had pledged themselves to his rebellion in the hopes of the realisation of their own aspirations. Ironically he had to face the fact that Bligh's laws on the rum trade were the most sensible, and he thereby ordered

[1] *HRNSW*, Vol. 6, p. 832, Abbott to King, 13 February-4 April 1808; the trial is reported in *ibid.*, pp. 465-510.

[2] *HRNSW*, Vol. 6, pp. 648-9.

[3] George Crossley had been sent to New South Wales after conviction in Britain for forgery (he had had the temerity to place a fly in a dead man's mouth and then forge a will arguing that there was still life in the deceased when the will was made out). He had had legal training and became a part-time legal adviser to Bligh, who excused his use of this man on the ground that nobody else in the colony had knowledge of law. His lack of character still did not make proper his imprisonment for supporting Bligh against MacArthur. For biography, *see* Bonwick Transcripts, Mitchell Library MS A2000-1.

[4] A look through issues of the *Sydney Gazette* after it began to appear again in 1808 (its publication was interrupted during the rebellion by lack of paper) shows that the sentencing in the courts under Johnston's regime was extremely severe. *See* e.g. issues for June 5, 12, 19, 1808.

that they be continued, much to the dismay of many of the officers and rankers, as well as merchants and captains who had brought new supplies into the harbour. Commanding a colony as troublesome as New South Wales was a new and exacting experience, and Johnston turned to MacArthur to assist him. He did this by creating a new post, 'Colonial Secretary'.[5] By placing MacArthur in this position he handed him the colony, a position which MacArthur had last exercised to his own substantial benefit under Grose. The position was to be without pay, but a man as rich as MacArthur was unlikely to be deterred by such an imposition, especially as the post gave him opportunities to widen his already extensive commercial empire.

Within a short time complaints, arguments and disputes began to increase in tempo, and the regime ran towards its first crisis. Two problems that had to be dealt with at the beginning of the new administration were the rum trader, *Jenny*, which had been turned away from the port by Johnston, and another vessel, the *Brothers*, in which MacArthur's partner, Hullets' of London, had an interest. The *Jenny* was eventually sent away, though not without some of its cargo leaking out to the thirsty populace,[6] while the *Brothers* split the new leaders into camps. The dispute over the *Brothers* concerned its captain, Oliver Russell, whom Blaxland, a Sydney merchant, wanted to sack. MacArthur did not agree to this action, for some reason now unknown but probably because the whole affair was part of one of his schemes to frustrate a rival. Johnston did not agree either. Failing to get 'legal' sanction for their wishes, the Blaxlands attempted an unofficial eviction of Russel and ended up in court. Revolutionary justice looks after its own; in this case the luckless Captain and his Mate, instead of getting exoneration and redress for illegal entry and assault, found themselves sentenced to seven years' transportation. This was too much both for MacArthur, who was widely believed to have been behind the whole affair from the start, and for Johnston.[7]

Grimes, the judge-Advocate who had handled the case, in Atkins' place, was summarily dismissed from office by Johnston. This placed Grimes in the anti-Macarthur camp, where as before he had been wholly committed to his interests. Two of the magistrates, Dr Harris and Lieutenant Symons, were also dismissed. Russell and his Mate were immediately released from custody.[8] The manipulation of the legal system in so blatant a manner, within weeks of the rebellion for 'liberty', is indicative of the hypocritical cant of the anti-Bligh forces. If proof was needed that the entire episode was geared to creating a situation in the colony judged beneficial to the interests

---

[5] *HRNSW*, Vol. 6, p. 519; Johnston's reasons for appointing MacArthur are interesting: 'As there was no Office vacant to which I could appoint him, and as it was necessary that he should have some public character, I created an Office which has never before existed here, and I appointed him Secretary to the Colony. This unauthorized innovation I trust will not be disapproved, when my peculiar situation is considered, more particularly as it entails no additional expense upon the publick.' Johnston to Castlereagh, Letter, 11 April 1808, *HRA*, Vol. 6, pp. 217-19.

[6] *HRA*, Vol. 6, pp. 218 and 553-4.

[7] *See ibid.*, pp. 378-516, for details of trials of Russell and the Blaxland brothers.

[8] Johnston to Castlereagh, Letter, 30 April 1808, *HRA*, Vol. 6, p. 456.

of traders, monopolists, farmers and bureaucrats, the actions of the court on this occasion go a long way to providing it. Johnston knew that his case would not stand up to examination by London, and wrote to Castlereagh attempting to justify himself.[9]

Johnston did the next best thing to reconsidering his position; he decided to eliminate opposition by the expedient of sending people out of the colony. He had the perfect excuse for this: the need to send despatches to Britain as quickly as possible regarding the extraordinary measures he had taken in deposing Bligh. He knew that Bligh would be sending despatches to London with his version. The 'requisition', which was by this time signed by large numbers of people (it did not pay to be seen to be neutral regarding the new Government, especially with MacArthur in charge), gave him some cover against accusations that he had acted rashly in a mutinous manner. By implicating dozens of citizens he hoped to spread the opprobrium, if there was any, and the guilt, if there was retribution. He ordered Grimes and Harris to Britain. Lieutenant Minchin was sent in the *Brothers* and Lieutenant Symons and John Blaxland took passage in Campbell's ship, *Rose*.[10] The one man he could not get rid of was William Bligh, who was sitting it out at Government House, waiting for word from London.

The Commander of the Corps, Lieutenant-Colonel Paterson, during this time was stationed with a detachment of the troops at Port Dalrymple where a small penal colony and settlement existed. Both factions, Bligh's and Johnston's, were anxious to find out what his attitude to the rebellion would be. If he decided to order the re-instatement of Bligh this would place Johnston in a perilous position; if he decided otherwise it made Bligh's case hopeless. Paterson decided to do nothing. He had the excuse that he could not leave his post immediately and travel to Sydney, as he had the hardest and wildest prisoners to contend with. It was bad news for Bligh. It was not necessarily good news for Johnston because it did nothing to relieve him of sole responsibility for his actions.[11]

The next possible source of better news for Bligh was the expected arrival of Lieutenant-Colonel Foveaux from Britain with a party of troops. He was due to arrive in a few months' time to take up the post of Lieutenant-Governor to Bligh. He was, as we know from Mrs Bligh's letter of January

[9] Johnston pointedly castigated the persons involved by telling Castlereagh that there 'are a few persons in the Colony who are more influenced by Mr Lord and his associates than by a regard to justice' and that there was 'abundance of Evidences to be found here who will swear anything'.

[10] Bligh was able to get a message to the Cape of Good Hope about Symons, who was a Lieutenant in the navy and therefore responsible to Bligh. As he had left without Bligh's permission he was treated as a deserter by the naval commanders at the Cape. Both he and Blaxland were arrested and taken as prisoners on board a British ship and sent on to Britain. *See HRNSW*, Vol. 7, pp. 227, 555, Blaxland's 'Memorial', 26 October 1809; Macquarie referred to the Blaxland brothers as 'the most discontented, unreasonable and troublesome persons in the whole country'. *HRA*, Vol. 7, p. 560.

[11] *HRA*, Vol. 6, pp. 635-7, Johnston to Paterson, 18 April 1808, pp. 635-7 and Paterson to Johnston, 18 May 1808; *HRNSW*, Vol. 6, pp. 538-9, Paterson to Castlereagh. By avoiding travelling to Sydney, Paterson also avoided making the illegal step of assuming the Government; *see* Bligh's opinion, *HRA*, Vol. 6, p. 528.

1808, no friend to Bligh's interests. He was specifically described by her as being 'very ill disposed towards you'; she was acting on information arising from the attempt by Bligh's critics in London to remove him during December-January 1808. There was not much hope that Foveaux would support Bligh on the grounds that the coup was illegal, but to countenance it would implicate himself in its consequences.

MacArthur was coming under increasing fire from his many opponents and competitors. A rather clever ploy to get rid of him in early February came to nothing. Acting on the wave of popularity felt for MacArthur by the Establishment, some of his 'friends' decided it would be useful to raise a fund for the purposes of sending a messenger from the colony to London with despatches and an agreed account of why they had removed Bligh. Who better to carry this message than John MacArthur? To prove their sincerity a fund was started, which quickly climbed to over £1,000. But MacArthur, while happy to accept the honour and the wild cheers that greeted his nomination at the heady meeting in the town, was no fool. He was vulnerable on two counts if he accepted the mission: first, he might be arrested for treason in Britain, and second, he would be leaving his commercial interests, at a time when they were beginning to bear fruit, to the mercies of a regime consisting of people who, he knew, were not over-anxious to protect his interests. After the cheers had died down and the over-happy 'friends' had dispersed, MacArthur soon made it plain he had no intention of going. In fact, he was appointed by Johnston to his new post not long after this. Instead of getting him out of the colony, his rivals, by publicly showing him to be popular, got him placed over them. If MacArthur had a sense of humour he must have been laughing all the sixteen miles back to Elizabeth Farm.[12]

Criticism of MacArthur mounted and came in from all sides. Whoever was 'Governor' of the colony was inevitably the butt of all the problems and grievances that arose; people identified the cause of their problems with whoever was in charge. Just as governments tend to suffer mid-term unpopularity, so revolutionary leaders become a victim of their own propaganda. His critics had blamed Bligh for everything; but no Governor is to blame for everything, and when they assumed command and the problems continued, along with new ones discovered, they became implicated in the disappointment of the constituents. Settlers, for example, issued a petition which was sent to Patterson. It said, in part: 'The whole government appears to be put into the hands of John McArthur Esqr., who seems a very improper person, he having been a turbulent and troublesome character, constantly quarrelling with His Majesty's Governors, and other principal officers, from Governor Phillip to Governor Bligh; and we believe him to be the principal agitator and promoter of the present alarming and calamitous state of the colony.'[13] They were even more unrestrained in their condemnation of

---

[12] *HRNSW*, Vol. 6, p. 513; Messers Lord, Kable, Underwood, Blaxland, Bayly and Blaxcell were among those offering to contribute, and a total sum of £1,095 5s. was promised.
[13] *HRNSW*, Vol. 6, p. 596.

MacArthur to Johnston as 'the Scourge of this Colony' and accused him by 'his monopoly and extortion' of having been 'highly injurious to the Inhabitants of every description'.[14] Paterson had every reason to believe every word of these charges, as he had clashed with MacArthur before and had personal experience of his nature.[15]

Johnston had to act and he decided the best thing to do was to confront the critics of MacArthur among his officers. He invited any officer with a specific charge against MacArthur to present it to him in writing, and addressed the letter personally to each of MacArthur's critics. 'If he has committed any offence, it is not my intention to shut my ears against the proof of it. If anything improper in his conduct can be made appear he shall immediately be dismissed from his Office.' But Johnston went on to put a most onerous condition on the critics if their charges led to MacArthur's dismissal: 'I hope some one of you Gentlemen will have public spirit sufficient to supply his place and to perform the laborious duties Mr. McArthur now discharges without reward or emolument.'[16] By siding with MacArthur so eloquently and decisively, Johnston did not stem the disaffection. That continued to spread.

MacArthur was not immune to these pressures. In his private correspondence there is a letter which shows him to be depressed by the turn in events. He wrote to his friend Piper: 'If Foveaux arrives safe there will be a pretty scenery here. One Governor in arrest, and two rival Lieut.-Governors laying claim to the command.' MacArthur was not alone in anticipation of what would happen when Foveaux arrived. But his main concerns were more local. He had a long list of names of people with whom he was in conflict:[17]

I am sorry to resport to you that some of your old acquaintance have behaved most scurvily – Abbott among the worst. Minchin *sent* home with the Despatches – not from any confidence placed in him; Grimes on the same errand – only for telling a few lies, &c.; Bayly, for whom every proper thing has been done, is become a violent oppositionist – the assigned reason, some *information* he received *from Grimes* of my finding fault with him:– but the real one, because I would not advise Johnston to make Laycock a Magistrate and Police Officer – with some other little disappointments respecting men, cows, &c. in short I am of opinion, that, had they been given way to, the whole of the publick property would not have satisfied them.

[14] *HRA*, Vol. 6, pp. 572-3, Address of 11 April 1808.

[15] Paterson had been MacArthur's apponent in the duel which got him sent home to Britain in 1801; *see* p. 340.

[16] Onslow (ed.), 1914, pp. 160-1; with suitable verbiage the named people signed a reply which declared them 'unanimously of opinion that they do not feel themselves justified nor would they presume to call in question the Right of Propriety of his consulting any person he may think proper either publickly or privately' (p. 162). This did not, of course, answer the main contention in Johnston's letters to them. Of interest, we might note that John MacArthur acted as Notary in signing the letters as 'true copies'.

[17] MacArthur to Piper, 24 May 1808, Piper Papers, ML MS A254, pp. 137-9; *HRNSW*, Vol. 6, p. 643.

This last remark is indicative of the mood among the victors at the lack of spoils.

The quarrels among the factions that formed the administration between the coup of 26 January and the arrival of Foveaux on 28 July were never resolved. Johnston could complain of the failure to annihilate the 'Party Spirit that has unfortunately too much prevailed almost ever since the day when you all urged me to assume the Government',[18] but this is one of the penalties of unconstitutional action: it provokes lack of reverence for legal process and therefore further unconstitutional action. With Foveaux's arrival the issue was resolved: Johnston and MacArthur ceased to form the Government, which was assumed by Foveaux himself.

Foveaux arrived in the *Lady Madeleine Sinclair* transport, the same vessel in which Bligh had made his journey to Australia. He was closeted with the leaders of the rebel government from the moment he arrived and decided that his best option was to assume the government himself as Lieutenant-Governor, continue Bligh's arrest and persuade him to go back to Britain. This, of course, infuriated Bligh.[19] If he was not to be helped by lawful authority when faced with a mutiny, he was certainly not going to oblige them by removing himself from the colony without instructions to that effect from London.[20] From this time on Bligh's stubbornness came to the fore. He was to suffer many indignities and privations during the next twenty-two months, but he stuck to his original position that only the King could relieve him of his command and the rest of them could go to hell.

Bligh decided to appeal formally to Paterson as the Commander-in-Chief of the Corps to travel to Sydney and restore him to office. Paterson replied that Bligh should go back to Britain and seek redress there.[21] The last thing that Paterson wanted was to get involved if he could help it. But he could not remain indefinitely in Port Dalrymple without compromising himself with London. As the senior British Commander in the colony next to Governor Bligh, he could not pretend that the affair in Sydney was of insufficient significance to justify his journey. So he eventually arrived in Sydney in January 1809. Foveaux had ruled the colony during the previous six months, basically continuing the measures adopted by Johnston's Government. Once Paterson arrived, Foveaux had to step aside for the senior man. However, protocol in seniority did not interfere with convenience in administration. Foveaux continued as before, with Major Johnston as effective administrator.

Paterson's main task, as he saw it, was to remove Bligh from the Colony, preferably on the next ship going to Britain. To summarise adequately the machinations between the two sides would take up considerable space.

---

[18] Onslow (ed.), 1914, p. 161.

[19] For Bligh's reaction to Foveaux's decision *see* Bligh to Castlereagh, Letter, 31 August 1808, *HRA*, Vol. 6, pp. 588-602; Bligh also wrote to the Earl of Minto, Governor-General of India, about Foveaux's betrayal. It was unlikely that Minto would send troops from his colony to interfere in another's.

[20] Foveaux to Castlereagh, Letter, 4 September 1808, *HRA*, Vol. 6, pp. 623-6, for Foveaux's explanation of his conduct and his views of the state of the colony when he arrived.

[21] Bligh to Paterson, 8 August 1808, *HRNSW*, Vol. 6, p. 701.

Notes, letters, commands, petitions and memorials abounded in every quarter, each person in the drama carefully recording his dissent with the next with a view to establishing judicial prudence if the necessity arose in the future. This led to the most extravagant language and accusations, to justify to London and the Colonial office their admittedly difficult and unique situation.[22]

Paterson arrived back in Sydney on 9 January 1809, nearly a year after the coup. He proceeded to initiate the process by which Bligh was to be forced to leave for Britain. Bligh had remained in Government House for the entire period since the coup, a virtual prisoner, kept away from other people in the colony. Paterson decided that, by removing him from the comforts of Government House, Bligh might be forced to make the journey home. He misjudged the man who had led his party for forty-six days in the open boat; comfort and luxury were things Bligh would gladly forgo if he thought the situation demanded it. For Bligh the important thing was to make things hard for the military in carrying out their intentions. To this end he refused to co-operate with the orders to remove him from his official residence. Once again, he insisted, only the Sovereign could do that. Johnston and Abbott were chosen by Paterson to handle the removal, and Bligh later claimed that this was the first time he had seen or dealt with them since 26 January 1808.[23]

Bligh was forcibly removed from Government House on 30 January 1809, and taken to the barracks. He was confined to a two-room 'suite', accompanied by Mrs Putland.[24] He was told to be ready to embark on the *Estramina*. But Bligh had no intention of embarking on any vessel other than the *Porpoise*. His reasoning was simple. The *Porpoise* was a naval vessel and as such under his command. He knew that, no matter what the military did to him ashore, there was no question of the naval officers disobeying his orders, as he was plainly gazetted as Commander of all naval vessels in the colony, was clearly Senior Captain over the officers of the *Porpoise* and had recently been promoted to Commodore by London. Naval officers would not want to get entangled in the shore mutiny. They had no part in what was going on ashore and were trying their best to remain aloof from the whole business. In this situation Bligh knew that if he could get onto the *Porpoise* he would have command of the ship.

After considerable arguing between Bligh and his jailers Paterson agreed to allow Bligh to join H.M.S. *Porpoise*. At the same time Johnston and

[22] It was alleged that there was a plot by Bligh supporters to kidnap Paterson, but this is so out of character that it must not be taken seriously; Paterson was encouraged to believe there was a plot, and it had the desired effect on the new 'Governor'; he wrote indignantly to Castlereagh to complain about Bligh, *see HRA*, First Series, Vol. 7, pp. 16-17, Paterson to Castlereagh, Letter, 12 March 1809. In one of the exchanges, Bligh was accused of having 'concubines' in Sydney; an outrageous suggestion in Bligh's case, especially as he had his daughter with him throughout his governorship. Any and every charge was being bandied about.

[23] For an account of these transactions *see HRNSW*, Vol. 7.

[24] At Johnston's trial it was testified by the military that Bligh had been well treated in his new abode; *see* Bartrum, 1811, p. 215.

MacArthur were negotiating with Paterson to be allowed to quit the colony and take passage to Britain in the *Admiral Gambier*, then in Sydney. They were anxious to travel to Britain, both to explain themselves to the Government in reply to whatever Bligh would report (it being believed at the time that Bligh's departure for Britain was finally settled), and to avoid unpleasant circumstances arising for themselves if the expected relief for Bligh arrived in the colony and found them still there.

Bligh's removal from the barrack rooms to the *Porpoise* was conditional on a pledge that he would take the ship to Britain and not stop at any other port in the colony nor return unless the King sent him back. Bligh pledged to keep these conditions on his 'honor as an officer and a gentleman'.[25] Paterson took him at his word. But Bligh, much to the consternation of his critics, reneged on his word as soon as he got on board. The officers and crew, instead of getting an early voyage back home, were told that Bligh intended to remain in the colony in command of the ship until told otherwise by the King. Disappointment at missing an early home voyage was added to some feelings of sympathy for the military. Life under Bligh, in the mood which he was in after thirteen months of virtual house arrest and the frustration of all his plans to restore his command, was not the most enticing prospect for any of them. Lieutenant Kent, with whom Bligh had been in dispute over his non-support for him in the past year as the next senior naval officer in the colony, was immediately placed under arrest by Bligh and confined to the ship until he was court-martialled.[26]

The arguments about the morality of Bligh's actions when he regained command of a Navy ship must not be seen in isolation. The game being played in New South Wales was deadly serious. Men could hang for what they did in this dispute. The borderline between treason and indiscretion would greatly depend on how things were viewed from London. Bligh had every right to feel he was dealing with usurpers and rebels against the King's representative. How far he treated with them, what he told them and what he agreed to was a matter for him to decide in the light of his overall objective, which was in no circumstances to act in any way which would compromise the validity of the King's writ and authority. He viewed it as absolutely essential that he give no credence whatsoever to the rebels' authority by co-operating with them, or accepting any of their wishes. As an unarmed man he did not consider personal resistance as being productive or necessary. As long as he stood firm on the principle that they had no authority or right to override him as Governor, he was convinced that in the long run London would support him and recognise that he had done his duty.[27] For that

[25] *HRNSW*, Vol. 7, p. 17.

[26] *HRNSW*, Vol. 7, pp. 74, 103, 494. He was confined for 23 months and tried by court martial on 8 January 1811 on H.M.S. *Gladiator*. He was acquitted. Bligh was under enormous emotional strain at this time and began to behave with slight paranoia (he even believed he might be poisoned, which is less far-fetched when one remembers that with several hardened criminals on hand it would have been quite possible to engineer an assassination); *HRNSW*, Vol. 7, p. 175.

[27] This was indeed the view of the British Government through Castlereagh, until he was forced to resign for fighting a duel with Canning. The incoming administration took a more liberal view of the proceedings.

principle Bligh was prepared to be criticised for his contravention of his word. Others might have acted differently, and could have been judged on the basis that they put their own honour above that of the King. It is difficult today to grasp the viewpoint of a man like Bligh over this issue, but it ought to be remembered that duty as perceived by such men in that age was a very powerful controller of their behaviour. This is said neither in praise nor in criticism of such attitudes, but only in order to help understand them.

Bligh's resolve did not falter during the next year, which he spent on the *Porpoise* sailing between Sydney and Derwent in Tasmania. He used his command of the vessel to stop ships from London to find what messages had been sent to the colony, to raise victuals for himself and the crew and to remind the rebels that while deposed he was not defeated.[28] Johnston and MacArthur sailed on 29 March in the *Admiral Gambier* for Britain.[29] Paterson was left in command of the colony. It was soon clear to him that Bligh was going to insist on remaining in the vicinity and he therefore issued a proclamation debarring any person in the colony from any form of contact with Bligh or the *Porpoise*.[30] It was a measure of the discord between the two men that this extreme measure was taken. Bligh had issued his own proclamation, printed by friends in Sydney, denouncing the military government for being in a state of mutiny and forbidding any ship to take the rebel leaders to Britain. But the blast and counterblast were confined to paper.

Paterson's administration was notable for its official plunder of the territory in the form of largesse in land granting. He managed in twelve months to grant more land to whoever asked for it than even the generous Governor King managed in almost six years. The fact that grants to military officers, their wives and children and to the civilian friends of the Johnston regime predominated in his gifts suggests the real nature of the military regimes between those of Bligh and Macquarie; namely, that they were regimes calculated to increase the wealth and privilege of the Establishment in the colony over the heads and interests of the ordinary settlers.[31]

The next year, then, was spent in waiting for a decision from London.

[28] While at Derwent Bligh clashed with the local military commander, David Collins, after Paterson wrote to Collins and gave him orders regarding the treatment of Bligh. *See HRNSW*, Vol. 7, pp. 101-201 for details of the Bligh-Collins relationship.

[29] The *Admiral Gambier* was bound for Rio and they had to take another ship to complete their journey. Before leaving, MacArthur advertised some stock and one of his farms (2,000 acres at the Hawkesbury) for sale in the *Sydney Gazette* in issues between 15 January and 2 April 1809.

[30] The Proclamation was published in the *Sydney Gazette*, 19 March 1809; it reproduced the agreement entered into between Bligh and Paterson and demanded of the citizens of the colony that they should 'not ... hold, countenance, or be privy to any communication or correspondence, by personal interview, Letter, Message, Signal or otherwise, with the said William Bligh Esq., or any person belonging to his Family, Establishment or Retinue ...'. Two of Bligh's supporters, Palmer and Hook, were sentenced to jail for helping him. They were referred to in the Proclamation as 'wicked and evil disposed Persons implicated in the high crimes and misdemeanours' of Bligh.

[31] *HRA*, Vol. 7, p. 804; *see* Mackaness, 1951, p. 495 for further details. In his period of office Bligh granted 2,180 acres, compared to 5,660 acres under George Johnston, 8,325 acres under Foveaux, 68,101 under Paterson. In the military interregnum under Grose between Phillip and Hunter, Paterson managed to grant 4,965 acres as well. *See* Mackaness, 1951, p. 496 and note.

Meanwhile in London news of the overthrow of the Governor caused a considerable stir in and around Government and the Admiralty.[32] The country was, however, somewhat distracted by the wars with Napoleon and it was some time before thought was given as to what to do about the situation. The Government considered, probably correctly, that, whatever the merits and demerits of the situation, it was plainly impossible for Governor Bligh to continue in office by being restored to it. It did not seem that the rebellion was aimed at the integrity of the King, except in so far as it condemned his wish to have Bligh as Governor; it was not considered that the rebellion was a version of the American War of Independence. It was merely the ever-factious colony getting out of hand and crossing the line of discretion. It was clear that a replacement for Bligh had to be found. The first choice fell not on any of the petitioners (mainly naval men) but on Brigadier-General Nightingale, Commander-in-Chief of the 73rd Regiment. The idea of sending out a soldier instead of a naval captain was a good one; it recognised belatedly that the colony was no longer an appendage to naval exploration but a shore posting requiring military experience.

The legal opinions that the Government had taken about the insurrection came down fairly clearly on the side of Bligh in the strict sense that the actions of the officers of the Corps were contrary to their duty and that they were in jeopardy of trial for mutiny.[33] This jeopardy extended to Foveaux who was deemed liable on the grounds that he had continued the detention of Bligh. In the case of MacArthur it was felt that he too was in legal jeopardy, but that as the colony was outside the Kingdom he should be tried in the Criminal Court in Sydney. Johnston, however, was liable to trial in Britain, but the fact that he was bringing MacArthur with him as a witness meant that MacArthur escaped the threat of a local trial. With a purge in the colony this was unlikely to be the farce that his earlier trials had turned out to be. Such was MacArthur's delicate position in a legal sense, and such was his fear of a court appearance, that he did not return to the colony until 1817, accepting instead the forcible separation from his wife and business interests throughout the years in between.

Nightingale eventually withdrew from the nomination as Governor owing to illness, and as it had been decided to post the 73rd Regiment to New South Wales and recall the Corps the alternative choice fell on Lachlan

---

[32] Edward MacArthur had arrived in Britain with news of the rebellion in September 1808. He wrote to his father: 'Our late affairs make little impression on the public mind, and excite still less attention at the offices, for Spain and Portugal attract all their attentions – all their thoughts', Onslow (ed.), 1914, p. 167; some part of the lack of interest in the colony's affairs was probably occasioned by a lack of willingness to discuss important affairs of state with the son of someone who appeared to be a rebel. In a later letter to his father he wrote: 'From all I can learn I fear you will find yourself necessitated to return to England, for the Government will, I fear, to the very last, support Bligh; but it is of no use, for up he must be given at length. A gentleman told me to-day that although Governor Bligh's conduct was most flagrant, yet the Government would look with great jealousy on his suspension, on account of precedent; but justice must be done, for Major Johnston has a friend who has the power in a certain degree to enforce it', *ibid.*, p. 172.

[33] *HRNSW*, Vol. 7, pp. 229-30.

Macquarie, the second-in-command.[34] He accepted the appointment and received his orders on 9 May 1809. Macquarie's instructions were specific and augured ill for the rebels. Castlereagh instructed him:[35]

> take immediate measures for placing Major Johnston in close arrest, and for sending him Home in order that he may be tried for his conduct on his return to England; and as Gov'r Bligh has represented that Mr McArthur has been the leading promoter and instigator of the mutinous measures which have been taken against His Majesty's Governor, you will, if examinations be sworn against him charging him with criminal acts against the Governor and his authority, have him arrested thereupon and brought to trial before the Criminal Court of the settlement.

Further instructions required Macquarie to cancel all official appointments made subsequent to Bligh's arrest, to restore to office those who had been deposed, with the exception of Atkins, who was to be sent home, to cancel all land grants made since Bligh's deposition, to send the Corps, including all its officers, home and to hand back to Bligh all papers belonging to him. His orders also included the nominal re-appointment of Bligh as Governor for twenty-four hours, to confirm the King's writ in effect. He was then to assume command of the colony himself.

When Macquarie arrived in Sydney on 28 December 1809, he was unable to implement the restoration of Bligh as Governor because at this time Bligh was with the *Porpoise* off Tasmania. Restoration to office would have done wonders for Bligh's dignity and gone some way to mending his pride after his experiences as a 'fugitive' and 'exile' over the previous year. When he heard news of Macquarie's arrival he arrived back in Sydney as soon as he could cover the distance from Tasmania. He landed to an official reception and a guard of honour made up of the 73rd Regiment on 17 January 1810, nearly two years after the coup. It was a triumph of a sort and Bligh made the most of it.[36]

Macquarie had arrived with his regiment in H.M.S. *Dromedary* and H.M.S. *Hindostan*. His second-in-command, Lieutenant-Colonel O'Connell, later married Bligh's daughter the widowed Mrs Putland. Relations between Bligh and Macquarie were at first cordial, but they became not a little strained when Macquarie, acting on his judgement of the needs of the situation, became reliant on Foveaux for advice and administration of the colony. This mortally offended Bligh, who regarded Foveaux as part of the mutinous gang of usurpers, and he took it as a slight to himself that Macquarie should act in this way.[37] Matters were not made any better by the inevitable fraternising that went on between the rank and file of the Corps

[34] Lachlan Macquarie had dined with Bligh when their ships met at the Cape of Good Hope in 1788; Bligh, of course, was commanding the *Bounty* at that time and Macquarie was going to India with his regiment.

[35] Castlereagh to Macquarie, Letter, 14 May 1809, *HRNSW*, Vol. 7, pp. 143-4.

[36] *See ibid.*, p. 252 for Macquarie's account of Bligh's arrival and his formal arrangements to welcome him.

[37] Bligh to Elizabeth Bligh, 8 March 1810, Bligh Family Correspondence, ML MS Safe 1/45.

and the new arrivals. A soldier's lot in the British army in the nineteenth century was rough enough without involving himself in the quarrels of state and the sensitivity of those in high office. Fraternisation was inevitable, even if it was not encouraged, and measures to stop it would have reopened many wounds and, more important from Macquarie's point of view, would have continued the tensions of the past into his administration. He wanted tranquillity and a break with the past. The fact that his inability to prevent the Corps mixing with citizens and soldiers offended Bligh and his supporters was of less concern to him than the probable consequences of involving himself in dispute between Bligh and the Corps, which was strictly a matter for the courts in Britain to decide. As far as he was concerned, his presence guaranteed that both sides in the dispute could carry on as normal without fear of intimidation. To this end he involved Bligh socially in the affairs of Government House and permitted others to do likewise.[38]

It was Bligh's intention to see that those civilian persons who had remained in Sydney after Johnston and MacArthur had left, and who had been active in opposition to his Governorship during the coup, should be prosecuted in the criminal courts. Unfortunately for this plan his orders from London did not specify such an action. They referred to a local trial for MacArthur, but not for others. He complained in the letter to his wife of 8 March of 'the insufficiency of my Instructions' and that 'through that cause [I have] been very much embarrassed ever since to know how to act in bringing the offenders here to justice.' Faced with this legal dilemma, which was of course brought to his attention by Bligh, Macquarie took advice from his own Judge-Advocate and then resorted to the well-worn device of seeking further instructions from London. In this case I believe he had little alternative.

The last public airing of the controversy between Bligh and his critics took place in April. Bligh's supporters in the colony wanted to signify their public support for him before he left and they chose the form of an address of condolence and congratulation to be voted on at two public meetings, one in Sydney and one in the Hawkesbury district.[39] In both places Bligh had considerable popular support; so had MacArthur and Johnston. As all public meetings had to receive official permission and be chaired by the Provost-Marshal (in this case Gore, whom Macquarie had restored to office), the new Governor faced the usual problem. If he permitted the meetings

[38] Macquarie wrote to his brother a confidential letter regarding Bligh. He said, in part: 'Governor Bligh certainly is a most disagreeable Person to have any dealings, or Publick business to transact with; having no regard whatever to his promise or engagements however sacred, and his natural temper is uncommonly harsh, and tyrannical in the extreme'. He also said that it was 'an undoubted fact that he is a very improper Person to be employed in any situation of Trust or Command and he is certainly very generally detested by high, low, rich and poor, but more specially by the higher Classes of People', *Journal of the Royal Australian Historical Society*, Vol. 16, Part 1 (1930), p. 27. Bligh claimed that he was under strain because of the treatment by Macquarie of the loyalists in Sydney and the affront to them, especially those that had suffered at the 'justice' of the military governments, by his intimacy with the insurrectionists. He had remarked on 8 March in his letter to Mrs Bligh: 'It is a hard trial of my temper to be here just now.'

[39] *HRNSW*, Vol. 7, p. 311.

would they cause trouble between the two factions? If he did not permit the meetings would he appear to be opposing a declaration of support for ex-Governor Bligh? No doubt with some misgivings, Macquarie gave his permission for the meetings.

The first one was held in Sydney and attracted a huge crowd. Both factions had drummed up everybody they could get, including officers of the New South Wales Corps. The address to Bligh was in the fulsome language in which these things were normally written and made particularly biting comments on Johnston and MacArthur.[40] The meeting broke up in uproar as each side claimed it had the majority. Gore announced that the address was carried and persons were invited to sign it individually at their convenience. In the end 460 citizens signed it, which in view of the discord, the delay of two years since Bligh's overthrow, and the fact that they stood to gain nothing by supporting a finished regime, suggests that Bligh's support was deeper and more widespread than some critics have conceded.

The meeting itself was over but the supporters of Johnston and MacArthur were not finished. Bligh's supporters, having achieved their object, left the meeting. His opponents demanded that Gore put alternative motions to the vote. This Gore refused to do, on the ground that the Governor had given permission to discuss the address to Bligh and that precluded other matters being discussed. Blaxland and Lord (two signatories of the 'requisition' to Johnston) went to Macquarie and complained of Gore's ruling. This put Macquarie on the spot. He sent for Gore and ordered him to be impartial and present the other motions. Thus a further meeting was called for that afternoon. This was strictly illegal. Notice of meetings had to be carried in the *Gazette* and notice of the motion had to be handed to the Government. To get round this problem it was decided to call the afternoon meeting as an 'adjourned' continuation of the morning's meeting, but this was also strictly improper because no notice of the motions had been given. Macquarie was forced into this position by the tension that the first meeting had created among the rebels' supporters, and rather than have a rebirth of discord in the town he had to give them their say. In the afternoon meeting their four resolutions were carried without dissent (Bligh's supporters holding to the view that the meeting was improper). The gist of the resolutions was contained in the first one, namely that the morning's meeting was conducive to disharmony in the colony.[41] The last resolution was the most strange in that it declared that all the resolutions were carried 'unanimously'. Even so, the participants refused Gore's invitation to sign their names to any of them. Macquarie had the last say and he refused permission for the motions of either meeting to be printed in the *Gazette*. Bligh was presented with his address by his supporters before he left Sydney.

The last duty that Bligh undertook before returning home was to give his daughter away at her wedding to Lieutenant-Colonel O'Connell. The engagement came as a surprise to him. One of his letters to his wife gives us a

[40] *See* Bartrum, 1811, p. 448.
[41] *ibid.*, p. 459.

brief look into his most intimate family life and it is worth quoting from. He wrote to his wife from Rio de Janeiro, where the *Hindostan* called on its voyage home.[42] He was writing to tell her that he was not bringing Mary home with him and at the same time announcing her wedding. He obviously felt this was not the easiest thing to do, as Elizabeth Bligh had not seen her daughter for four years and did not even know her new husband. Moreover, the rigours of the journeys to and from Australia meant that she would never see her daughter again. Bligh writes the letter as a father torn between love for his daughter and his wife, and tries to justify his decision and re-assure her against the natural alarm which she would feel on reading it. 'My Dearest Love,' he wrote:

> Providence has ordained certain things which we cannot account for; so it has happened with us. My perfect reliance that everything which occurs is for the best is my great consolation. In the highest feelings of comfort & pride of bringing her, to England, altho I thought she could be under no guidance but my own – my heart devoted to her, – in the midst of the most parental affections and conflicting passions of adoration for so good and admired child, I at the last found what I the least expected; – Lieut-Colonel O'Connel commanding the 73 Regt. had unknown to me won her affections.

Bligh was probably so busy completing his affairs that he did not notice the relationship developing between Mary and O'Connell. Their introduction had taken place on Bligh's return to Sydney in the *Porpoise* and O'Connell had had the Blighs to dinner on their second night back in the colony. Mary was, according to several accounts, an attractive woman who was a social success even in the dark days of the revolution. She was passionately loyal to her father – she tried single-handed to stop Johnston's troops entering Government House to arrest him – and after her first husband's death remained at his side, suffering all the discomforts of his wanderings on the *Porpoise*.

Bligh gives O'Connell a glowing reference to reassure Betsy that Mary has married a man of standing. 'Nothing can exceed the esteen & high Character he has. – He is likewise Lt. Govr. of the Territory.' Then he goes on to describe how he was informed of the intentions of the couple just before he and Mary were due to board the ship for the journey home.

> A Few days before I sailed, when everything was prepared for her reception, & we had even embarked, he then opened the circumstance to me – I gave him a flat denial for I could not believe it. I retired with her, when I found she had approved of his addresses & given her Word to him. What will you not my Dear Betsy feel for my situation at the time, & when you know that nothing I could say had any effect; at last overwhelmed with a loss I could not retrieve I had only to make the best of it – My consent could only be

---

[42] Bligh to Elizabeth Bligh, 11 August 1810, *Hindostan*, Rio de Janero, Bligh Family Correspondence, ML MS Safe 1/45. Bligh's convoy at Rio missed by a few weeks Captain Peter Heywood's visit in H.M.S. *Nereus*, in October 1810.

extorted, for it was not a free gift; however, on many proofs of the Honor, Goodness and high Character of Colonel O'Connel, and his good sense which had passed under my own trial, I did, like having no alternative, consent to her marriage, & gave her away at the ceremony consumated at Government House, under the most public tokens of respect & veneration – the whole Colony, except a few Malcontents, considering it the first blessing ever bestowed upon them – every creature devoted to her service, by her excellence, with respect and adoration. Thus my Dear Love, when I thought nothing could have induced our dear Child to have quitted me, have I left her behind in the finest climate in the World, which to have taken her from into the tempestuous Voyage I have performed I now believe would have caused her death. – Every thing honorable & affectionate has been performed by Col. O'Connel, which I soon hope to communicate to you – they remain persons of the utmost importance, & consequence to the Wellfare of the Colony, and the admiration & respect of Govr & Mrs Macquarie who did the honors at the Ceremony at Government House with an extraordinary degree of pleasure & even exultation.

He added at the end of the letter:

I have now only to hope I shall be able to console you for our Dear Mary remaining behind – if I had forced her away & I had lost her on the Voyage I could never have survived it – she remains as a Pattern of Virtue and admired by every one.

Mary was twenty-seven years old at the time of her second wedding; the fact that her suitor had to ask her father's permission is not without interest nowadays. As she had inherited her father's determination it is not surprising that, once she had consented to the proposal privately, she would not let her father talk her out of it.

He boarded the *Hindostan* alone and sailed in the convoy for Britain on 12 May 1810. The *Porpoise* and the *Dromedary* sailed in the convoy, each carrying the officers and men of the New South Wales Corps, now renamed the 102nd Regiment of Foot. With their departure the Rum Corps was separated from the only home it knew. That it had managed to disgrace itself in its twenty years' tenure did not lessen the emotionalism of the departure. With the men of the regiment went their wives and children, many of whom were to perish on the voyage or soon afterwards in the colder and damper climate of southern England. Colonel Paterson died at sea off Cape Horn. He finally succumbed to the years of heavy drinking which had marred his judgement and government. The *Hindostan* landed its passengers at Spithead on 25 October 1810. Bligh travelled to London to see his wife and family, to prepare to answer any charges brought against him and to prosecute Johnston for mutiny.

30

Journey's End

Bligh returned to Britain, after what was to be his last sea voyage, to face the final public challenge to his conduct. This time he was facing formidable forces. When he had stood up to the Christian family in 1792-5 he had had a singular advantage in that the men ranged against him were in the main of inferior calibre and that the sponsors of the opposition, who were of greater standing, had to fight at second-hand through these people. The Johnston-MacArthur faction, held together by a common fear that if one fell so would the other, were of altogether different stock. Of the two MacArthur was the stronger and the cleverer. He was also over-confident of the impending success of his business.

At Rio, where he was changing ships from the *Admiral Gambier* to the *Lady Warburton*, MacArthur wrote to his wife:[1] 'In two months I hope to be in England, and in three months after on my way back; but however short my stay there may be, or speedy the returning voyage, it will yet be to me a dreary and comfortless time.' His confidence was born of the reception that his son Edward had received from friends of Johnston's in Britain, in particular from the Duke of Northumberland.[2] This pleasant news was topped up by the opinions on Bligh's conduct that he was given by British officers he met in Rio. They seemed to suggest, if their opinions were general among the British Establishment, that Bligh was going to come off worse in the enquiry and trial.[3] His optimism was short-lived. He had lived too long in a parochial community where he held disproportionate power and where he was a major personality to be reckoned with. In Britain, the cities and country were full of 'John MacArthur's' and in the main they were bigger and more powerful than he was. Bligh had many important friends on his side too – men like Sir Joseph Banks whose views and interest still counted in and around Government.[4]

[1] MacArthur to Elizabeth MacArthur, 30 July 1809, Rio de Janero, in Onslow (ed.), 1914, pp. 180-2.

[2] The Duke of Northumberland was a protector of George Johnston; they had served together in the Americas; Bligh went so far as to suggest that Johnston was the Duke's son in a pencil note on his copy of Bartrum's *Trial of Johnston* in the Mitchell Library (ML MS 344/4A3). For an account of the reception of Edward MacArthur by the Duke *see* Onslow (ed.), 1914, pp. 165-76.

[3] *See* MacArthur to Elizabeth MacArthur, 22 and 30 July, Rio de Janerio, Onslow (ed.), 1914, pp. 177-82; Admiral De Courcy 'loudly reprobated the conduct of Bligh – as indeed every man does who speaks of him'.

[4] MacArthur noted with sarcasm that 'Sir Joseph Banks still continues to advocate his friend's cause, and speaks of him as a much injured meritorious character – fortunately no one believes him', MacArthur to Elizabeth MacArthur, 3 May 1810, London, Onslow (ed.), 1914, p. 195.

His visit, far from taking a matter of months, as MacArthur had asserted confidently that it would, became an exile of eight years. Bligh's arrival home brought the main characters in the drama within reach of London and they set about manoeuvring and petitioning with all the intensity of their factional battles in Sydney. The difference, this time, was that London was no isolated village on the edge of the world; it was the centre and metropolis of an enormous Empire. The whole country was fully committed to the great wars of Europe, and the capital sported several dozen faction fights on all kinds of issues against which the quarrels of Sydney looked relatively minor and unimportant. It took some time for MacArthur and his friends to get a sense of their own stature in the queue of problems facing Government at the time.[5]

The first really good news for MacArthur was the fall of Castlereagh. Less notice has been taken of the other great political change of the day, namely the succession to the Prime Minister's post of Spenser Percival in place of the ailing Duke of Portland. Percival was linked from years past with the friends of the Christian family; he was an intimate friend of Samuel Romilly, the radical lawyer who had helped Edward Christian conduct his enquiry into the *Bounty*. He had followed Edward Law as Attorney-General. Law was a close family friend of the Christians. All of them had a common interest in legal matters and we might remember that Edward Christian was Professor of Law and editor of *Blackstone's Commentaries*. I have no documentary evidence that Spenser Percival was interested or active in the 'party spirit' that broke out over the Bligh-Johnston campaign. But it seems to me that his coming into the highest office under the King at this opportune moment was not without its consequences for the anti-Bligh forces on the broad conduct of the fight.

I have mentioned that there were events about this time which might explain why Heywood did not proceed with publication of Morrison's Journal (if he had it) in 1808-10.[6] One was his sighting of Fletcher Christian in Fore Street, Plymouth, around 1808-10 (see p.254). Heywood believed he saw Fletcher Christian, and Barrow vouched for the authenticity of the report.[7] When he lost sight of the man who ran away as he approached Heywood declined to make enquiries, considering that it would be 'prudent to let the matter drop'. In this case it would not be prudent, after all, to publish any account of Morrison's Journal.

This would also explain his failure to contact MacArthur and Johnston, who faced the same kind of tribulation that he had gone through and for what to him must have seemed familiar reasons, and might also suggest a reason why Edward Christian did not appear on the scene with help or support. It could not have been that he was unaware that a major trial was about to take place. Edward Christian's interest in law would assure him that knowledge as well as his interest in its protagonist. If Fletcher Christian

[5] *See ibid.*, p. 195: 'In such a state of things it would be weak indeed to expect that the affairs of our insignificant Colony should create much interest.'

[6] His decision to publish in 1825 may also have been connected with the appearance of Byron's poem on the mutiny, which was regarded as pro-Bligh. See Chapter 19, n. 22.

[7] Barrow, 1961, p. 279n.

was alive and in Britain none of his family would want to remind the public
of the case: interest might beget 'Bounty' hunters and encourage gossip. The
apparent lack of contact[8] between the MacArthur/Johnston camp – who
were combing the country looking for aid and interest – and
Heywood/Christian families, who were surely still looking for revenge, is
remarkable. I cannot accept that they had lost interest. It could be that they
were in league with the MacArthur/Johnston campaign, either directly or
indirectly, and that they kept their participation a total secret. As yet there is
no evidence either way, and this must remain another mystery until
something definite turns up.

With Bligh's arrival in London in October 1810, the legal proceedings
could get under way. This delay in Bligh's return caused Johnston and
MacArthur to fret away the time fruitlessly fuming at their predicament.
They had arrived a year earlier, unasked and unwelcome, and the
government refused to proceed without the presence of the former Governor,
who would be principal witness for the prosecution of Major Johnston.
MacArthur told his wife in February 1810 'it is useless to repine, and indeed
improper'.[9] His correspondence details some of the measures his faction were
taking in their campaign and shows that he was fully cognisant of the
implications of the fall of Castlereagh. 'How it might have been,' he wrote,
'had Lord Castlereagh and that Northern Bear Mr. Cook remained in office I
cannot say, for certain it is they had both declared themselves adverse to us;
and had they retained their authority they would have increased our
difficulties, and perhaps, in the end, have crushed us altogether. – We ought,
therefore, to think ourselves very fortunate that these men are removed, for
from what I hear and know of their characters, it is not trifles that would
deter them from executing any plan which they might conceive their interest
required them to pursue.'[10] When he heard the news of Bligh's arrival
MacArthur declared that he was going to sue him for £20,000. 'I am
continually engaged from morning until night with my lawyers in arranging
the plan of a formidable attack upon Mr. Bligh,' he wrote to his wife.[11]

The first public move came through Johnston in November, a month after
Bligh returned. It was in the form of an address by Johnston to the Earl of
Liverpool, calling for an opportunity to prove his case. He offered to 'produce
incontestible evidence of his [Bligh's] tyranny and oppression of the people
he was sent to govern; – of gross frauds and shameful robberies committed
upon the public property entrusted to his care; and lastly I will prove, that he
has been guilty of heretofore unheard of and disgraceful cowardice.'[12] A week

---

[8] I have found no references to Christian or Heywood in the MacArthur papers of the time;
there may, however, be other papers extant. Heywood rescued survivors of the *Isabella*, one of
MacArthur's ships which sank off South America in 1812, and they had a mutual friend in the
person of Mr Charles Runcker. Heywood got Runcker a post as astronomer at Parramatta and he
became a visiting neighbour of the MacArthurs.
[9] MacArthur to Elizabeth MacArthur, Letter, 14 February 1810, London, Onslow (ed.),
1914, p. 189.
[10] *ibid.*, p. 183, 28 November 1809.
[11] *ibid.*, p. 207, 5 December 1810.
[12] Lieutenant-Colonel Johnston to Earl of Liverpool, Memorial, 16 November 1810,

later he wrote again to the busy Earl asking for permission to move to London to prepare his case against Bligh (even though he had had a whole year to do just that) and leave his regimental duties to a second-in-command. The Earl replied, through a secretary, to his second letter with a polite refusal.[13]

Matters stood still until January 1811, when Lieutenant Kent requested a court martial on the charges by Bligh that had kept him under arrest since he left Sydney. Kent's request for a court martial was granted and it took place on 8 January on H.M.S. *Gladiator*. The charges against him were that he had sailed H.M.S. *Porteous* from Sydney without Governor Bligh's permission, that he had unlawfully removed Bligh's broad pennant from the mast and that he had let Lieutenant Symons leave the colony without Bligh's permission. In effect he had carried out the interests of the usurpers of lawful government in New South Wales.

The trial was of significance to the pending court martial of Johnston; it was a dry run, so to speak, for the legality of the post-Bligh government. If Kent was convicted, which seemed likely, Bligh's position would be strengthened and Johnston's weakened. MacArthur was Kent's chief adviser during the trial. Victory in this relatively minor skirmish was probably part of his 'plan of a formidable attack' on Bligh. Bligh took the view that Kent was guilty of breaches of the Articles of War and that he only needed to prove that for a conviction. By restricting the issues to technicalities, Bligh was not doing sufficient to overcome sympathy for the prisoner who had, after all, spent twenty-three months in close detention while awaiting trial. True, Bligh offered to call a long list of witnesses to the wider issues of the illegal overthrow of his Government, but he told the court that he would only call them if the defendant raised these wider issues himself. Kent was advised by MacArthur not to raise any other issues than the technical ones, presumably because from his point of view this would be to his benefit. The trial, which lasted three days, made heavy work of the three main charges without discussing the legalities of Bligh's Government. Its verdict was bad news for Bligh: Kent was acquitted.[14]

The final decision on the insurrection could only be made by a court martial of Johnston. MacArthur and Johnston had been clamouring for some months for a trial, if only because they knew that they could not keep their witnesses indefinitely in Britain. MacArthur also wanted to leave Britain and get back to his estates in Australia. Johnston, who had recently been promoted to Lieutenant-Colonel in the 102nd Regiment of Foot (the old New South Wales Corps), had a more pressing need for a trial; if his witnesses deserted him to attend to their own affairs he was liable to the mercy of a

---

reproduced in Onslow (ed.), 1914, pp. 208-10; the charge of 'cowardice' apparently refers to the absurd charge of hiding under a bed. The Memorial has a touch of MacArthur about it and may have been the first product of his long consultations with his lawyers referred to earlier.

[13] *ibid.*, p. 211.

[14] *See Naval Chronicle*, Vol. 25, 1811; Marshall's *Naval Biography*, Vol. 4, Part 1, p. 162; *HRNSW*, Vol. 7, pp. 495-6.

future court martial which might take a very serious view of his actions. Bligh
was back in his home territory and he would never give up the effort to get
him convicted. In the short time he had been in Britain Johnston had come to
appreciate the extent of Bligh's influence in government, even if he was
convinced that he had no standing with the public.

The court martial of Lieutenant-Colonel George Johnston began on 7 May
1811 at Chelsea Barracks. Lieutenant-General Keppel was President and
Charles Manners-Sutton was Judge-Advocate General. Bligh was
represented by a new advocate, Frederick Pollock (later Sir Frederick). The
trial lasted until 5 June 1811, and a parade of witnesses passed through the
room telling their tales and answering questions as best they could.
Bartrum's report on the trial covered 484 pages. It would not be productive
to summarise it here.[15] The decision of the court was: 'That *Lieut.-Col.
Johnston* is *Guilty* of the act of Mutiny as described in the Charge, and do
therefore sentence him to be Cashiered.'[16] With this verdict everybody won
something. Bligh was vindicated but not avenged. Johnston was convicted
but not punished. Only MacArthur was left in legal jeopardy by the verdict.
If Johnston was convicted in a trial after all the interest and influence he
could muster through the Duke of Northumberland, it did not look too good
for MacArthur if he returned to New South Wales and to a certain trial for
his part as a civilian in the mutiny. If a British court judged the action a
mutiny then a colonial court would start off from that point to decide on the
guilt of MacArthur. As he had never concealed his role in the affair he was
certain to be convicted and placed at the mercy of the Governor. That this is
not exaggeration on my part is proved by the conduct of MacArthur after the
trial: he refused to return to Australia until he was given proper assurance in
Britain that he would not be placed on trial. He had to wait until 1817 for
that assurance.[17]

After the trial the participants dispersed. Mr Johnston, as he now was,
took passage back to New South Wales and his farm. Before he went the
Prince Regent made his own comments on the case. He said: 'The Court, in
passing a sentence so inadequate to the enormity of the crime of which the
prisoner has been found guilty, have apparently been actuated by a
consideration of the novel and extraordinary circumstances, which, by the
evidence on the face of the proceedings, may have appeared to them to have
existed during the administration of Gov. Bligh, both as affecting the
tranquillity of the colony, and calling for some immediate decision.' He
continued, with a touch of regret about the Court's sentence: 'No
circumstances whatever can be received by His Royal Highness in full
extenuation of an assumption of power, so subversive of every principle of
good order and discipline.'[18] This made it even more difficult for MacArthur

---

[15] Bartrum, 1811. Bligh's personal copy with his notes in the margin is in the Mitchell
Library, 344/4A3.
[16] The sentence was posted as a General Order, 2 July 1811; Bartrum, 1811, pp. 408-9.
[17] Details of MacArthur's exchanges with the Government in 1816-17 on conditions for his
return are in Onslow (ed.), 1914, pp. 268-85.
[18] Bartrum, 1811, pp. 408-9.

to proceed home. Governor Macquarie was bound to take note of the Prince Regent's observations, more so, as it was plainly felt in some circles that the wrong man was being tried for rebellion. Johnston was only the instrument of MacArthur. But MacArthur's view would also have been that it was Bligh who should have been tried and, indeed, he went to some effort to get him impeached in order to bring him to trial.

James MacArthur was to complain about the trial some years later:

> Johnston had a tribunal knowing little or nothing of Bligh, and it was exceedingly difficult, if not impossible, to adduce evidence, at such a distance both as to time and place, of the state of things which induced him to resort to the extreme measures of deposing the Governor. Corruption, rapacity, violent language and conduct though causes for deposing a Governor, after the trial or enquiry before a competent authority, could not in the eye of the Law, or of ordinary expediency justify such a step ... But a staid military Court sitting at Chelsea could not comprehend the extraordinary and exceptional state of things which had existed on the 26th January 1808 at the Antipodes, in the then insignificant Town of Sydney, constituted too of so peculiar and anomalous a population. Could Bligh have been brought to trial the matter would have been very different. Evidence might probably have been brought to criminate him though it was unavailable as a defence for Colonel Johnston.[19]

What MacArthur's son is really complaining about is the fact that MacArthur was prevented from using the courts in the same careless and irreverent manner as he had used them in Sydney. If Bligh was protected from persecution by his critics, it was in fact the same law and circumstances that protected MacArthur. The MacArthurs found it impossible to get Bligh into a court, but then neither could the Blighs put MacArthur into a court while he remained in Britain. His £20,000 civil suit planned against Bligh was dropped and not heard of again, presumably on legal advice that Bligh could only be sued in Australia on such an action. Neither Bligh nor MacArthur had the slightest intention of going to Australia, certainly not together, to test the legal issues, and so the matter rested.

Another problem for the Johnston camp was the great difficulty in finding a just cause for their actions after the event. He had been manoeuvred by MacArthur into arresting Bligh on the emotional issues in the dispute and not the legal ones. Once the emotional turmoil dissipated they were left justifying an action that was not justifiable. Manners-Sutton, when cross-examining MacArthur at Johnston's trial, summed up the absurdity of the rebellion when he told him: 'It seems the first cause of grievance was the detention of that ship of yours, and the forfeiture of the bond for 900£; the next is about a post that was taken away from your ground; and these seem to have been the principal part of all the causes of the revolution.'[20] It is,

[19] Onslow (ed.), 1914, pp. 221-2.
[20] Bartrum, 1811, p. 213.

when all is said and done, a fair summary of the magnitude of the merits of Johnston's deposition of Bligh. He may have believed sincerely that he was fighting the tyranny of Government House for 'liberty' and 'justice' against a 'monster of depravity' and so on, but in fact all it boiled down to was the petty interests of the merchant-farmer, John MacArthur.

But what of Bligh? The decision of the Court was not satisfactory from his point of view. He would have preferred a hanging. He believed that the 'Northumberland interest' had saved Johnston and he may well have been right. Sir David Baird, a member of the court martial, wrote to Governor Macquarie a couple of years later: 'I was a member of the CourtMartial that tried the late commander of New South Wales (Col. Johnston). – I was able to attend untill the day that *sentence* was to be passed & on that day I was so ill (from my wound) as to be obliged to have an operation performed – this I believe was very fortunate for Johnston for I never heard as connected an evidence proving him guilty of Mutiny – without the least palliation that was in my Mind worthy of consideration.'[21] Baird might have tipped the balance the other way, and the full majesty of the law might have been imposed. This suggests some thoughts on the outcome of the judicial process: if Castlereagh had remained in office and Northumberland had been frustrated, the vindication of Bligh as Governor would have been complete.

As it was, Bligh came out of the affair with some gratification. The rebellion against him had been confirmed as judicial mutiny, which made his position legally secure. It was the nearest he could get to an acquittal from the charges mounted against him by MacArthur and Johnston. With his legal position secure, he was safe from retribution and disgrace and consequent loss of pension rights. He was fifty-seven years old and a senior Captain in the Navy. By his seniority he was due for promotion. He had applied for his Admiral's flag in December 1810, but this had been held back pending the enquiry into the rebellion. After the trial and the verdict his promotion went ahead. On 31 July 1811, he was gazetted Rear-Admiral of the Blue Squadron, which, with a particular mark of official approval, was also back-dated to July 1810. (At that time he was at sea on his way back to Britain.) This shows that the Admiralty regarded his service in Australia as being continuous through the period of his arrest and his time on H.M.S. *Porpoise*. This arrangement had been made prior to his going out as Governor and his tribulations did not compromise his naval service.

He was not engaged in official service after the trial and consequently, for the first time in his life, had considerable time to spend with his family and to visit his circle of friends. Unfortunately, Elizabeth Bligh did not live very long afterwards to enjoy a peaceful domestic life with her husband. She died on 15 April 1812 and was buried in the family grave at Lambeth Churchyard. Bligh soon after moved himself and his unmarried daughters to an imposing manor house in Farningham, Kent.

By seniority (generally occasioned by the deaths of those higher on the list)

---

[21] Baird to Macquarie, Letter, 30 March 1813, Macquarie Letterbooks, ML MS A797, p. 79; quoted in Ellis, 1955, p. 401.

he was promoted twice more. In 1812 he became a Rear-Admiral of the White and in 1814 Vice-Admiral of the Blue, but he did not get an opportunity to fly his flag on a ship. He was consulted by the Admiralty and the House of Commons on various matters to which his expertise might contribute something of value. In 1812 the problem of transportation of convicts to New South Wales was one such subject; he managed to describe some features of his Governorship germane to the problem.[22] He advised the Admiralty on the functioning of Vice-Admiral courts, from his experience in Sydney of commanding one, and then he took on a consultancy role with Rear-Admiral Thomas Hamilton to advise on the viability of a new design of 74-gun ship. He wrote enthusiastically about the design to Sir Joseph Banks.[23]

Almost nothing is known about his activities during the next few years; this is surprising after the inordinate amount of notice his life received in the previous forty years. Like many another old soldier he retired gracefully and quietly. He had much to attend to on the domestic front, with four daughters living in the house with him, including the epileptic Anne, who required constant attendance. He continued to travel up to London as business and health permitted. On 7th December 1817 he collapsed and died. He was buried next to his wife at St. Mary's, Lambeth. The inscription on the tomb reads:

Sacred
to the Memory of
William Bligh Esquire, F.R.S.
Vice Admiral of the Blue
the celebrated navigator
who first transplanted the Bread fruit tree
from Otaheite to the West Indies
bravely fought the battles of his country
and died beloved, respected and lamented
on the 7th day of December 1817
aged 64

It is interesting that the inscription makes no reference at all to his being Governor of New South Wales. This may have been his decision and instruction or his family's.

Bligh's death did not end the controversies of his life. Some of these have already been tackled in earlier chapters. The rediscovery of Pitcairn was to some extent responsible for these issues' remaining alive, and the growing contact between the mutineers' settlement and the world at large called attention to their origins and added romance to their existence. The saga of the *Bounty*, for that is what it became, has gone on ever since. Interest in it has been both scholarly and commercial. Every generation throws up its

---

[22] *Report of the Select Committee on Transportation*, 1812, pp. 29-47.
[23] Bligh to Banks, 2 September 1813. Quoted in Mackaness, 1951, pp. 527-8.

champions and critics of Bligh, Christian and the others. This is remarkable, considering the rather trivial circumstances in which the mutiny took place and its pathetic causes. But legend and romance are part of the human condition and must be treated as such. My only complaint is that authors have picked up the legends and repeated them carelessly until the legends have come to be believed. Folk myths are deeply ingrained, and those referring to William Bligh are treated as settled facts, incontrovertible and immune from criticism.

Yet William Bligh was not the ogre he has been made out to be. The roots of the myths about Bligh are found in the personal vendettas pursued by Edward Christian, Peter Heywood, James Morrison, John Fryer, William Purcell, John Frazier, and John MacArthur. The allusions and charges were not objectively assessed by impartial judges (if they could be found!) but were made by people partisan to the cause of ruining Bligh and his reputation. This is not to say that Bligh was more worthy than his critics or that he was a paragon of virtue. Bligh was a lot of the things his critics said he was. He was violent in speech and abrasive in command. The extent to which he stepped across the line into tyranny is a matter of opinion and one on which it is very difficult for us, a hundred and seventy years later, to make secure pronouncements. To say he was accused of these things by people throughout his life and therefore must have been a tyrant is a methodology vulnerable to the choice of witness.

Many men have had harsh dispositions. Cook, for example, had a foul temper and a violent streak when it came to flogging. Nelson, a man adored by his men, treated mutineers with a violence that would have done Judge Jeffries credit. William Bligh was not a harsh man of that kind. Critics are hard put to show that he engaged in brutality on the *Bounty*; the records of official violence by flogging show a ship comparatively softly treated for the eighteenth century. On the *Director* Bligh fought for his men, including mutineers, who were threatened by the summary justice of the Admiralty after the Nore mutiny. If his reputation was anything like the truth he would gladly have sent as many as he could for trial and hanging. His kindness was always apparent when the people he dealt with treated him politely and deferentially. When they were insolent or disobedient, they brought out the worst in him. People like John Fryer, William Purcell, John Frazier and John MacArthur saw how to send him into paroxysms of rage and set about it with gusto. That they made life hell for everybody else and difficult for Bligh was a side-issue in the personal disputes they pursued against him. But they never defeated him nor broke his spirit. It is a remarkable fact, but in all the correspondence I have read written by Bligh there is not a single sign that he felt doubts about what he was doing when he fought these people. Every move they made seemed to fuel him for new bursts of action against them.

Observers of these personal battles between Bligh and his baiters were sometimes appalled at the ferocity of sentiment that flared up. James Morrison's record of Bligh's outbursts was coloured by his grievance that Bligh believed him to be a mutineer. Others took them in their stride and did not lose a sense of proportion about Bligh. In all his life Bligh never failed to find friends who would testify for him and friends who would stand by him. He may not have been acclaimed a hero or a saint, but there were many who would swear he was the best there was when other men (more saintly perhaps) would have been overwhelmed. He was a fighter, a survivor, a man of intense personal conviction and also a man of considerable courage. His critics claimed he was a bully, a tyrant, a coward and a thief. I am one observer who firmly believes that they were unjust.

Bibliography

Allen, Edward W. 1959. *The Vanishing Frenchman: The Mysterious Disappearance of Lapérouse*. New York.

Allen, Kenneth S. 1976. *That Bounty Bastard*. London.

Almy, Charlotte, 1923. *Two Years in Southern Seas*. London.

Anderson, Isobel W. 1967. *Notes on the Heywood Family of Locarbine, Devonshire, Hampshire and the Isle of Man, Collected by me, 1966-67 from Victoria County History, Oliver Heywood's Diaries, Foster Lancashire Pedigrees and Burke's Peerage*. (Typescript, Mitchell Library MS Doc 1259).

Anon. 1794. *Voyage to the South Seas in H.M. Ship Bounty under the Command of Lieut. Wm. Bligh, for the purpose of conveying the Bread Fruit Tree from the South-Sea Island to the West Indies ... With the Journal of Bligh, Surgeon Ledward, Fryer, and Nelson, &c., more Accurate and Full than any hitherto published*. London.

Anon. 1808. *A Letter etc Addressed to the Right Honourable The Viscount Castlereagh, His Majesty's Principal Secretary of State for Colonial Affairs*. London. (Proof copy with marginal notes by MacArthur family, Mitchell Library MS C475.)

Anon. 1808. *Statements of the loss of His Majesty's new ship the Bounty, W. Bligh, Esq. commander, by a conspiracy of the crew, including the wonderful escape of the captain and about twelve men in an open pinnace; also the adventures of the mutineers, as communicated by Lieutenant Christian, the ringleader, to a relation in England*. London.

Anon. 1809. 'Mutineers of the Bounty', *Naval Chronicle*, Vol. 21, January-June, pp. 454-5.

Anon. 1809. 'Visit of the Topaz to Pitcairn's Island', *The Times*, 1 July, 1 September.

Anon. 1810. 'Topaz discovery', *Quarterly Review*, Vol.10, no.5, September, pp. 23-4.

Anon. 1811. *Naval Economy exemplified in conversation between a member of parliament and the officers of a man-of-war during a winter's cruise*. London.

Anon. 1815. 'Account of the Descendants of Christian and Other Mutineers of the Bounty', *Naval Chronicle*, Vol. 33, January-June, pp. 217-18, 377.

Anon. 1816. 'Missionary Needs of Pitcairn', *Quarterly Review*, Vol. 16, no. 31, p. 82.

Anon. 1816. *Songs etc. in Pitcairn Island: a new, romantick, operatick ballet spectacle founded on the recent discovery of a numerous colony, formed by and descended from the mutineers of the Bounty frigate first performed at the Theatre Royal, Drury Lane*. London.

Anon. 1818. *An Account of the Dangerous Voyage, performed by Captain Bligh, With a part of the Crew of His Majesty's Ship Bounty, in an Open Boat, Over twelve hundred Leagues of the Ocean, With an Appendix, In which is contained an Account of the Island of Otaheite, &c.* London.

Anon. 1820. *Dangerous Voyage of Captain Bligh in an Open Boat, over 1200 Leagues of the Ocean, in the year 1789. With an Appendix containing an Account of Otaheite, and some of the Productions of that Island*. Dublin.

Anon. 1824. *The Dangerous Voyage performed by Captain Bligh, with a part of the crew of His Majesty's Ship Bounty, in an Open Boat, Over Twelve Hundred Leagues of the Ocean; in the year 1789. To Which is Added An Account of the Sufferings and Fate of the Remainder of the Crew of said Ship*. Dublin.

Anon. 1831. 'Obituary Notice for Captain Peter Heywood', *The United Service Journal and Naval and Military Magazine*, London, April 1831, Part 1, pp. 468-81.

Anon. 1880. *The Story of the Good Ship Bounty and Her Mutineers and Mutinies in Highland Regiments*. London.

Anon. 1880. 'Bligh on the Mutiny of the Bounty', *Sydney Mail*, 10, 24 April.

Anon. 1885. *The Mutiny of the Bounty and Other Narratives*. London/Edinburgh.

Anon. 1939. 'Almost certainly the anchor of the *Bounty*', *Illustrated London News*, 26 August, p. 349.

Anon. 1941. '*Bounty* Anchor for Auckland Museum', *Pacific Islands Monthly*, August, p. 9.

Anon. 1949. 'Relics of the *Bounty*', *Pacific Islands Monthly*, Vol. 19, February.

Anon. 1971. 'The indomitable Captain Bligh', *Early Governors of Australia*. Sydney.

Anson, George. 1748. *A Voyage Round the World In The Years MDCCXL, I, II, III, IV. By George Anson, Esq; later Lord Anson*. London.

Anthony, Irvin. 1935. *The Saga of* The Bounty: *Its Strange History as related by the Participants Themselves*. New York.

Australiana Society. 1952. *Bligh's Narrative of the Mutiny on Board H.M. Ship Bounty …* (1790); *Minutes of the Court Martial … with an Appendix.* (1794); *Bligh's Answers to Certain Assertions* (1794); *Edward Christian's Reply* (1795). Melbourne. Facsimiles of original pamphlets (limited edition).

Baarslag, Karl. 1940. *Islands of Adventure*. New York.

Ball, Ian M. 1973. *Pitcairn: Children of the Bounty*. London.

Barney, Stephen. 1794. *Minutes of the Proceedings of the Court-Martial held at Portsmouth, August 12, 1792* [sic] *on ten persons charged with mutiny on board His Majesty's ship Bounty*. [With an 'Appendix' by Edward Christian] London.

Barrow, Sir John. 1831. *The Eventful History of the Mutiny and Piratical Seizure of H.M.S. Bounty: its Cause and Consequences*. London.

Barrow, Sir John. 1834. 'Recent Accounts of the Pitcairn Islanders', *Journal of the Royal Geographical Society*, Vol. 3, 1833, pp. 156-67. London.

Barrow, Sir John. 1914. *The Mutiny & Piratical Seizure of H.M.S. Bounty*. With an Introduction by Admiral Sir Cyprian Bridge, G.C.B. (The World's Classics). Oxford.

Barrow, John. 1961. *The Mutiny of the 'Bounty'*. London/Glasgow.

Bartrum, — (ed.). 1811. Proceedings of A General Court-Martial, held at Chelsea Hospital, Which commenced on *Tuesday, May 7, 1811*, and continued by Adjournment to *Wednesday, 5th of June* following, for The Trial of Lieut.-Col. Geo. Johnston, *Major of the 102d Regiment, late the New South Wales Corps*, on A Charge of Mutiny, Exhibited against him by the Crown, for Deposing On the 26th of January, 1808, William Bligh, Esq. F.R.S. Taken in short hand By Mr. Bartrum, of Clement's Inn, *Who attended on behalf of Governor Bligh, by Permission of the Court*.

Beach, Susan Emily Hicks. 1956. *The Yesterdays Behind the Door*. Liverpool.

Beaglehole, J.C. 1955, 1961, 1967. *The Journals of Captain Cook on his Voyages of Discovery edited from the original manuscripts*. 4 vols. Cambridge.

Beaglehole, J.C. 1967. *Captain Cook and Captain Bligh*. D.E. Collins Lecture, University of Wellington, N.Z.

Beaglehole, J.C. 1974. *The Life of Captain James Cook*. London.

Beard, William. 1956. '*Valiant Martinet*', or *The Adventures on Sea and Land of Captain William Bligh*. (Foreword by Dr George Mackaness, O.B.E., M.A.) Sydney, N.S.W.

Bechervaise, Edward. 1911. 'The Mutiny of the 'Bounty' – Lieut. Bligh's Voyage in the Ship's Boat to Timor', *Victorian Geographical Journal*, Vol. 28, 1910-11, Melbourne, Victoria, pp. 78-87.

Bechervaise, John. 1839. *Thirty-Six Years of a Seafaring Life*. By An Old Quarter Master. Portsea.

Becke, Louis, and Jeffrey, Walter. 1898. *The Mutineer: a Romance of Pitcairn Island*. London.

Becke, Louis, and Jeffrey, Walter. 1899. *Bligh and the Mutiny on the Bounty*. London.

Becke, Louis, and Jeffrey, Walter. 1899. *The Naval Pioneers of Australia*. London.

Beechey, Captain F.W. 1831. *Narrative of a Voyage to the Pacific and Beering's Strait, to co-operate with the Polar Expeditions: performed in His Majesty's Ship Blossom, under the command of Captain F.W. Beechey, R.N., F.R.S. &c, in the Years 1825, 26, 27, 28*. 2 vols. London.

Belcher, Sir Edward. 1848. *Narrative of the Voyage of H.M.S. Samarang, during the Years 1843-46; employed surveying the Islands of the Eastern Archipelago; accompanied by a brief vocabulary of the principal languages*. 2 vols. London.

Belcher, Lady [Diana]. 1870. *The Mutineers of the Bounty and their Descendants in Pitcairn and Norfolk Islands*. London.

Berckman, Evelyn. 1962. *Nelson's Dear Lord: A Portrait of St Vincent*. London.

Bigge, J.T. 1822. *The Report of the Commissioner of Inquiry into the state of the Colony of New South Wales, 6 May, 1822*. London.

Bladen, F.M. 1908. 'The Deposition of Governor Bligh', *Royal Australian Historical Society, Journal and Proceedings*, Vol. 1, June, pp. 192-200.

Blewitt, Mary. 1967. *Surveys of the Sea*. London.

Bligh, William. 1790. *A Narrative of the Mutiny, on board His Majesty's Ship* Bounty; *and the subsequent voyage of part of the crew, in the ship's boat, from Tofoa, one of the Friendly Islands, To Timor, a Dutch Settlement in the East Indies*. London.

Bligh, William. 1792. *A Voyage to the South Sea, undertaken by command of His Majesty, for the purpose of Conveying the Bread-Fruit Tree to the West Indies, in His Majesty's Ship the Bounty, commanded by Lieutenant William Bligh. Including an account of the mutiny on board the said ship, and the subsequent voyage of Part of the Crew in the Ship's Boat, From Tofoa, one of the Friendly Islands, To Timor, a Dutch Settlement in the East Indies, with seven charts, diagram and a portrait*. London. Republished New York, 1965 as *The Mutiny on the Bounty*.

Bligh, William. 1794. *An Answer to Certain Assertions contained in the Appendix to a Pamphlet, entitled Minutes of the Proceedings on the Court-Martial held at Portsmouth, August 12th, 1792, on Ten Persons charged with Mutiny on Board his Majesty's Ship the Bounty*. London.

Bligh, William. 1898-1901. 'Miscellaneous Letters', in *Historical Records of New South Wales*, Vols. 6, 7. Sydney, N.S.W.

Bligh, William. 1901. *A Narrative of the Mutiny on Board His Majesty's Ship Bounty and the subsequent voyage of part of the crew in the ship's boat from Tofoa, one of the Friendly Islands, To Timor, a Dutch settlement in the East Indies*. London. Published by George Nicol, Pall Mall, A.D. 1790. Re-published at the Sign of the Unicorn, A.D. 1901.

Bligh, William. 1937. *Bligh's Voyage in the Resource from Coupang to Batavia, together with the Log of his subsequent Passage to England in the Dutch Packet Vlydt and his Remarks on Morrison's Journal. All Printed for the first time from the Manuscripts in the Mitchell Library of New South Wales, with an Introduction and Notes by Owen Rutter, & Engravings on Wood by Peter Barker-Hill*. Golden Cockerel Press, London (limited edition).

Bligh, William. *The Log of the Bounty*. See Rutter (ed.), 1937.

Bligh, Capt. W. 1975. *The Log of H.M.S. Bounty, 1787-1789*. London (facsimile of Admiralty copy, PRO Adm. 55/151; limited edition).

Bligh, Capt. W. 1976. *The Log of H.M.S. Providence*. London (facsimile of Admiralty copy; limited edition).

Blount, Charles (ed.). 1937. *Memorandoms* [sic] *by James Martin*. Cambridge.

Brenton, Edward Pelham. 1837. *The Naval History of Great Britain from the Year 1783 to 1836*. 2 vols. London.

Brian, Rev. T.H. 1824. *History of New South Wales from the Settlement to the close of the year 1824*. London.

Brodie, Walter. 1851. *Pitcairn's Island, and the Islanders, in 1850*. London.

Bryant, Rev. J. 1914. 'A Lonely Isle and a Curious People' [Pitcairn Island], *The Scottish Geographical Magazine*, Vol. 30, no. 2, February, pp. 83-7.

Buck, P.H. 1954. *Vikings of the Sunrise*. Christchurch, N.Z.

Buffet, John. 1846. 'A Narrative of Twenty Years' Residence on Pitcairn's Island', *The Friend*, Vol. 4, pp. 2-3, 20-1, 27-8, 34-5, 50-1, 66-8.

Bullocke, J.G. 1938. *Sailor's Rebellion: A century of naval mutinies*. London.

Burke, Peter. 1866. *Celebrated Naval and Military Trials*. London.

Burrows, M. 1853. *Pitcairn's Island*. London.

Byron, Lord. 1823. *The Island; or Christian and his comrades. A poem; based partly on the account of the mutiny of the Bounty, and partly on Mariner's Account of the Tonga Islands. With appropriate Extracts from the Voyage, by Capt. Bligh*. London.

Callender, Geoffrey. 1936. 'The Portraiture of Bligh', *The Mariner's Mirror*, Vol. 22, no. 2, April, pp. 172-8.

Campbell, Gordon. 1936. *Captain James Cook R.N., F.R.S.* London.

Campbell, John. 1812-1817. *Lives of the British Admirals: containing also a new and accurate Naval History, from the Earliest Periods*. By Dr John Campbell. Continued to the year 1779, by Dr. Berkenhout. In Eight Volumes. London.

Campbell, J. 1840. *Maritime Discovery and Christian Missions*. London.

Camperdown, Earl of. 1898. *Admiral Duncan*. London.

Casey, Robert J. 1932. 'Pitcairn: The Breed of the "Bounty" Mutineers', *Easter Island: Home of the Scornful Gods*. London.

Chamier, Frederick. 1838. *Jack Adams, the mutineer*. 3 vols. London.

Chauvel, Charles. 1933. *In the Wake of 'The Bounty' to Tahiti and Pitcairn Island*. Sydney, N.S.W.

Chomley, C.H. 1903. *Tales of Old Times*. Melbourne, Victoria.

Christian, Edward. 1794. 'An Appendix', in Stephen Barney, *Minutes of the Proceedings ...* London.

Christian, Edward. 1795. *A Short Reply to Captain Bligh's Answers*. London.

'Christian, Fletcher' (?). 1796. *Letters from Mr. Fletcher Christian, containing a narrative of the transactions on board* His Majesty's Ship Bounty, *Before and After the Mutiny, with his subsequent voyages and travels in South America*. London.

'Christian, Fletcher' (?). 1798. *Voyages and Travels of Fletcher Christian, and a Narrative of the Mutiny On Board His Majesty's Ship Bounty, at Otaheite. With a succinct account of the Proceedings of the M̶.̶.̶ ̶.̶.̶.̶.̶.̶ with a Description of the Manners, Customs, Religious Ceremonies, Diversions, Fashions, Arts, Commerce; Method of Fighting; the Breadfruit, and every interesting particular relating to The Society Islands. Also His Shipwreck on the coast of America, and travels in that extensive Country; with a history of the Gold Mines and general account of the possessions of The Spaniards. In Chili, Peru, Mexico &c.* London.

Clowes, Sir William Laird. 1877-1903. *The Royal Navy: a History From the Earliest Times to the Present*. 7 vols. London.

Clune, Frank. 1967. *Journey to Pitcairn*. Sydney, N.S.W.

Collins, David. 1798, 1802. *An Account of the English Colony in New South Wales: with Remarks on the Dispositions, Customs, Manners, &c. of the Native Inhabitants of that Country. To which are added, Some Particulars of New Zealand; compiled, by permission, from the MSS. of Lieutenant-Governor King*. 2 vols. London.

Cook, James, and King, James. 1784. *A Voyage to the Pacific Ocean; Undertaken by Command of his Majesty, for making Discoveries in the Northern Hemisphere; performed under the Direction of Captains Cook, Clerke, and Gore, In the Years 1776, 1777, 1778, 1779, and 1780. Being a copious, comprehensive, and satisfactory Abridgement of the Voyage written by Captain James Cook, F.R.S. and Captain James King. LL.D. and F.R.S. Illustrated with Cuts*. In Four Volumes. London.

Copplestone, B. 1925. *The Boat Voyage of Bounty Bligh*. Oxford.

Couper, J.M. 1969. *The Book of Bligh*. Melbourne, Victoria.

Cullen, A.H. 1916. *Blazing the Trail*. London.

Cunningham, C. 1829. *A Narrative of Occurrences that took place during the Mutiny at the Nore, in the Months of May and June, 1797; with a few Observations upon the Impressment of Seamen, and the Advantages of those who are employed in His Majesty's Navy; also on the*

Necessity and useful Operations of the Articles of War. Chatham.

Currey, C.H. 1958. 'An Outline of the Story of Norfolk Island and Pitcairn's Island 1788-1857', *Royal Australian Historical Society, Journal and Proceedings*, Vol. 44, Part 6, Sydney, N.S.W., pp. 325-74.

Danielsson, Bengt. 1962. *What Happened on the Bounty*. Trans. Alan Tapsell. London.

Darby, Madge. 1965. *Who Caused the Mutiny on the* Bounty? Sydney, N.S.W.

Darby, Madge. 1966. *The causes of the Bounty mutiny; a short reply to Mr. Rolf Du Rietz's comments.* (*Studia Bountyana*, vol. 2) Uppsala.

David, Andrew C.F. 1976. *The Surveyors of the Bounty: A preliminary study of the hydrographic Surveys of William Bligh, Thomas Heywood and Peter Heywood and the charts published from them.* Taunton.

David, Andrew C.F. 1977a. 'Broughton's schooner and the *Bounty* mutineers', *Mariner's Mirror*, Vol. 63, pp. 207-13.

David, Andrew C.F. 1977. 'The surveys of William Bligh', *Mariner's Mirror*, Vol. 63, No. 1, February, pp 69-70.

Daws, Gavan, 1968. 'Kealakekua Bay Re-visited', *Journal of Pacific History*, vol. 13, pp. 21-3.

Dawson, Warren R. (ed.). 1958. *The Banks Letters: A Calendar of the manuscript correspondence of Sir Joseph Banks preserved in the British Museum, the British Museum (Natural History) and other collections in Great Britain*. London.

Delano, Amasa. 1817. *A Narrative of Voyages and Travels, in the Northern and Southern Hemispheres: comprising Three Voyages round the World; together with a Voyage of Survey and Discovery, in the Pacific Ocean and Oriental Islands*. Boston, Mass.

Dillon, Peter. 1829. *Narrative and Successful Result of a Voyage in the South Seas, Performed by Order of the Government of British India, to ascertain the actual fate of La Pérouse's Expedition, interspersed with accounts of the Religion, Manners, Customs, and Cannibal Practices of the South Seas Islanders*. By the Chevalier Capt. P. Dillon. 2 vols. London.

Dugan, James. 1966. *The Great Mutiny*. London.

Duncan, Archibald. 1811. 'Narrative of the loss of the *Bounty* through a conspiracy', *The Mariner's Chronicle*, Vol. IV, pp. 21-35, and 'Narrative of the total loss of His Majesty's Ship the *Bounty*, including the transations of the mutineers, after they gained possession of the vessel. Extracted from the letters of Lieutenant Christian', pp. 49-62. Also 'Loss of the Pandora Frigate', Vol. V, pp. 271-3.

Du Rietz, Rolf. 1963. 'Three Letters from James Burney to Sir Joseph Banks; a contribution to the history of William Bligh: *A Voyage to the South Sea.*' *Ethnos*, 1-4, pp. 115-25.

Du Rietz, Rolf. 1964. 'The Voyage of H.M.S. *Pandora*, 1790-1792: Some Remarks upon Geoffrey Rawson's Book on the Subject', *Ethnos*, 1963: 2-4, pp. 210-18. Stockholm.

Du Rietz, Rolf. 1966. *The causes of the Bounty mutiny: some comments on a book by Madge Darby.* (*Studia Bountyana*, vol. 1). Uppsala.

Dyall, Valentine. 1957. *A Flood of Mutiny*. London.

Edmonds, I.G. 1964. *The Bounty's Boy*. London.

Edwards, Bryan. 1818, 1819. *The History, civil and commercial, of the British Colonies in the West Indies*. 5th edn. 6 vols. London.

Edwards, Edward, and Hamilton, George. 1915. *Voyage of H.M.S. 'Pandora', despatched to arrest the mutineers of the 'Bounty' in the South Seas, 1790-91, being the narratives of Captain Edward Edwards, R.N., the commander, and George Hamilton, the surgeon; with introduction and notes by Basil Thomson*. London.

Elder, John Rawson (ed.). 1932. *The Letters and Journals of Samuel Marsden, 1765-1838*. Dunedin, N.Z.

Ellis, M.H. 1947. *Lachlan Macquarie; his Life, Adventures and Times*. Sydney, N.S.W.

Ellis, M.H. 1955. *John MacArthur*. Sydney, N.S.W.

Evatt, Herbert Vere. 1938. *Rum Rebellion: A Study of the Overthrow of Governor Bligh by John MacArthur and the New South Wales Corps*. Sydney, N.S.W.

Ellis, M.H. 1963. 'The mutiny on the Bounty: Bligh whitewashed again', *The Bulletin* (Sydney), 16 February.

Ferguson, John Alexander. 1941, 1945, 1951. *Bibliography of Australia*. 7 vols. Volume 1: *1784-1830*; Volume 2: *1831-1838*; Volume 3: *1839-1845*. Sydney, N.S.W.

Flanagan, Roderick. 1862. *The History of New South Wales; with an account of Van Diemen's Land* [Tasmania], *New Zealand, Port Phillip* [Victoria], *Moreton Bay, and other Australasian Settlements. Comprising a Complete View of the Progress and Prospects of Gold Mining in Australia. The Whole Compiled from Official and other Authentic and Original Sources*. 2 vols. London.

Fletcher, William. 1867. 'Fletcher Christian and the mutineers of the "Bounty"', *Transactions of the Cumberland Association for the Advancement of Literature and Science*, Part II, 1876-7, Carlisle.

Flinders, Matthew. 1814. *A Voyage to Terra Australis; undertaken for the purpose of completing the discovery of that vast country, and prosecuted in the Years 1801, 1802, and 1803, in His Majesty's Ship the Investigator, and subsequently in the Armed Vessel Porpoise and Cumberland Schooner. With an account of the Shipwreck of the Porpoise, Arrival of the Cumberland at Mauritius, and Imprisonment of the Commander during six Years and a half in that Island*. 2 vols. London.

Folger, Mayhew. Letter to Admiralty, London, from Nantucket, 1 March 1813, in *Quarterly Review*, April 1815, pp. 376-7; also in *Annual Register*, 1815, pp. 515-16, and *The Naval Chronicle*, January 1816.

Folger, Mayhew. Letter to Amasa Delano, *Quarterly Review of Science and Arts*, Vol. 1, 1819, pp. 263-71.

Fox, U. 1935. 'Bounty's Launch', in *Sailing, Seamanship and Yacht Construction*, Book 2, pp. 137-9. London.

Friendly, Alfred, 1977. *Beaufort of the Admiralty*. London.

Fryer, Mary Ann. 1938. *John Fryer of the Bounty: Notes on his Career written by his daughter Mary Ann. With an Introduction and Commentary by Owen Rutter and Wood-Engravings by Averil Mackenzie-Grieve. Printed at The Golden Cockerel Press*. See also *Mariner's Mirror*, Vol. 26. January, pp. 117-19.

Fullerton, W.Y. 1923. *The Romance of Pitcairn Island*. London.

Gilbert, Davies. 1938. *The Parochial History of Cornwall, founded on the manuscript histories of Mr. Hals and Mr. Tonkin; with additions and various appendices*. 4 vols. London.

Gill, Conrad. 1913. *The Naval Mutinies of 1797*. Manchester.

Godwin, George. 1930. *Vancouver: A Life 1757-1798*. London.

Goldhurst, William. 1963. 'Martinet or Martyr', *Horizon* (New York), vol. 5, no. 7, September, pp. 42-8.

Gould, R.T. 1928. 'Bligh's Notes on Cook's Last Voyage', *The Mariner's Mirror*, vol. 14, no. 4, October, pp. 371-85.

Gould, R.T. 1935. *Captain Cook*. London. (New edition 1978.)

[Greatheed, S.] 'Authentic History of the Mutineers of the Bounty', *The Sailor's Magazine and Naval Miscellany*, London, 1820, vol. 1, pp. 402-6, 449-56; 1821, vol. 2, pp. 1-8.

Gunning, Henry. 1854. *Reminiscences of the University, Town, and County of Cambridge, from the Year 1780*. 2 vols. London.

Hall, James Norman. 1935. *Shipwreck: An Account of a Voyage in the Track of the Bounty from Tahiti to Pitcairn Island in 1933*. London.

Hamilton, George. 1793. *A Voyage Round the World in His Majesty's Frigate Pandora, Performed under the Direction of Captain Edwards In the Years 1790, 1791, and 1792*. Berwick.

Hamond, Captain. 1792. 'Account of the Proceedings of the Bounty Court Martial', *Gentleman's Magazine*, December.

Hannay, David. 1900. *Some Naval Mutinies*. London.

Hattersley, Roy. 1974. *Nelson*. London.

Hawkey, Arthur. 1975. *Bligh's Other Mutiny*. London.

Hawkesworth, John. 1773. *An Account of the Voyages undertaken by Order of His Present Majesty for making Discoveries in the Southern Hemisphere, And successfully performed by Commodore Byron, Captain Wallis, Captain Carteret and Captain Cook. In the Dolphin, the*

Swallow, and the Endeavour: Drawn up From the Journals which were kept by the several Commanders. And from the Papers of Joseph Banks, Esq; by John Hawkesworth, LL.D. In Three Volumes. London.

Hay, R.G. 1935. 'One Aspect of the Deposition of Governor Bligh', *Journal and Proceedings of the Paramatta and District Historical Society*, vol. 4, pp. 180-94.

Henderson, G.C. 1933. *The Discoverers of the Fiji Islands: Tasman, Cook, Bligh, Wilson, Bellingshausen*. London.

Herbert, David. 1876. *Great Historical Mutinies, comprising the story of the Mutiny of the Bounty, the Mutiny at Spithead, the Mutiny at the Nore, Mutinies in Highland Regiments and the Indian Mutiny*. London/Edinburgh.

Holt, Joseph, 1838. *Memoirs of Joseph Holt, General of the Irish Rebels in 1798*. 2 vols. London. (Edited by T. Crofton Croker.)

Home, Rev. C.S. 1894. *The Story of the London Missionary Society 1795-1895*. London.

Hough, Richard. 1972. *Captain Bligh & Mr Christian: The Men and the Mutiny*. London.

Houston, Neal B. 1965-6. 'Fletcher Christian and the Rime of the Ancient Mariner', *The Dalhousie Review*, vol. 45, no. 55, Winter, pp. 431-46.

Houston, Neal B. 1969. 'The Mutiny On the Bounty: An Historical and Literary Bibliography', *Bulletin of Bibliography and Magazine Notes*, vol. 26, no. 2, April-June, pp. 37-41. Westwood, Mass.

Howay, F.W. 1944. 'Some Lengthy Open-boat Voyages in the Pacific Ocean', *American Neptune*, January, pp. 53-7. Salem, Mass.

Howe, F.H. 1865. *Life and Death on the Ocean*. Cincinnati, Ohio.

Howell (Rev.) Wm. 1792. *Original Autograph ms Sermon preached on the Sunday after the Execution of Three Mutineers on the text: Hebrew 13v. 17*. 16pp. 4to. Portsmouth.

Hughes, E.A. (ed.). 1928. *Bligh of the Bounty: Being The Narrative of the Mutiny of the Bounty and The Voyage in the Open Boat*. London.

Humble, Richard. 1976. *Captain Bligh*. London.

Hunter, John. 1793. *An Historical Journal of the Transactions at Port Jackson and Norfolk Island, with the Discoveries which have been made in New South Wales and in the Southern Ocean, since the publication of Phillip's Voyage, compiled from the Official Papers; Including the Journals of Governors Phillip and King, and of Lieut. Ball; and the Voyages From the first Sailing of the Sirius in 1787, to the Return of that Ship's Company to England in 1792*. London.

Ingleton, Geoffrey Chapman. 1952. *True Patriots All, or News from Early Australia, as told in A Collection of Broadsides, garnered & decorated by Geoffrey Chapman Ingleton*. Sydney, N.S.W.

Ingram, B.T. 1937. *Masters of Maritime Art*. London.

Jack, Robert Logan. 1921. *Northmost Australia: Three Centuries of Exploration, Discovery, and Adventure in and around the Cape York Peninsula, Queensland; With a Study of the Narratives of all Explorers by Sea and Land in the light of Modern Charting, many Original or hitherto unpublished Documents, Thirty-Nine Illustrations, and specially prepared Maps*. 2 vols. London.

Jackson, T. Sturges. 1899, 1900. *Logs of the Great Sea Fights 1794-1805*. (Publications of the Navy Records Society, Vols. XVI, XVIII.) London.

James, William. 1837. *The Naval History of Great Britain, from the Declaration of War by France in 1793 to the Accession of George IV*. 6 vols. London.

Jarman, Robert. 1838. *Journal of a Voyage to the South Seas in the 'Japan'*. London.

'Jenny', 'Narrative', *Sydney Gazette*, 17 July 1819; *Bengal Hurkaru*, 2 October 1826.

Johnston, Sir Harry. 1913. *Pioneers in Australasia*. London.

Jose, Arthur W. 1929. *History of Australia from the Earliest Times to the Present Day*. Sydney, N.S.W.

Kemp, Peter (ed.). 1969. *History of the Royal Navy*. London.

Kennedy, Gavin. 1978. *The Death of Captain Cook*. London.

Kent, W.G.C. R.N. 1811. *Courtmartial on Charges Exhibited Against Him by Captain William Bligh, R.N.* Portsmouth.

King, Agnes Gardner. 1920. *Islands Far Away*. London.

King, Henry. 1820. 'Extract from the Journal of Captain Henry King of the *Elizabeth*' [Visit to Pitcairn Island], *Edinburgh Philosophical Journal*, vol. III, no. VI, article XXII, pp. 380-8.

Kippis, Andrew. 1788. *A Narrative of the Voyages Round the World, Performed by Captain James Cook. With an account of his life, during the previous and intervening periods*. 2 vols. London.

Knight, C. 1936. 'H.M. Armed Vessel *Bounty*', *The Mariner's Mirror*, vol. 22, no. 2, April, pp. 183-99.

Labillardière, J.J. Houtou de. 1800. *An Account of a Voyage in search of La Pérouse, undertaken by order of the Constituent Assembly of France, and performed In the Years 1791, 1792, and 1793, in the Recherche and Espérance, Ships of War, under the command of Rear-Admiral Bruni D'Entrecasteaux*. Translated from the French of M. Labillardière. 2 vols. London.

Langdon, Robert. 1959. *Island of Love*. London.

Laughton, John Knox (ed.). 1886. *Letters and Despatches of Horatio, Viscount Nelson, K.B., Duke of Bronte, Vice-Admiral of the White Squadron*. London.

Laughton, John Knox (ed.). 1907. *Letters and Papers of Charles Lord Barham, 1758-1813*. 3 vols. London.

Ledward, Thomas D. 'Letters to his Family' in *Notes and Queries*, 9th series, vol. XII, 26 December 1903, pp. 501-2.

Lee, Ida. 1920. *Captain Bligh's Second Voyage to the South Sea*. London.

Lees, Ida. 1939. 'The Morrison Myth' (review), *The Mariner's Mirror*, vol. 25, no. 4, October, pp. 433-8.

L'Estrange, Alfred G.L. (ed.). 1891. *The Friendships of Mary Russell Mitford, as recorded in Letters from her Literary Correspondents*. 2 vols. London.

L'Estrange, A.G.L. 1891. *Lady Belcher and Her Friends*. London.

Lewis, Michael. 1939. *England's Sea-Officers: The Story of the Naval Profession*. London.

Lewis, Michael. 1960. *A Social History of the Navy, 1793-1815*. London.

Lindsay, Philip. 1931. *Ruffians Hall*. London.

Lloyd, Christopher. 1963. *St Vincent & Camperdown*. London.

Lloyd, Christopher. 1968. *The British Seaman 1200-1860: A Social Survey*. London.

Lloyd, Christopher. 1970. *Mr Barrow of the Admiralty: a Life of Sir John Barrow 1764-1848*. London.

London Missionary Society. 1818. *Narrative of the Mission at Otaheite and the other islands in the South Seas*. London.

Lord, Clive. 1922. 'Notes on Captain Bligh's visits to Tasmania,' *Papers and Proceedings of the Royal Society of Tasmania*.

Lovett, Richard. 1899. *The History of the London Missionary Society 1795-1895*. 2 vols. London.

MacArthur, John. 1792. *A Treatise of the Principles and Practice of Naval Courts-Martial, with an Appendix, containing Original Papers and Documents illustrative of the text, opinions of Counsel upon remarkable cases, the forms preparatory to Trial, and proceedings of the Court to Judgment and Execution*. By John M'Arthur. London. 4th ed. 1813.

MacArthur, John. 1808. *The Trial of John MacArthur, Esquire*. London.

McFarland, A. 1884. *Mutiny in the Bounty and the Story of the Pitcairn Islands*. Sydney, N.S.W.

McGilchrist, J. 1859. *The Mutineers: A Poem*. Edinburgh.

Mackaness, George. 1931. *The Life of Vice-Admiral William Bligh, R.N., F.R.S.* 2 vols. Sydney, N.S.W. New and revised ed., 1 vol., 1951 (this is the edition quoted throughout this book).

Mackaness, George. 1936. *Sir Joseph Banks: His Relations with Australia*. Sydney, N.S.W.

Mackaness, George (ed.). 1938. *A Book of the 'Bounty', by William Bligh and Others*. (Everyman's Library, no. 950). London.

Mackaness, George (ed.). 1943. *Captain William Bligh's Discoveries and Observations in Van Diemen's Land*. Sydney, N.S.W.

Mackaness, George (ed.). 1949. *Some Correspondence of Captain William Bligh, R.N., with John and Francis Godolphin Bond 1776-1811.* (Australian Historical Monographs, No. 19). Sydney, N.S.W.

Mackaness, George (ed.). 1953. *Fresh Light on Bligh: Being Some Unpublished Correspondence of Captain William Bligh, R.N., and Lieutenant Francis Godolphin Bond, R.N., with Lieutenant Bond's Manuscript Notes made on the Voyage of H.M.S. 'Providence', 1791-1795.* (Australian Historical Monographs, No. 29). Sydney, N.S.W.

McKee, Alexander. 1961. *The Truth about the Mutiny on the Bounty.* London.

McKinnes, George. 1931. *Biography of William Bligh.* Sydney, N.S.W.

Maiden, J.H. 1909. *Sir Joseph Banks, the 'Father of Australia'.* London/Sydney, N.S.W.

Mann, D.D. 1811. *The Present Picture of New South Wales; illustrated with large coloured views, from drawings taken on the spot, of Sydney, the Seat of Government: with a Plan of the Colony, taken from actual survey by public authority. Including the present state of agriculture and trade, prices of provisions and labour, internal regulations, state of society and manners, late discoveries in natural history. And other interesting subjects: with Hints for the Further Improvement of the Settlement.* London.

Manwaring, G.E. 1931. *My Friend the Admiral: The Life, Letters and Journals of Rear-Admiral James Burney, F.R.S. the Companion of Captain Cook and Friend of Charles Lamb.* London.

Marden, Luis. 1957. 'I Found the Bones of the Bounty', *National Geographic Magazine,* vol. 112, no. 6, December, pp. 725-89.

Marden, Luis. 1962. 'Huzza for Otaheite!' *National Geographic Magazine,* vol. 121, no. 4, April.

Marks, Percy J. 1935. *Norfolk Island and The Bounty Mutiny.* Sydney, N.S.W. [privately printed].

Marsden, J.B. (ed.). 1958. *Memoirs of The Life and Labours of the Rev. Samuel Marsden, of Paramatta, Senior Chaplain of New South Wales; and of his Early Connexion with the Missions to New Zealand and Tahiti.* London.

Marshall, James Stirrat & Carrie. 1955. *Vancouver's Voyage.* Vancouver, B.C.

Marshall, John. 1823-1835. *Royal Naval Biography; or, Memories of the Services of all the Flag-Officers, Superannuated Rear-Admirals, Retired-Captains, Post-Captains, and Commanders, Whose names appeared on the Admiralty List of Sea Officers at the commencement of the present year, or who have since been promoted; Illustrated by a Series of Historical and Explanatory Notes, Which will be found to contain an account of all the Naval Actions, and other important Events, from the Commencement of the late Reign, in 1760, to the present period. With Copious Addenda.* London.

Masefield, John. 1905. *Sea Life in Nelson's Time.* With an Introduction by Professor C.C. Lloyd. (The 1971 edition is used throughout this book.)

Massachusetts Sabbath School Society. 1855. *Aleck and the Mutineers of the Bounty.* Boston, Mass.

Maude, H.E. 1958. 'In Search of a Home: From the Mutiny to Pitcairn Island (1789-1790)', *The Journal of the Polynesian Society,* vol. 67, no. 2, June, pp. 106-16.

Maude, H.E. 1959. 'Tahitian Interlude: The Migration of the Pitcairn Islanders to the Motherland in 1831', *The Journal of the Polynesian Society,* vol. 68, no. 2, June, pp. 115-40.

Maude, H.E. 1964. 'The Voyage of the Pandora's Tender', *The Mariner's Mirror,* vol. 50, no. 8, August, pp. 217-35.

Miller, Stanley. 1973. *Mr Christian: The Journal of Fletcher Christian, Former Lieutenant of His Majesty's Armed Vessel 'Bounty'.* (A novel.) London.

Mitchell, R. Else. 1939. 'George Caley: His Life and Work', *Royal Australian Historical Society, Journal and Proceedings,* vol. 25, esp. pp. 523-8: 'The Bligh Rebellion'.

Mitford, Mary Russell. 1811. *Christina, The Maid of the South Seas; A Poem.* London.

Mitford, Mary Russell. 1852. *Recollections of a Literary Life; or, Books, Places, and People.* 3 vols. London.

Montgomerie, H.S. 1937. *William Bligh of the 'Bounty', in Fact and in Fable.* London.

Montgomerie, H.S. 1938. *The Morrison Myth: a pendant to* William Bligh of the Bounty in Fact and in Fable. London. [privately printed].

Moore-Robinson, J. 1922. 'Tasmanian State Records', *Papers & Proceedings of the Royal Society of Tasmania, for the Year 1921*, pp. 156-65. Hobart, Tasmania.

Morrison, James. 1935. *The Journal of James Morrison Boatswain's Mate of The Bounty describing the Mutiny & subsequent Misfortunes of the Mutineers together with an account of the Island of Tahiti. With an Introduction by Owen Rutter and five engravings by Robert Gibbings. Printed & made in Great Britain by The Golden Cockerel Press.*

Mortimer, George. 1791. *Observations and Remarks made during a Voyage to the Islands of Teneriffe, Amsterdam, Maria's Islands near Van Diemen's Land; Otaheite, Sandwich Islands; Owhyhee, the Fox Islands on the North West Coast of America, Tinian, and from thence to Canton, in the Brig Mercury.* London.

Mudie, James. 1837. *The Felonry of New South Wales: being a Faithful Picture of the Real Romance of Life in Botany Bay. With anecdotes of Botany Bay Society, and a Plan of Sydney.* London.

Muir, H. 1950. 'The Literature of the Bounty', in Charles Barnet, *The Pacific: Ocean of Islands.* Melbourne, Victoria.

Murray, Hugh. 1827. *Adventures of British Seamen in the Southern Ocean, displaying the Striking Contrasts which the Human Character exhibits in an uncivilized state.* Edinburgh.

Murray, Thomas Boyles. 1853. *Pitcairn: the Island, the People, and the Pastor; with a short account of the Mutiny of the Bounty.* London.

Nichols, G.R. 1904-18. *Historical Notes on the Hawkesbury.* Sydney, N.S.W.

Nicholson, Joyce. 1961. *Man Against Mutiny: the Story of Vice-Admiral William Bligh.* London.

Nicolas, N.H. (ed.). 1844-6. *The Dispatches and Letters of Vice-Admiral Lord Viscount Nelson, with Notes by Sir Nicholas Harris Nicolas, G.C.M.G.* 7 vols. London.

Nicolson, Robert B. 1966. *The Pitcairners.* Sydney, N.S.W.

Nield, R.A. n.d. *Mutiny of the Bounty and Story of Pitcairn Island, 1790-1824.* London [?].

Nordhoff, Charles, and Hall, James Norman. 1933. *Mutiny!* London.

Nordhoff, Charles, and Hall, James Norman. 1934. *Men Against the Sea.* London.

Nordhoff, Charles, and Hall, James Norman. 1935. *Pitcairn's Island.* London.

O'Brien, Frederick. 1922. *Atolls of the Sun.* London.

Oman, Carola. 1947. *Nelson.* London.

Onslow, Sibella MacArthur (ed.). 1914. *Some Early Records of the MacArthurs of Camden.* Sydney, N.S.W.

Padfield, Peter. 1973. *Guns at Sea.* London.

Paine, Ralph D. 1921. *Lost Ships and Lonely Seas.* London.

Pears, Randolph. 1960. *Young Sea Dogs: Some Adventures of Midshipmen of the Fleet.* London.

Phillip, Arthur. 1789. *The Voyage of Governor Phillip to Botany Bay; with an Account of the Establishment of the Colonies of Port Jackson & Norfolk Island; compiled from Authentic Papers, which have been obtained from the several Departments; to which are added The Journals of Lieuts Shortland, Watts, Ball, & Capt Marshall; with an Account of their New Discoveries.* London.

Phillips, Marion. 1909. *A Colonial Autocracy: New South Wales under Governor Macquarie 1810-1821.* London.

Pipon, Philip. 1834. 'The Descendants of the Bounty's Crew', *United Service Journal*, vol. 63. [abridged version].

The Pitcairn Island Register Book; edited with an Introduction by Sir Charles Lucas. London, S.P.C.K., 1929.

Polwhele, R. 1826. *Traditions and Recollections; Domestic, Clerical, and Literary; in which are included Letters of Charles II, Cromwell, Fairfax, Edgecumbe, Macaulay, Wolcot, Opie, Whitaker, Gibbon, Buller, Courtenay, Moore, Downman, Drewe, Seward, Darwin, Cowper, Hayley, Hardinge, Sir Walter Scott, and other Distinguished Characters. By the Rev. R. Polwhele.* 2 vols. London.

Polwhele, R. 1831. *Biographical Sketches in Cornwall.* 3 vols. Truro.

Pool, Bernard. 1966. *Navy Board Contracts 1660-1832: Contract Administration under the Navy Board.* London.

Pope, Dudley. 1963. *The Black Ship*. London.

Pope, Dudley. 1972. *The Great Gamble*. London [Nelson at Copenhagen].

Portlock, Nathaniel. 1789. *A Voyage Round the World; but more particularly to the North West Coast of America: performed in 1785, 1786, 1787, and 1788, in The King George and Queen Charlotte, Captains Portlock and Dixon*. London.

Postgate, R.W. 1920. *Revolution from 1789 to 1906: Documents selected and edited with Notes and Introductions*. London.

Raine, J. 1821. 'Captain Raine's Narrative of a Visit to Pitcairn's Island in the ship Surry, 1821', *The Australian Magazine; or, Compendium of Religious, Literary, and Miscellaneous Intelligence*, vol. 1 for 1821, pp. 80-4, 109-14. Sydney, N.S.W.

Rawson, Geoffrey. 1930. *Bligh of the 'Bounty'*. London.

Rawson, Geoffrey. 1963. *Pandora's Last Voyage*. London.

Renouard, David T. 1842. 'Pandora's Tender 1791', in *The United Service Magazine*, part 3, pp. 1-3; also in *The Mariner's Mirror*, vol. 50, no. 3, 1964.

Robinson, A.H.W. 1952. 'Captain William Bligh R.N., hydrographic surveyor'. *Empire Survey Review*, vol. XI, no. 85, pp. 301-6.

Robinson, A.H.W. 1962. *Marine Cartography in Britain*. Leicester.

Ross, Alan S.C., and Moverley, A.W. 1964. *The Pitcairnese Language*. London.

Rutter, Owen. 1930. *Cain's Birthday* (A novel based on the character of Fletcher Christian.) London.

Rutter, Owen (ed.). 1931. *The Court-Martial of the 'Bounty' Mutineers*. London.

Rutter, Owen. 1932. 'Travels of Fletcher Christian', *Blue Peter*, June.

Rutter, Owen. 1933. 'Vindication of William Bligh', *Quarterly Review*, October.

Rutter, Owen (ed.). 1934. *The Voyage of the Bounty's Launch as related in William Bligh's despatch to the Admiralty and the Journal of John Fryer*. London.

Rutter, Owen. 1936. 'Bligh's Log', *The Mariner's Mirror*, vol. 22, no. 2, April, pp. 179-82.

Rutter, Owen. 1936. *The True Story of the Mutiny in the 'Bounty'*. London.

Rutter, Owen. 1936a. *Turbulent Journey: A Life of William Bligh, Vice-Admiral of the Blue*. London.

Rutter, Owen (ed.). 1937. *The Log of the Bounty, being Lieutenant William Bligh's Log of the proceedings of His Majesty's Armed Vessel 'Bounty', on a voyage to the South Seas to take the breadfruit from the Society Islands to West Indies, now published for the first time from the manuscript in the Admiralty records*. 2 vols. London.

Samwell, David. 1786. *A Narrative of the Death of Captain James Cook*. London.

Schomberg, Isaac. 1802. *Naval Chronology; or, An Historical Summary of Naval & Maritime Events, from the Time of The Romans, to the Treaty of Peace 1802. With an Appendix*. 5 vols. London.

Scott, Ernest. 1912. *La Perouse*. Sydney, N.S.W.

Scott, Ernest. 1914. *The Life of Captain Matthew Flinders, R.N.* Sydney, N.S.W.

Scott, Ernest. 1916. *A Short History of Australia*. London.

Serle, Percival. 1949. *Dictionary of Australian Biography*. 2 vols. London.

Shapiro, H.L. 1936. *The Heritage of the Bounty: The Story of Pitcairn through Six Generations*. London.

Shapiro, H.L. 1938. 'Pitcairniana – A Commentary on the Mutiny of the *Bounty* and its Sequel on Pitcairn Island', *Natural History*, vol. 41, January, pp. 34-45.

Shillibeer, J. 1817. *A Narrative of The Briton's Voyage, to Pitcairn's Island*. London.

Shorter, Alfred H. 1957. *English Paper Mills and Paper Makers in England 1495-1800*. Hilversum.

Silverman, David. 1967. *Pitcairn Island*. Cleveland, Ohio.

Slocum, V. 1926. 'Voyage of the Bounty's Launch', *Yachting*, vol. 40, July, pp. 37-40.

Smith, Bernard. 1956. 'Coleridge's *Ancient Mariner* and Cook's Second Voyage', *Journal of the Warburg and Courtauld Institutes*, vol. XIX, no. 1-2, pp. 117-54.

Smith, D. Bonner (ed.). 1922, 1927. *Letters of Admiral of the Fleet the Earl of St Vincent whilst First Lord of the Admiralty 1801-1804*. (Publications of the Navy Records Society. London.

Smith, D. Bonner. 1936. 'Some Remarks about the Mutiny of the *Bounty*', *The Mariner's Mirror*, vol. 22, no. 2, April, pp. 200-37.

Smith, D. Bonner. 1937. 'More Light on Bligh and the *Bounty*', *The Mariner's Mirror*, vol. 23, no. 2, April, pp. 210-28.

Spence, S.A. 1970. *Captain William Bligh, R.N. (1754-1817) & Where to Find Him: Being a Catalogue of works wherein reference is contained to this remarkable seaman*. London. [privately printed, 75 copies].

Spruson, J.J. 1885. *Norfolk Island: Outline of its History from 1788 to 1884*. Sydney, N.S.W.

Squire, John. 1953. 'Was Fletcher Christian the Ancient Mariner?', *Illustrated London News*, vol. 222, 9 May, p. 732.

Stackpole, Edouard A. 1953. *The Sea-Hunters: The New England Whalemen during Two Centuries 1635-1835*. New York.

Staines, J., and Pipon, Philip. n.d. *Interesting Report on the Only Remaining Mutineers of His Majesty's Ship Bounty, Resident on Pitcairn's Island in the Pacific Ocean*. London.

Steven, M.J.E. 1962. *Robert Campbell and the Bligh Rebellion 1808*. (Canberra and District Historical Society: Typescript Paper delivered on 27 March 1962). Sydney, N.S.W.

Suttor, W.H. 1887. *Australian Stories Retold, and Sketches of Country Life*. Bathurst, N.S.W.

'Taffrail' [H.T. Dorling]. 1928. 'The Mutiny of the "Bounty"', *Chamber's Journal*, seventh series, vol. 18, pp. 711-14, 733-6, 748-51; 6, 13, 20 October.

Tagart, Edward. 1832. *A Memoir of the late Captain Peter Heywood R.N., with extracts from his Diaries and Correspondence*. London.

Taylor, A.H. 1937. 'William Bligh at Camperdown', *The Mariner's Mirror*, vol. 23, no. 4, October, pp. 417-34.

Tench, Watkin. 1793. *A Complete Account of the Settlement at Port Jackson, in New South Wales, including an accurate description of the situation of the colony; of the natives; and of its natural productions: taken on the spot, by Captain Watkin Tench, of the Marines*. London.

Thomas, Marcel. 1958. *L'Affaire du Bounty. Documents originaux traduits et presentés*. [Limited Edition].

Thomas, Marcel. 1958. *L'Affaire du Bounty*. Paris.

Thomson, Basil (ed.). 1915. *E. Edwards and G. Hamilton, Voyage of HMS Pandora, despatched to arrest the mutineers of the Bounty in the South Seas, 1790-91 being the narratives of Captain Edwards, R.N., the commander, and George Hamilton, surgeon, Introduction and notes by Basil Thomson*. London.

Topliff, Samuel. 1821. 'Visit of Sultan to Pitcairn, 1817', *New-England Galaxy*, vol. 4, January.

Tucker, Jedediah Stephens. 1844. *Memoirs of Admiral the Right Hon. the Earl of St. Vincent, G.C.B. &c*. London.

Turnbull, John. 1813. *A Voyage round the World, in the years 1800, 1801, 1802, 1803, and 1804: in which The Author visited Madeira, the Brazils, Cape of Good Hope, the English Settlements of Botany Bay and Norfolk Island; and the Principal Islands in the Pacific Ocean. With a Continuation of their History to the Present Period*. Second Edition. London.

Vancouver, George. 1798. *A Voyage of Discovery to the North Pacific Ocean, and Round the World; in which the Coast of North-West America has been carefully examined and accurately surveyed. Undertaken by His Majesty's Command, principally with a view to ascertain the existence of any navigable communication between the North Pacific and North Atlantic Oceans; and performed in the Years 1790, 1791, 1792, 1793, 1794, and 1795, in the Discovery Sloop of War, and Armed Tender Chatham, under the Command of Captain George Vancouver*. 3 vols. London.

Vancouver, George. 1908. 'Letter, March 2, 1794', *Hawaiian History Society Report*, no. 16, pp. 18-19.

Vaucaire, Michel. 1947. *Les Revoltes de la Bounty recit historique*. Paris.

Verne, Jules. 1882. 'Bounty Mutiny', *Bekannte und unbekannte Welten*, vol. 37-8, pp. 250-3.

Verne, Jules. 1880. *The Begun's Fortune; with an Account of The Mutineers of the 'Bounty'*. Translated by W.H.G. Kingston. London.

Vidil, Charles. 1932. *Histoire des mutins de la Bounty et de l'Ile Pitcairn, 1789-1930*. Paris.

Villiers, Alan. 1962. *Men, Ships, and the Sea*. Washington, D.C.

Walker, C.F. 1938. *Young Gentlemen: the Story of Midshipmen from the XVIIth Century to the present day*. London.

Walker, J.B. 1902. *Early Tasmania*. Hobart, Tasmania.

Walters, Stephen. 1976. 'The literature of Bligh', *Sea Breezes: The Magazine of Ships and the Sea*, vol. 50, no. 370, October, pp. 608-11.

Warren, Samuel. 1855. 'The Paradise in the Pacific', in *Works*, vol. 5, pp. 154-78. London/Edinburgh.

Waters, D.W., R.N. 1966. 'Navigational Instruments and Timekeepers', in Gervis Frere-Cook (ed.), *The Decorative Arts of the Mariner*, Chapter X, pp. 165-92. London.

Watson, James. 1959. 'The Mutiny on the "Bounty" ', in *Stamps and Ships*, Chapter 4. London.

Weate, Philip, and Chapman, Caroline. 1972. *Captain William Bligh*. Sydney, N.S.W.

Webb, A.J. 1885. *The History of Fiji*. Sydney, N.S.W.

Welsby, T. 1913. 'Bounty mutiny', in *Discoverers of the Brisbane River*, London.

Whymper, T. 1878-80. 'Mutiny of the Bounty', *The Sea*, vol. 1, pp. 236-49. London.

Wilkie, A. 1930. *Governor Bligh: a tale of old Sydney*. Sydney, N.S.W.

Wilkinson, C.S. 1953. *The Wake of the Bounty*. London.

Wilson, Erle. 1958. *Adams of the Bounty*. Sydney, N.S.W.

Wilson, William. 1799. *A Missionary Voyage to the Southern Pacific Ocean, performed in the Years 1796, 1797, 1798, in the Ship Duff, Commanded by Captain James Wilson. Compiled from Journals of the Officers and the Missionaries; and Illustrated with Maps, Charts, and Views, Drawn by Mr. William Wilson, and engraved by the most eminent Artists*. London.

Wood, Arthur Skevington. 1957. *Thomas Haweis 1734-1820*. London.

Yexley, Lionel. 1911. *Our Fighting Sea Men*. London.

Yonge, C.D. 1863. *The History of the British Navy: From the Earliest Period to the Present Time*. 2 vols. London.

Young, Sir George. 1928. 'H.M.S. Bounty', in *Young of Formosa*, London.

Young, Rosalind Amelia. 1894. *Mutiny of the Bounty and Story of Pitcairn Island, 1790-1894*. Oakland, California.

Index